DBS Library

22534

C++ for Business Programming

Second Edition

)BS Library

13/14 Aungier Street

Dublin 2

This book is due for return on or before the last date shown below.

Phone: 01-4177572

CANCELLED

APR 2007

2 0 APR 2007

1 0 MAY 2007

John C. Molluzz

Pace University, N

Library of Congress Cataloging-in-Publication Data

Molluzzo, John C.
  C++ for business programming / John C. Molluzzo.-- 2nd ed.
    p. cm.
  Includes bibliographical references and index.
  ISBN 0-13-046700-6
  1. C++ (Computer program language) 2. Business--Computer programs.
I. Title.
  HF5548.5.C125M65 2006
  005.13'3--dc22   2005014365

Vice President and Editorial Director, ECS: *Marcia J. Horton*
Senior Acquisitions Editor: *Tracy Dunkelberger*
Editorial Assistant: *Christianna Lee*
Executive Managing Editor: *Vince O'Brien*
Managing Editor: *Camille Trentacoste*
Director of Creative Services: *Paul Belfanti*
Managing Editor, AV Management and Production: *Patricia Burns*
Art Editor: *Gregory Dulles*
Cover Design Director: *Jayne Conte*
Cover Designer: *Kiwi Designs*
Manufacturing Manager, ESM: *Alexis Heydt-Long*
Manufacturing Buyer: *Lisa McDowell*
Executive Marketing Manager: *Pamela Shaffer*
Marketing Assistant: *Barrie Reinhold*

DUBLIN BUSINESS SCHOOL
LIBRARY
RECEIVED

2 4 MAY 2008

PEARSON   © 2006 Pearson Education, Inc.
Prentice Pearson Prentice Hall
Hall   Pearson Education, Inc.
          Upper Saddle River, NJ 07458

All rights reserved. No part of this book may be reproduced in any form or by any means, without permission in writing from the publisher.

Pearson Prentice Hall® is a trademark of Pearson Education, Inc.

The author and publisher of this book have used their best efforts in preparing this book. These efforts include the development, research, and testing of the theories and programs to determine their effectiveness. The author and publisher make no warranty of any kind, expressed or implied, with regard to these programs or the documentation contained in this book. The author and publisher shall not be liable in any event for incidental or consequential damages in connection with, or arising out of, the furnishing, performance, or use of these programs.

Printed in the United States of America

10 9 8 7 6 5 4 3 2 1

ISBN: 0-13-046700-6

Pearson Education Ltd., *London*
Pearson Education Australia Pty. Ltd., *Sydney*
Pearson Education Singapore, Pte. Ltd.
Pearson Education North Asia Ltd., *Hong Kong*
Pearson Education Canada, Inc., *Toronto*

Pearson Educación de Mexico, S.A. de C.V.
Pearson Education—Japan, *Tokyo*
Pearson Education Malaysia, Pte. Ltd.
Pearson Education, Inc., *Upper Saddle River, New Jersey*

Contents

6. ARRAYS   234

7. POINTERS AND C-STRINGS   266

13. INHERITANCE   600

14. FILES   664

15. SPECIAL TOPICS: FRIENDS, OPERATOR OVERLOADING, MACROS, AND INLINE FUNCTIONS

Preface

C++ for Business Programming, Second Edition is an introduction to C++ programming. The power of C++ lies in its object-oriented extensions of the C language. However, we believe that for beginning students it is best to learn the basics of programming without the extra encumbrance of having to learn object-oriented concepts. Therefore, the book is divided into two sections. Part I, "Basic C++," covers the procedural parts of C++. Part II, "Object-Oriented Programming," covers all the essential object-oriented ideas through inheritance and polymorphism.

Unlike most books on C++, which emphasize applications to computing or mathematics, this book emphasizes business applications. Therefore, the book is most appropriate for business and information systems students. The entire book can be covered in one semester in a class of students who have a good background in programming in another language. In such a class, it is possible to quickly cover the essential programming constructs from Part I and then concentrate on object-oriented concepts and programming in Part II. For students who have little programming experience, we suggest covering Part I in one semester and Part II in a second semester. The material in Part I can be supplemented as needed by material from Appendix A, "Computers and Data," and Appendix B, "Program Control."

Throughout the book, we emphasize good pedagogy.

- Each chapter begins with a set of learning objectives.
- Each chapter ends with a review section that includes important terms, a chapter summary, and review exercises.
- Concepts are explained in clear, understandable language and are illustrated by many fully worked-out examples.
- Important definitions, concepts, and rules are appropriately highlighted in notes.
- Programming tips and pitfalls are noted in the margins of the text.
- One of the best ways to learn a programming language is to read programs in that language. Therefore, every important idea is illustrated in an example program and accompanying output. There are approximately 150 complete programs in the text, each of which we very carefully explain.

- The book contains over 800 exercises of varying types and levels of difficulty. These exercises are placed at the end of each section rather than at the end of each chapter so students can immediately reinforce their new knowledge. These exercises include exercises, experiments, and programming problems.
    o Almost every section contains exercises on the syntax and semantics of C++. Most of these are of the paper and pencil type, although some require writing a simple program.
    o The experiments, which ask the student to investigate various aspects of the C++ language, are a unique feature of the exercise sections. The experiments improve the student's understanding of the finer points of C++ and help the student avoid common errors made by beginning programmers.
    o The programming problems, which range from 10-20-line programs to full-scale projects that require the use of several user-defined functions and/or classes, are found in most sections of the book. The chapter-illustrative programs and programming problems emphasize the business applications of C++.
- The book conforms to the ANSI C++ standard. All illustrative programs, however, can easily be adapted to nonstandard compilers. Therefore, the book can be used with any C++ compiler.
- Topics are introduced on a need-to-know basis to provide motivation for the student. Therefore, the book is not encyclopedic in its coverage of C++. In some cases, all the relevant ideas surrounding a topic are spread throughout several sections or chapters.
- Appendix A, "Computers and Data," and Appendix B, "Program Control," provide supplementary material for students who have a weak background in computing. Appendixes A and B contain exercises.

CHANGES FROM THE FIRST EDITION

- The terminology and program constructs used have been updated to conform to current practice.
- Several sections have been labeled as optional to improve the flow of the exposition and enable the reader and instructor to concentrate on the more important concepts.
- In some chapters, notably Chapters 2 and 5, material has been rearranged to improve readability.
- A section on the C++ Math Library functions has been added to Chapter 5.
- Chapter 12 in the first edition, "Friends and Operator Overloading," has been moved to the end of the book (Chapter 15) and has been renamed "Special Topics."
- The section titled "Macros and Inline Functions," has been moved from Chapter 5 to "Special Topics," Chapter 15.
- The book now distinguishes C-style strings from objects in the `string` class.

- To help students transition from Part I to the object-oriented concepts in Part II, we include a transition chapter, Chapter 10, on the C++ `string` class. Object-oriented concepts are introduced in this chapter so that students can begin instantiating, using, and manipulating `string` objects without having to worry about how to define a class.

CHAPTER OVERVIEW

Chapters 1–9 constitute Part I, "C++ Basics." Chapter 1, "Introduction to C++," introduces the student to the basic anatomy of a C++ program. It covers the input and output objects `cin` and `cout`, variables, integer data types, and arithmetic. Chapter 2, "Real Numbers," introduces the `float` and `double` data types, the compound assignment, and increment and decrement operators.

Chapters 3 and 4 discuss the basic control structures of programming. Chapter 3, "Iteration," begins by covering relation conditions. Then it proceeds to discuss indefinite iteration (the `while` and `do` statements), definite iteration (the `for` statement), and nested loops. Chapter 4, "Decision Making," covers the `if` statement, the logical operators, nested `if` statements, and the `switch` statement.

Chapter 5 introduces the important concept of functions. Because the function is new to most students, the concept is developed gradually—first with functions that do not return a value, then functions having arguments, and, finally, functions that return a value. We also include a discussion of scope and duration. An entire section is devoted to discussing three programs that use functions. Special care is taken to show how the program logic is modularized into functions. The chapter ends with a discussion of the C++ Math Library functions.

Chapter 6, "Arrays," shows how to properly define an array and reference its elements. Care is taken to show how to use a `for` loop to process the elements of an array. We also cover in some detail how to sort an array using the standard bubble sort. Finally, we show how to declare and process multidimensional arrays.

Chapter 7 introduces pointers. To help the student understand this important topic, we quickly put pointers to work by applying them to C-style strings. Illustrative programs show how to count characters in a string, display a string in reverse, and count words in a string. We also discuss arrays of strings and arrays of pointers.

Chapter 8, "Pointers, Arrays, and Functions," reinforces the student's knowledge of strings and pointers. Call by address using pointers, call by reference, passing arrays as function arguments, and functions that return pointers are discussed in detail. We also cover some useful string library functions and character classification and conversion functions. We also discuss the use of dynamic memory allocation using the `new` and `delete` operators.

Chapter 9, "User-Defined Data Types and Tables," discusses `typedef`, enumerated types, and structures. Special attention is given to the use of structures in defining tables. A major application involves sorting and searching a table (an array of structures), including both sequential and binary searches. The chapter also discusses pointers to structures and using them as function arguments. This chapter can be omitted if time is a consideration.

Chapters 10–15 comprise Part II, "Object-Oriented Programming." Chapter 10, "The `string` Class: An Introduction to Classes and Objects," serves as a transition from the emphasis on procedural programming of Part I to object orientation. The chapter begins with a general discussion of object-oriented concepts. Then it illustrates those concepts using the built-in `string` class. Sections discuss how to perform operations on `string` objects, how to manipulate `string` objects and make decisions with `string` objects, and how to use `string` objects with functions. Upon completion of this chapter, students should be comfortable with the object paradigm.

The material in Chapters 11–13 is unified through the gradual development of a Savings Account class. As new object-oriented programming (OOP) concepts are introduced, they are added to the Savings Account class. Chapter 11 introduces the reader to user-defined classes and objects. We discuss how to declare a class, instantiate objects, and code methods, constructors, and destructors. The chapter ends with a thorough discussion of function overloading and default method arguments.

Chapter 12, "Manipulating Objects," is the longest chapter in the book. Some of the topics, as outlined in the chapter introduction, can be omitted at first reading. The chapter begins by discussing how to include array and pointer instance variables in a class and how to use dynamic memory allocation in a constructor and destructor. Next, the chapter discusses the copy constructor and when it is used. The many ways of using the keyword `const` in C++ are then covered in detail. We also discuss functions that return objects as well as how to pass objects to functions by value, pointer, and reference. Several of the issues relating to the dynamic allocation of objects are covered along with the uses of `static` class data members and methods.

Chapter 13 covers the important concept of inheritance and related ideas. We use one major example throughout most of the chapter to unify the material. After introducing the basic terminology of inheritance and how to construct a class hierarchy, the chapter discusses the uses of methods in such a hierarchy and the concept of polymorphism. Pure virtual methods and abstract base classes complete the chapter.

Chapter 14 gives a thorough treatment of file processing in C++. The chapter begins with a discussion of input/output (I/O) streams, the standard I/O class hierarchy, and how to process simple text files. We then show how to process a file one character at a time. Next, we discuss binary files and the random-access methods. These ideas are then applied to the problems of processing a binary sequential file of records and to randomly processing a binary file of records. The chapter culminates with a random-file-access update program.

Chapter 15 covers several special topics. First we discuss the concepts of `friend` functions and operator overloading. We emphasize the extensibility of the C++ operators by showing how to overload the arithmetic operators, assignment, the insertion and extraction operators, the compound assignment operators, the relational operators, and the unary operators. We conclude the chapter with a discussion of the use of macros and inline functions.

I thank Laura Steele and Alan Apt of Prentice Hall, who made the first edition of this book possible. I also thank Kate Hargett and Mike Giacobbe for guiding me through the second edition. A special thanks to Dean Susan Merritt of Pace University who gave this project and me her enthusiastic support for the many years it took to complete. Thanks also to Chin-Mei Huang for her helpful comments on an early version of the manuscript, Anna Kristoferitsch for helping to solve some of the chapter exercises and, especially, Kenyata Millet, who spent many long hours solving the programming problems and exercises. I also thank Esther Amiri for the work she did on the exercises and programming problems in chapter 10. I thank Professor Gerald Wohl of Pace University for having the courage to use the first draft of this book in his C++ courses, for catching many errors and typos, and for providing me with many helpful comments about the book, and the many readers and reviewers who provided valuable input to the second edition. Finally, I thank my family—my wife, Maria, and my sons, John and Charles—for the help and love they have given me.

A note about the typefaces used in this book: In the program outputs, data that the user inputs in response to program prompts is set in boldface to distinguish it from output produced by the programs.

Reviewers for this edition:
Dennis D. Howard, University of Alaska Anchorage
Nitin Kale, University of Southern California
Dan Calderwood, College of the Redwoods
Safoora Fatima, Devry University

Part I *C++ Basics*

Chapter 1

Introduction to C++

OBJECTIVES

- To write a simple C++ program
- To use comments in a program
- To declare variables of different integer data types and decide when to use them
- To use the `cout` output stream to display strings and variable values
- To use the `cin` input stream to input data
- To use the arithmetic operators
- To understand and use the operator precedence rules
- To solve simple problems involving integers

WHY STUDY C++?

C++, pronounced "C plus plus," is one of the most popular programming languages used to develop computer applications. Many corporate computing departments have adopted C++ as the language in which to develop in-house applications. Many software vendors use C++ to write their application software. Why is C++ so popular and why is learning it important?

- *C++ is a "middle-level" language.* Programming languages can be categorized as high-level or low-level. Assembly languages are low-level languages. An assembly language allows the programmer maximum control over the computer system. The programmer can directly interface with and control the computer's hardware and operating system. This control comes at a price, however. Assembly languages are hard to learn because they are highly symbolic and the programmer must take care of all the details of the program. Assembly-language programs are also difficult to maintain and debug. Perhaps most important, assembly-language programs are not portable. An assembly-language program is

1

specific to the hardware and operating system of the computer platform on which it is developed. Thus, you cannot directly execute a PC assembly language program on a Macintosh.

By contrast, high-level languages, such as COBOL, Visual Basic, and Java, are easier to learn, maintain, and debug than assembly languages. The program statements in such languages use English words and familiar mathematical symbols to express instructions to the computer. Typically, each such instruction replaces several equivalent assembly-language instructions. Thus, using a high-level language is easier than using an assembly language. However, the price for this ease of use is the loss of direct control over the computer system that you have in an assembly language.

C++, although it is a middle-level language (and, therefore easier to learn and use than an assembly language), contains many of the low-level capabilities of an assembly language. Thus, C++ is sometimes called a "middle-level" language. It is possible through C++ to attain almost as much control over the computer as you can achieve with an assembly language.

- *C++ is portable.* Most high-level languages are portable in the sense that a program written in a high-level language should execute, with minor modifications, on several different computer systems. C++ is one of the most portable of all the high-level languages. Properly written, a C++ program can run on several computer systems with no modifications. Portability is important because it is now common for a business to have several different types of computer systems (a mainframe, minicomputers, workstations, PCs, and Macintoshes). A properly written application in C++ should be portable to most, if not all, these systems. Thus, portability eliminates the cost of developing the application several times for different platforms.

- *C++ is small.* The C++ language does not contain many of the built-in features present in other programming languages (such as in Visual Basic), which further enhances its portability. For example, Visual Basic has about 150 **keywords**. (A keyword is a word that has special meaning in the language.) C++, on the other hand, has about 60 keywords. Visual Basic includes extensive capabilities to help the programmer write programs. However, this greatly increases the complexity of the Visual Basic language. In contrast, the designers of C++ tried to keep the language as simple as possible by not building things into the language. Instead, the programmer must use programmer-defined and built-in functions and classes. This gives the C++ programmer great flexibility and allows the language to be highly portable.

- *C++ is an object-oriented extension of the C programming language.* Dennis Ritchie developed C at Bell Laboratories in 1972 to help write the UNIX operating system for the PDP-11 minicomputer. Today many mainframes and most minicomputers, including Reduced Instruction Set Computing (RISC) workstations, and many Intel-based PCs and servers use the UNIX or Linux operating system. All versions of UNIX/Linux contain a version of C as their native language. In other words, UNIX/Linux speaks C. Why is this important?

Before C, a systems programmer on such a computer system needed to use assembly language to directly communicate with the computer. Now, along with the applications programmer, the systems programmer can use C. In the early 1980s, Bjarne Stroustrup of AT&T Bell Labs developed C++, which is an object-oriented extension of C.

C is an example of a procedure-oriented programming language. Thus, to develop a C program to accomplish a task, the programmer breaks down the task into a series of steps. On the other hand, to develop an object-oriented C++ program, the programmer views the problem as a set of interacting objects, each with its own properties and behaviors.

This book is divided into parts. In Part I, Chapters 1 through 9, we concentrate on the non-object-oriented aspects of C++. This will enable you to learn the basic constructs of C++ without the additional burden of learning object-oriented terminology and concepts. Chapter 10, in Part II of the book, introduces you to object-oriented ideas through the C++ built-in string class. We then cover all the important object-oriented constructs that make C++ one of the most powerful tools for development of object-oriented software.

Finally, it is important for you to learn C++, even if you do not intend to become a professional programmer. As a person who is professionally involved with computers, it is important that you know a little of the language that many programmers speak. Not to do so would be like beginning your professional career in a foreign country not knowing a word of the native language. You would quickly find out that you must learn some of the native tongue to perform efficiently on the job. In a similar way, so that you can communicate effectively with your colleagues, you should learn at least some of the "native tongue" of the modern programmer—C++.

1.1 OUR FIRST C++ PROGRAM

One of the best ways to learn about the basic features of a programming language is to study a small program written in that language. In this section, we discuss a simple C++ program that displays a two-line message on the computer screen. Before we do so, we discuss some general ideas about how to develop a program.

1.1.1 The Program Development Cycle

You must take several steps each time you develop a program. The following six steps are typical when developing a C++ program. See Figure 1.1.

Step 1: Define the Problem   It is very important that you understand the problem you are trying to solve. Make sure you read the problem specifications carefully. Know what data is to be input into the program and what form that data should be in. Also, know what processing has to be done to that data. Finally, determine what the expected output is supposed to be and what form the output must take.

For example, suppose you are asked to write a simple program that simulates a calculator. The program is to ask the user (the person running the program)

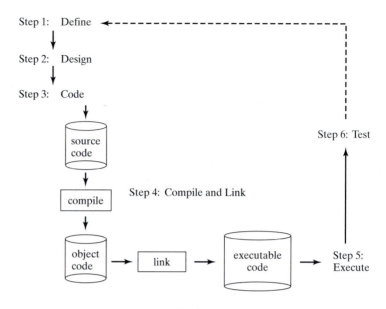

Figure 1.1

to enter two numbers, then the program is to output the sum of the numbers. Before you start doing anything, you have to define this problem more completely. For example, should the program ask the user to enter the numbers? If so, how should the program ask? What kind of numbers are to be input? Must they be whole numbers or can they be decimal numbers? Should the numbers be input one number per line, or can they both be input on one line? After the numbers are input and added, how should the result be displayed? Do you want the input numbers output along with the sum, or do you just want to output the sum? If you want the input numbers as well as the sum to be output, how do you want it done—in column format or on one line?

As you can see, there are many questions to ask even in this simple problem—and we did not ask any questions about the processing, because adding is a simple calculation. Imagine how complex it would be to calculate a person's income tax!

The important point here is to ensure that you solve the correct problem. Make sure that you understand exactly what you have to do before you start the next step in the development cycle. If you are not sure what you need to do, ask the person who wants you to develop the program. If you are writing the program for yourself, then you have to make all the decisions. Do not waste time solving the wrong problem.

Step 2: Design the Program   There are several ways of describing program design. Two common methods are by flowcharts and pseudocode. A **flowchart** is a graphic description of a program design that uses combinations of various standard flowchart symbols. Figure 1.2 shows some standard symbols and the operations they represent. We shall use flowcharts to represent only the basic program control structures.

Pseudocode (literally, "false code") describes program design using English. Pseudocode avoids the syntax of a programming language and, instead, emphasizes

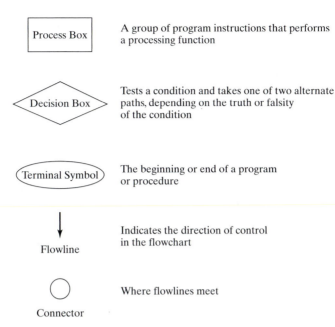

Figure 1.2

the design of the problem solution. There is no standard form of pseudocode—you make up your own rules. The only guideline is that the meaning of the pseudocode should be clear to anyone reading it. We shall include a description of the pseudocode of each program control structure that we introduce in the text. We shall design most programs in Part I of this book using pseudocode.

When you design a program, it is important to check its logic before you start to write the program code itself. If possible, have a friend or coworker check your program design. The program designer is frequently too close to his or her design to see some errors.

Step 3: Code the Program   Note that in some cases, you do steps 3, 4, 5, and 6 (which follow) in an **Integrated Development Environment (IDE)**. Examples of IDEs are Visual Studio.NET and Borland Enterprise Studio for C++ for the Windows platform, and Code Forge for the Linux environment and KDevelop for the UNIX environment. All the steps are performed selecting from pull-down menus or clicking icons. All compiler error messages are listed in a window separate from the edit window (see step 4). When you execute your program (see step 5), it executes in a separate window. At no time do you have to leave the IDE.

After you complete and check the program design, code the program. To **code** a program means to translate the design from step 2 into a computer programming language (C++, in our case). Code the program by entering it into your IDE's text editor, or any text editor on your computer system. Make sure that you save the program to disk before proceeding to the next step.

In the next step of the program development cycle, you will submit the program code, called the **source program** or the **source code**, to the computer for compilation.

Step 4: Compile and Link the Program   The only language a given computer understands is its own **machine language**. A machine language instruction is a binary-coded instruction (consisting of zeros and ones) that commands the computer to do one specific task, such as add 1 to a register. Each computer has its own machine language. The machine language for a Sun workstation is different from the machine language of a Macintosh, which is different from the machine language of an IBM PC, and so on. Because machine language is in binary, it is difficult to write and find errors in machine language programs.

Because a computer understands only its own machine language, it cannot execute high-level or middle-level language instructions directly. The computer, using a program called a **compiler**, must translate **middle-level** and **high-level** language programs into equivalent machine language programs. A compiler is a specialist. It translates only one high-level or middle-level language into a specific machine language. A PC-based C++ compiler translates C++ into PC machine language. The compiler cannot translate a different language (such as Java) and cannot be used on a different type of computer (such as a Macintosh.)

A compiler has two main functions. First it checks the source program for syntax errors. **Syntax errors** are errors in the grammar of the programming language. If there are any fatal syntax errors (that is, errors so severe that the compiler does not understand the statement and cannot translate the statement into machine language), the compiler will stop and notify you of the errors it found. If the compiler finds no fatal errors, it translates each high-level language instruction into one or more machine language instructions. This machine language version of the source program is the **object program**.

Although it is in machine language, the object program may not be ready to execute. The program may contain references, called **external references**, to other programs that a user may have written or that the C++ compiler provides for use by all system users. In either case, you must use a program called a **linker** to **resolve** these external references. The linker finds the other programs and makes them part of your program. We call this process **linking**. The linker resolves external references and combines the object code with these other programs to produce the **executable code**. It is the executable code that the computer executes.

The steps necessary for you to compile and link a program depend on the computer system and compiler on which you develop the program, and the IDE you use. Some IDEs simply require selecting the compile and link options from pull-down menus. Some IDEs require that you create a project in which to run your program. Other IDEs require executing one or two statements at command level to compile and link a program. Consult your program IDE's manual or online help for instructions on the procedure you must follow.

Step 5: Execute the Program   Once you have compiled and linked the program, you are ready to execute the program. Executing the program is usually quite simple. In some IDEs, all you need to do is select the execute option from a menu or click an icon. On other systems, you need to execute the program at command level. Consult your program development environment user's guide for the procedure you must follow.

Step 6: Test and Debug the Program   Even if a program executes, it does not mean that the program is correct. Even if a program gives correct results using some data, it does not mean that the program will give correct results using another set of data. Make sure that you test your program under as many conditions as possible to try to catch errors.

1.1.2 Errors in the Cycle

The six steps in developing a program form a cycle—the **program development cycle**. An error at any step can force you to go back to an earlier step and begin over. Following are some errors that can occur in the cycle.

Errors in Step 1: An error at the problem definition stage can affect the entire program; make sure that you understand the problem you are supposed to solve. Errors can arise in most of the following steps because of a faulty understanding of the problem.

Errors in Step 2: After the initial program design, you or a friend might discover a flaw in the design. If this is the case, you have to redesign part or the entire program.

Errors in Step 3: Errors in step 3, coding the program, can be caught by the IDE. Many IDEs color code different syntactic elements of a program. This makes it easier to catch obvious mistakes in your coding. Make sure that you save your program after each correction that you make. Some coding errors, however, are not highlighted by the IDE. Therefore, after you have entered your program in the IDE's text editor, read the entire program. It is also a good idea to check a printed version of the program.

Errors in Step 4: If the compiler finds any fatal errors in your program, it will not complete the translation of your program into machine language. You will receive a list of error messages detailing the type and location of each error the compiler found. Then, you must go back to step 3, correct your errors, and start the process over. Besides fatal errors, the compiler also may advise you of what it thinks are mistakes. The compiler usually calls these **warnings**. Warnings are not serious enough to stop the translation, but the compiler thinks you should be made aware of them. If the compiler issues warnings, the compilation will take place. However, you should try to correct the source of these warnings before you execute the program unless you coded the source of the warning on purpose. Statements that cause the compiler to issue warnings can cause some very subtle errors in program output when you execute the program. In short, do not execute your program until you have removed all syntax errors.

   After a successful compile, there can be an error in the linking process. Usually, a linker error is caused by the inability of the linker to resolve an external reference. The most common cause of this error is the misspelling of the name of an external program. The linker cannot find the misspelled program because it does not exist. Whatever the cause of the linker error, you must find and correct it.

Errors in Step 5: Assuming the compilation and linking are successful, you can execute your program. Two types of errors can now occur. First, the program may end during execution because it cannot execute a particular instruction. This is a **run-time error**. When a program abnormally ends, the computer displays a message showing the type of error that occurred. You must now locate the cause of the error (which could be in the data processed by your program, not in the program itself) and make the necessary changes. Many compilers have techniques that you can use to locate run-time errors. These techniques include step-by-step tracing of program instructions and the ability to stop the program at a predetermined place to inspect the values of variables. Consult your compiler's user's guide or on-line help for instructions on how to locate run-time errors.

Errors in Step 6: While testing your program with different sets of data, errors can occur that are difficult to detect. In fact, they could go unnoticed. Although a program executes, produces output, and ends successfully, it is not necessarily correct. Check your output to see if it is unreasonable or if it contains obvious errors. If so, you must find the cause of the error. At this point in the program development cycle, the error is probably a **logic error**. The compiler checks the program for syntax errors, but it cannot check for errors in logic. Faulty program design causes most logic errors. If your program contains a logic error, you must find its cause (which is sometimes very difficult), go back to step 2, redesign, recode, reenter, recompile, relink, and retest the program (and hope that you do not introduce new errors along the way).

Occasionally, **faulty coding** causes logic errors. Faulty coding is code that is syntactically correct but incorrectly translates the program design into program code. If your program contains faulty coding, locate and correct the faulty code, and then reenter, recompile, relink, and retest the program. As we work through this book, we shall point out some common errors caused by faulty coding.

The general rule of program development is *catch errors early.* A mistake in step 2 might not show until step 6. If this happens, you must go back to step 2 and start the cycle again. This wastes your time, computer time, and money. Be cautious, and work slowly and deliberately. If you are careful at the beginning of program development, your efforts will pay off in the end.

1.1.3 Displaying a Two-Line Message: dem01-1.cpp

The following is our first C++ program, dem01-1.cpp, followed by its output. The program contains features of C++ that we will use throughout this book. Read the program carefully. After the program code, we explain each line of the program.

```
// dem01-1.cpp

// John C. Molluzzo

#include <iostream>

using namespace std;
```

```
int main()
{
  cout << "This is our first C++ program." << endl;
  cout << "It works!!!" <<endl;

  cout << endl;
  return 0;
}
```

Program Output

```
This is our first C++ program.
It works!!!
```

1.1.4 Comments

The first two nonblank lines of dem01-1.cpp are **comments**. A comment begins with the two characters // and continues to the end of the line. The first comment gives the name of the program and the second gives the author of the program. A comment is not an executable statement. That is, a comment does not result in the computer taking any action. Comments, which can appear anywhere in a C++ program, help to describe parts of the program and are a valuable documentation tool. For example, comments might describe what a program's variables represent or the purpose of a section of the program. Remember that comments are not executable statements and, therefore, the C++ compiler ignores everything from // to the end of the line.

Comment your programs to explain their code. You can follow the style that we use in the programs in this book, although programmers frequently use other commenting styles. Be sure to include at least the name of the program and your name as comments in your own programs.

The first comment shows that the name of this program is dem01-1.cpp. We use the convention that a C++ source-code program name should be eight or fewer characters in length (the characters can be letters, digits, and the hyphen), followed by the .cpp file-name extension. This naming convention conforms to the requirements of most C++ compilers. (Note: Many UNIX/Linux C++ compilers require the extension .C on the name of a C++ source-code file.)

There is a blank line separating the two comment lines in dem01-1.cpp. You can insert blank lines anywhere in a C++ program. We shall separate the important parts of each program by one or more blank lines to enhance the readability of our program code.

Comments can span several lines, as shown by the following.

```
// This is our first C++ program.  This line is a comment line.
// It is common practice to write multiple-line comments
// like this.
```

Before explaining the #include and using lines in dem01-1.cpp, we discuss the remainder of the program.

1.1.5 The Function `main()`

A C++ program is a collection of **functions** that work together to solve a problem. We shall not discuss the exact nature of a C++ function until Chapter 5. For now, think of a function as a part of a program that performs a single task. The collection of functions that make up a C++ program must contain exactly one function called **`main()`**. The function `main()` controls the C++ program by executing C++ statements and other functions. A C++ program automatically begins execution at the first executable statement of the function `main()`.

A function in C++ can either produce, or *return*, a value that can be used by the system or it can produce no value at all. The word `int` that precedes the word `main()` tells the C++ compiler that `main()` produces an integer value. In Chapter 5, we shall discuss how to write functions that do not produce a value. For now, place the word `int` before the word `main()`.

The statements in `main()` must be enclosed in braces {...}. Thus the name `main()` is followed by a left brace {, which begins the function `main()`. The left brace is followed by the program statements. The program ends with the matching right brace }. When program execution reaches this matching right brace, the program stops. Code the left and right braces in `main()` in column one and indent the program statements two spaces. This indenting convention, which we use throughout the book, makes the program easier to read.

Each `cout` statement in dem01-1.cpp ends in a **semicolon.** Semicolons are very important in C++, as stated in Note 1.1.

Note 1.1   Semicolons

Each statement in a C++ program must end in a semicolon. Omitting a required semicolon will cause a compiler syntax error.

A common error is to code a colon rather than a semicolon at the end of a statement, so be careful to use the correct punctuation.

A statement in C++, which can span several lines, ends with a semicolon in much the same way as an English sentence ends with a period. Omitting a required semicolon would be like omitting a period in English—you would be writing the equivalent of a run-on sentence.

Because C++ is statement oriented, we can code the function `main()` of dem01-1.cpp as follows and cause no syntax errors.

```
int main(){ cout << "This is our first C++ program." << endl;
cout << "It works!!!" <<endl; cout << endl; return 0;}
```

This code, however, is hard to read. Note 1.2 gives a good rule of thumb to use when coding a C++ program.

It is very important to keep in mind that C++ is **case sensitive**. That is, when coding C++ statements there is a difference between uppercase and lowercase letters. Coding

```
int Main()
```

is incorrect because we used an uppercase M instead of a lowercase m in the word `main`. When a C++ program begins executing, it looks for a function named `main()`, not a

> **Note 1.2 Coding Statements**
>
> Code one statement on each line unless
>
> - The statement is too long to fit on one line, or
> - Writing the statement over several lines clarifies the meaning of the statement.

function named `Main()`. Later, we shall adopt conventions for naming various C++ program elements. These conventions will allow the use of uppercase letters to help us recognize the type of element each name represents. Until then, use lowercase letters for everything except what appears inside double quotes `"..."`, where you can use whatever combination of letters you require.

The function `main()` can execute any of the following:

1. A built-in C++ statement. The program dem01-1.cpp does not contain any built-in C++ statements. Much of this book is devoted to discussing the built-in C++ statements.
2. A function. The function `main()` can use any function whether it is a **user-defined function** (one that the programmer defines and codes) or a **standard library function** (a precoded function that is part of the C++ system). We shall learn about C++ functions throughout the rest of the book.
3. Operations on C++ streams, which we explain in the next section.
4. Other operations, which we shall encounter in later chapters.

1.1.6 The Output Stream cout

In C++, output is written to a **data stream**, which you can think of as a sequence of characters. The stream **cout** (for "console output" and read as "see-out") represents the standard output stream, which is automatically "attached" to the user's monitor when the C++ program begins. Data can be sent to, or inserted into, the output stream cout using the **insertion operator**, `<<`, which you can read as "is sent" or "gets". Thus, read

```
cout << "Hello";
```

as "cout gets 'Hello'" or "cout is sent 'Hello'".

Because the output stream is attached to the monitor, the data appears on the screen. See Figure 1.3.

To insert a **string** (that is, a set of characters) into the **output stream**, enclose the string in quotation marks. (Remember that you must end the statement with a semicolon.) Thus,

```
cout << "This is our first C++ program.";
```

inserts the words `"This is our first C++ program."` into the output stream, which, in turn, makes the words appear on the monitor, beginning at where the cursor was when the statement was executed. If we follow the above `cout` by

```
cout << "It works!!!";
```

Use the output stream cout and the insertion operator << to send data to
the output stream.

Figure 1.3

the following would appear on the monitor:

```
This is our first C++ program.It works!!!
```

> After the first cout executes, the cursor is left following the period after the word
> program. Therefore, when the second cout is executed, the characters it sends to the
> output stream appear beginning at the current location of the cursor, that is, immedi-
> ately after the period.
> To correct this problem, we use **endl** (end-of-line). When endl is sent to cout, it
> forces the cursor to the beginning of the next line. Note that the last character in endl
> is a lowercase l, NOT a 1 (the digit one).

```
cout << "This is our first C++ program." << endl;
cout << "It works!!!" << endl;
```

> After the string "This is our first C++ program." is sent to cout, the state-
> ment sends endl, which causes the screen cursor to move to the beginning of the next
> line. Thus, more than one thing can be sent to cout in one statement by "cascading" the
> << operator. When several insertion operators are used in the same cout statement,
> read the first one as "gets" or "is sent" and the subsequent ones as "followed by".

```
This is our first C++ program.
```

> The second of the two statements in our program displays "It works!!!" and then
> sends endl to cout, which causes the cursor to move to the beginning of the next line.

```
It works!!!
```

The net effect is the following output.

```
This is our first C++ program.
It works!!!
```

> One cout statement can display data on several lines. For example, the following
> cout produces the same output as the two cout statements of dem01-1.cpp.

```
cout << "This is our first C++ program." << endl << "It works!!!" << endl;
```

To obtain double spacing between the displayed lines, code the following.

```
cout << "This is our first C++ program." << endl << endl;
cout << "It works!!!" << endl;
```

```
This is our first C++ program.

It works!!!
```

1.1.7 The return Statement

The last statement executed by main() should be the return statement. As noted previously, we declare the function main() to produce an integer value. The return 0; statement does two things. First, it ends the execution of main(). Second, it sends the integer value 0 back to the operating system to indicate that the program ended normally. In Chapter 5, we shall see how to construct functions that return other types of values or no value at all.

1.1.8 The Preprocessor Directive #include

Compiling a C++ program is a two-step procedure. First, a program called the **preprocessor** analyzes the C++ source-code program and carries out all **preprocessor directives**. Each preprocessor directive begins with a # character in the first position of a line. Therefore, in dem01-1.cpp, the line

```
#include <iostream>
```

is a preprocessor directive. The preprocessor carries out its directives before the second step in the compilation procedure, which translates your program into machine code. Preprocessor directives usually occur before the main() statement, as in dem01-1.cpp.

The #include directive causes the preprocessor to replace the line containing the #include directive with the text of the named **header file** (so-called because it usually appears at the beginning of the program) that appears inside the angle brackets < >. Thus, the text of the named header file effectively becomes part of your program and is subsequently compiled along with your program statements.

Header files usually contain information about constants, functions, classes, and other C++ elements that frequently appear in C++ programs. (We shall learn about these as we proceed through this book.) The header file **iostream**, which stands for "input/output stream", is one of a standard set of **system header files** that every C++ compiler provides. The header file iostream contains information about the standard input/output streams. In particular, it contains information about the object cout, which appears in dem01-1.cpp. Therefore, if you omit #include <iostream> from your program, the compiler will not recognize cout and will generate an error. See Experiment 1.1.

We use the header file iostream so often that we shall adopt the rule of Note 1.3. Note that the preprocessor directive

```
#include <iostream>
```

does not end with a semicolon because a preprocessor directive is not a C++ language statement. A preprocessor directive is an instruction that the preprocessor carries out prior to the compilation of the program. See Note 1.4.

Note 1.3   The `iostream` Header File

Always code

        #include <iostream>

in all your programs. Code it before `main()`.

Note 1.4   Preprocessor Directives and Semicolons

Preprocessor directives *do not* end with a semicolon.

As we learn how to use other features of C++, we shall introduce other standard header files. We also shall learn other preprocessor directives.

1.1.9 The `using` Directive

The C++ language compiler uses many files to build a C++ executable program. In addition to the source file, which is the C++ program that you code, the compiler uses one or more header files, such as iostream, and libraries of standard and user-defined functions to create the executable program. Therefore, many programmers, including you, have been involved in writing the code that goes into making your program work. It is, therefore, possible that two or more people might have used the same name for two entirely different things. This would lead to a compiler error. To avoid such conflicts, C++ provides the mechanism of the **namespace**, which divides the names that programmers can use into named scopes. The directive

        using namespace std;

allows us to code in our programs `cout` (and later `cin`) without having to qualify these by coding `std::cout` (and `std::cin`). The `using` directive basically says that we can use all names within the `std` namespace (`cout` and `cin` are two such names) without qualification.

Perhaps an analogy will help clarify the use of namespaces. Suppose I am at a meeting of 40 people, two of which, besides me, are named John. If the committee chairperson says "John, did you finish your report?", there would be confusion about which of the three Johns she is talking to. Therefore, the chairperson must qualify the name by saying "John Molluzzo, did you finish your report?" However, when I am home in my own "standard namespace" and my wife wants me to take out the garbage, all she needs to say is "John, please take out the garbage." Since I am in my own house (my "standard namespace"), there is no need for her to qualify my name.

Note that the `using` directive is a requirement of the C++ standard, which was approved in 1998. Older compilers will not recognize the `using` directive. If the `using` directive causes errors when you compile dem01-1.cpp, you probably have an older compiler that does not conform to the new standard. In that case, remove the using directive and recompile your program. It will then be necessary to make the same change to all the sample programs in the book.

1.1.10 Execution of dem01-1.cpp

Now enter, compile, and execute the program dem01-1.cpp. How you do this depends on the particular C++ compiler you use. Refer to your C++ language manual, your instructor, or a local expert. Some chapter exercises ask you to make slight changes to dem01-1.cpp or to write your own simple C++ program. To do this, you must be familiar with the editor that accompanies your compiler or a word processor that produces ASCII text files. Again, refer to the appropriate language manual or your instructor.

1.1.11 Keywords, Multiline Comments, and Escape Sequences

Keywords. The word int as well as using, namespace, and return are examples of **keywords** (or **reserved words**), which are words that have special meaning in the C++ language. Table 1.1 lists the C++ keywords. You will learn the meanings of many of these keywords as you work through this book.

Multiline Comments. Earlier in this section, we mentioned that you can make multiline comments by prefixing each line with the double slash // as follows.

```
//This is the first of a multi-line comment.
//This is the third line.
//This is the final comment line.
```

Some programmers prefer to make multiline comments by using the /*...*/ pair. C++ considers everything between the /* and the */ to be a comment. Therefore, the previous comment can be coded as follows.

```
/*
This is the first of a multi-line comment.
This is the third line.
This is the final comment line.
*/
```

TABLE 1.1

asm	do	if	return	typedef
auto	double	inline	short	typeid
bool	dynamic_cast	int	signed	typename
break	else	long	sizeof	union
case	enum	mutable	static	unsigned
catch	explicit	namespace	static_cast	using
char	export	new	struct	virtual
class	extern	operator	switch	void
const	false	private	template	volatile
const_cast	float	protected	this	wchar_t
continue	for	public	throw	while
default	friend	register	true	
delete	goto	reinterpret_cast	try	

All three lines between the /* and */ are considered comments. This technique is convenient when you want to comment out an entire block of code for debugging purposes. However, be careful if you use this technique—remember to end the comment with the */. Failure to do so will cause the compiler to treat everything from the /* to the end of the file as a comment.

Escape Sequences. Using endl, as we did in dem01-1.cpp, is the most common way to control line spacing in C++. A second, but less common way to control line spacing is by using the newline **escape sequence**. Each escape sequence begins with the backslash character \. The escape sequence that causes the cursor to move to the beginning of a new line on the monitor screen is \n, the **newline character**. Therefore, the first of the following statements displays the string "This is our first C++ program." and then causes the cursor to move to the beginning of a new line. The two lines produce exactly the same output as dem01-1.cpp.

```
cout << "This is our first C++ program.\n";
cout << "It works!!!\n";
```

There are many escape sequences that you can use in a string that you send to cout. Experiments 10, 11, and 12 ask you to experiment with some escape sequences. Table 1.2 lists the common escape sequences. *To use an escape sequence in a* cout *statement, the escape sequence must be contained in a quoted string.*

1.1.12 About the Exercises, Experiments, and Programming Problems

At the end of each section of this book is some combination of exercises, experiments, and programming problems. You can do most of the exercises with paper and pencil, although some may require you to write a short program. The exercises reinforce the ideas discussed in the chapter. Try to complete as many as possible before going on to the next chapter.

The experiments usually ask you to modify a program discussed in the text or ask you to code and execute a simple program and interpret the output. Working with computers is an experimental science. You can treat each of your programs as an experiment: will the program work as you expect? To answer this question, carefully examine

TABLE 1.2

Escape Sequence	Meaning
\a	alert (bell)
\b	backspace
\f	form feed
\n	new-line
\r	carriage return
\t	horizontal tab
\v	vertical tab
\'	single quotation mark
\"	double quotation mark
\\	single back slash
\?	question mark

and interpret the output of the program (the result of the experiment) and decide whether the program (the experiment) worked correctly. Chemists, physicists, and biologists learn from both successful and failed experiments. You also can learn a great deal about programming from programs that work as required and from programs that do not work as required. In addition, the experience gained from doing the experiments will help you avoid making mistakes when writing your own programs. Try to do as many experiments as possible. The more you do, the more you will learn.

The programming problems range in difficulty from simple, straightforward problems to problems that require considerable time to design, code, and test. Attempt at least one programming problem in each chapter. In each programming problem, design the program, write the code, compile the program, and then test the program with sample input data.

Exercises 1.1

1. What is wrong with the attempt at a multiline comment in `main()`?

```
//   dem01-1.cpp
//   John C++. Molluzzo

#include <iostream>

using namespace std;

int main()
{   // This is the body of the
        function main()
   cout << "This is our first C++ program." << endl;
   cout << "It works!!!" << endl;

return 0;
}
```

2. What, if anything, is wrong with the following `cout` statement?

```
cout  >>  "My name is Maria; << endl
```

3. What, if anything, is wrong with the following program?

```
#Include <iostream>       main(){     cout << "Is there something
wrong " << endl << endl   cout << "with this program"?;    }
```

Experiments 1.1

For each experiment concerning dem01-1.cpp, start with a fresh copy of dem01-1.cpp and make the indicated changes.

1. Delete the `#include <iostream>` preprocessor directive from dem01-1.cpp. Attempt to compile and execute the resulting program. What message does your compiler issue?

2. As mentioned in this section, C++ is case sensitive. Replace the i in the pre-processor directive #include by I and compile the resulting program. What message does your compiler issue? Now replace the word cout by COUT. What message does the compiler issue?

3. Every C++ statement must end with a semicolon. Intentionally omit the semi-colon at the end of the first cout statement in dem01-1.cpp and compile the re-sulting program. What message does your compiler issue?

4. A preprocessor directive must not end with a semicolon. Put a semicolon at the end of the #include directive in dem01-1.cpp and compile the resulting pro-gram. What message does your compiler issue?

5. The body of the function main() must be enclosed in braces {}. Omit either the left brace {or the right brace} in dem01-1.cpp and compile the resulting pro-gram. What message does your compiler issue?

6. If you are not sure if your compiler conforms to the new C++ standard, write a program that will find out.

7. If your compiler conforms to the new C++ standard, remove the using statement from dem01-1.cpp and compile the program. What happens?

8. If your compiler conforms to the new C++ standard, remove the using statement from dem01-1.cpp and replace all occurrences of cout by std::cout. Recompile the resulting program. What happens?

9. If your compiler conforms to the new C++ standard, add the .h in the #include directive in dem01-1.cpp. Recompile the resulting program. What happens?

10. A useful escape sequence is the horizontal tab \t. It works like the tab stops on a typewriter. Enter, compile, and execute the following program. What does the tab escape sequence do?

```
// Tabs
#include <iostream>
using namespace std;
int main()
{
    cout << "One\tTwo\tThree\tFour" << endl;
    cout << "\tFive\tSix\tSeven" << endl;
    cout << "\t\tEight\tNine" << endl;
    cout << "\t\t\tTen" << endl;

    return 0;
}
```

Based on the output, at what positions are your computer's tabs set?

11. Another useful escape sequence is the alert \a, also called the bell or audible tone. Enter, compile, and execute the following program. What does the alert es-cape sequence do?

```
// Alert
#include <iostream>
using namespace std;
```

```
int main()
{
  cout << "\a\a\aWake up!" << endl;
  cout << "The program ran!!" << endl;

  return 0;
}
```

12. When outputting a string with the cout statement, the double quote " indicates the beginning or end of a character string and the backslash \ denotes the beginning of an escape sequence. If you want the character string you are displaying to contain either of these characters, you must use a corresponding escape sequence. Enter, compile, and execute the following program. What do the \" and \\ escape sequences do?

```
// Quotes and Backslashes

#include <iostream>

using namespace std;

int main()
{
  cout << "The following is enclosed in double quotes: \"Quote\""
       << endl << endl;
  cout << This is a backslash: \\" << endl;

  return 0;
}
```

Why are there two double quotes near the end of the first cout statement?

Programming Problems 1.1

1. Write a program that displays the following lines triple-spaced.

```
Hello!
This is your computer.
What is your name?
```

2. Write a program that has the same output as the program of Programming Problem 1, but uses just one cout statement.

3. Write a program that displays the following.

```
***********       * Welcome *       ***********
```

4. Write a program that displays your first initial in block form using asterisks. For example, the program that John writes would display the following.

```
*********
    *
    *
    *
    *
*****
```

1.2 INTEGERS AND ARITHMETIC

The simplest type of numeric data that a programmer can define in a C++ program is integer data. This section discusses how to declare and name integer variables, assign values to them, and how to do arithmetic with them.

1.2.1 Identifiers

All programming languages, including C++, require that the programmer name various items that a program uses. We refer to the names of these items as **identifiers**. An identifier can be any name you choose as long it conforms to the rules of Note 1.5.

Note 1.5   Identifier Naming Rules

An identifier consists of up to 31 characters subject to the following rules:

1. The characters can be letters (uppercase or lowercase), digits, and under-scores (_).
2. An identifier cannot begin with a digit.
3. An identifier cannot have the same spelling as a keyword.

The following identifier names are valid.

salary	employee_discount	_name4
x	total_cost	margin
Tax_Rate	VAR	Margin

Good programming practice requires that an identifier name reflect the purpose or meaning of what the identifier represents. Thus, do not use the identifier p to represent the price of a computer. Instead, use either the identifier price or the identifier computer_price.

An identifier cannot contain a space. Therefore, to improve readability, we shall use the underscore to separate words. The identifier total_cost is easier to read than the identifier totalcost. Although an underscore can be the first character in an identifier, we suggest that you avoid doing so to avoid conflict with identifiers used in system header files. (Some programmers capitalize the second and subsequent words of multi-word identifiers instead of using underscores. This naming method is called using "in-caps" notation. For example, such programmers would use totalCost instead of total_cost and totalGrossReceipts instead of total_gross_receipts.)

Do not forget that C++ is case sensitive. Therefore, the identifier profit_margin is different from the identifier Profit_Margin.

1.2.2 Variables

A **variable** is a named location in the computer's main memory that stores a particular type of data. Because it is a location in computer memory, a variable can assume any one of a set of permissible values. This is why we call such a location a variable.

In a C++ program, we define a variable in a **declaration**. A variable declaration begins with the variable's **data type**, which tells the kind of data that a program can store at the location named by the variable. There are many data types in C++, including built-in data types and user-defined data types. The data type is followed by the name of the variable, which is followed by a semicolon.

The name of a variable is an identifier and, as such, is subject to Note 1.5. However, we shall adopt the variable naming convention of Note 1.6. Remember that this is just a convention, that is, a rule that is used in this book, and is not a rule of the C++ language.

Note 1.6   Variable Names

We use only lowercase letters and the underscore for names of variables.

For example, the following is a variable declaration.

```
int i1;
```

In this declaration, the keyword `int` means that the named variable, `i1`, is of the integer data type. Depending on a particular platform (a **platform** consists of the computer hardware, operating system, and C++ compiler being used), an integer can be two bytes (16 bits) or four bytes (32 bits). If two bytes (16 bits) are used to represent an integer, $2^{16} = 65536$ integers (positive, negative, and zero) can be represented in an integer variable. Half the integers in this range are negative (that is, less than zero) and half are nonnegative (that is, greater than or equal to zero). Therefore, such an integer variable would have a value in the range -32768 to $+32767$. (In computers that store `int`-type variables in four bytes, the range for an `int` variable is the same as that for a `long`. We discuss the type `long` and its range of values later in this chapter.) Experiment 4 at the end of this section shows how to use the **sizeof** operator (which determines how many bytes a data type occupies) to find out how many bytes an integer variable occupies on your computer.

Note that in many of the examples and demonstration programs in this book, we shall use short names for some variables to shorten the code. For example, it is common practice to use i, i1, i2, j, and k, and so on, to represent generic integer variables, and r, s, t, x, y, and z to represent generic double variables (see Chapter 2). However, in our longer programs, we will use meaningful names for our variables as you should in all your program solutions to the programming problems.

It is possible to declare more than one variable in one declaration. For example, the following declares three integer variables `i1`, `i2`, and `sum`.

```
int i1,
    i2,
    sum;
```

Alternatively, you can write all the variables on one line as follows.

```
int i1, i2, sum;
```

Note in both cases that there is a comma after each instance of i1 and i2, and that the declaration ends with a semicolon after the last variable name. You can declare any number of variables of the same type by separating their names by commas and ending the declaration by a semicolon.

A variable can be declared anywhere in a C++ program. However, a variable must be declared before it is used. Although not required by C++, we shall adopt the practice of placing each variable declaration at the beginning of main() on a separate line. This improves the readability of our programs and allows us to place a comment after a variable's name to explain its function in the program. In later chapters, we shall discuss when it is appropriate to declare a variable elsewhere in the program.

The **value of a variable** is the data stored at that location in computer memory. Declaring a variable does not give the variable any specific value. A declaration simply reserves storage for that variable in the computer's memory and associates the declared name with that storage. Before the program places data into a variable, the value of the variable is meaningless to the program. In this case, we say that the variable contains **garbage**. It is up to the programmer to make sure that the program places meaningful data into each variable.

1.2.3 Using Integer Variables: dem01-2.cpp

The second program that we discuss in this chapter asks the user to input values for the integers, does arithmetic on these values, and displays the results. To write this program, you need to learn how to input values into the variables, how to do arithmetic, and how to display the results.

The program dem01-2.cpp has the following four-part structure.

1. Declare the variables.
2. Obtain the data from the user.
3. Do the required calculations with the data.
4. Output the results.

Many programs in the first part of this book have this four-part structure. We discuss the new features of the program after the program code.

```
// dem01-2.cpp

// This program demonstrates the use of integers in C++.
// The user enters two integers.  The program adds, subtracts,
// multiplies, and divides the integers and outputs the
// results of the calculations.

#include <iostream>

using namespace std;

int main()
{
   // Declare the variables
    int i1,
       i2,
```

```
    sum,
    difference,
    product,
    quotient,
    remainder;
// Obtain the data from the user
cout << "Input an integer followed by a return: ";
cin  >> i1;

cout << "Input an integer followed by a return: ";
cin  >> i2;

// Do the arithmetic
sum = i1 + i2;
difference = i1 - i2;
product = i1 * i2;
quotient = i1 / i2;
remainder = i1 % i2;

// Output the results
cout << endl;
cout << "The sum of " << i1 << " and " << i2 << " is " << sum << endl;
cout << "The difference of " << i1 << " and " << i2 << " is "
    << difference << endl;
cout << "The product of " << i1 << " and " << i2 << " is "
    << product << endl;
cout << "The quotient of " << i1 << " and " << i2 << " is "
    << quotient << endl;
cout << "The remainder when " << i1 << " is divided by " << i2
    << " is " << remainder << endl;

return 0;
}
```

Program Output

```
Input an integer followed by a return: 15
Input an integer followed by a return: 6

The sum of 15 and 6 is 21
The difference of 15 and 6 is 9
The product of 15 and 6 is 90
The quotient of 15 and 6 is 2
The remainder when 15 is divided by 6 is 3
```

1.2.4 Variable Declarations

The declaration in dem01-2.cpp reserves storage for seven integer variables but does not place values into the seven storage locations. The program needs the variables i1 and i2 to store the integers input by the user. It also needs the variables sum, difference, product, quotient, and remainder to store the results of each arithmetic calculation. Remember that because each of these variables is an integer, each of their values must be in the range of an integer variable. Experiment 4 addresses the question of what happens if one of these numbers is outside the permissible range.

1.2.5 Asking the User for Input: Prompts

The first cout statement in dem01-2.cpp, which is called a **prompt**, asks the program user to enter an integer followed by a return. A program should always prompt the user for the data that the program expects the user to enter. The prompt should be short and should clearly specify the kind of data the user is to enter. Because the prompt ends in a colon followed by a space, the cout leaves the cursor after this blank space. The prompt looks like the following on the screen.

```
Input an integer followed by a return: _
```

1.2.6 The Input Stream cin

Just as output in C++ is done via the output stream, input is done via the input stream. The input stream cin (for "console input" and read as "see-in") is to input what cout is to output: cin obtains the next data item from the input stream, which is attached to the keyboard, and places it into the variable following the **extraction operator**, >>. When we use the extraction operator on cin, cin obtains the next data item from the input stream, that is, the next data item you type at the keyboard, and places a copy of it into the variable that follows >>. See Figure 1.4. The statement cin >> i1; gets the integer that the user enters at the keyboard in response to the prompt and places the integer's value into the variable i1.

The second cout statement in dem01-1.cpp prompts the user for the second integer. The statement cin >> i2; obtains the integer the user enters and places its value into the variable i2.

The integer that the user enters can be preceded by a + or −sign, but it cannot contain a comma or a decimal point. After retrieving the sign, if present, cin retrieves only digits from the input buffer up to but not including the first non-digit it encounters. Thus, if the user enters 13,708 in response to the first prompt, cin will retrieve only 13 and assign it to i1. See Experiment 2.

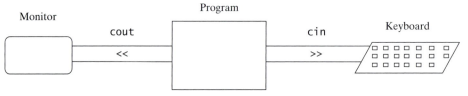

Use cin and the extraction operator >> to remove data from the input stream (the keyboard.)

Figure 1.4

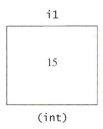

(int)

Figure 1.5

As Figure 1.5 shows, we shall diagram a variable by a square. The name of the variable is at the top of the square. The data type of the variable is in parentheses at the bottom of the square, and the value of the variable is in the square.

Assume that the user enters 15 in response to the first prompt and 6 in response to the second. After the program executes the `cin` statements, we have the situation shown in Figure 1.6.

1.2.7 The Input Buffer

The integers that the user enters at the keyboard are not immediately sent to the program for processing. Instead, the computer places the characters in a temporary storage location called the **input buffer**. The computer sends these characters to the program when the user presses the return key. We call this action **flushing the input buffer**.

In response to the first prompt of dem01-2.cpp, if the user enters an integer and does not press the return key, the program will do nothing. When the user presses the return key, the computer flushes the buffer and sends its contents to the program for processing.

Remember that a variable does not have a valid value until the program in some way assigns a value to the variable. Using `cin` and the extraction operator is one way to assign a value to a variable. Next, we discuss another way to place a value into a variable.

1.2.8 The Assignment Operator and Integer Constants

Recall that until the program assigns a value to a variable, the variable does not have a valid value. That is, the variable contains garbage. After the `cin` statements execute, the

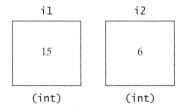

Figure 1.6

variables i1 and i2 have valid values. However, at this point, the variables sum, difference, product, quotient, and remainder contain garbage. We give values to these variables by using arithmetic expressions and the assignment operator.

After the program inputs the integers and places their values into the variables i1 and i2, the program can do its calculations. The statements in this part of the program are all similar. Each statement begins with a variable name, followed by the =, followed by an arithmetic expression, followed by a semicolon.

```
sum = i1 + i2;
difference = i1 - i2;
product = i1 * i2;
quotient = i1 / i2;
remainder = i1 % i2;
```

The **assignment operator** = (read "becomes" or "is replaced by") works as follows: The computer evaluates the expression to the right of = (we shall see how very shortly) and assigns the resulting value to the variable on the left of =. A variable name must appear on the left side of the assignment operator. Thus, the following assignment gives the variable sum the value 2345.

```
sum = 2345;
```

The expression on the right of the preceding assignment is an **integer constant**. An integer constant is a whole number (positive, negative, or zero) written as a sequence of digits, the first of which is not zero. (The only exception to this rule is the integer constant 0.) An integer constant cannot contain a space, a comma, or a decimal point. An integer constant may be preceded by a + or a – to show its sign. If you omit a sign, the computer assumes the integer is positive. Thus,

$$0 \quad 2345 \quad -56 \quad +10782$$

are valid integer constants. The following are not valid integer constants.

$$034 \quad 5,678 \quad 93.0$$

The first begins with a 0, the second contains a comma, and the third contains a decimal point.

Note that you can assign an initial value to a variable in its declaration. For example, the declaration

```
int i  = 42;
```

defines the integer variable i and assigns it the value 42. Program statements can later change the value of i.

1.2.9 The Arithmetic Operators

In general, the expression to the right of the assignment operator involves one or more operators. The program dem01-2.cpp uses the five basic **arithmetic operators: addition** (+), **subtraction** (−), **multiplication** (*), **division** (/), and the **remainder** (or **modulus**) operator (%).

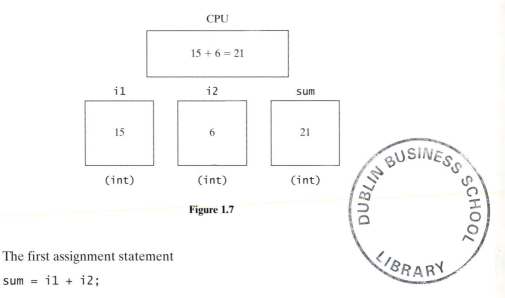

Figure 1.7

DUBLIN BUSINESS SCHOOL LIBRARY

The first assignment statement

```
sum = i1 + i2;
```

executes as follows. The computer's CPU adds the values of the variables i1 and i2, and assigns the result to the variable sum. If the user enters 15 and 6 for the two integers, the assignment has the result shown in Figure 1.7.

It is important to note that the assignment operator in C++ is different from equality in elementary algebra. In C++, and in most other programming languages, an assignment such as the following is legal and makes sense.

```
i1 = i1 + 1;
```

If i1 has the value 15, this assignment works as follows. The computer evaluates the expression to the right of the =. Since i1 has the value 15, the expression has the value 16. The computer assigns this result to the variable i1, which appears to the left of the operator =. The net effect of the assignment is to increase the value of i1 by one. Reading the assignment properly helps to understand its meaning—"The value of i1 becomes the value of i1 plus 1."

The second and third assignments of dem01-2.cpp behave similarly to the first. The second assignment subtracts the value of i2 from the value of i1 and assigns the result (9) to the variable difference. The third assignment multiplies the values of i1 and i2 and assigns the result (90) to the variable product.

The fourth assignment, which involves division, might not behave as you expect. Because i1 and i2 are integer variables, the division i1/i2 is an integer division. Therefore, the result of the division must be an integer. The computer discards any remainder resulting from the division. If the user enters the integers 15 and 6, the statement

```
quotient = i1/i2;
```

assigns the value 2 to quotient because 15 divided by 6 gives a quotient of 2 with a remainder of 3. The assignment discards the remainder 3. See Experiment 3 for what happens when you attempt to divide by zero.

You can assign the remainder produced by an integer division to a variable by using the remainder (or modulus) operator %. The assignment

```
remainder = i1 % i2;
```

divides the value of i1 by the value of i2 and assigns the remainder of the division to the variable remainder. If i1 and i2 have the values 15 and 6, the statement assigns 3 to the variable remainder.

Note that C++ does not have an exponentiation operator that allows you to raise a number to a power, such as 3^5. To do so in C++ requires use of the library function pow(), which we will discuss in Chapter 5.

1.2.10 Operator Precedence Rules

You can form more complicated arithmetic expressions by combining two or more arithmetic operators and using parentheses. For example, you could declare

```
int result;
```

and code the following assignment statement;

```
result = i1 * (i1 + i2);
```

As in elementary algebra, when an expression contains parentheses, you evaluate the expression in parentheses first. Thus, if i1 and i2 have the values 15 and 6, the computer evaluates the assignment as follows: first evaluate the expression in parentheses—the value of i1 + i2 is 21. Then multiply the value of i1, 15, by 21. Finally, assign the answer, 315, to the variable result.

Without parentheses, the computer evaluates an expression according to the operator precedence rules of Note 1.7.

Note 1.7   Arithmetic Operator Precedence Rules

Without parentheses, the computer evaluates the arithmetic operators in an expression according to the following.

1. Do multiplications, divisions, and remainder operations first. If there are more than one such operation, do them in order from left to right.
2. Next, do additions and subtractions. If there are more than one such operation, do them in order from left to right.

The operator precedence table, Table 1.3, summarizes the rules of Note 1.7 and includes the unary plus and minus operators.

The higher an operator appears in the table, the higher its precedence. The associativity rule determines how the computer applies operators on the same precedence level—either left to right (as is true for the arithmetic operators) or right to left, as is true for the unary plus and minus.

A unary minus might appear in an expression as follows.

```
result = -i1 + i2;
```

TABLE 1.3

Operators	Associativity
( )	left to right (i.e., from inside out)
+ (unary) - (unary)	right to left
* / %	left to right
+ -	left to right
=	right to left

Because there is no operand to the left of the minus sign, the minus is a unary minus and not the subtraction operator. Because the unary minus has higher precedence than addition, the computer first applies the unary minus and then does the addition. If i1 and i2 have the values 15 and 6, the current assignment gives the value –9 to result.

The C++ language has many operators and we shall study most of them in this book. As we do so, we will expand the operator precedence table to include the new operators.

To discuss several more examples of the precedence rules, we use the following declaration.

```
int    i = 14,
       j = 5,
       k = 3,
       r1,
       r2,
       r3;
```

What value does the following assignment place into r1?

```
r1 = i + j * 2 - i / 3;
```

The expression contains no parentheses. Therefore, the computer first executes the multiplications and divisions, from left to right.

```
i    +    j * 2    -    i / 3;
i    +     10      -     4
```

Next, the computer does additions and subtractions, from left to right.

```
i    +      10     -     4
   24               -     4
         20
```

Thus, the statement assigns 20 to the variable r1.

As a second example, what value does the following assignment place into r2?

```
r2 = (i + j) * 2 - i / 3;
```

The computer executes the expression inside parentheses first.

```
(i + j)    *    2    -    i / 3;
   19      *    2    -    i / 3
```

Next, the computer executes multiplications and divisions, from left to right. Finally, the computer does the subtraction.

```
19      *    2    -    i / 3
   38             -        4
      34
```

Thus, the statement assigns 34 to the variable r2.

As a final example, what value does the following assignment place into r3?

```
r3 = i % j + k * 5;
```

There are no parentheses in the expression. The computer does multiplications and remainders, from left to right, and then does the addition.

```
i   %   j   +   k   *   5;
    4           +      15
        19
```

Thus the assignment places 19 into the variable r3.

1.2.11 The Object cout Revisited

The first cout statement in the final part of the program

```
cout << endl;
```

makes the cursor skip one line before the program outputs the results of the arithmetic.

Besides displaying a character string, as we did in dem01-1.cpp and in the prompt of dem01-2.cpp, cout also can display the values of variables. Consider the first of the last five cout statements of dem01-2.cpp.

```
cout << "The sum of " << i1 << " and " << i2 << " is " << sum
     << endl;
```

This statement sends a string to the output stream followed by the value of i1, followed by another string, followed by the value of i2, followed by a third string, followed by the value of sum. The space after the word *of* places a space between that word and the value of the variable i1, and similarly with the other strings. The variable values are not automatically followed by a space. Thus, the output appears as follows.

```
The sum of 15 and 6 is 21
```

Note that a cout statement can span several lines as in the last three cout statements in dem01-2.cpp. In each case, the semicolon at the end of the second line ends the cout statement.

Exercises 1.2

In Exercises 1–16, find the value assigned to the variable on the left of the assignment operator =. Work each problem independently of the others. Assume the following declarations.

```
int i = 2,
    j = 3,
    k = 4,
    result;
```

1. `result = 5 * i - j;`
2. `result = 5 * (i - j);`
3. `result = 33 / i * j;`
4. `result = 33 / (i * j);`
5. `result = 33 % i * j;`
6. `result = i - j + k;`
7. `result = i - (j + k);`
8. `result = 17 % k - i * j + 6;`
9. `result = 17 % (k - i) * j + 6;`
10. `result = i * (7 + (j + 3) / 2) - k;`
11. `j = j + k;`
12. `i = i * 2;`
13. `i = i % 3;`
14. `i = i / j + k;`
15. `k = k - 5;`
16. `k = (i + j) * k / 4;`

Experiments 1.2

1. Compile and execute dem01-2.cpp.
2. Execute dem01-2.cpp and enter 13,708 for the first integer (include the comma) and 14.2 for the second integer. What happens and why?
3. Execute dem01-2.cpp and enter 0 for the second integer. What happens and why? Can you suggest a way to help the user avoid this mistake?
4. The `sizeof` operator yields the number of bytes in a data type. In this experiment, you will use `sizeof` to find out how many bytes are used in your computer to store an integer. Then you will test dem01-2.cpp with very large numbers. (We shall use `sizeof` in later chapters.)
   a. Enter and compile the following simple program.

   ```cpp
   #include <iostream>
   #include <iomanip>

   using namespace std;

   int main()
   {
      cout << "On this computer an Integer has " << sizeof(int)
           << " bytes." << endl;

      return 0;
   }
   ```

   b. If the program of part (a) shows that your computer stores an integer in 2 bytes, do the following: Execute dem01-2.cpp and enter 20000 and 15000 for the two integers. Are the results of the arithmetic correct?
   c. If the program of part (a) shows that your computer stores an integer in 4 bytes, do the following: Execute dem01-2.cpp and enter 200000 and 150000 for the two integers. Are the results of the arithmetic correct?

5. In dem01-2.cpp, one `cin` statement can obtain both integers. Replace the two `cout`/`cin` pairs in dem01-2.cpp by the following.

```
cout << "Enter two integers: ";
cin >> i1 >> i2;
```

Note that the input prompt does not specify how to enter the integers. Compile the resulting program and execute it twice as follows.

a. Enter the integers 19 and 7 separated by a space and then hit the return.

b. Enter the integer 19, hit the return, enter the integer 7, and hit the return.

Is there any difference in the resulting output? Explain why or why not.

Programming Problems 1.2

1. An arithmetic expression, rather than a variable, can appear in the variable list of a `cout` statement. For example, you can replace the first `cout` statement of dem01-2.cpp by

```
cout << "The sum of " << i1 << " and " << i2 << " is "
    << i1 + i2 << endl;
```

With this change to dem01-2.cpp, you can eliminate the variable sum from the program and eliminate the assignment statement that gives `sum` the value of `i1 + i2`.

Recode dem01-2.cpp by (a) eliminating the variables `sum, difference, product, quotient,` and `remainder,` (b) eliminating the associated assignments, and (c) replacing the `cout` statements by statements, such as the previous one, that contain the required arithmetic operations. Compile and execute the program. Does it work in the same way as dem01-2.cpp?

2. Write a program that asks the user to enter two integers. The program should divide the first integer by the second and then display the resulting quotient and remainder.

1.3 SOLVING A PROBLEM WITH INTEGERS

In this section, we develop a program to calculate the charge for parts and labor done by mechanics at an automobile service outlet.

1.3.1 Problem 1.1

An automobile service outlet charges its customers for the parts it uses to repair customer vehicles and for the labor required for the repair. The labor charge is $44 per hour. Write a C++ program that prompts the user to enter the total cost of parts for a customer and the number of hours of labor required for the repair. Assume the total cost of parts and the number of hours are integers. The program should display the cost of the parts, the charge for labor, and the total charge for the repair (the sum of the cost of parts and labor).

Discussion of Problem 1.1

To solve this problem, we first design a high-level solution using pseudocode. Pseudocode (literally, "false code") describes program design using English. Pseudocode avoids the syntax of a programming language and, instead, emphasizes the design of the problem solution. There is no standard form of pseudocode—you make up your own rules. The only guideline is that the meaning of the pseudocode should be clear to anyone reading it.

Pseudocode for Problem 1.1:

   Obtain the input data from the user.

   Calculate the labor and total charges.

   Display the results.

   The pseudocode does not specify the variables to use, or how to obtain the input data, calculate the charges, or display the results. We shall fill in these details when we code the program. At this point in the solution design, the pseudocode specifies what the program must do and the order in which the program must do it.

1.3.2 The Program prb01-1.cpp

Before considering the code, we select the variables necessary to solve our problem. The user is to input two numbers—the cost of parts and the number of hours worked. Therefore, we declare a variable for each of these quantities. Suppose we call these variables `parts` and `hours`. Because the program must calculate the labor charge and the total charge of the repair, we also declare the variables `labor` and `total`.

   What range of values can these variables assume? The largest number the program will produce is the total cost of the repair. The total cost should not exceed the largest possible value for an integer variable, at least 32767 (if `int` variables are two bytes) or over 2 billion (if `int` variables are four bytes.) Therefore, we declare all four of the variables as type `int`.

   Following is the program code that solves our problem.

```cpp
// prb01-1.cpp

// This program calculates the total charge for parts and labor

#include <iostream>
#include <iomanip>

using namespace std;

int main()
{
   const int HOURLY_RATE = 44;

   int parts,          // Cost of parts
       hours,          // Number of hours worked
       labor,          // Labor charge
       total;          // Total charge to customer
```

```
            // Obtain the input data

            cout << "Enter the cost of parts: ";
            cin >> parts;
            cout << endl;

            cout << "Enter the number of hours worked: ";
            cin >> hours;
            cout << endl;

            // Do the calculations

            labor = HOURLY_RATE * hours;
            total = parts + labor;

            // Display the results

            cout << "Cost of parts: " << setw(5) << parts << endl;
            cout << "Labor charge: " << setw(6) << labor << endl;
            cout << "---------------" << endl;
            cout << "Total charge: " << setw(6) << total << endl;

            return 0;
        }
```

Program Output

```
Enter the cost of parts: 239
Enter the number of hours worked: 2
Cost of parts:    239
Labor charge:      88
--------------------
Total charge:     327
```

1.3.3 Header Files

We include the iostream header file as usual. The header **iomanip** is included for the **setw()** I/O manipulator, which we shall discuss shortly.

1.3.4 Defined Constants

A variable declaration preceded by the keyword **const** declares a "constant variable." As any other variable, such a variable can be initialized in its declaration. However, once so initialized, no statement in the program can change the value of a const variable. The variable thus becomes a constant in the program. Thus, the declaration

        const int HOURLY_RATE = 44;

defines the variable HOURLY_RATE, which represents the hourly labor rate of $44 per hour, as a constant. We shall use the convention (this is not a rule of C++, but a convention that we use in this book) that defined constant names are in uppercase letters. This makes it easier to distinguish between defined constants and ordinary variables.

    Using defined constants makes program maintenance easier. If the hourly labor rate should change next week, then to update the program, all we need to do is change the value assigned to the defined constant HOURLY_RATE in its declaration. It is not necessary to search through the program for the line or lines in which the hourly rate of 44 appears.

1.3.5 Declaration of Variables

As stated earlier, the four variables the program uses are of type int. Each declaration line contains a comment that describes the quantity that the variable stores.

1.3.6 The Prompts and Calculations

The program statements are in three sections—Obtain the input data, Do the calculations, and Display the results. The program obtains input data by prompting the user and retrieving the input by cin statements.

The calculations are straightforward. The cost of labor is HOURLY_RATE (remember, this has a value of 44) multiplied by the number of hours worked.

```
labor = HOURLY_RATE * hours;
```

The total charge to the customer is the sum of the cost of parts and the cost of labor.

```
total = parts + labor;
```

1.3.7 The Output: I/O Manipulators

The cout statements that display the results contain a new feature, the **setw() I/O manipulator**. You can think of an I/O manipulator as a message to the output stream cout to display the output in a particular way. The setw() manipulator sets the width of the display field of the next item output. The item is displayed right-justified; that is, it is displayed in the right-most positions of the field. For example, the cout statement

```
cout << "Cost of parts: " << setw(5) << parts << endl;
```

first displays the string "Cost of parts: ". Then the setw(5) manipulator tells cout to display the next item in a field of width 5. Thus, the value of the variable parts, 239, is displayed in the right-most three positions of the five-position field as follows.

| field of width 5

C	o	s	t		o	f		p	a	r	t	s	:				2	3	9

Likewise, the second cout statement

```
cout << "Labor charge: " << setw(6) << labor << endl;
```

displays the value of the variable labor in a field of width 6. This field is one position larger than the field set by the previous setw() because the string "Labor charge: " contains one fewer character than the string "Cost of parts: ". Thus, the value of the variable labor, 88, is displayed as follows.

| field of width 6

L	a	b	o	r		c	h	a	r	g	e	:						8	8

In this way, we can use setw() to align the numbers on the right as numbers usually are when displayed in column form.

To use the manipulator setw(), you must place the #include <iomanip> statement at the beginning of your program. In the next chapter, we introduce several other I/O manipulators that are of use in displaying numbers that contain decimal points.

Note 1.8   The iomanip Header File

To use an I/O manipulator, you must place the following preprocessor statement at the beginning of your program.

    # include <iomanip>

Exercises 1.3

1. Code a defined constant that represents the number of feet in a mile.
2. Code a defined constant that represents the number of people enrolled in your class.

Programming Problems 1.3

1. Write a program that asks the user to enter the dollar amount of the opening balance of an account, the dollar amount of deposits to the account, and the dollar amount of withdrawals from the account during the past month. The program should then display the closing balance (opening balance plus deposits minus withdrawals) in the account.

2. Write a program that asks the user to enter the integer lengths (in centimeters) of the dimensions of a box that will hold gum drops. The program should then display the volume of the box (the product of the three dimensions) in cubic centimeters.

3. Write a program that asks the user to enter the duration of a baseball game by first asking for the number of hours and then asking for the number of minutes. The program should display the total number of minutes that the game lasted.

1.4 OTHER INTEGER DATA TYPES[1]

In this section, we introduce the other integer data types and solve a problem that requires these types.

1.4.1 Unsigned, Long, and Short Integers

Recall that on some computers a variable of type int might assume values in the range -32768 to $+32767$. Sometimes, this range is inadequate to store the values of

---

[1]This section is optional and may be omitted without loss of continuity.

the variables a program requires. For example, if the variable nyc_pop is to store the population of New York City, it would have to assume a value of more than 8,000,000.

The C++ programmer can use other kinds of integer variables that can have a larger range of values than type int. If a variable can assume only nonnegative values, then you could declare it as type unsigned int or, equivalently, unsigned. The declaration

    unsigned i1;

declares i1 to be of type unsigned integer. An unsigned integer variable must be non-negative. Therefore, if an unsigned integer variable occupies two bytes of storage, its value can be in the range from 0 to +65535.

To guarantee a wider range of positive and negative values, you can declare the variable to be of type long int or, equivalently, long. On most computers, a variable of type long occupies four bytes (that is, 32 bits). Such a variable, therefore, can assume any of $2^{32} = 4,294,967,296$ values. Because half these values represent negative numbers and half represent nonnegative numbers, a variable of type long has a range of values from $-2,147,483,648$ to $+2,147,483,647$. Therefore, if we declare

    long nyc_pop;

then the variable nyc_pop could store the value of New York City's population.

Finally, if an integer variable, by virtue of what values it represents, cannot assume a negative value, you can declare it as an **unsigned long**. If an unsigned long variable occupies four bytes, it can assume a value in the range from 0 to 4,294,967,295. Because the value of New York City's population cannot be negative, it is safe to make the following declaration for the variable nyc_pop.

    unsigned long nyc_pop;

C++ also permits variables of the data type short int or, equivalently, short. Depending on the computer platform, a variable of type short occupies one or two bytes of storage and, therefore, has a value range from -128 to $+127$ or -32768 to $+32767$. Also, an **unsigned short int** or, equivalently, unsigned short has a range from 0 to 255 (1 byte) or from 0 to 65,535 (2 bytes).

Experiment 1 at the end of this section uses the sizeof operator to show how to determine exactly how many bytes are required to store the data types we have discussed. The only thing required of the C++ compiler relative to the number of bytes in which the different data types are stored is that sizeof(short) $\leq$ sizeof(int) $\leq$ sizeof(long).

The specific data type you choose for an integer variable depends on the kind (nonnegative only or not) and the range of values the variable can assume. Ensure that you choose the correct data type and be consistent in your program.

1.4.2 Mixing Data Types

C++ allows variables of different data types to appear in the same expression. To do arithmetic on the values of such an expression, C++ converts all the data to a common data type. The rules that C++ uses to decide this common data type are complex. Therefore, we shall not consider them. For now, however, the rule of Note 1.9 will suffice for our work.

> **Note 1.9   Expressions with Mixed Data Types**
>
> If an arithmetic expression contains mixed data types, to do the arithmetic, C++ converts all values to that of the most general type, that is, the type that will store the most values.

For example, suppose the following declarations.

```
short k = 3;
int   i = 8;
long  j = 56;
```

To evaluate the expression, i + j + k, C++ converts the value of i, which is an int, to the equivalent long because a long can store more values than an int. Then, C++ converts the value of k, which is a short, to the equivalent long. Finally, C++ adds the resulting values to the value of j.

The variable on the left of an assignment also can be of a different type than the expression on the right. For example, suppose we have the following declarations.

```
int    int1,
       int2;
long   long1,
       long2;
```

Then, the following assignment is valid.

```
long1 = int1 + int2;
```

C++ automatically attempts to convert the value of the expression on the right to the type of variable on the left of the assignment operator. The conversion is successful if the value of the expression on the right of the assignment is within the range of the variable type on the left of the assignment. The previous assignment is always valid because it is always valid to convert an int to a long.

However, the following assignment is valid only if the value of the expression on the right is within the range of an int variable.

```
int1 = long1 + long2;
```

If the value of long1 + long2 is not within the range of an int variable, an invalid result will be assigned to int1. The previous assignment will cause some compilers to issue a warning message.

1.4.3 Using the Other Integer Types: Problem 1.2

A taxi cab company has awarded a contract to the automobile repair outlet of Problem 1.1 to service its fleet of 103 taxi cabs. The repair company will bill the taxi company once a month for all the repairs it makes for the month. Change the program prb01-1.cpp so the user can enter the total cost of parts for the taxis for the entire month and the total number of hours for the month spent repairing the taxis.

Discussion of Problem 1.2

We can use the same prompts and calculations as those of prb01-1.cpp. However, we need to change the variable declarations. Over the period of one month the cost of parts for a fleet of 103 taxi cabs could exceed $32,767. Therefore, we should declare the variable parts as type long, which can store a value more than two billion. The other variables in prb01-1.cpp must also be redeclared as type long.

```cpp
// prb01-2.cpp
// This program calculates the total charge for parts and labor

#include <iostream>

using namespace std;

int main()
{
    const int HOURLY_RATE = 44;

    long parts,          // Cost of parts
         hours,          // Number of hours worked
         labor,          // Labor charge
         total;          // Total charge to customer

    // Obtain the input data

    cout << endl;
    cout << "Enter the cost of parts: ";
    cin >> parts;
    cout << endl;
    cout << "Enter the number of hours worked: ";
    cin >> hours;

    // Do the calculations

    labor = HOURLY_RATE * hours;
    total = parts + labor;

    // Display the results

    cout << endl;
    cout << "Cost of parts: " << setw(9) << parts << endl;
    cout << "Labor charge: " << setw(10) << labor << endl;
    cout << "-------------------------"       << endl;
    cout << "Total charge: " << setw(10) << total << endl;

    return 0;
}
```

Program Output

```
Enter the cost of parts: 52731
Enter the number of hours worked: 97
Cost of parts:      52731
Labor charge:        4268
-------------------------
Total charge:       56999
```

Exercises 1.4

In Exercises 1–5, state the type (or types) of integer variable that would be appropriate for storing the given quantity.

1. The number of cars that pass a given intersection during a 24-hour period
2. The yearly salary of a major-league baseball player
3. The temperature, to the nearest degree, outside your house at 12:00 noon on any given day of the year
4. The enrollment at your school during a typical fall semester
5. The balance, to the nearest dollar, in a checking account that has overdraft privileges of up to $2,000 (that is, you can write checks to a total of $2,000 more than your balance).

Experiments 1.4

1. Compile and execute the following program to determine how many bytes are required on your computer to store each of the data types discussed in this chapter.

```cpp
#include <iostream>
#include <iomanip>

using namespace std;

int main()
{
   cout << "On this computer a Short has " << sizeof(short)
        << " bytes." << endl;
   cout << "On this computer an Integer has " << sizeof(int)
        << " bytes." << endl;
   cout << "On this computer a Long has " << sizeof(long)
        << " bytes." << endl;
   return 0;
}
```

2. Consider the following program.

```cpp
#include <iostream>

using namespace std;

int main()
{
   int i1;
   long lg1, lg2;

   lg1 = 5000000;
   lg2 = 5000000;
   i1 = lg1 * lg2;

   cout << "The product of the longs " << lg1 << " and " << lg2
        << " is the int " << i1 << endl;

   return 0;
}
```

a. Compile and execute the program. Does your compiler issue any warning messages? What does the program display?

b. Try assigning the sum of two unsigned integers to a long, two integers to an unsigned, and so on. Does your compiler issue any warning messages? What does the program display in each case?

Programming Problems 1.4

In each program, be sure to use a type of integer variable that is suitable for the values it can assume. Also, use symbolic constants where appropriate.

1. Write a program that asks the user to enter the integer lengths (in inches) of the dimensions of a refrigerator shipping crate. The program should display the volume of the box in cubic inches.

2. A swimming-pool maintenance company resurfaces the inside surfaces of an inground concrete pool for $2 per square foot of surface area. Write a program to calculate what the company should charge to resurface a pool. The program should ask the user to input the length, width, and depth of the pool, each to the nearest foot. The program should display the cost of resurfacing the pool. The following formula gives the inside surface area of a pool.

$$\text{surface} = 2 * \text{depth} * (\text{length} + \text{width}) + \text{length} * \text{width}$$

3. Your pulse rate is the number of times your heart beats each minute (usually about 70 per minute for an adult and higher for children). Write a program that asks the user to enter his/her approximate age; first ask for the number of years, then the number of months. The program should display the approximate number of times the person's heart has beat since his or her birth. To do this, first calculate the approximate number of minutes the person has lived (2160 times the number of months entered, plus 525600 times the number of years entered). Then multiply the result by 80, which is the approximate average number of heartbeats per minute for a person throughout his or her lifetime. Make sure that the program gives valid results, even for a senior citizen.

4. A cattle feed company has two grades of feed, A and B. Feed A costs $2 per 100 pounds and feed B costs $3 per 100 pounds. Ranchers can order a mixture of feeds A and B. Write a program that calculates the charge for a feed order. The program should ask the user to enter the number of hundreds of pounds of feed A ordered and the number of hundreds of pounds of feed B ordered. The program should display the amount of each type of feed ordered and its cost, and the total cost of the order.

5. A minor-league baseball stadium has three types of seats. Bleacher seats cost $3 each, reserved seats cost $8 each, and box seats cost $12 each. Write a program that calculates the total revenue from gate receipts at the ballpark (that is, the total amount received by selling seats). The program should ask the user to enter the number of bleacher seats sold, the number of reserved seats sold, and the number of box seats sold. The program should display the total amount of revenue from the gate receipts.

6. Your city's parking violation bureau wants you to write a program to compute fines for parking violations. There are four types of violation: type A carries a fine of $10, type B carries a fine of $20, type C carries a fine of $30, and type D carries a fine of $50. The program should ask for the number of type A violations, the number of type B violations, and so on. The program should display the total fine for the person.

CHAPTER REVIEW

T E R M I N O L O G Y

Describe the meaning of each of the following terms.

keyword	`int`
flowchart	`endl`
Integrated Development Environment (IDE)	preprocessor
pseudocode	preprocessor directives
code	header file
syntax error	system header files
source program	name space
source code	`iostream`
machine language	reserved words
high-level language	`using namespace std;`
compiler	escape sequence
object program	newline character
external reference	identifiers
linker	variable
resolve	declaration
linking	data type
executable code	platform
program development cycle	`sizeof`
warnings	value of a variable
run-time error	value
logic error	garbage
faulty coding	prompt
comment	`cin`
function	extraction operator (>>)
`main ()`	input buffer
semicolon	flushing the input buffer
case sensitive	assignment operator
user-defined function	integer constant
standard library function	arithmetic operators
string	addition
data stream	subtraction
output stream	multiplication
`cout`	division
insertion operator (<<)	modulus/remainder

```
const                          long
setw()                         unsigned short
iomanip                        unsigned long
unsigned
short
```

SUMMARY

- Every C++ program contains a function `main()` that controls execution of the program.
- Every C++ statement must end in a semicolon (Note 1.1).
- Use the output stream `cout` and the insertion operator `<<` to display strings and variable values.
- Always code the preprocessor directive `#include <iostream>` in all your programs (Note 1.3).
- Always code the `using namespace std;` directive if your program conforms to the C++ standard.
- Send `endl` to the output stream to force the cursor to the beginning of a new line.
- An identifier can consist of up to 31 characters (uppercase and lowercase letters, digits, and the underscore). An identifier cannot begin with a digit nor can it be a keyword (Note 1.5).
- A variable is a named location in computer memory that stores a particular type of data.
- A variable declaration must begin with the variable's data type.
- The integer types are `int`, `unsigned`, `long`, `unsigned long`, `short`, and `unsigned short`.
- A nonzero integer constant cannot begin with the digit zero, nor contain a decimal point or a comma.
- Use `cin` and the extraction operator `>>` to obtain a datum from the input stream (that is, the keyboard) and place it into a variable.
- The arithmetic operators are +, -, *, /, and %.
- The arithmetic operators follow the usual precedence rules (Note 1.7).
- Use `const` to declare defined constants.
- The `setw()` I/O manipulator determines the width of the field in which `cout` places the next data item. To use `setw()`, use the preprocessor directive `#include <iomanip>` (Note 1.8).

REVIEW EXERCISES

1. Describe the steps in the program development cycle and the errors that can occur at each step.
2. How can you insert a comment in a C++ program?
3. What is a C++ program?
4. What is a keyword in C++?
5. What is the purpose of the word `int` before `main()`?
6. In what punctuation mark must each C++ statement end?
7. What is meant by saying that C++ is case sensitive?

8. What data stream can you use to output data? What operator should you use with that data stream?

9. What is the preprocessor and what is it used for? What is a preprocessor directive and how do you code one?

10. What is a header file and which one should you include in each of your C++ programs?

11. What is an identifier and what are the rules for naming an identifier?

12. What is a variable and how do you declare one?

13. What data stream can you use to input data? What operator should you use with that data stream?

14. What are the five basic arithmetic operators in C++?

15. What are the arithmetic operator precedence rules?

16. What is pseudocode and how is it useful in program development?

17. What is the purpose of the keyword `const`?

18. What is an I/O manipulator? What header file do you have to include to use one?

19. What are the integer data types and how do they differ?

Chapter 2

Real Numbers

OBJECTIVES

- To declare `float` and `double` variables
- To use `cin` to input and `cout` to display decimal numbers nicely formatted
- To solve problems involving decimal numbers
- To use mixed-mode arithmetic expressions and type casts
- To understand the value of a C++ expression
- To use the compound assignment, increment, and decrement operators

Besides integers, C++ also allows variables to store real numbers. Dollar and cents amounts, which are used in most business programs, are examples of real numbers. This chapter shows how to declare and use real numbers in a C++ program.

The C++ programming language has many operators. Chapter 1 discussed the basic arithmetic operators of addition, subtraction, multiplication, and division of integers. In this chapter, we extend the use of these operators to real numbers. We also discuss several additional arithmetic operators that enable the programmer to code some common types of statements more compactly.

2.1 REAL NUMBERS

2.1.1 Real-Number Variables and Constants

A **real**, or **floating point**, **number** is one that has a fractional part. That is, a floating point number is one that has a decimal point. There are two floating point data types in C++—`float` and `double`. The following declarations define the variable f1 to be of type `float` and the variable db to be of type `double`.

```
float f1;
double db;
```

The two floating point types differ in their **precision** (that is, the number of significant digits that each type stores) and in the amount of storage each type requires. On most computers, a variable of type float occupies four bytes and has a precision of seven digits. A variable of type double occupies eight bytes and has a precision of 15 digits. See Experiment 1 at the end of this section.

The following are examples of valid **floating point constants**.

8.45

–1298.45678

+0.68

15.

Just as for integer constants, a floating point constant may be preceded by a + or – to show its sign. If you omit the sign, C++ considers the sign to be plus. Also, like integer constants, a floating point constant cannot contain a comma. However, a floating point constant must contain a decimal point, even if the decimal point is not followed by a digit as in the last constant listed.

The following are examples of invalid floating point constants.

3,620.78

195

The first number contains a comma and is, therefore, invalid. The second number does not contain a decimal point and so is not a floating point constant. However, the number is a valid integer constant. The C++ compiler always stores floating point constants as type double.

You can initialize a floating point variable in its declaration with the value of a floating point constant. For example,

```
float   fl =   3.14159;
double db = -0.0023156;
```

Note that the preceding declaration of fl will usually result in a compiler warning message about possible truncation. See "Metric Conversion—Problem 2.3" in Section 2.2 for a way to avoid the message.

Floating point variables can appear in arithmetic statements in the same way as integer variables. For example, consider the following declarations and assignment.

```
double db1 = 3.14159,
       db2 = -83.01267,
       db3;
db3 = 2 * db1 + db2;
```

The assignment gives the value –76.72949 to the variable db3. The expression on the right of the assignment operator contains mixed data types. Before it carries out the arithmetic, the computer automatically converts the integer 2 appearing in the expression on the right of the assignment to a floating point 2.0. Then the computer multiplies the value of db1 by 2.0, which gives 6.28318. Finally, the computer adds this result to the value of db2, which gives –76.72949. The computer then assigns the result to db3. (See the discussions of Problems 2.2 and 2.3 for further information on mixed data types in arithmetic expressions.)

Because we are interested mostly in business applications in the text, we will always use type `double`. Type `float` has only about seven-digit precision, so you cannot accurately store a dollar-and-cents amount value greater than 99,999.99. Because most modern business transactions involve numbers larger than $100,000.00, type `float` is inadequate. Type `double`, having about 15-digit precision, can store accurately even the national debt.

2.1.2 Input and Output of Real Numbers

To input a real number, use `cin` with a variable of type `float` or `double`. The user must enter a number (optionally preceded by a + or –) that can include a decimal point, but cannot include a comma. If the number the user enters does not contain a decimal point, for example 216, `cin` automatically converts the integer to the equivalent floating point number, 216.0.

Consider the following simple example. Suppose that a program contains the following declaration and code, and that the user enters 356.091 in response to the prompt.

```
double db;
cout << "Enter a floating point number: ";
cin >> db;
```

Suppose we now want to display the value of db. The `cout` statement

```
cout << "The value of db is " << db << endl;
```

displays the following.

```
The value of db is 356.091
```

2.1.3 Outputting Decimal Numbers

Because decimal numbers can be displayed in various ways (different number of digits to the right of the decimal, trailing zeros, and so on), outputting decimal numbers is more involved than outputting integers. Because most of our programs will involve dollar-and-cents amounts, we shall adopt the contents of Note 2.1. Section 2.4 at the end of this chapter explains the purpose of each line of code in Note 2.1.

Note 2.1   Displaying Dollar-and-Cents Amounts

Include the following statement at the beginning of any program that displays dollar-and-cents amounts.

```
cout << setprecision(2)
     << setiosflags(ios::fixed)
     << setiosflags(ios::showpoint);
```

To use this statement, you must also include the header file `iomanip` with the following statement at the beginning of your program.

```
#include <iomanip>
```

The single, three-line cout statement of Note 2.1 will ensure nice, readable output from the programs we write that output dollar-and-cents amounts. See dem02-1.cpp, which follows.

2.1.4 Calculating Sales Tax—dem02-1.cpp

The following program illustrates the ideas we have discussed so far. A retailer wants to know how much an item's selling price will be after adding the sales tax. Assume that the sales tax rate is 8.25%. The program dem02-1.cpp uses floating point arithmetic to do the necessary calculations.

```cpp
// dem02-1.cpp
// This program calculates the sales tax and price of an item.

#include <iostream>
#include <iomanip>

using namespace std;

int main()
{
    const double TAX_RATE = 0.0825;
    double base_price,          // The price of the item
           tax,                 // The tax on the item
           price;               // The selling price (price + tax)

    //Set up output stream for currency output
    cout << setprecision(2)
         << setiosflags(ios::fixed)
         << setiosflags(ios::showpoint);

    cout << "Enter the price of the item: ";
    cin >> base_price;

    tax = base_price * TAX_RATE;
    price = base_price + tax;

    cout << endl;
    cout << "The base price is" << setw(11) << base_price << endl;
    cout << "The tax is" << setw(18) << tax << endl;
    cout << "The price is" << setw(16) << price << endl;

    return 0;
}
```

Program Output

```
Enter the price of the item: 100.00

The base price is      100.00
The tax is               8.25
The price is           108.25
```

The sales tax rate of 8.25% as a decimal is 0.0825. The program uses `const double` to declare the defined constant TAX_RATE, whose value equals 0.0825.

The program requires three variables. The variable `base_price` stores the number input by the user. The variables `tax` and `price` store the amount of the sales tax and the total price of the item (`base_price + tax`).

Because all three variables store dollar-and-cents amounts (that is, decimal numbers), we declare all three variables as type `double`. We use type `double` instead of type `float` for two reasons. First, a type `double` has more precision than a type `float`. Therefore, arithmetic with variables of type `double` is generally more accurate than arithmetic with variables of type `float`. Second, most computers automatically convert floats to doubles, then do the arithmetic, and finally convert the result from type `double` back to type `float`. Using type `double` in the first place avoids these conversions.

Inputting the base price and doing the calculations are straightforward. Note the use of the defined constant TAX_RATE in the first assignment statement.

The `setw(11)` in the `cout` that displays the base price creates a field that can hold a number with as many as eight digits to the left of the decimal. (The decimal point and the two digits to the right of the decimal account for the other three positions in the field.) Therefore, a number as large as 99999999.99 can appear in the field. The `setw(18)` and `setw(16)` in the next two `cout` statements force the alignment of the decimal points of the three numbers. See Figure 2.1. Remember that if a number has more digits than the field width allows, `cout` displays the number in its entirety. In this case, the numbers may not align correctly when `cout` displays them. See Experiment 3. In Section 3.4, "Definite Iteration," we show how to use `setw()` to arrange output in column form.

Exercises 2.1

In Exercises 1–10, find the value that the expression assigns to the variable on the left of the assignment operator. Work each problem independently of the others. Assume the following declarations.

```
double d1 =    3.167,
       d2 = -41.823,
       d3 =    0.2513,
       result;
```

1. `result = 2.4 + 3.1 * d1;`
2. `result = d1 - (d2 - d3);`

The base price is	100. 00	Field of width 11
The tax is	8.25	Field of width 18
The price is	108.25	Field of width 16

Figure 2.1

3. `result = d2 / d1 + 4 * d3;`

4. `result = d1 * d2 * d3;`

5. `result = d1 * d1 * d1;`

6. `d1 = d1 + 2.089;`

7. `d1 = d2 - d3;`

8. `d2 = d2 * d2;`

9. `d2 = d1 * 4.53 + 47.1;`

10. `d3 = d3 - d3;`

In Exercises 11–15, find exactly what each `cout` statement displays. Assume the following declarations and `cout` statement.

```
double d1 = 285.3451,
       d2 = -51.768465,
       d3 =   0.0036245;

cout << setprecision(2)
     << setiosflags(ios::fixed)
     << setiosflags(ios::showpoint);
```

11. `cout << d1 << d2;`

12. `cout << d1 << " " << d2;`

13. `cout << setw(10) << d1 << setw(10) << d2;`

14. `cout << setw(11) << d1 << setw(11) << d3;`

15. `cout << setprecision(4) << setw(11) << d1 << setw(11) << d3;`

Experiments 2.1

For each experiment concerning dem02-1.cpp, start with a fresh copy and make the indicated changes.

1. Compile and execute the following program to see how many bytes variables of type `float` and `double` occupy on your computer.

```
#include <iostream>
using namespace std;
int main()
{
   cout << "On this computer a float occupies this many bytes "
        << sizeof(float) << endl;
   cout << "On this computer a double occupies this many bytes "
        << sizeof(double) << endl;

   return 0;
}
```

2. Defining the sales tax rate as a defined constant limits the program dem02-1.cpp. Different localities have different sales tax rates even within the same state.

Recode dem02-1.cpp so it prompts the user for the sales tax rate. Use this sales tax rate in the calculation of the tax.

3. In dem02-1.cpp, enter 950000000.00 in response to the prompt. What happens to the output? Recode the program so that if the user enters 950000000.00 in response to the prompt, the program vertically aligns the displayed numbers on the right. Compile and execute the resulting program.

4. Algebraically, what should the following program display? Compile and execute the program. What does the program display? Can you explain why?

```
#include <iostream>
#include <iomanip>

using namespace std;

int main()
{
   cout << setprecision(8)
        << setiosflags(ios::fixed)
        << setiosflags(ios::showpoint);

   double db;
   db = 3.0 * (1.0 / 3.0);
   cout << "db = " << setw(10) << db << endl;
   return 0;
}
```

5. Not all real numbers are representable on a computer because of the limited precision of floating point numbers. Compile and execute the following program.

```
#include <iostream>
#include <iomanip>

using namespace std;

int main()
{
   cout << setprecision(12)
        << setiosflags(ios::fixed)
        << setiosflags(ios::showpoint);

   float fl1 = 1.2345678,
         fl2 = 1.2345679;

   cout << "fl1 = " << setw(15) << fl1 << endl;
   cout << "fl2 = " << setw(15) << fl2 << endl;

   return 0;
}
```

What numbers are output? Can you explain why? What does the output tell you about the number of digits stored in a float-type variable?

6. Code, compile, and execute a program similar to the one of Experiment 4 that will enable you to decide how many digits your computer stores in a variable of type double.

Programming Problems 2.1

1. Write a program that asks the user to enter the prices of two items. The program should then apply a 7.5% discount to the sum of the prices. The program should display the two prices, the sum of the two prices, the discount (7.5% of the sum of the prices) and the discounted price (the sum of the prices minus the discount).

2. Write a program that asks the user to enter a student's grades on four exams. The program should display the four grades and the average of the four grades, rounded to the nearest tenth.

3. The State Highway Traffic Violations Bureau wants you to write a program to compute the amount of a moving violation. The program should prompt the user to enter the illegal speed in miles per hour at which the person was driving. Calculate the fine as follows: $50.00 plus $5 for each mile per hour over the legal limit of 55.

4. Write a program that asks the user to enter a student's mid-term and final exam scores. The program should display the mid-term and final exam scores and the final grade of the student. Compute the final grade by taking the sum of 40% of the mid-term exam score and 60% of the final exam score.

5. A bank teller needs a program to total the amount of money in his coin tray. Write a program that asks the user to enter the number of each type of U.S. coin (half-dollars, quarters, nickels, dimes, and pennies) and that displays the total value of the coins in dollars and cents.

6. An account executive must keep track of her expenses on a business trip. Write a program that totals the executive's expenses. The program should ask the user to enter the number of miles driven (calculate this expense by multiplying the number of miles driven by 0.30, that is, 30 cents per mile), the amount spent on highway tolls and parking, the amount spent on meals, the amount spent on lodging, and the amount spent on entertainment.

2.2 SOLVING PROBLEMS WITH REAL NUMBERS

In this section, we state and solve three problems that involve real numbers. In doing so, we discuss how C++ evaluates expressions that contain variables of different data types. We also discuss how to alter the data type of a constant or variable by using a type cast.

2.2.1 Simulating a Cash Register—Problem 2.1

The C++-Side Restaurant wants you to write a program that simulates a simple cash register. The program should ask the user to enter the price of the meal. The program should calculate the sales tax (8.25% of the meal price) and add it to the price to obtain the total price, which it should display for the user. The program is then to ask for the amount tendered, that is, the amount the customer gives to pay the bill. After the user enters the amount tendered, the program should display the amount tendered, the total price of the meal, and the change.

2.2.2 Program Design

The program design follows the steps outlined in the statement of the problem. Following is a pseudocode solution to the problem.

Pseudocode for Problem 2.1

> Obtain the meal price.
>
> Calculate the tax and total price of the meal.
>
> Display the price, tax, and total.
>
> Obtain the amount tendered.
>
> Calculate the change.
>
> Display the amount tendered, total price, and change.

This program requires five variables. Because the variables store dollar-and-cents amounts, they will all be floating point variables. As we did in dem02-1.cpp, all the variables will be declared as type `double`. We need the variable `meal_price` to store the price of the meal. The variables `sales_tax` and `total` store the amount of the sales tax (8.25% of `meal_price`) and the total price of the meal (`meal_price + sales_tax`). Finally, the variable `amt_tendered` stores the amount the customer gives to pay for the meal and the variable `change` stores the change (`amt_tendered - total`) that the customer receives.

2.2.3 The Program prb02-1.cpp

Following is the program solution to Problem 2.1.

```cpp
// prb02-1.cpp
// This program simulates a simple cash register.
#include <iostream>
#include <iomanip>

using namespace std;

int main()
{
   const double SALES_TAX_RATE = 0.0825;

   double meal_price,       // Price of meal entered by user
          sales_tax,        // Amount of sales tax
          total,            // Total bill: meal_price + sales_tax
          amt_tendered,     // Amount received from customer
          change;           // Change: amt_tendered - total

   // Set up output stream for currency output
   cout << setprecision(2)
        << setiosflags(ios::fixed)
        << setiosflags(ios::showpoint);

   // Display banner and obtain price
   cout << "*** C++-Side Restaurant ***" << endl << endl;
   cout << "Enter the price of the meal: $";
```

```
cin >> meal_price;
cout << endl;

// Calculate tax and total price
sales_tax = meal_price * SALES_TAX_RATE;
total = meal_price + sales_tax;

// Display price tax and total
cout << endl;
cout << "Price of Meal: " << setw(6) << meal_price << endl;
cout << "Sales Tax: " << setw(10) << sales_tax << endl;
cout << "---------------------" << endl;
cout << "Total Amount: " << setw(7) << total << endl;

// Obtain amount tendered
cout << endl;
cout << "Enter amount tendered: $";
cin >> amt_tendered;
cout << endl;

// Calculate change
change = amt_tendered - total;

// Display amounts and change
cout << endl;
cout << "Amount Tendered: $" << setw(7) << amt_tendered
        << endl;
cout << "Total Amount:       $" << setw(7) << total << endl;
cout << "-------------------------" << endl;
cout << "Change:             $" << setw(7) << change << endl;

// Print closing banner
cout << endl << endl;
cout << "*** Thank You ***" << endl;

return 0;
}
```

Program Output

```
*** C++-Side Restaurant ***

Enter the price of the meal: $52.95

Price of Meal:   52.95
Sales Tax:        4.37
---------------------
Total Amount:    57.32

Enter amount tendered: $70.00

Amount Tendered: $   70.00
Total Amount:    $   57.32
```

```
    ------------------------
Change:            $   12.68
*** Thank You ***
```

2.2.4 Discussion of prb02-1.cpp

The program code closely follows the pseudocode for the problem. First, the program displays an opening banner giving the name of the restaurant. Next, it prompts the user to enter the amount of the meal, and then calculates the sales tax and the total amount of the meal. Then, the program prompts the user to enter the amount tendered, calculates the amount of the change due the customer, and displays the results. Finally, the program displays a closing banner. Note that the program uses the setw() manipulator to force alignment of the decimal points.

If prb02-1.cpp were to be used commercially, users would soon notice several serious flaws in the program. First, the program does not check the amounts input by the user to see if they are valid. For example, suppose the user enters 2w.75 for the meal price instead of 23.75. How would the program behave? It certainly would not give the correct total price. See Experiment 1. What would happen if the amount tendered were less than the total cost of the meal? See Experiment 2.

The necessity of validating input data makes even simple problems a good deal more challenging. As we work through the book, we will discuss some data validation techniques. When writing a program that will be used by others, you must keep in mind to program defensively. Assume the user will make mistakes at every opportunity. Try to design your program so that it can recover from these mistakes.

2.2.5 Averaging Quiz Grades—Problem 2.2

Your instructor wants you to write a program that averages the three quiz grades you have taken this semester. Write a program that prompts the user for three integer quiz grades, calculates the average of the three grades, and displays the average to the nearest tenth.

2.2.6 Program Design—Mixed Types and Type Casts

At first, calculating an average appears to be a simple problem. Following is a pseudocode solution.

Pseudocode for Problem 2.2

      Obtain the three quiz grades.

      Calculate the quiz average.

      Display the quiz average.

The difficulty in the program lies in the types of variables it uses. The problem statement requires that each quiz grade be an integer and that the program display the average as a real number accurate to the nearest tenth. Therefore, the quiz grades should be of type `int` and the average of type `double`. Suppose we code the following declarations.

```
int     quiz1,          // Quiz 1 grade
        quiz2,          // Quiz 2 grade
        quiz3;          // Quiz 3 grade
double  average;        // Average of the three quiz grades
```

After obtaining the values of the quiz grades from the user, suppose the program calculates the average by the following assignment.

```
average = (quiz1 + quiz2 + quiz3) / 3;
```

The parentheses around the sum of the quiz grades are necessary because the program must add the quiz grades before dividing the sum by three. If the parentheses were not present—`quiz1 + quiz2 + quiz3 / 3`—by the order of operations rules, `quiz3` would be divided by three and then the values of `quiz1` and `quiz2` would be added to that result.

If the sum of the three quiz grades is not divisible by three, this assignment might not place the correct value into `average`. The three variables, `quiz1`, `quiz2`, and `quiz3`, and the constant that the sum is divided by, 3, are of type `int`. Therefore, the computer does integer arithmetic when evaluating the right side of the assignment. The computer discards any remainder that results from the division before making the assignment to `average`. If the user enters 78, 91, and 82 in response to the prompts, the actual average will be $(78 + 91 + 82)/3 = 251/3 = 83.66666$. However, in integer arithmetic, the result of 251 / 3 is the quotient 83. The remainder, 2, is discarded. Therefore, the computer assigns the result of the integer arithmetic, 83, to `average`. The specifications of the problem, however, require that this average be computed as 83.7, a decimal number rounded to the nearest tenth.

To correct this problem, we must force the computer to do floating point arithmetic when evaluating the expression to the right of the assignment operator. There are two ways to do this. One way is to mix the data types that appear in the expression. We cannot directly change the data types of the quiz grades. (We can change the type indirectly, as we shall see shortly.) However, we can change the data type of the constant that appears in the division. Suppose we recode the assignment as follows.

```
average = (quiz1 + quiz2 + quiz3) / 3.0;
```

Now, we have a **mixed-mode expression**, which is an expression containing mixed data types: an integer, namely the sum of the three quiz grades, divided by a floating point constant. The computer now carries out the arithmetic according to the rule of Note 2.2.

Note 2.2   Data Type Conversions in an Expression

When an arithmetic expression contains numbers of type `int` or `long` and numbers of type `float` or `double`, C++ automatically converts all the numbers to type `double` before doing the arithmetic. The result, therefore, is of type `double`.

Thus, because of the floating point constant 3.0 in the new expression, the computer automatically converts the sum of the quiz grades to a `double` before dividing the sum by 3.0. Then the computer assigns the result, which is of type `double`, to `average` with no loss of its fractional part. Using the grades 78, 91, and 82 as before, the number 83.66666 will be assigned to `average`. See Experiment 3.

The second way to force the computer to do floating point arithmetic in the arithmetic expression is to use a **type cast**. A type cast is one of C++'s data types followed by an expression enclosed in parentheses. A type cast changes the data type of the value of the expression in parentheses to the type specified. If we declare

```
int i = 5;
```

then `double(i)` casts the value of i, that is, converts the value of i to the `double` 5.0.

To correct the assignment involving the average, we could code the following.

```
average = double(quiz1 + quiz2 + quiz3) / 3;
```

The cast `double()` converts the value of the sum of the quiz grades to the equivalent floating point number before the computer divides this value by the integer constant 3. We now have an expression that contains mixed types, so Note 2.2 applies. The computer converts the integer constant 3 to the equivalent double 3.0 and then carries out the arithmetic.

We also can type cast a constant. The assignment to average could be coded as follows.

```
average = (quiz1 + quiz2 + quiz3) / double(3);
```

This is equivalent to the first way in which we corrected this problem. See Experiment 4. Type casting has several other important applications, which we shall encounter later.

Note that you can also type cast by enclosing the type in parentheses and placing the result before the expression. Therefore, `(double)sum` is equivalent to `double(sum)`, and `(double)3` is equivalent to `double(3)`.

Another way to solve the truncation problem is to disregard the requirement that the quiz grades be integers. We could declare the three quiz grade variables to be of type `double`. In this way, the `cin` statements would convert the integers entered by the user to the equivalent floating point numbers. Thus, according to Note 2.2, the computer would carry out the arithmetic in the following assignment statement in floating point.

```
average = (quiz1 + quiz2 + quiz3) / 3;
```

Although this solution works (see Experiment 5), it is not completely acceptable. The solution does not conform to the specifications of the problem, which require the grades to be integers. It is very important to conform to a problem's specifications unless you have a compelling reason not to do so. Deviating from a problem's specifications often leads programmers to solve a related, but wrong, problem. If you want to change a problem's specifications, get permission to do so from the person who gave you the problem.

2.2.7 The Program prb02-2.cpp

Following is the program code that solves Problem 2.2. We use the method of type casting the sum of the quiz grades to force floating point arithmetic. Note that we include statements at the beginning of `main()` to cause the average to be displayed to the nearest tenth.

```
#include <iostream>
#include <iomanip>

using namespace std;

int main()
{
    int  quiz1,          // Quiz 1 grade
         quiz2,          // Quiz 2 grade
         quiz3;          // Quiz 3 grade
    double average;      // Average of the three quize grades

    // Setup output stream for one decimal place

    cout << setprecision(1)
         << setiosflags(ios::fixed)
         << setiosflags(ios::showpoint);

    cout << "Enter the grade for Quiz 1: ";
    cin >> quiz1;
    cout << "Enter the grade for Quiz 2: ";
    cin >> quiz2;
    cout << "Enter the grade for Quiz 3: ";
    cin >> quiz3;

    // The type cast double() is required to convert the sum of the
    // quiz grades, which is an integer, to a floating point. Failure
    // to convert the expression on the right of the assignment would
    // result in the average being truncated to an integer.

    average = double (quiz1 + quiz2 + quiz3) / 3;

    cout << endl;
    cout << "The average of the three quizzes is " << average << endl;
    return 0;
}
```

Program Output

```
Enter the grade for Quiz 1: 84
Enter the grade for Quiz 2: 78
Enter the grade for Quiz 3: 95

The average of the three quizzes is 85.7
```

2.2.8 Metric Conversion—Problem 2.3

Many people have trouble thinking in terms of metric units. Write a program that converts a distance in miles and feet, entered as integers, to the equivalent distance in kilometers and meters. One mile equals 1.60935 kilometers. One foot equals 0.30480 meters. The program should ask the user to enter the number of miles and the number of feet to convert. The program should display the equivalent number of kilometers and meters as integers.

The solution to the preceding problem involves some complicated arithmetic with integers and floating point numbers. It also illustrates expressions having mixed data types and data conversions across the assignment operator.

2.2.9 Program Design

The design of this program is simple, as the following pseudocode illustrates.

Pseudocode for Problem 2.3.

Obtain the number of miles and feet from the user.

Convert miles and feet to kilometers and meters.

Display the equivalent number of kilometers and meters.

The difficult part of this problem is the arithmetic it requires. The integer variables `miles`, `feet`, `kilometers`, and `meters` will store the corresponding distances. Two `cin` statements will input values for the variables `miles` and `feet`. The problem is how to convert these to the equivalent number of kilometers and meters.

The strategy is first to convert the total distance to the equivalent number of meters. Then, convert the number of meters to kilometers and meters. To show how to do this, we consider an example.

In the following discussion, we use the abbreviations ft for feet, m for meters, and km for kilometers. Suppose the user enters 2 for the number of miles and 1000 for the number of feet. To convert the number of feet to meters, multiply the value of `feet` (1000) by the number of meters per foot, 0.30480. In our example this gives the following: 1000 ft $\times$ 0.30480 m/ft = 304.80 m. To convert the number of miles to meters, multiply the value of `miles` by the number of meters per mile. (The number of meters per mile is calculated as follows: 1.60935 km/mile $\times$ 1000 m/km = 1609.35 m/mile because there are 1000 meters in a kilometer.) In our example, therefore, the number of meters in 2 miles is 2 miles $\times$ 1609.35 m/mile = 3218.7 m. Now, add these two results and obtain the total distance in meters. This gives 3218.7 m + 304.80 m = 3523.50 m.

We store the answer to the previous calculation in the variable `total_meters`, which is of type `double`. The following assignment statement incorporates the calculations of the previous paragraph.

```
total_meters = miles * 1609.35 + feet * 0.30480;
```

Thus the value of `total_meters` is 3523.50m.

Now convert this number of meters to kilometers and meters. To convert from meters to kilometers, divide the number of meters by 1000. In our example, the result is 3523.50 m $\div$ 1000 m/km = 3.52350 km. We store this result in the variable `total_kilometers`, which is of type `double`. The following assignment statement does this calculation.

```
total_kilometers = total_meters / 1000;
```

Now convert the distance in kilometers, 3.52350km in our example, to the equivalent number of integer kilometers and meters. To do this, we take advantage of C++'s ability to convert types across the assignment operator.

When the data type of the value of the right side of an assignment differs from the data type of the variable on the left of the assignment, C++ tries to convert the right side's value to the type of the variable on the left. For example, suppose the following declarations.

```
int             i1 = 17,
                i2 = 5,
                i3;
double          d1 = 9.74,
                d2;
```

The assignment,

```
d2 = i1 + i2;
```

results in the double 22.0 being assigned to d2. The value of the right side is the integer 22. When this is assigned to the double d2, C++ converts the integer 22 to the equivalent double 22.0.

The assignment,

```
i3 = d1;
```

results in the integer 9 being assigned to i3. The value of the right side is the double 9.74. When this is assigned to the integer i3, C++ converts 9.74 into an integer. C++ does this by truncating the double to the integer 9.

Note 2.3   Data Type Conversions Across an Assignment

In arithmetic assignments, when the data type of the right side differs from the data type of the left side, C++ converts the value of the right side to the data type of the variable on the left side.

This conversion also takes place where you might not expect it to. Consider for example the following declaration and initialization:

```
float f = 1.23;
```

The variable f is of type float. However, the floating point constant 1.23 is automatically considered by C++ to be of type double. Therefore, the computer must convert the double 1.23 to the equivalent float. Also, some compilers will issue a warning that truncation can occur in such an initialization. To avoid having the computer make the conversion and avoid the possible compiler warning, postfix the constant with the type specifier F as follows.

```
float f = 1.23F;
```

Thus, 1.23F would be considered as type float so no conversion takes place and no compiler warnings are issued.

Recall that the variable `kilometers` is of type `int`. By Note 2.3 the assignment

```
kilometers = total_kilometers;
```

causes the computer to truncate the decimal part of `total_kilometers` before it assigns the equivalent integer to the variable `kilometers`. Thus, in our example, the above assignment gives `kilometers` the value 3.

Now convert the decimal part of `total_kilometers` to the equivalent number of meters. To get rid of the integer part of `total_kilometers`, subtract the value of `kilometers` from `total_kilometers`. In our example, this gives $3.52350-3 = 0.52350$ km. Multiplying this result by 1000 gives the equivalent number of meters: 0.52350 km $\times$ 1000 m/km $= 523.50$ m. To truncate the fractional part of this answer, assign it to a variable of type `int`. Experiment 6 shows how to round this answer to the nearest meter.

The following assignment statement gives the variable `meters` the value 523.

```
meters = (total_kilometers - kilometers) * 1000;
```

Thus, in our example, a distance of 2 miles, 1000 feet is equivalent to approximately 3 kilometers, 523 meters.

2.2.10 The Program prb02-3.cpp

Following is the program code that solves Problem 2.3. The program uses the formulas we developed in the previous subsection. Defined constants represent the conversion factors.

```cpp
// prb02-3.cpp
#include <iostream>
using namespace std;
int main()
{
    const double M_PER_MILE = 1609.35;
    const double M_PER_FOOT = 0.30480;

    int   miles,
          feet,
          kilometers,
          meters;
    double total_meters,
           total_kilometers;

    // Obtain data from user
    cout << "Enter the number of miles: ";
    cin >> miles;
    cout << "Enter the number of feet: ";
    cin >> feet;

    // Convert everything to meters
    total_meters = miles * M_PER_MILE + feet * M_PER_FOOT;

    // Calculate the number of kilometers
    total_kilometers = total_meters / 1000;
```

```
        kilometers = total_kilometers;        // truncates to integer
        // Convert decimal part of total_kilometers to meters
        meters = (total_kilometers - kilometers) * 1000;

        // Display results
        cout << endl;
        cout << "The distance is " << kilometers << " kilometers, "
            << meters << " meters." << endl;
        return 0;
    }
```

Program Output

```
Enter the number of miles: 2
Enter the number of feet: 1000

The distance is 3 kilometers, 523 meters.
```

Exercises 2.2

Use the following declarations in Exercises 1–6. Do each exercise independently of the others. In each case, find the value that the expression assigns to the variable on the left of the assignment operator.

```
    int     i = 5,
            j = 3,
            k;
    double x = 8.95,
           y = 15.4,
           z;
```

1. k = y * x;
2. k = int(y) * int(x);
3. k = i * j / 2;
4. z = i * j / 2;
5. z = double(i * j / 2);
6. z = double(i) * j / 2;

Experiments 2.2

1. Compile and execute prb02-1.cpp. Enter 2w.75 in response to the first prompt. What happens?
2. Compile and execute prb02-1.cpp. Enter 23.75 for the price of the meal and 20.00 for the amount tendered. What happens?
3. Change the assignment statement in prb02-2.cpp to the following.

```
    average = (quiz1 + quiz2 + quiz3) / 3.0;
```

Compile and execute the resulting program, entering 70, 94, and 87 as the three quiz grades. Does the program run correctly?

4. Change the assignment statement in prb02-2.cpp to the following.

```
average = (quiz1 + quiz2 + quiz3) / double(3);
```

Compile and execute the resulting program, entering 70, 94, and 87 as the three quiz grades. Does the program run correctly?

5. Change prb02-2.cpp by declaring all variables to be of type double. Compile and execute the resulting program, entering 70, 94, and 87 as the three quiz grades. Does the program run correctly?

6. The last assignment statement in prb02-3.cpp truncates the number of meters. Recode prb02-3.cpp so that the program rounds rather than truncates the number of meters. To do this, add 0.5 to the value appearing on the right of the assignment. Compile and execute the resulting program, inputting 2 miles and 1000 feet as the distance to convert. Does the program properly round the number of meters to 524? If so, explain why adding 0.5 works.

Programming Problems 2.2

1. Write a program that asks the user to enter the weight of a box of cereal to the nearest tenth of an ounce. The program should then display the equivalent weight of the box measured to the nearest tenth of a gram. One ounce is equivalent to 28.349527 grams.

2. Write a program that asks the user to enter his/her weight in pounds. The program should display the person's weight in kilograms. One pound equals 0.453592 kilograms.

3. If you invest P dollars, the principal, for t years in an account that earns simple interest at the annual interest rate of r, then the formula $I = P*r*t$ gives the total interest I that the investment earns. The total amount A in the account after t years is the principal plus the interest, or $A = P + I = P + P*r*t$. Write a program that asks the user to enter the principal, the interest rate as a percent (for example, 7.5), and the number of years at interest. The program should display the interest and the total amount in the account after the given number of years. Be sure to have the program convert the percent entered to the corresponding decimal before using it in the calculations.

4. Write a program that calculates the miles per gallon that the user gets on her car during a vacation trip. The program should ask the user to enter the number of miles traveled and the number of gallons of fuel consumed. The program should display the number of miles per gallon achieved on the trip.

5. Some self-service gas stations require that you pay for the gas before you pump it. If you want to fill your tank, you must estimate the cost of the amount of gas that you require. Suppose you know how many miles per gallon (mpg) your car gets on average and the number of miles (miles) you have traveled since your last fill-up. Then miles/mpg equals the number of gallons consumed and, therefore, the number of gallons you require for a fill-up. Multiply this number by the price

per gallon to obtain the estimate for the cost of filling up your gas tank. Write a program that calculates the cost of the gas required to fill your tank. The program should ask the user to enter the miles per gallon the car gets on average, the number of miles traveled since the last fill-up, and the price per gallon of gasoline. The program should display the cost of filling up the tank.

6. Write a program that converts pounds and ounces to kilograms and grams. One pound is 0.453592 kilograms or 453.592 grams. One ounce is 28.349527 grams. The program should ask the user to enter the number of pounds and ounces, and then should display the equivalent number of kilograms and grams. (Hint: Convert everything to grams first.)

2.3 MORE ON ARITHMETIC

2.3.1 The Value of an Expression

Note 2.4 states a very important principle of the C++ language.

Note 2.4   Every Expression Has a Value

Every expression in C++ has a numeric value.

The most basic application of Note 2.4 is that the expression on the right side of an assignment has a value. For example, suppose we have the following declaration and assignment statements.

```
int i1,
    i2,
    result;
i1 = 3;
i2 = 6;
result = i1 + 2 * i2;
```

The expression to the right of the assignment operator in the third assignment has the value 15, which the statement assigns to the variable `result`.

Note 2.4 also explains why we can send an arithmetic expression to cout. For example, using the previous declarations, consider the following cout statement, which displays the value of the expression `i1 + 2 * i2`, namely 15.

```
cout << "The value of result is " << i1 + 2 * i2 << endl;
```

An assignment is also an expression and, consequently, by Note 2.4, has a value.

Note 2.5   The Value of an Assignment

The value of an assignment is the value assigned.

Therefore, the entire assignment i1 = 3; has the value 3. The assignment i2 = 6 has the value 6. Note 2.5 allows us to code some odd-looking statements. For example, using the previous declarations, the following is a valid assignment statement.

result = (i1 = 9) + (i2 = 7);

The parentheses force the computer to make the assignment i1 = 9 first. The value of this assignment, by Note 2.5, is 9. Then the computer makes the second assignment i2 = 7, which itself has a value of 7. Next, the computer adds the values of the two assignments and assigns 16 to the variable result.

That you can code such assignment statements does not mean that you should! Statements like the preceding one are not easy to understand, so you should avoid coding them.

In the next section, and in several other places in this book, we shall discuss several important applications of Notes 2.4 and 2.5.

2.3.2 Multiple Assignment Statements

It is sometimes necessary to assign the same value to two or more variables. For example, suppose that a program must initialize the variables sum and count to zero. We could do this in two assignments as follows.

sum = 0;
count = 0;

Another way to make the assignments is to use a **multiple assignment statement** such as the following, which places the value zero into both variables, sum and count.

sum = count = 0;

Multiple assignments work because an assignment has a value (see Notes 2.4 and 2.5) and because of the right-to-left associativity of the assignment operator (see Table 1.3). In the multiple assignment statement

sum = count = 0;

the computer executes the right-most assignment first, which assigns 0 to count. By Note 2.5, the value of this assignment is the value assigned, namely 0. Therefore, the left-most assignment is equivalent to sum = 0. The net effect is to assign zero to both variables. See Figure 2.2.

sum   =   (count = 0)

                           0   value of right
                                          assignment

sum   =   0   which is used in
                                          the left assignment

Figure 2.2

You also can assign the same value to more than two variables in a multiple assignment statement. The following initializes the four integer variables i, j, k, and h to 3.

```
i = j = k = h = 3;
```

The following program, dem02-2.cpp, illustrates multiple assignment statements.

```cpp
// dem02-2.cpp
// This program illustrates multiple assignment statements
#include <iostream>
using namespace std;
int main()
{
  int h = 17,
      i,
      j,
      k;
  i = j = k = h;
  cout << "h = " << h;
  cout << " i = " << i;
  cout << " j = " << j;
  cout << " k = " << k << endl;
  return 0;
}
```

Program Output

```
h = 17   i = 17   j = 17   k = 17
```

2.3.3 The Compound Assignment Operators

Besides the basic arithmetic operators introduced in Chapter 1, C++ also has available the **compound assignment operators**, which simplify writing some common arithmetic expressions. Table 2.1 lists four of the compound assignment operators and how to read them, which also explains their meanings.

TABLE 2.1

Operator	Read As
+=	is increased by
-=	is decreased by
*=	is multiplied by
/=	is divided by

In programming, it is common to increase the value of a variable by the value of another variable. For example, suppose that a banking problem requires increasing the value of balance by the value of deposit. One way of coding this in C++ is as follows.

```
balance = balance + deposit;
```

When executing this statement, the computer adds the value of deposit (say, 300.00) to the current value of balance (say, 545.50) and assigns the result (845.50) to the variable balance.

An equivalent way of coding the previous assignment using the compound assignment operator += is as follows.

```
balance += deposit;
```

which we read as "balance is increased by deposit."

If a problem requires decreasing the balance in an account by the value of of withdrawal, the corresponding assignment in a C++ program could be

```
balance = balance - withdrawal;
```

Equivalently, using the compound assignment operator -=, we could code the assignment as

```
balance -= withdrawal;
```

which we read as "balance is decreased by withdrawal." Thus, if the value of balance is 845.50 and the value of withdrawal is 200.00, the previous compound assignment gives the value 645.50 to balance.

To replace a number by its square, we could code the statement

```
num = num * num;
```

Alternatively, we could use the compound assignment operator *= and code the statement as follows.

```
num *= num;
```

which we read as "num is multiplied by num." Thus, if the value of num is 7.5 before the assignment, its value is 56.25 after the assignment.

If we must replace the value of price by half its original value, we could code

```
price = price / 2.0;
```

Instead, we could use the compound assignment operator /= and code

```
price /= 2.0;
```

which we read as "price is divided by 2.0." If the value of price is 104.50 before the assignment, then its value is 52.25 after the assignment.

The following program, dem02-3.cpp, illustrates the compound assignment operators.

```
// dem02-3.cpp

// This program illustrates the compound assignment operators

#include <iostream>
#include <iomanip>
```

```
using namespace std;
int main()
{
   double balance    = 545.50,
          deposit    = 300.00,
          withdrawal = 200.00,
          num        =   7.5,
          price      = 104.50;

   cout << setprecision(2)
        << setiosflags(ios::fixed)
        << setiosflags(ios::showpoint);

   balance += deposit;
   cout << "The value of balance is " << balance << endl;

   balance -= withdrawal;
   cout << "The value of balance is " << balance << endl;

   num *= num;
   cout << "The value of num is " << num << endl;

   price /= 2.0;
   cout << "The value of price is " << price << endl;

   return 0;
}
```

Program Output

```
The value of balance is 845.50
The value of balance is 645.50
The value of num is 56.25
The value of price is 52.25
```

Assignment and all the compound assignment operators must take their places in the operator precedence rules. The compound assignment operators have the same precedence as the simple assignment operator =, which is lower than that of all the arithmetic operators. In addition, *all assignment operators associate from right to left.* Thus, if there is more than one assignment operator in an expression, the computer executes them from right to left. The operator precedence table, Table 2.2, summarizes these rules. We shall discuss the ++ and -- operators in the next section.

The low precedence of assignment makes an assignment work the way we expect. For example, in the assignment

```
result = i1 + 2 * i2;
```

the computer first evaluates the value of the right side of the assignment before giving this value to the variable `result`. The computer executes the assignment last because assignment has a lower precedence than the arithmetic operators.

TABLE 2.2

Operators	Associativity
( )	left to right (inside-out)
+ (unary) − (unary) ++ −−	right to left
* / %	left to right
+ −	left to right
= += −= *= /=	right to left

The next section discusses an important application of the right-to-left associativity of the assignment operator.

2.3.4 Increment and Decrement Operators

Two common assignments in programming increase the value of a variable by one and decrease the value of a variable by one. We can easily write statements to do either of these tasks with the operators we have learned so far. To increase the value of the variable count by one, we could code the following.

```
count = count + 1;
```

To decrease the value of the variable limit by one, we could code the following.

```
limit = limit - 1;
```

We could even use the compound assignment operators for these assignments as follows.

```
count += 1;
limit -= 1;
```

The C++ language, however, has still another way of coding these assignments using the **increment operator (++)**, and the **decrement operator (−−)**, as follows.

```
++count;
--limit;
```

Read the statement ++count as "count is increased by one" or "increment count"; the amount of the increment is understood to be one. Read the statement --limit as "limit is decreased by one" or "decrement limit"; the amount of the decrement is understood to be one.

The operators ++ and −− are **unary operators** because each operates on only one item. We can code the ++ operator either before the variable name, in which case it is a **preincrement**, or after the variable name, in which case it is a **postincrement**. Similarly, coded before the variable name, −− is a **predecrement**. Coded after the variable name, −− is a **postdecrement**. Thus, we can increase count by one and decrease limit by one by the following statements.

```
count++;
limit--;
```

Is there a difference between preincrementing and postincrementing a variable, and between predecrementing and postdecrementing a variable? Note 2.6 gives the answer to this question. See Experiment 1.

Note 2.6   Rules for Evaluating ++ and − −

The following rules apply to pre- and postincrementing and decrementing.

1. If the value produced by ++ or −− is not used in an expression, it does *not* matter whether it is a preincrement (predecrement) or a postincrement (or postdecrement).

2. If the value produced by ++ or −− is used in an expression, it *does* matter whether the ++ or −− is before or after the variable name.
   a. When ++ (or −−) is used *before* the variable name, the computer first increments (or decrements) the value of the variable and then uses this new value to evaluate the expression.
   b. When ++ (or −−) is used *after* the variable name, the computer uses the current value of the variable to evaluate the expression and then increments (or decrements) the variable

---

When it does not matter whether we use pre- or postincrement or decrement, we shall prefer preincrement and predecrement. We feel that placing the operator before the variable name, when possible, makes the operator more noticeable.

Rule 2 of Note 2.6 is a consequence of Note 2.4, namely, every expression has a value, and the following observations. Assume that j is an int variable. The expressions ++j and j++ have values. The value of the expression ++j is the value of j *after* adding one to the value of j. On the other hand, the value of the expression j++ is the value of j *before* the computer increases it by one. Likewise, the value of the expression −−j is the value of j *after* subtracting one from j. The value of j−− is the value of j *before* subtracting one from j. See Experiment 1.

The program dem02-4.cpp illustrates the second part of Note 2.6.

```
// dem02-4.cpp

// This program illustrates the difference between predecrement
// and postdecrement.

#include <iostream>
using namespace std;
int main()
{
   int i,
       j;

   i = 7;                            // Give i an initial value
   j = 4 + --i;
   cout << "Predecrementing i yields i = "
```

```
           << i << " and j = " << j << endl;
    i = 7;                          // Reinitialize i to 7
    j = 4 + i--;
    cout << "Postdecrementing i yields i = "
           << i << " and j = " << j << endl;
    return 0;
}
```

Program Output

```
Predecrementing i yields i = 6 and j = 10
Postdecrementing i yields i = 6 and j = 11
```

To explain the first line of the program's output, consider the statements

```
i = 7;
j = 4 + --i;
```

The value of the expression $--i$ is the value of i after decreasing it by one. Therefore, the program uses 6 in the addition, which results in 10 being assigned to j.

To explain the second line of the program's output, consider the statements

```
i = 7;
j = 4 + i--;
```

The value of the expression $i--$ is the value of i before the computer decreases it by one. Therefore, the program uses 7 in the addition, which results in 11 being assigned to j.

Table 2.3 summarizes the assignments of dem02-4.cpp.

The operators ++ and -- are unary operators and have the same precedence as the other unary operators, as shown in Table 2.2. In the chapters that follow, we shall make frequent use of the compound assignment operators, and the increment and decrement operators.

TABLE 2.3

	Expression	
	j = 4 + --i	j = 4 + i--
initial value of i is 7		
value of i used	6	7
value assigned to j	10	11
final value of i	6	6

Exercises 2.3

Use the following declarations in Exercises 1–6. Work each exercise independently of the others. State the values of each variable involved after the computer executes each statement.

```
int i = 6,
    j = 3,
    k = -2,
    h,
    m;
```

1. i += 3;
2. k *= 4;
3. k -= i;
4. j /= 2;
5. i += j + 4;
6. i -= j -= 1;

Use the following declarations in Exercises 7–13. Work each exercise independently of the others. State the values of each variable involved after the computer executes each statement.

```
int i = 6,
    j = 3,
    k = -2,
    h,
    m;
```

7. ++j;
8. k++;
9. h = j-- + i;
10. h = --j + i;
11. h = --j + ++i;
12. h = j-- + ++i;
13. h = ++i;
     m = i++;

In Exercises 14–17, rewrite the given statement using the increment, decrement, or a compound assignment operator.

14. i = i - 3;
15. j = j * i;
16. k = k + 9;
17. i = i / j;

In Exercises 18–19, replace the given statements by a single assignment that uses the increment, decrement, or a compound assignment operator.

18. i = i + 1;
     h = j + 2 * i;
19. i = j / 3 - k;
     k = k - 1;

Experiments 2.3

1. Enter, compile, and execute the following program. Explain the results in terms of Note 2.6.

```cpp
#include <iostream>
using namespace std;
int main()
{
   int i = 3;
   cout << ++i;

   int j = 3;
   cout << j++;

   return 0;
}
```

2. Run the following program.

```cpp
#include <iostream>
using namespace std;
int main()
{
   int i = 7;
   cout << "Given i = 7, the value of ++i is " << ++i << endl;

   i = 7;
   cout << "Given i = 7, the value of i++ is " << i++ << endl;

   return 0;
}
```

   How does the output explain Note 2.6? What is the final value of i?

3. Code, compile, and execute a short program that determines how your compiler interprets the expression i+++j. Initialize i to 2 and j to 3. Does the compiler interpret it as i++ + j or as i + ++j?

4. Code, compile, and execute a short program that determines what value your compiler gives the expression ++i + i++ after executing a statement that initializes i to 1. What value does i have after the computer evaluates the expression?

5. Compile and execute the following program. Try to determine the value that the program will display before you execute the program. The value that the program displays depends on the compiler you use. Why does your compiler give the answer it does?

```cpp
#include <iostream>
using namespace std;
int main()
{
   int i = 7;
```

```
    i = i++ + 1;
    cout << "i = " << i << endl;
    return 0;
}
```

Programming Problems 2.3

1. Write a program that asks the user to enter the dollar amount of the opening balance of an account. Then the program should ask the user to enter the dollar amount of deposits to the account. Use the += operator to add this amount to the balance. Next, ask the user to enter the dollar amount of withdrawals from the account during the last month. Use the -= operator to subtract this from the balance. The program should then display the closing balance in the account.

2. Write a program that asks the user to enter a student's grades on four exams. The program should display the four grades and the average of the four grades, rounded to the nearest tenth. To add the grades, use a variable called total_grade, which you should initialize to zero. As the program prompts for and obtains each grade, add the grade to total_grade using the += operator.

3. A bank teller needs a program to total the amount of money in his coin tray. Write a program that asks the user to enter the number of each type of U.S. coin (half-dollars, quarters, nickels, dimes, and pennies) and that displays the total value of the coins in dollars and cents. Use the variable total_amount, which you should initialize to zero, to total the value of the coins. As the number of each type of coin is input by the user, use the += operator to increase the value of total_amount.

4. Write a program that asks the user to enter the price of an item and the sales tax rate as a percent. The program should display the total price of the item (price plus sales tax.) After obtaining the input from the user, the program should use the *= operator to calculate the total price of the item using the equivalent of the following formula.
price = price * (1 + sales_tax_rate)

5. An account executive must keep track of her expenses on a business trip. Write a program that totals the executive's expenses. Use the variable total_expenses, which you must initialize to zero, to store the executive's total expenses. The program should ask the user to enter the number of miles driven (calculate this expense by multiplying the number of miles driven by 0.30, that is, 30 cents per mile), the amount spent on highway tolls and parking, the amount spent on meals, the amount spent on lodging, and the amount spent on entertainment. The program should use the += operator to add each expense to total_expenses as they are computed.

6. You want to estimate your income over the next three years. Write a program that asks the user to enter his/her annual salary and an estimated yearly rate of growth for the salary as a percent. For example the user's present salary might be $30,000.00 per year and she may estimate a rate of growth of 6% per year for the next three years. The program should display the estimated salary for each of the

next three years. Be sure to change the entered rate of growth to the corresponding decimal. Use the += operator to increment the salary.

7. Write a program to compute telephone bills for the local telephone company.
Each customer has a base charge of $12.95 per month and gets charged extra for
each local call and each long-distance call. The program should prompt the user
for the number of local calls made during the month. The charge for each local
call is $0.10. Use the += operator to add the cost of the local calls to the total bill.
Then the program should prompt the user for the total charge for long-distance
calls made during the month. Use the += operator to add the long-distance
charges to the total bill. Finally, the program should calculate the tax on the total
bill. The tax rate is 8.72%. Use the *= operator to add the tax to the total bill by
multiplying the total bill by 1.0872.

2.4 THREE DIFFICULTIES WHEN DISPLAYING DECIMAL NUMBERS WITH cout

In this section, we explain why we have included the following three lines of code in
the programs of this chapter.

```
cout << setprecision(2)
     << setiosflags(ios::fixed)
     << setiosflags(ios::showpoint);
```

Sometimes `cout` does not display a number the way you might expect. For example, the `cout` statement

```
cout << 356.70 << endl;
```

displays the number as 356.7, without the trailing zero.

Another problem with `cout` is that it sometimes displays a number in scientific
notation rather than in decimal notation. For example, the `cout` statement

```
cout << 3456789.70 / 2 << endl;
```

displays the result of the division as 1.72839 e + 006. This form of the answer would be
inappropriate for the output of a business application. Instead, we would want the answer to display as 1728394.85.

Finally, we would also like to control the number of digits that display to the right
of the decimal point. For example, if we calculate sales tax of 8.25% on an amount of
19.95, we would want `cout` to display the product 0.0825 * 19.95 to the nearest penny.
However, the following `cout` displays the product as 1.64588.

```
cout << 0.0825 * 19.95
```

The problems of losing trailing zeros, the switch to scientific notation, and the
control of the number of digits displayed to the right of the decimal point are interre-
lated. To solve them, we use **I/O** (or Input/Output) **manipulators**. Recall from Chapter 1
that you can think of an I/O manipulator as an instruction to the `cout` stream to display numbers in a certain way. The manipulators we shall use are `setprecision()`,
which sets the number of digits that display to the right of the decimal, and
`setiosflags()`, which controls various settings for `cout`. As mentioned in Note 2.1,
we include the following `cout` statement at the beginning of `main()` in any program

that displays dollar-and-cents amounts. Remember, to use the statement, you must include the header file iomanip using the preprocessor directive #include <iomanip>.

```
cout << setprecision(2) // two digits to right of decimal
     << setiosflags(ios::fixed)     // display in fixed form
     << setiosflags(ios::showpoint);  // print trailing zeros
```

The setiosflags() manipulator has a complicated syntax. In parentheses after the setiosflags manipulator name is the class name ios. We shall learn about classes in a later chapter. Right now, just follow the requirements of the syntax. The class name ios must be followed by two colons :: followed by what is called a **flag** name. The fixed flag tells the cout stream that floating point numbers are to be displayed in fixed point format as opposed to scientific format. The showpoint flag tells the cout stream to print trailing zeros. These settings remain in effect until they are changed by sending a different setiosflags() setting to cout.

When used in conjunction with setiosflags(ios::fixed), the setprecision(2) manipulator sets the number of digits that will display to the right of the decimal point to two. The number is displayed rounded to two places. If we had coded setprecision(3), then three digits would display to the right of the decimal point, appropriately rounded. Thus, the integer in parentheses after the setprecision name determines the number of digits that will display to the right of the decimal point. Whatever precision is set, it remains in effect until reset by sending another setprecision() message to the cout stream. (If you use setprecision() without using setiosflags(ios::fixed), then setprecision() determines the total number of digits displayed, not just the number of digits to the right of the decimal.)

Now, consider the following code.

```
cout << setprecision(2)
     << setiosflags(ios::fixed)
     << setiosflags(ios::showpoint);

cout << 3456789.70 / 2 << endl;
cout << 0.0825 * 19.95 << endl;
cout << 356.70 << endl;
```

The output of the preceding is the following.

```
1728394.85
1.65
356.70
```

Note that if the value of db is 356.091, displaying it to one decimal place does not affect the value stored in db. The actual value stored in db is still 356.091.

Note that the precision and the ios flag settings stay in effect until they are reset. To change the precision, simply use setprecision() again with a different value. To reset either the ios::fixed or the ios::showpoint flag, you must send **resetiosflags(ios::fixed)** or **resetiosflags(ios::showpoint)** to cout.

Experiments 2.4

1. The following program illustrates many floating point number concepts that we discussed in this section.

```
// This program demonstrates the use of variables of type
// float and of type double.

#include <iostream>
#include <iomanip>

using namespace std;

int main()
{
    // Declaration and initialization of float and double type
    // variables.

    cout << setprecision(2)
         << setiosflags(ios::fixed)
         << setiosflags(ios::showpoint);

    float   fl = 123.4567,
            fl1;
    double db = -.0000000000078945,
            db1;

    cout << "fl = " << fl << " db = " << db << endl;
    cout << "fl = " << setw(5) << fl << ", db = "
         << setw(5) << db << endl;
    cout << "fl = " << setw(10) << fl << ", db = "
         << setprecision(20) << setw(5) << db << endl;

    cout << endl;
    cout << "Enter a float: ";
    cin >> fl1;

    cout << endl;
    cout << "Enter a double: ";
    cin >> db1;

    cout << endl;
    cout << setprecision(5);
    cout << "The float you entered was " << fl1 << endl;
    cout << "The double you entered was " << db1 << endl;

    return 0;
}
```

Compile and execute this program on your computer. How do the `cout` statements display the values of `fl` and `db`, and `fl1` and `db1`?

2. By default, `cout` displays output right justified in each output field. You can control the type of justification `cout` uses by coding the `ios::left` and `ios::right` flags with `setioflags()`. Note that either of these flags causes the justification to stay in effect until it is changed by another call to `setiosflags()`. For example, the following code displays 3.14159 left justified in a field of width 10 and then displays 7.890 right justified in a field of width 10.

```
cout << setprecision(2)
     << setiosflags(ios::fixed)
     << setiosflags(ios::showpoint);
cout << setiosflags(ios::left);

cout << setw(10) << 3.14159 << endl;
cout << setiosflags(ios::right);
cout << setw(10) << 7.890 << endl;
```

Recode dem02-1.cpp and left justify all displayed output.

3. By default, `cout` does not show the plus sign when it displays positive numbers. Using the `ios::showpos` flag with `setiosflags()` causes `cout` to display positive numbers preceded by a plus sign. For example, the following code displays 3.14159 preceded by a plus sign in a field of width 10.

```
cout << setprecision(2)
     << setiosflags(ios::fixed)
     << setiosflags(ios::showpoint);
cout << setiosflags(ios::showpos);

cout << setw(10) << 3.14159 << endl;
```

Recode dem02-1.cpp with all numbers displayed with a plus sign. Note that to reset the `ios::showpos` flag, you must send `resetiosflags (ios::showpos)` to `cout`.

CHAPTER REVIEW

TERMINOLOGY

Describe the meaning of each of the following terms.

real number	compound assignment operators (+=, -=, *=, /=)
floating point number	
`float`	increment operator (++)
`double`	decrement operator (−)
floating point constant	unary operator
`setprecision()`	pre- and postincrement operators
`setiosflags(ios::fixed)`	pre- and postdecrement operators
`setiosflags(ios::showpoint)`	manipulators
mixed-mode expression	`resetiosflags(ios::fixed)`
type cast	`resetiosflags(ios::showpoint)`
multiple assignment statement	

SUMMARY

- The two floating-point number types are `float` (7-digit precision) and `double` (15-digit precision.)
- Floating point constants must contain a decimal point but cannot contain a comma.

- Use the I/O manipulators `setprecision()` and `setiosflags()` to control the format of decimal numbers displayed using `cout` (Note 2.1).
- If integer and decimal types appear in the same arithmetic expression, C++ converts all numbers to type `double` before doing the arithmetic (Note 2.2).
- A type cast (a C++ data type followed by an expression in parentheses) changes the data type of the value of the enclosed expression to the specified type.
- When the data type of the right side of an assignment differs from the data type of the variable on the left side, C++ converts the value of the right side to the data type of the variable on the left side (Note 2.3).
- Every expression in C++ has a numeric value (Note 2.4). The value of an assignment is the value assigned (Note 2.5).
- The compound assignment operators +=, -=, *=, /=, combine assignment with the indicated arithmetic operator.
- The increment operator, ++, increases a variable by one. The decrement operator, --, decreases a variable by one.
- The increment and decrement operators can be used before or after the variable on which they operate (Note 2.6).

REVIEW EXERCISES

1. What are the two floating point types in C++ and how do they differ?
2. How can you use the `setprecision()` and `setiosflags()` manipulators to control the output of decimal numbers?
3. Explain how C++ handles an arithmetic expression that contains different numeric data types.
4. What is a type cast and how do you make one? Why is a type cast sometimes necessary?
5. How are data types converted across the assignment operator?
6. What is the value of an assignment expression?
7. Explain how a multiple assignment works.
8. What are the compound assignment operators and how do they work?
9. What are the increment and decrement operators and how do they work?
10. What is the difference between pre- and postincrement?

Chapter 3

Iteration

OBJECTIVES

- To write relation conditions using the relational operators
- To use the `while` statement to code indefinite iteration loops
- To declare and use `char` type variables
- To use `cin.get()` to obtain a character from the input buffer
- To use embedded assignment in the condition of a `while` loop
- To use the `do` statement to code an indefinite iteration loop
- To use counters and accumulators
- To use the `for` statement to code definite iteration loops
- To code nested `while` and `for` loops

Most of a computer's power lies in its ability to repeatedly execute the same set of instructions. This process, called **iteration**, or **looping**, is the subject of this chapter. We assume that the reader is familiar with the basic iteration control structures, namely the **while** loop, the **do** loop, and the **for** loop. The reader who is not familiar with this material is referred to Appendix B.

To stop an iteration requires testing a condition. Therefore, before we learn how to code the while, do, and for loops in C++, we must learn how to code simple conditions.

3.1 RELATION CONDITIONS

The simplest type of condition is the **relation condition**, which compares the values of two operands. You code relation conditions in C++ by using the **relational operators**. Table 3.1 lists the relational operators and their meanings.

Note that the operator that tests for equality is ==, not =, which is the assignment operator. The C++ compiler may not detect the mistake of incorrectly substituting = for ==. (Some compilers will issue a warning message that a conditional expression is

TABLE 3.1

Relational Operator	Meaning
==	Equal to
!=	Not equal to
<	Less than
<=	Less than or Equal to
>	Greater than
>=	Greater than or Equal to

expected.) Therefore, it is very important to use = when you want an assignment and ==
when you want to test for equality. See Experiment 1, Section 3.2.

Each relational operator compares the values of the expressions that appear on
either side of the operator for the indicated relation and yields either true or false. Suppose, for example, that we have the following declarations.

```
int i = 10,
    j = 10,
    k = 15;
```

The relation condition i == j is true because the value of the expression to the
left of the == operator equals the value of the expression to its right. Similarly, the relation condition i >= 15 is false.

Recall that Note 2.4 stated that every expression in C++ has a value.

Note 3.1   The Value of a Relation Condition

In C++, if a relation condition is true, the whole condition has the numeric value
1. If a relation condition is false, the whole condition has the numeric value 0. In
fact, C++ considers any nonzero value to be true and 0 to be false.

Thus, the condition i == j has the value 1 because it is true. Table 3.2 shows the
precedence of the relational operators relative to the other operators that we have discussed so far.

We see from Table 3.2 that the equality operator and the inequality operator (!=)
have a lower precedence than the other relational operators. Also, all the relational operators have a lower precedence than all the arithmetic operators.

Using the previous declarations of j and k, the condition j != k - 5 has the
value 0 because it is false. The computer evaluates the expression j != k - 5 as follows.
Of the two operators appearing in the expression, subtraction has higher precedence.
Therefore, the computer first evaluates k - 5, which gives 10. Then the computer performs the second operation, namely the inequality test, and determines that the condition is false. See Experiments 1 and 2.

TABLE 3.2

Operators	Associativity
( )	Left to Right (Inside-Out)
+ (unary) – (unary) ++ ––	Right to Left
* / %	Left to Right
+ –	Left to Right
< <= > >=	Left to Right
== !=	Left to Right
= += –= *= /=	Right to Left

Exercises 3.1

Translate the statements of Exercises 1–5 into valid C++ relation conditions. Assume the following declarations.

```
int i,
    j,
    k;
```

1. The value of i is greater than the value of j multiplied by the value of k.
2. The value of j is not less than 300.
3. The value of k is less than or equal to the value of i.
4. Twice the value of i is not greater than three less than the value of k.
5. Five more than the value of j is greater than the value of i.

Determine whether the relation conditions in Exercises 6–9 are true or false. Assume the following declarations.

```
int  i = 12,
     j = 9,
     k = 21;
```

6. (i == j + 3)
7. (2 * j >= k)
8. (j – i != k 2 18)
9. (k – j + i < 20)

Experiments 3.1

1. Compile and execute the following program. Explain its output.

```
#include <iostream>

using namespace std;

int main()
{
```

```
int i = 3,
    j = 8,
    k;

k = (i >= 0) + (i == j);
cout << "k = " <<  k << endl;

return 0;
}
```

2. Compile and execute the following program. Explain its output.

```
#include <iostream>

using namespace std;

int main()
{
  int i = 3,
      j = 8,
      k = 5,
      result;

  result = (i < j < k);
  cout << "result = " << result << endl;

  return 0;
}
```

3.2 INDEFINITE ITERATION: THE while AND do STATEMENTS

3.2.1 The while Statement

Figure 3.1 shows how to express indefinite iteration, or looping, in flowchart and pseudo-code forms.

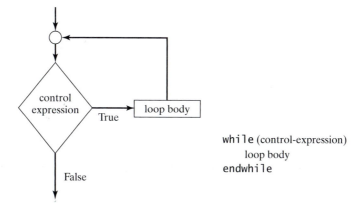

while loop: Flowchart Form   while Loop: Pseudocode Form

Figure 3.1

To code the **indefinite iteration** loop, or `while` loop, of Figure 3.1 in C++, we use the `while` statement, which has the following form.

```
while (control-expression)
   loop-body
```

The control-expression, which must be enclosed in parentheses, can be any valid C++ expression. For now, we assume that the control-expression is a simple relation condition and concentrate on how the `while` statement works. The loop body can be a single C++ statement ending with a semicolon or it can be a compound statement. We shall learn about compound statements shortly.

Consider the following declaration and code.

```
int count = 0;

while (count < 5)
      ++count;
cout << "The value of count is " << count << endl;
```

The code begins by declaring and initializing the integer variable `count` to zero. Next, the `while` statement executes. The `while` statement first tests the loop condition. Because the value of `count` is 0, the loop condition is true. Therefore, the loop body, which consists of the one statement

```
++count;
```

executes. This statement increases the value of `count` by one, making its value 1. Now the program tests the loop condition again. The condition is still true because the value of `count`, 1, is less than 5. Therefore, the loop body executes again and increases the value of `count` by 1, making it 2. The program continues to execute the loop body as long as the loop condition is true.

Table 3.3 shows a **trace** of the values of `count` and the loop condition. Tracing a section of a program's code or tracing the entire program is one of the simplest techniques for understanding or debugging a program.

Thus the loop condition is false when the value of `count` is 5. At this point, the program exits the loop and executes the `cout` statement. The `cout` statement displays the current value of the variable `count` as follows.

```
The value of count is 5
```

TABLE 3.3

Value of count	Loop Condition (count <5)
0 (initial value)	True
1	True
2	True
3	True
4	True
5	False

We can arrive at this same conclusion without doing the trace by remembering that the loop condition (count < 5) is false when the program exits the loop. Therefore, the value of count must be greater than or equal to 5 when the program executes the cout statement. Because the program initializes count to zero and increases its value by one each time through the loop, the first value of count that makes the loop condition false is 5. Therefore, the cout statement displays the value 5.

The body of a while loop can be a **compound statement**—a set of statements enclosed in braces {}. We have been using braces since we discussed our first C++ program, dem01-1.cpp. Because braces enclose the statements of the function main(), the body of main() is a compound statement.

Now consider the following declaration and code.

```
int count = 0;

while (count < 5)
{
   ++count;
   cout << "Hello" << endl;
}

cout << endl;
cout << "Hello was displayed " << count << " times." << endl;
```

The initial value of count and the loop condition are exactly as they were in the previous example. The body of this while loop is a compound statement that consists of two simple statements. Code the opening brace under the reserved word while and indent the statements in the compound statement two places beyond the brace. The closing brace is coded in the same column as the opening brace. The C++ language does not require this method of indentation. However, the program is easier to read because the indentation emphasizes the body of the while loop. Note also that each statement in the compound statement ends in a semicolon, but there is no semicolon after the closing brace of the compound statement.

As in the first example, the loop body executes five times. Therefore, the program code displays the following.

```
Hello
Hello
Hello
Hello
Hello

Hello was displayed 5 times.
```

3.2.2 An Example of Indefinite Iteration: The char Data Type

Coding an indefinite iteration using the while statement is most appropriate when you do not know how many times the loop body will execute. This is why such a loop is called indefinite. Suppose we want to write a program that counts the number of characters the user enters on one line at the computer keyboard. A line is a stream of characters ended by a return. The return is not part of the line and does not count as a character. The program does not know the number of characters that the user will enter. Therefore, an indefinite iteration loop is appropriate.

To write such a program, we need a variable that keeps a tally of the characters as the program counts them. This variable, which we shall call num_chars for "number of characters", is an example of a **counter variable**, or **counter**. A counter is a variable that counts the number of times an event occurs during program execution. The event we wish to count in our program is the typing of a character by the user.

It is very important that your programs handle counters correctly. Note 3.2 states how you should use them.

Note 3.2   How to Use a Counter

To use a counter variable properly, the program must execute the following steps.

1. Initialize the counter, usually to zero.
2. Increment the counter, that is increase the counter by one, when the event it counts occurs.
3. Use the counter. You are using the counter variable for a purpose. Make sure you use it for that purpose.

Step 1 in Note 3.2 is especially important. If a counter is not initialized, it will contain garbage—that is, some unknown number. Therefore, the counter will have an invalid value and will be meaningless. See Experiment 2.

The steps outlined in Note 3.2 apply to the counter num_chars. Before the program begins, the user has not entered any characters. Therefore, the program should initialize num_chars to zero. Whenever the program obtains a character from the user, it will increase num_chars by one. Finally, after the user inputs the line, the program displays the value of num_chars.

As stated in the previous paragraph, whenever the program obtains a character from the user, it increases num_chars by one. This is obviously an iterative process— obtain a character, increment num_chars; obtain a character, increment num_chars; and so on, until the user ends the line by entering a return. Because we do not know how many characters the user will enter, this is an indefinite iteration, which calls for the use of a while loop.

We shall also need a variable in which to store a character when the program obtains it. We use the char data type to declare a variable that will store a single character. You cannot store two or more characters in a variable of type **char**. Thus, the following declares the variable ch in which we can store a single character.

```
char ch;
```

A **character constant** is a single character enclosed in apostrophes. Thus, 'A' and ';' are character constants. You can assign a character constant to a **character variable** in the same way that you assign a numeric constant to a numeric variable. Thus, the following assigns the character constant 'A' to the character variable ch, which was declared previously.

```
ch = 'A';
```

You can also initialize a character variable in its declaration.

```
char ch = 'A';
```

3.2.3 Using cin.get()

Recall that when the user enters data from the keyboard, it is entered into the input stream cin. Instead of extracting an entire number from cin as we did in Chapters 1 and 2, we can extract the characters from the cin input stream one character at a time. To do this, we use cin.get(). Appending .get() to cin essentially asks cin to extract the next character from the input stream. (We will explain the nature of the dot (.) notation in Chapter 11.) To use cin.get(), declare a character variable, say, ch.

```
char ch;
```

Then, the following statement assigns the next character from the input stream to the variable ch.

```
ch = cin.get();
```

Suppose, for example, that the user enters Mt into the input stream as a response to a prompt and then hits the enter key. Then, executing

```
ch = cin.get();
```

obtains the character M from the input stream and assigns it to the variable ch. If we execute

```
ch = cin.get();
```

again, it extracts the next available character, namely t from the input stream, and assigns it to ch; Note that you do not use the >> operator when using cin.get().

3.2.4 The Program dem03-1.cpp

The while statement's condition determines when the loop stops executing. In our program, we want the loop to stop executing when the character the user enters, which the program stores in the variable ch, is equal to the newline character '\n'. Therefore, we want the loop to execute as long as the character that the user enters is <u>not</u> equal to the newline character; that is, the loop condition should be (ch != '\n').

The first time the program tests the loop condition, the variable ch must have a valid value. Therefore, before it executes the while statement, the program must input the first character by executing the assignment

```
ch = cin.get();
```

Following is the code of dem03-1.cpp.

```
// dem03-1.cpp

// This program counts the number of characters input
// by the user on one line.  The line is terminated by
// a return.  The return is not counted as a character.

#include <iostream>

using namespace std;

int main()
{
   char ch;                    // Used to store the input character
   int  num_chars = 0;        // Counts the number of characters
   cout << "Enter any number of characters terminated by return."
        << endl << endl;

   ch = cin.get();  // Obtain the first character

   while (ch != '\n')
   {
      ++num_chars;
      ch = cin.get();
   }

   cout << endl;
   cout << "You entered " << num_chars << " characters." << endl;

   return 0;
}
```

Program Output

Enter any number of characters terminated by return.

aaB1, 34

You entered 8 characters.

The program stores each character it obtains in the character variable ch. The integer counter num_chars, which the program initializes to zero in its declaration, stores the number of characters input by the user.

The program prompts the user to enter characters. When the user hits the return key, the computer transmits the entire line (including the return character) to the input stream. The first execution of cin.get() retrieves the first character from the input stream and stores it in ch. The while statement now tests the condition (ch != '\n'). If the user did not enter a return as the first character, this condition is true and the body of the loop executes.

The loop body is a two-statement compound statement. Because program execution is now in the body of the while loop, the loop condition is true. This means that the user entered a character. To count this character, the program increases the variable `num_chars` by one. Before ending the body of the loop, the program obtains the next character from the input stream by the assignment statement

```
ch = cin.get();
```

After completing execution of the loop body, the program tests the loop condition again, but now with the new character that it obtained by executing `cin.get()` in the loop body. If this next character is not a newline character, the loop body executes again. The program counts the new character by increasing `num_chars` by one and then it obtains the next character from the keyboard input buffer by executing `ch = cin.get()`.

This process continues until executing `ch = cin.get()` in the loop body assigns the newline character, `'\n'`, to `ch`. Now, the loop condition is false. The loop stops executing and control falls through to the following `cout` statement, which displays the value of `num_chars`.

The process used in dem03-1.cpp occurs many times in computing. The program obtains the first character from the user before entering the loop. The body of the `while` loop processes the character. At the end of the loop body, the program obtains the next character from the user. Note 3.3 gives the general outline of this process.

Note 3.3 Processing an Unknown Number of Inputs

To process an unknown number of inputs using a `while` loop, structure your program as follows:

```
Obtain input data from the user           // the priming input
while (there is more data to process)
    {
        // loop body statements to process current data
        Obtain input data from the user
    }
```

How the program obtains input data from the user depends on the particular program. In dem03-1.cpp, the program obtains data from the user one character at a time. Therefore, the program obtains the input by executing `ch = cin.get()`. How you code the condition in the `while` loop of Note 3.3 also depends on how the program obtains the data from the user and in what form it stores the data. In dem03-1.cpp, there is more data to process if the character the program obtains from the user, which it stores in the variable `ch`, is not equal to `'\n'`. Thus, we coded the loop condition as `(ch != '\n')`. Finally, only after the program fully processes the current character in the body of the `while` loop, does it obtain the next character from the user.

See Experiments 4 and 5 for some variations of the outline of Note 3.3. The program prb03-1.cpp, which we develop in Section 3.3, also follows the outline of Note 3.3.

3.2.5 Embedded Assignment—Recoding dem03-1.cpp

Following is another version of dem03-1.cpp, which counts the number of characters entered by the user on one line at the computer keyboard. It illustrates another application of Note 2.4, which states that each C++ expression has a value.

```
// dem03-2.cpp

// This program counts the number of characters input
// by the user on one line.  The line is terminated by
// a return.  The return is not counted as a character.
// The program uses embedded assignment to obtain
// and test characters.

#include <iostream>

using namespace std;

int main()
{
    char ch;               // Used to store the input character
    int  num_chars = 0;    // Counts the number of characters
    cout << "Enter any number of characters terminated by return."
         << endl << endl;

    // The loop condition contains an embedded assignment

    while ( (ch = cin.get()) != '\n')
        ++num_chars;

    cout << endl;
    cout << "You entered " << num_chars << " characters." << endl;

    return 0;
}
```

Program Output

Enter any number of characters terminated by return.

aaBl, 34

You entered 8 characters.

The declaration and initial prompt are the same as in dem03-1.cpp. However, there is apparently no priming input and the program apparently does not obtain the next data from the user at the end of the loop body (see Note 3.3). Both of these seemingly missing elements are present in the loop condition in the form of an **embedded assignment**. We already know enough to understand this loop condition, so let us take a careful look at it.

```
while ( (ch = cin.get()) != '\n')
```

The control-expression is a **relational condition**—it tests to see if something is unequal to '\n'. See Figure 3.2.

Is this unequal to this?

(ch = cin.get ()) != '\n'

Figure 3.2

The left side of the relation condition is the assignment (ch = cin.get()). Thus, the program tests the value of this assignment to see if it is unequal to '\n'. To evaluate the assignment, the program executes ch = cin.get() (which obtains the next character from the input stream) and assigns this character to ch. By Note 2.4, the value of this assignment is the character assigned to ch. The computer tests this character against '\n' in the relation condition.

Now we explain how the loop works. When the program first encounters the while loop, it tests the loop condition. The act of testing the condition causes the statement ch = cin.get() to obtain the first character from the input stream and assign it to ch. This takes the place of the priming input. The computer then tests the value of this assignment, which is the value of the character obtained from the input stream, against '\n'. If they are unequal—that is, if the character obtained from the keyboard is not '\n'—then the loop body executes. The loop body contains one statement, which increments the counter num_chars.

The computer then tests the loop condition again. Doing so obtains the next character from the input stream (this is equivalent to obtaining the next character at the end of the loop body), assigns it to ch, and tests it against '\n'. The loop continues executing until the character obtained by ch = cin.get() equals '\n'.

3.2.6 The do-while Loop

A while loop tests the loop condition before it executes the loop body. Therefore, if the loop condition is false the first time it is tested, the program will never execute the loop body. Sometimes we want to guarantee that the program executes the body of a loop at least once. That is, we require the program to execute the loop body before it tests the loop condition. This type of loop is called a **do-while**, or **do**, loop. A flowchart depicting the do-while loop and the corresponding pseudocode appear in Figure 3.3.

In C++, you code the do-while loop by using the do **statement**, whose format is as follows.

```
do
 loop body
while (loop condition);
```

The loop body can be a single statement or a compound statement. Note that you must code a semicolon after the closing parenthesis of the loop condition. Following is a code fragment that displays the word "Hello" five times by using a do statement.

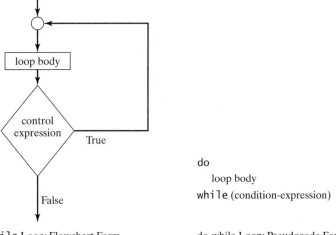

do
     loop body
whi1e (condition-expression)

do-whi1e Loop: Flowchart Form   do-while Loop: Pseudocode Form

Figure 3.3

```
int count = 0;
do
{
  ++count;
  cout << "Hello" << endl;
}
while (count < 5);

cout << endl;
cout << "Hello was displayed " << count <<  " times" << endl;
```

It is also possible to recode dem03-1.cpp using a do loop as follows.

```
// dem03-3.cpp

// This program counts the number of characters input
// by the user on one line.  The line is terminated by
// a return.  The return is not counted as a character.
// This program, which uses a do statement, is a version
// of dem03-1.cpp.

#include <iostream>

using namespace std;

int main()
{
  char ch;                // Used to store the input character
  int  num_chars = 0;  //  Counts the number of characters

  cout << "Enter any number of characters terminated by return."
       << endl << endl;

  do
  {
```

```
        ch = cin.get();
        ++num_chars;
    }
    while (ch != '\n');

    --num_chars;

    cout << endl;
    cout << "You entered " << num_chars << " characters." << endl;

    return 0;
}
```

Program Output

Enter any number of characters terminated by return.

aaB1, 34

You entered 8 characters.

Because the program does not test the loop condition until after it executes the loop body, it is not necessary to have the priming input as required by dem03-1.cpp. The do-loop body first obtains a character and then counts it by increasing num_chars by one. The loop condition tests this character to see if it is the newline character. If not, the loop body executes again. The only difficulty with the do loop is that the program counts the newline character that the user enters (and that ends the loop) as a character. Therefore, before displaying the value of num_chars, the program decreases the value of num_chars by one, using the statement

```
        --num_chars;
```

Although you must code a semicolon following the while condition in a do-while loop, do not code a semicolon after the while condition in a while loop—it could lead to an infinite loop. See Exercise 4.

Exercises 3.2

1. How many times does the following while loop display the word "Hello?"

```
    int count = 1;
    while (count < 10)
    {
        cout << "Hello" << endl;
        count += 2;
    }
```

2. How many times does the following while loop display the word "Hello?"

```
    int count = 1;
    while (count > 10)
    {
```

```
      cout << "Hello" << endl;
      count += 2;
   }
```

3. How many times does the following while loop display the word "Hello?"

```
int count = 0;
while (count != 10)
{
   cout << "Hello" << endl;
   count += 2;
}
```

4. What is the value of count after the following executes?

```
int count = 0;
while (count < 7) ;
   ++count;
```

5. What are the values of total and count after the following executes?

```
int count = 0,
    total = 0;
while (count < 7)
   total += count;
   ++count;
```

6. Rewrite the while loop of Exercise 1 as a do loop so that it displays the word "Hello" the same number of times.

7. Rewrite the while loop of Exercise 5 as a do loop so that total and count have the same final values as in Exercise 5.

Experiments 3.2

1. We mentioned in this chapter that the compiler does not usually detect the mistake of incorrectly replacing the **relational operator** == by the assignment operator =. This experiment shows what can happen if you do make this mistake. The following program asks the user to enter several Xs followed by a return. The program then displays the number of Xs the user entered.

```
#include <iostream>

using namespace std;

int main()
{
   char ch;
   int x_count = 0;
```

```
cout << "Enter several Xs, followed by a return." << endl << endl;
ch = cin.get();
while (ch == 'X')
{
  ++x_count;
  ch = cin.get();
}

cout << endl;
cout << "You entered " << x_count << " Xs." << endl;

return 0;
}
```

Compile and execute this program to ensure that it works properly. Now replace the == in the loop condition by =. Compile and execute the resulting program. Use the same number of Xs that you used to test the original program. After you enter a return, does the new program print the number of Xs that you entered? (If the program will not stop, hit the Break key while holding down the Ctrl key.)

2. In dem03-1.cpp, do not initialize the counter num_chars. Thus, just declare it—do not initialize it to 0. Compile and run the resulting program. What happens?

3. Recode dem03-1.cpp using cin and the extraction operator in place of cin.get().

4. See Note 3.3. Omit the priming input from dem03-1.cpp. Compile and execute the resulting program. Explain what happens.

5. A student writes the following program to count the number of characters the user enters on one line. Does the program work properly? Explain why or why not.

```
#include <iostream>

using namespace std;

int main()
{
  char ch = 'a'; // initialized to guarantee entry into loop
  int num_chars = 0;

  cout << "Enter any number of characters terminated by return."
       << endl << endl;

  while (ch != '\n')
  {
    ch = cin.get();
    ++num_chars;
  }

  cout << endl;
  cout << "You entered " << num_chars << " characters." << endl;
  return 0;
}
```

6. Predict the outcome of executing the following program. NOTE: If the program "hangs", hold down the Ctrl key and press the Pause/Break key.

```
#include <iostream>

using namespace std;

int main()
{
  int num = 1;
  while (num = 1)
  {
    cout << "The first three positive integers are " << num << ", "
         << num + 1 << ", and " << num + 2 << endl;
    num = 0;
  }

  return 0;
}
```

Compile and execute the program. Was your prediction correct? Explain why or why not.

3.3 SOLVING A PROBLEM WITH INDEFINITE ITERATION

The program prb02-3.cpp of Chapter 2 simulates a simple cash register, but processes only one customer. In this section, we discuss a program that processes many customers and displays summary information at the end of the day's business.

3.3.1 Problem 3.1

The C++-Side Restaurant (see Problem 2.1) wants you to write a program that simulates a simple cash register. The program should ask the user if a customer is to be processed. If the user responds yes, the program prompts the user to enter the price of the meal. Then the program calculates the sales tax and the total price, which it should display to the user. Next, the program asks the user to enter the amount tendered, and displays the amount tendered, the total price, and the customer's change. The program then asks the user if there is another customer to process. If the user responds yes, the program processes the next customer in the same way. This procedure continues indefinitely until the user responds no to the prompt for another customer. Finally, the program displays the total number of customers it processed and the grand total of all the meal prices.

3.3.2 Program Design

Because the program must process an indefinite number of customers, we use a while loop and apply Note 3.3, as shown in the following high-level pseudocode.

Prompt for a customer
while (there is another customer)
  Process the meal

    Prompt for a customer
  endwhile
  Display totals

Our program first asks the user if there is a customer to process (the priming input). The while loop's condition tests the user's response to this question. If the user indicates that there is another customer to process, the while loop's body executes, processing one customer's data. At the end of the loop body, the program asks the user if there is another customer to process.

To keep track of the number of customers that the program processes, we use a counter called num_customers. In addition, the program must keep a running total of the meal prices. When there are no more customers to process, the program must display the final value of the running total of the meal prices. This requires the use of an **accumulator**, which is a variable that totals the values that another variable assumes.

You use an accumulator to add numbers in much the same way as you use a calculator to add a set of numbers. The calculator's display acts as an accumulator. To use the calculator, you first clear the calculator display—that is, enter zero into the display. Clearing the display ensures that you rid the display of any numbers. Next, you add each number to the number in the display. Finally, after entering the last number, you press the equals key (=), and the final total appears in the calculator display.

An accumulator acts like a special calculator display for adding the values of a particular variable. Therefore, every accumulator must go through the three steps of Note 3.4, which follows. It is good programming practice to check that each accumulator goes through these three steps.

Note 3.4   How to Use an Accumulator

To use an accumulator properly, the program must execute the following steps.

1. Initialize the accumulator, usually to zero. Failure to do so may result in your program using a "garbage" initial value for the accumulator.

2. Increment the accumulator; that is, increase the accumulator by the value of the variable that the accumulator is totaling.

3. Use the accumulator. You are using the accumulator for a purpose. Make sure you use it for that purpose.

In the program we shall develop to solve Problem 3.1, the variable total stores the total cost of the meal, including tax. The program adds each meal total to the accumulator variable grand_total. This accumulator must go through the steps of Note 3.4. Before the user enters the price of the first meal, the value of grand_total should be zero. Therefore, we initialize grand_total to zero before using it.

To increase the accumulator, we code the following assignment statement.

```
grand_total += total;
```

This statement is the equivalent of adding a number (`total`) to the number in a calculator's display (`grand_total`). The program increases the value of `grand_total` by the current value of total. Following is a detailed pseudocode solution for Problem 3.1.

> Initialize the counter and accumulator
> Prompt for a customer
> while (there is another customer)
>   Obtain the meal price
>   Calculate the tax and total price of the meal
>   Display the price, tax, and total
>   Obtain the amount tendered
>   Calculate the change
>   Display the amount tendered, total price, and change
>   Increment the counter and accumulator
>   Prompt for a customer
> endwhile
> Display the counter and accumulator

3.3.3 The Program prb03-1.cpp

Following is the program solution to Problem 3.1.

```
// prb03-1.cpp

// This program simulates a simple cash register.  It processes
// an indefinite number of customers.  At the end of the program,
// the program prints the total number of customers processed and
// the grand total of the meal prices

#include <iostream>
#include <iomanip>

using namespace std;

int main()
{
   const double SALES_TAX_RATE = 0.0825;

   double meal_price,      // Price of meal entered by user
          sales_tax,       // Amount of sales tax
          total,           // Total bill: meal_price + sales_tax
          amt_tendered,    // Amount received from customer
          change,          // Change: amt_tendered - total
          grand_total;     // Grand total of total meal prices

   int    num_customers,   // Counts number of customers processed
          response;        // yes = 1, no = 0

   //Set up output stream for currency output
   cout << setprecision(2)
        << setiosflags(ios::fixed)
        << setiosflags(ios::showpoint);
```

```cpp
// Initialize counter and accumulator

grand_total = 0.0;
num_customers = 0;

// Display banner

cout << "*** C++ Side Restaurant ***" << endl << endl;

// Ask for a customer

cout << endl;
cout << "Do you want to process a customer?" << endl;
cout << "Enter 1 for Yes or 0 for No: ";
cin >> response;

// Main processing loop

while (response == 1)
{
  cout << endl;
  cout << "Enter the price of the meal: $";
  cin >> meal_price;
  cout << endl << endl;

  // Calculate tax and total price

  sales_tax = meal_price * SALES_TAX_RATE;
  total = meal_price + sales_tax;

  // Display price tax and total

  cout << "Price of Meal:  " << setw(6) << meal_price << endl;
  cout << "Sales Tax:      " << setw(6) << sales_tax << endl;
  cout << "----------------------" << endl;
  cout << "Total Amount:   " << setw(6) << total << endl << endl;

  // Obtain amount tendered

  cout << "Enter amount tendered: $";
  cin >> amt_tendered;
  cout << endl << endl;

  // Calculate change

  change = amt_tendered - total;

  // Display amounts and change

  cout << endl;
  cout << "Amount Tendered: $" << setw(6) << amt_tendered
       << endl;
  cout << "Total Amount:    $" << setw(6) << total << endl;
  cout << "------------------------" << endl;
  cout << "Change:          $" << setw(6) << change << endl;

  // Increment counter and accumulator
```

```
      ++num_customers;
      grand_total += total;

      // Ask for a customer

      cout << endl;
      cout << "Do you want to process a customer?" << endl;
      cout << "Enter 1 for Yes or 0 for No): ";
      cin >> response;
   }

   // Display total customers and grand total

   cout << endl;
   cout << "Grand Totals:" << endl << endl;
   cout << "Total Customers: " << num_customers << endl;
   cout << "Total Receipts:  " << grand_total << endl;

   // Print closing banner

   cout << endl;
   cout << "*** Thank You ***";

   cout << endl;

   return 0;
}
```

Program Output

```
*** C++-Side Restaurant ***

Do you want to process a customer?
Enter 1 for Yes or 0 for No: 1

Enter the price of the meal: $34.50

Price of Meal:   34.50
Sales Tax:        2.85
----------------------
Total Amount:    37.35

Enter amount tendered: $40.00

Amount Tendered: $ 40.00
Total Amount:    $ 37.35
-----------------------
Change:          $  2.65

Do you want to process a customer?
Enter 1 for Yes or 0 for No: 1

Enter the price of the meal: $75.23
```

```
Price of Meal:     75.23
Sales Tax:          6.21
-----------------------
Total Amount:      81.44

Enter amount tendered: $100.00

Amount Tendered: $100.00
Total Amount:     $ 81.44
-----------------------
Change:            $ 18.56

Do you want to process a customer?
Enter 1 for Yes or 0 for N): 1

Enter the price of the meal: $57.92

Price of Meal:     57.92
Sales Tax:          4.78
-----------------------
Total Amount:      62.70

Enter amount tendered: $70.00

Amount Tendered: $ 70.00
Total Amount:     $ 62.70
-----------------------
Change:            $  7.30

Do you want to process a customer?
Enter 1 for Yes or 0 for No: 0

Grand Totals:

Total Customers: 3
Total Receipts:  181.488

*** Thank You ***
```

Discussion of prb03-1.cpp

The program code follows the pseudocode exactly. Because the program declares the counter num_customers as an int and the accumulator grand_total as a double, it uses two separate assignment statements for the initializations. (Most compilers will accept the multiple assignment statement

```
        num_customers = grand_total = 0;
```

but issue a warning message that the statement involves incompatible data types.)
    The prompt that asks the user if there is a customer to process displays a message over two lines.

```
    // Ask for a customer
        cout << endl;
        cout << "Do you want to process a customer?" << endl;
```

```
cout << "Enter 1 for Yes or 0 for No): ";
cin >> response;
```

The second `cout` statement says that the user must enter 1 for a Yes or 0 for a No. The program stores the user's answer in the integer variable `response`. In a later chapter, we shall discuss how to allow the user to enter Y or N in response to such a prompt. For now, we ask the user to enter an integer response to yes/no questions. See Experiments 1 and 2 for variations of prb03-1.cpp.

3.3.4 More on Control-Expressions

In the programs of this chapter, the `while` loop control-expressions were simple relation conditions. However, a control-expression can be any valid C++ expression. Recall that Note 3.1 stated that C++ considers any nonzero value as true, and 0 as the only false value. Thus, when a program evaluates the control-expression in a `while` statement, if its value is nonzero, the program considers the expression true and the loop body executes once. If the value of the control-expression is 0, the expression is false and the program exits the loop. This is why the C++ compiler never catches it when you inadvertently replace = = by =.

> **Note 3.5   Control-Expressions**
>
> The control-expression in a `while` or do loop can be any valid C++ expression. If the value of the expression is 0, the expression is considered false. If the value of the expression is nonzero, the expression is considered true.

To illustrate, suppose that in prb03-1.cpp we replace the `while` statement's condition (`response == 1`) by the assignment (`response = 1`). No matter what value the user enters for `response`, the assignment gives the value 1 to `response`. Therefore, the assignment (which is the control-expression in this case) has the value 1, which is true. This causes the `while` loop to never terminate—a so-called **infinite loop**. If a program enters an infinite loop, the program will sometimes appear to do nothing (because it is processing the loop body and never stopping), or it may produce an endless stream of output (because the loop body contains one or more output statements). See Experiment 1.

Although it may seem strange that any C++ expression can be a control-expression, it does allow the C++ programmer to write more-compact code. For example, you can code the `while` loop's condition in prb03-1.cpp as follows.

```
while (response)
```

Remember that when the computer evaluates the control-expression, `response` has the last value the user entered. If the value of `response` is anything other than zero, the control-expression is true and the loop body executes once. If the value of `response` is zero, the control-expression is false and the program exits the loop. See Experiment 2.

To consider another example, in Section 3.2 we wrote the following simple program to display the word "Hello" five times.

```
int count = 0;
while (count < 5)
{
   ++count;
   cout << "Hello" << endl;
}

cout << endl;
cout << "Hello was displayed " << count << " times." << endl;
```

We can write the while loop more compactly as follows.

```
while (count++ < 5)
   cout << "Hello" << endl;
```

In the condition-expression, the variable count is postincremented. Therefore, the condition tests the current value of count and then count is incremented by one, which is what happens in the original code. However, the value of count after the program exits the while loop is different. What is the final value of count? See Experiments 3 and 4.

Experiments 3.3

1. In prb03-1.cpp, replace the while's condition by

   ```
   while (response = 1)
   ```

   Compile and execute the resulting program. Explain what happens and why.

2. In prb03-1.cpp, replace the while's condition by

   ```
   while (response)
   ```

   Compile and execute the resulting program. Explain why the program does or does not work.

3. How many times does the following loop display Hello? Carefully explain how the loop condition works.

   ```
   int count = 5;
   while (--count)
      cout << "Hello" << endl;
   ```

4. In Experiment 3, what would happen if count were initialized to –1? Try it by incorporating the code in a small program. Considering the range of int variables, is the loop really what it seems to be? Compile and execute the resulting program. Explain what happens and why.

Programming Problems 3.3

1. A swimming pool maintenance company wants you to write a program to estimate the cost of resurfacing the inside of in-ground pools. The program is to

process an indeterminate number of estimates. To make an estimate, the program should ask the user to input the length, width, and depth of the pool, each to the nearest tenth of a foot. The company charges $2.25 per square foot. The following formula gives the inside surface area of a pool.

2 * depth * (length + width) + length * width

Include a sales tax of 7.75% in the estimate. The program should display the dimensions of the pool and the estimated cost to the nearest penny for each customer it processes. Write the required program.

2. A cattle-feed company needs a program to help process feed orders. The program is to process an indeterminate number of orders. Each customer orders one or both of two types of feed, A and B. Feed A costs $2.50 per 100 pounds and feed B costs $3.15 per 100 pounds. Amounts less than 100 pounds are to be charged proportionally. For each customer, the program should ask the user to enter the actual number of pounds ordered for each of feeds A and B to the nearest tenth of a pound. The program should display the amount and cost of each type of feed and the total cost of the order. When no more customers are to be processed, the program should display the total number of customers processed, the total amount of feed A ordered, and the total amount of feed B ordered to the nearest tenth of a pound, and the total receipts. Write the required program.

3. A computer science instructor needs a program that averages the grades she receives on a quiz she gives to her class. Each grade is an integer between 0 and 100. She does not know the number of grades at this time. Write a program that asks the user to enter quiz grades one at a time. After the user has completed entering grades, the program should display the number of grades entered and the sum of the grades entered. The program should also display the average of the grades, rounded to the nearest tenth.

4. A computer science instructor wants you to write a program to compute final grades for her Introduction to Computers course. The program is to process an indeterminate number of students. For each student the program should ask the user to enter the mid-term and final exam scores and then display the student's final grade. The final grade is the sum of 45% of the mid-term exam score and 55% of the final exam score. After it processes all the students, the program should display the number of students it processed, and the average mid-term exam score, average final exam score, and average final grade all to the nearest tenth. Write the required program.

5. A bank wants you to write a program to calculate the amounts in accounts that earn simple interest. The program should process an indeterminate number of accounts. The following formula gives the amount in an account, in which the principal is the initial investment.

amount = principal + interest

The following formula gives the interest, in which the rate is the annual interest rate as a decimal and time is the number of years the principal is at interest.

interest = principal * rate * time

For each account, the program should ask the user to input the principal, the interest rate to the nearest tenth as a percent (for example, 7.7), and the number of years at interest. The program should then display the principal, the interest, and the amount in the account after the given number of years. When there are no more customers to process, the program should display the number of accounts processed and the total principal and total interest paid. Write the required program.

3.4 DEFINITE ITERATION

Indefinite iteration is appropriate whenever you do not know how often the program will execute a loop body. For example, in developing a program to count the number of characters input by the user, it is appropriate to use a while loop. However, sometimes during program design you know exactly how often the program will execute the loop body. We call such a loop a **definite iteration loop**.

3.4.1 The for Statement

The best way to code a definite iteration loop in C++ is by using the for statement, which we shall introduce by an example. While a user is interacting with a program, it is sometimes necessary to clear the monitor screen before continuing the exchange between the user and the program. A primitive way to do this (which is not the best way available to the C++ programmer) is for the program to display as many newline characters as are necessary to cause the contents of the monitor to "scroll" off the top of the screen. If your monitor displays 25 lines, displaying 25 newline characters accomplishes this task.

The following cout statement, which contains 25 newline characters enclosed in quotes, is a simple, but inelegant, way to scroll the screen. Unfortunately, counting is the only way to ensure that this statement displays exactly 25 newline characters.

```
cout << "\n\n\n\n\n\n\n\n\n\n\n\n\n\n\n\n\n\n\n\n\n\n\n\n\n";
```

Instead of treating the 25 newline characters as a unit, as in the previous cout statement, we can view this problem as an iteration: display one newline character 25 times using a loop. The following while loop accomplishes this.

```
int line_count = 1;

while (line_count <= 25)
{
  cout << endl;
  ++line_count;
}
```

The variable line_count counts the number of times the program displays a newline character. The program initializes line_count to 1 in its declaration, uses it in the condition of the while loop, and increments it by 1 in the loop body. When the value of line_count exceeds 25, that is, when the program has displayed 25 newline characters, the loop ends.

This loop differs from the loops of dem03-1.cpp and prb03-1.cpp. In dem03-1.cpp, we did not know before running the program how many characters the user would enter. In prb03-1.cpp, we did not know before running the program how many customers the user would process. Therefore, in both cases, we used a while statement (an indefinite iteration loop) to code the iteration. In our present problem, we know exactly how often the loop is to execute (25) as we are designing the program. This is an example of a **definite iteration loop**. Because a counter variable controls the loop, we also call such a loop a **counter-controlled loop**.

It is always possible to code a definite iteration loop using a while statement as we did earlier. However, C++'s for statement is specifically designed for definite iteration loops. The first line of a for statement contains all three things that a program must do to the counter—initialize, test, and increment. For example, the following for statement has the same effect as the previous while statement.

```
int line_count;

for (line_count = 1; line_count <= 25; ++line_count)
    cout << endl;
```

This for statement works as follows. When program execution first encounters the for statement, the computer executes the first statement inside the parentheses (in this case, line_count = 1). This is the **loop initialization**, which the program executes only once upon entering the loop. Next, the program evaluates the second statement inside the parentheses (in our case, the condition line_count <= 25). This expression is the **loop test**. If the expression evaluates to true (that is, any nonzero value), the loop body executes once. (In our example, executing the loop body displays one newline character.) Then the program executes the third statement inside the parentheses, the **loop adjustment** (in our case, ++line_count). Then the program again tests the loop condition; that is, it evaluates the second expression inside the parentheses. If the expression evaluates to true, the loop body executes again, and so on. Eventually, the loop test expression evaluates to false (in our example, the value of line_count will exceed 25) and the loop ends.

It is extremely important that you understand the flow of control in a for statement. The dashed line in Figure 3.4 traces the flow of control of the previous for statement in a flowchart-like diagram, called a **definite iteration box**.

The program executes the loop initialization first and then makes the loop test. If the test is true, the loop body executes once, the computer adjusts the counter, and makes the test again. If the test is false, the loop ends.

Following is the definite iteration in pseudocode form.

```
for (each line_count from 1 to 25)
    print '\n'
endfor
```

The phrase "from 1 to 25" shows that the counter variable is to range from 1 to 25. The word "each" means that line_count is incremented by 1 for each loop iteration. The pseudocode word endfor indicates the end of the loop body.

Following is the general form of the for statement in C++. The semicolons are required after both the loop initialization and loop test statements. There must not be a semicolon after the loop adjustment statement.

```
for (loop initialization; loop test; loop adjustment)
    loop body
```

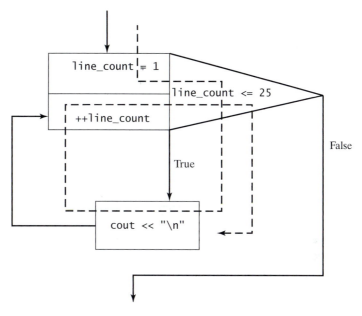

Figure 3.4

Following are five important facts about the `for` statement.

1. When execution exits the loop, the loop condition is false. In the loop that displays 25 newline characters, the loop condition is (`line_count <= 25`). Therefore, when the program exits the loop, the value of `line_count` is greater than 25. The program initializes `line_count` at one and increments `line_count` by 1 each time through the loop. Therefore, when control exits the loop, the value of `line_count` must be 26.

2. In a `for` loop, the counter can be initialized to any number, and the counter can be incremented by any number. For example, the following displays all the multiples of 5 from 5 to 95 on one line.

```
int multiple;

cout << endl;
for (multiple = 5; multiple <= 95; multiple += 5)
   cout << setw(3) << multiple;
cout << endl;
```

The first `cout` statement causes the cursor to start on a new line. The `for` statement initializes `multiple` to 5. Because this value is less than or equal to 95, the loop body executes once, which displays the value of the variable `multiple` in a three-character field. The loop adjustment statement increases `multiple` by 5, making it 10. In this way, `multiple` takes the values 5, 10, 15, 20, ..., 95. When the loop increases `multiple` to 100, the loop condition is no longer true. The loop ends and the next `cout` statement places the cursor on a new line. Therefore, the loop produces the following output.

```
5 10 15 20 25 30 35 40 45 50 55 60 65 70 75 80 85 90 95
```

3. The loop counter can be decremented each time through the loop. The following displays the word "Hello" on five separate lines.

```
int count;

for (count = 5; count > 0; --count)
    cout << "Hello" << endl;
```

This loop initializes the counter variable count to 5 and decreases it by one each time through the loop. The loop condition (count > 0) remains true as long as the value of count is positive. Therefore, when count has the values 5, 4, 3, 2, 1, the loop body executes. When count becomes 0, the loop condition is false and the loop ends. Therefore, the loop produces the following output.

```
Hello
Hello
Hello
Hello
Hello
```

4. The loop counter can be a non-integer. For example, consider the following code, which displays the tax on amounts ranging from $2.50 to $3.00 in increments of $0.10. (What is the purpose of the cout statement that follows the for statement?)

```
double price;

cout << setprecision(2)
     << setiosflags(ios::fixed)
     << setiosflags(ios::showpoint);

for (price = 2.50; price <= 3.00; price += 0.10)
    cout << "Tax on " << setw(4) << price
         << " is " <<  setw(4) << price * 0.0825 << endl;
cout << endl;
```

This code fragment initializes the variable price to 2.50. Each time through the loop, the statement increases the value of price by 0.10. The loop ends when the value of price exceeds 3.00. Therefore, the loop produces the following output. What is the value of price when the loop ends?

```
Tax on 2.50 is 0.21.
Tax on 2.60 is 0.21.
Tax on 2.70 is 0.22.
Tax on 2.80 is 0.23.
Tax on 2.90 is 0.24.
Tax on 3.00 is 0.25.
```

Using a non-integer to control a `for` loop can lead to unexpected results. See Experiment 3.

5. The body of a `for` loop can be a compound statement. The following produces the same output as the previous loop.

```
double price,
       tax;

cout << setprecision(2)
     << setiosflags(ios::fixed)
     << setiosflags(ios::showpoint);

for (price = 2.50; price <= 3.00; price += 0.10)
{
   tax = price * 0.0825;
   cout << "Tax on " << setw(4) << price
        << " is " << setw(4) << tax << endl;
}
cout << endl;
```

The difference between this loop and the previous one is that this loop computes the tax in a separate assignment statement inside the loop body. Therefore, the loop body, which now consists of two statements, must be a compound statement. See Experiment 4 for more variations on the `for` loop.

3.4.2 An Example of Definite Iteration

The program dem03-4.cpp uses `for` loops to display the following banner.

```
*******************************************************************
**                                                             **
**                                                             **
**                     Welcome to C++                          **
**                                                             **
*******************************************************************
```

The design of the program is simple, as the following pseudocode shows.

Clear the screen.
Display line 1.
Display line 2.
Display line 3.
Display line 4.
Display line 5.
Move the banner up 10 lines.

To display a line requires use of one or more `for` statements. For example, we can expand the pseudocode statement "Display line 2" by the following pseudocode.

print '**'
for (each position from 3 to 58)
    print ' '
endfor
print '**'

We leave as an exercise how to expand the pseudocode for displaying lines 1 and 3. Following is the program code for dem03-4.cpp.

```cpp
// dem03-4.cpp

// This program prints a welcome banner.

#include <iostream>

using namespace std;

int main()
{
  const char SYMBOL = '*';
  int i,
      position;

  // Clear screen
  for (i = 1; i <= 25; ++i)
    cout << endl;

  // Print line 1
  for (position = 1; position <= 60; ++position)
    cout << SYMBOL;

  // Print line 2
  cout << endl << SYMBOL << SYMBOL;
  for (position = 3; position <= 58; ++position)
    cout << " ";
  cout << SYMBOL << SYMBOL;

  // Print line 3
  cout << endl << SYMBOL << SYMBOL;
  for (position = 3; position <= 24; ++position)
    cout << " ";
  cout << "Welcome to C++";
  for (position = 37; position <= 58; ++position)
    cout << " ";
  cout << SYMBOL <<  SYMBOL;

  // Print line 4
  cout << endl << SYMBOL << SYMBOL;
  for (position = 3; position <= 58; ++position)
    cout << " ";
  cout << SYMBOL << SYMBOL;

  // Print line 5
  cout << endl;
  for (position = 1; position <= 60; ++position)
    cout << SYMBOL;

  // Move display up 10 lines
  for (i = 1; i <= 10; ++i)
    cout << endl;

  return 0;
}
```

Program Output

```
************************************************************
**                                                        **
**                   Welcome to C++                       **
**                                                        **
************************************************************
```

The character that the program uses to make the border (SYMBOL) is a symbolic constant. This allows us later to use a different symbol for the banner's border.

A simple for loop clears the screen. Another for loop displays the first line of the banner by printing 60 asterisks. The value of the variable position keeps track of where the cursor is on the line. Thus, in the for loop, position ranges from 1 to 60.

The cout statement in the body of this loop

```
cout << SYMBOL;
```

displays one copy of the character represented by SYMBOL.

To display line two, a single cout displays a newline character and two SYMBOLs to begin the line.

```
cout << endl << SYMBOL << SYMBOL;
```

Then, a for loop displays blanks in positions 3 through 58. Finally, a cout displays the last two SYMBOLs.

To display line three, a cout displays a newline character and two SYMBOLs. Then a for loop displays the blanks (in positions 3 through 24) that appear before the message. A single cout then displays the message. Another for loop displays the blanks (in positions 37 through 58) that appear after the message. Finally, a cout displays the two SYMBOLs that end the line.

Line four is exactly like line two and line five is exactly like line one. Displaying ten newline characters moves the banner up ten lines. See also Experiments 1 and 2.

3.4.3 Calculating Interest on a CD—Problem 3.2

The following problem uses a for loop to construct an interest table for a local bank that needs a program to calculate the monthly interest on a Certificate of Deposit (CD). The user is to enter the amount of the deposit, the term of the certificate in months, and the annual interest rate as a percent. The interest is to be compounded monthly. The program should display a table that lists the interest for each month, the total interest accumulated up to each month, and the balance in the account at the end of each month. After the program lists the table, it should display summary information listing the amount of the initial deposit, the total interest accumulated, and the final total amount in the CD account.

The interest earned on a CD is **compound interest**. The interest that a compound-interest account earns each month is added to the account balance. The new account balance then earns interest for the next month. Thus, in a compound-interest account, the interest earns interest.

The interest rate that the user provides to the program is an annual interest rate in percent form. Before using it in calculations, the program must convert the rate to a percent by dividing it by 100. This gives the annual rate as a decimal number. Then, the program must divide the annual rate by 12 to give the monthly interest rate.

For example, suppose you make a deposit of $10,000 in a CD that earns 9% interest annually. The annual rate as a decimal is $9/100 = 0.09$. The monthly rate is $0.09/12 = 0.0075$. The interest for the first month is $(10000.00) * (0.0075) = 75.00$. The program adds this interest to the balance. Therefore, the opening balance at the beginning of the second month is 10075.00. The interest for the second month is $(10075.00) * (0.0075) = 75.56$. The program adds this interest to the balance giving an opening balance of 10150.56 for the third month. This process continues for the life of the CD.

Following is the pseudocode for Problem 3.2.

Obtain deposit amount, term, and annual rate from user
Calculate monthly interest rate
Initialize total interest accumulator to 0
Initialize account balance to deposit amount
Display table headings.
for (each month from 1 to term)
   Calculate interest for current month
   Increment account balance
   Increment total interest
   Display data for current month
endfor
Display deposit amount, total interest, final balance

After obtaining the input data from the user, the program converts the annual interest rate to the equivalent decimal monthly interest rate. The program initializes the total interest accumulator to zero and the account balance to the value of the deposit. The for loop does its calculations once for each month of the term of the CD. In the for loop's body, the program calculates the interest for the current month, increments the account balance and the total interest accumulator, and displays the required information for the current month. When the program exits the for loop, it displays the summary data.

Following is the program code for prb03-2.cpp.

```
/// prb03-2.cpp

// This program illustrates the use of a for-loop to calculate
// the monthly interest on a CD.
// The user enters the amount deposited, the term, and the
// interest rate.  The program outputs a table listing the
// interest, accumulated interest, and account balance for
// each period.

#include <iostream>
#include <iomanip>
```

```cpp
using namespace std;

int main()
{
  double annual_rate,       // Annual interest rate as a percent
         monthly_rate,      // Per period interest rate
         deposit,           // Amount of deposit
         acct_balance,      // Monthly account balance
         interest,          // Monthly interest
         total_interest;    // Total interest
  int    month,             // Counts the periods of the CD
         term;              // Term of the CD in months

  // Set output for currency

  cout << setprecision(2)
       << setiosflags(ios::fixed)
       << setiosflags(ios::showpoint);

  cout << "Enter amount deposited in CD: ";
  cin >> deposit;
  cout << endl;
  cout << "Enter term of CD in number of months: ";
  cin >> term;
  cout << endl;
  cout << "Enter the annual CD interest rate in %: ";
  cin >> annual_rate;

  monthly_rate = (annual_rate / 100) / 12;
  total_interest = 0.00;
  acct_balance = deposit;

  cout << endl << endl;
  cout << "PERIOD    INTEREST  TOTAL INTEREST  NEW BALANCE" << endl;
  cout << "---------------------------------------------------" << endl;

  for (month = 1; month <= term; ++month)
  {
    interest = monthly_rate * acct_balance;
    acct_balance += interest;
    total_interest += interest;

    cout << endl << setw(4) << month
         << setw(14) << interest
         << setw(13) << total_interest
         << setw(15) << acct_balance;
  }

  cout << endl;
  cout << "---------------------------------------------------" << endl << endl;
  cout << "\tSummary" << endl << endl;
  cout << "Initial Deposit:" << setw(8) << deposit << endl;
```

```
cout << "Interest:        " << setw(8) << total_interest << endl;
cout << "Final Total:     " << setw(8) <<   acct_balance << endl;

return 0;
}
```

Program Output

Enter amount deposited in CD: **1000.00**

Enter term of CD in number of months: **12**

Enter the annual CD interest rate in %: **7.5**

PERIOD	INTEREST	TOTAL INTEREST	NEW BALANCE
1	6.25	6.25	1006.25
2	6.29	12.54	1012.54
3	6.33	18.87	1018.87
4	6.37	25.24	1025.24
5	6.41	31.64	1031.64
6	6.45	38.09	1038.09
7	6.49	44.58	1044.58
8	6.53	51.11	1051.11
9	6.57	57.68	1057.68
10	6.61	64.29	1064.29
11	6.65	70.94	1070.94
12	6.69	77.63	1077.63

          Summary

Initial Deposit: 1000.00
Interest: 77.63
Final Total: 1077.63

The program code closely follows the pseudocode. One assignment calculates the monthly_rate.

```
monthly_rate = (annual_rate / 100) / 12;
```

The parentheses in the expression on the right of the assignment are not necessary, but we include them to clarify the purpose of the expression. After the program initializes acct_balance and total_interest, it displays the heading line of the table.

The counter variable month controls the for loop and ranges from one to the value of term. In the body of the for loop, the program calculates the interest as monthly_rate * acct_balance. At this point in the loop body, acct_balance is the opening balance for the month currently being processed by the loop. After calculating the interest, the program increases acct_balance and total_interest by the value

PERIOD	INTEREST	TOTAL INTEREST	NEW BALANCE
4	14	13	15

Field Widths

Figure 3.5

of interest. This new updated value of acct_balance is the closing balance at the end of the current month.

Finally, the cout statement displays the row of the table that contains the data for the current month. The setw() manipulators align the variable values in the columns of the table. Each setw() defines a field on the output line into which a value is placed. We selected the field widths so that the values align vertically with the column headings. See Figure 3.5. Recall that the values appear right-justified in each field.

Exercises 3.4

In Exercises 1–7, assume the following declarations.

```
int i;
double f;
```

For each for statement, find the number of times the loop body executes and the value of the loop counter when the program exits the loop.

1. for (i = 1; i <= 27; ++i)
   cout << endl << i;

2. for (i = 0; i < 27; ++i)
   cout << endl << i;

3. for (i = 3; i <= 27; i += 2)
   cout << endl << i;

4. for (i = 25; i > 10; --i)
   cout << endl << i;

5. for (f = 1.05; f <= 2.0; f += 0.10)
   cout << endl << f;

6. for (f = 2.0; f <= 100.0; f *= 2.0)
   cout << endl << f;

7. for (i = 1; i <= 10; ++i)
   cout << endl << i++;

8. Write a while loop and associated statements that are equivalent to the for loop of Exercise 1.

9. Write a while loop and associated statements that are equivalent to the for loop of Exercise 5.

10. Write a do loop and associated statements that are equivalent to the for loop of Exercise 3.

11. Write a `for` loop that is equivalent to the following `while` loop.

```
int count = 0;
while (count < 20)
{
   cout << "Hello" << endl;
   ++count;
}
```

12. Write a `for` loop that is equivalent to the following `while` loop.

```
int count = 1;
while (count < 10)
{
   cout << "Hello" << endl;
   count += 2;
}
```

Experiments 3.4

1. Change dem03-4.cpp so that it asks for the symbol that the user wants to use for the border around the welcome banner. The program should display the banner with the indicated border.

2. Place the following `for` statement between the first two `for` statements in dem03-4.cpp. What effect does it have?

```
for (i = 1; i <= 10000 ; ++i)  ;
```

The body of the previous `for` statement is the **empty statement**, that is, a semicolon by itself. Can you think of a practical use for such a `for` statement?

3. Inspect the following `for` loop. How many times should the loop display the word "Hello?"

```
double d;
for (d = 0.0; d <= 1.0; d += 0.2)
   cout << "Hello" << endl;
```

If you answered "six times," you are correct. Now inspect the following `for` loop. How many times should the loop display the word "Hello?" Test the correctness of your answer by embedding the code in a program. Can you explain the results?

```
double d;
for (d = 0.0; d <= 1.0; d += 0.05)
cout << "Hello" << endl;
```

4. The comma is a C++ operator. When the comma separates two statements, the statement to the left of the comma executes, then the statement to the right of the statement executes. The value of the whole expression is the value of the last statement executed. The comma operator can be used effectively in the `for` statement. What is the value of `j` after each of the following `for` loops ends? Assume the `i` and `j` are `int` type variables.

a. for (i = 1, j = 3; i < 5; ++i)
　　j += i;
b. for (i = 1, j = 3; i < 5; ++i, ++j)
　　j += i;
c. for (i = 1, j = 3; i < 5, j < 10; ++i, ++j)
　　j += i;

Programming Problems 3.4

1. Write a program that displays all the even integers between 1 and 100, inclusive.
2. Write a program that prompts the user to enter the number of times he/she wants to display the word "Hello." The program should then display Hello the requested number of times.
3. Write a program that asks the user to enter an integer between 1 and 10, sums the squares of the integers from 1 to the number entered, and displays the sum. Thus, if the user enters 5, the program should display the following.

   `The sum of the squares of the integers from 1 to 5 is 55.`

4. Write a program that displays a table of integers from 1 to 20 with their squares and cubes. The columns of the table should have appropriate headings.
5. Write a program that displays a conversion table for degrees Fahrenheit to degrees Celsius beginning with 20°F through 100°F in steps of 5°. The conversion formula is celsius = 5 * (fahrenheit −32)/9.

   The columns of the table should have appropriate headings. Round each Celsius value to the nearest integer.
6. The factorial of the integer n, denoted by n!, is the product of all the integers from 1 to n. Thus, 3! = (1)*(2)*(3) = 6 and 5! = (1)*(2)*(3)*(4)*(5) = 120. 0! is defined to be 1. Write a program that asks the user to enter an integer between 1 and 10 and then displays the factorial of the integer entered.
7. Write a program that performs multiplication of integers by repeated addition. The program should ask the user to enter two integers, which the program stores in num1 and num2. Using an accumulator, the program should then add num1 to itself num2 times. Finally, the program should display the resulting product.
8. Write a program that raises an integer to a positive integer power. The program should prompt the user to enter the base and the exponent. The program should calculate the power by multiplying base by itself exponent times. Finally, the program should display the result. Test your program by making it calculate 2^5 and 5^4.
9. Write a program that displays the following.

```
   *    *    *    *    *
   *              *
   *              *
   *              *
   *    *    *    *    *
```

10. See Programming Problem 9. Write a program that asks the user for the size of the square to be displayed (up to 24 × 24). The program should display a square of that size.

11. See Programming Problem 10. Write a program that asks the user for the size of the square to be displayed (up to 20 × 20) and for the character to use in the display. The program should then display a square of the required size, bordered by the required character.

3.5 NESTED LOOPS

The body of a loop can contain any C++ statement. Loops are **nested** when the body of a loop contains another loop.

3.5.1 Nested while Loops

The program dem03-1.cpp counted the number of characters entered by the user on one line. We now consider a program that uses nested while loops to count the number of characters entered by the user over several lines. The program asks the user to enter characters. The user may enter as many lines and as many characters on each line as he/she wishes. Thus, we do not know how many lines the user will enter nor do we know how many characters the user will enter on each line. This suggests that the program should use indefinite iteration to process the input data. We consider the user's input to be an iteration of an unknown number of lines.

    while (there is another line)
      process the line
    endwhile

To process a line, the program must count an unknown number of characters on the line.

    while (there is another character on the line)
      count the character
    endwhile

Placing the second loop inside the first, we have the complete pseudocode.

    while (there is another line)
      while (there is another character on the line)
        count the character
      endwhile
    endwhile

Because we are using two while loops, we must decide exactly how to code each loop's condition. The inner while loop is very much like the while loop in dem03-1.cpp. To count the number of characters on a line, the program gets and counts each character until it encounters a newline character.

How do we signal the program that we no longer want to enter characters? We cannot use one of the usual characters, such as a period or comma, to signal the end of the input because we want to count all such characters. C++ provides the special symbolic constant EOF to signal the end of input. EOF is a mnemonic that means "end of file." The standard header file iostream contains the definition of EOF. Therefore, if your program contains the #include <iostream> preprocessor directive, there is no need for you to define EOF in your program. The value of EOF is system dependent, although most systems use the int value –1.

Entering the value of EOF from the keyboard is not straightforward. You cannot enter the characters EOF because the program would count them as three separate characters. Neither can you directly enter the numeric value of EOF, namely –1, because the program would consider –1 as two separate characters. In Windows, to enter the correct value of EOF from the terminal, you must enter ^Z; that is, hold the Ctrl key down and press Z. This transmits the correct value of EOF to the program. In UNIX/Linux, enter ^D for the value of EOF.

Following is the program code for dem03-5.cpp.

```
// dem03-5.cpp

// This program uses nested while-loops to count the number
// of characters input by the user on several input lines.

#include <iostream>

using namespace std;

int main()
{
   int ch;              // Stores the character entered by the user
   int num_chars = 0;   // Counts the number of characters entered

   cout << "This program counts the number of characters" << endl
        << "you enter on each input line and outputs the" << endl
        << "total number of characters entered.  Terminate" << endl
        << "each line with Enter.  Terminate the program by" << endl
        << "pressing Enter, [Ctrl]+Z, and Enter." << endl << endl;
   while ((ch = cin.get()) != EOF)
   {
      ++num_chars;
      while ((ch = cin.get()) != '\n')
         ++num_chars;
   }
   //cout << endl;
   cout << "You entered " << num_chars << " characters." << endl;

   return 0;
}
```

Program Output

This program counts the number of characters
you enter on each input line and outputs the
total number of characters entered. Terminate
each line with Enter. Terminate the program by
pressing Enter, [Ctrl]+Z, and Enter.

abc
defg
hijkl
^Z

You entered 12 characters.

The variable ch, which stores the character that the user enters, is type int instead of type char. A character is actually stored as a binary integer. The only difference in storing a character, say 'a', in an int type variable instead of a char type variable is that the int variable requires two or four bytes of storage whereas the char type variable requires one or two bytes (two bytes for Unicode characters) of storage. In either case, the character 'a' is stored as the integer value 97 (see Table A.3) in binary form. Whatever value your computer system uses to represent EOF, it cannot be a value that represents a character. Because the program declares ch as an int, ch can represent any character value as well as the value of EOF.

Note 3.6   Storing EOF

If a variable is to store EOF as well as other characters, the variable should be declared as type int instead of type char.

The variable num_chars is a counter that sums the number of characters the user enters. As usual, the program initializes the counter to zero.

The outer while loop's condition

```
while ((ch = cin.get()) != EOF)
```

contains an embedded assignment. The computer executes the cin.get() and returns the next character from the input stream. Then the program assigns this character to the variable ch and tests the value of the expression (ch = cin.get()), which is the value assigned to ch, against EOF. If the character is not equal to EOF, the program executes the body of the outer while loop.

The first statement in the body of the outer while loop increments the variable num_chars by one. This is necessary to count the character that was entered and tested by the cin.get() that was executed in the outer while loop's condition. After the program counts this character, the inner while loop counts characters up to but not including the newline character that ends the line. This completes one iteration of the outer while loop. Testing the outer while loop's condition now retrieves the first character on the next line. If the character is not EOF, then the program processes the rest of the line as described above. If the character is EOF, then the outer loop ends and the program displays the value of num_chars.

Since the program tests only the first character of each line against EOF, to end the program properly $^\wedge$Z must be the first character on the line. See Experiments 1 and 2.

Table 3.4 shows a trace of the program when the following three lines are input by the user.

```
abcd
123
^Z
```

3.5.2 Nested for Loops

In this section, we consider a program that uses nested for loops to display a staircase.

Suppose we want to display the staircase depicted in Figure 3.6.

We can view the staircase as an iteration of 22 steps, as shown in the pseudocode:

```
for (each step from 1 to 22)
  produce a step
endfor
```

Each step is an iteration of Xs. However, the number of Xs in each row is not fixed. The number of Xs in a step equals the number of the step, as you count from the top of the staircase. The top step has one X; the second step from the top has two Xs; the third step from the top has three Xs; and so on. Thus, to produce a step, we have:

```
for (each position from 1 to the step number)
  print 'X'
endfor
```

TABLE 3.4

Character Processed (Value of ch)	num_chars	Keyboard Input Buffer
		abcd\n
a	1	bcd\n
b	2	cd\n
c	3	d\n
d	4	\n
\n		123\n
1	5	23\n
2	6	3\n
3	7	\n
\n		^Z \ n
^Z		\n

Figure 3.6

Placing this loop inside the previous one, we have the pseudocode solution to the problem.

```
for (each step from 1 to 22)
  for (each position from 1 to the step number)
    print 'X'
  endfor
endfor
```

Following is the code for dem03-6.cpp.

```cpp
// dem03-6.cpp

// This program illustrates nested for loops by displaying
// steps consisting of Xs.  The number of iterations
// of the inner for loop depends on the value of the counter
// that controls the outer for loop.

#include <iostream>

using namespace std;

int main()
{
  const int SCR_SIZE = 22;
  int step_number,
      x_count;

  for (step_number = 1; step_number <= SCR_SIZE; ++step_number)
  {
    cout << endl;
    for (x_count = 1; x_count <= step_number; ++x_count)
```

```
            cout << "X";
        }
        cout << endl;
        return 0;
    }
```

Program Output

```
X
XX
XXX
XXXX
XXXXX
XXXXXX
XXXXXXX
XXXXXXXX
XXXXXXXXX
XXXXXXXXXX
XXXXXXXXXXX
XXXXXXXXXXXX
XXXXXXXXXXXXX
XXXXXXXXXXXXXX
XXXXXXXXXXXXXXX
XXXXXXXXXXXXXXXX
XXXXXXXXXXXXXXXXX
XXXXXXXXXXXXXXXXXX
XXXXXXXXXXXXXXXXXXX
XXXXXXXXXXXXXXXXXXXX
XXXXXXXXXXXXXXXXXXXXX
XXXXXXXXXXXXXXXXXXXXXX
XXXXXXXXXXXXXXXXXXXXXXX
```

The variable step_number controls the outer loop. One iteration of the outer loop, that is one execution of its loop body, produces one line of Xs. The first statement in the loop body is a cout that moves the cursor to the next line. The second statement in the loop body is the inner for loop. The variable x_count is the counter for the inner loop. The inner loop displays Xs, one at a time on the same line. The program initializes the counter x_count to 1 and increments it by 1 as long as x_count <= step_number. Thus, the number of Xs that the program displays equals the current value of the variable step_number. Table 3.5 shows the values of step_number and x_count for the first few iterations.

Our examples of **nested loops** included nesting a while loop inside a while loop and nesting a for loop inside a for loop. You can, of course, nest a while loop inside a for loop, or nest a for loop inside a while loop. Any combination of nesting is possible.

TABLE 3.5

step_number	x_count	
1	1	First iteration of outer loop
2	1	Second iteration of outer loop
	2	
3	1	Third iteration of outer loop
	2	
	3	
4	1	Fourth iteration of outer loop
	2	
	3	
	4	
.....	.....	.....

Experiments 3.5

1. Change the type of ch in dem03-5.cpp to char. Compile and execute the resulting program. Does the program run correctly? Why or why not?

2. Test dem03-5.cpp by entering ^Z at the end of a line, before hitting enter. Can you explain what happens? Look very carefully at the program code and trace it with the data you enter.

3. Adjust dem03-6.cpp so that each step contains two more Xs than the previous step. Compile and execute the resulting program.

4. Adjust dem03-6.cpp so the user can enter the character that the program is to use to make the steps. Compile and execute the resulting program.

Programming Problems 3.5

1. Adjust dem03-5.cpp so that it counts the number of characters and the number of lines the user enters and displays the total number of characters and the total number of lines. Compile and execute the resulting program.

2. A wholesale book dealer needs a program to write invoices for book orders that he takes over the phone. Each order usually consists of multiple copies of several book titles. The program should ask the user if there is an order to process. If the user responds yes, the program should then ask for the price of the first book in the order and the number of such books. The program should then display the cost of these books, including a 7.5% sales tax. Then it should ask for the price of the second book in the order and the number of such books, and display the cost of these books. The program should continue in this way, processing the books in the first order. When there are no more books in the order, the program should display the total cost of the order. Then the program should ask if there is another order. If there is one, the program should process it as just described. If there are no more orders, the program should display the total number of orders

processed, the total number of books sold, and the total receipts. Use nested `while` loops.

3. Suppose you deposit $1 into an account this month, $2 into the account the second month, $4 the third month and so on, doubling your deposit each month. Write a program that displays the first month that your deposit exceeds $1,000,000.

4. Typically, the trade-in value of a car is about 70% of its value one year ago. Suppose that you buy a new car whose value is $30,000. Write a program that asks the user to enter the current value of a car. For a new car, it is the selling price of the car. The program should display the number of years it takes for the car's trade-in value to be below $1000.

5. Write a program to display the following tree.

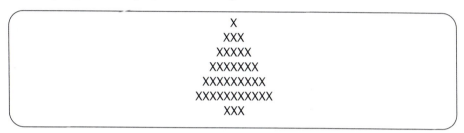

```
                    X
                   XXX
                  XXXXX
                 XXXXXXX
                XXXXXXXXX
               XXXXXXXXXXX
                  XXX
```

Center the tree both vertically and horizontally on the terminal screen.

5. Write a program that displays a line with 26 As, a second line with 26 Bs, a third line with 26 Cs, and so on to a 26th line with 26 Zs.

6. Write a program that displays a tax rate table in the following form.

Amount		Tax Rate					
	4.0%	4.5%	5.0%	5.5%	6.0%	6.5%	7.0%
100.00							
200.00							
300.00							
1000.00							

Use nested `for` loops to produce the body of the table.

7. A paper products manufacturer needs a program to forecast its sales over a six-month period. To do so requires knowing the value of the sales growth rate and how the sales grow over that period. Write a program that asks the user to enter the minimum assumed growth rate (as a percent) and the sales for the current month. Assume a linear growth; that is, the sales for a month is a fixed percent (the growth rate) over the previous month. The program should display, in a table, the projected sales for the minimum growth rate and for growth rates up to 4% greater than the minimum. The table should look like the following if the user enters 7 for the minimum growth rate and 30000 for the current month's sales.

Sales Projection

Current Month's Sales: 30000

Growth
Rate in %   Month

	1	2	3	4	5	6
7						
8						
9						
10						
11						

CHAPTER REVIEW

TERMINOLOGY

Discuss the meaning of each term.

iteration	embedded assignment
looping	do-while loop
while loop	do statement
do loop	relational operator
for loop	accumulator
definite iteration loop	infinite loop
indefinite iteration	counter-controlled loop
trace	loop initialization
compound statement	loop test
char	loop adjustment
character constant	definite iteration box
character variable	compound interest
cin.get()	empty statement
priming input	nested loops
relational condition	

SUMMARY

- The relational operators (Table 3.1) can be used to code simple relation conditions.
- If a relation condition is true, its numeric value is 1; otherwise, its value is 0 (Note 3.1).
- Any nonzero value is considered true; 0 is considered false (Note 3.1).
- Use the while statement to code indefinite iteration loops.
- Use a counter variable to keep track of how many times an event occurs in a program. A counter must be initialized (usually to 0), incremented (usually by 1), and used (Note 3.2).
- A char type variable can store a single character. A character constant is a single character enclosed in apostrophes.

- The member function `cin.get()` returns a single character from the input buffer.
- To process an unknown number of inputs, use a priming input before the `while` loop and then another input at the end of the `while` loop body (Note 3.3).
- Embedding an assignment in a `while` loop condition, for example `while ((ch = cin.get()) != '\n')`, is an effective way to process all characters in the input buffer.
- Use an accumulator to add the values that a variable takes on. An accumulator must be initialized (usually to 0), incremented (usually by the value of the variable it is totaling), and used (Note 3.4).
- The control-expression in a `while` or do loop can be any valid C++ expression (Note 3.5).
- Use the `for` statement to code definite, or counter-controlled, iteration loops.
- If a variable is to store characters and possibly EOF (the end-of-file character), the variable should be declared as type `int` (Note 3.6).
- You can nest `while`, do, and `for` loops (that is, a `while`, do, or `for` statement can be in the loop body of a `while`, do, or `for` statement).

REVIEW EXERCISES

1. What are the six relational operators in C++?
2. What is the value of a relation condition?
3. What is the precedence of the relational operators relative to the arithmetic and assignment operators and relative to each other?
4. Explain how the `while` statement works.
5. How can you enclose more than one statement in the body of a `while` loop?
6. What are the rules for the correct use of a counter variable?
7. What function can you use to obtain one character from the input buffer?
8. Describe the structure of a loop that processes an unknown number of inputs.
9. What is embedded assignment and how does it work?
10. Explain how the execution of a `do-while` loop differs from that of a `while` loop.
11. What are the rules for the correct use of an accumulator variable?
12. What can appear as the control expression in a `while` or `do-while` loop?
13. Explain how a `for` loop executes.
14. How can you enter the end-of-file character from the terminal?

Chapter 4

Decision Making

OBJECTIVES

- To code an `if` statement to make a simple decision
- To write a program that makes simple decisions
- To code compound conditions using the logical operators not: !, and: &&, and or: | |
- To use the precedence rules for the logical operators
- To code a nested `if` statement to make complex decisions
- To write a program that uses a nested `if`
- To code a `switch` statement to make a multi-way decision
- To write a program that makes a multi-way decision
- To use `break` to exit prematurely from a loop
- To use `continue` to end the current iteration of a loop

Most programs make decisions according to the truth or falsity of conditions. This chapter discusses decision making in C++. We start by considering simple conditions and how to code simple `if` statements. We discuss how to code compound conditions and how to write `if` statements based on them. Then we show how to place a decision within a decision (nested `if` statements). Finally, we discuss how to make multi-way decisions using the `switch` statement.

4.1 BASIC DECISION MAKING

Basic decisions are coded in C++ using the `if` statement. This section discusses how to translate a decision into the corresponding C++ code.

4.1.1 The `if` Statement

You code a decision in C++ by using the `if` statement, whose general form follows.

```
if (control-expression)
   true-part
else
   false-part
```

The words **if** and **else** are C++ keywords. You also must enclose the control-expression in parentheses. The control-expression can be any valid C++ expression. The true and false parts of an if statement can be any simple statement ended by a semicolon or a compound statement.

Note 4.1 describes how the if statement works.

Note 4.1   How the if Statement Works

A program executes an if statement as follows. First, it evaluates the control-expression. If the control-expression is true (that is, has a nonzero value), the program executes the true part; it skips the false part, and then executes the statement that follows the if. If the control-expression is false (that is, has the value zero), the program skips the true part and executes the false part. After the program executes the false part, it executes the statement that follows the if statement.

To translate a decision into C++ code, follow the procedure of Note 4.2.

Note 4.2   How to Code an if Statement

To code an if statement:

1. Code the keyword if.
2. Code the control-expression. Be sure to enclose the expression in parentheses.
3. Code the true part, namely everything to be done when the control-expression is true. If the true part is one statement, end it with a semicolon. If the true part consists of several statements, write them as a compound statement (that is, enclose the set of statements in braces).
4. If there is a false part, code the keyword else. If there is no false part, code nothing and skip step 5.
5. Code the false part, namely everything to be done when the control expression is false. This must be a simple statement or a compound statement as described in step 3.

As an example, we translate the following into C++ code: If the value of the variable balance exceeds $500.00, then add 1 to large_balance. If the value of balance does not exceed $500.00, then add 1 to small_balance.

Following Note 4.2, we have the following code segment.

```
if (balance > 500.00)
   ++large_balance;
else
   ++small_balance;
```

For a second example, we translate the following into C++ code: If the value of balance exceeds $500.00, then add 1 to large_balance and display the message "Large Balance". If the value of balance does not exceed $500.00, then add 1 to small_balance and display "Small Balance".

The true part of this test requires two actions—increment a variable and display a message. If the true or false part of an if consists of two or more statements, you must code that part as a compound statement. Note that we align the braces with the if and else keywords and indent the statements inside the braces two spaces.

```
if (balance > 500.00)
{
   ++large_balance;
   cout << "Large Balance";
}
else
{
   ++small_balance;
   cout << "Small Balance";
}
```

What would happen if we omit a pair of braces in the solution of the previous example as follows?

```
if (balance > 500.00)
{
   ++large_balance;
   cout << "Large Balance";
}
else
   ++small_balance;
   cout << "Small Balance";
```

The true and false parts of an if statement in C++ are single statements—either a simple statement or a compound statement. Therefore, in the previous if statement, the false part consists only of the statement

```
++small_balance;
```

The cout statement that follows this increment is not inside the if statement. Therefore, the code displays the message "Small Balance" no matter what the value of balance. See Experiments 1 and 2 for further discussion.

It is possible for the false part of an if statement to be empty, as shown in the flowchart of Figure 4.1.

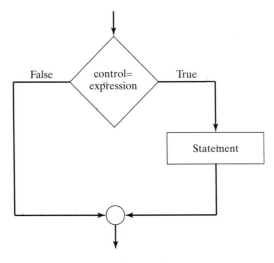

Figure 4.1

To code this in C++, simply omit the keyword `else` and the false-part statements. Again, the true part can be a single statement ended by a semicolon, or a single compound statement. Therefore, you would code the statement as follows.

```
if (control-expression)
    true-part
```

As a final example of coding decisions, suppose we translate the following. If the value of the `char` variable `pay_code` equals R, then set the value of the `double` variable `pay_rate` equal to 4.25 and set the value of the `double` variable `health_rate` equal to 0.024.

The following code translates the decision into C++.

```
if (pay_code == 'R')
{
    pay_rate = 4.25;
    health_rate = 0.024;
}
```

4.1.2 Calculating a Payroll with Overtime—Problem 4.1

A bookstore owner wants you to write a program that calculates the store's weekly payroll. The store's employees are paid by the hour. The program should prompt the user to enter for each employee the number of hours worked for the week and the hourly pay rate. The program is to calculate each employee's gross pay, including the possibility of overtime pay. Regular pay is the number of hours the employee worked (up to 40 hours) times the hourly pay rate. The program is to pay overtime if the employee worked more than 40 hours. The overtime pay equals the number of hours the employee worked over 40 hours, multiplied by 1.5 (the overtime pay factor), multiplied by the hourly pay rate. The program should output the worker's regular pay, overtime pay, and gross pay (the sum of the regular pay and overtime pay). Then the program should ask the user if he/she wants to process another employee. If there is another employee to process, the program should calculate the pay as described earlier. When the user responds that there are no more employees to process, the program should display the number of employees it processed and the total payroll, that is, the sum of the gross salaries of the employees.

The pseudocode solution to this problem is straightforward.

Initialize total payroll and employee count accumulators
do
  Obtain hours and rate from the user
  if (hours > 40)
   Calculate regular pay and overtime pay
  else
   Calculate regular pay, overtime pay = 0
  endif
  Calculate gross pay
  Increment total payroll and employee count accumulators
  Display regular pay, overtime pay, gross pay
  Prompt the user for another employee
  Obtain response
while (response is yes)
  Display employee count and total payroll

A do-while loop is appropriate because we assume that the user wants to process at least one employee. Recall that, in a do-while loop, the loop body executes at least once.

An employee's pay is determined by the if statement. A worker earns overtime pay only if the number of hours worked is greater than 40. Therefore, the if statement in the pseudocode checks the value of hours.

If the value of hours is greater than 40, the program calculates the regular pay and the overtime pay. In this case, the regular pay equals the pay rate multiplied by 40 because the first 40 hours worked earn pay at the regular rate. To calculate the overtime pay, the program first calculates the number of overtime hours, which is the number of hours worked minus 40. Then, it multiplies the number of overtime hours by 1.5 to obtain the number of equivalent regular hours. Finally, the program multiplies the number of equivalent regular hours by the pay rate to obtain the overtime pay.

If the value of hours does not exceed 40, the regular pay equals the number of hours worked multiplied by the pay rate, and the overtime pay is zero. Whether or not the person worked overtime, the gross pay is the regular pay plus the overtime pay (which is zero if the person did not work more than 40 hours).

The program requires two accumulators; one for counting the number of employees processed, and another for accumulating the total payroll. We initialize both accumulators to zero at the beginning of the program. The program increments the accumulators near the end of the loop body after the calculation of the gross pay.

At the end of the loop body, the program prompts the user for another employee. If there is another employee to process, the loop body executes again. If there are no more employees to process, the loop ends and the program displays the totals.

Following is the program code for prb04-1.cpp.

```cpp
// prb04-1.cpp

// This program calculates a payroll.  For each employee, it
// calculates the gross pay including overtime
// paid at 1.5 times the hourly rate.  The program also
// calculates the total payroll.  The program illustrates
// the use of the if statement.

#include <iostream>
#include <iomanip>

using namespace std;

int main()
{
  const double OT_PAY_FACTOR = 1.5;
  const double NORMAL_HOURS = 40.0;
  int    employee_count,
         another_employee;        // 1 if another employee; 0 if not
  double hours,
         rate,
         regular_pay,
         ot_pay,
         gross_pay,
         total_payroll;

  total_payroll = 0.00;
  employee_count = 0;

  cout << setprecision(2)
       << setiosflags(ios::fixed)
       << setiosflags(ios::showpoint);

  do
  {

      // Prompt the user
    cout << endl << endl;
    cout << "Enter number of hours worked: ";
    cin >> hours;
    cout << "\nEnter pay rate: ";
    cin >> rate;

     // Calculate the pay
    if (hours > NORMAL_HOURS)
    {
      regular_pay = NORMAL_HOURS * rate;
      ot_pay = (hours - NORMAL_HOURS) * OT_PAY_FACTOR * rate;
    }
```

```
      else
      {
        regular_pay = hours * rate;
        ot_pay = 0.00;
      }
      gross_pay = regular_pay + ot_pay;
      total_payroll += gross_pay;
      ++employee_count;

        // Display the pay

      cout << endl << endl;
      cout << "REGULAR PAY  OVERTIME PAY  GROSS PAY";
      cout << endl << setw(11) << regular_pay
             << setw(14) << ot_pay
             << setw(11) << gross_pay << endl;
      cout << "----------------------------------" << endl;

        // Ask the user if he/she wants to continue

      cout << endl << endl;
      cout << "Do you want to process another employee?" << endl;
      cout << "Enter 1 for Yes or 0 for No: ";
      cin >> another_employee;
    }
    while (another_employee);

    // Print the total

    cout << endl << endl;
    cout << "Payroll for " << employee_count
           << " employees is " << total_payroll << endl;

    return 0;
  }
```

Program Output

```
Enter number of hours worked: 53

Enter pay rate: 6.50

REGULAR PAY  OVERTIME PAY  GROSS PAY
    260.00        126.75     386.75
-----------------------------------

Do you want to process another employee?

Enter 1 for Yes or 0 for No: 1

Enter number of hours worked: 36

Enter pay rate: 4.00
```

```
REGULAR PAY   OVERTIME PAY   GROSS PAY
     144.00          0.00      144.00
-----------------------------------------

Do you want to process another employee?
Enter 1 for Yes or 0 for No: 1

Enter number of hours worked: 45.5

Enter pay rate: 10.00

REGULAR PAY   OVERTIME PAY   GROSS PAY
     400.00         82.50      482.50
-----------------------------------------

Do you want to process another employee?
Enter 1 for Yes or 0 for No: 0

Payroll for 3 employees is 1013.25.
```

The program follows the pseudocode exactly. The condition expression in the `while` statement contains just the name of the variable `another_employee`. If the user enters 1 in response to the prompt for another employee's data, the value of `another_employee` is 1, which C++ considers true, and the program processes the employee in the loop body. If the user enters 0 in response to the prompt, the value of `another_employee` is 0, which C++ considers false. This terminates the loop. Note that because C++ considers any nonzero value to be true, entering any nonzero number (not just 1) will cause another iteration of the loop.

The overtime pay factor and the number of regular hours worked are symbolic constants because these could change from one program run to another. A new labor contract, for example, could reduce the number of regular hours to 35 and increase the overtime pay factor to 1.75. Then it would be a simple matter to change the corresponding values in the declarations.

Exercises 4.1

In Exercises 1–3, translate the pseudocode into valid C++ code.

```
1. set valid_flag to 1
   if (balance >= 0)
      set balance_hold to balance
      display balance
   else
      set valid_flag to 0
   endif

2. if (tax_code == 'S')
      set local_tax_flag to 1
      set state_tax_flag to 1
```

```
   endif
   add 1 to local_taxpayers
```

3.
```
   add 1 to line_number
   if (line_number > 50)
      set page_break to 1
   endif
   if (key_a == key_save)
      display regular_line
   else
      display other_line
   endif
   add group_accum to total_accum
```

In Exercises 4–7, use the following declarations. In each exercise, state which variable the code increases.

```
int    a = 1,
       b = 2;
double d1 = 32.6,
       d2 = 27.9;
```

4.
```
   d2 *= 3;
   if (d1 > d2)
      ++a;
   else
      ++b;
```

5.
```
   if (d1 <= d2)
      ++a;
   else
      ++b;
```

6.
```
   if (2 * d2 < d1 + 10.0)
      ++a;
   else
      ++b;
```

7.
```
   if (d1 != d2)
      ++a;
   else
      ++b;
```

In Exercises 8–12, translate the given statements into C++ code.

8. Calculate gross_pay as hours_worked multiplied by pay_rate. If gross_pay is less than 100.00, calculate tax as 12% of gross_pay. If gross_pay is greater than or equal to 100.00, calculate tax as 15% of gross_pay. In either case, calculate net_pay as tax subtracted from gross_pay.

9. Assume num is an integer. If num is even, display "The number is even." If num is odd, display "The number is odd." (Hint: Use the remainder operator % to test num.)

10. If `quantity_on_hand` is less than 200, add 1 to `below_level` and display "Quantity on hand is low."; otherwise, display "Quantity on hand is acceptable."

11. If `age` is greater than 18, set `dues` equal to 2.50 plus 0.50 multiplied by the number of years that `age` exceeds 18. If `age` is less than or equal to 18, set `dues` equal to 2.50.

12. If `grade` is greater than or equal to 65, set the character variable `mark` equal to 'P' and display "Passed."; otherwise, set `mark` equal to 'F' and display "Failed."

Experiments 4.1

Base your answers to Experiments 1 and 2 on the following code.

```
if (balance > 500.00)
{
   ++large_balance;
   cout << "Large Balance" << endl;
}
else
{
   ++small_balance;
   cout << "Small Balance" << endl;

}
```

1. Code a program containing the above `if` statement, but omit both braces in the true part of the `if` statement. What message does your compiler issue and why? Exactly which statements are contained in the `if` statement?

2. Code a program containing this `if` statement, but omit the parentheses that enclose the condition (`balance > 500.00`). What message does your compiler issue and why?

Programming Problems 4.1

1. Write a program that defines a symbolic constant `CONSTANT` whose value is 10. The program should prompt the user to enter an integer. If the integer is greater than the value of `CONSTANT`, then the program should display "The number entered is larger than `CONSTANT`."; otherwise, the program should display "The number entered is not larger than `CONSTANT`."

2. Write a program that prompts the user to enter two `doubles`. The program should decide which number is larger, the first or the second, and display an appropriate message.

3. Write a program that prompts the user to enter the number of nuts sold and the number of bolts sold. If the numbers are the same, the program should display "The numbers of nuts and bolts are the same." If the numbers are different, the program should display the message "The numbers of nuts and bolts are different." The program also should decide which number is greater, and advise the user how many of the lesser type will make the numbers the same. For example,

if the number of nuts sold is 500 and the number of bolts sold is 455, the program should display the following.

```
The numbers of nuts and bolts are different.

The number of nuts sold exceeds the number of bolts sold.

You need 45 bolts.
```

4. Write a program that asks the user to enter an integer, decides if the integer is even or odd, and displays an appropriate message. See Exercise 9.

5. Write a program that asks the user to enter an integer, decides if the integer is divisible by six, and displays an appropriate message.

6. Write a program that asks the user to enter a single character, decides if the character is an uppercase letter, and displays an appropriate message.

7. The State Highway Traffic Violations Bureau wants you to write a program to compute the amount of a moving violation. The program should prompt the user to enter the illegal speed in miles per hour at which the person was driving. Calculate the fine as follows: If the illegal speed was less than 70 miles per hour, the fine is $50.00 plus $5 for each mile per hour over the legal limit of 55. If the illegal speed was greater than 70 miles per hour, the fine is $125 plus $10 for each mile per hour over 70.

8. A small airline company needs a program to compute baggage charges. Write a program that asks the user to enter the weight of a passenger's baggage. The program should display the baggage charge, which is calculated as follows. If the baggage weight is 50 pounds or less, the program should display "No Charge". If the baggage weight is greater than 50 pounds, the baggage charge is $5.00 plus $0.95 for each pound over 50.

9. A real estate company needs a program to help decide commissions due an agent when the agent sells a property. Write a program that prompts the user for the selling price of the property and the property class of the property. If the class equals 1, the commission rate is 4.5%. If the class is 2, the commission rate is 5.0%, and if the class is 3, the commission rate is 6.0%. The commission equals the appropriate commission rate multiplied by the selling price of the property. The program should display the selling price, the property class, the commission rate, and the commission.

10. Redesign, code, and execute the solution to Problem 4.1 to take income tax into consideration. Assume that the income tax rate is 15% of the gross salary for gross salaries of $500.00 or less. If the gross salary is greater than $500.00, the tax is $75.00 plus 20% of the gross salary over $500.00. The program should display the regular pay, overtime pay, gross salary, tax, and net salary (gross salary minus the tax) for each employee. After processing all the employees, the program should display the number of employees it processed, and totals for the gross salary, tax, and net salary.

4.2 COMPOUND CONDITIONS—THE LOGICAL OPERATORS

Sometimes a program must test a condition that is a combination of other, simpler conditions. We can combine simple conditions to form compound conditions by using the **logical operators**, which are listed in Table 4.1.

4.2.1 The not Operator, !

Recall that the **truth value** of an expression is either true (any nonzero value) or false (value zero). The **not**, or **negation**, operator, !, reverses the truth value of its operand. Suppose we have the following declarations and if statement.

```
int i = 7;
char ch;

if (!(i == 3))
    ch = 'A';
else
    ch = 'B';
```

Because the value of i is 7, the condition (i == 3) is false. The not operator ! reverses the truth value of the condition to true. Therefore, the if statement assigns the value 'A' to the variable ch.

4.2.2 The and Operator, &&

The **and** operator && (also called **conjunction**) combines two conditions as follows: (condition 1) && (condition 2). The truth value of conjunction is true only if both conditions are true; otherwise, the truth value is false. Table 4.2 shows the truth value of a conjunction in terms of the truth values of the conditions that it combines. In the table, T represents true and F represents false.

TABLE 4.1

Operator	Meaning
!	not
&&	and
||	or

TABLE 4.2   TRUTH TABLE FOR (CONDITION 1) && (CONDITION 2)

	&&	condition 1 T	F
condition 2	T	T	F
	F	F	F

Conjunction is useful in many situations. For example, suppose that a payroll program must set the tax rate to 22% for any salary between $500.00 and $999.99. To be in this range, the salary must be greater than or equal to 500.00 and less than 1000.00. The following if statement makes the test and sets the tax rate accordingly.

```
if ( (salary >= 500.00) && (salary < 1000.00) )
    tax_rate = 0.22;
```

Note the use of parentheses. A pair of parentheses, which the if statement requires, surrounds the entire compound condition. A pair of parentheses also surrounds each simple condition. Although C++ may not always require them, you should parenthesize each simple condition to help clarify the compound condition.

4.2.3 Testing for a Digit—dem04-1.cpp

The program dem04-1.cpp, which follows, asks the user to enter a single character followed by a return. The program tests the character to see if it is a digit and, displays an appropriate message.

```
// dem04-1.cpp

// This program demonstrates the use of a compound if-statement
// that decides whether a key depressed by the user is numeric.
// The program uses cin.get() to input a character at a time.

#include <iostream>

using namespace std;

int main()
{
    char ch;

    cout << "Please press a key, then press enter: ";

    ch = cin.get();

    cout << endl;

    if ( (ch >= '0') && (ch <= '9'))

        cout << "The key you pressed was a digit." << endl;
    else
        cout << "The key you pressed was not a digit." << endl;

    return 0;
}
```

Program Output

```
Please press a key, then press enter: a
The key you pressed was not a digit.
```

The program uses `cin.get()` to obtain the character from the user and places it in the char variable ch. The `if` statement's control-expression is a compound condition. To be a digit, the character that the user enters must be between 0 and 9, inclusive. Therefore, the condition that the program tests is `(ch >= '0') && (ch <= '9')`.

It is important to understand how the program refers to zero and nine in this condition. The `cin.get()` obtains the character that the user types and transmits it to the program as an alphanumeric character. The program stores this character in the character variable ch. In the condition of the `if` statement, the program compares the value of ch to the characters 0 and 9, not the integers 0 and 9. (The character 0 and the integer 0 have different bit representations. See Appendix A.) Therefore, we must enclose the character 0 and the character 9 in single quotes so the program makes a character comparison instead of a numeric comparison. See Experiment 1.

4.2.4 The or Operator, ||

The **or** operator || (or **disjunction**) combines two conditions as follows: (condition 1) || (condition 2). The truth value of disjunction is true if either or both conditions are true; otherwise, the truth value is false. In other words, the only time a disjunction is false is when both conditions are false. Table 4.3 shows the truth value of a disjunction in terms of the truth values of the conditions that it combines. In the table, T represents true and F represents false.

4.2.5 The Program dem04-2.cpp

Following is dem04-2.cpp, which, like dem04-1.cpp, tests a character entered by the user to see if it is a digit. However, instead of using && to test if the character is in the valid range, it uses || to test if the character is outside the valid range. The character the user enters is invalid if it is less than '0' or if it is greater than '9'. Note that the error message is now in the true part of the `if` statement.

```
// dem04-2.cpp
```

```
// This program demonstrates the use of a compound if-statement
// that decides whether a key depressed by the user is numeric.
// The program uses cin.get() to input a character at a time.
```

```
#include <iostream>
```

```
using namespace std;
```

TABLE 4.3   TRUTH TABLE FOR
(CONDITION 1) || (CONDITION 2)

		condition 1	
||		T	F
condition 2	T	T	T
	F	T	F

```
int main()
{
  char ch;

  cout << "Please press a key, then press enter: ";

  ch = cin.get();

  cout << endl;
  if ( (ch < '0') || (ch > '9'))
    cout << "The key you pressed was not a digit." << endl;
  else
    cout << "The key you pressed was a digit." << endl;

  return 0;
}
```

Program Output

```
Please press a key, then press enter: 7
The key you pressed was a digit.
```

4.2.6 Precedence Rules

We have already discussed the precedence and associativity rules for the arithmetic operators, the assignment operators, and the relational operators. We also must fit the logical operators into this hierarchy. Table 4.4 shows the complete precedence and associativity rules for all the operators we have discussed so far.

Negation is at the highest precedence level along with the other unary operators. The conjunction operator && has a higher precedence than disjunction ||, and both associate from left to right.

To consider an example, suppose we have the following declaration and code.

```
int i = 7,
    result;

if ( (i != 0) && (i <= 10) || (i == 17) )
  result = 1;
else
  result = 0;
```

Because && has a higher precedence than ||, the computer evaluates the conjunction first. The condition (i != 0) is true and the condition (i <= 10) is true. Therefore, the conjunction of the two conditions is true. The computer uses this truth value in the disjunction with the condition (i == 17). Because the disjunction of a true with a false is true, the entire condition in the if statement is true. Therefore, the code sets the value of result to 1. Figure 4.2 shows the evaluation of the truth value of the compound condition.

TABLE 4.4

Operators	Associativity
( )	Left to Right (Inside-Out)
! + (unary) – (unary) ++ – –	Right to Left
* / %	Left to Right
+ –	Left to Right
< <= > >=	Left to Right
== !=	Left to Right
&&	Left to Right
||	Left to Right
= += -= *= /=	Right to Left

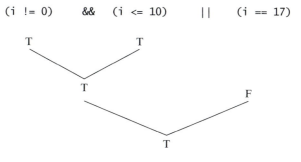

Figure 4.2

This last example shows an interesting aspect of how C++ evaluates logical expressions; C++ uses **"short-circuit" evaluation**. When the computer can decide the truth value of an expression, it stops evaluating the expression. When C++ evaluates the expression that we discussed previously, it knows that the conjunction (i != 0) && (i <= 10) is true. Therefore, it knows that the disjunction of this truth value with the condition (i == 17) must be true no matter what is the truth value of (i == 17). Therefore, the computer will not test the value of i to see if it equals 17. There is no need to make this test, so the computer does not make it. See Experiment 2.

Exercises 4.2

In Exercises 1–4, use the following declarations. Find the final value of the variable result.

```
    double a = 32.6,
           b = 27.9;
    int    result = 0;
```

1. if ((a > 20.0) && (b <= 30.0))
```
      ++result;
   else
      --result;
```

2. ```
if ((a > 40.0) || (b > 30.0) || (2 * b > a))
   ++result;
else
   --result;
```

3. ```
if ( (a == 30.0) && (3 * b > 50.0) || (2 * b > a) )
   ++result;
else
   --result;
```

4. ```
if ((a == 30.0) && ((3 * b > 50.0) || (2 * b > a)))
   ++result;
else
   --result;
```

In Exercises 5–8, translate the given statements into C++ code.

5. If the value of the integer variable score is less than 40 or greater than 100, increment out_of_range by one.

6. If the value of the double variable income is greater than 20000.00 but less than 25000.00, then assign 0.225 to tax_rate.

7. If the value of the character variable credit_code is 'N' and the value of the double variable account_balance is greater than 1000.00, then assign 'Y' to the character variable credit_message.

8. If the value of the integer variable employee_code is 1, 3, or 6, assign the value of 'h' to the character variable hospitalization_code.

## Experiments 4.2

1. In dem04-2.cpp, replace the compound condition by the following.

   ```
   if ( (ch >= 0) && (ch <= 9) )
   ```

   Test the resulting program by entering the digit 7 and then by entering the character A. Explain the actions of the program.

2. To show that C++ uses short-circuit evaluation in compound conditions, consider the following program.

   ```
   #include <iostream>

   using namespace std;
   int main()
   {
      int i = 3,
          j = 5;

      if ( (i == 3) || (++j > 0) )
         cout << "i = " << i << ",  j = " << j << endl;

      return 0;
   }
   ```
   ```

What do you think the output should be? Remember how the preincrement operator works. When you execute the program, is the output what you expect? If not, explain what happens.

3. Devise a small program to find out how C++ interprets the condition !i == 3. Give i the value 1 and test the conditions (!i == 3) and !(i == 3).

Programming Problems 4.2

1. Write a program for The Department of Motor Vehicles (DMV) to calculate the registration fees for automobiles. The DMV classifies automobiles as type 1, for luxury, or as type 2, for all others. The registration fee for an automobile is $35.00. If the automobile is a luxury vehicle, add a surcharge of $15.00. The DMV also classifies automobiles as city vehicles (class 1) or non-city vehicles (class 2). An automobile that is registered in the city of Metropolis must pay an additional surcharge of $20.00, no matter what its type. Your program should prompt the user for the luxury type (either 1 or 2) and for the city class (either 1 or 2) of the automobile. The program should display the total registration fee for the vehicle. Design the program to process any number of automobiles.

2. Write a program for a mail-order software company to calculate shipping and handling charges for its orders. The program should prompt the user for the weight of the order in ounces. If the weight is eight ounces or less, then there is a flat rate charge of $1.50. If the weight of the order is more than eight ounces but less than 32 ounces, the charge is $1.50 plus $0.50 for each ounce over eight. If the weight of the order is 32 ounces or greater, the charge is $13.50 plus $0.75 for each ounce over 32. The program should display the weight of the order and the shipping and handling charge. Design the program to process any number of orders. At the end of the program, display the total number of orders processed and the total of the shipping and handling charges.

3. The mail-order company of Programming Problem 2 requires a program to calculate discounts that it is giving to all its customers during a sales campaign. Write a program that asks the user to enter the total price of an order. If the order price is $200.00 or less, the discount rate is 10%. If the order price is greater than $200.00, the discount rate is 15%. The net price of the order is the price minus the discount. The program should display the price of the order, the discount amount, and the net price of the order. Design the program to process any number of orders. When there are no more orders to process, the program should display the number of orders it processed, the total of the prices, the total of the discounts, and the total of the net prices.

4. Write a program that combines the requirements of Programming Problems 2 and 3. Thus, the program should prompt the user for the price of the order and its weight. The program should discount the price according to the specifications of Programming Problem 3. Then the program should calculate the shipping and handling charges according to the specifications of Programming Problem 2. For each order, the program should display the price and weight, the discount amount, the discounted price, the shipping and handling charges, and the net

price (price – discount + shipping and handling charge). Design the program to process any number of orders.

5. A bank's vice president in charge of small loans needs a program to help her approve or disapprove loans. Write a program that meets the following requirements. The program should prompt the user for the annual income of the loan applicant, the amount of the loan, and the number of years of the loan. The program should display an approval or rejection message, as appropriate. Approve the loan in either of the following cases: if the amount of the loan is less than $5,000.00 and the applicant's annual income is at least $30,000.00; or if the amount of the loan is greater than or equal to $5,000.00 and less than $20,000.00, and the applicant's annual income is at least $75,000.00. In all other cases, reject the application.

4.3 NESTED if STATEMENTS

Sometimes it is necessary to test a condition only if a previously tested condition is true or false. This section discusses how to make such a test using a nested if statement.

4.3.1 Coding a Nested if Statement

Consider the flowchart of Figure 4.3. The flowchart tests the value of state_code only if the value of employee_code is 'A'. Thus, the true part of the test of employee_code contains the test for state_code. This is an example of a **nested if**, that is, the true or false part of an if structure (sometimes called the **outer if**) contains another if (sometimes called the **inner if**).

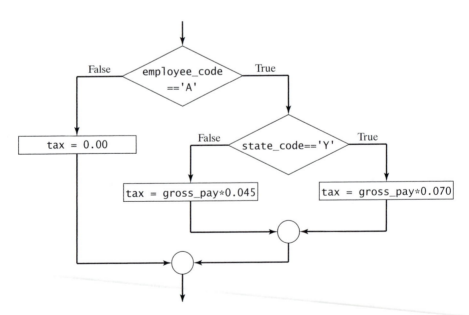

Figure 4.3

To code the nested if of Figure 4.3, follow the steps of Note 4.2. First, code the keyword if followed by the condition (employee_code == 'A'). Next, code what the program must do when the condition is true, namely make another test. To code this second test, again use the steps of Note 4.2.

The following code translates the flowchart of Figure 4.3 into C++ code.

```
if (employee_code == 'A')
  if (state_code == 'Y')
    tax = gross_pay * 0.07;
  else
    tax = gross_pay * 0.045;
else
  tax = 0.00;
```

We align the if-else pairs in a nested if on the same vertical column and indent the true and false parts of each if-else two spaces. This coding technique helps to identify the parts of the nested if.

In the preceding code, it is not necessary to surround the inner if by braces because the if-else statement is one statement, not a compound statement. However, it is sometimes necessary to enclose the true or false parts of a nested if in braces. To consider an example, we translate the flowchart of Figure 4.4 into C++ code.

The true part of the outer if consists of two statements—an if statement and an assignment statement. The false part of the outer if consists of two assignment statements.

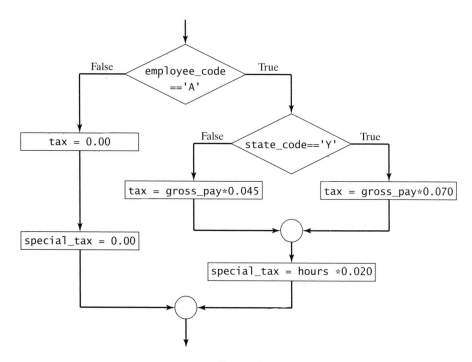

Figure 4.4

Therefore, in both cases, we must use braces to form a compound statement. Following is the corresponding C++ code.

```
if (employee_code == 'A')
{
  if (state_code == 'Y')
     tax = gross_pay * 0.07;
  else
     tax = gross_pay * 0.045;
  special_tax = hours * 0.02;
}
else
{
  tax = 0.00;
  special_tax = 0.00;
}
```

Braces do not follow the else part of the inner if. Therefore, the else part of the inner if consists of only the following statement.

```
tax = gross_pay * 0.045;
```

Thus, the C++ compiler knows that the assignment statement

```
special_tax = hours * 0.02;
```

is not part of the inner if. The computer makes the assignment to special_tax no matter what is the value of state_code.

C++ uses the rule of Note 4.3 to match if-else pairs in a nested if.

Note 4.3 Rules for Nested if Statements

Without braces, the compiler matches each else in a nested if with the most recent if that is not already matched with an else.

You must be very careful when you omit braces. For example, some people incorrectly translate the flowchart of Figure 4.5 as follows. Before your read beyond the code, try to decide why it is incorrect.

```
if (employee_code == 'A')
   if (state_code == 'Y')
      tax = gross_pay * 0.07;
else
   tax = 0.00;
```

This code does not correctly translate Figure 4.5 because the C++ compiler matches the else with the second if, not the first if.

Using the rule of Note 4.3, the compiler scans the if statement looking for elses to match with ifs. It first encounters the if that tests employee_code, then it encounters

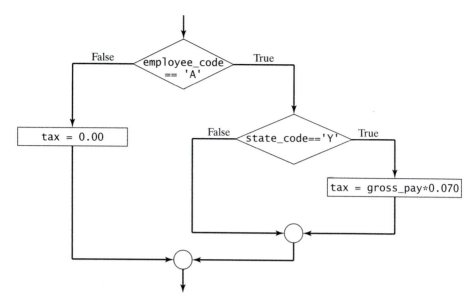

Figure 4.5

the if that tests `state_code`. Next, the compiler meets an `else` and matches this `else` with the most recent if that it has not already matched with an `else`, namely, the if that tests `state_code`. Therefore, if we use proper indentation, the previous code should be as follows.

```
if (employee_code == 'A')
   if (state_code == 'Y')
      tax = gross_pay * 0.07;
   else
      tax = 0.00;
```

This code is equivalent to the flowchart of Figure 4.6, not the flowchart of Figure 4.5.

To correctly translate the flowchart of Figure 4.5 into C++ code, force the compiler to match the `else` with the first if by enclosing the inner if in braces.

```
if (employee_code == 'A')
{
   if (state_code == 'Y')
      tax = gross_pay * 0.07;
}
else
   tax = 0.00;
```

Braces now enclose the true part of the outer if. Therefore, the compiler does not match the `else` with the if that tests `state_code`.

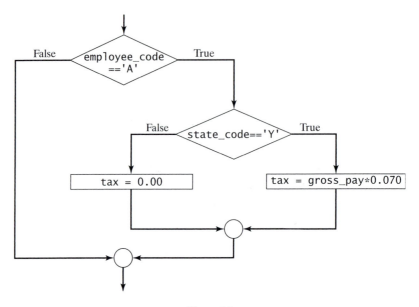

Figure 4.6

4.3.2 Calculating a Payroll—Problem 4.2

The following problem uses a nested `if` to calculate the tax on employee pay and discusses how to input single characters in response to program prompts.

An automobile repair shop wants you to write a payroll program for its employees. The program must calculate each employee's net salary, that is, the salary after taxes. Prompt the user for the employee's pay rate, hours worked, employee code (either 'A' for full time or 'B' for part-time), and state code (either 'Y' for New York or 'J' for New Jersey). Allow the user to enter either uppercase or lowercase letters. The program should display the regular pay, the overtime pay, the gross pay, the tax, and the net pay.

Calculate the gross pay as follows. If the employee worked 40 hours or less, the regular pay is the pay rate times the hours worked and overtime pay is zero. If the employee worked over 40 hours, the regular pay is the pay rate times 40 and the overtime pay is 1.5 times the pay rate times the hours worked over 40.

Calculate the tax as follows. If the employee code is 'A' and the state code is 'Y', the tax is 7% of the gross pay. If the employee code is 'A' and the state code is not 'Y', the tax is 4.5% of the gross pay. If the employee code is not 'A', the tax is zero. The net pay is the gross pay minus the tax.

After the program processes the last employee, it should display the total number of employees it processed and the total gross pay, tax, and net pay.

4.3.3 Program Design

A pseudocode solution to Problem 4.2 follows.

> Display program banner
> Initialize accumulators

do
　Obtain pay rate, hours, employee code, and state code
　Calculate gross pay
　Calculate tax
　Calculate net pay
　Increment accumulators
　Display results
　Prompt for another employee
　Obtain response
while (response is yes)
Display final totals

We now expand the high-level pseudocode statements "Calculate gross pay" and "Calculate tax." First, to calculate the gross pay, we have the following pseudocode.

if (hours > 40)
　calculate regular pay
　calculate overtime pay
else
　calculate regular pay
　overtime pay = zero
endif
gross pay = regular pay + overtime pay

To calculate the tax, we use a nested if structure as follows.

if (employee code = 'A')
　if (state code = 'Y')
　　tax = gross pay * 0.07
　else
　　tax = gross pay * 0.045
　endif
else
　tax = 0.00
endif

4.3.4 Character Input

Problem 4.2 requires the user to input three characters: A or B in response to the prompt for the employee code; Y or J in response to the prompt for the state code; and Y or N in response to the prompt for another employee. We must be careful about the contents of the keyboard input buffer when a program inputs characters and numbers.

According to the pseudocode, the program first obtains the employee's pay rate and number of hours worked. The program obtains these values by executing cin statements. When retrieving a number from the keyboard input buffer, cin skips all whitespace (newline characters, tabs, and blanks) and retrieves the next number it encounters. The newline character that the user enters after entering the number remains in the keyboard input buffer. Figure 4.7a shows the keyboard input buffer after the

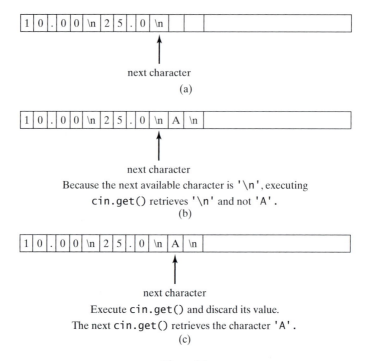

next character

(a)

next character

Because the next available character is '\n', executing

`cin.get()` retrieves '\n' and not 'A'.

(b)

next character

Execute `cin.get()` and discard its value.

The next `cin.get()` retrieves the character 'A'.

(c)

Figure 4.7

user enters 10.00 and 25.0 in response to the first two prompts. An arrow shows the next character that is available to the program (a newline character).

According to the pseudocode, the program now prompts for the employee code. Assume the user enters the character 'A' and then a newline character. Suppose the program obtains the next character from the input buffer by executing `cin.get()`. It would then retrieve the newline character that it left in the buffer after the user entered the number of hours worked. The program would not retrieve the character 'A'. See Figure 4.7b. To get rid of this newline character, we make the program execute `cin.get()` and discard the character it returns. The program will execute `cin.get()` again and place the returned character into the variable `employee_code` so the program can test its value later. See Figure 4.7c. Following is the code to accomplish this.

```
cin.get();
employee_code = cin.get();
```

The first `cin.get()` statement obtains the next available character from the input buffer, but does not assign this value to any variable. This, in effect, discards the newline character that precedes the employee code.

The program prb04-2.cpp, which follows, uses this technique to obtain values for the other two character variables that the program requires.

4.3.5 The Program prb04-2.cpp

Following is the program code, prb04-2.cpp.

```cpp
// prb04-2.cpp

// This program processes a payroll for a small company.  It
// calculates gross pay including the possibility of overtime.
// It also calculates payroll tax depending on the employee
// code and state code.  The program displays the gross salary,
// tax, and net salary for each employee.  When there are no more
// employees to process, the program displays summary information.

#include <iostream>
#include <iomanip>

using namespace std;

int main()
{
  const double RESIDENT_RATE = 0.070;
  const double NON_RESIDENT_RATE = 0.045;

  int   employee_count;
  char employee_code,
       state_code,
       response;
  double    pay_rate,
            hours,
            regular_pay,
            overtime_pay,
            gross_pay,
            tax,
            net_pay,
            total_gross_pay,
            total_tax,
            total_net_pay;

  cout << setprecision(2)
       << setiosflags(ios::fixed)
       << setiosflags(ios::showpoint);

      // Display banner

  cout << "This program calculates the net pay for each employee."
       << endl << endl;
  cout << "At each prompt, enter the requested data.";

      // Initialize accumulators

  employee_count = 0;
  total_gross_pay = total_tax = total_net_pay = 0.00;

            // Main processing loop
```

```
do
{
    // Obtain input data

  cout << endl << endl << "Enter the pay rate: ";
  cin >> pay_rate;
  cout << endl << "Enter the number of hours worked: ";
  cin >> hours;
  cout << endl<< "Enter the employee code (A or B): ";
  cin.get();                    // Discard the \n
  employee_code = cin.get();
  cout << endl << "Enter the state code (Y or J): ";
  cin.get();                    // Discard the \n
  state_code = cin.get();

    // Calculate the gross pay

  if (hours > 40.0)
  {
     regular_pay = 40.0 * pay_rate;
     overtime_pay = (hours - 40.0) * 1.5 * pay_rate;
  }
  else
  {
     regular_pay = hours * pay_rate;
     overtime_pay = 0.00;
  }

  gross_pay = regular_pay + overtime_pay;

    // Calculate the tax

  if ((employee_code == 'A') || (employee_code == 'a'))
     if ((state_code == 'Y') || (state_code == 'y'))
       tax = gross_pay * RESIDENT_RATE;
     else
       tax = gross_pay * NON_RESIDENT_RATE;
  else
     tax = 0.00;

    // Calculate net pay
  net_pay = gross_pay - tax;

    // Display results

  cout << endl << endl;
  cout << "Regular Pay:  " << setw(7) << regular_pay << endl;
  cout << "Overtime Pay: " << setw(7) << overtime_pay << endl;
  cout << "Tax:          " << setw(7) << tax << endl;
  cout << "Gross Pay:    " << setw(7) << gross_pay << endl;
  cout << "----------------------" << endl;
  cout << "Net Pay:      " << setw(7) << net_pay << endl;

// Increment accumulators
```

```
            ++employee_count;
            total_gross_pay += gross_pay;
            total_tax += tax;
            total_net_pay += net_pay;

              // Prompt for another employee

            cout  << endl << endl;
            cout << "Do you want to process another employee?(y/n): ";
            cin.get();                      // Discard the \n
            response = cin.get();
        }
    while ( (response == 'y') || (response == 'Y') );

          // Display summary information

    cout  << endl << endl << endl;
    cout << "Total number of employees processed: " << employee_count
          << endl;
    cout << "Total gross pay:" << setw(9) << total_gross_pay << endl;
    cout << "Total tax:       " << setw(9) << total_tax << endl;
    cout << "Total net pay:   " << setw(9) << total_net_pay << endl;

    return 0;
}
```

Program Output

This program calculates the net pay for each employee

At each prompt, enter the requested data.

Enter the pay rate: **7.25**

Enter the number of hours worked: **47**

Enter the employee code (A or B): **A**

Enter the state code (Y or J): **Y**

```
Regular Pay:    290.00
Overtime Pay:    76.12
Tax:             25.63
Gross Pay:      366.12
--------------------
Net Pay:        340.50
```

Do you want to process another employee?(y/n): **y**

Enter the pay rate: **8.50**

Enter the number of hours worked: **30**

Enter the employee code (A or B): **A**

```
Enter the state code (Y or J): J

Regular Pay:    255.00
Overtime Pay:     0.00
Tax:             11.47
Gross Pay:      255.00
--------------------
Net Pay:        243.53
Do you want to process another employee?(y/n): y

Enter the pay rate: 6.00

Enter the number of hours worked: 50

Enter the employee code (A or B): B

Enter the state code (Y or J): Y

Regular Pay:    240.00
Overtime Pay:    90.00
Tax:              0.00
Gross Pay:      330.00
--------------------
Net Pay:        330.00

Do you want to process another employee?(y/n): n

Total number of employees processed: 3
Total gross pay:    951.12
Total tax:           37.10
Total net pay:      914.02
```

The program very closely follows the pseudocode. We declare the three variables that store single characters as type int according to Note 3.5 of Chapter 3.

The conditions in the nested if that decide the tax and the condition in the do-while loop test for either a lowercase or an uppercase letter. This is good practice because some users inadvertently enter a lowercase letter when your program expects an uppercase letter, or the other way around.

As a final comment on prb04-2.cpp, note that the body of the do-while loop is very long (about 60 lines). Because it is sometimes difficult to understand a long piece of code, we commented each section of the body of the loop and separated the sections by spaces. It would be far better if we could modularize this part of the code so that it looks more like the high-level pseudocode that we developed earlier. This is exactly what we shall do in Chapter 5 when we discuss how to write our own functions and how to code modular C++ programs.

Exercises 4.3

1. Translate the flowchart of Figure 4.8 into C++ code using a nested if.

2. Translate the flowchart of Figure 4.9 into C++ code using a nested if.

Figure 4.8

Figure 4.9

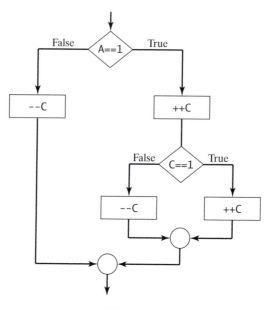

Figure 4.10

3. Translate the flowchart of Figure 4.10 into C++ code using a nested if.

4. Translate the flowchart of Figure 4.11 into C++ code using a nested if.

5. The following nested if is correct. Recode the statement using proper indentation.

```
if (a > b) if (c == d) {y = x; s = t;} else u = t; else if (e >
    f) ++g;
```

6. The following is indented correctly but not is not coded the way the indentation suggests. Correct the code.

```
if (read_code == 2)
   ++record_count_1;
   ++record_count_2;
else
   ++record_count_3;
```

Experiments 4.3

1. The first example in this section contained the following nested if statement.

```
if (employee_code == 'A')
{
   if (state_code == 'Y')
      tax = gross_pay * 0.07;
```

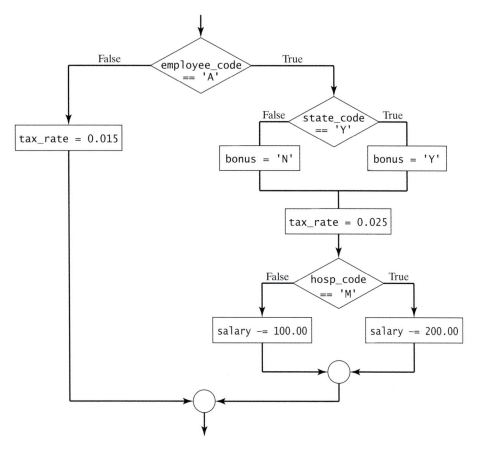

Figure 4.11

```
    else
        tax = gross_pay * 0.045;
    special_tax = hours * 0.02;
}
else
{
    tax = 0.00;
    special_tax = 0.00;
}
```

Write short programs to see what happens if you omit the first pair of braces. Does the resulting program compile? If the program does compile, what does the nested if assign to tax and special_tax?

2. Using the code segment of Experiment 1, write a short program to see what happens if you omit the second pair of braces. Does the resulting program compile?

If the program does compile, what does the nested if assign to tax and special_tax?

3. Using the code segment of Experiment 1, write a short program to see what happens if you omit both pairs of braces. Does the resulting program compile? If the program does compile, what does the nested if assign to tax and special_tax?

Programming Problems 4.3

1. Suppose that the automobile repair shop of Problem 4.2 has a maximum pay rate of $25.00. Recode prb04-2.cpp so that it issues an error message if the user enters a pay rate greater than 25.00. The program should prompt the user for a valid pay rate until the user enters a rate of $25.00 or less.

2. Recode dem04-1.cpp using a nested if to test the character that the user inputs.

3. The loan officer at Humongus National Bank wants you to write a program to help her decide whether to approve small loan applications. The program should prompt the user for the customer's yearly income, the number of years of the loan (the loan period), the amount of the loan (the principal), and the customer status (1 for preferred, or 0 for ordinary). To approve a loan, the customer must satisfy one of the following conditions.

   a. The principal divided by the period must be less than or equal to 1/12 of the customer's income.

   b. If the customer is a preferred customer (that is, the customer status is 1), the principal divided by the period need only be less than or equal to 1/10 of the customer's income.

   The program should display an appropriate approval or disapproval message for each customer it processes. When there are no more customers to process, the program should display the total number of approvals and disapprovals it processed.

4. At Humongus National Bank, the vice president in charge of credit cards decides to issue a new type of credit card, the Platinum Card. Write a program to help the bank decide which of its customers it will offer a Platinum Card. The program should prompt the user for the customer's present credit limit and account balance. If a customer has a credit limit of at least $2000.00 and an account balance of $500.00 or less, issue the customer a Platinum card. If a customer has a credit limit of at least $2000.00 and an account balance of more than $500.00, send a letter to the customer stating that if their balance falls below $500.00 he or she will receive a Platinum Card. If a customer does not fall into either of these categories, take no action.

   For each customer, the program should display a message that shows the action that the bank should take—issue a Platinum Card, send a letter, or no action. When there are no more customers to process, the program should display the total number of customers in each category.

5. The Big Racket Tennis Club wants you to write a program to calculate the yearly dues for its members. The program should prompt the user for the membership

type (either 'I' for individual, or 'F' for family) and the number of years the person has been a member. Calculate the dues as follows: If the person is a family member and has been a club member for more than three years, the dues are $2400.00. If the person is a family member and has been a club member for three years or less, the dues are $3000.00. If the person is an individual member and has been a club member for more than five years, the dues are $1500.00. If the person is an individual member and has been a club member for five years or less, the dues are $1900.00.

For each member, the program should display the type of membership, the number of years the person has been a member, and the dues.

When there are no more members to process, the program should display the total number of family members and individual members, and the total amount of dues.

4.4 THE switch STATEMENT

The C++ language switch statement implements the case structure of structured programming, which effects multi-way branching. Thus, the switch statement can be used in certain circumstances in place of a nested if statement.

The switch statement has the following general format.

```
switch (integer-expression)
{
    case    case-value-1:
        statement-body-1
    case    case-value-2:
        statement-body-2

        .
        .
        .

    case    case-statement-n
        statement-body-n
    default:
        default-statement-body
}
```

The integer-expression following the keyword switch must evaluate to an integer data type. Most often the integer expression is a simple int or char variable. The body of the switch statement must be enclosed in braces as shown.

The body of the switch statement consists of a set of cases. Each case begins with the case label. A **case label** begins with the keyword **case**, followed by a case value, followed by a colon. The case value is a possible value that the integer-expression can take on. The case value must be of the same type as the value of the integer-expression. The statement body for that case follows the case label. The program executes the statements in the statement body if the integer-expression equals the case value that is in the case label. Note that the statement body can consist of no statements, in which case nothing will be done. See the discussion of Problem 4.3, which follows shortly.

The **default** label body of the switch contains the statements that the program is to execute if the value of the integer-expression is not equal to any of the case label values. The default case label is optional and need not appear last in the body of the switch statement.

The switch statement works as follows. The program evaluates the integer-expression and compares this value to each case value. If the value of the expression equals a case value, the computer executes all the statements in that case label's statement body. The computer then executes all the following statement bodies, unless otherwise directed (for example, by a **break** statement as we shall see shortly). We call this behavior **fall through**.

If the value of the integer-expression is not equal to any of the case values, the program executes the **default** statement body. If you do not include the default case in the switch statement and the integer expression is unequal to any case value, switch takes no action. Then, the program executes the statement that follows the switch.

To see how the switch statement works, we consider a real estate commission program.

4.4.1 Calculating Real Estate Commission—Problem 4.3

A real estate broker sets fees for selling properties according to the property type as shown in Table 4.5.

The broker wants you to write a program that prompts the user for the sale price of the property and the property type code. The program should then display the dollar amount of the broker's commission (the sale price multiplied by the appropriate commission rate). If the user enters an invalid property code, the program should display an appropriate error message and stop. Allow the user to enter uppercase or lowercase letters.

4.4.2 Program Design

The pseudocode solution for Problem 4.3 follows.

Obtain the sale price from the user
Obtain a property code from the user
Determine the commission rate based on property code
Calculate the commission
Display the commission

TABLE 4.5

Property Type	property_code	Rate
Residential	R	0.060
Multi-Dwelling	M	0.050
Commercial	C	0.045

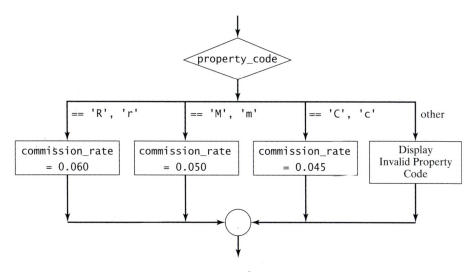

Figure 4.12

To determine the commission rate based on the property code, we shall use a switch statement. To decide the commission rate, the program must take one of four possible paths depending on the value of property_code. There are three possible valid values for the property code. The fourth alternative is any value other than these three valid values. Thus, the problem requires a multi-way branch, that is, a **case structure**, as shown in the flowchart of Figure 4.12

In the flowchart, the program takes the path appropriate to the value of property_code. Thus, if property_code equals 'm', the program will flow down the second arrow and assign the value of 0.050 to commission_rate.

Following is the switch statement that translates the flowchart of Figure 4.12.

```
switch (property_code)
  {
    case 'R':
    case 'r':
      commission_rate = 0.060;
      break;
    case 'M':
    case 'm':
      commission_rate = 0.050;
      break;
    case 'C':
    case 'c':
      commission_rate = 0.045;
      break;
    default:
      cout << endl << endl
           << "Invalid Property Code! Try Again." << endl;
      break;
  }
```

This `switch` statement first evaluates the variable `property_code`. The program branches to the case label that equals the value of `property_code`. If `property_code` is not equal to any case-label value, the program branches to the `default` label. For example, suppose that the value of `property_code` is 'M'. The program branches to the case label

```
case 'M':
```

and executes the statements that follow. The statement that immediately follows this case label (`case: 'M'`) is another case label (`case: 'm'`), which is not an executable statement. Therefore, the program "falls through" the case label and executes the next statement, which is

```
commission_rate = 0.050;
```

followed by the `break` statement. The `break` statement causes program control to **exit** the `switch` statement. If the `break` statement were not there, the program would fall through the next two case labels and assign 0.045 to `commission_rate`, which would be incorrect. See Experiment 3.

Thus, in some circumstances, we want fall through to occur, such as when multiple values lead to the same actions. In other circumstances, we do not want fall through to occur, such as when we want to exit the `switch` statement. The `break` statement causes an immediate exit from the body of the `switch` statement.

If the value of `property_code` does not equal any of the case-label values, then the `default` case is executed and an error message is displayed. We explain the use of `exit(0)` in the discussion of prb04-3.cpp, which follows.

4.4.3 The Program prb04-3.cpp

Following is the program code. Note that in the program we must include the requirement that the program end if the user inputs an invalid property code.

```
// prb04-3.cpp

// This program determines the commission on real estate sales
// depending on the type of property sold.

#include <iostream>
#include <iomanip>
#include <cstdlib>

using namespace std;

int main()
{
    const double    RESIDENTIAL_RATE = 0.060;
    const double    MULTIDWELLING_RATE = 0.050;
    const double    COMMERCIAL_RATE = 0.045;

    int       property_code;
    double    sale_price,
              commission_rate,
              commission;
```

```
        cout << setprecision(2)
            << setiosflags(ios::fixed)
            << setiosflags(ios::showpoint);

        cout << "Enter the property's selling price: ";
        cin >> sale_price;

        cout << endl;
        cout << "Enter the property code according to the following."
            << endl << endl;
        cout << "Residential,       enter R" << endl;
        cout << "Multiple Dwelling, enter M" << endl;
        cout << "Commercial,        enter C" << endl << endl;
        cout << "Please make your selection: ";

        cin.get();              // Discard the \n
        property_code = cin.get();

        switch (property_code)
        {
          case 'R':
          case 'r':
            commission_rate = RESIDENTIAL_RATE;
            break;
          case 'M':
          case 'm':
            commission_rate = MULTIDWELLING_RATE;
            break;
          case 'C':
          case 'c':
            commission_rate = COMMERCIAL_RATE;
            break;
          default:
            cout << endl << endl
                 <<"Invalid Property Code! Try Again" << endl;
            exit(1);
            break;
        }

        commission = sale_price * commission_rate;

        cout << endl << endl;
        cout << "The commission is " << commission << endl;

        return 0;
    }
```

Program Output

```
Enter the property's selling price: 270000

Enter the property code according to the following.
```

```
Residential,          enter R
Multiple Dwelling, enter M
Commercial,           enter C

Please make your selection: R

The commission is 16200.00
```

After obtaining the sale price of the property, the program displays a menu of property codes and asks the user to enter a menu option. A cin.get() statement skips the newline character that is in the keyboard input buffer because of the user entering the sale price. The next cin.get() places the entered code into the variable property_code.

The switch statement decides the value of commission_rate depending on the value of property_code as explained previously. If the user enters an invalid code, the program displays an error message and then executes the standard library function exit(). When a program executes the exit() function, the program ends and returns control of the computer to the operating system. See Experiment 4. The exit() function takes a single argument of type int. Therefore, a call to exit() can take the form exit(0); or exit(1); or exit(2);, and so on. By convention, an argument value of 0 means that the program ended normally; a nonzero argument value means that the program ended abnormally. The programmer can use a nonzero value for the argument to indicate the reason the program did not end successfully. An operating system program can then use this value to act appropriately.

To use the function exit(), the program must include a third header file, cstdlib, which stands for the "C++ standard library" header file.

4.4.4 More on break

In addition to its use in the switch statement, the break statement can alter the flow of control in a C++ program when used inside the body of a loop. Execution of the break statement causes the program to end the smallest enclosing while, do, or for statement. The program then transfers control to the point just beyond the completed while, do, or for statement. Thus, the break statement causes a premature exit from a loop.

The program dem04-3.cpp illustrates the break statement used in a loop. The program counts the number of characters the user enters before the first @ character.

```
// dem04-3.cpp

// This program counts the number of characters that the user
// enters on a line to the left of the first @ character.

#include <iostream>

using namespace std;

int main()
{
```

```
    int ch,            // The input character
        count = 0;  // Count of the characters before @

    cout << "Enter a line containing @" << endl;

    while ( (ch = cin.get()) != '\n')
    {
      if (ch == '@')
        break;
      ++count;
    }

    if (ch == '\n')
    {
      cout << endl;
      cout << "You did not enter a @ character." << endl;
      cout << "You entered " << count << " characters."  << endl;
    }

    else
    {
      cout << endl;
      cout << "You entered " << count
           << " characters before the first @"
           << endl;
    }

    return 0;
}
```

Program Output

Enter a line containing @
asd,1@34

You entered 5 characters before the first @

The program prompts the user to enter a line that contains the character @. The while loop's condition, which we have seen several times before, obtains a character from the keyboard input buffer and tests to see if it is not the newline character. If the character is not the newline character, the program enters the loop body. The if statement in the loop body checks to see if the character that the user entered equals the @ character. If it is, the break statement executes. This causes the program to exit the while loop and execute the if statement that follows the while. If the character that the user entered is not the @ character, the program increments the variable count and the next iteration of the while loop obtains the next character from the keyboard input buffer.

When the program reaches the if statement that follows the while, we know that the loop ended for one of two reasons—either an @ character was met and the break statement caused the loop to end, or the user did not enter an @ character and the loop ended by encountering the newline character. In either case, the character that caused the loop to end is stored in the variable ch. The if statement tests the value of ch to determine why the loop ended.

4.4.5 The continue Statement

The continue statement is another way to alter the flow of control within a while, do-while, or for loop, and may appear only inside such loops. However, instead of ending the enclosing loop as break does, execution of continue ends only the current iteration. The next loop iteration then begins immediately.

The program dem04-4.cpp counts the number of uppercase characters that the user enters on one line.

```
// dem04-4.cpp

// This program counts the number of upper-case characters that
// the user enters on one line.

#include <iostream>

using namespace std;

int main()
{
   int ch,          // The character entered
       count = 0; // The number of upper-case characters

   cout << "Enter a line of characters:" << endl;

   while ( (ch = cin.get()) != '\n')
   {
      if ( (ch < 'A') || (ch > 'Z') )
         continue;
      ++count;
   }

   cout << endl;
   cout << "You entered " << count << " upper-case characters." << endl;

   return 0;
}
```

Program Output

```
Enter a line of characters:

asDvFF,a12BBa

You entered 5 upper-case characters.
```

The while loop's condition obtains a character from the input buffer and places it into the variable ch. If the value of ch is not '\n', then the loop body executes. The if statement in the loop body tests whether the value of ch is not an uppercase letter. If the value of ch is not an uppercase letter, the continue statement executes. This causes the current loop iteration to end. The ++count statement does not execute, and the program executes the next loop iteration. Therefore, the while loop's condition obtains the next character from the keyboard input buffer and the process repeats. If the value of ch is an uppercase letter, the continue statement does not execute and count is incremented by one. The while loop's condition then obtains the next character from the keyboard input buffer.

Exercises 4.4

1. A program is to use the integer variable years_employed to define three groups of employees. The groups and the required processing follow in Table 4.6.
   a. Write a nested if statement that tests years_employed and does the appropriate processing.
   b. Write a switch statement that tests years_employed and does the appropriate processing.
2. Recode dem04-3.cpp without using the break statement.
3. Recode dem04-4.cpp without using the continue statement.

Experiments 4.4

1. Place the default case in the switch statement of prb04-3.cpp before all the case labels. Compile and test the resulting program. Does placing the default label first have any effect on the program?
2. Omit the default case in the switch statement of prb04-3.cpp. Compile and execute the resulting program. When prompted by the program, enter the value A for the property code. What does the program do?
3. In the switch statement of prb04-3.cpp, remove the break statement in the case 'M' section. Recompile the resulting program. Execute the program and enter 'M' or 'm' for the property code. Does the program compute the commission correctly? If not, explain why.
4. Execute prb04-3.cpp and enter an invalid value for the property code. What happens?

TABLE 4.6

years_employed	Processing
0–3	add 1 to j_count
4–10	add 1 to r_count
11 or more	add 1 to s_count

Programming Problems 4.4

1. The Easy Living resort hotel wants you to write a program to calculate the base charge for its guests. The program should prompt the user for the room type ('G' for garden view, 'P' for pool view, or 'L' for lake view) and the number of days the guest is to stay. The program also should prompt for whether the guest is to have a refrigerator in the room and whether there is to be an extra bed in the room.

   The daily room rates are as follows. A garden-view room is $125.00 each day; a pool-view room is $145.00 each day; a lake-view room is $180.00 each day. A refrigerator costs $2.50 extra each day. An extra bed costs $15.00 extra each day for either a garden-view room or a pool-view room, but costs $20.00 extra each day for a lake-view room. Calculate the total bill by multiplying the room rate (adjusted for a refrigerator and extra bed, if necessary) by the number of days the guest is to stay.

   The program should display the room type, the number of days of the stay, the basic daily room rate, the daily charge for the refrigerator and bed (only if the guest requests these), and the total charge for the stay.

2. The PCs-R-US computer rental company wants you to write a program to calculate the charge for renting a computer. The program should prompt the user for the type of computer ('F' for a 586 or 'P' for a 586-P), whether the customer rented a monitor, and whether the customer rented a printer, and the number of days the customer rented the computer system. Table 4.7 gives the daily rate for renting a computer system, depending on the configuration. An X in a box means that the customer selected that option. For example, the daily rate for renting a 586 with a monitor and no printer is $12.50.

   The charge to the customer is the appropriate rate multiplied by the number of days the customer rented the computer. For each customer, the program should display the daily rental charge, the number of days of the rental, and the total rental charge.

   When there are no more customers to process, the program should display the total number of customers processed, the number of 586 systems rented, the number of 586-P systems rented, and the total of all the rental charges.

TABLE 4.7

586	585-P	Monitor	Printer	Rate
X				10.50
X		X		12.50
X			X	13.50
X		X	X	15.00
	X			15.50
	X	X		18.50
	X		X	19.00
	X	X	X	21.00

3. Write a program that asks the user to enter the number of a month of the year and the year. For example, if the user wants to enter June, 2005, he/she would enter 6 and then enter 2005. The program should then display the number of days in that month. Be sure to take leap years into account.

4. After many years of being frustrated by a checkbook that just will not balance, you decide to write a program to help balance your money market checking account. The program should begin by asking the user for the month's opening account balance. Then the program should display a menu that lists the following choices: D for a deposit, C for a check, W for a withdrawal, and Q for quit. If the user selects D, ask the user to enter the amount of the deposit, and add the amount to the account balance. If the user enters C, ask the user for the amount of the check, and subtract the check amount from the balance. If the user enters W, ask the user for the amount of the withdrawal, and subtract the amount from the balance. When the user enters Q, the program should display the opening balance, the total amount deposited, the total amount withdrawn, the total amount of the checks, and the final balance. If the user enters something other than D, W, C, or Q, the program should issue an error message and redisplay the menu. Allow the user to enter either uppercase or lowercase letters.

5. Redo Programming Problem 4 with the following change. If at anytime during the program a withdrawal or a check results in a negative balance, warn the user that the account is overdrawn. Display the amount by which the account is overdrawn, and end the program as described in Programming Problem 4.

6. Redesign and recode prb04-3.cpp so that it processes any number of real estate transactions. In addition, after the program finishes processing all transactions, the program should display the total amount of sales, the total commissions for each property type, the grand total of all the sales, and the grand total of all the commissions.

7. A commodities broker requires a program to calculate brokerage commissions. Write a program that asks the user if the transaction was a sale or a purchase and then asks for the amount of the transaction. The program should then ask the user where the transaction was made. The user should enter E for the Commodity Exchange, C for the New York Cotton Exchange, or M for the Mercantile Exchange. If the amount was a sale, and was made at the Commodity Exchange, the commission rate is 5.0% of the amount. If a sale is made at the New York Cotton Exchange, the commission rate is 3.7% of the amount. If a sale is made at the Mercantile Exchange, the commission rate is 4.2% of the amount. If the transaction was a purchase at the Commodity Exchange, the rate commission is 6.3% of the amount. If a purchase is made at the Cotton Exchange, the commission rate is 4.3% of the amount. If a purchase is made at the Mercantile Exchange, the commission rate is 5.7% of the amount. The program should process any number of transactions.

8. Your city's Parking Violation Bureau wants you to write a program to compute fines for parking violations. There are four types of violation: type A carries a fine of $10, type B carries a fine of $20, type C carries a fine of $30, and type D carries a fine of $50. The program should ask for the number of type A violations, the

number of type B violations, and so on. If the number of type A, B, or C violations exceeds 10, impose an additional fine of $50 for each category that exceeds 10. If the total number of type A, B, or C exceeds 20 but none of types A, B, or C individually exceeds 10, impose an additional fine of $75. If the number of type D violations exceeds three, impose an additional fine of $20 for each type D violation over three. The program should display the total fine for the person. The program should process any number of persons.

CHAPTER REVIEW

TERMINOLOGY

Discuss the meanings of the following terms.

`if`	inner `if`
`else`	case structure
logical operators	`case`
truth value	`switch`
and (`&&`)	case label
negation (`!`)	`break`
conjunction (`&&`)	`default`
disjunction (`||`)	fall through
"short-circuit" evaluation	`exit()`
nested `if`	`cstdlib`
outer `if`	`continue`

SUMMARY

- Use the `if` statement to code a simple decision (Note 4.1 and Note 4.2).
- Use the not, and, and or operators, `!`, `&&`, `||`, respectively, to code compound conditions.
- The `&&` operator has higher precedence than the `||` operator (Table 4.4).
- The `if` statement can contain other `if` statements; that is, you can code nested `if`s (Note 4.3).
- Use `cin.get()` to remove an unwanted newline character from the input buffer.
- The `switch` statement implements the case structure for multi-way decisions.
- The `break` statement causes exit from the `switch` statement. If a `case` does not contain a `break` statement, fall through occurs to the next `case`.
- The `break` statement causes a premature exit from the smallest enclosing `while`, `do`, or `for` statement.
- The `continue` statement ends the current iteration of the smallest enclosing `while`, `do`, or `for` statement.
- Executing the function `exit(1)` terminates a program.

REVIEW EXERCISES

1. Explain how the `if` statement works.
2. How do you code an `if` statement?
3. How can you enclose more than one statement in the true or false part of an `if` statement?
4. What are the logical operators and how do they work?
5. How does the precedence of the logical operators compare to that of the other operators we have covered to this point? Which has higher precedence, `&&` or `||`?
6. How can short-circuit evaluation affect the results of a logical expression?
7. What are the rules for coding a nested `if` statement?
8. What must you be careful of when mixing character input with the input of numbers?
9. Explain how the `switch` statement works. What is the function of the `break` statement in a switch statement?
10. What is the difference between a `break` statement and a `continue` statement in the body of a loop?

Chapter 5

Functions

OBJECTIVES

- To understand how functions work in C++
- To declare a function using a prototype
- To code and use a function having no arguments and no return value
- To code and use a function having arguments and no return value
- To understand how arguments are passed by value
- To code and use a function that returns a value
- To understand and use local and global variables
- To understand and use static variables
- To design and code a program that uses functions
- To define and use a macro
- To use the conditional operator
- To define and use inline functions

Many large projects are often divided into a set of smaller, more manageable tasks to reduce the project's complexity and allow specialists to work on these tasks. A large program is also often divided into smaller pieces called modules. A **program module** is a part of a program that performs a single, well-defined task. One of the modules is the main, or control, module. The main module calls, or executes, the other modules of which the program is composed. So far, our programs have consisted of only the main module, coded as the function main(). In C++, a module is usually coded as a function. In this chapter, we shall learn how to define and use our own functions and how to use them to help write programs.

5.1 THE FUNCTION CONCEPT

Functions are central to all the work that we shall do in the rest of this book. In this section, we discuss the nature of a function and learn how to declare, define, and use simple functions.

5.1.1 How Functions Work

To construct a building, a general contractor calls upon the services of subcontractors who specialize in certain areas. For example, to lay the foundation of the building, the contractor hires a company that specializes in laying foundations. The contractor has only to give the foundation company the information (size, shape, and so on) necessary to do its work. The foundation company already knows how to build the foundation, so the contractor need not be concerned with how to perform this task. All the contractor needs to do is tell the foundation company to start. The foundation company, in turn, must tell the contractor when it has completed its task and how long the contractor must wait to begin the next phase of construction. (The foundation must harden properly, so a certain time must pass before any work can be resumed on the building.) To complete the rest of the building, the contractor will hire other subcontractors in much the same way. Electrical, plumbing, carpentry, and more will be done by appropriate subcontractors. It is even possible that one of the subcontractors will, in turn, hire another subcontractor. For example, the carpentry subcontractor might itself hire a subcontractor to install the interior walls of the building.

Many programming problems can be approached in much the same way as the contractor approaches constructing a building. The function main() can act as the contractor. When it is necessary to perform a task, main() can call upon the services of another function (subcontractor) that performs that task. Such a function may require some information to perform its task, just as the foundation company needs to know the size and shape of the foundation it is to build. The function, also like the foundation company, has to notify main() when it is done and might have to pass back some data for main() to use in its processing. Continuing the analogy with the carpentry subcontractor, it is possible for a function to call upon still another function to perform an even more specialized task.

Generally, a function that calls upon, or executes, another function is known as the **calling function**. The function that the calling function executes is known as the **called function**. Thus, if main() executes a function named Func1(), main() is the calling function and Func1() is the called function. Note that if Func1() then executes a function named Func2(), Func1() is then the calling function and Func2() is the called function. Figure 5.1 shows a diagram of a generalized function.

A function should perform a single, well-defined task. To accomplish this task, the function might require zero or more values, called **arguments**, that are passed to it by the calling function. When the function has completed its task, it can return no or one value, called the **return value**, to the calling function. The calling function can then use the return value in any of its statements.

For example, suppose that in a purchase-order processing program we need to calculate the sales tax on the amount of the purchase. Figure 5.2 shows a diagram of a function Calc_Sales_Tax() that could perform this task.

A Generalized Function

Figure 5.1

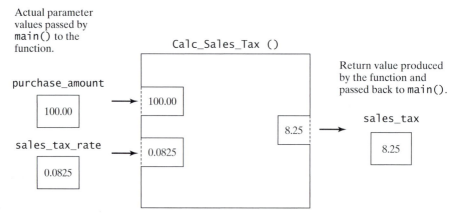

Figure 5.2

The function Calc_Sales_Tax() requires two arguments because the function must be given the value of the purchase and the applicable sales tax rate. The function main(), which is the calling function in this case, passes the values of purchase_amount and sales_tax_rate to the function. The function uses these values, namely 100.00 and 0.0825, to calculate the sales tax. The function then passes the value of the sales tax back to main(), which assigns it to the variable sales_tax. Exactly how the function computes the sales tax and returns its value is not important right now. We shall learn how to do these things later in this chapter.

It is also possible to construct a function to either require no arguments and/or return no value. Because this is the easiest type of function to write, we begin our examples with a function that requires no arguments and returns no value.

5.1.2 A Function with No Arguments and No Return Value

We want to write a program that displays the following pattern on the monitor screen.

```
XXXXXXXXXX
XXXXXXXXXX
XXXXXXXXXX
XXXXXXXXXX
XXXXXXXXXX
```

The pattern consists of five rows of 10 Xs. Because the rows are identical, a `for` loop that executes its loop body five times, each iteration producing a row of ten Xs, is the appropriate control structure. Following is the pseudocode solution for the problem.

```
main()
        Display newline
        for (i = 1; i <= 5; ++i)
          Print_10_Xs()
          Display newline
        endfor
Print_10_Xs()
        for (i = 1; i <=10; ++i)
        Display 'X'
        endfor
        return
```

The solution consists of two functions that work together. The body of `main()`'s `for` loop executes five times. On each iteration, when `main()` executes the function `Print_10_Xs()`, `main()` passes control to the function, which carries out its task of displaying ten Xs. When the function finishes this task, it passes control back to `main()`. Then, `main()` continues execution at the statement that follows the statement `Print_10_Xs()`, which is the statement that displays a newline character. This ensures that on the next iteration, the ten Xs begin on a new line. Because this is the end of the loop body, `main()` increments the loop counter, tests the loop counter, and executes the loop body again. This calls the function `Print_10_Xs()` a second time, and so on.

To translate the pseudocode into C++ code requires several new features of C++.

5.1.3 The Function Prototype and Definition

Just as we must declare a variable before using it in a program, we also must declare a function before using it in a program. In C++, we declare a function in a **function prototype**. Note 5.1 shows the format of a function prototype.

For example, the function `Calc_Sales_Tax()` that we considered earlier accepts two decimal numbers as its arguments (the purchase amount and the sales tax rate) and returns a decimal number (the sales tax) to `main()`. Therefore, the prototype for this function is as follows.

```
double Calc_Sales_Tax(double, double);
```

This prototype tells the C++ compiler that the function `Calc_Sales_Tax()` requires two arguments, each of which is a `double`, and returns a value that is a `double`.

Note 5.1   Declaring a Function

To declare a function, use a function prototype. A prototype has the following format.

return-type function-name(argument type, argument type, . . .);

The return-type is the data type of the value that the function returns. In parentheses after the function name is a list of the data types of the arguments that are passed to the function.

The prototype does not say what the function does or how it accomplishes its task. The prototype gives the compiler information about the function so the compiler can verify that the program uses the function correctly. For example, each time the function appears in the program, the compiler checks that there are exactly two arguments and that they are both of type double.

Note that we capitalize the first letter of each word in the function name. This is another naming convention that we shall use in this book. This convention is not a rule of the C++ language. The convention makes it easier to pick out user-defined function names when reading a program. The only functions whose names <u>cannot</u> be capitalized are main() and the standard library functions (such as exit()), which you must spell exactly as C++ expects.

As another example, consider the following prototype.

```
int Func(char, double, int);
```

This prototype tells the C++ compiler the following. The function Func() returns a value of type int. The function has three arguments. The first argument must be of type char, the second must be of type double, and the third must be of type int.

The function Print_10_Xs(), whose pseudocode we developed earlier, has no return value and does not require any arguments. Note 5.2 shows what to do in this case.

Note 5.2   Using void in a Declaration

If a function does not return a value, use the keyword void as the return type in its prototype. If a function has no arguments, then either use the keyword void for its argument type list or omit the argument type list.

Thus, the prototype for the function Print_10_Xs() can be either of the following. The second of these prototypes is the most-used style in C++ and is the one that we shall use in this book.

```
void Print_10_Xs(void);
```

or

```
void Print_10_Xs();     //The style we shall use in this book
```

Note that in the C programming language, to specify that a function takes no arguments, you must use void for the argument type list. If you omit the argument list in C, it gives the computer no information about the number or types of arguments.

As we proceed in this chapter, we shall discuss more examples of function prototypes. We can now write the code for main(). We shall write the code for the function shortly.

```
// dem05-1.cpp

#include <iostream>

using namespace std;

void Print_10_Xs();

int main()
{
  int i;

  cout << endl;

  for (i = 1; i <= 5; ++i)
  {
    Print_10_Xs();
    cout << endl;
  }

  cout << endl;
  return 0;
}
```

Note that we code the prototype for Print_10_Xs() before the code for main() because the compiler must be aware of the function before it sees it in main(). Because Print_10_Xs() has return type void, to cause main() to execute the function, all we need to do is code the function's name. Because there is no argument type list, we follow the function's name by an empty set of parentheses (). Thus, when main() encounters the statement

```
Print_10_Xs();
```

it passes control to the function. When the function finishes its task, it passes control back to main(), which resumes by executing the statement that follows the function call.

We now consider how to write the code for the function Print_10_Xs(). The code for a function is separate from the code of main(). Some programmers prefer to place the code of their functions before main() and some prefer to place the code of their functions after main(). We shall place the code of all our functions after main() to emphasize that main() controls all the other functions in our program.

Note 5.3 gives an outline of how to write the code of a function.

> **Note 5.3   Format of a Function Definition**
>
> A function definition has the following format.
>
> return-type function-name(type parameter, type parameter, ...)
> {
>   function body
> }

The first line of the function definition is the **function definition header**, which looks very much like the function prototype. Note that the header does not end in a semicolon. The difference between the header and the prototype is in the parameter list. The function definition header specifies the name that the function uses for each parameter in addition to the parameter type. In the next section, we shall explain exactly what a parameter is and see examples of the use of parameters and the parameter list.

The **function body** contains the statements that enable the function to perform its task. You code the function body in the same way that you code the body of the function main(). If necessary, you can declare variables and use any C++ language statement or library function that you wish.

The function Print_10_Xs() does not return a value and has no arguments. Therefore, just as in its prototype, its definition header specifies the return type as void and has no parameter list.

Following is the definition of the function Print_10_Xs().

```
void Print_10_Xs()
{
  int j;

  for (j = 1; j <= 10; ++j)
    cout << 'X';

  return;
}
```

The function displays ten Xs using a for loop. Each iteration of the for loop displays one X. The last statement in the function body is the C++ language statement return. The return statement passes control of the computer back to the function that executed Print_10_Xs(), namely the calling function, which is the function main().

Our program dem05-1.cpp is the function main() together with the function Print_10_Xs().

```
// dem05-1.cpp

#include <iostream>

using namespace std;

void Print_10_Xs();
```

```
int main()
{
  int i;

  cout << endl;

  for (i = 1; i <= 5; ++i)
  {
    Print_10_Xs();
    cout << endl;
  }

  cout << endl;
  return 0;
}

void Print_10_Xs()
{
  int j;

  for (j = 1; j <= 10; ++j)
    cout << 'X';

  return;
}
```

Program Output

```
XXXXXXXXXX
XXXXXXXXXX
XXXXXXXXXX
XXXXXXXXXX
XXXXXXXXXX
```

It is important that you know how main() and Print_10_Xs() work together. After displaying a newline character, main() begins executing its for loop. When the loop body executes, main() executes the function Print_10_Xs().

Control of the computer now passes to the function Print_10_Xs(). The function's for loop then displays ten Xs. When the loop finishes, the function executes the return statement, which passes control of the computer back to main().

The function main() resumes execution at the statement following the function call, which is the cout << endl; statement. This ends one iteration of the for loop's body in main(). The next four iterations behave in a similar fashion.

5.1.4 A Function with Arguments and No Return Value

The function Print_10_Xs() is not very versatile because it displays a fixed character, X, exactly ten times. In this section, we develop a function Print_Char(), which can display any character any number of times. We shall pass as argument values to Print_Char() the character to display and the number of times to display the character.

We want to write a program that will first ask the user to enter a character. Suppose the user enters Z. Then the program should ask the user in how many rows to display the character. Suppose the user enters 5. Then, the program should display the following on the monitor screen.

```
Z
ZZ
ZZZ
ZZZZ
ZZZZZ
```

We can easily solve this problem using nested for loops. However, instead we shall use functions to solve the problem. The program must display five lines. Each line has one more character than the preceding line. We shall use one function, Print_Char(), to produce each of these lines. Thus, we need to pass information to the function, namely, the character the user wants to display and the number of times to display the character.

We pass information to a function that requires data by means of the function's arguments. Each data item we pass to a function requires its own argument. The function Print_Char() needs to know the character to display and the number of times to display it. Therefore, main() must pass two arguments to Print_Char()—one of type char and one of type int. Print_Char(), on the other hand, needs to store the argument values it receives. The values that a function receives from the calling function are stored in the function's **parameters**, which are variables declared in the function's definition header. When the function is called, the function initializes its parameters to the arguments that the calling function passed. The parameters, therefore, must be of the same data type as the arguments that are passed.

The pseudocode solution for our problem is as follows.

```
main()
    Prompt for and obtain character ch.
    Prompt for and obtain the number_of_rows.
    Display newline
    for (i = 1; i <= number_of_rows; ++i)
       Print_Char(ch, i)
       Display newline
    endfor
Print_Char(display_char, count)
    for (j = 1; j <= count; ++j)
       Display display_char
    endfor
```

After obtaining a character from the user and storing it in ch, and obtaining an integer and storing it in number_of_rows, main() displays a newline character. This ensures that the first line of characters that the program displays begins a newline. The for loop in main() executes five times. The first statement in the loop body executes the function `Print_Char()`. This function needs two arguments to accomplish its task. The first argument is the value of the character to display, which is stored in the variable `ch`. The second argument is the number of times to display the character, which is stored in the variable `i`. In the first execution of the `for` loop, the value of `i` is one. Therefore, on the first iteration, the value of the character that the user entered and the value of `i`, namely one, are passed to `Print_Char()`. `Print_Char()` then displays the character once, and returns control of the computer to `main()`.

The next statement that `main()` executes displays a newline character so the next displayed line begins on a new line. This ends the `for` loop body in `main()`, which causes the `for` statement to increment `i`. Because the new value of `i` is two, which is less than or equal to `number_of_rows`, the loop body executes again.

On the second iteration, the value of `i` is two. Therefore, when the program executes `Print_Char()`, it passes the value of the character that the user entered and the value of `i`, namely two, to the function. `Print_Char()` then displays the character twice and returns control of the computer to `main()`.

Similarly, on the third iteration, `Print_Char()` displays the character three times, on the fourth iteration it displays the character four times, and so on until it displays the character `number_of_row` times.

The arguments `main()` uses in the function call to `Print_Char()`, namely `ch` and `i`, contain the actual values that `main()` passes to the function. The pseudocode for `Print_Char()` names the two parameters it uses. The first parameter, `display_char`, is the character the function must display. The second parameter, `count`, is the number of times the function displays the character. A parameter is like a variable in the sense that it is declared in the function header. However, a parameter is unlike a variable because it receives its value from outside the function. The value that a parameter receives is the value of the corresponding argument that `main()` passes to the function. Thus, inside the function, the parameters represent the values that `main()` passed to the function. The parameter `display_char` receives the value of `ch` passed by `main()`. The parameter `count` receives the value of `i` passed by `main()`.

This example illustrates two important points about arguments and parameters. First, the order of the arguments and parameters must be consistent. The function expects the first argument to be the character and the second argument to be the number of times the character is to print. Therefore, when the function is called, `Print_Char(ch, i)`, the first argument must be a character and the second an integer. Likewise, in the function definition, the first parameter must represent the character to be displayed and the second parameter must represent the number of times the character is to be displayed. When the arguments are passed, the first argument is assigned to the first parameter and the second argument is assigned to the second parameter. Arguments and parameters are matched on a positional basis only and not on their meaning.

Second, as this example shows, the names that `Print_Char()` uses for its parameters are not necessarily the same as the names `main()` uses for the arguments. The function `main()` passes the values of `ch` and `i` to `Print_Char()`. These values are assigned to the corresponding parameters in `Print_Char()`. Therefore, in `Print_Char()`, we use the parameters `display_char` and `count` as ordinary variables whose values are assigned when `main()` calls the function. See Note 5.4.

Note 5.4   Argument/Parameter Order and Naming

1. When the arguments are passed to a function, the first argument is assigned to the first parameter in the function definition and the second argument is assigned to the second parameter in the function definition and the second argument is assigned to the second parameter in the function definition, and so on. Thus, arguments and parameters are matched on a positional basis only and not on their meaning.

2. The names a function uses for its parameters need not be the same as the names main() uses for the function's arguments.

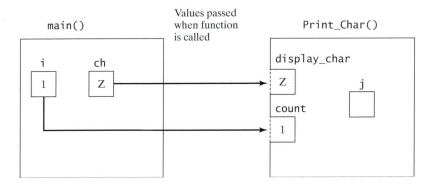

Figure 5.3

In Figure 5.3, we represent ordinary variables, such as ch, i, and j by closed squares. We represent parameters by squares with one side open to the outside of the function box. This suggests that parameters receive their values from outside the function.

The number of times the loop body executes in Print_Char() depends on the value of count. The loop body displays the value of display_char.

5.1.5 Defining and Using a Function that Has Arguments

Following is the prototype for the function Print_Char().

```
void Print_Char(char, int);
```

The function does not return a value, so the return type is void. The function requires two arguments. The first argument is of type char and the second is of type int. This reflects the use of the function in the pseudocode. The first argument that we shall pass to the function will be the character that we want the function to print. The second argument will be the number of times we want the function to display the character.

The code for dem05-2.cpp closely follows the pseudocode.

```
// dem05-2.cpp
#include <iostream>
using namespace std;
void Print_Char(char, int);
int main()
{
  int i,
      number_of_rows;
  char ch;

  cout << "Enter the character you want to display: ";
  cin >> ch;

  cout << endl;
  cout << "Enter the number of rows you want to display: ";
  cin >> number_of_rows;

  cout << endl;
  for (i = 1; i <= number_of_rows; ++i)
  {
    Print_Char(ch, i);
    cout << endl;
  }

  cout << endl;
  return 0;
}
void Print_Char(char display_char, int count)
{
  int j;

  for (j = 1; j <= count; ++j)
    cout << display_char;

  return;
}
```

Program Output

```
Enter the character you want to display: Z
Enter the number of rows you want to display: 5

Z
ZZ
ZZZ
ZZZZ
ZZZZZ
```

We use `Print_Char()` in `main()` in much the same way as we used `Print_10_Xs()` in dem05-1.cpp. Because the function does not return a value, to execute the function, we simply code the function name. However, we must pass two arguments to `Print_Char()`, namely, the character to display and the number of times to display it. These are the values of `ch` and `i`. Note that we enclose the arguments in parentheses after the function name and separate them by a comma.

You must be careful to pass the arguments in the correct order. The function expects the first argument to be the value of the character to display and the second to be the number of times to display it. If you mistakenly reverse the order of the arguments and code

```
Print_Char(i, ch);
```

either the compiler will catch the error, or the program will produce incorrect results. See Experiment 2.

The function `Print_Char()` has two parameters. The parameter `display_char` holds the value of the character that the function is to display. The parameter `count` holds the number of times that the function is to display the character. The variable `j` declared in the function serves as the loop counter. The `for` loop in the function displays the character stored in `display_char` exactly `count` times. Then the function returns control back to `main()`.

5.1.6 Passing Arguments by Value

In dem05-2.cpp, `main()` communicated with `Print_Char()` by passing argument values to the function. It is important that you understand that these arguments were **passed by value**. Passing by value means that the argument's value is passed to a function, and not to the argument itself. In dem05-2.cpp, `main()` passes the value of `ch` to `Print_Char()`. This value is assigned to `Print_Char()`'s parameter `display_char`. Because only the value of `ch` was passed, `Print_Char()` can alter the value of `display_char` with no effect on the value of `ch`.

The following program, dem05-3.cpp, illustrates passing arguments by value. In this program, the increment of `parm` in the function `PreInc()` has no effect on the value of `i` in `main()`.

```
// dem05-3.cpp

// This program demonstrates how an argument
// is passed by value in C++.

#include <iostream>

using namespace std;

void PreInc(int);

int main()
{
  int i;
```

```
    // The variable i is initialized to 5.

  i = 5;

  cout << "Before calling PreInc(), i = " << i << endl;

// The value of i is passed to the function PreInc(), where
// the value is assigned to the parameter parm (see the definition
// of PreInc() below).  The function increases the value of its
// parameter by one and returns to main().
// The value of the variable i is not affected by the function
// call to PreInc().

  PreInc(i);

  cout << "After calling PreInc(), i = " << i << endl;

  cout << endl;
  return 0;
}
void PreInc(int parm)
{

// The value passed to the function is assigned
// to the parameter parm.  The function increases the value
// of parm and returns control to main().

  ++parm;
  return;
}
```

Program Output

```
Before calling PreInc, i = 5
After calling PreInc, i = 5
```

Figure 5.4 illustrates how i is passed by value in dem05-3.cpp. When PreInc(i) is executed in main(), the value of i, namely 5, is passed to PreInc() and is assigned to its parameter parm. In PreInc(), the statement ++parm; increases the value of parm. Therefore, the value of i in main() remains unchanged.

C++ also allows **passing arguments by reference**. When an argument is passed by reference, the argument's address in main memory is passed to the function. Thus, the function can change the value of the argument in the calling program. We shall discuss the use of passing arguments by reference and the use of pointers as arguments in Chapter 8.

In the next section, we discuss functions that return a value to the calling program and several concepts that relate to where a variable is declared in a program that contains several functions.

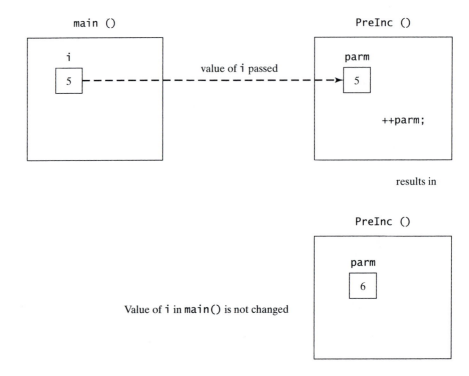

Figure 5.4

Exercises 5.1

In Exercises 1–6, code the appropriate function prototype.

1. A function called `Func1()` that does not return a value and that has two arguments. The first argument is a `double` and the second is an `int`.
2. A function called `Func2()` that returns an `int` and that has one argument, which is of type `double`.
3. A function called `Func3()` that returns a `double` and that has no arguments.
4. A function called `Func4()` that returns a `char` and that has one argument that is also of type `char`.
5. A function called `Func5()` that returns a `double` and that has three arguments, all of which are of type `double`.
6. A function called `Func6()` that returns an `int` and that has three arguments. The first and third arguments are of type `double`. The second argument is of type `int`.
7. Given the following function prototype, is there anything invalid about the use of the function in `main()`? If there is anything invalid, correct it.

```
int Func8(int, double);
int main()
{
    int i = 5,
```

```
        j;
    double db = 8.70;

    j = Func8(db, i);

    return 0;

}
```

8. Given the following function prototype, is there anything invalid about the use of the function in `main()`? If there is anything invalid, correct it.

```
void Func9(int, int);

int main()
{
   int i = 4,
       j = 9,
       k;

   k = Func9(j, i);

   return 0;

}
```

9. Code a function `Stars()` that displays a line of 26 asterisks at the beginning of a line.

10. Code a function `Num_Stars()` that takes one integer argument. The function should display as many asterisks as indicated by the value of its argument beginning on a newline. Therefore, `Num_Stars(14)` displays 14 asterisks at the beginning of a new line.

11. Code a function `Rectangle_Area()` that takes two `double` arguments representing the length and width of a rectangle. The function should display the area (length * width) of the rectangle.

12. Code a function `Rectangle_Perim()` that takes two `double` arguments representing the length and width of a rectangle. The function should display the perimeter (2 * length + 2 * width) of the rectangle.

13. Code a function `Circle_Area()` that takes one `double` argument that represents the radius of a circle. The function should display the area (3.14159 * radius * radius) of the circle.

14. Code a function `Circle_Circum()` that takes one `double` argument that represents the radius of a circle. The function should display the circumference (3.14159 * 2 * radius) of the circle.

Experiments 5.1

1. Recode dem05-2.cpp so that the program prompts the user for the number of steps to display in addition to the character to display.

2. In dem05-2.cpp, intentionally reverse the order of the arguments. Thus, code `Print_Char(i, ch)` in `main()`'s for loop. Explain what happens.

3. Write a program that displays the following.

```
a
bb
ccc
dddd
.
.
.
zzzzzzzzzzzzzzzzzzzzzzzzzzz
```

Use the function `Print_Char()` in the program.

4. Use the function `Print_Char()` to recode dem05-1.cpp.

5. Recode dem05-2.cpp using nested `for` loops instead of a function.

Programming Problems 5.1

1. Write a program that displays the following.

```
CCCCCCCCCCCC
CC
CC
CC
CC
CC
CC
CCCCCCCCCCCC
```

Use a function `Cee()` to display the letter.

2. Write a program that displays the following on the screen.

```
**************************
*                        *
*  I can write functions!  *
*                        *
**************************
```

The program should use three functions to accomplish its task. The function `Stars()` should display a line of 26 asterisks. The function `Bar()` should display an asterisk, 24 blanks, and an asterisk. The function `Message()` should display the middle line. None of the functions should return a value.

3. Write a program that draws a rectangle of Xs. Ask the user to enter the dimensions of the rectangle. Then use the function Rectangle() to draw a rectangle of the requested size consisting of Xs. Rectangle() should have two arguments— the length and width of the rectangle, which must be integers. The function should not return a value.

4. A manufacturer needs a program to display a table of costs of manufacturing certain numbers of her product. She wants to input the cost of producing one unit, the smallest number of products produced, and the largest number of products produced, each in hundreds. For example, she might input 3.46 for the unit cost, and 300 and 700 as the range of numbers. The resulting table should look like the following.

```
                    Product Cost Table
----------------------------------------------------------
Number Produced                                     Cost
----------------------------------------------------------
----------------------------------------------------------
     300                                         1038.00
     400                                         1384.00
     500                                         1730.00
     600                                         2076.00
     700                                         2422.00
```

Use a function Heading() to display the table heading lines. Heading() should receive no arguments and return no value. Use another function, Table(), to produce the table. Table() should have three arguments—the unit cost, the smallest number produced, and the largest number produced. Table() should not return a value.

5.2 USER-DEFINED FUNCTIONS THAT RETURN A VALUE

We now discuss functions that return a value to the calling program, and the concepts of scope and duration. The scope of a variable determines which functions in a program that can use the variable. The duration of a variable determines when the variable comes into and passes out of existence.

5.2.1 Calculating Grades Using a Function

Suppose an English teacher wants you to write a program that calculates her students' final grades. The program should prompt the user for the Midterm Exam grade and the Final Exam grade. The Final Grade is 40% of the Midterm Exam grade plus 60% of the Final Exam grade. The teacher wants the Final Grade correctly rounded to the nearest integer. For now, write the program to process one student's grade.

Following is the pseudocode solution for this problem.

main()

> Prompt for and obtain midterm_exam and final_exam grades
> final_grade = Calc_Grade(midterm_exam, final_exam)
> Display the final_grade

Calc_Grade(midterm_exam, final_exam)
> Calculate the rounded_grade
> Return rounded_grade

We use a function, Calc_Grade(), to calculate the final grade. This function requires two arguments to accomplish its task—the value of midterm_exam and the value of final_exam. The function returns the value of final_grade to main().

To evaluate the right side of the assignment statement, main() calls the function Calc_Grade() and passes to the function the values of the midterm exam and the final exam. The function then uses these values to calculate the rounded grade and returns the value of the rounded grade to main(). When the program resumes executing in main(), main() uses the value returned by the function in place of the function call. Thus, the rounded grade is assigned to final_grade.

Exactly how the function Calc_Grade() computes the rounded final grade, we shall leave for the discussion of the function code in the next section.

5.2.2 Calculating Grades—The Program dem05-4.cpp

Using a function that returns a value is different from using a function that does not return a value. If a function does not return a value, encountering the function's name causes main() to execute the function. The called function performs its task and returns control to main(). If, however, a function returns a value, main() uses the returned value in place of the function's call (the function name followed by the appropriate arguments).

Translating the pseudocode of main() into C++ code is straightforward. The return type in the function prototype for Calc_Grade() is int because the final grade is to be an integer. Because the midterm and final grades are also integers, we declare the two arguments as type int. We also declare two symbolic constants representing the weights given to the midterm and final exam grades in the body of the function Calc_Grade(). This allows us to change these values easily later. Following is the code for dem05-4.cpp, which closely follows the pseudocode of the previous subsection.

```
// dem05-4.cpp

// This program calculates a final grade based on the midterm and
// final exam scores.   It uses a function Calc_Grade() to calculate
// the final grade.   The function returns a value to main().

#include <iostream>

using namespace std;

int Calc_Grade(int, int);
```

```cpp
int main()
{
  int midterm_exam,
      final_exam,
      final_grade;

  cout << "Enter the Midterm Exam score: ";
  cin >> midterm_exam;
  cout << endl;

  cout << "Enter the Final Exam score: ";
  cin >> final_exam;

  final_grade = Calc_Grade(midterm_exam, final_exam);

  cout << endl;
  cout << "The Final Grade is " <<  final_grade << endl;

  cout << endl;
  return 0;
}

int Calc_Grade(int midterm, int final)
{
  const double MIDTERM_WEIGHT = 0.40;
  const double FINAL_WEIGHT   = 0.60;

  double grade;
  int rounded_grade;

  grade = MIDTERM_WEIGHT * midterm + FINAL_WEIGHT * final;
  rounded_grade = grade + 0.5;

  return rounded_grade;
}
```

Program Output

Enter the Midterm Exam score: **77**

Enter the Final Exam score: **80**

The Final Grade is 79

To execute the assignment statement in main(), the program first executes the function Calc_Grade(). Then, main() passes the values of midterm_exam and final_exam to the function. The function calculates the grade and returns this value to main(). The returned value is the value of the function call, which main() then assigns to final_grade.

It remains to explain how Calc_Grade() calculates the final grade. The function receives the midterm and final exam scores as parameter values. The midterm exam is

40% of the final grade and the final exam is 60% of the final grade. Thus, the function should use the following assignment to calculate the grade.

    grade = 0.40 * midterm + 0.60 * final;

Using the symbolic constants declared at the beginning of the function, the assignment becomes the following.

    grade = MIDTERM_WEIGHT * midterm + FINAL_WEIGHT * final;

The problem with this assignment is that the expression on the right is of type double with a fractional part that could be greater than or equal to 0.5. The fractional part would then be truncated when the number is converted to an integer by the assignment. For example, if the value of midterm is 77 and the value of final is 80, the value of the right side of the assignment is 78.8. If we declare grade as type int, then the assignment will truncate the fractional part of the answer. This would place 78 into grade, not the correctly rounded answer of 79. Therefore, we declare grade to be of type double so that the assignment places 78.8 into grade. To round the value of grade to the nearest integer, we add 0.5 to the value of grade and assign the result to the integer variable, rounded_grade. Thus, if the value of grade is 78.8, adding 0.5 results in 79.3. Assigning this value to rounded_grade truncates the fractional part and stores 79 into rounded_grade.

Note again that the names of the parameters in Calc_Grade() are different from the names of the arguments used in main(). The parameter names and the argument names need not be the same. However, remember that the names you use should be meaningful and reflect their use in the program.

The return statement in Calc_Grade()contains an identifier, rounded_grade. The return statement has the following general form.

        return expression;

The expression in the return statement, which is optional (there should be no expression in the return statement if the return type of the function is void), can be any legal C++ expression. Execution of the return statement causes the function to stop and return control to the calling program. If the return statement contains an expression, the return statement passes the value of the expression back to the calling program for use in place of the function call. The data type of the expression should be the same as the return type declared in the function prototype. In dem05-4.cpp, the return type of Calc_Grade() is int. Thus, the expression in the return statement of Calc_Grade() is also of type int.

5.2.3 Variable Attributes

In this section, we consider some technical aspects of functions, and where and how we declare variables. In C++, each variable has two attributes that determine the variable's scope and duration. The **scope** of a variable is the part of the program that has access to the variable. The **duration** of a variable is the time that the program allocates storage for the variable.

5.2.4 Scope

A variable declared inside a function has **local scope**—the variable is known only in-side the function. No statement outside the function in which it is declared can change the value of a variable with local scope. A variable declared outside a function body has **global scope**—the variable is known to all functions <u>defined</u> after the point of the variable's declaration. Thus, any function whose definition comes after the declaration of a global variable can change the value of a global variable.

Program dem05-5.cpp illustrates the ideas of local and global scope.

```cpp
// dem05-5.cpp

// This program demonstrates local and global variables.

#include <iostream>

using namespace std;

int global1,      // Global variable declarations
    global2;

void Func();

int main()
{
  // The following assignments are valid because
  // the variables global1 and global2 are global and were
  // declared before main().

  global1 = 88;
  global2 = 99;

  // Display the values of the global variables global1 and global2

  cout << "Initial values of the global variables:" << endl;
  cout << "global1 = " << global1
       << " global2 = " << global2 << endl;

  // Call the function Func()

  Func();

  // Display the values of the global variables
  // global1 and global2.  Either of these variables could
  // have been changed when the function Func() was executed.

  cout << endl;
  cout <<"After the call to Func(), the global variables are:"
       << endl;
  cout << "global1 = " << global1
       << " global2 = " << global2 << endl;

  return 0;

}

int global3;          // A global variable accessible to Func()
```

```
void Func()
{
    int global1,    // Variables local to Func().
        local1;         // The local variable global1 is different than
                    // global variable global1 declared before main().

    global3 = 1;      // Give a value to the global variable global3

    local1 = 2;       // Initialize the local variable local1

    global1 = 3;      // Does not change the value of main()'s global1.

    global2 = 4;      // Since global2 was not declared in this function,
                    // this is the global variable declared before
                    // main().  Therefore, this assignment changes
                    // the value of global2 in main().

    //Display the values of the local variables global1 and local1
    // and the global variables global2 and global3.

    cout << endl << endl;
    cout << "In Func(), the global variables are:" << endl;
    cout << "global2 = " << global2
         << " global3 = " << global3 << endl << endl;

    cout << "In Func(), the local variables are:" << endl;
    cout << "global1 = " << global1
         << " local1 = " << local1 << endl;
}
```

Program Output

```
Initial values of the global variables:
global1 = 88 global2 = 99

In Func(), the global variables are:
global2 = 4 global3 = 1

In Func(), the local variables are:
global1 = 3 local1 = 2

After the call to Func(), the global variables are:
global1 = 88 global2 = 4
```

The variables global1 and global2 are declared before main(). Therefore, global1 and global2 are global variables whose values are accessible to all the functions defined in the program. The program initializes these variables in main() to 88 and 99 and displays their values.

The variable global3 is declared outside main() and before the function Func(). The variable gobal3 is a global variable, but is accessible only to the function Func(). Therefore, it is valid for Func() to reference global3, which it does by assigning it the value one.

The variables global1 and local1 are declared inside the function Func(). Although the local variable global1 has the same name as the global variable global1, it is a different variable. Whenever Func() refers to the variable global1, it references the local variable global1 and not the global variable global1. Thus, later in the function, when global1 is given the value 3, the assignment has no effect on the value of the global variable global1.

The function Func() assigns the value 4 to global2. This assignment is valid because global2 is global and known to all the functions in the program. When control returns from Func() to main(), the value of global2 is 4, not the original value of 88.

Figure 5.5 illustrates the use of variables in dem05-5.cpp. Squares that lie outside the function boxes represent global variables. Squares inside function boxes represent local variables.

Any function whose <u>definition</u> comes after the declaration of a global variable can access that variable. This makes using global variables dangerous. A function can change the value of a global variable that another function assumes will not change. You should always try to avoid using global variables unless it is absolutely necessary to do so. When data must be shared among functions, do so by means of arguments and return values.

> **Note 5.5   Avoid Using Global Variables**
>
> Avoid using global variables. Share data among functions by means of arguments and return values.

Because local variables are known only to the functions in which they are declared, in a program we can declare variables with the same name in different functions. For example, we can code dem05-1A.cpp as follows.

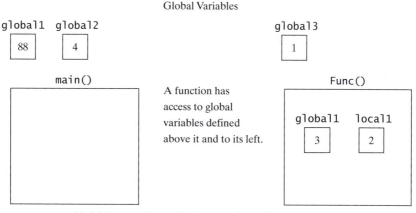

Global Variables

global1   global2   global3

| 88 | | 4 | | 1 |

main()   Func()

A function has
access to global
variables defined   global1   local1
above it and to its left.
                              | 3 | | 2 |

Variable values immediately before Func() returns
control to main()

Figure 5.5

```
// dem05-1A.cpp
#include <iostream>
using namespace std;
void Print_10_Xs();
int main()
{
  int i;

  cout << endl;
  for (i = 1; i <= 5; ++i)
  {
    Print_10_Xs();
    cout << endl;
  }

  cout << endl;
  return 0;
}
void Print_10_Xs()
{
  int i;

  for (i = 1; i <= 10; ++i)
    cout << 'X';

  return;
}
```

The variable i declared in main() is known only to main() and the variable i declared in Print_10_Xs() is known only to Print_10_Xs(). Each variable i is a different memory location in the computer. When main() changes the value of its variable i, it has no effect on the value of the variable i in Print_10_Xs(). When Print_10_Xs() changes its variable i, it has no effect on the value of the variable i in main().

Figure 5.6 illustrates the use of variables in dem05-1A.cpp.

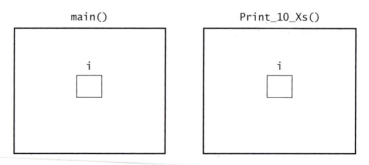

Figure 5.6

We represent a local variable by a square that lies completely inside the function box in which it is declared. A function knows only the variables inside its own function box. Print_10_Xs() is unaware of the existence of the local variables in main(), as main() is unaware of the local variables in Print_10_Xs(). Thus, main() cannot change the value of a local variable in Print_10_Xs(), and Print_10_Xs() cannot (at least, directly) change the values of the local variables in main().

5.2.5 Duration—Storage Class

The **storage class** of a variable determines its duration. The storage class of a variable can be either auto or static. (The words auto and static are C++ language key-words.) A local variable, which by default has storage class auto, (and is sometimes called an **automatic variable**) is allocated storage when the function in which it is de-clared begins executing. When a variable is allocated storage, the computer sets aside a certain amount of storage (depending on the variable type) for that variable and binds the variable name to that location. This enables us to use the name of the variable to represent the storage location. When the function stops executing, the storage set aside for an automatic variable is deallocated; the storage space can be reused by the com-puter and the variable name no longer is bound to that location in computer memory. Thus, the variable in effect ceases to exist. If main() calls the function again, the vari-able is re-created, possibly in a different location in computer memory.

A static **variable** is allocated storage when the program begins. A static vari-able stays in existence as long as the program is executing, independent of which func-tion happens to be active. A global variable has static storage class by default. It is possible to create a local static variable by including the keyword static in the vari-able's declaration. Such a variable is accessible only in the function in which it is de-clared. However, because its storage class is static, the variable stays in existence and retains its value after the function in which it is declared stops executing.

As an example, consider the program dem05-6.cpp.

```cpp
// dem05-6.cpp

#include <iostream>

using namespace std;

void Loop_Count();

int main()
{
   int i;

   for (i = 1; i <= 5; ++i)
     Loop_Count();

   cout << endl;
   return 0;
}

void Loop_Count()
{
```

```
        static int count = 0;

        ++count;

        cout << "Iteration " << count << endl;

        return;
}
```

Program Output

```
Iteration 1
Iteration 2
Iteration 3
Iteration 4
Iteration 5
```

The function main() consists of a for loop that executes the function Loop_Count() five times. In the function Loop_Count(), the variable count is declared as static and is given an initial value of 0. The first time main() calls Loop_Count(), count is initialized to zero and incremented by one. Then the cout statement displays the value of count, which is one, and returns control to main(). Because count is a static variable, it remains in existence and retains its value when control resumes in main(). The second time main() executes Loop_Count(), the variable count is not reinitialized. Instead, the current value of count is incremented by one, giving count the value two. The cout statement then displays the value of count, namely two, and returns control to main(). This process repeats a total of five times, resulting in the output shown.

Exercises 5.2

For Exercises 1–4 assume the following program outline.

```
int i1 = 9;

int main()
{
   int i2 = 5,
       i3;

   i3 = i1 + 7;
   i1 = Func12a(i1,i2);
   Func12b(i2,i3);

   return 0;
}

int i3 = 2;

int Func12a(int i1, int i3)
```

```
{
    static int i2 = 4;

    return i1 + i2 + i3;
}

Func12b(int j, int k)
{
    int i3 = 1;

    j = i3 + i2 + k;
}
```

1. Identify those variables that are local and those that are global.
2. State which functions have access to each global variable.
3. State which variables are of storage class `auto` and which are of storage class `static`.
4. State which assignment statements are valid and which are invalid.
5. Code a function `Rectangle_Area()` that takes two `double` arguments representing the length and width of a rectangle. The function should return the area (length * width) of the rectangle.
6. Code a function `Rectangle_Perim()` that takes two `double` arguments representing the length and width of a rectangle. The function should return the perimeter (2 * length + 2 * width) of the rectangle.
7. Code a function `Circle_Area()` that takes one `double` argument that represents the radius of a circle. The function should return the area (3.14159 * radius * radius) of the circle.
8. Code a function `Circle_Circum()` that takes one `double` argument that represents the radius of a circle. The function should return the circumference (3.14159 * 2 * radius) of the circle.
9. Code a function `Min()` that takes two `double` arguments and that returns the value of the smaller of the two arguments.
10. Code a function `Sgn()` that takes one `double` argument and returns +1 if the argument is positive; returns–1 if the argument is negative; and returns 0 if the argument is zero.
11. Code a function `Calc_Discount()` that has two `double` arguments representing the price of an item and a discount amount as a percent. The function should apply the discount to the price and return the discount amount.

Experiments 5.2

1. Remove the declaration of the variable `global1` from the function `Func()` in dem05-5.cpp. Compile and execute the resulting program. In what way does this affect the output of the program?
2. Remove the qualifier `static` from the declaration of the variable `count` in the function `Loop_Count()` in the program dem05-6.cpp. Compile and execute the resulting program. In what way does this affect the output of the program?

Programming Problems 5.2

1. Write a program that asks the user to enter two decimal numbers. The program should calculate and display the product and quotient of the two numbers. Use a function Product() to calculate the product. The function should have two arguments, which are the two numbers that the user inputs. The function should return the product of the numbers. Use a function Quotient() that has two arguments, which are the numbers input by the user. The function should return the quotient of the first number divided by the second. If the second number is zero (recall that division by zero is not allowed), display an error message and exit the program.

2. Write a program that asks the user to enter two decimal numbers. The program should display the larger of the two numbers. Use a function Max() to find the larger number. Max() should have two arguments, which are the numbers that the user input. Max() should return the larger of the two numbers.

3. Write a program that raises an integer to a positive integer power. The program should prompt the user to enter the base and the exponent, and the program should display the corresponding power. Use a function Power() to calculate the power. Pass the base and the exponent to the function. Power() should calculate the power by multiplying base by itself exponent times. The function should return the value of the power.

4. Write a program that calculates the mileage you get on your car. The program should ask the user for the number of miles traveled and the number of gallons consumed. Use the function Mileage() to calculate the mileage. Mileage() should take two arguments—the number of miles traveled and the number of gallons consumed. The function should return the mileage. The program should then display the mileage.

5. Write a program that computes the cost of a taxi cab ride. A taxi charges a fixed charge of $2.50 plus an additional charge of $5.50 per mile. The program should ask the user to enter the length of the trip in miles. The program should use the function Taxi_Charge() to calculate the fare. Taxi_Charge() should have one argument, the length of the trip, and should return the total fare for the ride. The program should display the total fare.

6. Write a program that asks the user to input a grade that he or she received on an exam. The grade is an integer from 0 to 100 inclusive. The program should convert the numeric grade into the equivalent letter grade. Do the conversion by using a function Letter_Grade() that converts a numeric grade in the range 0–100 to the equivalent letter grade. The function should have one parameter, the integer grade. The return value of the function should be A if the grade is 90 to 100; B if the grade is 80 to 89; C if the grade is 70 to 79; D if the grade is 65 to 69; and F if the grade is 64 or lower. After converting the grade, the program should display the numeric grade and the equivalent letter grade.

7. Write a program to compute a person's weekly wage. The program should ask the user to enter the person's pay rate and the number of hours worked. The program should display the person's gross pay, income tax, and net pay. Use a function

Gross_Pay() to calculate the gross pay. Pass two arguments to the function—the pay rate and the hours worked. The function should return the gross pay, including overtime. Overtime is paid at 1.5 times the regular rate for hours worked over 40. Use a function Tax() to calculate the person's tax. Pass one argument to the function—the person's gross pay. Tax() should calculate the tax as 15% of the gross pay. The function should return the tax. Use a function Net_Pay() to calculate the net pay. Pass two parameters to the function—the gross pay and the tax. The function should return the net pay. The net pay is the gross pay minus the tax. Use a function Display_Results() to display the gross pay, tax, and net pay, which you should pass to the function as arguments. Display_Results() should not return a value.

8. Write a program that validates a date input by the user. The program should ask for the year, the month number (1 for January, 2 for February, and so on), and the day of the month. Use a function Valid_Date() that takes three arguments—the year, the month number, and the day—to validate the date. The function should validate the date as follows. The day must be greater than 0 and must not exceed the correct number of days in the month (remember to check for leap year—a year that is divisible by 4—in which February has 29 days). The month number must be from 1 to 12. The year must not be less than 1900 nor greater than 2100. If the date is valid, Valid_Date() should return 1; otherwise it should return 0.

5.3 PROGRAMS THAT USE FUNCTIONS

In this section we discuss three problems whose solutions involve the use of functions. The problems are longer than those we have considered so far. However, by dividing each problem into a set of modules, we can design reasonably simple solutions.

5.3.1 Problem 5.1—Moving Costs

A moving contractor wants you to write a program that he can use to estimate the cost of moving a residential customer. The charge for moving is based on two factors. First, the labor cost is estimated by charging $4.00 for every 100 pounds of furniture to be moved. Second, the travel charge is $50.00 plus $1.75 for each mile the furniture is to be moved. The program should prompt the user for the estimated weight of the furniture and the distance the furniture is to be moved. Finally, the program should display the labor charge, the travel charge, and the total charge.

5.3.2 Program Design

The program design is straightforward. The pseudocode solution for the problem is as follows.

Prompt for and obtain the weight and distance.
Calculate the labor charge.
Calculate the travel charge.
Calculate the total charge.
Display the results.

The program shall obtain the input data in the usual way. To calculate the labor charge and the travel charge, the program will use the functions `Calc_Labor()` and `Calc_Travel()`. Similarly, the program will use the function `Display_Charges()` to display the results of the program.

5.3.3 The Program prb05-1.cpp

Following is the code for prb05-1.cpp, the solution to Problem 5.1.

```cpp
// prb05-1.cpp

// This program estimates the charge for moving furniture.  It
// uses functions to do calculations and output the results.

#include <iostream>
#include <iomanip>

using namespace std;

double Calc_Labor(int);
double Calc_Travel(int);
void Display_Charges(double, double, double);

int main()
{
   int    weight,         // Estimated weight
          distance;       // Estimated distance
   double labor_charge,   // Estimated labor charge
          travel_charge,  // Estimated travel charge
          total_charge;   // Estimated total charge

   cout << setprecision(2)
        << setiosflags(ios::fixed)
        << setiosflags(ios::showpoint);

   cout << "Enter the weight in pounds: ";
   cin >> weight;

   cout << endl;
   cout << "Enter the distance in miles: ";
   cin >> distance;

   labor_charge = Calc_Labor(weight);
   travel_charge = Calc_Travel(distance);
   total_charge = labor_charge + travel_charge;

   Display_Charges(labor_charge, travel_charge, total_charge);

   cout << endl;
   return 0;

} // End of main()

double Calc_Labor(int weight)
{
```

```
    const double LABOR_RATE = 4.00;

    double labor_charge;

    labor_charge = (weight / 100) * LABOR_RATE;

    return labor_charge;
}  // End of Calc_Labor()

double Calc_Travel(int distance)
{
    const double MILEAGE_RATE     = 1.75;
    const double FLAT_TRAVEL_COST = 50.00;

    double travel_charge;

    travel_charge = FLAT_TRAVEL_COST + distance * MILEAGE_RATE;

    return travel_charge;
}  // End of Calc_Travel()

void Display_Charges(double labor_charge, double travel_charge,
                     double total_charge)
{
    cout << endl;
    cout << "The estimated charges are as follows:" << endl << endl;
    cout << "Estimated Labor:  " << setw(9) << labor_charge << endl;
    cout << "Estimated Travel: " << setw(9) << travel_charge << endl;
    cout << "----------------------------" << endl;
    cout << "Total Estimate:   " << setw(9) << total_charge << endl;
}  // End of Display_Charges()
```

Program Output

```
Enter the weight in pounds: 7400

Enter the distance in miles: 230

The estimated charges are as follows:

Estimated Labor:    296.00
Estimated Travel:   452.50
-----------------------------
Total Estimate:     748.50
```

The program begins by declaring the three functions that it uses. Calc_Labor() returns the labor cost, so we declare the function as returning a double. Its only argument is of type int because the weight is entered in pounds. Calc_Travel()'s prototype also declares it to return a double. The only argument that Calc_Travel uses, the distance the contractor is to move the furniture, is of type int. Finally, Display_Charges() takes three arguments, namely the labor cost, the travel cost, and the total cost. Because `Display_Charges()` does not return a value, its return type is `void`.

The program begins by prompting for and obtaining the weight of the furniture and the distance it is to be moved. The assignment statement

```
labor_charge = Calc_Labor(weight);
```

causes execution of the function `Calc_Labor()`. The function calculates the labor charge based on the weight of the furniture, which is passed as an argument value, and returns the labor charge to `main()`. Then, the program assigns the returned value to `labor_charge`.

The next assignment statement works similarly, assigning the travel charge returned by `Calc_Travel()` to the variable `travel_charge`. Finally, the `total_charge` is calculated as the sum of the labor and travel charges.

The program then passes the values of `labor_charge`, `travel_charge`, and `total_charge` to `Display_Charges()`, which displays the program's output.

The code for each of the functions that `main()` uses is straightforward. Note that in `Calc_Labor()` the labor rate, LABOR_RATE, is defined as a symbolic constant, as are MILEAGE_RATE and FLAT_TRAVEL_COST in the function `Calc_Travel()`.

5.3.4 Problem 5.2—Calculating Simple Interest

The BigDeal Finance Company wants you to write a program that will help to service its customers who use their automatic teller machines (ATMs). The program is to allow the user to determine the monthly payments, total interest, and total amount on a personal loan.

First, the program should display a greeting that announces the name of the program and what the program does. The greeting should be as follows.

```
*****************************************************************
              Welcome to the Personal Loan Program

This program will determine the interest, total amount
and monthly payment of your loan.

Please follow the instructions carefully.
*****************************************************************
```

After displaying the greeting, the program is to ask the user for the amount of the loan (the `principal`), the annual interest rate of the loan as a percent (the `rate`), and the number of years of the loan (the `term`). Because the program is to handle only personal loans, the loan amount cannot be smaller than $1,000.00 and cannot be greater than $20,000.00. If the loan amount is outside this range, the program should display an appropriate message and terminate. The annual interest rate of the loan cannot be greater than 18.7% as mandated by state law. If the entered interest rate is greater than

18.7%, the program should display an appropriate message and terminate. Finally, the longest term possible is five years. If the entered term is greater than five years, the program should display an appropriate message and terminate.

If all the input data is valid, the program should calculate the interest for the full term of the loan, the total amount of the loan, and the monthly payment by using the following formulas.

```
interest = principal * (rate/100) * term

total = principal + interest

monthly payment = total / (12 * term)
```

It is necessary to divide the value of `rate` by 100 in the first formula because the user enters the rate as a percent. If the user enters 10.7 as the rate, the rate we use in the formula must be 10.7/100 = 0.107.

In the third formula, the expression (12 * term) is the number of months of the loan. Dividing this into the total amount of the loan gives the monthly payment.

Finally, the program should output the data that the user entered, the interest on the loan, the total amount of the loan, and the amount of the monthly payment.

5.3.5 Program Design

The top-level design of this program is straightforward, as the following hierarchy chart shows.

We shall implement the module `Display_Greeting` as a function because the greeting involves displaying many lines. We divide the module `Obtain_Data` into three submodules, each of which we shall implement as a function. It is common programming practice to obtain each input value using a separate function. This enables you to localize in the corresponding function any input data verification that the program must do.

Because the interest calculations involve three simple formulas, we shall not implement the `Do_Calculations` module as a function. Instead, the three formulas will appear in `main()`. Also, the `cout` statements necessary to implement the `Display_Results` module will appear in `main()` and not as a separate function.

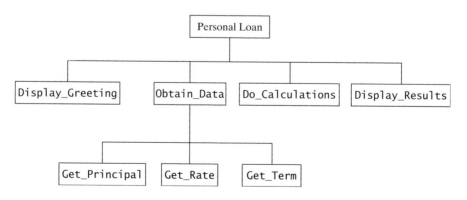

Figure 5.7

The pseudocode for the program based on the hierarchy chart is as follows.
Pseudocode for Problem 5.2

Display_Greeting
Obtain_Data:
      Get_Principal
      Get_Rate
      Get_Term
Do_Calculations
Display_Results

The three modules that obtain the input from the user are similar in structure. Therefore, we shall develop the pseudocode for `Get_Principal` and leave the pseudocode for the other two as exercises.

The principal cannot be less than 1000.00 or greater than 20000.00. To test that the principal is in this range, we use a nested `if` statement.

Pseudocode for `Get_Principal`

Prompt for and get principal
  if (principal < 1000.00)
    Display error message
    Exit program
  else
    if (principal > 20000.00)
    Display error message
    Exit program
  else
    return principal
  endif
endif

After obtaining the principal, the pseudocode tests to see if the value of `principal` is less than 1000.00. If it is, the program displays an error message and exits the program as required. If `principal` is not less than 1000.00, the pseudocode tests to see if it is greater than 20000.00. If it is, the program displays an error message and exits the program. If the `principal` is not greater than 20000.00, it must be in the range 1000.00 to 20000.00. In this case, the pseudocode returns the value of the `principal` to `main()`.

5.3.6 The Program prb05-2.cpp:

Following is the code for prb05-2.cpp, our solution to Problem 5.2.

```
// prb05-2.cpp

// Simple Interest Program

#include <iostream>
#include <iomanip>
#include <cstdlib>
```

```cpp
using namespace std;

void    Display_Greeting();
double  Get_Principal();
double  Get_Rate();
int     Get_Term();

int main()
{
  double interest,
         principal,
         rate,
         total,
         monthly_payment;
  int    term;

  cout << setprecision(2)
       << setiosflags(ios::fixed)
       << setiosflags(ios::showpoint);

// Display Greeting

  Display_Greeting();

// Obtain Data

  principal = Get_Principal();
  rate      = Get_Rate();
  term      = Get_Term();

// Do Calculations

  interest        = principal * (rate/100) * term;
  total           = principal + interest;
  monthly_payment = total / (12 * term);

// Display Results

  cout << endl;
  cout << "Interest Rate:    " << setw(5) << rate << "%" << endl;
  cout << "Term of Loan:     " << term << " Years" << endl << endl;
  cout << "Amount Borrowed:  $" << setw(9) << principal << endl;
  cout << "Interest on Loan: $" << setw(9) << interest << endl;
  cout << "---------------------------" << endl;
  cout << "Amount of Loan:   $" << setw(9) << total << endl;
  cout << "Monthly Payment:  $" << setw(9) << monthly_payment << endl;

  cout << endl;
  return 0;

} // End of main()

void Display_Greeting()
{
  int position;
```

```
   cout << endl << endl;
   for (position = 1; position <= 70; ++position)
        cout << "*";

   cout << endl << endl;
   cout << "\t\tWelcome to the Personal Loan Program" << endl << endl;
   cout << "This program will determine the interest, total amount"
        << endl;
   cout << "and monthly payment of your loan." << endl << endl;
   cout << "Please follow the instructions carefully." << endl << endl;

   for (position = 1; position <= 70; ++position)
     cout << "*";
   cout << endl << endl << endl;
} // End of Display_Greeting
double Get_Principal()
{
   const double MIN_PRINCIPAL = 1000.00;
   const double MAX_PRINCIPAL = 20000.00;

   double principal;

   cout << "Enter amount of the loan: $";
   cin >> principal;

   if (principal < MIN_PRINCIPAL)
   {
     cout << endl;
     cout << "Sorry, we do not make loans for under $1,000.00." << endl;
     exit(1);
   }
   else
     if (principal > MAX_PRINCIPAL)
     {
       cout << endl;
       cout << "Sorry, we do not make personal loans";
       cout << " in excess of $20,000.00" << endl << endl;
       cout << "Please try our Home Equity Loan\n";
       exit(1);
     }
     else
       return principal;
} // End of Get_Principal()
double Get_Rate()
{
   const double MAX_RATE = 18.70;

   double rate;

   cout << endl;
   cout << "Enter current annual interest rate (in %): ";
```

```cpp
  cin >> rate;
  if (rate > MAX_RATE)
  {
     cout << endl;
     cout << "Sorry, the rate exceeds the legal maximum of "
          << MAX_RATE << "%" << endl;
     exit(1);
  }
  else
     return rate;
} // End of Get_Rate()
int Get_Term()
{
  const int MAX_TERM = 5;

  int term;

  cout << endl;
  cout <<"Enter the number of years of the loan: ";
  cin >> term;

  if (term > MAX_TERM)
  {
     cout << endl;
     cout << "Sorry, the term of your loan cannot exceed "
          << MAX_TERM << " years" << endl;
     exit(1);
  }
  else
     return term;
} // End of Get_Term()
```

Program Output

```
****************************************************************
            Welcome to the Personal Loan Program

This program will determine the interest, total amount
and monthly payment of your loan.

Please follow the instructions carefully.

****************************************************************

Enter amount of the loan: $10000.00
Enter current annual interest rate (in %): 10.7
Enter the number of years of the loan: 4
Interest Rate:      10.70%
Term of Loan:       4 Years
```

```
Amount Borrowed:     $ 10000.00
Interest on Loan:    $  4280.00
------------------------------
Amount of Loan:      $ 14280.00
Monthly Payment:     $   297.50
```

5.3.7 Discussion of the Program

The program begins with the function prototypes for the four functions that main()
uses. Because Display_Greeting() only displays information on the screen, it does
not require any arguments and does not return a value to main(). None of the three
functions that obtain the input data requires an argument to do its work. If the data
that the user enters is acceptable, each of these functions returns that data to main().
Thus the return type of each function corresponds to the type of data the user enters.
Because the principal and rate are decimal numbers, the functions Get_Principal()
and Get_Rate() return a double. Because the term is an integer, Get_Term() returns
an integer.

To display the greeting, main() executes the function Display_Greeting().
The next three assignments execute the functions that obtain the input data and
place the appropriate values into the variables principal, rate, and term. Remember that the user enters the rate as a percent.

Next, three assignments place the appropriate values into interest, total, and
monthly_payment using the formulas described in the previous section. Finally, a series of seven cout statements displays the results.

The code for Get_Principal() closely follows the pseudocode we developed
earlier. The values of the minimum and maximum principals are defined as symbolic
constants. The function prompts for and obtains the input value for the principal.
Then, it uses a nested if to decide if the value is in the valid range for the principal (between MIN_PRINCIPAL [1000.00] and MAX_PRINCIPAL [20000.00]). If not, a cout
statement displays an appropriate message and the exit(1) function ends the program. If the value is in the valid range, the function returns the value of principal.
See the exercises for some extensions of the program.

The code for Get_Rate() and Get_Term() work similarly to that of
Get_Principal().

5.3.8 Testing the Program

Whenever you design a program to catch input errors, you should test for each of those
input errors. The program output that accompanied the program in the previous section was produced by valid input values. Following are four program runs that test each
input error that the program checks for.

Test 1: Principal Too Small

```
*****************************************************************

          Welcome to the Personal Loan Program

This program will determine the interest, total amount
and monthly payment of your loan.

Please follow the instructions carefully.

*****************************************************************

Enter amount of the loan: $750.00

Sorry, we do not make loans for under $1,000.00.
```

Test 2: Principal Too Large

```
*****************************************************************

          Welcome to the Personal Loan Program

This program will determine the interest, total amount
and monthly payment of your loan.

Please follow the instructions carefully.

*****************************************************************

Enter amount of the loan: $30000.00

Sorry, we do not make personal loans in excess of $20,000.00

Please try our Home Equity Loan.
```

Test 3: Rate Too Large

```
*****************************************************************

          Welcome to the Personal Loan Program

This program will determine the interest, total amount
and monthly payment of your loan.

Please follow the instructions carefully.

*****************************************************************
```

```
Enter amount of the loan: $10000.00

Enter current annual interest rate (in %): 20.0

Sorry, the rate exceeds the legal maximum of 18.70%
```

Test 4: Term Too Large

```
********************************************************************

            Welcome to the Personal Loan Program

This program will determine the interest, total amount
and monthly payment of your loan.

Please follow the instructions carefully.

********************************************************************

Enter amount of the loan: $10000.00
Enter current annual interest rate (in %): 10.7
Enter the number of years of the loan: 7

Sorry, the term of your loan cannot exceed 5 years.
```

5.3.9 Problem 5.3—Calculating Commissions: Data Validation

This program demonstrates the use of a prompting function whose return value controls the main processing loop and how to construct a data validation function that continually prompts the user for valid data.

The Pickering Paper Products Company wants you to write a program to calculate the total income of its sales personnel. The program should prompt the user for the following data: the sales person number, which must be between 000 and 999; the salesperson salary, which must be between 0.00 and 200.00; the amount of the salesperson's sales, which must be between 0.00 and 10,000.00. If the user enters invalid data, the program should display an error message and prompt the user to enter correct data. The program should continue to prompt until the user enters valid data.

The salesperson's income is the sum of the salary, the straight commission, and the bonus commission. The straight commission is the sales multiplied by the commission rate of 5.0%. If the sales exceeds the sales quota for the salesperson, the bonus commission is the amount by which the sales exceeds the quota multiplied by the bonus commission rate of 8.5%. The sales quota for a salesperson is five times the salary of the salesperson.

For each salesperson that the program processes, display the salesperson number, salary, sales, and income. After the program processes the last salesperson, it should display the total number of salespersons that it processed.

5.3.10 Program Design

The pseudocode for the main module of the program is as follows. We defer to the discussion of the program code in the next section to see exactly how to make the test for another salesperson.

Pseudocode for Problem 5.3

    while (another salesperson)
      Process_Salesperson
      ++salesperson_count
    endwhile
    Display salesperson_count

The module `Process_Salesperson` requires obtaining valid data from the user, calculating the salesperson income, and displaying the salesperson data.

    Process_Salesperson
            Get_Valid Sales_No
            Get_Valid_Salary
            Get_Valid_Sales
            Calculate_Income
            Display_Salesperson_Data

The three modules that obtain valid data from the user have essentially the same design. Following is a generalized pseudocode that we shall use to develop the data validation modules.

    Data Validation Module
            do
              Get data from user
              If (data is invalid)
                invalid_data = true
                display error message
              else
                invalid_data = false
              endif
            while (invalid_data is true)
            return data

The pseudocode uses the variable `invalid_data` as a flag. A **flag** is a variable whose value signals the occurrence of an event in a program. If the user enters invalid data, the `if` statement sets the flag `invalid_data` to `true`; otherwise (that is, the user enters valid data), the `if` statement sets `invalid_data` to `false`. Thus, the value of `invalid_data` tells the program whether the user entered invalid data. The do loop's condition shows that the program will stay in the loop as long as the user enters invalid data. When the program exits the loop, the data that the user entered was valid. Therefore, the module returns the valid data to the program.

A flag is an example of a **Boolean variable**—a variable that takes only the values `true` and `false`. The program prb05-3.cpp, which we will discuss shortly, uses the Boolean data type `bool`. A variable of type `bool` can assume only one of two values, `true` and `false`, both of which are C++ keywords. For example, the following code declares the Boolean variable `invalid_data` and initializes it to `false`.

```
bool invalid_data = false;
```

Recall from Chapter 3 that any nonzero value (in particular, 1) is considered by C++ to be true and 0 is considered false. C++ treats the values `true` and `false` as the integers 1 and 0 respectively. Note that older C++ compilers do not have the `bool` data type. In that case, instead of using a `bool` variable, you must use an `int` variable and use the values 1 and 0 for `true` and `false`. If possible, however, it is better to use a `bool` variable rather than an `int` for a flag. A `bool` variable can have only one of two possible values, whereas an `int` variable can assume any integer value (all of which are considered true, except 0). See Experiment 9.

Note 5.6 Boolean Variables

Use the Boolean data type `bool` to declare a Boolean variable. A Boolean variable can have only the values `true` and `false`.

Normally, `cin` and `cout` are connected to the standard input and output streams—the keyboard and the monitor, respectively. At command level, the user can redirect either one or both `cin` and `cout` to system files. Therefore, the user can force `cin` to obtain its data from a file and force `cout` to place its data into a file. In our data validation modules, we will have to display error messages to the monitor when the program obtains invalid data. We do not want these error messages to be redirected to a file, where we will not see them. To make sure that our error messages are sent to the monitor and cannot be redirected to another device, we will send all error messages to the `cerr` output stream. You use `cerr` in exactly the same way as `cout`. The only difference is that the data sent to `cerr` must go to the monitor.

Note 5.7 The cerr Output Stream

Use the `cerr` output stream to display error messages on the monitor. The `cerr` stream cannot be redirected.

The pseudocode for the `Calculate_Income` module is straightforward.

Calculate_Income
    quota = salary * 5
    straight_commission = sales * 0.05

if (sales > quota)
  bonus_commission = (sales − quota) * 0.085
else
  bonus_commission = 0.00
endif
income = salary + straight_commission + bonus_commission
return income

Finally, the pseudocode for Display_Salesperson_Data.

Display_Salesperson_Data
        Display salesperson_number
        Display salary
        Display sales
        Display income

We now discuss the actual program code.

5.3.11 The Program prb05-3.cpp

Following is the code for the program prb05-3.cpp.

```cpp
// prb05-3.cpp

// This program calculates commissions based on salary and
// sales quota.  It validates input data before doing the
// calculations.

#include <iostream>
#include <iomanip>

using namespace std;
int     Another_Salesperson();
void    Process_Salesperson();
void    Display_Salesperson_Data(int, double, double, double);
int     Get_Valid_Sales_No();
double Get_Valid_Sales();
double Get_Valid_Salary();
double Calculate_Income(double, double);

int main()
{
   int salesperson_count = 0;

   cout << setprecision(2)
        << setiosflags(ios::fixed)
        << setiosflags(ios::showpoint);

   while (Another_Salesperson())
   {
     Process_Salesperson();
     ++salesperson_count;
   }
```

```cpp
   cout << endl << endl;
   cout << "Number of Salespersons Processed: " << salesperson_count;

   cout << endl;
   return 0;

}   // End of main()

int Another_Salesperson()
{
   int response;

   cout << endl << endl;
   cout << "Do you want to process a salesperson income?" << endl;
   cout << "Enter 1 for Yes, 0 for No: ";
   cin >> response;

   return response;

}   // End of Another_Salesperson()

void Process_Salesperson()
{
   int     salesperson_number;
   double sales,
          salary,
          income;

   salesperson_number = Get_Valid_Sales_No();
   salary             = Get_Valid_Salary();
   sales              = Get_Valid_Sales();
   income             = Calculate_Income(sales, salary);

   Display_Salesperson_Data(salesperson_number, salary, sales, income);

}   // End of Process_Salesperson()

int Get_Valid_Sales_No()
{
   int salesperson_number;
   bool invalid_data;

   do
   {
      cout << endl;
      cout << "Enter the Salesperson Number (000-999): ";
      cin >> salesperson_number;

      if ((salesperson_number < 0) || (salesperson_number > 999))
      {
         cerr << endl;
         cerr << "Salesperson Number must be between 000 and 999.";
         invalid_data = true;
      }
      else
         invalid_data = false;
   }
```

```cpp
    while (invalid_data);

    return salesperson_number;

}  // End Get_Valid_Sales_No()

double Get_Valid_Salary()
{
    bool invalid_data;
    double salary;

    do
    {
        cout << endl;
        cout << "Enter salary (0 - 200): ";
        cin >> salary;

        if ( (salary < 0.00) || (salary > 200.00) )
        {
            cerr << endl;
            cerr << "Salary is invalid - Please reenter";
            invalid_data = true;
        }
        else
            invalid_data = false;
    }
    while (invalid_data);

    return salary;

}  // End Get_Valid_Salary()

double Get_Valid_Sales()
{
    bool   invalid_data;
    double sales;

    do
    {
        cout << endl;
        cout << "Enter sales (0 - 10,000): ";
        cin >> sales;

        if ( (sales < 0.00) || (sales > 10000.00) )
        {
            cerr << endl;
            cerr << "Sales is invalid - Please reenter";
            invalid_data = true;
        }
        else
            invalid_data = false;
    }
    while (invalid_data);

     return sales;

}  // End Get_Valid_Sales()
```

```
double Calculate_Income(double sales, double salary)
{
   const double COMMISSION_RATE = 0.050;
   const double BONUS_RATE      = 0.085;
   const int    QUOTA_FACTOR    = 5;

     double quota,
            income,
            straight_commission,
            bonus_commission;

   quota = salary * QUOTA_FACTOR;

   straight_commission = sales * COMMISSION_RATE;

   if (sales > quota)
      bonus_commission = (sales - quota) * BONUS_RATE;
   else
      bonus_commission = 0.00;

   income = salary + straight_commission + bonus_commission;

   return income;
}  // End Calculate_Income()

void Display_Salesperson_Data(int sp_no, double salary, double sales,
                              double income)
{
   cout << endl;
   cout << "Data - Salesperson #" << sp_no << endl << endl;
   cout << "Salary: " << setw(10) << salary << endl;
   cout << "Sales:  " << setw(10) << sales << endl;
   cout << "Income: " << setw(10) << income << endl;
} // End Display_Salesperson_Data()
```

Program Output

```
Do you want to process a salesperson income?
Enter 1 for Yes, 0 for No: 1

Enter the Salesperson Number (000-999): 123

Enter salary (0 - 200): 150.00

Enter sales (0 - 10,000): 3500.00

Data - Salesperson #123

Salary:    150.00
Sales:    3500.00
Income:    558.75
```

```
Do you want to process a salesperson income?
Enter 1 for Yes, 0 for No: 1

Enter the Salesperson Number (000-999): 826

Enter salary (0 - 200): 375.00

Salary is invalid - Please reenter
Enter salary (0 - 200): 75.00

Enter sales (0 - 10,000): 2700.00

Data - Salesperson #826
Salary:      75.00
Sales:    2700.00
Income:     407.63

Do you want to process a salesperson income?
Enter 1 for Yes, 0 for No: 1

Enter the Salesperson Number (000-999): 373

Enter salary (0 - 200): 75.00

Enter sales (0 - 10,000): 12000.00

Sales is invalid - Please reenter
Enter sales (0 - 10,000): 2000.00

Data - Salesperson #373

Salary:      75.00
Sales:    2000.00
Income:     313.13

Do you want to process a salesperson income?
Enter 1 for Yes, 0 for No: 1

Enter the Salesperson Number (000-999): 6789

Salesperson Number must be between 000 and 999.

Enter the Salesperson Number (000-999): 678

Enter salary (0 - 200): 90.00

Enter sales (0 - 10,000): 1500.00

Data - Salesperson #678

Salary:      90.00
Sales:    1500.00
Income:     254.25

Do you want to process a salesperson income?
Enter 1 for Yes, 0 for No: 0

Number of Salespersons Processed: 4
```

5.3.12 Discussion of the Program

Note that the user made several input-data errors in the program run that follows the listing.

All the functions closely follow the pseudocode that we developed in the previous section. Note the use of the `bool` variable `invalid_data` in the data validation functions and the use of the `cerr` output stream to display the error messages on the monitor.

The only function that we did not discuss is `Another_Salesperson()`. When the `while` statement executes, it evaluates its control expression, which causes the function `Another_Salesperson()` to execute. The function prompts the user for a 1 or 0 answer to the prompt for another salesperson. It then places the user's answer into the variable `response` and returns this value to `main()`. Thus, evaluating the `while` loop's condition causes the program to prompt the user and obtain the response. If the user responded by entering 1, which C++ considers true, the `while` statement's condition expression is true and the loop body executes.

Experiments 5.3

1. Add a function `Display_Greeting()` to prb05-1.cpp that displays the purpose of the program. After displaying the greeting, the function should pause and display

   `Press any key to continue`

   (Hint: use `cin.get()`.) The program should then proceed as in the text. Use the function in the program. Recompile, execute, and test the resulting program.

2. Add the function `Calc_Total_Charge()` to prb05-1.cpp. The function should take two arguments representing the labor charge and the total charge. The function should return the sum of its arguments. Use the function in the program. Recompile, execute, and test the resulting program.

3. Add the function `Calc_Payment()` to prb05-2.cpp. The function should calculate the monthly payment as done in the original program. Replace the `Do_Calculation` section of the program by a call to the `Calc_Payment()` function. Recompile, execute, and test the resulting program.

4. In prb05-2.cpp, the principal, rate, and term must all be positive. Include in the functions `Get_Principal()`, `Get_Rate()`, and `Get_Term()` a test to see if the entered data is positive. If the data is not positive, display an error message and exit the program. Use the new functions in the program. Recompile, execute, and test the resulting program.

5. In prb05-3.cpp, validate the response obtained by the function `Another_Salesperson()`. If the response is not 0 or 1, continually prompt until the person enters either 0 or 1. Use the new function in the program. Recompile, execute, and test the resulting program.

6. In prb05-3.cpp, if the user enters invalid data, the program continually prompts for another value until the user enters a valid value. Change all the data validation functions so they prompt the user for valid data a maximum of three times. If

the user enters invalid data three times the program should issue a polite message and end.

7. In prb05-3.cpp, why is `salesperson_count` declared in `main()` and incremented in `main()`'s while loop and not declared and incremented in `Process_Salesperson()`?

8. In prb05-3.cpp, would it be a good idea to declare the global constants

   `const int TRUE = 1;`

   `const int FALSE = 0;`

   instead of making three pairs of such declarations (one for each validation function), if the bool data type is not used.

9. Write a small program that outputs the values of two `bool` type variables, one of which has the value `true` and the other of which has the value `false`. How does C++ store the values of `true` and `false`?

Programming Problems 5.3

1. The Big Racket Tennis Club wants you to write a program to calculate the yearly dues for its members. The program should prompt the user for the membership type (either 'I' for individual or 'F' for family) and the number of years the person has been a member. Use a function `Get_Member_Type()` that prompts the user for his or her membership type, obtains the type from the user and returns the type to `main()`. Use a function `Years()` that prompts the user for the number of years he or she has been a member and returns that number to `main()`.

   Use a function `Dues()` to calculate the member's dues. Pass the member type and number of years to the function. Calculate the dues as follows: If the person is a family member and has been a club member for more than three years, the dues are $2400.00. If the person is a family member and has been a club member for three years or less, the dues are $3000.00. If the person is an individual member and has been a club member for more than five years, the dues are $1500.00. If the person is an individual member and has been a club member for five years or less, the dues are $1900.00. The function `Dues()` should return the dues to `main()`.

   Use a function `Display_Member_Info()` to display the type of membership, the number of years the person has been a member, and the dues, all of which should be passed to the function as arguments.

2. At Humongus National Bank, the vice president in charge of credit cards decides to issue a new type of credit card, the Platinum Card. Write a program to help the bank decide to which of its customers it will offer a Platinum Card. Use a function `Get_Credit_Limit()` to prompt the user for the customer's present credit limit. The function should return the credit limit. Use a function `Get_Acc_Bal()` to prompt the user for the customer's account balance. The function should return the account balance.

   Use a function `Determine_Action()` whose arguments are the customer's credit limit and account balance. `Determine_Action()` should return 0, 1, or 2 according to the following. If a customer has a credit limit of at least $2000.00 and an account balance of $500.00 or less, the bank will issue the customer a Platinum card. In this case, the function should return 2. If a customer has a credit limit of at least $2000.00 and an account balance of more than $500.00, the bank will send a letter to the customer. This letter will state that if the customer's balance falls below $500.00, he or she will receive a Platinum Card. In this case, the function should return 1. If a customer does not fall into either of these categories, the bank will take no action. In this case, the function should return 0.

Use a function `Display_Action()` to display the action that the bank will take for the customer. Pass to `Display_Action()` the value that `Determine_Action()` returned. Based on this value, `Display_Action()` should display a message that shows the action that the bank should take: issue a Platinum Card, send a letter, or take no action.

3. After many years of being frustrated by a checkbook that just will not balance, you decide to write a program to help balance your money market checking account. The program should begin by asking the user for the month's opening account balance. Use a function to obtain and validate the input data. The balance cannot be negative.

   Then the program should use a function to display a menu that lists the following choices: D for a deposit, C for a check, W for a withdrawal, and Q for quit. Use a function to obtain and validate the user's choice. If the user enters something other than D, W, C, or Q, the program should issue an error message and redisplay the menu. Allow the user to enter either uppercase or lowercase letters.

   If the user selects D, use a function to ask the user to enter the amount of the deposit, and add the amount to the account balance.

   If the user enters C, use a function to ask the user for the amount of the check, and subtract the check amount from the balance. However, if the amount of the check exceeds the balance, issue a warning message and exit the program.

   If the user enters W, use a function to ask the user for the amount of the withdrawal, and subtract the amount from the balance. However, if the amount of the withdrawal exceeds the balance, issue a warning message and exit the program.

   When the user enters Q, the program should use a function to display the opening balance, the total amount deposited, the total amount withdrawn, the total amount of the checks, and the final balance.

4. Generalize the program of Programming Problem 1 as follows. The function `Get_Member_Type()` should validate the membership type. Anything other than 'I' or 'F' is an invalid membership type. Continually prompt the user to enter a valid membership type until he or she does so. The function `Years()` should validate the number of years that the user enters. The number of years should be nonnegative and less than 37, which is the age of the tennis club. Continually prompt the user to enter a valid number of years until he or she does so. The program should also process any number of members.

5. Generalize the program of Programming Problem 2 as follows. Write the program so that it will process any number of customers. The function

`Get_Credit_Limit()` should validate the credit card limit that the user entered. The credit card limit must be between 500.00 and 20,000.00, inclusive. If the user enters an invalid credit card limit, prompt the user again. If the user enters an invalid limit again, the program should stop processing that customer and go on to the next customer. The function `Get_Acc_Bal()` should validate the account balance. The balance must be nonnegative and less than the validated credit limit. If the user enters a negative account balance, prompt the user again for an account balance. If the user enters an invalid account balance again, the program should stop processing that customer and go on to the next customer. If the user enters an account balance that is greater than the validated credit limit, the program should display a message to that effect, and go on to the next customer.

6. A piece of equipment, such as a computer, loses value over time. The amount of this lost value is called **depreciation**. The simplest way to determine depreciation is by the **straight-line** method. If the asset has a useful life of n years, the straight-line method of depreciation assumes a depreciation of 1/n of the item's value each year. Assume a particular $3,000 computer has a useful life of five years. At the end of the five years, assume it has a **scrap value** of $500. Thus, the net cost of the computer is $3000 - 500 = 2500. Using the straight-line method, the computer depreciates $500 ($= 2500 \times 1/5$) each of the five years of its useful life. After two years, the computer depreciates $1,000. Thus, the **book value** of the computer after two years (the difference between the cost of the item and the depreciation to date) is $2,000 ($= 3000 - 1000$).

Write a program that calculates the depreciation of an asset using the straight-line method. The program should ask the user for the initial cost of the item, the scrap value of the item, and the item's useful life in years. Use a function `Depreciation()` that calculates and displays a table that shows the book value of the item after each year of its useful life. The function should have three arguments—the initial cost, the scrap value, and the life of the item. The function should not return a value.

7. An automobile part supplier decides to give discounts to this week's customers to help improve customer relations. Write a program to calculate a customer's discount. The discount is based on the value of the customer's order (the invoice amount) and the customer code, which is a single character. If the customer code is A, the discount rate is 5%. If the customer code is B, the discount rate is 8%. Finally, if the customer code is C, the discount rate is 12%. A customer code other than A, a, B, b, C, or c is invalid. The discount amount is the amount multiplied by the discount rate. The net invoice amount is the amount minus the discount amount. The program should display the invoice amount, the discount amount, and the net invoice amount.

8. A credit card company wants a program to calculate updates on its customers' accounts. The program should prompt for the previous month's balance, the amount of the new purchases, and the amount of the payments received.

The program should use a function to calculate the customer's finance charge by first subtracting the payments received from the previous month's balance. Then multiply the result by 1/12 the annual interest rate of 16 percent to get the finance charge.

Next, use a function to calculate the late charge, if any. If the payments received amount is less than 12% of the previous month's balance, the late charge is 0.5% of the difference between the previous month's balance and the payments received. The minimum late charge is $3.00. If the payments received amount is 12% or more of the previous month's balance, there is no late charge.

The program should use a function to calculate the new balance. To calculate the new balance, first subtract the payments received from the previous month's balance. From the result, add the finance charge, the late charge, and the new purchases amount to give the new balance.

Finally, use a function to calculate the minimum payment. If the new balance is less than or equal to $100.00, the minimum payment is the new balance. If the new balance is greater than $100.00, the minimum payment is 20% of the new balance.

9. Your county government wants you to write a program that computes the property tax on commercial and residential properties. The program should prompt the user for the type of property (1 for a home, 2 for a commercial property). If the property is a home, the program should ask if the property is a residence (1 for primary residence, 2 for non-primary residence). If the property is commercial, the program should ask if the property contains a building (1 for building, 2 for land only). Finally, the program should ask for the property tract number and for the assessed value of the property. Use functions to obtain all input values. Invalid input values should be rejected.

The property tax should be calculated according to the following. If the property is a home used for a primary residence, the tax rate is 3.2% of the assessed value. If the property is a home that is a non-primary residence, the tax rate is 4.1% of the assessed value. If the property is commercial and is land only, the tax rate is 5.3% of the assessed value. If the property is a commercial building, the tax rate is 6.2% of the assessed value. Use a function to decide the tax rate.

The program should output the property tract number, the type of property, the assessed value of the property, the tax rate, and the amount of the property tax.

10. A garment manufacturer requires a program to calculate the payroll of his piecework employees. A piecework employee receives a guaranteed wage, which is based on the seniority of the person. However, a worker can receive incentive pay instead of the guaranteed wage. Incentive pay is determined by the number of units the worker produces. For all units produced up to and including 100 , the incentive pay is $3.50 per unit. For all units produced in excess of 100, the incentive pay is $4.50 per unit. An employee cannot receive both a guaranteed wage and incentive pay. Instead, an employee receives the greater of the two. Write a program to compute the payroll.

The program should use a function to obtain the employee's guaranteed wage, and a function to obtain the number of units produced. Use a function to calculate the pay based on the guaranteed wage and the number of units produced. Finally, use a function to display the employee's wage and whether it is the guaranteed wage or the incentive pay.

The program should process any number of employees.

11. Your city's Parking Violation Bureau wants you to write a program to compute fines for parking violations. There are four types of violation: type A carries a fine of $10, type B carries a fine of $20, type C carries a fine of $30, and type D carries a fine of $50. The program should ask for the number of type A violations, the number of type B violations, and so on. Use four separate functions to obtain the number of violations of each type. If the number of type A, B, or C violations exceeds 10, impose an additional fine of $50 for each category that exceeds 10. If the total number of type A, B, or C exceeds 20 but none of types A, B, or C individually exceeds 10, impose an additional fine of $75. If the number of type D violations exceeds 3, impose an additional fine of $20 for each type D violation over three. Use a function to calculate the total fine. Pass to this function the number of fines of each type. The function should return the total fine. Finally, use a function to display the total fine for the person. The program should process any number of persons.

5.4 THE C++ MATH LIBRARY FUNCTIONS[1]

Some business calculations involve evaluating expressions that involve operations other than the four basic operations of addition, subtraction, multiplication, and division. C++ contains a library of mathematical functions that are sometimes useful in these situations. These functions include the standard trigonometric functions (such as `sin()`, `cos()`, and `tan()`), and exponential and logarithmic functions (such as `exp()` and `log()`). Because we are primarily concerned with business applications, discussing these would take us beyond the scope of this book. However, there are several functions in the math library that can prove useful in some business problems. To use the math library functions, you must include the header file `<cmath>`.

5.4.1 The Library Function pow()

As mentioned in Chapter 1, C++ does not have an exponentiation operator as do several other programming languages (such as Visual Basic). Suppose we have the following:

$$p = b^e$$

We call the number b the **base**, e the **exponent**, and the value of the base raised to the exponent, namely p, the **power**.

To raise a base to an exponent in C++, you can use one of two techniques. If the exponent is an integer, you can use a `for` loop to calculate the power. For example, to raise the value stored in the variable `base` to the exponent 8, that is, to compute the power $base^8$, which means `base` multiplied by itself 8 times, use the following loop.

```
for(int exponent = 1, int power = 1; exponent <= 8; ++exponent)
    power *= base;
```

[1]This section may be omitted.

The loop essentially multiplies power, which begins with a value of 1, by the value of base exactly 8 times. This gives power the final value of base^8. See Experiment 1.

If the exponent that we want to raise the base to is not an integer, then we cannot use a for loop because we cannot execute the body of a loop a fractional number of times. Therefore, using a for loop, we cannot compute $3^{1.35}$. This is where the C++ library function pow() comes in handy. The function **pow(base, exponent)** raises the first argument, base, to its second argument, exponent. Both arguments must be doubles and the value returned is also a double. Therefore, to display the value of $3^{1.35}$, we can code

```
cout << pow(3.0, 1.35);
```

The cout will display the value 4.4067.

5.4.2 The Library Function sqrt()

To find the square root of a number, say $\sqrt{30}$, you can use the fact that the square root of a number is the same as raising the number to the 0.5 power. Therefore, to find the square root, you can use pow() as follows:

```
pow(30.0, 0.5).
```

However, there is another math library function that calculates square roots more directly. The function **sqrt()** returns the square root of its argument. The argument should be a double and the function returns a double. For example, the following statement will display 11.1803.

```
cout << sqrt(125.0);
```

The program dem05-7.cpp demonstrates the use of pow() and sqrt().

```
//dem05-7.cpp

//This program demonstrates the use of pow()
//and sqrt()

#include <iostream>
#include <cmath>

using namespace std;

int main()
{
    double base;
    double exponent;

    double num;

    cout << "Enter a base: ";
    cin >> base;

    cout << "Enter an exponent: ";
    cin >> exponent;

    cout << base << " raised to the " << exponent
```

```
            << " is " << pow(base, exponent) << endl << endl;
        cout << "Enter a number to find its square root: ";
        cin >> num;

        cout << "The square root of " << num
             << " is " << sqrt(num) << endl;

        return 0;
    }
```

Program Output

```
Enter a base: 4.2
Enter an exponent: 6.49
4.2 raised to the 6.49 is 11088.9

Enter a number to find its square root: 873.47
The square root of 873.47 is 29.5545
```

Note 5.8 summarizes the main points of this section.

Note 5.8   The C++ Math Library

- To use the functions in the C++ math library, you must include the header file cmath.
- The C++ math library contains useful mathematical functions—trigonometric, logarithmic, exponential, and others.
- The function pow(base, exponent) raises the number that is its first argument, base, to its second argument, exponent. Both arguments must be doubles. The function returns a double.
- The function sqrt() returns the square root of its argument. The argument must be a double. The function returns a double.

Exercises 5.4

1. Write each of the following mathematical expressions using either pow() or sqrt().

    a. 19^2

    b. $\sqrt{59.63}$

    c. $2.73^{9.53}$

    d. $9.4^{0.5}$

Experiments 5.4

1. Use the following for loop to write a program to compute 2.3^8. In the same program, use the function pow() to compute the same number. Do the results differ?

```
for(int exponent = 1, int power = 1; exponent <= 8; ++exponent)
    power *= base;
```

Programming Problems 5.4

1. Write a function called my_pow() that takes two arguments. The first should be a double and the second should be an integer. The function my_pow should use a loop similar to the one in Experiment 1 to raise the first argument to the exponent that is its second argument. Write a program to test your function.

2. An IRA (individual retirement account) is an example of an annuity. The holder of an IRA can deposit money into the account each year. The amount is usually withdrawn when the depositor is age 65. However, it can be withdrawn when the depositor is age 59.5 without incurring a penalty. A bank wishes to show its customers the difference between what they will have in their accounts at age 65 and what they will have in their accounts at age 59.5, if equal annual payments are made to the account. Write a program to do this.

   The program should prompt for the annual deposit (which should not exceed $2,000), the annual interest rate, and the customer's age when the account was opened. Use a function to obtain each input datum. The function that obtains the interest rate should allow the user to enter the interest rate as a percent (for example, 4.7) but should return the decimal equivalent of the entered percent (for example, 0.047.)

   The amount in an IRA after n years of equal annual deposits of R dollars at an annual interest rate of r is given by the following formula.

   $$A = R(((1 + r)^n - 1)/r)$$

   To calculate the value of an IRA when the customer is 65, first subtract the customer's age at the time the account was opened from 65. This gives the value of n to use in the formula. The values of R and r are obtained from the user. To calculate the value of an IRA when the customer is 59.5, proceed in the same manner, but subtract the customer's age from 59.5 to obtain the value of n.

   The program should output the value of the IRA at age 65, the value of the IRA at age 59.5, and the difference between these values.

3. A bank wishes to calculate the monthly payment required to pay off (or amortize) personal loans that it will make to customers. Write a program to do this.

   The program should prompt the user for the amount of the loan (the principal), the annual interest rate, and the length of the loan in years. The principal cannot exceed $100,000 and the length of the loan cannot exceed five years. Allow the user to enter the interest rate as a percent. Use a function to obtain each input value.

The monthly payment M on an N-year loan with a principal of P at a monthly interest rate of r is given by the following formula.

$$M = Pr/(1 - (1 + r)^{-12N})$$

Calculate the monthly interest rate by dividing the yearly interest rate by 12.

The program should output the amount of the loan, the annual interest rate, the length of the loan in years, and the monthly payment.

CHAPTER REVIEW

TERMINOLOGY

Discuss the meanings of the following terms.

program module	automatic variable
return	auto
calling function	static
called function	static variable
return value	flag
argument	Boolean variable
function prototype	bool
user-defined function	cerr
void	depreciation
function definition header	straight-line
function body	scrap value
parameter	book value
arguments passed by value	<cmath>
arguments passed by reference	base
scope	exponent
duration	power
local scope	pow()
global scope	sqrt()
storage class	

SUMMARY

- A function is a program module that performs a specific, well-defined task.
- A function can have zero or more arguments (inputs), and zero or one return value.
- A function must be defined in a prototype, which specifies the function name, return type (void if none), and the argument types (Note 5.1 and Note 5.2).
- Specify what the function does in the function definition (Note 5.3).
- The function parameters, which are initialized to the values of the arguments passed to the function, are declared in the function definition header.
- When the arguments are passed to a function, the first argument is assigned to the first parameter in the function definition and the second argument is assigned to the second parameter

in the function definition, and so on. Thus, arguments and parameters are matched on a positional basis only and not on their meaning (Note 5.4).

- The names a function uses for its parameters need not be the same as the names main() uses for the function's arguments (Note 5.4).
- By default, arguments are passed by value.
- A variable declared inside a function has local scope; that is, it is known only inside that function.
- A variable declared outside a function definition has global scope; that is, it is known to all functions whose definition follows that of the variable. You should avoid using global variables (Note 5.5).
- An automatic variable (local variables are automatic by default) ceases to exist when the function in which it is declared ends.
- A static variable (global variables are static by default; a local variable can be declared static using the keyword static in its declaration) is allocated storage when the program begins executing and remains in existence as long as the program is running.
- Use a Boolean variable of type bool for a program flag. A bool variable can assume only the values true and false (Note 5.6).
- Use the cerr output stream for error messages. The cerr output stream cannot be redirected (Note 5.7).
- The math library contains mathematical functions. To use the functions in the math library, you must include cmath (Note 5.8).
- The math library function pow() can raise a number to an exponent (Note 5.8).
- The math library function sqrt() takes the square root of the number that is its argument (Note 5.8).

REVIEW EXERCISES

1. What is a function? What is the difference between the calling function and the called function?
2. How many arguments can a function have and how many return values?
3. What is the purpose of a function prototype and how do you code one?
4. How do you code the fact that a function has no arguments? How do you code the fact that a function has no return value?
5. How does a function pass control back to the calling function?
6. What is the purpose of a parameter in a function definition?
7. What is the default method that C++ uses to pass arguments to a function?
8. What is the scope of a variable?
9. What is the difference between local and global scope?
10. What kind of variable has local scope by default?
11. What kind of variable has global scope by default?
12. Why should you avoid using global variables?
13. What is the difference between the auto and static storage classes?

14. What kind of variable is `auto` by default?

15. What kind if variable is `static` by default?

16. How can you declare a local variable to be `static`? Why can such a variable be useful?

17. What is the purpose of a program flag?

18. What is the `bool` data type and when should it be used?

19. What is the difference between the `cout` and `cerr` output streams?

20. What function allows you to compute exponential expressions?

21. What function allows you to compute square roots?

Chapter 6

Arrays

OBJECTIVES

- To properly declare an array
- To use subscripts to access array elements
- To initialize an array
- To use a `for` loop to process an array
- To code an array search
- To code a bubble sort on an array
- To properly declare a two-dimensional array
- To initialize a two-dimensional array
- To use nested `for` loops to process a two-dimensional array

Sometimes it is convenient to store related data together as an array. This chapter begins by showing how to declare, initialize, and process the elements in an array. Then, we discuss several applications of arrays, including searching an array. We also cover how to pass an array as a function argument, and we use functions in several applications, including sorting an array using the bubble sort. Finally, we close the chapter by discussing multidimensional arrays.

6.1 BASIC CONCEPTS

Sometimes it is advantageous to store a collection of data together as a unit. For example, in a program to compute shipping charges on mail orders, you might want to store the shipping rates for the five shipping regions that your company uses. You could use five different variables to store the rates: `rate1, rate2, rate3, rate4, rate5`. However, because the five numbers represent shipping rates, it makes more sense to store all five rates in one "variable" called `rate`. This object called `rate` is not a variable in the sense

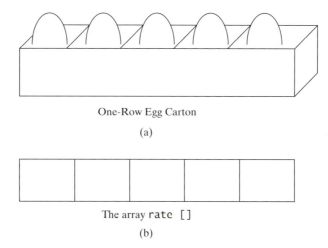

One-Row Egg Carton

(a)

The array `rate []`

(b)

Figure 6.1

that we have used the term so far. It is what we shall call an **array**. An array stores values similarly to the way in which a one-row egg carton holds eggs. We can view the egg carton of Figure 6.1a as a single object. We can also consider the array of Figure 6.1b as a single object. The egg carton of Figure 6.1a stores five individual items, which you can process (fry, boil, scramble, poach) individually. Likewise, the array of Figure 6.1b stores five shipping rates, which a program can individually process.

6.1.1 Definition of an Array

An **array** is a collection of a <u>fixed number</u> of objects all of the <u>same type</u>, which are <u>stored sequentially</u> in computer memory. The objects in an array are the array's **elements**.

The three underlined parts of the definition are important. First, once you decide on the number of elements in an array, that number, the **array size**, stays fixed during the program. However, the values of the individual elements in the array can change as much as the program demands.

Second, the elements in an array must all be the same type. Therefore, they must all be of type `int`, or all of type `char`, or all of type `double`, and so on. The common type of the array's elements is the **array type**. This property of an array ensures that each element in a given array requires the same amount of storage.

Finally, the computer stores the elements in an array sequentially, one after the other, in memory. Therefore, if the computer knows the location of the first element of an array, it knows that the second element immediately follows the first, the third immediately follows the second, and so on. Figure 6.1b illustrates how **array elements** are stored. This property of an array is why some refer to an array as a **linear data structure** or **one-dimensional data structure**—the computer stores the elements of an array in the same way as points appear on a line.

6.1.2 Declaring an Array

To use an array in a program, you first must declare the array. The declaration specifies the name of the array, the array type, and the size of the array. Following is the format of an array declaration.

array-type array-name [array-size];

Thus, the following declares an array of type `double` called `rate` that can store five shipping rates.

```
double rate[5];
```

To read the declaration of an array, follow the rule of Note 6.1.

Note 6.1   Reading an Array Declaration

Begin reading an array declaration at the array name and proceed clockwise through the declaration to the array type. Read the left bracket as "is an array of".

Using Note 6.1, we read the previous declaration as "`rate` is an array of five doubles." Also, read the declaration

```
int grade[10];
```

as "`grade` is an array of ten integers."

6.1.3 Referencing and Initializing Array Elements

Each element in an array is numbered by its **offset**, or **displacement**, from the beginning of the array. Thus, the first element of an array is numbered 0 because it is zero elements from the beginning of the array. The second element of an array is numbered 1 because it is one element from the beginning of the array, and so on. Some people call the offset of an element the element's **subscript** or **index**.

In a program, to refer to a particular element of an array, code the array name and enclose the offset of the element in brackets. Thus, the elements of the array `rate[]` that we declared earlier are `rate[0]`, `rate[1]`, `rate[2]`, `rate[3]`, and `rate[4]` as shown in Figure 6.2. Note that the largest valid offset is one less than the size of the array. The array name and the left bracket can be separated by one or more spaces, although we shall not generally do so.

Note 6.2   Subscript Range

In an array of size N, the valid offset range (subscript values) is from 0 to N–1.

---

rate[0] rate[1] rate[2] rate[3] rate[4]

Figure 6.2

0.075	0.080	0.082	0.085	0.088

rate[0] rate[1] rate[2] rate[3] rate[4]

Figure 6.3

It is now an easy matter to code assignment statements to initialize the elements of an array. For example, to initialize the five elements of the array `rate[]` to 0.075, 0.080, 0.082, 0.085, and 0.088, we could code the following. See Figure 6.3.

```
rate[0] = 0.075;
rate[1] = 0.080;
rate[2] = 0.082;
rate[3] = 0.085;
rate[4] = 0.088;
```

However, instead of coding five separate lines to initialize the array, we can place initial values into the array in the array's declaration. To declare and initialize the array `rate[]` with the values we gave previously, code the following.

```
double rate[5] = {0.075, 0.080, 0.082, 0.085, 0.088};
```

Note 6.3   Initializing an Array

To initialize an array in its declaration, list the elements' initial values in braces. Follow each listed value, except the last value, with a comma.

   If you do not list enough values, the compiler will fill the remaining elements with zeros.

   If you list too many elements when initializing an array, the compiler ignores the extra elements.

   If you initialize an array in its declaration, you can omit the size of the array.

For example, consider the following declaration.

```
double rate[5] = {0.075, 0.080, 0.082};
```

Figure 6.4

The C++ compiler creates the array `rate[]` and allocates enough storage for exactly five doubles. Then, the compiler initializes the first three elements to 0.075, 0.080, and 0.082, and places the double 0.0 into the remaining array elements. See Figure 6.4.

Note that you can initialize an array by setting it equal to the initialization list only in the declaration, not later in an assignment. Thus, the following assignment is illegal.

```
double rate[5];

rate[] = {0.075, 0.080, 0.082, 0.085, 0.088}; // Illegal assignment
```

As a second example, the following declaration initializes all the elements of the array grade to zero. We list one grade in the initialization. The compiler places zero in the other nine array elements.

```
int grade[10] = {0};
```

In the following declaration, seven values are listed in the initialization list, but the array is of size five. Thus, the compiler places only the first five numbers in the array `customer_count[]`.

```
int customer_count[5] = {3, 4, 5, 6, 7, 8, 9};
```

If you initialize an array in the array declaration and omit the size of the array, the compiler will infer the size from the list of elements. For example, the following declaration declares the array `customer_count[]` of size five because we list five elements.

```
int customer_count[] = {3, 4, 5, 6, 7};
```

Note that if you omit the size of the array, you must initialize the array. Thus, the following declaration is illegal because the compiler cannot determine how much memory to allocate for the array.

```
int customer_count[];  // Illegal array declaration
```

6.1.4 Accessing Array Elements by Subscript

The primary advantage of using an array to store data is the ability to refer to the array's elements by number. This allows us to use a variable, usually called a **subscript**, to reference the elements in an array. For example, consider the following declarations.

```
double rate[5] = {0.075, 0.080, 0.082, 0.085, 0.088};
int    i;
```

If we execute the assignment,

```
i = 3;
```

then `rate[i]` refers to the element `rate[3]`, which has the value 0.085. If we now execute the assignment

```
i = 1;
```

then `rate[i]` refers to the element `rate[1]`, which has the value 0.080.

The following program, dem06-1.cpp, shows how to initialize an array and how to use a subscript to access the elements in an array. The program calculates shipping charges based on the price of an item and the shipping region, and calculates the total price of the item. The total price is the sum of the item's price and the item's shipping charge. The program asks the user to enter the price of an item and the shipping region. If the user enters a valid region number (1 to 5), the program calculates the shipping charge by multiplying the price of the item by the shipping rate for the region. If the shipping region that the user entered is invalid, the program issues an error message and asks the user to reenter a valid shipping region.

```cpp
// dem06-1.cpp

// This program calculates shipping charges for mail orders
// based on price and sales region.   This program
// uses the region number to access the array elements.

#include <iostream>
#include <iomanip>

using namespace std;

int Get_Valid_Region();

int main()
{
    // The following declaration defines the integer array rate[] as
    // having 5 elements.

    double rate[5] = {0.075, 0.080, 0.082, 0.085, 0.088};
    int    region;
    double price,
           charge,
           total_price;

    cout << setprecision(2)
         << setiosflags(ios::fixed)
         << setiosflags(ios::showpoint);

    cout << "Enter the price of the item: $";
    cin >> price;
    region = Get_Valid_Region();

    charge = price * rate[region - 1];
    total_price = price + charge;
```

```
    cout << endl << endl;
    cout << "Item Price:        " << setw(9) << price << endl;
    cout << "Shipping Charge:  " << setw(9) << charge << endl;
    cout << "Total Price:       " << setw(9) << total_price << endl;

    return 0;
} //End of main()

int Get_Valid_Region()
{
    bool invalid_data;
    int region;

    do
    {
      cout << endl;
      cout << "Enter shipping region (1-5): ";
      cin >> region;
      if (region < 1 || region > 5)
      {
        cerr << endl;
        cerr << "Region in invalid - Please reenter.";
        invalid_data = true;
      }
      else
         invalid_data = false;
    }
    while(invalid_data);

    return region;
}
```

Program Output

```
Enter the price of the item: $100

Enter shipping region (1-5): 4

Item Price:         100.00
Shipping Charge:      8.50
Total Price:        108.50
```

The program begins with the declaration and initialization of the array rate[]. The program prompts the user for the price of the item and obtains a valid shipping region from the function Get_Valid_Region(). The function uses the same type of data validation do loop that we developed in Chapter 5. After prompting for the shipping region, the if statement checks the validity of the shipping region. If the region is invalid, that is, less than one or greater than five, the program displays an error message using the cerr output stream, the if statement completes, and the loop executes again. If the region is valid, the loop ends and the function returns the value of the region to main().

After receiving a valid region number from Get_Valid_Region(), the program calculates the shipping charge. The shipping charge is the item price multiplied by the shipping rate for the entered shipping region. The region number is an integer in the range 1–5. However, the offset that accesses the array elements must be in the range 0–4. The shipping rate for region one is located in rate[0]. The shipping rate for region two is located in rate[1], and so on. Thus, to access the proper array element, we must subtract one from the region number. Therefore, we access the shipping rate by the expression rate[region - 1]. Note that we can use an expression, such as region - 1, as the subscript in an array reference.

Note 6.4   Expressions as Subscripts

In C++, it is valid to use an expression as an array subscript if the expression evaluates to an integer type.

Finally, the total charge for the item is the price plus the shipping charge. The cout statements display the item's price, shipping charge, and total price.

As a final comment, keep Note 6.5 in mind when using arrays.

Note 6.5   Validating Subscripts

The C++ compiler does not check that subscripts are in the valid range of offsets for the array. You must write code to check for valid subscript values.

For example, suppose that we incorrectly code the following in dem06-1.cpp.

```
charge = price * rate[region];
```

If the user enters 3 for the region, this assignment would incorrectly access rate[3], which is the rate for region four. As if this weren't bad enough, suppose the user enters 5 for the region. Then the assignment would access rate[5], which is not an element in the array! Instead, rate[5] would access a garbage value and the program would produce incorrect results.

In the next section, we show how to use a subscript to apply the same processing to all the elements in an array.

Exercises 6.1

1. Declare an array that will store the annual salaries of a typical 25-member major league baseball team. (Most teams have players that earn over $1,000,000 each year.)

2. Declare an array that will store the attendance at each major league baseball park on July 4th. There are 30 such parks and many of them can seat over 50,000 people.

3. Declare an array that will store the prices of the 50 stocks of the Dow-Jones Industrial Averages Stock Index.

4. The manager of an automobile dealership wants to store the number of cars each of her 14 salespeople sell in one month. Declare an array that will store the data.

5. Declare an array `subscr[]` and initialize each of its ten elements to the value of its subscript.

Use the following declarations in Exercises 6–8.

```
int arr_1[7] = {3, 4, 6, 12};
int arr_2[]  = {9, 6, 7, 3, 5, 2};
int arr_3[7];
int i;
```

6. What are the values of `arr_1[4]`, `arr_2[6]`, `arr_1[0]`, and `arr_2[5]`?

7. If we execute `i = 3;`, what is the value of the expression
`arr_1[i] * arr_2[i + 2]`?

8. If we execute `i = 0;`, what is the value of the expression
`arr_1[i] * arr_2[i + 2]`?

6.2 PROCESSING AN ARRAY: for LOOPS

In this section, we discuss how to use a `for` loop to apply the same processing to the elements of an array.

6.2.1 Using for Loops

A `for` loop is the ideal control structure to use to process an array. The array subscript acts as the loop counter. Each time through the loop, the loop body processes the array element that the subscript specifies. To clarify the procedure, we consider a simple example.

In a program she is writing to process student grades, a teacher wants to enter the ten quiz grades that a student receives during the semester. The program is to display the student's average to the nearest tenth. The teacher decides to store the grades in the ten-element array `grade[]`. To verify that she entered the grades correctly, the teacher wants to display the ten grades on one line before the program displays the average grade.

We shall discuss the `for` loop that displays the grades first because it is simpler than the `for` loop that inputs the grades. Suppose the ten grades have already been loaded into the array `grade[]`. The following loop displays the elements of the array on one line.

```
for (quiz = 0; quiz < 10; ++quiz)
    cout << setw(6) << grade[quiz];
```

There are several things to note about this `for` statement. First, the beginning value for `quiz` is zero because the first element in the array is element number zero.

Second, the loop test is quiz < 10. Thus the program stays in the loop for the following values of quiz: 0, 1, 2, 3, 4, 5, 6, 7, 8, and 9, which are the valid offsets for the array. We use the test quiz < 10 instead of quiz <= 9 because 10 is the size of the array. Third, the subscript quiz is incremented by one each time through the loop so the loop processes every array element. Finally, the loop body processes the element determined by the value of quiz. Thus, in the loop body we refer to the array element as grade[quiz].

To input the array elements into the array grade[], we can use the following for loop.

```cpp
for (quiz = 0; quiz < 10; ++quiz)
{
   cout << "\nEnter grade for quiz " << quiz + 1 << ": ";
   cin << grade[quiz];
}
```

The for loop prompts the user for the ten quiz values and enters the values into the array grade[]. In the cout statement, we have the opposite problem to that of dem06-1.cpp. The value of the subscript quiz is one less than the number of the quiz grade for which we prompt. When quiz is zero, we want to prompt for the grade on quiz one. When quiz is one, we want to prompt for the grade on quiz two, and so on. Therefore, the number that we want to display in the prompt is the value of quiz + 1. The cin statement places the value that the user enters into the array element grade[quiz].

```cpp
// dem06-2.cpp

// This program shows how to find the average of the elements
// in an array.

#include <iostream>
#include <iomanip>

using namespace std;

int main()
{
   const int NUM_QUIZZES = 10;
   int grade[NUM_QUIZZES]; // The array to store the quiz grades
   int quiz,               // The array subscript
       grade_sum = 0;
   double grade_avg;

   cout << setprecision(1)
        << setiosflags(ios::fixed)
        << setiosflags(ios::showpoint);

   cout << "Please enter " << NUM_QUIZZES
        << " integer quiz grades." << endl << endl;

   for (quiz = 0; quiz < NUM_QUIZZES; ++quiz)
   {
      cout << endl;
      cout << "Enter grade for quiz " << quiz + 1 << ": ";
      cin >> grade[quiz];
   }
```

```
        cout << endl;
        cout << "The grades you entered are:";
        for (quiz = 0; quiz < NUM_QUIZZES; ++quiz)
            cout << setw(5) << grade[quiz];

        for (quiz = 0; quiz < NUM_QUIZZES; ++quiz)
            grade_sum += grade[quiz];

        grade_avg = double(grade_sum) / NUM_QUIZZES;
        cout << endl << endl;
        cout << "The average quiz grade is " << grade_avg << endl;

        return 0;
    }
```

Program Output

```
Please enter 10 integer quiz grades.

Enter grade for quiz 1: 55

Enter grade for quiz 2: 66

Enter grade for quiz 3: 77

Enter grade for quiz 4: 88

Enter grade for quiz 5: 99

Enter grade for quiz 6: 100

Enter grade for quiz 7: 100

Enter grade for quiz 8: 99

Enter grade for quiz 9: 88

Enter grade for quiz 10: 77

The grades you entered are:    55   66   77   88   99   100   100   99   88   77

The average quiz grade is 84.9
```

First, we define the number of quizzes as a symbolic constant, NUM_QUIZZES. It is good programming practice to do so. It makes changing the program easier. We use NUM_QUIZZES in the cout that labels the output to reflect the number of quizzes that the program processes. We shall follow the advice of Note 6.6 in all our programs.

Note 6.6   Defining the Size of an Array

It is good programming practice to define the size of an array as a symbolic constant.

The program declares the accumulator `grade_sum`, which is initialized to zero, to hold the sum of the grades that the user enters into the array `grade[]`. The `double` variable `grade_avg` will store the average of the ten grades.

First, the program inputs the ten quiz grades. The second `for` loop adds each grade in the array to the accumulator `grade_sum`. Then, the assignment statement computes the grade average. A type cast converts the value of the integer variable `grade_sum` to the equivalent `double`. Finally, the `cout` statement displays the value of `grade_avg`.

6.2.2 Searching an Array

Suppose that our teacher wants to display the quiz number and corresponding grade of the first quiz, if any, on which the student achieved a grade of 85 or better. This is an example of an **array search**—we want our program to find a particular array element. To do this, the program will test each array element beginning with the first. If the grade that the program is testing satisfies the condition (the grade is 85 or greater), it displays the grade and the quiz number and ends the program. If there is no grade equal to or greater than 85, the program should display a message to that effect. This method of searching, namely beginning at the first array element and proceeding through the entire array one element at a time, testing as we go along, is called a **linear**, or **sequential**, **search**.

To keep the program as simple as possible, dem06-3.cpp prompts the user for the grades and then displays the first grade of 85 or greater, if any.

```cpp
// dem06-3.cpp

// This program shows how to find the first element in an array
// that satisfies a condition. The condition tested in this
// program is that the quiz grade is greater than or equal to 85.

#include <iostream>
#include <iomanip>

using namespace std;

int main()
{
   const int NUM_QUIZZES = 10;
   const int MIN_GRADE = 85;

   int grade[NUM_QUIZZES];       // The array to store the quiz grades
   int quiz;                     // The array subscript

   cout << "Please enter " << NUM_QUIZZES
        << " integer quiz grades." << endl << endl;

   for (quiz = 0; quiz < NUM_QUIZZES; ++quiz)
   {
      cout << endl;
      cout << "Enter grade for quiz " << quiz + 1 << ": ";
      cin >> grade[quiz];
   }
```

```
for (quiz = 0; quiz < NUM_QUIZZES; ++quiz)
  if (grade[quiz] >= MIN_GRADE)
  {
    cout << endl;
    cout << "The first grade of at least " << MIN_GRADE
         << " is:" << endl << endl;
    cout << "Quiz #" << quiz + 1 << "  Grade: "
         << setw(3) << grade[quiz] << endl;
    break;
  }

if (quiz >= NUM_QUIZZES)
{
  cout << endl;
  cout << "No grade greater than " << MIN_GRADE
       << " was found." << endl;
}

return 0;
}
```

Program Output

Test Run 1

Please enter 10 integer quiz grades.

Enter grade for quiz 1: **40**

Enter grade for quiz 2: **50**

Enter grade for quiz 3: **80**

Enter grade for quiz 4: **70**

Enter grade for quiz 5: **80**

Enter grade for quiz 6: **94**

Enter grade for quiz 7: **85**

Enter grade for quiz 8: **68**

Enter grade for quiz 9: **73**

Enter grade for quiz 10: **90**

The first grade of at least 85 is:

Quiz #6 Grade: 94

Test Run 2

Please enter 10 integer quiz grades.

Enter grade for quiz 1: **40**

Enter grade for quiz 2: **50**

Enter grade for quiz 3: **60**

Enter grade for quiz 4: **70**

Enter grade for quiz 5: **80**

Enter grade for quiz 6: **70**

Enter grade for quiz 7: **60**

Enter grade for quiz 8: **70**

Enter grade for quiz 9: **80**

Enter grade for quiz 10: **84**

No grade greater than 85 was found.

First, note that we define a symbolic constant MIN_GRADE with a value of 85. This makes it easier to change this minimum grade later.

A for loop prompts the user to enter the ten quiz grades. The for loop that does the **linear search** is next. The body of this loop consists of a single if statement. If the grade on the quiz being processed is greater than or equal to MIN_GRADE, the search is successful. Then, the program displays a message that shows the quiz number and the grade on that quiz. In this case, the break statement executes, which causes the program to exit the loop.

When the program exits the second for loop, it does so for one of two reasons. If the search is successful, as described in the previous paragraph, the break statement causes the program to exit the loop before the loop condition (quiz < 10) is false. If the search is unsuccessful, the program exits the loop because the loop condition is false, not because of the break statement. The if statement that follows the second for loop decides which condition caused the program to exit the loop. If the search was unsuccessful, the value of quiz must be greater than or equal to 10 because the loop condition must be false. Therefore, if quiz >= 10, the program displays a message that no grade was found that satisfies the condition. If quiz is not greater than or equal to 10, then it must be less than 10. In this case, the program exited the loop because the search was successful. Thus, if the condition in the if statement is false, the program does nothing.

Exercises 6.2

1. Is there anything wrong with the following for loop that attempts to add each element of arr_1[] to the corresponding element of arr_2[] and place the result

in the corresponding element of arr_3[]?

```
for (i = 0; i < 7; ++i)
   arr_3[i] = arr_1[i] + arr_2[i];
```

2. What does the following code display?

```
int arr[9];
int i;

for (i = 0; i < 9; ++i)
   arr[i] = i + 3;

cout << endl;
for (i = 0; i < 9; ++i)
   cout << setw(4) << a[i];

cout << endl << endl;
for (i = 8; i >= 0; --i)
   cout << setw(4) << a[i];
```

Use the following declarations in Exercises 3–8.

```
double d_array[10] = {3.4, 12.8, 9.5, 2.0, 1.7, 3.8};
char letters[26];
int i;
```

3. Write a for loop to display only the elements of d_array[] having an even subscript.

4. Write a for loop to display only the elements of d_array[] having an odd subscript.

5. Write a for loop to display only the first element of d_array[] that is less than 3.0.

6. Write a for loop to display all the elements of d_array[] that are greater than 5.0.

7. Write a for loop that sets each element of letters[] to a blank.

8. Write a for loop that places the lowercase letters of the alphabet into the array letters[].

Experiments 6.2

1. What does the following program display?

```
#include <iostream>

using namespace std;

int main()
{
   int arr[] = {3, 4, 5, 6, 7};
   int i;

   for (i = 0; i < 6; ++i)
      cout << endl << arr[i];

   return 0;
}
```

2. Recode dem06-3.cpp so that it finds the last element in the array that is at least 85.

3. Suppose the teacher of dem06-2.cpp does not know how many grades she will have at the end of the semester. However, she does know that she will not give more than 12 quizzes. Recode dem06-2.cpp so that it inputs up to 12 quiz grades. To do this, you need a counter that counts each grade as it is entered. After the user finishes entering the grades, sum the grades that were entered and calculate the average grade by dividing the grade sum by the number of grades.

Programming Problems 6.2

Be sure to use modular design and functions where appropriate.

1. Bluebird Airlines has flights from Phoenix to six other cities in Arizona. The cities are referred to by number, 1 to 6. The price for a round-trip ticket to each of the cities is shown here.

City	1	2	3	4	5	6
Price	56.79	105.69	93.49	155.99	87.49	73.99

Write a program that computes the total price of tickets that a customer orders. The program should prompt the user for the number of the destination city and the number of tickets desired. If the user enters an invalid city number, the program should display an error message and terminate. The program should display the total price of the ticket order. Use an array to store the ticket price table.

2. Rewrite the program of Programming Problem 1 so that it processes any number of ticket orders. The program also should continually prompt the user for a valid city number. When the user indicates that there are no more customers to process, the program should display the total number of tickets sold to each of the six cities, the total price of the tickets sold to each city, and the grand total of all the ticket prices. Use an array of accumulators to store the number of tickets sold to each city.

3. A bookstore owner wants you to write a program to calculate the store's weekly payroll. The store's employees are paid hourly. Overtime is to be paid at the rate of 1.5 times the normal rate for hours an employee worked over 40. The program should prompt the user to enter the number of hours the employee worked and the pay rate for the employee. The program should display the regular pay, overtime pay, and gross pay for that employee. Then the program should prompt the user to enter the data for another employee. When the user responds that there are no more employees to process, the program should display the number of employees it processed and the total payroll, that is, the sum of the gross salaries of the employees.

The program should validate the pay rate as it is entered. The only valid hourly pay rates are the following: 5.50, 6.00, 6.50, 6.75, 7.00, 7.25, 7.50, 7.75, 8.00. Store the rates in an array. When a pay rate is entered, search the array for a match. If there is a match, continue the rest of the calculations. If there is no match, display an error message, a list of the valid pay rates, and prompt for another pay rate.

4. Bluebird Airlines needs a program to assign boarding passes on its only plane, which has a seating capacity of 30. The seats in the plane are numbered from 1 to 30. The first ten seats are first class and the remaining twenty are business class. The program should prompt the user to enter the class of the ticket (1 for first class, 2 for business class). Store the seating information in an array. If a seat is empty, the corresponding array element is zero. If a seat is reserved, the corresponding array element is one. Assign the seats numerically on a first-come-first-serve basis. If a passenger requests a seat and there are no more seats of that class, the program should check to see if there are any seats available in the other class. If other seats are available, ask the user if he/she wants a seat in the other class and proceed appropriately. If no other seats are available, display an appropriate message. When there are no more passengers to process (the plane may not be full when it takes off), display the total number of passengers in each class.

5. Write a program that prompts the user to enter text at the terminal. When the user finishes entering text, he/she should enter the appropriate end-of-file character to terminate input. The program should count the frequency of each letter of the alphabet. The program should not distinguish an uppercase letter from a lowercase letter. When the user finishes inputting text, the program should display each letter and its count.

Hint: Declare an array of counters, one for each letter. Use the letter itself as the subscript that determines which array element to increment. To do this, the program must convert the letter to the corresponding subscript. Remember that the decimal ASCII values of the lowercase letters are 97–122 and the uppercase letters are 65–90.

6. The marketing department of a large book club wants to analyze the geographical distribution of its customers by categorizing customers by zip code. Write a program that prompts the user to enter the five-digit zip code of a customer. Store the zip codes in an array of integers, and store the counts of the customers in a corresponding array of integers. Assume a maximum of 100 zip codes. When a zip code is entered, search the zip code array for the zip code. If it is not in the array, add it to the end of the array and set the corresponding count array element to one. If the entered zip code is in the zip code array, increment the corresponding count array.

When the user completes entering zip codes, the program should display a table that lists the zip codes with their corresponding counts and the percent that count is of the total number of customers. The total number of customers should display at the bottom of the table.

6.3 SORTING AN ARRAY

This section introduces array sorting. To sort an array means to arrange the elements of the array in either increasing or decreasing order.

6.3.1 Sorting

Suppose that after inputting the ten grades for a student, our teacher wants to display the grades in increasing order. To do this, the program must arrange the numbers that it stores in the array `grade[]` into increasing order. We call this process **sorting** the array. Among the techniques for sorting an array is the **bubble sort**, which programmers frequently use for sorting small arrays. There are several variations of the bubble sort. The one that we shall describe here is not the most efficient bubble sort, but it works and illustrates the basic technique.

The key idea of the bubble sort is to compare adjacent elements in the array. Begin by comparing the first two array elements. We assume that we want the array in nondecreasing order. If the elements are in order (that is, the first element is less than or equal to the second), leave them alone. If the elements are not in order (that is, the first is greater than the second), interchange them in the array. Then, compare the second and third array elements. Again, if they are out of order, interchange them; otherwise, leave them alone. Continue this process until you compare the last pair of array elements. This completes the first pass over the array.

To illustrate, suppose we start with the following array of five integers.

> 7   3   4   8   6

The first pass does the following. Because 7 and 3 are not in order, interchange them.

> 3   7   4   8   6

Compare 7 and 4. They are not in order, so interchange them.

> 3   4   7   8   6

Compare 7 and 8. They are in order, so leave them alone and go on to the next pair.
Compare 8 and 6. They are not in order, so interchange them.

> 3   4   7   6   8

This completes the first pass. What does the first pass accomplish? The first pass moves the largest number in the array into the right-most position, which is where we want it when the array is completely sorted. This is why we call this sort the bubble sort. The largest array element "bubbles" up to the top of the array.

Now we make a second pass over the array. This time, however, we do not have to go to the end of the array because the first pass moved the largest array element into the right-most position. The second pass moves the second largest array element into the next-to-last position. Following is a trace of pass two.

Start with:	3	4	7	6	8	
Begin:	3	4	7	6	8	Leave 3 and 4 alone
	3	4	7	6	8	Leave 4 and 7 alone
	3	4	6	7	8	Interchange 7 and 6

Likewise for pass three and pass four.

Trace of Pass Three:

Start with:	3	4	6	7	8	
Begin:	3	4	6	7	8	Leave 3 and 4 alone
	3	4	6	7	8	Leave 4 and 6 alone

End of Pass Three.

Trace of Pass Four:

Start with:	3	4	6	7	8	
Begin:	3	4	6	7	8	Leave 3 and 4 alone

End of Pass Four. The array is sorted.

After the fourth pass, the array is sorted. Note that the array is sorted at the end of pass two, but the procedure keeps going. It would be more efficient if the procedure recognizes at some point that the array is sorted and ends. See Programming Problem 2.

An important part of the bubble sort is interchanging two array elements. To interchange the values of two variables requires the use of a third variable. For example, consider the following declarations.

```
int i = 5,
    j = 7,
    temp;
```

The following assignments interchange the values of i and j.

```
temp = i;       // Places 5 into temp
i = j;          // Places 7 into i, destroying its contents
j = temp;       // Places 5 into j
```

6.3.2 A Sort Program—dem06-4.cpp

The following program, dem06-4.cpp, prompts the user to enter a ten-element array and displays the array. Then, the program uses the bubble sort to sort the array in increasing order. Finally, the program displays the sorted array.

```
// dem06-4.cpp

// This program shows how to sort the elements
// in an array using the bubble sort.

#include <iostream>
#include <iomanip>
```

```cpp
using namespace std;

int main()
{
  const int NUM_QUIZZES = 10;

  int grade[NUM_QUIZZES];       //The array to store the quiz grades
  int quiz,                     // Subscript for the array grade[]
      temp,                     // For swapping array elements
      pass,                     // The number of the pass
      limit;                    // Keeps track of how far to go on a pass

  // Get the grades
  cout << "Please enter " << NUM_QUIZZES
       << " integer quiz grades." << endl << endl;

  for (quiz = 0; quiz < NUM_QUIZZES; ++quiz)
  {
    cout << endl;
    cout << "Enter grade for quiz " << quiz + 1 << ": ";
    cin >> grade[quiz];
  }

  // Display the quiz grades
  cout << endl << endl;
  cout << "The grades you entered are as follows:" << endl;

  for (quiz = 0; quiz < NUM_QUIZZES; ++quiz)
    cout << setw(6) << grade[quiz];

  cout << endl;

  // Do the bubble sort
  limit = NUM_QUIZZES - 2;

  for (pass = 1; pass <= NUM_QUIZZES - 1; ++pass)
  {
    for (quiz = 0; quiz <= limit; ++quiz)
      if (grade[quiz] > grade[quiz + 1])
      {
        temp = grade[quiz];
        grade[quiz] = grade[quiz + 1];
        grade[quiz + 1] = temp;
      }

    --limit;
  }

  // Display the sorted quiz grades
  cout << endl << endl;
  cout << "The grades in increasing order are as follows:" << endl;
```

```
    for (quiz = 0; quiz < NUM_QUIZZES; ++quiz)
      cout << setw(6) << grade[quiz];

    cout << endl;

    return 0;
}
```

Program Output

```
Please enter 10 integer quiz grades.
Enter grade for quiz 1: 40
Enter grade for quiz 2: 50
Enter grade for quiz 3: 80
Enter grade for quiz 4: 70
Enter grade for quiz 5: 80
Enter grade for quiz 6: 94
Enter grade for quiz 7: 85
Enter grade for quiz 8: 68
Enter grade for quiz 9: 73
Enter grade for quiz 10: 90
The grades you entered are as follows:
    40    50    80    70    80    94    85    68    73    90
The grades in increasing order are as follows:
    40    50    68    70    73    80    80    85    90    94
```

The program needs the integer array grade[] to store the student grades. The variable quiz is the array subscript. The program uses the variable temp for swapping array elements, the variable pass to count the number of passes that the bubble sort makes, and the variable limit to keep track of how far to go on a pass.

The program obtains the ten quiz grades from the user in a for loop and stores them in the array grade[]. Then, a for loop displays the grades in the order in which the user entered them. Now the program uses the bubble sort to arrange the elements of the array into increasing order.

The variable limit keeps track of how far to go on a pass. Recall, from our discussion, that the first pass of the bubble sort compares pairs of adjacent elements up to the last pair. Therefore, in an array with NUM_QUIZZES elements, it compares elements 0 and 1, elements 1 and 2, elements 2 and 3, ..., elements NUM_QUIZZES - 2 and NUM_QUIZZES - 1. Therefore, because the sort always compares an element to the next element, we initialize limit to NUM_QUIZZES - 2. At the end of a pass, limit is decreased by one, so that the next pass considers one less element. Remember that a pass places the next highest element at the right of the array so the sort does not have to consider this element again.

The bubble sort is done in a nested `for` loop. The outer `for` loop initializes the value of `pass` to one. The sort makes a total of `NUM_QUIZZES` - 1 passes over the array, which is reflected in the loop test. The `if` statement in the inner loop's body tests to see if the pair of adjacent array elements is out of order. If they are out of order, the elements are interchanged. If they are in order, nothing is done to the pair.

When the bubble sort finishes sorting the array, the elements of `grade[]` are in increasing order. Then, the program uses a `for` loop to display the elements of the array `grade[]`, which are now in increasing order.

Exercises 6.3

1. Trace the bubble sort using the following integers, which represent the elements in an array.
   5, 7, 3, 8, 6, 7, 3
2. Trace the bubble sort using the following integers, which represent the elements in an array.
   98, 76, 54, 34, 22, 50

Experiment 6.3

1. Recode dem06-4.cpp to sort the array in decreasing order.

Programming Problems 6.3

1. A survey organization telephones 20 homes and records the household income of each family surveyed. Write a program that inputs the 20 incomes into an array and then sorts the array into decreasing order. The program should display the following statistics: the maximum income, the minimum income, the average income, and the median income. The median of a set of sorted numbers is the middle number, if there is an odd number of numbers. If there is an even number of numbers, the median is the average of the two middle numbers.

2. The bubble sort of dem06-4.cpp is inefficient for sorting large arrays because it does not recognize when the array is sorted. The function makes `size` - 1 passes on an array with `size` elements even if the array is already sorted. The function will be more efficient if, when making a pass over the array, it recognizes if the array is sorted and stops. Recode dem06-4.cpp to do this.

   Hint: Use a flag called `sorted`. Set `sorted` equal to zero immediately before making a pass over the array. If the flag equals one, the array is sorted. In this case, exit the loop and return to the calling function. If the flag equals zero, the array is not sorted. In this case, the program must make a pass over the array. In the inner loop of the nested `for` loop, when the function swaps two array elements, set the flag to one.

6.4 MULTIDIMENSIONAL ARRAYS

Multidimensional arrays are a way of organizing data that you can classify according to two or more categories. This section shows how to define and use multidimensional arrays in C++. We concentrate on two-dimensional arrays because they are the most widely used by programmers and are easy to describe.

6.4.1 Declaring Multidimensional Arrays

As we mentioned in Section 6.1, you can use an array to store a collection of related data. Data are related if you categorize them into a common class. For example, the grades that a student receives on a set of ten quizzes forms a category. You can consider the ten grades as belonging to a common class of data.

Sometimes, you can classify data according to two or more categories. For example, suppose that our teacher now wants to find the average quiz grade of the five students in her class. We now have ten quiz grades for five students—a total of 50 integers. We can classify each grade according to two categories: the student to whom the grade belongs and the quiz on which the grade was achieved. You can arrange such data in a **two-dimensional array**, or **matrix**. Figure 6.5 shows the class grades stored in the two-dimensional array `class_grades`.

The data are arranged into rows and columns. The five rows represent the five students in the class. The ten columns represent the ten quiz grades. The **array size** is 5 × 10, meaning that the array has five rows and ten columns. In keeping with the way in which C++ refers to array elements, we number the rows from 0 to 4 and the columns from 0 to 9.

Referring to a specific element in the two-dimensional array requires two subscripts. The first subscript specifies the row (that is, the student). The second subscript specifies the column (that is, the quiz). We enclose each subscript in brackets. Thus, `class_grades[2][3]` refers to the grade of student 2 (the third student) on quiz 3 (the fourth quiz).

The 5 × 10 Two-Dimensional Array `class_grades[][]`

Figure 6.5

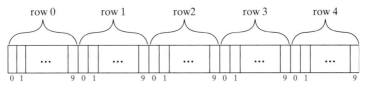

Storage Layout of a 5 × 10 Two-Dimensional Array

Figure 6.6

To declare a two-dimensional array, specify the array type and the size of the array. Place the number of rows and the number of columns each in its own brackets. For example, the following declares a two-dimensional array of integers of size 5 × 10.

```
int class_grades[5][10];
```

To read this declaration, use the rule of Note 6.1. Remember to read a left bracket as "is an array of." Therefore, read the declaration as follows: "class_grades is an array of five elements, each of which is an array of ten integers." Thus, the two-dimensional array class_grades is an array, each of whose elements is an array of integers. This fact has implications in the way C++ stores the elements of the array and the way in which you can reference parts of the array.

Figure 6.6 shows how C++ stores the 50 grades. All 10 grades of student 0 are followed by the 10 grades of student 1, and so on. We call this way of storing the grades **row major order**.

It is possible to initialize a two-dimensional array in the array declaration. The following initializes the elements of class_grades[][].

```
int class_grades[5][10] = { {50, 56, 87, 67, 98, 90, 68, 54, 67, 30},
                            {70, 68, 64, 78, 97, 57, 68, 90, 67, 74},
                            {64, 76, 87, 67, 95, 67, 56, 83, 60, 78},
                            {76, 65, 84, 47, 86, 65, 46, 66, 87, 65},
                            {76, 57, 65, 45, 90, 76, 76, 44, 67, 82}};
```

We enclose the entire set of values in braces. We also enclose the values in each row in another set of braces. Note the comma after each set of inner braces. The final set of inner braces is not followed by a comma. This technique of organizing the initial values in a two-dimensional array mirrors the logical row-by-column structure of the array. The inner braces help to distinguish one row from the next row. In addition, if too few numbers are enclosed in the inner braces, the compiler automatically sets the remaining row elements to zero. If there are too many elements in the inner braces, the compiler ignores the extra elements in the row. See Experiment 8.

The C++ language does not require this bracing technique to initialize a two-dimensional array. The important thing is that the elements appear in the initialization in the order in which C++ stores them, that is, in row major order. See Experiment 3.

Note 6.7 summarizes the rules for initializing a two-dimensional array.

Although we shall not have much use for higher-dimensional arrays, you can define them in C++ in much the same way as two-dimensional arrays. For example, suppose our teacher wants to store the ten quiz grades for the five students in each of her

> **Note 6.7   Initializing a Two-Dimensional Array**
>
> To initialize a two-dimensional array, enclose the elements of each row in braces. Separate each row's elements by commas. Follow each set of row braces by a comma, except the last row. Enclose the entire set of row initializers by braces.
>
> If a row initializer contains too few elements, the remaining elements of the row are automatically initialized to zero.
>
> If a row initializer contains too many elements, the compiler ignores the extra elements.

four classes. We can classify the data into three categories—class, student, and quiz number. We can store all 200 grades in a three-dimensional array `student_grades` of size 4 × 5 × 10. The following declaration defines the storage for the array.

```
int student_grades[4][5][10];
```

The first subscript, which refers to the class, ranges from 0 to 3. The second subscript, which refers to the student, ranges from 0 to 4. The third subscript, which ranges from 0 to 9, refers to the quiz. Thus, the element `student_grades[2][3][4]` contains the grade on quiz 4 (that is, the fifth quiz) of student 3 (that is, the fourth student) in class 2 (that is, the third class). See Programming Problem 6.

6.4.2 Processing a Two-Dimensional Array

The major tool for processing a two-dimensional array is the nested `for` loop. Assume the following declaration.

```
int array[NUMBER_ROWS][NUMBER_COLUMNS];
```

To process each element in this two-dimensional array, we use a nested `for` loop structured as follows.

```
for (row = 0; row < NUMBER_ROWS; ++row)
    for (column = 0; column < NUMBER_COLUMNS; ++column)
        {process the array element array[row][column]}
```

The outer `for` loop steps through the rows of the array one at a time. When the subscript `row` equals zero, the nested loop processes row number zero; when the subscript `row` equals one, the nested loop processes row number one, and so on. The inner loop processes each element in the row determined by the subscript `row`. Thus, the nested loop processes the elements of the array in row major order. For example, when `row` equals zero, the `for` loop runs the subscript `column` from zero to one less than `NUMBER_COLUMNS`. Table 6.1 shows how the nested loop varies the subscripts and to which element `array[row][column]` refers in the body of the loop.

Thus, the following displays all the grades in the 5 × 10 array `class_grades[][]` that we declared and initialized earlier.

TABLE 6.1

row	column	Element Processed in Loop Body
0	0	array[0][0]
	1	array[0][1]
	2	array[0][2]
	.	
	.	
	.	
	NUMBER_COLUMNS - 1	array[0][NUMBER_COLUMNS - 1]
1	0	array[1][0]
	1	array[1][1]
	2	array[1][2]
	.	
	.	
	.	
	NUMBER_COLUMNS - 1	array[1][NUMBER-COLUMNS - 1]
	.	
	.	
	.	
NUMBER_ROWS - 1	0	array[NUMBER_ROWS][0]
	1	array[NUMBER_ROWS][1]
	2	array[NUMBER_ROWS][2]
	.	
	.	
	.	
NUMBER_ROWS - 1	NUMBER_COLUMNS-1	array[NUMBER_ROWS][NUMBER_COLUMNS - 1

```cpp
    int student,
        quiz;
    for (student = 0; student < 5; ++student)
      for (quiz = 0; quiz < 10; ++quiz)
        cout << "The grade of student " << student + 1
             << " on quiz " << quiz + 1
             << " is " << class_grades[student][quiz] << endl;
```

6.4.3 Finding Student Averages—dem06-5.cpp

We now write a program to find the average grade of each student in the five classes. The program will prompt the user for the ten grades of each student, one student at a time. The program will store the grades in a two-dimensional array. Then, it will calculate and display the average quiz grade for each student, rounded to the nearest tenth.

Following is the pseudocode solution for the problem.

```
    for (each student in the class)
      for (each quiz for a student)
       prompt for and get a quiz grade
      endfor
    endfor
```

```
      for (each student in the class)
        calculate the average quiz grade
        display the quiz grade
      endfor
```

Following is the code for dem06-5.cpp, our solution to the averaging problem.

```cpp
// dem06-5.cpp

// This program uses a two-dimensional array to store the
// quiz grades of students in several classes.  The program
// then calculates the average quiz grade of each student.

#include <iostream>
#include <iomanip>

using namespace std;

int main()
{
  const int NUM_QUIZZES = 10;
  const int NUM_STUDENTS = 5;

  int class_grades[NUM_STUDENTS][NUM_QUIZZES];
  int student,
      quiz,
      quiz_sum;
  double quiz_average;

  cout << setprecision(1)
       << setiosflags(ios::fixed)
       << setiosflags(ios::showpoint);

  // Obtain and store the quiz grades for each student

  cout << "Enter exactly " << NUM_QUIZZES
       << " quiz grades for each student." << endl;
  cout << "Separate the grades by one or more spaces." << endl;

  for (student = 0; student < NUM_STUDENTS; ++student)
  {
    cout << endl << endl;
    cout << "Grades for Student " << student + 1 << ": ";
    for (quiz = 0; quiz < NUM_QUIZZES; ++quiz)
      cin >> class_grades[student][quiz];
  }

  // Calculate and display the average quiz grade for each student

  for (student = 0; student < NUM_STUDENTS; ++student)
  {
    quiz_sum = 0;
    for (quiz = 0; quiz < NUM_QUIZZES; ++quiz)
      quiz_sum += class_grades[student][quiz];
```

```
        quiz_average = (double) quiz_sum / NUM_QUIZZES;

        cout << endl << endl;
        cout << "Student: " << setw(3) << student + 1
             << "   Quiz Average: " << setw(5) << quiz_average;
    }

    cout << endl;

    return 0;
}
```

Program Output

```
Enter exactly 10 quiz grades for each student.
Separate the grades by one or more spaces.

Grades for Student 1: 50 56 87 67 98 90 68 54 67 30

Grades for Student 2: 70 68 64 78 97 57 68 90 67 74

Grades for Student 3: 64 76 87 67 95 67 56 83 60 78

Grades for Student 4: 76 65 84 47 86 65 46 66 87 65

Grades for Student 5: 76 57 65 45 90 76 76 44 67 82

Student:    1   Quiz Average:   66.7

Student:    2   Quiz Average:   73.3

Student:    3   Quiz Average:   73.3

Student:    4   Quiz Average:   68.7

Student:    5   Quiz Average:   67.8
```

The program defines the number of quizzes and the number of students as symbolic constants. In main(), we declare the two-dimensional array class_grades[][] as described earlier, the subscripts student and quiz, the accumulator quiz_sum, and the double variable quiz_average.

Because this program must obtain 50 grades, it does not prompt for each grade individually. Instead, the program asks the user to enter all ten grades for each student at once. First, the program tells the user how many grades to enter for each student and how to separate the grades. Then, the outer for loop prompts for the ten grades of one student. The inner for loop obtains the ten grades for the student and stores them in the array.

The next for loop calculates and displays the average of each student. To calculate the average of the student currently being processed, the body of the loop first initializes the accumulator quiz_sum to zero. Next, a for loop sums the quiz grades for the student being processed. After exiting the for loop, an assignment statement calculates the quiz average. To obtain the quiz average to the nearest tenth, it is necessary to type cast the variable quiz_sum to the type double. Failure to do so would cause the computer to do integer arithmetic when evaluating the right side of the assignment, which would result in the loss of the decimal part of the division. The last statement in the loop body displays the student number and the student's quiz average.

Exercises 6.4

1. Declare a two-dimensional array that contains 15 rows, each of which will store 12 integers.
2. Declare a two-dimensional array that contains 10 rows, each of which will store 4 doubles.

Use the following declarations in Exercises 3–4.

```
int arr_2d[3][4] = {{4, 5, 6, 7},
                     {2, 6, 1},
                     {8, 7, 2, 1}};
int row, col;
```

3. What are the values of arr_2d[2][2], arr_2d[0][0], arr_2d[3][4], and arr_2d [1][3]?
4. What does the following code display?

```
for (row = 1; row < 3; ++row)
{
   cout << endl;
   for (col = 0; col < 4; ++col)
      cout << setw(6) << arr_2d[row][col];
}
```

5. The commissioner of major league baseball wants you to write a program to analyze the salaries of all major league baseball players. As part of the program, you decide to store all the salaries in a two-dimensional array. Each row represents one of baseball's 30 teams. In each row are the salaries of the team's 25 players. Write the declaration of such an array.
6. Write a nested for loop to enter the salaries of all the players in major league baseball into the array declared in Exercise 5. The loop should prompt the user for each salary.
7. Write code that displays the total salary for each of the 30 major league baseball teams whose player salaries are stored in the array of Exercise 5.
8. Write code to do the following. Declare a three-dimensional array arr_3d[][][] of size 3 × 4 × 5 and initialize each array element to the sum of its subscripts.

Experiments 6.4

1. Dem06-5.cpp displays the average of each student on the ten quizzes. Recode that program so it displays the average grade on each of the ten quizzes.
2. Execute the following program and explain what it displays.

```
#include <iostream>
using namespace std;
```

```
int main()
{
  int arr_3d[4][3] = {{1},
                      {1, 2},
                      {1, 2, 3},
                      {1, 2, 3, 4}};
  int row, col;

  for (row = 0; row < 4; ++row)
  {
    cout << endl;
    for (col = 0; row < 3; ++col)
      cout << setw(3) << arr_3d[row][col];
  }

  return 0;
}
```

3. Write a program to see if there is any difference between the following array declarations.

```
int arr1[2][3] = { {1, 2, 3},
                   {4, 5, 6}};

int arr2[2][3] = {1, 2, 3, 4, 5, 6};
```

Programming Problems 6.4

1. A sweatshirt manufacturer wants to take inventory of the college logo sweatshirts that it has in stock. The company makes sweatshirts for seven colleges. Refer to the colleges by number, 1–7. Sweatshirts come in four sizes: small, medium, large, and x-large. An employee gathers the inventory information by hand. Write a program that prompts the employee to enter the number of sweatshirts in stock for each of the seven colleges in each of the four sizes. Store the inventory information in a two-dimensional array. After inputting the inventory data, the program should display an inventory report in the following format.

```
                             Inventory Report
                                College
                    1    2    3    4    5    6    7    Total
           Small
           Medium
Size
           Large
           XLarge
College Total
Total Quantity On Hand
```

At the end of each row should be the total inventory for that size. At the bottom of each column should be total inventory of each college. The Total Quantity On Hand should be the total inventory of all sweatshirts.

2. Our teacher wants a program to store the ten quiz grades of each of the five students in her four classes in a 4 × 5 × 10 three-dimensional array. Write a program that prompts the user to enter the grades on a class-by-class basis. Within each class, the program should prompt the user for the grades of each student. After all the grades are entered, the program should display the following: the average grade of each student on a class-by-class basis and the average grade of the entire class on the ten quizzes.

3. Recode Programming Problem 2 so it displays the average grade on each of the ten quizzes.

CHAPTER REVIEW

TERMINOLOGY

Describe the meanings of the following terms.

array	array search
array type	linear search
array element	sequential search
linear data structure	sorting
one-dimensional data structure	bubble sort
offset	two-dimensional array
displacement	matrix
subscript	array size
index	row major order

SUMMARY

- An array is a collection of a fixed number of objects of the same type, which are stored sequentially in computer memory. The number of elements in an array is the array size.
- To read an array declaration, start at the name and proceed counterclockwise through the declaration to the array type (Note 6.1).
- Each element in an array is numbered (beginning at zero) by its offset from the first element in the array. The largest valid offset is one less than the array size (Note 6.2).
- You can initialize an array in its declaration by setting the array equal to a comma-separated list of initial values enclosed in braces (Note 6.3).
- Any expression that evaluates to an integer can be used as an array subscript (Note 6.4).
- C++ does not check a subscript for validity (Note 6.5).
- Use a for loop to process array elements. Use a subscript as the for loop counter.
- In a program, define the size of an array as a symbolic constant (Note 6.6).

- The bubble sort works by comparing pairs of adjacent elements. If the elements are out of order, they are interchanged.
- Use a two-dimensional array to store elements that can be classified according to two categories. Two subscripts are required to reference an element in a two-dimensional array. The first subscript references the row, and the second subscript references the column.
- A two-dimensional array can be initialized (Note 6.7).
- Use nested `for` loops to process a two-dimensional array.

REVIEW EXERCISES

1. What is an array and how do you declare one?
2. What is the valid subscript range in an array of N elements? What happens if you use a subscript outside this range?
3. How do you initialize an array? What happens if you do not list enough elements? What happens if you list too few elements?
4. What C++ statement is best used to process an array?
5. Why should you define the size of an array as a symbolic constant?
6. Explain how a sequential search works.
7. Explain how a bubble sort works.
8. How do you code the declaration for a multidimensional array?
9. Some people say that in C++ there is no such thing as a true multidimensional array. Why do they have this opinion?
10. How do you initialize a two-dimensional array?
11. What C++ statement is best used to process a two-dimensional array?

Chapter 7

Pointers and C-Strings

OBJECTIVES

- To declare a pointer
- To properly read a pointer declaration
- To use the address operator to initialize a pointer in a declaration
- To use the indirection operator to dereference a pointer
- To use the name of an array as a constant pointer
- To perform pointer arithmetic
- To declare and use strings
- To code string input and output
- To design and code programs that use pointers and strings
- To store strings using a two-dimensional character array
- To store strings using an array of character pointers
- To design and code programs that use arrays of strings

Pointers are central to understanding the C++ language. In this chapter, we introduce pointers and use pointers to manipulate strings, which are sequences of characters. We discuss how to process strings and how to use the string-manipulation library functions. Finally, we show how an array of stings can store a table of names.

7.1 POINTERS

This section introduces the idea of pointers and how to declare and initialize them. We also discuss how to use a pointer to change the value of a variable.

7.1.1 Declaring and Initializing Pointers

Every variable has an **address**, which is a number that specifies the location of the variable in the computer's main memory. A variable's address functions like the address of your house. The post office uses your house address to locate your house for the delivery of mail. In much the same way, the computer uses the address of a variable to locate the variable so that it can place a value in that location or copy the value that is already stored in that location. A **pointer** is a variable whose value is the address of another variable. In Figure 7.1a, i is an integer variable having a value of 5. We assume that the address of i is 004800. The variable i_ptr is a pointer whose value is the address of i, namely 004800. Because i_ptr contains the location of the variable i, i_ptr in effect points to the variable i. Therefore, we say that i_ptr **points to** i.

Normally, we do not know the actual numeric address of a variable. Therefore, to show that a pointer points to a variable, we draw an arrow from the pointer to the variable it points to, as in Figure 7.1b.

The pointers of Figure 7.1 are depicted as circles rather than squares, which we have been using to symbolize ordinary variables throughout the book. A circle emphasizes that the value of a pointer is an address.

A memory address is not the same as the value of an ordinary variable. Normally, we can think of the address of a byte as a number that uniquely identifies the location of that byte in computer storage. See Figure 7.1. Bytes are numbered with addresses from 0 to one less than the number of bytes in the computer's memory. This simple concept of computer storage is useful in understanding most of what goes on inside a computer. In some computers, however, the address of a byte consists of several numbers that identify the location of the byte. A good analogy is the address of a typical house, which is not a simple number like 2345. A house address has several parts— house number, street, city, state—that together identify the location of the house. Similarly, the address of a byte may have several parts.

Recall that variables of different types can occupy different amounts of storage. Thus, when declaring a pointer, we must specify the type of the variable whose address the pointer contains. A pointer has a type just as an ordinary variable has a type. There are pointers to variables of type int, pointers to variables of type double, and so on.

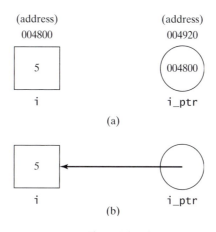

(a)

(b)

Figure 7.1

Because an address might not be a simple integer, we cannot declare a pointer as an ordinary integer. To declare a pointer, we begin with the data type of a variable to which it will point, followed by an asterisk, *, followed by the name of the pointer. Thus, the following declares two pointers—one of type `int` and one of type `double`.

```
int*    i_ptr;
double* d_ptr;
```

To read these declarations, use the rule of Note 7.1, which is similar to Note 6.1 for reading array declarations.

Note 7.1 Reading a Pointer Declaration

Begin reading a pointer declaration at the pointer name and proceed clockwise through the declaration. Read the * as "pointer."

Thus, read the first pointer declaration previously noted as "`i_ptr` is an `int` pointer" and read the second as "`d_ptr` is a `double` pointer." We use the suffix `_ptr` on pointer names to remind us that these variables are pointers.

We append the asterisk in a pointer declaration immediately after the data type to emphasize that the pointer is a data type. The data type `int*`, that is, the integer pointer data type, is a different type of object than that of an integer. Placing the asterisk in the declaration does not modify the `int` data type, but instead actually refers to a completely different type. Note, however, that it is not required to append the asterisk after the data type. The following declarations are equivalent to that of `i_ptr`. Some programmers use these styles of declaring pointers.

```
int  *  i_ptr;      //Declares i_ptr as an integer pointer

int  *i_ptr;        //Declares i_ptr as an integer pointer
```

Declaring a pointer, like declaring an ordinary variable, does not give the pointer a valid value. Thus, referring to the previous declarations, `i_ptr` and `d_ptr`, although valid pointer variables, do not yet have valid values. Before using a pointer, make sure you give it a valid value by assigning the address of a variable to the pointer. The unary **address of operator**, &, returns the address of the variable to which it is applied. For example, if `i` is an integer variable, then `&i` is its address.

Note 7.2 The Address of Operator &

1. The address of operator & is a unary operator. Thus, it has the same precedence and right-to-left associativity as the other unary operators.

2. Read the address of the operator as "the address of."

The following declarations and assignments declare and initialize the pointers i_ptr and d_ptr to point to the variables i and d.

```
int      i = 5;
double   d = 3.14;
int*     i_ptr;
double*  d_ptr;

i_ptr = &i;
d_ptr = &d;
```

The value of the right side of the assignment i_ptr = &i is the address of i. Therefore, the assignment places the address of the variable i into the pointer i_ptr. Similarly, the assignment d_ptr = &d places the address of the variable d into the pointer d_ptr. See Figure 7.2.

You can also assign a value to a pointer in the pointer's declaration. The following is equivalent to the previous declarations and assignments.

```
int      i = 5;
double   d = 3.14;
int*     i_ptr = &i;
double*  d_ptr = &d;
```

When assigning the address of a variable to a pointer in the pointer's declaration, you must observe the rule of Note 7.3.

Note 7.3   Initializing a Pointer in Its Declaration

When assigning the address of a variable in a pointer's declaration, the variable must have been previously declared.

Thus, the following is illegal because i is declared after the declaration and initialization of i_ptr. At the time i_ptr is declared and initialized, the variable i is not known to the compiler.

```
int* i_ptr = &i;        // invalid initialization
int  i;
```

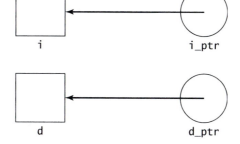

Figure 7.2

No matter how you initialize a pointer, you must initialize it before you use it.

Note 7.4   Initializing a Pointer

Make sure that you initialize a pointer to a valid address before using the pointer. Failure to do so will not be caught by the compiler and can lead to unpredictable results.

Be sure that the address type matches the pointer type. For example, the following pointer initialization is illegal.

```
int     i;
double* d_ptr = &i;        // illegal pointer initialization
```

You cannot assign the address of an integer variable to a pointer to a double. Normally, the compiler will detect all such type mismatches. However, do not rely on the compiler. Do not make the mistake in the first place.

Assigning a pointer the address of a variable using the & operator is one way to give a pointer a valid value. With one exception, you cannot directly assign an integer value to a pointer. Thus, the following declaration is illegal.

```
int* i_ptr = 004600;       // illegal pointer assignment
```

The one exception is the value 0, which is called the **null pointer**. You can also use the predefined constant NULL in place of zero. NULL is defined in several header files including iostream. Thus, the following are legal.

```
int* i_ptr = 0;            // Legal pointer assignment

int* j_ptr = NULL;         // Legal pointer assignment
```

Initializing a pointer to zero, although giving it a valid value, in effect makes the pointer point to nothing. You can assign the value 0 to a pointer of any type. Thus, the following declarations are legal.

```
double* d_ptr = NULL;
char*   c_ptr = NULL;
```

7.1.2 The Indirection Operator

A pointer allows you to indirectly access the value of the variable to which it points. To begin explaining how, we again use the house address analogy. Suppose that you want to give a letter to the President of the United States. One way to do so is to hand deliver the letter and give it to the President directly (if you could get that close!). Another way, is to give the President the letter by mailing the letter to Resident, 1600 Pennsylvania Ave., Washington, D.C. This second method gives the letter to the President, but gives it indirectly through the President's address.

The following declarations set up memory as shown in Figure 7.3.

Figure 7.3

```
int    i;
int*   i_ptr = &i;
```

We could place the value 17 into the integer variable i by the following direct assignment.

```
i = 17;
```

Another way to place a value into i is indirectly through the pointer i_ptr using the **indirection operator** *. The following assignment also places the value 17 into the variable i but does so indirectly through the pointer i_ptr.

```
*i_ptr = 17;
```

Read the left side of this assignment as "the value of the target of i_ptr" or, simply, "the target of i_ptr." The target of i_ptr is the variable to which i_ptr points, namely i. Therefore, the assignment places 17 into the variable i.

Note 7.5 states two important rules about the indirection operator.

Note 7.5   The Indirection Operator

1. The indirection operator * is a unary operator. Thus, it has the same precedence and right-to-left associativity as the other unary operators.

2. Read the indirection operator as "the target of." The target of a pointer is the variable to which it points.

Program dem07-1.cpp illustrates the ideas we have discussed so far.

```
// dem07-1.cpp

// This program illustrates the use of pointers and the indirection
// operator.

#include <iostream>

using namespace std;

int main()
{
    int    i;
    int* i_ptr = &i;
```

```
cout << "The address of i is   " << &i << endl;
cout << "The value of i_ptr is " << i_ptr << endl << endl;

// Place a value into i using indirection

*i_ptr = 17;

cout << "The value of i is   " << i << endl << endl;
cout << "The value of *i_ptr is " << *i_ptr << endl;

return 0;
}
```

Program Output

```
The address of i is   0012FF7C
The value of i_ptr is 0012FF7C

The value of i is   17
The value of *i_ptr is 17
```

The values that the first two cout statements display depend on the particular system on which you run the program. We ran dem07-1.cpp on a PC running Windows XP. The address is displayed in hexadecimal format. See Appendix A if you are unfamiliar with the hexadecimal numeration system. If you run dem07-1.cpp under another operating system, you will probably receive different results for the address of i. The important thing is that the address of i and the value of i_ptr are the same. Thus, i_ptr is pointing to i. Also, the program shows that you can reference the value of i either directly through i or indirectly through the pointer i_ptr.

7.1.3 Pointers and Arrays

We begin with a very important fact about arrays.

Note 7.6   The Name of an Array is a Pointer

The name of an array is a pointer to the first element in the array.

Consider, for example, the following declarations.

```
int  nums[5] = {3, 4, 5, 6, 7};
int* nums_ptr;
```

The identifier nums, which is the name of the array, is an integer pointer to the first element of the array. Thus, *nums, the target of the pointer, is the array element nums[0], which has the value 3. Because nums is a pointer to an integer, the following assignment is legal.

```
nums_ptr = nums;        // A legal pointer assignment
```

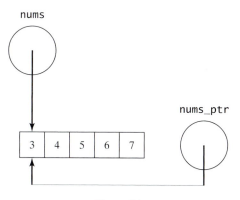

Figure 7.4

After making this assignment, *nums_ptr also refers to the first element of the array nums[], namely nums[0]. See Figure 7.4.

However, you must be careful not to make an assignment like the following.

```
nums_ptr = nums[2];     // Illegal pointer assignment
```

The left side of this assignment is an integer pointer. The right side is an integer. Therefore, the assignment is invalid.

Although we now have two pointers to the first element of the array nums[], there is an important difference between how we can use nums and nums_ptr. The name of an array is a **constant pointer** in the sense that no C++ statement can change its value. Therefore, the following assignment is illegal.

```
nums = nums_ptr;        // Illegal assignment
```

Note 7.7   The Name of an Array Is a Constant Pointer

The name of an array is a constant pointer. It is, therefore, illegal to try to change the value of the name of an array.

You can do simple integer arithmetic on pointers. For example, assume the following assignment.

```
nums_ptr = nums;
```

We can now execute ++nums_ptr. This causes the value of num_ptr to point to the next integer value, namely nums[1], or 4. See Figure 7.5. Note, however, that ++nums is illegal because it is an attempt to change the value of the name of an array, which is a constant pointer.

It is important to note that pointer arithmetic within an array is scaled to the type of the array. For example, suppose the following declaration.

```
double  d_array[4] = {3.2, 4.3, 5.4, 6.5};
double* d_ptr = d_array;
```

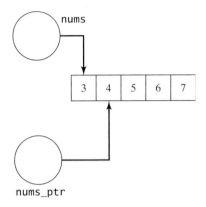

Figure 7.5

Thus, d_ptr points to the first element of d_array, namely 3.2. The statement ++d_ptr causes d_ptr to point to the next double in the array, namely 4.3. If we again execute ++d_ptr, d_ptr will point to the next double in the array, namely 5.4.

You can use pointer arithmetic on an array name if it does not result in changing the value of the array name. The following is a valid assignment.

```
nums_ptr = nums + 2;        // Valid pointer assignment
```

This assignment causes the pointer nums_ptr to point to the array element nums[2]. See Figure 7.6. In general, the expression nums + i is a pointer to the array element nums[i]. Therefore, *(nums + i) is the same element as nums[i]. Anywhere that you can use nums[i] in a program it is legal to use *(nums + i) in its place. (To what does *nums + i refer?)

When using a pointer and pointer arithmetic to access array elements, you must take care that you do not cause the pointer to increase beyond the limits of the array. For example, in the previous example of Figure 7.6, if we execute nums_ptr += 3, the

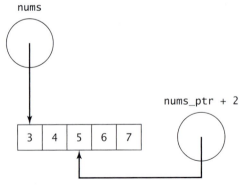

Same as nums[2]

Figure 7.6

pointer will be pointing to the next integer location after the array. There is no way to tell what is stored in that location. The C++ compiler will not warn you if you make this mistake. The program will simply access the memory locations after the end of the array, whether they have been allocated or not. Accessing such locations could cause a run-time error in the program or could cause the program to produce incorrect results. See Experiment 2.

Program dem07-1A.cpp demonstrates the ideas discussed so far.

```cpp
// dem07-1A.cpp

//This program demonstrates pointer arithmetic and arrays.

#include <iostream>
#include <iomanip>

using namespace std;
int main()
{
        int   nums[5] = {3, 4, 5, 6, 7};
        int* nums_ptr;
        int   i;

        cout << "The array using nums[i] notation" << endl;

        for (i = 0; i < 5; ++i)
           cout << setw(4) << nums[i];

        cout << endl << endl;

        cout << "The array using *(nums + i) notation" << endl;

        for (i = 0; i < 5 ; ++i)
            cout << setw(4) << *(nums + i);

        cout << endl << endl;

        cout << "The array using nums_ptr" << endl;

        for (nums_ptr = nums; nums_ptr < nums + 5; ++nums_ptr)
            cout << setw(4) << *nums_ptr;

        cout << endl << endl;

        return 0;
}
```

Program Output

```
The array using nums[i] notation
   3    4    5    6    7

The array using *(nums + i) notation
   3    4    5    6    7

The array using nums_ptr
   3    4    5    6    7
```

The first for loop displays the five array elements using the usual array notation introduced in Chapter 5. The second for loop uses the fact that the name of an array is a pointer. The reference to *(nums + i) is the same as the reference to nums[i]. The third for loop uses the pointer nums_ptr to march through the array. Each time through the loop, nums_ptr is increased by one, which causes nums_ptr to point to the next array element. The loop continues as long as nums_ptr < nums + 5. The address nums + 5 is the address of the first integer *after* the last integer in the array.

To understand pointers completely, you must see them in action and use them in programs. Section 7.2 introduces the idea of strings, which are sequences of characters. Section 7.3 shows how strings, arrays, and pointers are related and discusses several programs that use pointers to manipulate strings.

Exercises 7.1

1. Code declarations for the following.
   a. A pointer to a float variable.
   b. A pointer to a long integer variable.
   c. A pointer to the unsigned integer variable u and initialize the pointer to the address of u.
   d. A pointer to the unsigned long integer variable u1 and initialize the pointer to the address of u1.

   Use the following declarations for Exercises 2–5.

   ```
   int i = 9,
       j = 4,
       k,
       l;
   int* i_ptr = &i;
   int* j_ptr = &j;
   int* k_ptr = &k;
   int* l_ptr = &l;
   ```

2. What are the values of the following?
   a. *j_ptr
   b. i_ptr
   c. *(&i)

3. Give the values of i, j, k, and l after execution of the following assignments.

   ```
   *k_ptr = *i_ptr + *j_ptr;
   l = k + *j_ptr;
   (*l_ptr)++;
   ```

4. Is the following assignment legal?

   ```
   i_ptr = 9;
   ```

5. Is the following assignment legal?

   ```
   *j_ptr = &j;
   ```

In Exercises 6–11, use the following declarations. In each exercise, state the value of the given expression.

```
int arr[] = {1, 2, 3, 4, 5, 6, 7, 8, 9};
int* arr_ptr = arr;
```

   6. `*(arr_ptr + 4)`
   7. `*arr_ptr + 4`
   8. `arr_ptr[4]`
   9. `(*arr_ptr)++`
   10. `*(arr_ptr++)`
   11. `*space_ptr++`

Experiments 7.1

   1. In dem07-1.cpp, remove the initialization of `i_ptr` to the address of `i`. Execute the resulting program. Explain what happens.
   2. Compile and execute the following program. Explain the output.

```
#include <iostream>

using namespace std;

int main()
{
   int arr[] = {1, 2, 3, 4, 5, 6, 7, 8, 9};
   int* arr_ptr = arr;

   arr_ptr += 9;

   cout << *arr_ptr;

   return 0;
```

7.2 C-STRINGS

This section introduces strings, that is, sequences of characters. We begin with basic ideas and techniques for manipulating strings.

7.2.1 Defining and Initializing a String

Colloquially, a string is a sequence of characters. For example, the previous sentence is a string. In C++, strings can be implemented in two ways. In this chapter, we shall define a **string** as an array of characters that ends with the **null character**. The null character is a byte all of whose bits are zero. We denote the null byte by the escape sequence '\0'. The null character denotes the end of the string. If a character array does not end in a null character, the array does not contain a string.

Strings defined in this way are sometimes referred to as **C-strings** because this is the way in which strings are defined in the C programming language. (Recall that C++ is based on C and contains all the capabilities of C.) In Chapter 10, we shall see how strings can be implemented using the string class. For now, we use C-strings primarily to make you familiar with this way of implementing strings (the technique is still important and used) and to illustrate the use and power of pointers. Throughout the rest of this chapter, we shall use the simpler term "string" to refer to a C-string.

The following declaration and initialization create a string consisting of the word "Hello". To hold the null character at the end of the array, the size of the character array containing the string is one more than the number of characters in the word "Hello."

```
char greeting[6] = {'H', 'e', 'l', 'l', 'o', '\0'};
```

This method of declaring and initializing a string is tedious because we must enclose each character in apostrophes and separate the characters by commas. The C++ language gives another way to initialize a string by using a **string constant,** which is a sequence of characters enclosed in quotation marks. Thus, the following declaration and initialization are equivalent to the previous one.

```
char greeting[6] = "Hello";
```

You do not place the null character at the end of a string constant. The C++ compiler automatically places the '\0' at the end of the string when it initializes the array. Therefore, the preceding declaration causes the compiler to initialize storage as shown in Figure 7.7.

Also, recall that if you initialize an array in its declaration, you do not have to state the size of the array. The C++ compiler will infer the array size from the initialization value. Thus, the following is equivalent to the previous declaration.

```
char greeting[] = "Hello";
```

7.2.2 String Input and Output

So far in this book, we have not input strings into our programs. Suppose we wish to write a simple program that asks the user for the name of an item and its price. The program will then display the item name, the tax on the price, and its final cost (the price plus the tax). The only new feature of this program is obtaining the name of the item and displaying the name.

Recall from Chapter 3 that to obtain a single character from the keyboard input buffer, we use cin.get(). Similarly, to obtain a string from the keyboard input buffer, we code **cin.getline().** The getline() member function requires two arguments. The first argument must be the name of the array in which to store the string. The second argument should be the size of the array that is the first argument. The getline()

greeting

Figure 7.7

member function extracts all characters available in the keyboard input buffer up to and including the newline character, or to one less than the number of characters specified as the second argument, whichever comes first. The extra position is left for the terminating null character. The function places the characters, terminated by the null character, into the array named as its first argument. The result of executing `cin.getline()`, therefore, is to place the line that the user enters into a character array with the null character appended to the end.

For example, suppose the following declaration and statement.

```
char buffer[6];
```

```
cin.getline(buffer, 6);
```

The `cin.getline()` statement reads all the characters the user types up to and including the newline character or up to five (5) characters, whichever comes first. The function places the string, with a null character appended, into the array buffer []. If the `'\n'` is read by `cin.getline()`, it is not placed into the buffer.

The program dem07-2.cpp shows how to use `cin.getline()`.

```cpp
// dem07-2.cpp

// This program demonstrates the use of cin.getline() to input a string
// and cout to display strings in several ways.

#include <iostream>
#include <iomanip>

using namespace std;

int main()
{
   double const TAX_RATE = 0.0825;
   char item_name[51];
   double price,
          tax,
          total;

   cout << setprecision(2)
        << setiosflags(ios::fixed)
        << setiosflags(ios::showpoint);

   cout << "Enter the name of the item: ";
   cin.getline(item_name, 51);
   cout << endl;
   cout << "Enter the item price: ";
   cin >> price;

   tax = price * TAX_RATE;
   total = price + tax;

   cout << endl;
   cout << "Item: " << item_name << endl << endl;;
   cout << "Price: " << setw(9) << price << endl;
   cout << "Tax:   " << setw(9) << tax << endl;
   cout << "----------------" << endl;
```

```
    cout << "Total: " << setw(9) << total << endl;

    return 0;
}
```

Program Output

```
Enter the name of the item: System Unit

Enter the item price: 1459.95

Item: System Unit

Price:    1459.95
Tax:       120.45
----------------
Total:    1580.40
```

We assume that the item name is, at most, fifty characters. Therefore, the size of the array item_name[] is 51. (Remember, we must have room for the null character.) After prompting for the name, the program obtains the name from the keyboard input buffer by executing cin.getline(item_name, 51). Figure 7.8 shows the contents of the array item_name[] after cin.getline() executes.

Next, the program prompts for the item price and calculates the tax and total price. The program uses cout to display the item name. When the program sends a character string to cout, cout recognizes it as a string and outputs it accordingly.

A problem that can occur with getline() is when the user enters the maximum number of characters or more than the allowable number of characters. In this case, cin.getline() stops further input and leaves characters in the input buffer. See Experiment 2.

7.2.3 String Constants as Pointers

An important relationship between pointers and strings (remember that a C-string is an array of characters terminated by a null character) is that a string constant, such as "Hello", is actually a pointer to a character array. When the C++ compiler encounters a string constant in a program, it stores the string (with the null character appended) somewhere in memory. Whenever the compiler encounters the string constant, it treats the string constant as a pointer to the base of the string. Therefore, the following declaration and initialization are legal.

```
    char* greeting_ptr = "Hello";
```

item_name

S	y	s	t	e	m		U	n	i	t	\0			. . .	

Figure 7.8

The C++ compiler treats the string constant "Hello" as a character pointer to the base of the string "Hello". Hence, the assignment gives the character pointer greeting_ptr the value of another character pointer. The expression *(greeting_ptr + 4) references the character 'o' in the string. See Figure 7.9.

In the following sections, we discuss several programs that use pointers and pointer arithmetic to manipulate strings.

7.2.4 Counting Characters in a String

It is sometimes important to know how many characters are in a string. The program dem07-3.cpp counts the number of characters in a string entered by the user by using a while loop and a pointer to move through the array and to count the characters in the string.

```cpp
// dem07-3.cpp

// This program counts the number of characters input by the
// user on one line. It uses a pointer to move through the string
// and uses a while loop to count the characters.

#include <iostream>

using namespace std;

int main()
{
  char line[81];
  char* ch_ptr = line;
  int  count = 0;

  cout << "Enter a line of characters:" << endl << endl;
  cin.getline(line, 81);

  while ( *ch_ptr != '\0' )
  {
    ++count;
    ++ch_ptr;
  }

  cout << endl;
  cout << "The string you entered has " << count << " characters." << endl;

  return 0;
}
```

DUBLIN BUSINESS SCHOOL LIBRARY

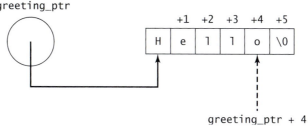

Figure 7.9

Program Output

```
Enter a line of characters:
```
Now is the time for good people to come to the aid of their country.
```
The string you entered has 68 characters
```

Because the normal width of a monitor screen is 80 characters, we declare the array `line[]` to be of size 81. We declare a character pointer `ch_ptr`, which we initialize to point to the base of the array `line[]`, and initialize `count` to zero in its declaration. After prompting for, and obtaining, the string from the user, the `while` loop counts the characters in the string. The loop condition tests the target of `ch_ptr` against the null character. Initially, `ch_ptr` points to the first character in the string that is stored in the array `line[]`. If this is not the null character, the program executes the loop body. The first statement in the loop body increments the variable `count` to count the character. The next statement increments the pointer `ch_ptr` so that it points to the next character in the string. The next time the program tests the loop condition, it tests the next character. The loop executes until the target of `ch_ptr` is the null character. At this point, the counter `i` equals the number of characters in the string.

In Chapter 8, we shall discuss several built-in C++ functions that allow us to manipulate C-strings. Among them is the function `strlen()`, which returns the length of a C-string.

7.2.5 Displaying a String in Reverse

The following program asks the user to enter a string and then displays the string in reverse.

```cpp
// dem07-4.cpp

// This program asks the user to enter a string and then displays
// the string in reverse.

#include <iostream>

using namespace std;
int main()
{
    char line[81];
    char* ch_ptr = line;

    cout << "Enter a line of characters:" << endl << endl;
    cin.getline(line, 81);

    // Find the end of the string

    while ( *ch_ptr != '\0' )
        ++ch_ptr;

    // ch_ptr now points to the null character
```

```
    --ch_ptr;

    // ch_ptr now points to the last character in the string

    cout << endl;
    cout << "The line in reverse is:" << endl << endl;

    // The while loop displays all but the first character

    while ( ch_ptr != line )
    {
       cout << *ch_ptr;
       --ch_ptr;
    }

    // Display the first character

    cout << *ch_ptr;

    cout << endl;
    return 0;
}
```

Program Output

```
Enter a line of characters:
```
abcd efgh ijkl
```
The line in reverse is:
```
lkji hgfe dcba

The program uses the array `line[]` to store the string that the user enters. The pointer `ch_ptr` keeps track of where the program is in the string. Therefore, the declaration of `ch_ptr` initializes it to point to the first character of `line[]`. See Figure 7.10a. Next, the program prompts for and obtains a string from the user. The first `while` loop "slides" the pointer to the end of the string. By this, we mean that the loop increments the pointer until the target of the pointer is the null character. Thus, when the loop ends, `ch_ptr` is pointing to the null character that ends the string. See Figure 7.10b. Therefore, before displaying a character, the program backs up the pointer to the last character in the string by executing `--ch_ptr`. See Figure 7.10c.

The second `while` loop backs up the pointer to the beginning of the string and displays each character as it does so. Because `ch_ptr` is not equal to `line` (remember that `line` is a pointer to the first character in the string) the loop body displays the target of the pointer and then decrements the pointer. This `while` loop ends when `ch_ptr` equals `line`. Therefore, the loop does not display the first character in the string. See Figure 7.10d. The last `cout` statement displays the first character in the string.

(a) Initial setting of ch_ptr

(b) Setting of ch_ptr when first while loop ends

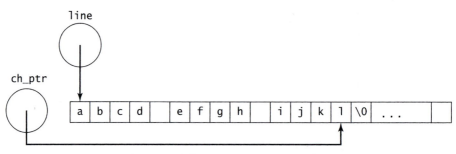

(c) Setting of ch_ptr after executing --ch_ptr

(d) Setting of ch_ptr after executing second while loop

Figure 7.10

7.2.6 Counting Words in a String

A little more difficult than counting the number of characters in a string is counting the number of words in a string. We shall consider a word to be any sequence of non-blank characters. Thus, one or more blanks separate words. The only exception is that the null character, which is the end of the string, also signifies the end of a word.

Following is the pseudocode for the program.

```
prompt for and obtain the string
skip leading blanks
while (there is a character)
  count the word
  skip the word
  skip the blanks after the word
endwhile
display the word count
```

For the program to count words, it must count the number of sequences of non-blank characters (words). Because blanks separate words, whenever the program encounters blanks, it skips them. When the program hits a non-blank character, that character is either the beginning of a word or the end of the string (the null character). If the non-blank character is not the null character, the program increments the word counter and then skips all the characters in the word. The program comes to the end of a word when it encounters either a blank or the end of the string. This process continues until the program hits the null character.

The program dem07-5.cpp counts the number of words in a string entered by the user.

```cpp
// dem07-5.cpp

// This program counts the number of words in a string entered
// by the user.

#include <iostream>

using namespace std;

int main()
{
   char line[81];
   char* ch_ptr;
   int  word_count = 0;

   cout << "Enter a line of words:" << endl << endl;
   cin.getline(line, 81);

   // Skip any blanks at the beginning of the line
   for (ch_ptr = line; *ch_ptr == ' '; ++ch_ptr)
      ;

   // Process rest of line
   while (*ch_ptr != '\0')
   {
```

```
        ++word_count;                        // Count the word

        // Skip the word
        for ( ; (*ch_ptr != ' ') && (*ch_ptr != '\0'); ++ch_ptr)
            ;

        // Skip blanks after the word
        for ( ; *ch_ptr == ' '; ++ch_ptr)
            ;
    }

    cout << "\nThe line you entered has " << word_count << " words."
        << endl;

    return 0;
}
```

Program Output

```
Enter a line of words:
  Now is the time for good people to come to the aid of their country.
The line you entered has 15 words.
```

It is important to keep in mind throughout this discussion that the pointer ch_ptr keeps track of which character in the string the program is processing. After prompting for and obtaining the line from the user, the program executes the first for loop. (This program shows that you can use for loops just as effectively as while loops to process strings. See Experiment 3.) This first loop skips any blanks that may be at the beginning of the line. The loop initializes ch_ptr to point to the beginning of the string. As long as the target of ch_ptr equals a blank, the loop increments the pointer. The body of this loop is empty because the for statement does all the work that we need.

At the end of this loop, therefore, ch_ptr points to the position of the first non-blank character in the string. See Figure 7.11a.

The while loop processes the rest of the line. As long as the character that the program is processing, namely the target of ch_ptr, is not the null character, the while loop keeps processing characters. The first statement in the loop body increments word_count because the program is at the beginning of a word. The first for loop in the while loop body skips the word. Note that the initialization part of the for statement is empty. The program does not reinitialize ch_ptr because we want ch_ptr to retain the value it had when the program exited the previous for loop. Remember that ch_ptr keeps track of the program's position in the string.

The for loop skips all the characters in the word by incrementing ch_ptr as long as the character being processed, namely *ch_ptr, is non-blank and not the null character. Therefore, when the program exits this loop, the character being processed is either a blank or the null character. See Figure 7.11b. If the character being processed is

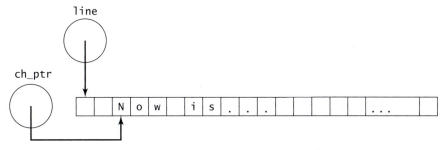

(a) Setting of ch_ptr after executing first for loop

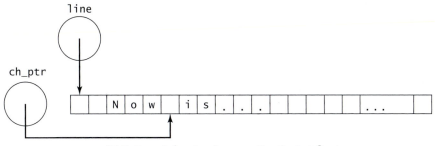

(b) Setting of ch_ptr after executing the first for loop
in the body of the while loop

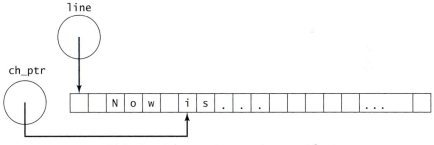

(c) Setting of ch_ptr after executing second for loop
in the body of the while loop

Figure 7.11

a blank, the second for loop in the while loop body skips that blank and any others that immediately follow. Thus, when the program exits the second for loop, the character being processed is non-blank. See Figure 7.11c.

The program then tests the condition in the while loop. If the character being processed is not the null character, the program has encountered another word and it executes the while loop body again. If the character being processed is the null character, the program has reached the end of the string. Then, the while loop stops, and the program displays the number of words in the string.

Exercises 7.2

1. Declare a string called my_name and initialize it with your name.
2. Declare a string called my_state and initialize it with the name of the state in which you live.
3. Declare a string called birthday_month and initialize it with the name of the month in which you were born.
4. Declare a string called your_city. Code statements that prompt the user to enter the name of the city in which he or she lives and place the city name into the string your_city.
5. Declare a string called birth_date that is to hold a date in the form xx/xx/xx. Code statements that prompt the user to enter his/her birth date in the form xx/xx/xx and place the birth date into the string birth_date.

Experiments 7.2

1. In dem07-5.cpp, replace the two for loops in the body of the while loop by equivalent while loops. Compile, execute, and test the resulting program.
2. Execute the following program:

```
#include <iostream>

using namespace std;

int main()
{
    char buffer[6];

    cout << "Enter five character string: ";
    cin.getline(buffer, 6);

    cout << endl << endl;
    cout << "The string you entered was " << buffer << endl;

    cout << "Enter another five character string: ";
    cin.getline(buffer, 6);

    cout << endl << endl;
    cout << "The string you entered was " << buffer << endl;

    return 0;
}
```

At the first prompt, enter six characters. What happens? Run the program again. At the first prompt, enter seven characters. What happens? How can you program around this? (Hint: Think of using cin.get() and/or a loop.)

Programming Problems 7.1

1. Write a program that prompts the user to enter a string of up to 80 characters. The program should display the middle character in the string if there is an odd

number of characters in the string. If there is an even number of characters in the string, the program should display the middle two characters.

2. Write a program that prompts the user to enter a string and then prompts the user to enter a character. The program should display the number of times the character occurs in the string.

3. Write a program that prompts the user to enter a string and then prompts the user to enter a character. The program should display the location of the first occurrence of the character in the string. For example, if the user enters the string "asfrdbrt" and the character d, the program should say that the character d is character number 5 in the string. If the character does not occur in the string, the program should display an appropriate message.

4. Write a program that prompts the user to enter two strings. The program should display "The strings are identical" if the strings are exactly the same and "The strings are not identical" if the strings are not exactly the same.

5. Write a program that prompts the user to enter a string. The program should output the number of vowels (a, e, i, o, u) contained in the string. For example, the previous sentence contains 26 vowels.

6. Modify the program of Programming Problem 5 to display the number of times each vowel appears in the string input by the user.

7. Write a program that prompts the user to enter a string and then copies the string into another array. The program should display the array in which the string was originally stored and the array in which the copy was placed.

8. Write a program that prompts the user to enter a string. The program should display the string one word per line. Hint: See dem07-5.cpp.

9. Write a program that inserts one string into another. The program should prompt the user for a string. Then the program should prompt the user to enter another string that is to be inserted into the first string. Finally, the program should prompt the user for the position at which to insert the second string. The program should then do the insertion and display the new string. For example, suppose the user enters for the first string "I left my heart in Francisco", for the second string "San" and for the position 20. Then, the program should output "I left my heart in San Francisco".

10. Encoding messages is important in many industries to keep important information out of the hands of "industrial spies." Write a program that prompts the user to enter a line of text, and then displays the line in code. The program should use the following simple coding scheme. Store the alphabet in two different orderings in two different arrays. For example,

```
char source[] = "qazwsxedcrfvtgbyhnujmikolp";
char target[] = "lkjhgfdsaqwertyuiopmnbvcxz";
```

For each character input by the user, search the source[] array for that character and note its subscript. Then encode that character by the character with the corresponding subscript in the target[] array. For example, suppose the user enters v. The letter v has subscript 11 in the source[] array. Therefore, the letter v gets encoded as the letter e because e has subscript 11 in the target[] array. The word "computer" would get encoded as "acnzprdq". Treat uppercase characters the same as lowercase characters. Characters that are not letters of the alphabet should be unchanged.

11. An International Standard Book Number (ISBN) is a code of ten characters that uniquely identifies a book. The right-most digit of such a number is a check digit, which helps detect errors in case the number is copied incorrectly. For example, in the ISBN 0132261197, the check digit is 7. The check digit is computed from the other nine digits as follows: First compute the sum of the first digit plus two times the second digit, plus three times the third digit, ..., plus nine times the ninth digit. The check digit is the remainder when this sum is divided by 11. If the remainder is ten, the check digit is X. For example, the sum for the ISBN 0132261197 is

$$1*0 + 2*1 + 3*3 + 4*2 + 5*2 + 6*6 + 7*1 + 8*1 + 9*9 = 161$$

The remainder when 161 is divided by 11 is 7, which is the last character of the ISBN. When copying an ISBN, if a digit is copied incorrectly, or the order of two digits is reversed, the check digit can be used to detect the error. For example, suppose that the above ISBN is incorrectly written as 0132621197. If you attempt to calculate the check digit from the first nine digits, you obtain the sum:

$$1*0 + 2*1 + 3*3 + 4*2 + 5*6 + 6*2 + 7*1 + 8*1 + 9*9 = 157$$

The remainder when you divide 157 by 11 is 3. Because this does not agree with the check digit of 7, we know that the ISBN has been incorrectly transcribed. Write a program that asks the user to enter the name of a book and its ISBN. The program should validate the ISBN and print a message that states that the ISBN is correct or it is incorrect. Store the ISBN in a character array. To do the summation with the ISBN characters, use the fact that the numeric value of a digit character can be had by subtracting the character 0 from the character. For example, the value of 4–0 is 4.

12. See Programming Problem 11. The ISBN is usually written with dashes as follows: 0-13-226119-7. Redo Programming Problem 11 to take the dashes into account. In other words, let the user enter the ISBN with the dashes. The program should validate the number as in Programming Problem 11.

7.3 ARRAYS OF STRINGS AND POINTERS

In C++, the elements in an array can be any data type. In this section, we consider arrays of strings and arrays of pointers, and several applications.

7.3.1 Defining an Array of Strings

Recall that a two-dimensional array is actually an array, each of whose elements is an array. For example, the array

```
char day_names[7][10];
```

is an array of seven elements, each of which is an array of ten characters. An array of characters can store a string. Therefore, a two-dimensional array of characters, such as day_names[][], is capable of storing strings. Consider, for example, the following declaration and initialization.

```
char day_names[7][10] = {"Monday", "Tuesday", "Wednesday",
                         "Thursday", "Friday", "Saturday","Sunday"};
```

The 7×10 character array day_names[][] can hold seven strings, each up to nine characters long. The longest name of the days of the week is Wednesday, which has nine characters. The tenth position is for the null character. Figure 7.12 shows what the declaration places into storage.

Now that we have placed the names of the days of the week into storage, how can we refer to them in a program? Each element of the array day_names[][] is an array of characters. Therefore, the reference day_names[3] accesses element number three of the array, which is the array of characters containing the string "Thursday." Thus, to refer to a particular string in the array, use the array name followed by a single subscript.

Note 7.8   String References in a Two-Dimensional Array

When strings are stored in a two-dimensional array, use the array name followed by one subscript to refer to the individual strings.

7.3.2 Using an Array of Strings

A sales manager wants to total the sales for each salesperson in her department and find the day of the week on which the salesperson had the highest sales. Write a program to perform this task. The program should ask the user for the sales of the salesperson for each day of the week. The prompt should include the name of the day of the week. The program should then total the weekly sales. Finally, the program should

day_names

0	M	o	n	d	a	y	\0			
1	T	u	e	s	d	a	y	\0		
2	W	e	d	n	e	s	d	a	y	\0
3	T	h	u	r	s	d	a	y	\0	
4	F	r	i	d	a	y	\0			
5	S	a	t	u	r	d	a	y	\0	
6	S	u	n	d	a	y	\0			

Figure 7.12

display the total weekly sales, the name of the day of the week that the salesperson had the highest sales, and what the highest sales amount was.

Following is a pseudocode solution to the problem.

Prompt for and get the name of the salesperson
Prompt for and get the sales amounts for each day
Calculate the total sales
Find the highest sales amount
Display the total sales, name of the day of the highest
    sales, and the highest sales amount

The program prb07-1.cpp, which follows, is the solution to this problem.

```cpp
// prb07-1.cpp

// This program totals weekly sales amounts and finds the highest
// sales for the week.  It uses an array of strings to store the
// names of the days of the week.

#include <iostream>
#include <iomanip>

using namespace std;
int main()
{
  char day_names[7][10] = {"Monday", "Tuesday", "Wednesday",
                    "Thursday", "Friday", "Saturday", "Sunday"};
  double sales[7];
  char    salesperson[41];
  double max_sales,
         total_sales;
  int     day,
          max_day;

  cout << setprecision(2)
       << setiosflags(ios::fixed)
       << setiosflags(ios::showpoint);

  cout << "Enter the name of the salesperson: ";
  cin.getline(salesperson, 41);

  for (day = 0; day < 7; ++day)
  {
    cout << endl << endl;
    cout << "Enter the sales for "<< day_names[day] << ": ";
    cin >> sales[day];
  }

  total_sales = 0;
  max_day = 0;
  max_sales = sales[0];

  for (day = 0; day < 7; ++day)
  {
```

```
    if (sales[day] > max_sales)
    {
      max_sales = sales[day];
      max_day = day;
    }

    total_sales += sales[day];
  }
  cout << endl << endl;
  cout << "The total sales for " << salesperson
       << " is " << total_sales << "." << endl << endl;
  cout << "The highest sales was " << max_sales << "." << endl << endl;
  cout << "The highest sales occurred on "
       << day_names[max_day]<< "." << endl;

  return 0;
}
```

Program Output

```
Enter the name of the salesperson: Joseph Harris

Enter the sales for Monday: 379.90

Enter the sales for Tuesday: 2877.95

Enter the sales for Wednesday: 2661.90

Enter the sales for Thursday: 178.45

Enter the sales for Friday: 3066.20

Enter the sales for Saturday: 0.00

Enter the sales for Sunday: 2904.77

The total sales for Joseph Harris is 12069.17.

The highest sales was 3066.20.

The highest sales occurred on Friday.
```

The declarations begin with the two-dimensional array day_names[][], which is initialized to the names of the days of the week. The array sales[] stores the seven sales amounts. The character array salesperson[] stores the name of the salesperson. The double variable max_sales stores the highest sales and the variable total_sales is the accumulator for totaling the sales amounts. The integer variable day acts as the subscript for both the day_names[][] array and the sales[] array.

The program begins by prompting for and obtaining the name of the salesperson. Next, a for loop prompts for and obtains the seven sales amounts and stores them in the array sales[]. The cout statement displays the name of the day of the week by displaying day_names[day], which is the name of the day corresponding to the day number.

The program prepares to total the sales amounts and find the day of the highest sales by initializing three variables. The accumulator `total_sales` is initialized to zero. To begin the process of finding the highest sales amount, we assume that the highest sale occurs on day zero. Therefore, the program initializes `max_day` to zero and `max_sales` to the sales on the first day, namely `sales[0]`.

The next `for` loop totals the sales and finds the highest sales amount. For each of the seven days, the loop tests the sales of the day being processed, `sales[day]`, against `max_sales`, the highest sales found so far. If `sales[day]` is greater than `max_sales`, the current day's sales is greater than the highest sales seen so far. Therefore, the program replaces the value of `max_sales` by the value of `sales[day]` and replaces the value of `max_day` by the value of the current day, namely `day`. If the value of `sales[day]` is not greater than `max_sales`, no adjustment needs to be made to either `max_sales` or `max_day`. In either case, the value of `total_sales` is increased by the value of `sales[day]`. When the program exits the `for` loop, `total_sales` contains the sum of the seven days' sales, `max_sales` contains the highest sales amount, and `max_day` contains the number of the day on which the highest sales occurred.

The `cout` statements display the results of the program. The first `cout` displays the salesperson's name and the total sales for the week. The second `cout` displays the value of the highest sales. The third `cout` displays the name of the day on which the highest sales occurred. The name of the day is accessed by `day_names[max_day]` because `max_day` is the number of the day of the highest sales.

7.3.3 Using an Array of Pointers to Store Strings

The method we used in the previous section to store strings in a two-dimensional array can be very inefficient. The 7×10 array `day_names[][]` occupies 70 bytes of storage. Each row of the array had to be ten characters long to accommodate the longest name. However, most of the rows are not completely filled. See Figure 7.12. Only 57 of the 70 bytes are actually occupied by the names. Thus, approximately 19 percent of the array is wasted. In other situations, this waste of storage space can be even greater. If you use a two-dimensional array to store the last names of people, the number of columns in the array must be large enough to store the longest last name. If the longest last name is Dimitripopadopolous, each row would have to contain 20 characters. If the average last name is only eight characters long, this means that on average you waste 12 characters per row. If you must store 1000 names, this means wasting about 12,000 bytes of storage.

A more memory-efficient way of storing the names of the days of the week is to define the array of names as an array of character pointers. Consider the following declaration.

```
char* day_names [7] =   {"Monday", "Tuesday", "Wednesday",
                         "Thursday", "Friday", "Saturday", "Sunday"};
```

First, be sure to read the declaration correctly. Remember the rule of Note 6.1 for reading array declarations. Begin reading the declaration at the array name and proceed clockwise through the declaration. Thus, `day_names` is an array of seven character

day_names

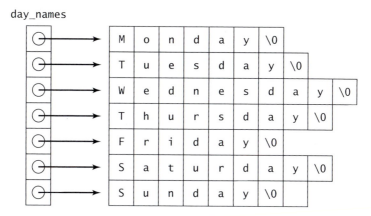

Figure 7.13

pointers. Each element of the array is a pointer to a character. The initialization list contains seven character strings. Recall that a character string is really a pointer to the first character of the string. Figure 7.13 shows what the declaration does.

This declaration of day_names[] as an array of pointers saves storage because each string takes up only as much memory as needed. This declaration requires 57 bytes to store the names of the days of the week, not 70 as in the two-dimensional declaration.

To illustrate the use of an array of pointers, consider prb07-2.cpp, which is another version of prb07-1.cpp.

```
// prb07-2.cpp

// This program totals weekly sales amounts and finds the highest
// sales for the week.  It uses an array of pointers to store the
// names of the days of the week.

#include <iostream>
#include <iomanip>

using namespace std;

int main()
{
   char* day_names[7] = {"Monday", "Tuesday", "Wednesday",
                    "Thursday", "Friday", "Saturday", "Sunday"};
   double sales[7];
   char    salesperson[41];
   double max_sales,
          total_sales;
   int     day,
           max_day;

   cout << setprecision(2)
        << setiosflags(ios::fixed)
        << setiosflags(ios::showpoint);
```

```cpp
   cout << "Enter the name of the salesperson: ";
   cin.getline(salesperson, 41);
   for (day = 0; day < 7; ++day)
   {
      cout << endl << endl;
      cout << "Enter the sales for " << day_names[day] << ": ";
      cin >> sales[day];
   }

   total_sales = 0;
   max_day = 0;
   max_sales = sales[0];

   for (day = 0; day < 7; ++day)
   {
      if (sales[day] > max_sales)
      {
         max_sales = sales[day];
         max_day = day;
      }

      total_sales += sales[day];
   }

   cout << endl << endl;
   cout << "The total sales for " << salesperson
        << " is " << total_sales << "." << endl << endl;
   cout << "The highest sales was " << max_sales << "." << endl << endl;
   cout << "The highest sales occurred on "
        << day_names[max_day] << "." << endl;

   return 0;
}
```

Program Output

```
Enter the name of the salesperson: Joseph Harris
Enter the sales for Monday: 379.90
Enter the sales for Tuesday: 2877.95
Enter the sales for Wednesday: 2661.90
Enter the sales for Thursday: 178.45
Enter the sales for Friday: 3066.20
Enter the sales for Saturday: 0.00
Enter the sales for Sunday: 2904.77
The total sales for Joseph Harris is 12069.17.
The highest sales was 3066.20.
The highest sales occurred on Friday.
```

The difference between prb07-2.cpp and prb07-1.cpp is the declaration of the array of day names as an array of pointers. The references to `day_names` are the same as in prb07-1.cpp because only one subscript was used in prb07-1.cpp to access a day name.

Exercises 7.3

1. Declare a two-dimensional array of characters that is initialized to the names of the months of the year.
2. Declare an array of character pointers that is initialized to point to the names of the months of the year.
3. Declare a two-dimensional array of characters that is initialized to the names of the Presidents who were elected to office after 1950.
4. Declare an array of character pointers that is initialized to point to the names of the Presidents who were elected to office after 1950.

Experiments 7.3

1. Execute dem07-2.cpp and enter an item name that is longer than 50 characters. What happens?
2. Recode dem07-5.cpp by replacing all the `for` loops by equivalent `while` loops. Execute and test the resulting program.

Programming Problems 7.2

1. Write a program that asks the user to enter his/her birthday as three integers in the form month, day, year, for example 7 10 81. The program should output the date in the form month name, day, year. Using the previous example input, the program would output July 10, 1981. Use an array of character pointers to store the month name.
2. A software company has seven service representatives who are identified in the payroll system by the ID numbers 1 through 7. Write a program that prompts the user to enter the representative ID number, hours worked, and pay rate. The program should display the representative's name and gross pay (hours*rate.) Store the representatives' names in an array of character pointers.

CHAPTER REVIEW

TERMINOLOGY

Describe the meanings of the following terms.

address	string
pointer	null character
points to	`'\0'`
address of operator &	C-string
`Null` pointer	string constant
indirection operator	`cin.getline()`
constant pointer	

SUMMARY

- A pointer is a variable whose value is the address of another variable.
- Use the asterisk, *, to declare a pointer. For example, int* i_ptr; declares i_ptr as an integer pointer (Note 7.1).
- Use the address operator, &, to initialize a pointer. For example, i_ptr = &i; initializes the integer pointer i_ptr to the address of the integer variable i (Note 7.2, Note 7.3, and Note 7.4).
- Use the indirection operator, *, to dereference a pointer. Thus, *i_ptr is the value of the target of the pointer i_ptr (Note 7.5).
- The name of an array is a constant pointer to the first element of the array (Note 7.6 and Note 7.7).
- You can do simple integer arithmetic on pointers. This arithmetic is scaled to the size of the pointer type.
- A string is a character array that ends in the null character, '\0'.
- You can initialize a character array to a character string in its initialization.
- The member function cin.getline() returns an entire line from the input buffer.
- A string constant is a character pointer to the string's first character.
- You can store strings in a two-dimensional character array. In this case, the array name followed by one subscript refers to an individual string (Note 7.8). This way of storing strings can waste memory.
- A more efficient way of storing strings is to use an array of character pointers.

REVIEW EXERCISES

1. What is a pointer and how do you declare one?
2. If all pointers occupy the same amount of storage, why do you have to include a data type in a pointer declaration?
3. Why must you make sure that a pointer is initialized to point to a valid address?
4. What is the null pointer?
5. How do you use the indirection operator?
6. How must you treat the name of an array?
7. What is a string?
8. What function should you use to obtain a string from the input buffer?
9. What function can you use to discard unwanted characters from the input buffer?
10. What is the data type of a string constant?
11. Describe two ways to declare an array of strings. What are the advantages and disadvantages of each?

Chapter 8

Pointers, Arrays, and Functions

OBJECTIVES

- To code a function whose argument is passed by address
- To code a function whose argument is passed by reference
- To code a function that has an array as an argument
- To code the bubble sort using a function
- To code a function whose argument is a string
- To code a function that returns a pointer
- To use the standard string library functions, including `strlen()`, `strcpy()`, `strcmp()`, and `strcat()`, to manipulate strings
- To use the character classification and conversion functions to manipulate characters
- To use the functions `atoi()`, `atol()`, and `atof()` to convert numeric strings to their numeric equivalent
- To use the `new` operator to dynamically allocate memory on the heap
- To use the `delete` operator to deallocate memory on the heap

In this chapter, we discuss how to use functions that have pointers and arrays as arguments and functions that return pointers. We also discuss several string and character functions in the C++ standard library.

8.1 POINTERS, REFERENCE VARIABLES, AND FUNCTIONS

A function can have a pointer as an argument and can return a pointer to the calling function. This section discusses how to use such functions.

8.1.1 Call By Address—Pointers as Function Arguments

By default, arguments to C++ functions are passed by value. This means that the value of the argument, not the argument itself, is passed to the function. Consider the following program.

```cpp
// dem08-1.cpp

// This program demonstrates passing an argument by value.

#include <iostream>

using namespace std;

int Neg_By_Value(int);

int main()
{
    int i = 4;

    i = Neg_By_Value(i);

    cout << "i = " << i << endl;

    return 0;
}
int Neg_By_Value(int a)
{
    return -a;
}
```

Program Output

```
i = -4
```

When main() executes the assignment statement, it calls the function Neg_By_Value() and passes the value of the variable i, namely 4, to the function. The function returns the negative of the value of its argument. Thus, Neg_By_Value() has not changed the value of its argument. The function returns the value–4. The assignment statement in main() then assigns–4 to the variable i. Thus, the assignment statement in main() places a new value into the variable i. See Figure 8.1.

In C++, anything can be passed as a function argument, even a pointer. When a pointer to a variable is passed as a function argument, the function receives the address of the variable. Using the indirection operator, the function can manipulate the value of the variable as though the variable were local to the function. The program dem08-2.cpp also negates the value of an integer, but uses a function that has a pointer argument.

```cpp
// dem08-2.cpp

// This program demonstrates passing an argument by address.

#include <iostream>

using namespace std;
```

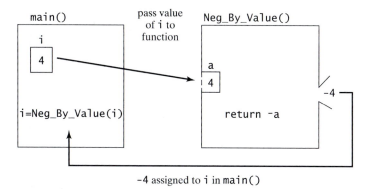

-4 assigned to i in main()

Figure 8.1

```
void Neg_By_Address(int*);
int main()
{
   int i = 4;
   Neg_By_Address(&i);
   cout << "i = " << i << endl;
   return 0;
}
void Neg_By_Address(int* a_ptr)
{
   *a_ptr = -(*a_ptr);
}
```

Program Output

```
i = -4
```

The function Neg_By_Address() negates its integer argument. The type (int*) in the function prototype tells the compiler that the argument is an integer pointer. Thus, when we use the function, the argument must be the address of an integer. Note that the function does not return a value.

To negate the value of i, main() executes the following statement.

```
Neg_By_Address(&i);
```

This function call passes the address of the variable i, not the value of i, to the function Neg_By_Address(). In the function Neg_By_Address(), the parameter a_ptr is declared as an integer pointer. Thus, when main() calls the function, the function

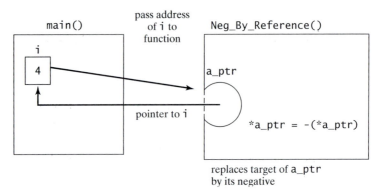

Figure 8.2

places the address that main() passed into the pointer a_ptr. Figure 8.2 shows the parameter a_ptr as a circle to show that it is a pointer.

The pointer a_ptr now points to the variable i. Therefore, the function can use the indirection operator to manipulate the target of a_ptr, namely i. The body of the function contains only the following statement.

```
*a_ptr = -(*a_ptr);
```

This statement replaces the value of the target of a_ptr, namely the value of i, by the negative of the target of a_ptr. Thus, the function Neg_By_Address() changes the value of i in main().

Passing the address of a variable to a function is referred to as **call by address**.

8.1.2 Swapping Variable Values—An Example of Call by Address

A function can return, at most, one value to the calling function. However, using call by address, it is possible to make a function change two or more variables in the calling function. Recall that an important part of the bubble sort, which we discussed in Chapter 6, is swapping the values of two integer variables. The program dem08-3.cpp uses the function Swap_Int() to interchange the values of two integer variables. Later in this chapter, we shall use Swap_Int() in another version of the bubble sort program that uses functions for all major operations.

```
// dem08-3.cpp
#include <iostream>
using namespace std;
void Swap_Int(int*, int*);
int main()
{
    int i = 3,
        j = 5;
```

```
    cout << "Before swapping: i = " << i<< " j = " << j << endl;
    Swap_Int(&i, &j);

    cout << "After swapping: i = " << i<< " j = " << j << endl;

    return 0;

}
void Swap_Int(int* a_ptr, int* b_ptr)
{
    int temp;

    temp = *a_ptr;
    *a_ptr = *b_ptr;
    *b_ptr = temp;
}
```

Program Output

```
Before swapping: i = 3, j = 5
After swapping: i = 5, j = 3
```

The function prototype for Swap_Int() declares its return value to be void because the function does not return a value. Instead, Swap_Int() exchanges the values of two integer variables in the calling function using pointers. The function's arguments are both declared as integer pointers. Thus, we must pass the addresses of two integers to the function.

The declaration of the variables i and j in main() initialize the variables to 3 and 5, respectively. A cout statement displays the initial values of i and j. Then, main() executes the Swap_Int() function by executing the following statement, which passes the addresses of i and j to Swap_Int(). See Figure 8.3.

```
    Swap_Int(&i, &j);
```

The function Swap_Int() assigns these addresses to the parameters a_ptr and b_ptr. Swap_Int() uses the indirection operator to interchange the values of the targets of a_ptr and b_ptr, namely i and j. Thus, the function has the effect of changing the values of two variables in main().

8.1.3 Reference Variables and Call by Reference

Reference variables and arguments are sometimes an alternative to pointers. A **reference variable** is an alias, that is, another name for an already existing variable. For example, suppose we have the following declarations.

```
    int    i = 7;
    double d = 1.2;
```

When main() calls Swap_Int()

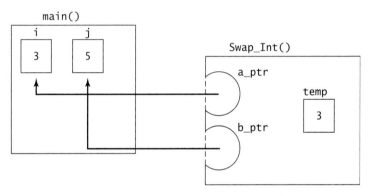

After executing temp = *a_ptr in Swap_Int()

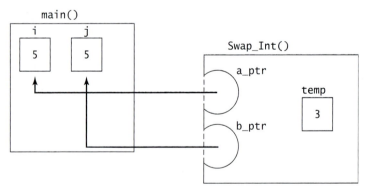

After executing *a_ptr = *b_ptr in Swap_Int()

Figure 8.3

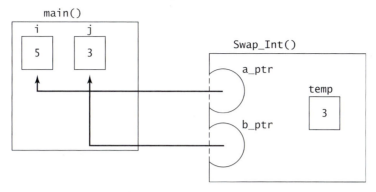

After executing *b_ptr = temp in Swap_Int()

Figure 8.3 (*Continued*)

We can declare reference variables for i and d as follows.

```
int&    r = i;
double& s = d;
```

Read the & in these declarations as "reference." Thus, read the first declaration as "r is an integer reference initialized to i" and read the second declaration as "s is a double reference initialized to d."

Think of a variable name as a label attached to the variable's location in memory. You can then think of a reference as a second label attached to that memory location. Therefore, you can access the contents of the variable through either the original variable name or the reference. See Figure 8.4.

We can change the contents of the variable i by using the identifier i or the reference r. For example, either of the following assignments will change the value of i to 9.

```
i = 9;
r = 9;
```

Just as for pointers, we append the & in a reference declaration to the end of the data type to emphasize that the reference is another type. However, the ampersand can be placed anywhere between the data type and the name of the reference variable. Therefore, the following are legal declarations.

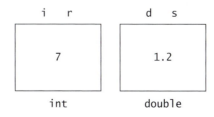

Figure 8.4

```
double & s = d;          //Legal reference declaration
int  &r = i;             //Legal reference declaration
```

In many cases, it is easier to use references rather than pointers as function arguments. In this case, we are passing arguments by reference or using **call by reference**. As an example of call by reference, consider the following variation of the program dem08-2.cpp.

```
// dem08-2R.cpp

// This program demonstrates passing an argument by reference

#include <iostream>

using namespace std;

void Neg_By_Reference(int&);

int main()
{
    int i = 4;

    Neg_By_Reference(i);

    cout << "i = " << i << endl;

    return 0;
}

void Neg_By_Reference(int&  a)

{

    a = -a;
}
```

Program Output

```
i = -4
```

The function `Neg_By_Reference()` has an integer reference as an argument and does not return a value. When the function calls `Neg_By_Reference()` it passes i to the function. Then i is assigned to the reference parameter a in the function. This is equivalent to the declaration and assignment

```
int& a = i;
```

Thus, in the function `Neg_By_Reference()`, a is an alias for i. Any change to a is, therefore, a change to i. Thus, we do not need the dereference operator, *, as we did in dem08-2.cpp. The function `Neg_By_Reference()` replaces a by the negative of a. Therefore, the function replaces i, which is a variable declared in main(), by the negative of i.

As another example of call by reference, consider the following variation of dem08-3.cpp

```cpp
// dem08-3R.cpp

//This program illustrates passing arguments by reference.

#include <iostream>

using namespace std;

void Swap_Int(int&, int&);

int main()
{
  int i = 3,
      j = 5;

  cout << "Before swapping: i = " << i<< " j = " << j << endl;

  Swap_Int(i, j);

  cout << "After swapping: i = " << i<< " j = " << j << endl;

  return 0;
}
void Swap_Int(int& a, int& b)
{
  int temp;

  temp = a;
  a    = b;
  b    = temp;
}
```

Program Output
```
Before swapping: i = 3, j = 5
After swapping: i = 5, j = 3
```

The prototype for the `Swap_Int()` function specifies that the two arguments are integer references. When the function is called, `Swap_Int(i, j)`, the arguments are simply i and j. (We do not pass the addresses as we did in dem08-3.cpp.) Recall that when a function is called, the arguments are, in effect, assigned to the function's parameters. Within the function, therefore, we have the equivalent of the following declarations and initializations.

```cpp
int& a = i;
int& b = j;
```

Thus, within the body of the function, the parameters a and b are aliases for i and j. See Figure 8.5. Therefore, we do not need the dereference operator, *, as we did in the `Swap_Int()` function of dem08-3.

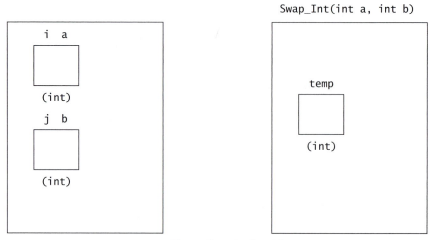

a and b are aliases for i and j.

Figure 8.5

Exercises 8.1

In Exercises 1–5, code the prototype for the given function.

1. A function `Swap_Char()` that interchanges the values of two characters. The function has two arguments, both of which are addresses of characters. The function does not return a value.

2. A function `Sort_Int()` that takes three arguments. Each argument is the address of an integer. The function does not return a value.

3. A function `Calc_Fed_Tax()` that takes four arguments. The first two arguments are the addresses of `doubles`, the third is the address of an integer, and the fourth is the address of a`double`. The function does not return a value.

4. A function `Calc_Weight()` that takes two arguments and returns a `double`. The two arguments are references to `doubles`.

5. A function `Total_Price()` that takes two arguments and returns a `double`. The first argument is a reference to an integer. The second argument is a reference to a `double`.

Experiments 8.1

1. Rewrite dem08-3.cpp so that it swaps two `doubles`.

2. Write and compile a short program in which you declare but do not initialize a reference variable. Does the compiler issue any error messages?

Programming Problems 8.1

1. Write a program to calculate a person's net pay after subtracting federal income tax. The program should ask the user to enter the person's name, social security

number, gross pay, and the number of dependents. The program should first determine the tax rate according to the following schedule.

Weekly Income	Tax Rate
0.00–300.00	0.085
300.01–500.00	0.120
500.01–1000.00	0.185
1000.01 and over	0.220

Use a function Tax_Rate() to determine the schedule. Pass the gross pay to Tax_Rate() and have the function return the rate.

Next, use the function Calc_Fed_Tax() to calculate the federal tax. The first argument should be the address of the gross income. The second argument should be the address of the tax rate (as returned by Tax_Rate()). The third argument should be the address of the number of dependents. The amount of the federal tax should be returned in the target of the fourth argument.

Finally, the program should calculate the net pay by subtracting the federal tax from the gross income. The program should display the person's name, social security number, gross pay, number of dependents, federal tax, and net pay.

2. Code a solution to Programming Problem 1 in which the arguments to the function Calc_Fed_Tax() are passed by reference.

8.2 ARRAYS AND FUNCTIONS

An array name is a pointer to the base of the array. A C-string is a character pointer. Thus, passing an array or a C-string to a function is equivalent to passing a pointer. This section and the next discuss how to pass arrays and strings to functions.

Because an array name is a pointer to the base of the array, you can use an array name in the same way that you use a pointer as an argument in a function. However, because an array has a fixed number of elements, we must take a few special steps when using an array as a function argument. This section discusses how to pass an array to a function and applies this to array sorting.

8.2.1 Passing an Array to a Function

To pass an array to a function, you must do two things in your program, one in the function prototype and one in the function definition header.

Suppose that the function Avg() is to find the average of the integers in an array. We pass the array to the function as one of the function's two parameters. The second parameter is the size of the array that we pass as the first parameter. The following would be the function's prototype.

```
double Avg(int [], int);
```

Avg() returns a value of type double and has two parameters. The first parameter is an array of type int. The brackets [] in the type list tell the compiler that the first parameter is an array. The data type preceding the [] determines the array type. Avg()'s second parameter, which is the array size, is of type int.

The function definition header corresponding to the previous prototype is as follows.

```
double Avg(int arr[], int size)
```

Avg() returns a value of type double and has two parameters. The first parameter, arr, is an array of type int. The brackets [] after the formal parameter name tell the compiler that the parameter is an array. You do not specify the size of the array in this parameter declaration. The second parameter, size, is of type int. This second parameter is the size of the array.

The following program, dem08-4.cpp, does the same thing as dem06-2.cpp—it finds the average of a set of 10 grades input by the user. However, it uses the function Avg() to calculate the average of the grades.

```cpp
// dem08-4.cpp

// This program shows how to find the average of the elements
// in an array.  It finds the average by passing the array
// to a function that computes the average.

#include <iostream>
#include <iomanip>

using namespace std;

double Avg(int [], int);

int main()
{
  const int NUM_QUIZZES = 10;

  int    grade[NUM_QUIZZES]; // The array to store the quiz grades
  int    quiz;               // The array subscript
  double grade_avg;

  cout << setiosflags(ios::fixed)
       << setiosflags(ios::showpoint)
       << setprecision(1);

  cout << "Please enter " << NUM_QUIZZES << " integer quiz grades."
       << endl << endl;

  for (quiz = 0; quiz < NUM_QUIZZES; ++quiz)
  {
    cout << "\nEnter grade for quiz " << quiz + 1 << ": ";
    cin >> grade[quiz];
  }

  grade_avg = Avg(grade, NUM_QUIZZES);

  cout << endl;
  cout << "The average quiz grade is " << grade_avg << endl;

  return 0;

}   // End of main()
```

```
double Avg(int arr[], int size)
{
   int    i,                    // The array subscript
          sum = 0;              // The accumulator
   double avg;                  // The array average

   for (i = 0; i < size; ++i)
      sum += arr[i];

   avg = double(sum) / size;

   return avg;
}    // End of Avg()
```

Program Output

```
Please enter 10 integer quiz grades.

Enter grade for quiz 1: 67

Enter grade for quiz 2: 55

Enter grade for quiz 3: 83

Enter grade for quiz 4: 75

Enter grade for quiz 5: 57

Enter grade for quiz 6: 86

Enter grade for quiz 7: 58

Enter grade for quiz 8: 100

Enter grade for quiz 9: 86

Enter grade for quiz 10: 96

The average quiz grade is 76.3
```

The program begins with the prototype declaration of the function Avg(), as we described previously. The function's first argument is an array of integers. The second argument is an integer that holds the size of the array. You may wonder why we pass the size of the array as an argument since we know that the array has 10 elements. Passing the array size to a function that manipulates an array makes the function more versatile. You can use the same function for finding the average of any array of integers, no matter how many elements are in the array.

Note 8.1   Pass the Size of an Array to a Function

When you pass an array to a function, also pass the size of the array to the function. Doing so makes the function more useful because it will be able to handle arrays of any size.

The only variables that `main()` needs are the array `grade[]`, the subscript variable `quiz`, and the variable `grade_avg`. It does not need an accumulator, as in dem06-2.cpp, because the function `Avg()` sums the array elements.

When the program begins, it prompts the user for the 10 quiz grades, which it places into the array `grade[]`. To calculate the average of the numbers in the array `grade[]`, `main()` calls the function `Avg()` by executing the following assignment.

```
grade_avg = Avg(grade, NUM_QUIZZES);
```

`Avg()`'s first argument is the name of the array of integers that we want to pass. Note that you should use only the name of the array because we are passing a pointer to the function `Avg()`. Do not put brackets after the name. The second argument is the number of elements in the array, namely NUM_QUIZZES. `Avg()` returns the average of the numbers in the array `grade[]`. The assignment statement places the return value into the variable `grade_avg`. Finally, `main()` displays the value of `grade_avg`.

`Avg()`'s parameters, which are declared in the function header, are `arr` for the array and `size` for the array size. Therefore, in the function body, we refer to the array by the name `arr` and the size of the array as `size`. `Avg()` uses three local variables. The variable `i` is the array subscript. The variable `sum` is the accumulator that the program uses to add the array elements. The `double` variable `avg` stores the average of the array elements.

`Avg()` begins by summing the elements in the array using essentially the same loop as the one used in dem06-2.cpp. The only difference is that the loop test is `i < size` because the number of elements in the array is stored in the parameter `size`.

Next, the function computes the average of the array elements. The type cast `double(sum)` converts the value of `sum` to the equivalent `double` for use in the calculation. Finally, the function returns the value of `avg` to the calling program.

When we pass an array name to a function, we pass the address of the array, which is a pointer to the base of the array. We do not pass the value of an array element or a copy of the entire array. When dem08-4.cpp calls the function `Avg(grade, NUM_QUIZZES)`, it passes to `Avg()` the address of the array `grade[]` and the value of NUM_QUIZZES. In the function `Avg()`, the formal parameter `arr` takes on the value of the address of the array `grade[]` in the function `main()`. Thus, in `Avg()`, using `arr[]` is equivalent to using `grade[]` in `main()`. See Figure 8.6.

8.2.2 Sorting an Array

The function `Avg()` in dem08-4.cpp does not change any value in the array. However, if it did change a value in the array `arr[]`, it would change the corresponding value in the array `grade[]` back in the function `main()`.

Note 8.2   Passing an Array to a Function

Pass an array to a function by using the array name as an argument. Doing so passes the address of the array to the function. Therefore, any change that the function makes to the parameter array changes the array in the calling function.

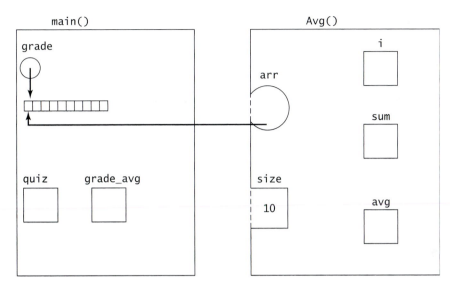

Figure 8.6

The following program, dem08-5.cpp, does the same thing as dem06-4.cpp. It prompts the user to enter a 10-element array and displays the array. Then, the program uses the bubble sort to sort the array in increasing order. Finally, the program displays the sorted array. However, dem08-5.cpp uses functions to obtain the grades from the user, display the grades, and do the bubble sort.

```cpp
// dem08-5.cpp
// This program shows how to sort the elements
// in an array.  It uses functions to do all array processing.
// The Swap_Int() function uses call by reference.

#include <iostream>
#include <iomanip>

using namespace std;

void Get_Grades(int [], int);
void Display_Array(int [], int);
void Bubble_Sort(int [], int);
void Swap_Int(int&, int&);
int main()
{
   const int NUM_QUIZZES = 10;

   // The array to store the quiz grades
   int grade[NUM_QUIZZES];

   Get_Grades(grade, NUM_QUIZZES);

   cout << endl << endl;
   cout << "The grades are as follows:";
```

```cpp
    Display_Array(grade, NUM_QUIZZES);

    Bubble_Sort(grade, NUM_QUIZZES);

    cout << endl << endl;
    cout << "The grades in increasing order are as follows:";
    Display_Array(grade, NUM_QUIZZES);

    cout << endl;
    return 0;


}    // End of main()
void Get_Grades(int arr[], int size)
{
  int quiz;

  cout << endl;
  cout << "Please enter " << size << " integer quiz grades."
        << endl << endl;

  for (quiz = 0; quiz < size; ++quiz)
  {
    cout << endl;
    cout << "Enter grade for quiz :" << quiz + 1 << ": ";
    cin >> arr[quiz];
  }

  return;

}    // End of Get_Grades()
void Display_Array(int arr[], int size)
{
  int i;

  cout << endl;
  for (i = 0; i < size; ++i)
    cout << setw(6) << arr[i];
  cout << endl;

  return;

}    // End of Display_Array()
void Bubble_Sort(int arr[], int size)
{
  int i,                         // The array subscript
      pass,                      // The number of the pass
      limit = size - 2;    // Keeps track of how far to go on a pass

  for (pass = 1; pass <= size - 1; ++pass)
  {
    for (i = 0; i <= limit; ++i)
      if (arr[i] > arr[i + 1])
        Swap_Int(arr[i], arr[i + 1]);
```

```
        --limit;
    }

    return;

}   // End of Bubble_Sort()
void Swap_Int(int& a, int& b)
{
    int temp;                   // Used for swapping integers

    temp = a;
    a = b;
    b = temp;

    return;
}   // End of Swap_Int()
```

Program Output

```
Please enter 10 integer quiz grades.

Enter grade for quiz 1: 40

Enter grade for quiz 2: 50

Enter grade for quiz 3: 80

Enter grade for quiz 4: 70

Enter grade for quiz 5: 80

Enter grade for quiz 6: 94

Enter grade for quiz 7: 85

Enter grade for quiz 8: 68

Enter grade for quiz 9: 73

Enter grade for quiz 10: 90

The grades are as follows:
    40    50    80    70    80    94    85    68    73    90

The grades in increasing order are as follows:
    40    50    68    70    73    80    80    85    90    94
```

The program uses four functions to do its work. The first argument in the first three functions is the name of the array that the function manipulates. Following the advice of Note 8.1 and how we defined the function Avg() in dem08-4.cpp, the second argument of these functions represents the size of the array. Remember that we do this to make the functions more useful. We can use these functions again should the need arise. The function Get_Grades() prompts for and obtains the grades from the user. Display_Array() displays the contents of an array. The function Bubble_Sort() sorts the array named as its first parameter. Finally, the fourth function, Swap_Int(), is the same function we used in dem08-3R.cpp. It interchanges the values of two integer variables using call by reference.

Besides the const integer variable NUM_QUIZZES, the only variable that main() needs is the integer array grade[]. Functions accomplish the program's processing. The first function call is to Get_Grades(). We pass the name of the array and the size of the array to this function. Get_Grades() prompts the user for 10 quiz grades and uses a for loop to obtain the grades. Recall from the previous section that when this function refers to the formal parameter arr[], it references the array grade[] in the function main(). Thus, the cout in the body of the for loop places the integer it obtains into the array grade[] in the function main(). See Figure 8.7.

Next, main() displays a message and calls the function Display_Array(). This function displays the elements in the array grade[], all on one line, in the order in which the user entered them.

Now main() calls Bubble_Sort(), which sorts the elements in the array grade[] into ascending order. Bubble_Sort() uses the variable i as the array subscript. The variable pass is a counter that keeps track of the number of the pass that the sort makes over the array. The for loop initializes the value of pass to one. The sort makes a total of size - 1 passes over an array having size elements. Therefore, the final value of pass is size - 1, which is reflected in the loop test condition.

The variable limit keeps track of how far to go on a pass. Recall from our discussion in Chapter 6 that the first pass of the bubble sort compares pairs of adjacent elements up to the last pair. Therefore, in an array with size elements, it compares elements 0 and 1, elements 1 and 2, elements 2 and 3, . . ., elements size - 2 and size - 1. Therefore, because the sort always compares an array element to the next array element, we initialize limit to size - 2. At the end of a pass, limit is decreased by

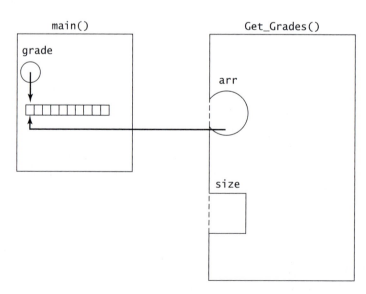

Figure 8.7

one, so that the next pass considers one less element. Remember that a pass places the next highest element at the right of the array so the sort does not have to consider this element again.

The if statement in the inner loop's body tests to see if the pair of adjacent array elements is out of order. If they are out of order, Swap_Int() interchanges the elements. If they are in order, the function does nothing to the pair.

When main() calls Bubble_Sort(), it passes the address of the array grade[]. Therefore, Bubble_Sort() manipulates the elements of the array grade[]. Thus, when Bubble_Sort() finishes sorting the array, the elements of grade[] are in ascending order. Then, main() displays a message and uses Display_Array() to display the elements of the array grade[], which are now in ascending order.

Exercise 8.2

In Exercises 1–3, code the prototype for the given function.

1. A function Avg() that has two arguments. The first argument is an array of doubles. The second argument is the size of the array. The function returns a double.

2. A function Max() that has two arguments. The first argument is an integer array and the second argument is the size of the array. The function returns an integer.

3. A function Find_It() that has three arguments. The first argument is an array of longs and the second argument is the size of the array. The third argument is the address of a long. The function returns an integer.

Experiments 8.2

1. Rewrite dem08-4.cpp so that it finds the average of the elements in an array of longs.

2. Rewrite the Swap_Int() function of dem08-5.cpp so that it uses call by address rather than call by reference. Compile, execute, and test the resulting program.

3. Rewrite dem08-5.cpp so that it sorts an array of doubles.

4. Rewrite dem08-5.cpp so that it sorts the array of integers into decreasing order instead of increasing order.

5. Rewrite dem08-5.cpp so that after it asks the user to enter the integers, it asks the user in which order the program is to display the array. The program should then sort the array in the given order. Recode the Bubble_Sort() function so that it takes a third parameter, which tells it the sort order (say, 1 for increasing, 0 for decreasing).

Programming Problems 8.2

1. Write a program that asks the user to enter three integers. The program should use the function Sort_Int() to sort the three integers into increasing order. Then the program should display the three integers in increasing order.

2. Write a program that asks the user to enter up to 20 integers. Store the integers in an array. Then the program should use the function Max() to find the largest integer in the array. Finally, the program should display the largest integer in the array.

3. Write a program that asks the user to enter up to 20 integers. Store the integers in an array of longs. Then, the program should ask the user to enter an integer. The program should use the function Find_It() to locate the integer in the array. The third argument in Find_It() is the address of the found integer. The function should return 1 if the integer is found and 0 otherwise. If the integer is found, the program should replace the integer by its negative and display the elements in the array. If the integer is not found, display an appropriate message.

8.3 STRINGS AND FUNCTIONS

Because a C-string is equivalent to a character pointer, passing a string to a function is equivalent to passing a pointer to a function. This section discusses how to pass strings to functions. We also discuss how to define and use a function that returns a pointer.

8.3.1 Using a Function to Count the Characters in a String

In this section, we discuss a program that asks the user to enter a string and then displays the number of characters in the string. The program uses a function Len_String() to count the number of characters in the string. Len_String() takes a string as its only argument and returns an integer equal to the number of characters in the string. Therefore, the following is the prototype for the function.

```
int Len_String(char*);
```

Following is the code for dem08-6.cpp.

```
// dem08-6.cpp

// This program calculates the number of characters input by the
// user on one line.  It uses the function Len_String() to count
// the characters.

#include <iostream>

using namespace std;

int Len_String(char*);

int main()
{
  char line[81];

  cout << "Enter a line of characters:" << endl;
  cin.getline(line,81);

  cout << endl;
  cout << "The string you entered has " << Len_String(line)
       << " characters" << endl;

  return 0;
}          // End of main()
```

```cpp
int Len_String(char* ch_ptr)
{
   int length = 0;

   while (*ch_ptr != '\0')
   {
      ++length;
      ++ch_ptr;
   }

   return length;
}        // End of Len_String()
```

Program Output

```
Enter a line of characters:
This is a test line.

The string you entered has 20 characters
```

The only variable main() requires is the array line[], which it uses to store the string entered by the user. The program prompts the user to enter a line of characters and obtains the line using cin.getline(). Finally, the program displays the length of the string by displaying the value returned by the function call Len_String(line).

The parameter declared in the function header for Len_String() is the character pointer ch_ptr. When main() executes the call Len_String(line), it passes the value of line (which is a pointer to the first element in the array line[]) to Len_String(). The value of line is assigned to ch_ptr. Thus, in Len_String(), ch_ptr initially points to the first character in the string that is stored in line[]. See Figure 8.8. The local variable length, which represents the length of the string, is initialized to zero.

The while loop in Len_String() tests the target of ch_ptr. If the target is not the null character, which is the end of the string, then the body of the loop counts that

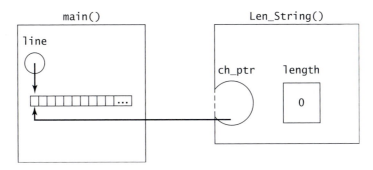

Figure 8.8

character by incrementing the variable length. Then, the loop increases the pointer by one. Thus, on the next iteration of the loop, ch_ptr points to the next character in the string. When the function exits the while loop, ch_ptr points to the null character and length equals the number of characters in the string. Therefore, the function returns the value of length.

8.3.2 Using a Function to Reverse a String in Place

In this section, we use a function to reverse a string in place, which means that the string is reversed in the array in which it is stored. The program does not make a copy of the string or merely display the string in reverse. Following is the code for dem08-7.cpp.

```
// dem08-7.cpp

// This program uses a function to reverse a string in place.

#include <iostream>

using namespace std;

void Reverse_String(char*);

int main()
{
    char line[81];

    cout << "Enter a string:" << endl;
    cin.getline(line, 81);

    Reverse_String(line);
    cout << endl;
    cout << "The string in reverse is as follows:" << endl;
    cout << line << endl;

    return 0;
}

void Reverse_String(char* ch_ptr)
{
    char* front;    // Points to the front of the string
    char* end;      // Points to the end of the string
    char temp;      // Required to exchange characters

    // Initialize pointers
    front = end = ch_ptr;

    // Find the end of the string
    while (*end != '\0')
        ++end;

    --end;

    // Exchange characters until pointers cross
    while (front < end)
    {
```

```
        temp    = *front;
        *front = *end;
        *end    = temp;
        ++front;
        --end;
    }

    return;
}
```

Program Output

```
Enter a string:
abcdefgh

The string in reverse is as follows:
hgfedcba
```

After obtaining the string from the user, the program makes the following function call.

```
Reverse_String(line);
```

The function `Reverse_String()` reverses the string in place. To do this, the function declares two character pointers, `front` and `end`. The function works as follows. The pointers `front` and `end` are initialized to point to the beginning of the string, which is pointed to by the parameter `ch_ptr`. Next, the function uses a `while` loop to set the pointer `end` to the end of the string. When the function exits the `while` loop, `end` points to the null character. Therefore, the pointer `end` is decreased by one to make it point to the last character in the string. See Figure 8.9a.

The second `while` loop reverses the string by exchanging the characters pointed to by `front` and `end`. If the pointer `front` is less than the pointer `end`, `front` points to a character to the left of the character pointed to by `end`. The loop body then exchanges the characters. Next, `front` is incremented and `end` is decremented. This readies `front` and `end` for the next exchange. See Figure 8.9b.

The loop terminates when `front` >= `end`. If `front` > `end`, the string has an even number of characters. Then, all the string's characters are reversed. See Figure 8.9c. If `front` = `end`, the string has an odd number of characters. Both `front` and `end` point to the middle character, which does not have to be moved. See Exercise 3.

8.3.3 A Function that Returns a Pointer

A function can return a pointer. Such functions are useful when processing strings. The next program, dem08-8.cpp, asks the user to enter a string. The function `Locate_Blank()` then attempts to find the first blank in the string. If it finds a blank, the function returns a pointer to the blank. If the function does not find a blank in the string, it returns the NULL pointer.

(a) After finding the last character in the string

(b) If front < end, swap characters, increment front and decrement end.

(c) Now, front > end. Therefore, all the characters have been swapped.

Figure 8.9

The prototype for Locate_Blank() shows that the return type is a pointer to a char. The only parameter is a pointer to a char, which is a string.

```
char* Locate_Blank(char*);
```

Following is the code for dem08-8.cpp

```
// dem08-8.cpp

// This program obtains a string from the user and replaces the first
// blank, if any, with a character obtained from the user.  It uses a
// function that returns a pointer to the first blank, or the NULL
// pointer if the string does not contain a blank.

#include <iostream>

using namespace std;

char* Locate_Blank (char*);

int main()
{
    char line[81];
    char* blank_ptr;
    char ch;

    cout << "Enter a string:" << endl;
    cin.getline(line, 81);

    blank_ptr = Locate_Blank(line);

    if (blank_ptr == NULL)
    {
        cout << endl;
        cout << "The string you entered does not contain a blank.";
    }
    else
    {
        cout << "\nEnter a character to replace the blank: ";
        ch = cin.get();
        *blank_ptr = ch;
        cout << "\nThe new string is as follows" << endl;
        cout << line;
    }

    cout << endl;
    return 0;
}

char* Locate_Blank(char* ch_ptr)

{
    while (*ch_ptr != '\0')

    {

        if (*ch_ptr == ' ')
```

```
        return ch_ptr;

    ++ch_ptr;

 }

 return NULL;
}
```

Program Output

Test Run 1

Enter a string:
asda sdvfsdv dffa

Enter a character to replace the blank: *

The new string is as follows

asda*sdvfsdv dffa

Test Run 2

Enter a string:
fsddfahfahfba

The string you entered does not contain a blank.

The function main() requires three variables. The character array line[] stores the string entered by the user. The character pointer ch_ptr will point to the first blank character in the string that is stored in line[]. The character variable ch stores the character that the user enters and that will be inserted in place of the first blank.

The program begins by prompting the user to enter a string and placing the string in the array line[]. The program then executes the following assignment.

```
blank_ptr = Locate_Blank(line);
```

Locate_Blank() returns a pointer to the first blank in the string if the string contains a blank. If the string does not contain a blank, the function returns the NULL pointer. In either case, the preceding assignment places the returned value into the pointer blank_ptr.

The if statement in main() tests the value of blank_ptr. If blank_ptr is NULL, the function did not find a blank in the string contained in line[]. Therefore, the program displays the appropriate message. If blank_ptr is not the NULL pointer, it points to the position of the first blank in the string that is stored in line[]. The program then prompts the user to enter a character. The cin.get() statement obtains the character, which is assigned to the variable ch. Then, the character in ch is assigned to the target of blank_ptr, which is the location of the first blank in the string. Finally, the program displays the new string.

The function Locate_Blank() works as follows. When main() calls the function, the formal parameter ch_ptr points to the first character in the array line[]. See Figure 8.10a. The while loop tests the characters in the string. If the target of ch_ptr is not the null character, the loop body tests the character. If the character is a blank, the function returns the value of ch_ptr, which points to the first blank in the string. See Figure 8.10b. If the target of ch_ptr is not a blank, the if statement does nothing, and ch_ptr is incremented to point to the next character. If the while encounters the null character, the string does not contain a blank. Therefore, the function returns the NULL pointer.

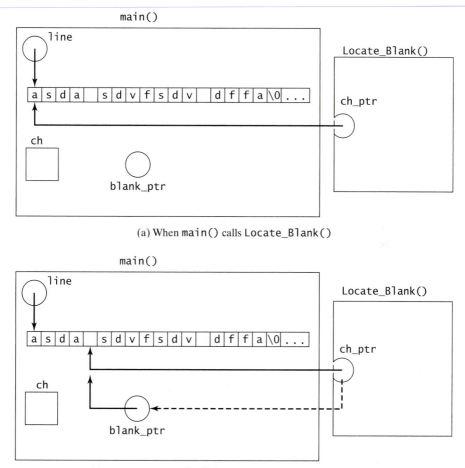

(a) When main() calls Locate_Blank()

(b) When Locate_Blank() finds a blank, the value of ch_ptr
is returned to main() and assigned to blank_ptr.

Figure 8.10

Exercises 8.3

In Exercises 1–2, code the prototype for the given function.

1. A function Count_Char() that has two arguments. The first argument is a string, and the second argument is a character. The function returns an integer.
2. A function Find_Char() that has two arguments. The first argument is a string, and the second argument is a character pointer. The function returns a character pointer.
3. Trace the values of the pointers front and end in dem08-7.cpp when the user enters a string with an odd number of characters such as "abcdefg".

Programming Problems 8.3

1. Write a program that first asks the user to enter a string and then asks the user to enter a character. The program should display the number of times the character appears in the string. Use the function Count_Char() of Exercise 1.
2. Write a program that first asks the user to enter a string and then asks the user to enter a character. The program should use the function Find_Char() (see Exercise 2) to determine the location of the first occurrence of the character in the string. The program should then ask the user for a replacement character. Then, the program should replace the original character by the replacement character and display the new string.

8.4 THE STANDARD LIBRARY STRING FUNCTIONS

The C++ language contains about twenty library functions that manipulate C-strings. These functions allow us to perform some common string operations such as finding the length of a string, assigning one string to another, or testing the equality of two strings. This section discusses some of the standard string functions.

The prototypes of all the string manipulation functions are in the header file **cstring**. (Note that in older implementations of C++, you had to use the header file string.h.) Thus, when writing a program that uses any of the functions introduced in this section, you must follow Note 8.3.

Note 8.3   The cstring Header File

A program that uses any of the string manipulation functions should contain the following preprocessor directive.

```
#include <cstring>
```

8.4.1 The Length of a String—The Function strlen()

The program dem08-6.cpp calculated the length of a string entered by the user, using the function Len_String(). We can also use the library function **strlen()** to find the length of a string. The function `strlen()` takes one argument, which must be a string (a character pointer), and returns the number of characters in the string. For example, consider the following declarations and assignment.

```
int length;
char greeting[6] = "Hello";
length = strlen(greeting);
```

The assignment places 5, the number of characters in the string, into the variable `length`. See Experiment 3, which asks you to rewrite dem08-6.cpp using `strlen()`.

8.4.2 String Assignment—The Function `strcpy()`

Using the following declarations, suppose we want to place a copy of the string `greeting1` into the string `greeting2`.

```
char greeting1[6] = "Hello";
char greeting2[10];
```

It is very tempting to code the following invalid assignment.

```
greeting2 = greeting1; // Invalid Assignment
```

However, this assignment causes a compiler error. Recall that the name of an array is a constant pointer whose value cannot change. The preceding assignment tries to assign a new value to the array name `greeting2`, which is invalid.

To assign one string to another in C++ requires the use of a function. The library function **strcpy()** assigns one string to another by copying the source string, character by character, to the target string. The `strcpy()` function has the following format.

```
strcpy(target-string-name, source-string-name)
```

The target string must be the first argument and the source string must be the second argument. When using `strcpy()` it is very important to keep Note 8.4 in mind.

> **Note 8.4   Make the Target of strcpy() Large Enough**
>
> It is the programmer's responsibility when using `strcpy()` to ensure that the target string is large enough to accommodate a copy of the source string. Failure to do so could cause `strcpy()` to overwrite other variables in the program.

Thus, to copy the string `greeting1` into the string `greeting2`, we can write the following statement.

```
strcpy(greeting2, greeting1);
```

The function `strcpy()` returns a pointer to the first character in the target string. Thus, assuming the following declaration at the beginning of the program,

```
char* ch_ptr;
```

the following assignment is valid.

```
ch_ptr = strcpy(greeting2, greeting1);
```

Thus, `ch_ptr` points to the first character of `greeting2[]`.
You could also code the following `cout` statement.

```
cout << strcpy(greeting2, greeting1));
```

This will display the string contained in `greeting2[]`.

We can use the fact that `greeting1` is a pointer to copy only a part of the string `greeting1` to `greeting2`. For example, the following statement copies the string "llo" to `greeting2`. See Figure 8.11a.

```
strcpy(greeting2, greeting1 + 2);
```

The `strcpy()` function begins copying characters at the address specified in its second argument and places the characters beginning at the address specified in its

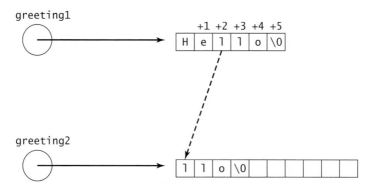

(a) After executing `strcpy(greeting2, greeting1 + 2);`

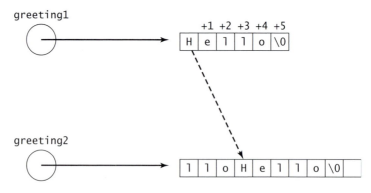

(b) After executing `strcpy(greeting2 + 3, greeting1);`

Figure 8.11

first argument. Thus, the following statements place the string "lloHello" into greeting2[]. See Figure 8.11b

```
strcpy(greeting2, greeting1 + 2);
strcpy(greeting2 + 3, greeting1);
```

8.4.3 Comparing Strings—The Function strcmp()

After copying the string greeting1 into the string greeting2, suppose that we want to verify that the strings are identical. Again, it is tempting to test for equality using the equality operator as follows.

```
greeting1 == greeting2
```

However, this expression tests the array names, which are pointers, for equality. An array name is a pointer to the address of the first element of the array. Because the arrays we are comparing are different, the comparison always yields false. See Experiment 1.

To compare two strings, we can use the library function strcmp(), which has the following format.

```
strcmp(string1, string2)
```

The arguments string1 and string2 must be strings, which are character pointers. The function strcmp() returns an integer based on the comparison of string1 to string2 according to Table 8.1.

The words "precedes" and "follows" in the previous table need some clarification. C++ stores a character as an integer (see Appendix A). The natural order of the integers gives an order to all the characters in the ASCII character set. One character precedes another if the decimal value of the first character is less than the decimal value of the second. Similarly, if the decimal value of one character is greater than the decimal value of a second character, the first character follows the second. We refer to this ordering of the characters in the ASCII character set as the **ASCII collating sequence**.

Referring to Table 8.2, we see that the character $ (decimal value 38) precedes the character + (decimal value 43). The character r (decimal value 114) follows character R (decimal value 52).

Table 8.2 shows that all the digits precede the uppercase letters, which precede the lowercase letters. Also the digits, the uppercase, and the lowercase letters retain their usual order—for the digits (numeric order) and for the letters (alphabetic order).

When strcmp() compares two strings, it begins comparing the first characters of each string. If the characters are equal, it compares the next pair of characters, and so on.

TABLE 8.1

Result of the Compare	Value Returned by strcmp()
string1 is identical to string2	0
string1 precedes string2	negative integer
string1 follows string2	positive integer

TABLE 8.2

Decimal	Hex	Symbol	Decimal	Hex	Symbol	Decimal	Hex	Symbol
32	20	(blank)	64	40	@	96	60	`
33	21	!	65	41	A	97	61	a
34	22	"	66	42	B	98	62	b
35	23	#	67	43	C	99	63	c
36	24	$	68	44	D	100	64	d
37	25	%	69	45	E	101	65	e
38	26	&	70	46	F	102	66	f
39	27	'	71	47	G	103	67	g
40	28	(	72	48	H	104	68	h
41	29	)	73	49	I	105	69	i
42	2A	*	74	4A	J	106	6A	j
43	2B	+	75	4B	K	107	6B	k
44	2C	,	76	4C	L	108	6C	l
45	2D	-	77	4D	M	109	6D	m
46	2E	.	78	4E	N	110	6E	n
47	2F	/	79	4F	O	111	6F	o
48	30	0	80	50	P	112	70	p
49	31	1	81	51	Q	113	71	q
50	32	2	82	52	R	114	72	r
51	33	3	83	53	S	115	73	s
52	34	4	84	54	T	116	74	t
53	35	5	85	55	U	117	75	u
54	36	6	86	56	V	118	76	v
55	37	7	87	57	W	119	77	w
56	38	8	88	58	X	120	78	x
57	39	9	89	59	Y	121	79	y
58	3A	:	90	5A	Z	122	7A	z
59	3B	;	91	5B	[	123	7B	{
60	3C	<	92	5C	\	124	7C	|
61	3D	=	93	5D	]	125	7D	}
62	3E	>	94	5E	^	126	7E	~
63	3F	?	95	5F	_			

The character-by-character comparison continues until either the end of one or both strings is encountered or until an unequal pair of characters is encountered. If an unequal pair of characters is encountered, the function returns a positive or negative number depending on how the unequal characters compare in the ASCII collating sequence. If each pair of characters is the same and the end of both strings has been encountered, the strings are identical. If each pair of characters is the same and only the end of one string has been encountered, then the string having more characters follows the other string. In this case, the function returns the appropriate value. Several examples should help to clarify how strcmp() compares strings.

Suppose the following declarations and initializations.

```
char string1[5] = "abcd";
char string2[5] = "abCd";
```

```
char string3[7] = "abcd  ";
char string4[5] = "abCd";
```

strcmp(string1, string2) returns a positive integer because the character c follows the character C in the ASCII collating sequence. Note that the order in which you compare strings affects the return value. For example, strcmp(string2, string1) returns a negative integer because C precedes c.

strcmp(string1, string3) returns a negative integer. Although the strings are identical up to the character d, string3 has more characters. Therefore, string1 precedes string3.

strcmp(string2, string4) returns zero because the strings are identical.

See Experiment 2 for some hints on the exact value that strcmp() returns when the strings it compares are unequal.

8.4.4 Pasting Strings Together—The Function strcat()

Sometimes it is necessary to paste one string onto the end of another—a process that we call **concatenation**. For example, suppose the following declarations and initializations.

```
char string1[27] = "abcdef";
char string2[27] = "ghij";
```

Now suppose that we want to paste the contents of string2 onto the end of the contents of string1. Therefore, after the pasting, string1 should contain the string "abcdefghij". The library function strcat() concatenates two strings. It has the following format.

```
strcat(target-string, source-string)
```

The function pastes the source string onto the end of the target string. It is the programmer's responsibility to ensure that the array that holds the target string is large enough to contain the result of the concatenation.

Note 8.5   Make the Target of strcat() Large Enough

It is the programmer's responsibility when using strcat() to ensure that the target string is large enough to accommodate a copy of the source string. Failure to do so could cause strcat() to overwrite other variables in the program.

Thus, to paste string2 onto the end of string1, we can execute the following.

```
strcat(string1, string2);
```

See Figure 8.12. The function strcat() places the first character of string2 where the null character in string1 was located and copies the null character of string2 into string1. The result is a valid string. Note also that strcat() does not place blanks after the original contents of string1. The function strcat() returns a pointer to the first character of the target string.

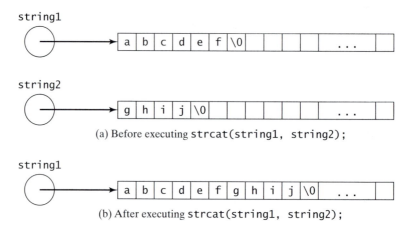

string1

(a) Before executing `strcat(string1, string2);`

string1

(b) After executing `strcat(string1, string2);`

Figure 8.12

8.4.5 Using the String Functions—dem08-9.cpp

The following program, dem08-9.cpp, uses the string functions that we introduced in this section. The program asks the user to enter his or her first name and last name. Then the program concatenates the first and last names to form the full name. Finally, the program asks the user to enter his or her full name. If the full name that the user enters equals the full name that the program constructed, then the program displays a congratulation message. Otherwise, the program asks the user to execute the program again.

```cpp
// dem08-9.cpp

// This program uses several string library functions.

#include <iostream>
#include <cstring>

using namespace std;

int main()
{
   char first_name[21];
   char last_name[31];
   char full_name[51];
   char full_name_chk[51];

   cout << "Please enter your first name: ";
   cin.getline(first_name, 21);

   cout << endl;
   cout << "Please enter your last name: ";
   cin.getline(last_name, 31);

   strcpy(full_name, first_name);
   strcat(full_name, " ");
   strcat(full_name, last_name);
```

```
cout << endl << endl;
cout << "Hello " << full_name << " Welcome to the program." << endl
     << endl;
cout << "Your first name has " << strlen(first_name)
     << " characters in it." << endl << endl;
cout << "Your last name has "<< strlen(last_name)
     << " characters in it." << endl << endl;

cout << "Now please enter your first and last names" << endl;
cout << "separated by one space: ";

cin.getline(full_name_chk, 51);

if (strcmp(full_name, full_name_chk) == 0)
{
  cout << endl;
  cout << "Congratulations! You followed the instructions." << endl;
}
else
{
  cout << endl;
  cout << "You did not follow the instructions!" << endl;
  cout << "Please try the program again." << endl;
}

return 0;
}
```

Program Output

Please enter your first name: **Adam**

Please enter you last name: **Zapple**

Hello Adam Zapple. Welcome to the program.

Your first name has 4 characters in it.

Your last name has 6 characters in it.

Now please enter your first and last names
separated by one space: **Adam Zapple**

Congratulations! You followed the instructions.

The program begins with the declarations of four character arrays—one to contain the first name, one to contain the last name, one to contain the full name that the program constructs, and one to contain the full name that the user will enter.

The program begins by prompting for and obtaining the first and last names of the user. Then the program constructs the user's full name. First, strcpy() copies first_name into full_name (Figure 8.13a). Then, strcat() pastes a blank onto the

(a) After executing strcpy(full_name, first_name);

(b) After executing strcat(full_name, " ");

(c) After executing strcat(full_name, last_name);

Figure 8.13

end of the contents of full_name (Figure 8.13b). Finally, strcat() pastes last_name onto the end of full_name (Figure 8.13c).

Next, the program greets the user using full_name and displays the number of characters in the user's first and last names. Then, the program asks the user to enter his or her first and last names separated by a space and places the name into full_name_chk[]. Then, strcmp() decides whether the contents of full_name_chk are the same as the contents of full_name, which the program constructed earlier. The program issues an appropriate message, depending on the outcome of this test.

Experiments 8.4

1. Write a short program that declares the following strings

```
char string1[] = "Hello";
char string2[] = "Hello";
```

and attempts to test the strings for equality by testing the following condition.

```
if (string1 == string2)
```

Attempt to compile the program. If it compiles successfully, try to execute the program. What are the results?

2. In this chapter, you learned that `strcmp()` returns a negative integer if its first argument precedes its second, and a positive integer if its first argument follows its second. Try to discover exactly what integer is returned by `strcmp()` when its arguments are not equal. As a hint, display the values `strcmp()` returns for the following pairs of strings.

   ```
   "abcde"   "abdde"
   "abcde"   "abede"
   "abcde"   "abbde"
   "abcde"   "abade"
   ```

3. Rewrite dem08-6.cpp using the library function `strlen()` instead of the user-defined function `Len_String()`.

Programming Problems 8.4

1. Write your own string assignment function `Copy_String()`. The function should copy the string that is its second argument to the string that is its first argument. The function should return a pointer to the first character of the first argument. Test your function by calling it from a simple program.

2. Write your own string compare function `Comp_String()`. The function should take two string arguments and return an integer. The function should return 0 if the strings that are its arguments are equal. If the first string follows the second, the function should return a positive number. If the first string precedes the second, the function should return a negative integer. (To help decide which number to return, see Experiment 2.) Write a program that thoroughly tests your function.

3. Write your own string concatenation function `Cat_String()`. The function should have two string arguments and should paste the second argument onto the end of the first. The function should return a pointer to the first character of the first argument. Write a program that thoroughly tests your function.

4. Write a program that constructs a user ID number from the user's first name, last name, and social security number. The program should prompt the user to enter his or her first name, last name, and social security number. Construct the ID number by taking the first two letters of the last name, followed by the second letter of the first name, followed by the middle three digits of the social security number. All characters are to be converted to uppercase. (For example, the ID number of Ron Zoni, who has social security number 123456789, is ZOO456.) The program should then display the newly constructed ID number. Finally, the program should prompt the user to enter the ID number. If the user correctly enters the number, congratulate the user and end the program. If the user does not enter the correct ID number, display it again and ask the user to memorize the ID number. Then end the program.

5. Write a program that asks the user to enter a list of words, one at a time. Store the words in a two-dimensional character array, one word in each row. Assume that no word is more than 20 characters long and that there are, at most, 100 words.

The program should then sort the array of words into increasing alphabetical order. Once the array is sorted, the program should display the alphabetized list.

6. Write a program that validates a date entered by the user. The program should ask the user to enter the month, day, and year. The month is to be entered by name and the day and year as integers. For example, the user might enter March 30, and 2005 for the month, day, and year. The function `Validate_Date()` should determine if the entered date is valid by returning `true` if the date is valid and `false` otherwise. For example, the date March 30, 1999 is valid, but the date February 29, 2006 is not. The program should display an appropriate message. Recall that a leap year is a year that is divisible by four. Remember to validate the month name.

8.5 CHARACTER CLASSIFICATION AND CONVERSION FUNCTIONS

The standard C++ library contains several functions that are useful in string manipulation programs. In this section, we consider two groups of such functions—the character classification functions and the character conversion functions.

8.5.1 The Character Classification Functions

It is sometimes necessary to classify characters according to common categories. For example, it may be necessary to decide whether a character is a punctuation character. Table 8.3 lists some C++ standard library character-classification functions. All the functions names begin with "is" and take a single argument of type `int`. Remember that you can store a character in a variable of type `int`. These functions also work properly if passed an argument of type `char`. Each function returns a nonzero (that is, true) value if the tested character is in the specified category, and returns zero (that is, false) if the character is not in the specified category. The prototypes of the functions are in the header file **cctype**.

TABLE 8.3 CHARACTER CLASSIFICATION FUNCTIONS

Prototypes in cctype

Function name	Category
`isalnum(ch)`	A digit or letter (either case)
`isalpha(ch)`	A letter (either case)
`isdigit(ch)`	The digits 0 through 9
`islower(ch)`	A lowercase letter
`ispunct(ch)`	A punctuation character (that is, a character that is not a space, not a digit, and not a letter)
`isspace(ch)`	A white-space character (blank, newline, carriage return, vertical tab, or form feed)
`isupper(ch)`	an uppercase letter

The following program, dem08-10.cpp, illustrates some character classification functions. It asks the user to enter a string and counts the number of characters in several categories.

```cpp
// dem08-10.cpp

// This program asks the user to enter a string.  It uses the
// character classification functions to count the number of
// characters in several categories and displays the results.

#include <iostream>
#include <cctype>
#include <iomanip>

using namespace std;

int main()
{
  char line[81];

  char* ch_ptr;
  int digit_count = 0,
      lower_count = 0,
      punct_count = 0,
      space_count = 0,
      upper_count = 0,
      total_chars;

  cout << "Enter a line of characters:" << endl;
  cin.getline(line, 81);

  ch_ptr = line;

  while (*ch_ptr != '\0')
  {
    if (isdigit(*ch_ptr))
      ++digit_count;
    else if (islower(*ch_ptr))
      ++lower_count;
    else if (ispunct(*ch_ptr))
      ++punct_count;
    else if (isspace(*ch_ptr))
      ++space_count;
    else if (isupper(*ch_ptr))
      ++upper_count;
    ++ch_ptr;
  }

  total_chars = digit_count + lower_count + punct_count
                 + space_count + upper_count;

  cout << endl;
  cout <<"The string contains the following:" << endl << endl;
  cout <<"Digits:                 "  << digit_count << endl;
  cout <<"Lowercase Letters:      " << setw(2) << lower_count <<endl;
```

```
cout <<"Punctuation Characters: " << setw(2) << punct_count << endl;
cout <<"White Space Characters: " << setw(2) << space_count << endl;
cout <<"Uppercase Letters:       " << setw(2) << upper_count << endl;
cout <<"--------------------------" << endl;
cout <<"Total Characters:        " << setw(2) << total_chars << endl;

return 0;
}
```

Program Output

```
Enter a line of characters:
ahlAd,,.>  B33@?,a    ;jjccMM.

The string contains the following:

Digits:                  3
Lowercase Letters:       8
Punctuation Characters:  9
White Space Characters:  3
Uppercase Letters:       4
--------------------------
Total Characters:        27
```

The program counts only three white-space characters. There are two blanks after the > character and there is a tab character after the ,a characters. Note also that the >, @, and ? are counted as punctuation characters.

The program itself is simple. After obtaining the string from the user, a while loop tests each character in the string. A nested if statement tests the character to see in which of the five categories the character belongs and increments the appropriate accumulator. When the loop ends, the program displays the results.

8.5.2 The Character Conversion Functions

The standard C++ library also contains several functions that are useful for converting individual characters.

If the int variable ch contains a lowercase letter, the function **toupper(ch)** returns the corresponding uppercase letter as an integer. If the int variable ch contains an uppercase letter, the function **tolower(ch)** returns the corresponding lowercase letter as an integer. In all other cases, the functions return the argument unchanged. Both function prototypes are contained in cctype.

The program dem08-11.cpp asks the user to enter a string and then displays the string in all uppercase and then in all lowercase.

```
// dem08-11.cpp

// This program asks the user to enter a string and then uses the
// functions toupper() and tolower() to display the string in all
// uppercase and all lowercase.
```

```cpp
#include <iostream>
#include <cctype>

using namespace std;

int main()
{
    char line[81];
    char* ch_ptr;

    cout <<"Enter a line of characters:" << endl;
    cin.getline(line, 81);

    cout << endl;
    cout <<"The line in all uppercase is:" << endl;
    ch_ptr = line;
    while (*ch_ptr != '\0')
    {
      cout << char(toupper(*ch_ptr));
      ++ch_ptr;
    }

    cout << endl;
    cout <<"The line in all lowercase is:" << endl;

    ch_ptr = line;
    while (*ch_ptr != '\0')
    {
      cout << char(tolower(*ch_ptr));
      ++ch_ptr;
    }

    cout << endl;

    return 0;
}
```

Program Output

```
Enter a line of characters:
abc123.;]XYZ

The line in all uppercase is:
ABC123.;]XYZ
The line in all lowercase is:
abc123.;]xyz
```

Both parts of the program work in essentially the same way, so we shall explain how the program displays the line in all uppercase. After obtaining the string from the user, the program initializes the pointer ch_ptr to the first character in the array line[]. The while loop then converts and displays each character in the string.

The function `toupper()` returns in integer form the uppercase version of the target of `ch_ptr` if the target is a lowercase letter. Otherwise, it returns the target of `ch_ptr` unchanged. Because the return value of `toupper()` is an integer, we must type cast the return value so that `cout` displays the value in character form rather than in integer form. See Experiment 2. After `cout` displays the returned character, the pointer `ch_ptr` is incremented so it points to the next character on the next loop iteration.

8.5.3 Putting the Functions to Work—Testing for a Palindrome

The words "otto" and "mom" are **palindromes**—they read the same forward and backward. A string can also be a palindrome if we ignore spacing, case, and punctuation. For example, the string "Madam, I'm Adam" is a palindrome. In this subsection, we develop program prb08-1.cpp, which asks the user to enter a string (up to 80 characters) and decides whether the string is a palindrome.

It is simple in principle to decide if a word is a palindrome. Check to see if the first and last characters are the same. If they are not equal, the string is not a palindrome. If they are equal, check the second and next-to-last characters. If they are unequal, the string is not a palindrome. If they are equal, move to the next pair of characters and continue checking. See Figure 8.14a. If you arrive at the middle of the word and all pairs of characters are equal, the word is a palindrome. See Figure 8.14b.

When checking a string to see if it is a palindrome, we must be aware that the string can contain blanks, mixed case letters, and punctuation characters. Therefore, to test a string, we must first rid the string of all blanks and punctuation characters, and then change all the characters to a common case. The pseudocode for the palindrome problem follows.

Prompt for and obtain a string.
Copy only the alphabetic characters to form a new string.
Convert the new string, which is a single word, to lowercase.
Test the resulting word for a palindrome.

Suppose that the user enters the string "Madam, I'm Adam!" and the program stores the string in the array `line[]`. See Figure 8.15a. To clear the string of blanks and punctuation characters, the program copies the string into another array, `buffer[]`. If the character to be copied is an alphabetic character, the program copies it. Otherwise, the program does not copy it and skips to the next character. See Figure 8.15b. Next, the program changes all the characters in `buffer[]` to lowercase. See Figure 8.15c. Finally, the program checks to see if the resulting word is a palindrome. See Figure 8.15d.

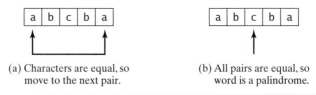

(a) Characters are equal, so move to the next pair.

(b) All pairs are equal, so word is a palindrome.

Figure 8.14

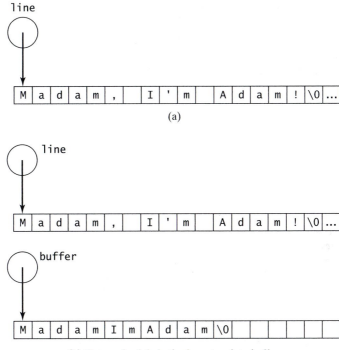

(a)

(b) Copy only alphabetic characters into buffer.
Do not copy nonalphabetic characters.

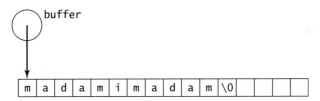

(c) All characters changed to lowercase.

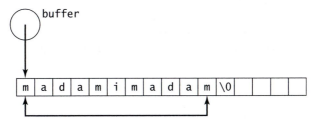

(d) Check all pairs of characters to test for palindrome.

Figure 8.15

Following is the code for prb08-1.cpp and a sample program run.

```cpp
// prb08-1.cpp

// This program uses the string and character library functions to
// decide whether a string entered by the user is a palindrome.
// A palindrome is a string that, disregarding case and punctuation,
// reads the same backward and forward.

#include <iostream>
#include <cctype>

using namespace std;

void Copy_Alpha(char*, char*);
void Convert_To_Lower(char*);
bool  Palindrome(char*);

int main()
{
  char line[81];
  char buffer[81];

  // Prompt for and obtain a string

  cout <<"Enter a string:" << endl;
  cin.getline(line, 81);

  // Copy only the alphabetic characters

  Copy_Alpha(buffer, line);

  // Convert the string to all lowercase

  Convert_To_Lower(buffer);

  // Test the result for a palindrome

  if ( Palindrome(buffer) )
  {
    cout << endl;
    cout <<"The string you entered is a palindrome." << endl;
  }
  else
  {
    cout << endl;
    cout <<"The string you entered is not a palindrome."  <<endl;
  }

  return 0;

} // End of main()

void Copy_Alpha(char* target, char* source)
{
  while (*source != '\0')
  {
    if (isalpha(*source))
```

```cpp
    {
      *target = *source;
      ++target;
    }

    ++source;
  }
  *target = '\0';

  return;

} // End of Copy_Alpha()

void Convert_To_Lower(char* source)
{
  while (*source != '\0')
  {
    *source = tolower(*source);
    ++source;
  }

  return;

}   // End of Convert_To_Lower()

bool Palindrome (char* source)
{
  char* start;
  char* end;

  start = end = source;

  while (*end != '\0')
    ++end;

  --end;

  while (start < end)
    if (*start != *end)
      return false;
    else
    {
      ++start;
      --end;
    }

  return true;
} // End of Palindrome()
```

Program Output

```
Enter a string:
Madam, I'm Adam!

The string you entered is a palindrome.
```

The header file `cctype` is included at the beginning of the program because the program's functions use several standard library character classification and conversion functions. The program handles each of the major steps in the pseudocode by executing a function. `Copy_Alpha()` takes the string that is its second argument and copies only the alphabetic characters into the string that is its first argument. Thus, the prototype for the function declares it as a `void` function with two arguments that are character pointers.

The function `Convert_To_Lower()` converts the string that is its argument to all lowercase. Thus, we declare it as a `void` function with a single argument that is a character pointer.

Finally, the function `Palindrome()` tests the string that is its only argument. It assumes that the string is a single word. If the string is a palindrome, the function returns `true`. If the string is not a palindrome, the function returns `false`. Thus, the function's return type is `bool`.

The program begins by prompting the user for a string and placing it in the array `line[]`. The program then executes the function `Copy_Alpha()`, which copies only the alphabetic characters from `line[]` and into the array `buffer[]`. To do this, the function tests each character in the string pointed to by `source`, which is the string stored in `line[]`. If the character is an alphabetic character, the target of `source` is assigned to the target of the pointer `target` and the pointer `target` is incremented. The pointer `source` is then incremented to point to the next character. Thus, if the character that was tested is not alphabetic, it is not copied. When the function exits the `while` loop, the "cleaned" string has been copied to the target string except for the null character. Therefore, the function assigns the null character to the target of the pointer `target`.

Next, `main()` executes the function `Convert_To_Lower()`, which converts all the characters in the array `buffer[]` to lowercase. The function does this by replacing each character in the string by its lowercase equivalent.

Finally, `main()` tests the returned value of the function `Palindrome()`. If the value is `true`, the string stored in `buffer[]` is a palindrome and the program displays an appropriate message. If the value is `false`, the string stored in `buffer[]` is not a palindrome and the program displays an appropriate message.

The `Palindrome()` function begins by initializing the character pointers `start` and `end` to point to the beginning of the string being tested. The first `while` loop slides the pointer `end` to the null character at the end of the string. Then, `end` is decremented so that it points to the last character in the string. Now, `start` points to the first character in the string and `end` points to the last character in the string. See Figure 8.16a. The `if` statement in the body of the next `while` loop tests the characters pointed to by `start` and `end`. If they are unequal, the string is not a palindrome and the function returns `false`. Otherwise, `start` is incremented and `end` is decremented. Thus, `start` and `end` point to the next pair of characters to be tested. See Figure 8.16b. The `while` loop continues as long as `start` is less than `end`. If at some point `start` equals `end`, there is an odd number of characters in the string. The middle character equals itself and all pairs of characters tested are equal. See Figure 8.16c. If at some point `start` exceeds `end`, there is an even number of characters in the string. In either case, all pairs of

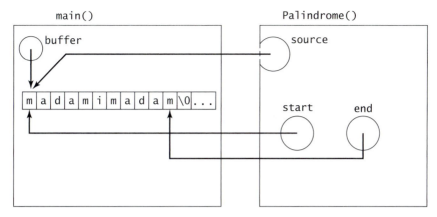

(a) Initially, start points to the first character and end points to the last character.

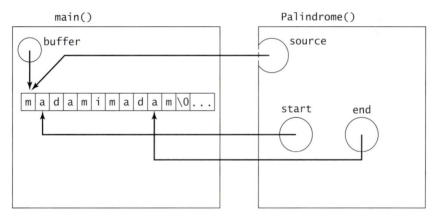

(b) If first pair are equal, increment start and decrement end to point to the next pair.

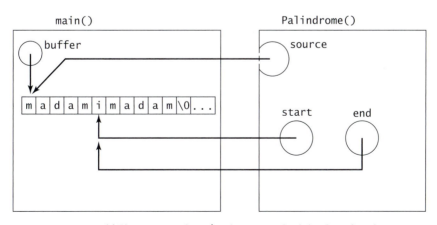

(c) If start equals end and no unequal pair has been found, the word is a palindrome.

Figure 8.16

characters tested are equal and, therefore, the string is a palindrome. The function then returns true.

8.5.4 Numeric Conversion Functions and Numeric Validation

Suppose the following declaration and statements.

```
int i;
cout << "Enter an integer: ";
cin >> i;
```

Consider what happens when the user enters an integer, for example, 173. The entered "integer" is actually a three-character string, which is stored in the input buffer. The cin statement converts the three-character string into the equivalent binary integer (10101101) and then stores the binary in the integer variable i. The conversion is completely automatic and transparent to the programmer and user.

Although using cin is very easy and intuitive, it is not very safe. If the user enters a non-integer in response to the prompt, the result is unpredictable, as shown in the output to dem08-12.cpp. You will probably obtain different output on your computer.

```
//dem08-12.cpp

#include <iostream>

using namespace std;

int main()
{
    int i;

    cout << "Enter an integer: ";

    cin >> i;

    cout << endl;
    cout << "The value of i is " << i << endl;

    return 0;
}
```

Program Output

Enter an integer: **ASD**

The value of i is   -858993460

If the user makes such a mistake in a program in which arithmetic is done on the entered value, the results of the program will be in error. To avoid this, the program can place the user's response into a character array, using, for example, cin.getline(), and then test the string to see if it represents an integer (or other type of data that the program requires). If the program decides that the entered data is a valid integer, then the program must convert the string into the equivalent number. There are three standard library functions that can make the conversion from a string into a number: atoi(), which converts a string into an integer; atol(), which converts a string into along; and atof(), which converts a string into a double. To use these functions, you must place #include **<cstdlib>** in your program.

Note 8.6   Numeric Conversion Functions

The following functions convert a numeric string into a number. In each case, the function returns the number that the numeric string represents. Each function stops converting the string when it encounters a nonnumeric character. If the function cannot convert the string into a number, the function returns zero. You must #include <cstdlib> to use the functions.

atoi() – converts a numeric string into an integer.
atol() – converts a numeric string into a long.
atof() – converts a numeric string into a double.

For example, consider the following declarations and assignment.

```
char char_int[] = "123";
char char_long[] = "50000";
char char_double[] = "67.89";

int i;
long long_i;
double db;

i = atoi(char_int);
long_i = atol(char_long);
db = atof(char_double);
```

In the first assignment, atoi(char_int)converts the character string "123" into the equivalent integer and stores it in the int variable i. The second assignment works in a similar way, converting the string "50000" into the equivalent long and storing it in long_i. The third assignment converts the string "67.89", which is stored in char_double[], into the equivalent double and stores the double in the variable db.

The following program illustrates the use of atoi(). Using atol() and atof() are similar.

```
//dem08-13.cpp

//This program illustrates the use of the function atoi().

#include <iostream>
#include <cstdlib>

using namespace std;
```

```
int main()
{
  char buffer[51];

  int i;

  cout << "Enter an integer: ";

  cin.getline(buffer, 51);

  i = atoi(buffer);

  cout << endl;
  cout << "The value of i is " << i << endl;

  return 0;
}
```

Program Output – Valid Data

```
Enter an integer: 173

The value of i is 173
```

Program Output – Invalid Data

```
Enter an integer: ASD

The value of i is 0
```

In the program, the input data is placed into the character array buffer[] using cin.getline(). Then the function atoi() converts the input string into the equivalent integer. Note how this works with valid input data and with invalid input data. With valid data, this program behaves like dem08-12.cpp. However, with invalid input data, the program places 0 into i because the atoi() function cannot convert the string into an integer.

The real power of this technique for inputting numeric data as a character string and then converting it into a number lies in the ability to validate the string as an integer (or decimal number) and then, if it is valid, convert the string into an integer (or double). Program dem08-14.cpp illustrates the technique.

```
//dem08-14.cpp

//This program illustrates the use of atoi() to validate user input

#include <iostream>
#include <cstdlib>
#include <cctype>

using namespace std;

bool Validate_Integer(char*);

int main()
{
  char buffer[51];
```

```
    int i;

    cout << "Enter an integer: ";

    cin.getline(buffer, 51);

    if (Validate_Integer(buffer))
    {
       i = atoi(buffer);
       cout << endl;
       cout << "The value of i is " << i <<endl;
    }
    else
    {
       cout << endl;
       cout << "You did not enter a valid integer." << endl;
    }

    return 0;
}
bool Validate_Integer(char* ch_ptr)
{

    //Skip initial white space
    while ( isspace(*ch_ptr) && *ch_ptr != '\0')
       ++ch_ptr;

    //If an empty line was input, return false
    if (*ch_ptr == '\0')
       return false;

    //Skip a leading plus or minus
    if (*ch_ptr == '-' || *ch_ptr == '+')
       ++ch_ptr;

    //Traverse string until a non-digit or end of the string
    while (isdigit(*ch_ptr) && *ch_ptr != '\0')
       ++ch_ptr;

    //If the end of the string was reached, the string is an integer
    if (*ch_ptr == '\0')
       return true;
    else
       return false;
}
```

Program Output – Valid Data

```
Enter an integer: -1234

The value of i is -1234
```

Program Output—Invalid Data—Run 1

Enter an integer: **ASD**

You did not enter a valid integer.

Program Output—Invalid Data—Run 2

Enter an integer: **123A**

You did not enter a valid integer.

The program uses the function `Validate_Integer()` to validate user input. The function's argument is the character array in which is stored the string to be tested. The function returns `true` if the string represents a valid integer, and returns `false` otherwise. In `main()`, the user is prompted for an integer. The input data is stored as a string in the array `buffer[]` using `cin.getline()`. The `if` statement tests the value returned by `Validate_Integer()`. If the integer string is valid, the string is converted into an integer and stored in the variable `i`. If the integer string is not valid, an error message is displayed.

The function `Validate_Integer()` works by testing the string one character at a time. First, a `while` loop skips all white space. It is possible that the user entered an empty line (that is, responded to the prompt by hitting the enter key). The `if` statement tests to see if the target of `ch_ptr` is the null byte. If it is, then the user did not enter any nonwhite space characters and the function returns `false`. Assuming the function did not return to the calling program, the target of the pointer `ch_ptr` must be a nonwhite space character. The next `if` statement skips a leading + or – sign. If no sign is present, the `if` statement does nothing. The next `while` loop moves through the string one character at a time until it reaches a non-digit or the end of the string. Recall that when a `while` loop ends, the loop condition is false. Therefore, either the target of `ch_ptr` is not a digit or the target of `ch_ptr` is the null character. The last `if` statement decides why the previous `while` loop stopped. If the target of `ch_ptr` is the null character, then the pointer went through the entire string without encountering a non-digit. Therefore, the user entered an integer and the function returns `true`. Otherwise, the string contains a non-digit and the function returns `false`.

Exercises 8.5

1. Write a function that returns 1 if its character argument is a digit, a letter, or a space, and returns 0 otherwise. Use as many library functions as you can.
2. Write a function `Invert_Case()` that has one argument, which is a string. The function should not return a value. The function should reverse the case of the characters in the string. Thus, a lowercase letter should get converted to uppercase and vice versa. A non-letter should not be changed.
3. Write a function `Validate_Double()` that validates a numeric string to see if it represents a valid decimal number. Remember that a decimal number can begin

with a leading sign and can contain only one decimal point. There can be any number of digits to the left and right of the decimal point. The function should return 1 if the string is valid; otherwise, it should return 0.

Experiments 8.5

1. Replace the nested `if` statement in dem08-10 by an equivalent `switch` statement. Compile, execute, and test the resulting program.
2. Remove the type casts from the `cout` statements in dem08-11.cpp. Compile and execute the resulting program. Explain the program's output.
3. Enter 17A in response to the prompt in dem08-13.cpp. What happens? Explain.
4. Recode dem08-14.cpp so that it asks for and validates a `double`.
5. Write a program that asks the user to enter a decimal number. Use the function `Validate_Double()` of Exercise 3 to validate the user's response.

Programming Problems 8.5

1. Recode Programming Problem 1, Section 5.3, to include validation of the number of years entered by the user. The entered value must be a valid integer.
2. Recode Programming Problem 2, Section 5.3, to include validation of the credit limit and account balance. Both must be valid decimal numbers. Use the function `Validate_Double()` of Exercise 3.
3. Take any program that you previously wrote and include validation of any integer and decimal input data.

8.6 DYNAMIC MEMORY ALLOCATION

8.6.1 The Heap

In program prb07-1.cpp of Chapter 7, we stored the names of the days of the week using a two-dimensional array. However, we saw in the program prb07-2.cpp that we could use memory more efficiently by using an array of pointers to store these names. This was possible because we knew the values of the strings that we wanted to store, namely, the names of the days of the week.

Now, suppose that we want to write a program that needs to store the names of five clients, which are to be entered into the program by the user. You could store the names in a two-dimensional array, one name in each row. The problem with this method is that all the rows must be the same size. Therefore, you must ensure that the rows are large enough to store the longest name. Suppose that the longest name that you can imagine is 80 characters long. Therefore, you must declare the array as follows.

```
char client[5][81];
```

The array `client[][]` requires 5 × 81 = 405 bytes of storage. However, the average name may have only 15 to 20 characters. Thus, you probably will waste about 300 or more of the 405 bytes allocated to the array `client[][]`. Emulating what we did in Chapter 7, can we save memory by using an array of pointers instead of a two-dimensional array? The problem we have if we try using an array of pointers is that we do not know in advance the values of the strings we need to store, as we did in Chapter 7 for the names of the days of the week. Somehow, we must have the user enter a name and then store this name in the computer's memory using an appropriate amount of storage.

It is possible in C++ to allocate memory for variables, arrays, and so on, from a special area of memory called the **heap** whenever the memory is needed by the program. Heap memory is completely under your control in the sense that you can allocate and deallocate the memory when you deem it necessary. The process of allocating and deallocating memory as a program is executing is called **dynamic memory allocation**.

The C++ operator new allocates heap memory, and the operator delete deallocates heap memory. The operator new takes one argument, the data type of the storage we want to allocate, and returns a pointer to the allocated space. For example, assume the following.

```
int* i_ptr;
i_ptr = new int;
```

The operator new allocates enough heap storage to store an integer and returns a pointer to that storage. The assignment statement then assigns that pointer to i_ptr. See Figure 8.17. If there is not enough free heap storage to satisfy the allocation request, new returns the null pointer.

As another example, the following assigns the pointer arr_ptr to point to enough heap space to store an array of 20 integers.

```
int* arr_ptr;
arr_ptr = new int [20];
```

To properly code a new statement, follow Note 8.7.

Note 8.7   How to Code the new Statement

To code a new statement,

1. Write an equivalent variable declaration.
2. Remove the variable name from the declaration.
3. Place the keyword new in front.
4. Assign the result to a pointer of the appropriate type.

Thus, to allocate space for an array of 20 integers:

1. Write an equivalent variable declaration for an array of 20 integers.

```
int arr[20];
```

The Heap

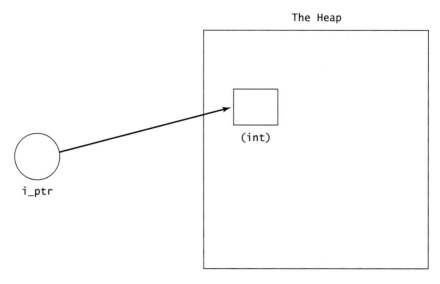

Figure 8.17

2. Remove the variable name from the declaration.

```
int [20];
```

3. Place the keyword new in front.

```
new int [20];
```

4. Assign the result to a pointer of the appropriate type.

```
arr_ptr = new int [20];
```

To deallocate space that has been previously allocated using new, use the operator delete. The operator delete takes one argument, namely, a pointer to the space on the heap that is to be deallocated. Thus, the following deallocates the heap space that was previously allocated by new.

```
delete i_ptr;
```

Take care to understand what delete does not do: delete does not delete the pointer that is its argument. It deallocates the space pointed to by the pointer so the space can be reused by the system. The pointer itself is still available for use in the program.

Note how to use delete to deallocate space for an array. Assuming that arr_ptr points to an array of 20 integers as shown previously, the following deallocates that space.

```
delete [] arr_ptr;
```

8.6.2 Static, Automatic, and Heap Memory

Heap memory is different from the other areas of memory that your C++ program uses, namely, static and automatic memory. If you declare a variable as static by using the `static` keyword or by declaring the variable outside a function, the space for the variable is allocated in static storage before the program begins. Only when `main()` ends does the computer deallocate space for static variables. An automatic variable, that is, a variable declared inside a block, is created in an area called the stack when the program enters the block. See Variable Attributes in Section 5.2. Such variables are deallocated when the program exits the block. Space for automatic variables is allocated and deallocated as the program is running. However, the allocation and deallocation are done automatically by C++. The programmer has no control over when to allocate and deallocate automatic variables. Heap storage, on the other hand, is completely under your control. You decide when to allocate and deallocate heap storage.

   Note also that storage allocated on the heap is independent of the block in which the storage is allocated. Thus, if a program allocates heap storage in a function, be sure to deallocate that storage before the function ends. Failure to deallocate the storage will result in the system being unable to reuse that storage later in the program. For example, consider the following program outline.

```
void Func()

int main()
{
   void Func();

   Func();

   return 0;
}

void Func()
{
   int* i_ptr;

   i_ptr = new int;

   *i_ptr = 17;
}
```

   The variable `i_ptr`, which points to space for an integer on the heap, is a local automatic variable. Therefore, `i_ptr` ceases to exist when the function `Func()` ends. Thus, the only way we had to access the heap storage in which we stored 17 is now lost. There is no way for `main()` to access or deallocate the heap storage that was allocated in `Func()`.

Note 8.8   Deallocate Heap Storage

Before exiting a function, be sure to use the operator `delete` to deallocate any heap storage that was allocated with the operator `new`.

8.6.3 The Program dem08-15.cpp

Suppose a program requires that you store the names of five clients. The program dem08-15.cpp shows how to dynamically allocate heap space to store the five names in such a way that no storage is wasted.

```cpp
// dem08-15.cpp

// This program illustrates the use of new and delete to dynamically
// allocate storage for an array.

#include <iostream>
#include <cstdlib>
#include <cstring>

using namespace std;

int main()
{
  const int SIZE = 5;

  char buffer[81];
  char* client[SIZE];
  int i;

  cout << "Enter " << SIZE << " names." << endl;

  for (i = 0; i < SIZE; ++i)
  {
    cout << endl;
    cout << "Name: ";
    cin.getline(buffer, 81);

    client[i] = new char [strlen(buffer) + 1];
    strcpy(client[i], buffer);
  }

  cout << endl;
  cout << "Following are the names you entered." << endl << endl;
  for (i = 0; i < SIZE; ++i)
    cout << endl << client[i];

  for (i = 0; i < SIZE; ++i)
    delete [] client[i];

  cout << endl;
  return 0;
}
```

Program Output

Enter 5 names.

Name: **Maria Ann**

Name: **Charles Anthony Thomas**

Name: **John Charles**

Name: **Amanda**

Name: **Jaqueline**

Following are the names you entered.

Maria Ann
Charles Anthony Thomas
John Charles
Amanda
Jaquiline

In the first for loop, the program asks for and stores five names. When the user enters a name, the program places it into the character array buffer[], which is large enough to hold the largest name. Then, the pointer client[i] is assigned the value returned by new, which allocates strlen(buffer) + 1 bytes on the heap for a character array. This is just enough heap space to store the string that is in buffer[]. Finally, the function strcpy() copies the string from buffer[] to the space pointed to by client[i].

To verify that the names are actually saved, the second for loop displays the five names in the order in which they are stored. The last for loop deallocates the space previously allocated by new.

8.6.4 A Second Example

Suppose that we must write a program that enters an unspecified number of doubles into an array. We could allocate space for a large number of doubles, say 100, and store the numbers in this array. If, however, we only enter a few numbers, the bulk of the space taken by the array is wasted. The following program, dem08-16.cpp, shows how to initially create the array of size 100, and then after the numbers are entered, replace the array with a smaller one that contains the same numbers.

```
// dem08-16.cpp

// This program demonstrates the use of new and delete to
// dynamically allocate heap storage.

#include <iostream>
#include <cstdlib>
#include <cctype>

using namespace std;

int main()
{
    double* numbers;      // pointer to an array of doubles
    double* temp_nums;    // pointer to a temporary array
    int     count;        // number of doubles entered
```

```cpp
int      i;
char     response;

// Allocate space for an array of 100 doubles
numbers = new double [100];

// Obtain doubles from the user
cout << "Do you want to enter a number(Y/N): ";
response = cin.get();

i = 0;
while (toupper(response) == 'Y')
{
   cout << endl;
   cout << "Enter a number: ";
   cin >> numbers[i];
   ++i;
   cin.get();      //To remove the newline character from the buffer
   cout << endl;
   cout << "Do you want to enter a number(Y/N): ";
   response = cin.get();
}

// Save the number of numbers in count
count = i;

// Allocate just enough space for the numbers entered
temp_nums = new double [count];

// Copy the numbers from the original array to the new array
for (i = 0; i < count; ++i)
   temp_nums[i] = numbers[i];

// Deallocate the old space
delete [] numbers;

// Set numbers to point to the smaller array
numbers = temp_nums;

// Display the numbers in the array
for (i = 0; i < count; ++i)
{
   cout << endl;
   cout << "numbers[" << i << "] = " << numbers[i];
}

cout << endl;
return 0;
}
```

Program Output

```
Do you want to enter a number(Y/N): y
Enter a number: 12.3
Do you want to enter a number(Y/N): y
Enter a number: 35.6
Do you want to enter a number(Y/N): y
Enter a number: 55.789
Do you want to enter a number(Y/N): y
Enter a number: 4
Do you want to enter a number(Y/N): n
numbers[0] = 12.3
numbers[1] = 35.6
numbers[2] = 55.789
numbers[3] = 4
```

The program begins by allocating enough space for an array of 100 doubles. See Figure 8.18a. Then, the program uses a loop to ask the user to enter numbers. The variable i counts the numbers as they are entered. When the program exits the loop, the value of i is stored in count. See Figure 8.18b. Next, the program allocates just enough heap storage to store an array of count doubles. The for loop then copies the numbers from the original array to the newly allocated array. See Figure 8.18c. The delete [] numbers statement deallocates the storage that numbers pointed to—the original array in which the numbers were stored. Then, the pointer numbers is set to point to the newly allocated space. See Figure 8.18d. Finally, the last for loop displays the numbers in the array. See Programming Problem 1 for another approach to this problem.

Exercises 8.6

1. Write C++ statements that declare a double pointer d_ptr and assign to that pointer space on the heap for storing an array of 100 doubles.
2. Write C++ statements that declare an integer pointer i_ptr and assign to i_ptr space on the heap for storing an array of 50 integers.
   In Exercises 3–6, locate and correct any syntax errors.
3. `int * i_ptr;`
   `i_ptr = new;`
4. `double db;`
   `db = new double;`
5. `int * i_ptr;`
   `i_ptr = new [] int;`
6. `int * i_ptr, i;`
   `i_ptr = new int;`
   `delete i;`

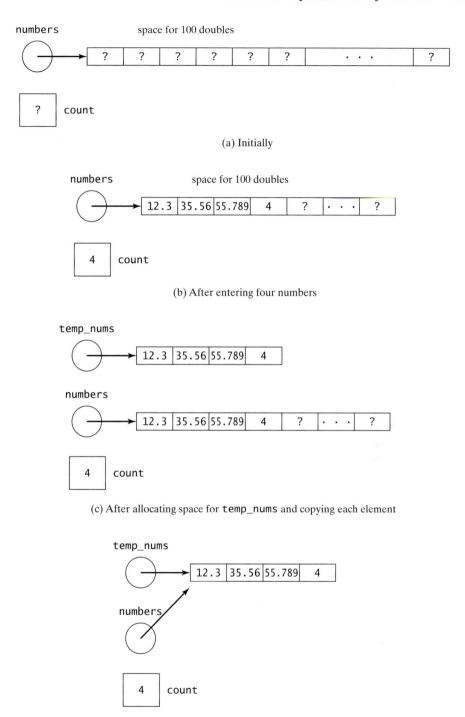

(a) Initially

(b) After entering four numbers

(c) After allocating space for `temp_nums` and copying each element

(d) After deallocating the original space and resetting
the pointer numbers

Figure 8.18

Experiments 8.6

1. Consider the following program segment.

```
char * ch_ptr;
ch_ptr = new char;

*ch_ptr = 'A';

ch_ptr = new char;

*ch_ptr = 'B';

cout << *ch_ptr;
```

What does the cout statement display? What happens to the character 'A'?

2. Recode dem08-12.cpp to include a check for new returning a null pointer.

Programming Problem 8.6

1. In dem08-13.cpp, we initially allocated space for 100 doubles, then allocated space just large enough to hold the numbers that the user entered and, finally, deallocated the original space. Another approach to this problem is to initially allocate very little space, say, enough for only five doubles. If the user enters a sixth number, allocate space for a larger array (say, an array of twice the size of the present one), copy the original array elements to the new array, and then deallocate the space for the original array. Rewrite dem08-13.cpp using this suggestion.

CHAPTER REVIEW

TERMINOLOGY

Describe the meanings of the following terms.

call by reference	ispunct()
call by address	isspace()
reference variable	isupper()
cstring	toupper()
strlen()	tolower()
strcpy()	palindrome
strcmp()	cstdlib
ASCII collating sequence	atoi()
concatenation	atol()
strcat()	atof()
cctype	heap
isalnum()	dynamic memory allocation
isalpha()	new
isdigit()	delete
islower()	

SUMMARY

- The address of a variable can be a function argument. In that case, use the indirection operator, *, in the function body to refer to the target of the pointer.
- A reference variable, declared by appending & to a data type, is another name for an already existing variable.
- Reference variables can be used as function arguments.
- An array can be a function argument. Always pass the array size as an additional argument (Notes 8.1 and 8.2).
- A string, that is, a character pointer, can be a function argument.
- A function can return a pointer.
- To use a function in the standard string library, you must `#include <cstring>` (Note 8.3).
- Use `strlen()` to find the length of a string.
- Use `strcpy()` to copy a string (Note 8.4).
- Use `strcmp()` to compare two strings. Strings are compared according to the ASCII collating sequence (Table 8.2).
- Use `strcat()` to append one string to the end of another (Note 8.5).
- To use the character classification functions (see Table 8.3) you must `#include <cctype>`.
- To use the character conversion functions `toupper()` and `tolower()`, you must `#include <cctype>`.
- To convert a numeric string to an integer, use `atoi()`; to a `long`, use `atol()`; to a `double`, use `atof()`. To use these functions, you must `#include <cstdlib>`.
- Use the `new` operator to dynamically allocate heap space (Note 8.6).
- Use the `delete` operator to deallocate heap space previously allocated by `new` (Note 8.7).

REVIEW EXERCISES

1. Explain the differences between passing an argument to a function by value, passing it by address, and passing it by reference.
2. What is a reference variable?
3. How can you pass an array to a function?
4. When you pass an array to a function, why should you also pass the size of the array to the function?
5. What do you have to do in a function prototype and the function definition so that one of the function's arguments is a pointer?
6. How do you code a function that returns a pointer?
7. Which header file must you include to use the string library functions?
8. What standard C++ library function returns the length of a string?
9. Which standard C++ library function allows you to copy a string? What must you be careful of when using this function?
10. Which standard C++ library function allows you to compare two strings?
11. What is the ASCII collating sequence?
12. Which standard C++ library function allows you to paste one string onto the end of another? What must you be careful of when using this function?

13. What header file must you include to use the standard library character classification functions?

14. Name as many of the character classification functions as you can and what they are used for.

15. What are the character conversion functions?

16. What are the numeric conversion functions and what does each do? Which header file must you include to use them?

17. What is meant by dynamic memory allocation?

18. What is the heap? How does heap storage differ from static and automatic storage?

19. How can you allocate memory from the heap? How can you deallocate memory from the heap?

Chapter 9

User-Defined Data Types and Tables

OBJECTIVES

- To use `typedef` to declare new data types
- To use `enum` to declare an enumerated type
- To use `struct` to declare a structure, and to declare a structure variable
- To use the member operator, `.`, to access a structure member
- To initialize a structure variable
- To assign one structure variable to another
- To define a table using an array of structures
- To code a program that loads and sorts a table
- To use a sequential search to do a table lookup
- To use a binary search to do a table lookup
- To code a function that has a structure as an argument
- To code a function that returns a structure
- To use the `->` operator to access a structure variable member through a pointer
- To code a function that has a structure pointer as an argument
- To code a function that has a structure reference as an argument

This chapter shows how to build other data types from the ones we already know. We start by discussing the `typedef` statement, which enables the programmer to define new data types from an existing data type. Next, we discuss the `enum` statement, which enables the programmer to define a data type having a small number of integer values.

The remainder of the chapter discusses the struct statement, which allows the programmer to define structures—compound data types created from preexisting data types. We show how to use structures to define and manipulate tables and how to use structures with pointers and functions.

9.1 THE typedef AND enum STATEMENTS

There are several ways in C++ to define new data types. In this section, we discuss typedef, which can be used to define a synonym for an existing type. We also discuss enum, which can be used to define a new type whose variables can assume a small number of integer values.

9.1.1 The typedef Statement

So far, we have discussed the built-in data types (char, int, long, float, double, etc.), pointers, and arrays of these types. The typedef statement allows you to define a synonym for an existing data type. (Thus, typedef does not define a new data type, but merely another name for an existing type.)

The typedef statement has the following format.

Note 9.1   Format of typedef

typedef *old_type   new_type*;

To understand how to use typedef, it is best to consider some examples. A program that manipulates money amounts would use variables of type double to represent these amounts. Such a program might contain the following declarations.

```
double value,
       amount;
```

A person reading this program might not know that the variables value and amount represent money amounts. If these values were output as negative numbers with six digits to the right of the decimal, the person might not suspect that something is wrong with the program.

Suppose instead that we declare the variables as follows.

```
typedef double MONEY_AMOUNT;
```

```
MONEY_AMOUNT value,
             amount;
```

The typedef statement makes the identifier MONEY_AMOUNT equivalent to the type double. Therefore, you are allowed to declare variables of type MONEY_AMOUNT. The C++ compiler translates a declaration of type MONEY_AMOUNT as though it is a declaration of type double. By using the type MONEY_AMOUNT, the variable declarations give information about the kind of number that the variables represent. Now, if the values of these variables are output incorrectly, a person reading the code is more likely to suspect that the program is in error.

You must declare a `typedef` before declaring a variable of that type. Exactly where you code the `typedef` is up to you. However, the scope rules that apply to variables also apply to types defined by `typedef`. Thus, a type defined by `typedef` within a function is accessible only within that function. A type defined by a `typedef` outside a function is accessible to all functions whose definitions occur after that `typedef`. Usually, programmers place all `typedef` statements before `main()`. This makes the types available to all functions in the program.

Another example of the use of `typedef` is in the declaration of character arrays that will store strings. If a program is to store a person's first and last names in arrays, we could code the following.

```
typedef char NAME[51];
```

Here, the new data type is NAME. The statement defines NAME as an array of 51 characters (to allow for a name of up to 50 characters—remember the `'\0'`.) Now, in the program, we can code the following, which declares `first` and `last` to be arrays of 51 characters.

```
NAME first,
     last;
```

Another example of the use of `typedef` is to define a synonym for a C-string data type. Suppose we code the following `typedef` statement.

```
typedef char* CSTRING;
```

Thus, CSTRING is equivalent to the type "character pointer", which is analogous to a C-string. We can then make the following declaration in a program.

```
CSTRING street_names [4] = {"Wall", "Spruce", "Cedar", "Pine"};
```

The data item `street_names` is an array of four CSTRINGs (that is, character pointers).

If you use CSTRING, be sure not to use an uninitialized pointer. For example, suppose we declare the following.

```
CSTRING emp_name;
```

It is dangerous to now execute the following statement.

```
cin.getline(emp_name, 51);
```

The variable `emp_name` is a character pointer and does not yet have an initial value. Therefore, it points to some unprotected location in memory. The call to `cin.getline()` will place the string entered by the user at that unprotected location. This could cause the `cin.getline()` to overwrite important program data or part of the operating system, which could cause a system crash.

In the next chapter, we shall see a much better and safer way to declare strings using the `string` class.

9.1.2 The enum Statement

An **enumerated type**, introduced by the keyword enum, defines a set of integer constants that are represented by identifiers.

Note 9.2   Format of enum

enum *enumerated-type-name* {*identifier list*}

For example, the following declares the enumerated type RESPONSE.

```
enum RESPONSE {cancel, ok};
```

The identifiers listed in braces have integer values beginning at 0 and are incremented by 1, unless otherwise specified. Thus, the identifiers cancel and ok in the foregoing declaration have the values 0 and 1. Once you declare an enumerated type, you can declare variables of that type. For example, we can code the following declaration.

```
RESPONSE result;
```

This declares the variable result as type RESPONSE, which is an enumerated type. Thus, result can be assigned the value cancel or ok.

```
result = ok;
```

We can also code the following while statement.

```
while (result == ok)
    {
    ...
    }
```

An enumerated type is considered a new type by the C++ compiler. For example, the compiler considers the previously declared RESPONSE to be a data type in the same way as int or double are types. This has implications in terms of the operations that you can perform on an enumerated type. For example, although the arithmetic operator ++ and the cin object are defined for variables of type int, they are not defined for enumerated types. Using ++ or cin on an enumerated type variable can lead to unpredictable results. Therefore, if you want to treat an enumerated type variable as an integer, you should type cast it as such. We shall see an example of this in dem09-1.cpp.

An enumerated type's values are integers (for example, in the RESPONSE type, ok has a value of 1). However, the C++ compiler will issue a warning message for the following statement.

```
result = 1;
```

The variable result is of type RESPONSE and the constant 1 is an integer. Although the assignment will assign the correct value to the variable result, the compiler issues a warning message that the types may not be compatible.

In the declaration of an enumerated type, you need not give the listed identifiers consecutive values from 0 on up. Consider the following declaration.

```
enum COLOR {red = 3, green, blue, white = 8, black};
```

Here, red is given the value 3. Because green is listed immediately after red and is not given a value, it automatically is given the next integer value, namely 4. Similarly, blue is given the value 5. The identifier white is explicitly given the value 8. Because black is listed immediately after white with no explicit initial value, it is automatically given the value 9.

9.1.3 An Example Using typedef and enum

The program dem09-1.cpp illustrates the uses of typedef and enum that we have discussed. It is based on the program prb07-2.cpp, which totals weekly sales amounts for a salesperson and finds the highest sales for the week. Note how this version of the program is more self-documenting than the original.

```cpp
// dem09-1.cpp

// This program totals weekly sales amounts and finds the highest
// sales for the week.  It uses an array of pointers to store the
// names of the days of the week.

// The program makes use of typedef and enum

#include <iostream>
#include <iomanip>

using namespace std;

typedef char* CSTRING;
typedef char NAME [41];
typedef double AMOUNT;
enum DAY {mon, tue, wed, thu, fri, sat, sun};

int main()
{
   CSTRING day_names[7] = {"Monday", "Tuesday", "Wednesday",
                           "Thursday", "Friday", "Saturday", "Sunday"};

   AMOUNT sales[7];
   NAME    salesperson;
   AMOUNT max_sales,
          total_sales;
   DAY    day,
          max_day;

   cout << setprecision(2)
        << setiosflags(ios::fixed)
        << setiosflags(ios::showpoint);

   cout << "Enter the name of the salesperson: ";
   cin.getline(salesperson, 41);
```

```
for (day = mon; day <= sun; day = (DAY)((int)day + 1))
{
  cout << endl << endl;
  cout << "Enter the sales for " << day_names[day] << ": ";
  cin >> sales[day];
}
total_sales = 0;
max_day = mon;
max_sales = sales[mon];

for (day = mon; day <= sun; day = (DAY)((int)day + 1))
{
  if (sales[day] > max_sales)
  {
    max_sales = sales[day];
    max_day = day;
  }

  total_sales += sales[day];
}
cout << endl << endl;
cout << "The total sales for " << salesperson
     << " is " << total_sales << "." << endl << endl;
cout << "The highest sales was " << max_sales << "." << endl << endl;
cout << "The highest sales occurred on "
     << day_names[max_day] << "." << endl;

return 0;
}
```

Program Output

```
Enter the name of the salesperson: Mack Adamia

Enter the sales for Monday: 345.76

Enter the sales for Tuesday: 239.89

Enter the sales for Wednesday: 100.00

Enter the sales for Thursday: 563.99

Enter the sales for Friday: 0.0

Enter the sales for Saturday: 789.99

Enter the sales for Sunday: 533.90

The total sales for Mack Adamia is 2573.53.

The highest sales was 789.99.

The highest sales occurred on Saturday.
```

The program begins with several `typedef` statements. The first `typedef` declares CSTRING as a character pointer. The program uses CSTRING to define an array of seven strings, which it initializes to the names of the days of the week. The second `typedef` declares NAME as an array of 41 characters. The program uses NAME to store a salesperson's name. The third `typedef` declares AMOUNT as a double. The program uses AMOUNT to declare the variables `max_sales` and `total_sales`, which store money amounts. Finally, the fourth declaration defines DAY as an enumerated type that gives values to the abbreviations of the names of the days of the week. The program uses DAY to declare the variables day and `max_day`, which store values corresponding to the days of the week.

The code of `main()` also takes advantage of the enumerated type values. The two `for` loops use the enumerated type values mon and sun to initialize and test the value of the DAY enumerated type variable day. Note that in both `for` loops, the variable day is incremented by the statement day = (DAY)((int)day + 1). Remember that the variable day is of type DAY. The arithmetic operators are not necessarily defined for variables of this type. Therefore, we type cast the variable to an integer and then add one. Before assigning this value to the variable day, we must recast the value to type DAY. Type casts are not necessary in the loop initializations or the loop tests. In the initializations we assign a DAY value to a variable of type DAY and in the tests we compare a DAY variable to a DAY value. The same is true in the assignment statements that initialize max_day to Monday and max_sales to Monday's sales.

You may think to use the expression ++day or ++((int)day) or day = day + 1 to increment the value of day in the `for` loops. See Experiment 3 to see that this does not work.

Exercises 9.1

In Exercises 1–6, use `typedef` and `enum` as appropriate.

1. Define a data type to store social security numbers.
2. Define a data type to store a table of 50 names, each of which contains, at most, 30 characters.
3. Define a data type to store an array of pointers.
4. Define an enumerated data type for the sizes small, medium, large, and xlarge.
5. Define an enumerated type for months of the year. Use the first three letters of each month as the value of the month name.
6. Define an enumerated type for the seating classes on an airplane. Use first, business, coach, and standby as the values.
7. Assume the following declaration.

   ```
   enum VEGIES {beans, carrots = 6, onions, tomatoes};
   ```

   What are the numeric values of beans, onions, and tomatoes?
8. (a) A corporation's Human Resources department rates applicants as Superior, Average, and SubAverage. Define an enumerated type that reflects this classification. Be sure to make the numeric values of the categories correspond to their relative standing. For example, Superior should be greater than Average and SubAverage.

(b) Using the data type defined in part (a), declare a variable called `rating` in which to store an interviewer's rating of an applicant.

(c) Using parts (a) and (b), write a statement that places the number 1 into the variable `decision` if the value of rating is Superior or Average.

9. **(a)** The Finance Department of a corporation is preparing an annual report. The company's revenues will be classified according to quarters. Define an enumerated type having values QTR1, QTR2, QTR3, and QTR4.

(b) Declare an array of `doubles` in which to store the company's revenues for the four quarters.

(c) Using the enumerated type defined in part (a), declare a variable `quarter` that will be used as a subscript for the array declared in part (b).

(d) Write a `for` loop that prompts the user to enter each of the four quarters' revenues and stores them in the array declared in part (b). Use the variable declared in part (c) as the loop counter. Be sure to use the values defined in the enumerated type.

Experiments 9.1

1. Compile the following program. What does your compiler do?

```
#include <iostream>

using namespace std;

void Func(void);

int main()
{
    typedef int NEW_TYPE;

    NEW_TYPE i = 0;

    Func();

    return 0;
}
void FUNC(void)
{
    NEW_TYPE j = 3;
}
```

2. In some C++ compilers, the values specified in an enumerated type are legal to use in place of the integer values they represent. Thus, using the DAY enumerated type of dem09-1.cpp, we could code the expression wed + thu. This expression has a value of 2 + 3, or 5. A variable of type DAY, for example day, can be assigned values such as mon and tue or numeric values such as 5 or 6. However, C++ does not check that the values you give to day are within the range 0–6. In dem09-1.cpp, replace the conditions in each of the for loops by day <= 6. Compile and run the resulting program. Does the compiler issue any errors? Does the program run correctly?

3. (a) In dem09-1.cpp, use the expression ++day to increment to the next day value in both for loops. Compile the program. What error message does the compiler give and why?

(b) In dem09-1.cpp, use the expression ++((int)day) to increment to the next day value in both for loops. Compile the program. What error message does the compiler give and why? What is an l value?

(c) In dem09-1.cpp, use the expression day = day + 1 to increment to the next day value in both for loops. Compile the program. What error message does the compiler give and why?

9.2 STRUCTURES

Arrays allow the programmer to define variables that combine several data items of the same kind. For example, an array of five integers combines five integer values that can be treated as a unit. In this section, we introduce the structure, which allows you to combine data items of different kinds.

9.2.1 Defining a Structure

Suppose we want to process inventory information on parts that are stored in a warehouse. For each part, we would like to store the part number (a seven-character code), the quantity on hand (an integer), and the unit price (a double). We could declare a variable for each of these quantities. However, doing so does not reflect that the three variables contain values that are associated with a particular part. We need a single variable in which we can store all three quantities. Most programming languages use a variable called a record for this purpose. In C++, the **structure** can provide this capability. In Chapter 11, we shall discuss classes, which is another way to accomplish the same thing.

The following defines a structure that we can use to solve our inventory problem.

```
struct PART_STRUCT
{
   char    part_no[8];
   int     quantity_on_hand;
   double  unit_price;
};
```

The definition begins with the keyword struct. The identifier PART_STRUCT gives a name to the structure. (We place the suffix _struct at the end of a structure name to remind us that the identifier is a structure. This is not required by C++, but is a useful programming practice.) Following the structure name are the **structure members** enclosed in braces. The structure members are the parts of the structure and they are declared in the same way as ordinary variables although they are not variables. The PART_STRUCT structure has three members. The first member, part_no, is a character array. The second member, quantity_on_hand, is an integer. The third member, unit_price, is a double. Note that the definition of the structure ends in a semicolon.

The PART_STRUCT template

Figure 9.1

It is important to realize that the definition of the PART_STRUCT structure does not declare a variable. It, therefore, does not reserve any space in computer storage. A structure definition defines a template for the compiler to use when we declare PART_STRUCT variables. As with enum, the struct statement actually defines another data type. By itself it does not declare a variable. Also, the part_no, quantity_on_hand, and unit_price members of the structure are merely names for the members of the structure and are not variables.

Figure 9.1 shows how we can think of the PART_STRUCT structure data type. The PART_STRUCT structure is divided into three pieces consisting of the three members, part_no, quantity_on_hand, and unit_price, in that order.

To declare a variable that is of the PART_STRUCT type, we can code the following.

    PART_STRUCT part;

This declaration defines a variable, part, that is of the data type PART_STRUCT. Internally, the variable part has the structure that we defined in the struct statement for PART_STRUCT. Figure 9.2 shows the variable part.

Although the PART_STRUCT data type does not reserve computer storage, the variable part does. The variable part requires whatever amount of storage is necessary to store an eight-character array, an integer, and a double.

9.2.2 Accessing Structure Members

Now that we have declared a structure variable, how can we access the members of that variable? For example, how can we assign the value 62 to the quantity_on_hand member of part? To access a member of a structure, we must use the **member operator**. The member operator is coded as a period between the structure variable name and the structure member that we wish to access. Thus, we refer to the quantity_on_hand member of part as part.quantity_on_hand. Read this reference from right to left as "the quantity_on_hand member of part". You can also read

part

The structure variable part

Figure 9.2

it as the possessive "part's quantity_on_hand." To assign 62 to this member, we would code the following.

```
part.quantity_on_hand = 62;
```

Again, read this assignment as "62 is assigned to the quantity_on_hand member of part", or as "part's quantity_on_hand becomes 62."

Note 9.3   Reading a Structure Reference

Read an expression that contains a structure member reference either from right to left (reading the member operator as "member of"), or as a possessive.

The following program, dem09-2.cpp, shows how to access the members of a structure.

```cpp
// dem09-2.cpp

// This program illustrates the declaration and use of structure
// variables and the member operator to access structure
// variable members.

#include <iostream>
#include <iomanip>

using namespace std;

struct PART_STRUCT
{
   char    part_no[8];
   int     quantity_on_hand;
   double  unit_price;
};

int main()
{
   PART_STRUCT part;

   cout << setprecision(2)
        << setiosflags(ios::fixed)
        << setiosflags(ios::showpoint);

   cout << "Enter the seven-character part number: ";
   cin.getline(part.part_no, 8);

   cout << endl;
   cout << "Enter the quantity on hand: ";
   cin >> part.quantity_on_hand;

   cout << endl;
   cout << "Enter the unit price: ";
   cin >> part.unit_price;
```

```
cout << endl;
cout << "You entered the following information:" << endl << endl;
cout << "Part Number:      " << part.part_no << endl;
cout << "Quantity On Hand: " << setw(7) << part.quantity_on_hand
     << endl;
cout << "Unit Price:       " << setw(7) << part.unit_price << endl;

return 0;
}
```

Program Output

Enter the seven-character part number: **AB12345**

Enter the quantity on hand: **62**

Enter the unit price: **34.95**

You entered the following information:

```
Part Number:      AB12345
Quantity On Hand:      62
Unit Price:         34.95
```

The program begins with the definition of the structure type that we discussed earlier. In main(), we declare the structure variable part. The program asks the user for a part number, quantity on hand, and unit price. When working with structures, it is important to keep Note 9.4 in mind.

Note 9.4   Data Type of a Structure Reference

The data type of a structure member reference is the same as the data type of the right-most element of that reference.

Thus, part.part_no has the same data type as part_no, which is the name of a character array, that is, a character pointer. Thus, any reference to part.part_no should be as the name of a character array, or character pointer. Also, part.quantity_on_hand is an integer because quantity_on_hand is an integer.

Because the seven-character part number is a string, the program obtains it by a call to cin.getline(). The cin.getline() function requires the name of a character array as its first argument. Thus, the required statement is

```
cin.getline(part.part_no, 8);
```

After prompting for, and obtaining, the data entered by the user, we can depict the contents of the structure variable part as shown in Figure 9.3.

The structure variable `part` with initial values

Figure 9.3

9.2.3 Initializing a Structure Variable

You can initialize a structure variable similarly to the way in which you initialize an array. For example, using the PART_STRUCT data type defined earlier, we can declare and initialize the variable old_part as follows.

```
PART_STRUCT old_part = {"XY98765", 17, 99.99};
```

Thus, to initialize a structure variable, enclose in braces a list of the structure member values. Separate the values by commas. You must take care that the types of the values in the list correspond to the data types of the members of the structure. Thus, in our example, the first listed value is a string, the second value is an integer, and the third value is a double.

9.2.4 More Complicated Structures

A structure can be simple or as complex as you like. A structure can consist of two or three members of simple types. For example, we could use the following structure to store the value of a standard playing card.

```
struct CARD_STRUCT
{
  int  value;
  char suit;
};
```

```
CARD_STRUCT card;
```

The structure variable `card` has two members, an `int` representing the face value of the card and a `char` representing the suit (S, H, D, C for spade, heart, diamond, and club). Thus, we can store the 7 of diamonds in the variable card as follows.

```
card.value = 7;
card.suit = 'D';
```

Figure 9.4 shows the contents of the variable `card` after these assignments.

A structure can also be complex, as was the PART_STRUCT structure of dem09-2.cpp. A structure can even contain other nested structures. For example, suppose that we want to store the following information on a company's employees: name, address, social security number, and hourly pay rate. The name is to consist of a first name, a middle initial, and a last name. The address is to consist of the street address, the city, the two-character state code, and the five-digit zip code. The social security number is

The structure variable `card`

Figure 9.4

to be stored as a character string. The hourly pay rate is a `double`. Because the name and address are subdivided into parts, it is logical to define structures for the name and the address. Then, we will define a structure consisting of the name and address structures, and the social security number. Following are such definitions.

```
struct NAME_STRUCT
{
  char first_name[31];
  char mid_initial;
  char last_name[31];
};

struct ADDRESS_STRUCT
{
  char st_adress[31];
  char city[31];
  char state[3];
  char zip[6];
};

struct EMPLOYEE_STRUCT
{
  NAME_STRUCT    name;
  ADDRESS_STRUCT address;
  char           soc_sec_no[10];
  double         pay_rate;
};

EMPLOYEE_STRUCT employee;
```

The structure variable `employee` has four members (see Figure 9.5.) The first member, `name`, is a structure of type `NAME_STRUCT`. The second member, `address`, is a structure of type `ADDRESS_STRUCT`. The third member, `soc_sec_no`, is a character array. The fourth member is a `double`.

You must be very careful when using the members of a complicated structure variable. For example, suppose we want to initialize the two-character state code of `employee` to "NY". The member `state` is a member of a member of the variable `employee`. Thus, we need to use the member operator twice. The following is how to make the reference.

```
employee.address.state
```

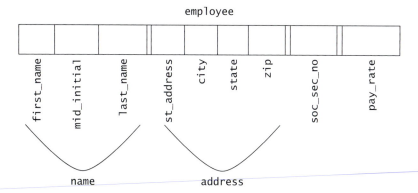

The EMPLOYEE_STRUCT variable employee

Figure 9.5

Following Note 9.3, we read the reference from right to left as "the state member of the address member of employee", or as "employee's address's state." Recall that the data type of this reference is the type of the right-most member. Thus, the reference is to the name of a character array, or a character pointer. To copy the string "NY" into the array, we would use the strcpy() function as follows.

```
strcpy(employee.address.state, "NY");
```

If we want to access the first letter of the state code, we would use the following reference.

```
employee.address.state[0]
```

Again using Note 9.3, you would read this reference from right to left as "element 0 of the state member of the address member of employee", or "employee's address's state element 0."

9.2.5 Assigning One Structure Variable to Another

A structure variable can be assigned to another structure variable of the same type. For example, consider the CARD_STRUCT structure defined in the previous subsection.

```
struct CARD_STRUCT
{
  int  value;
  char suit;
};
```

Suppose that we code the following declarations.

```
CARD_STRUCT card1 = {7, 'D'},
            card2;
```

Then, the assignment card2 = card1 is valid and is accomplished by a member-by-member copy. Therefore, the assignment results in the structure variable card2 having the same value as card1, namely, the seven of diamonds.

It is not valid to assign a structure variable of one type to a structure variable of a different type. This is true even if the number and data types of the members are the same. For example, suppose the following declarations and assignment.

```
struct NEW_CARD_STRUCT
{
   int value;
   char suit;
};

NEW_CARD_STRUCT new-card;
new_card = card;          //illegal assignment
```

The assignment is illegal because card is of type CARD_STRUCT and new_card is of type NEW_CARD_STRUCT.

Exercises 9.2

1. Define a structure type STUDENT_STRUCT described as follows: A 30-character name, a 9-digit student ID number, a 3-character student class, a 2-character grade, a 5-character course code, a 16-character course name.

2. Define a structure type JUROR_STRUCT described as follows. The first member is a structure containing the juror's name, street address, city, and zip code. The second member of JUROR_STRUCT is also a structure, which contains a five-character court code followed by a six-character date.

3. Define a structure type EMPLOYEE_STRUCT described as follows. The first member is a structure containing the employee's name, social security number, street address, city, and zip code. The second member of EMPLOYEE_STRUCT is also a structure. This structure contains the employee's initial date of employment in mm/yy/dd form, the employee's hourly pay rate, and the employee's number of dependents.

Experiments 9.2

1. Consider the following structures and variable declarations.

```
struct STRUCT1
{
   int i;
   double d;
};

struct STRUCT2
{
   float f;
   long  l;
};

STRUCT1 struct1_var = {3, 7.5};
STRUCT2 struct2_var;
```

Write a program containing these declarations and make the assignment `struct2_var` = `struct1_var`. What happens? Does the program compile? If it compiles, what gets assigned to `struct2_var`?

9.3 ARRAYS OF STRUCTURES: TABLES

A **table** is data organized into rows and columns. For example, Table 9.1 shows a list of parts. Each row of the table represents a part. The first column contains the part number; the second column contains the quantity on hand for the part; the third column contains the unit price for the part. We can use this table to look up a part number and find either the quantity on hand or the unit price. We might also want to update the information on a part. For example, it might be necessary to change the quantity on hand or the unit price.

We use data tables almost every day of our lives. When we look up a word in a dictionary, we use a table. You can think of the dictionary as a two-column table in which the first column contains the word and the second column the corresponding definition. The telephone book is also a table. It has three columns containing the name, address, and telephone number.

To look up a part in Table 9.1, or find a word in a dictionary, or look up a person's telephone number all require locating a particular row in a table. The column that you use to locate a table entry is the **table key**. In Table 9.1, the table key is the part number column. In a dictionary, the table key is the word column. The table key of a telephone book is the name column.

Sometimes, the table rows are in order based on the table key. For example, the dictionary and the telephone book are in order based on their table key. Such a table is **sorted**. On the other hand, some tables, like Table 9.1, are not sorted on the table key. In this case, you might want to sort the table before using it to look up the information on a part.

The most frequent operation performed on a table is to look up something in the table. For example, we use the dictionary to look up the definition of words. We use the telephone book to look up telephone numbers. The **search key** is the key value that you are looking for (for example, a particular word in a dictionary or a particular person in

TABLE 9.1

Part Number	Quantity on Hand	Unit Price
A123456	123	12.99
A987654	53	52.99
D001234	93	22.95
B109897	44	13.95
A035467	15	59.95
C837289	0	57.99
D346246	35	25.99
C253146	104	110.99
B194791	33	14.95
A826749	56	41.95

the telephone book.) The process of finding a match to the search key in the table key column is **table searching**.

This section shows how to use structures to define tables, how to sort a table, and how to do a table search.

9.3.1 Defining a Table Using Structures

A table in C++ is an array of structures. For example, consider the PART_STRUCT structure data type defined in Section 9.2.

```
struct PART_STRUCT
{
  char    part_no[8];
  int     quantity_on_hand;
  double unit_price;
};
```

We can define a table to store data on 10 parts as follows.

```
PART_STRUCT part_table[10];
```

Thus, part_table is an array of 10 elements, each of which is of type PART_STRUCT. Figure 9.6 shows how to view this table.

Each row of the table is a structure of type PART_STRUCT. Therefore, to access a particular entry in a particular row, you must use the member operator. For example, to assign 102 to the quantity_on_hand member of the fifth row of the table (remember, this is subscript 4), you would use the following.

```
part_table[4].quantity_on_hand = 102;
```

Using Note 9.3, read this assignment from right to left as "102 is assigned to the quantity_on_hand member of row 4 of part_table." Alternatively, read the assignment using a possessive as "part_table row 4's quantity_on_hand becomes 102."

	part_no	quantity_on_hand	unit_price
0	A123456	123	12.99
1	A987654	53	52.95
2	D001234	93	22.95
3	B109897	44	13.95
4	A035467	15	59.95
5	C837289	0	57.99
6	D346246	35	25.99
7	C253146	104	110.99
8	B194791	33	14.95
9	A826749	56	41.95

A table consisting of an array of
structures of type PART_STRUCT

Figure 9.6

9.3.2 Loading Table Values

To load a table means to store values in the table. It is possible to load a table with values when the table is declared. This technique is called **"hard coding" a table**. You can usually hard code a table in two circumstances. First, the table should be short. If the table has many rows, it would take too long to enter the table values by hand in the program code. Second, the table values should be stable in the sense that they should not be subject to frequent change. Every time a value in a hard-coded table changes, you must edit and recompile the program. If this happens frequently, for example four or five times daily, it can waste a great deal of time. Also, frequent changes to the program code increase the likelihood of introducing errors into the code.

Following is a hard-coded table containing the first four parts from Table 9.1.

```
PART_STRUCT partial_part_table[4] = { {"A123456", 123, 12.99},
                                      {"A987654",  53, 52.95},
                                      {"D001234",  93, 22.95},
                                      {"B109897",  44, 13.95}
                                    };
```

A program can also load a table interactively. The following program, dem09-3. cpp, shows how to interactively load `part_table`. After the program loads the table, it displays the table in table form with column headings and the total quantity on hand.

```cpp
// dem09-3.cpp

// This program shows how to define a table and how to interactively
// load the table with values.  To verify that the table is loaded
// correctly, the program also displays the table in table form
// with appropriate headings.

#include <iostream>
#include <iomanip>

using namespace std;

struct PART_STRUCT
{
   char    part_no[8];
   int     quantity_on_hand;
   double unit_price;
};

void Load_Part_Table(PART_STRUCT [], int);
void Display_Part_Table(PART_STRUCT [], int);

int main()
{
   const int TABLE_SIZE = 10;

   PART_STRUCT part_table[TABLE_SIZE];
   int row,
       total_on_hand = 0;
```

```
    cout << setprecision(2)
        << setiosflags(ios::fixed)
        << setiosflags(ios::showpoint);

    // Load the table
    Load_Part_Table(part_table, TABLE_SIZE);

    // Calculate the total on hand
    for (row = 0; row < TABLE_SIZE; ++row)
      total_on_hand += part_table[row].quantity_on_hand;

    // Display the table
    cout << endl << endl;
    cout << "This is the table you entered.";

    Display_Part_Table(part_table, TABLE_SIZE);

    cout << endl << endl;
    cout << setw(20) << "Total On Hand:"
        << setw(20) << total_on_hand << endl;

    return 0;
}

void Load_Part_Table(PART_STRUCT part_table[], int size)
{
    int row;

    cout << endl;
    cout << "Enter the table values as you are prompted:"
        << endl << endl;

    for (row = 0; row < size ; ++row)
    {
      cout << endl;
      cout << "For row #" << row + 1 << " enter:" << endl;
      cout << "Part Number (7 Characters): ";
      cin.getline(part_table[row].part_no, 8);

      cout << "Quantity On Hand: ";
      cin >> part_table[row].quantity_on_hand;

      cout << "Unit Price: ";
      cin >> part_table[row].unit_price;

      cin.get();   //remove the newline character from the input buffer

    }

} //End of Load_Part_Table()

void Display_Part_Table(PART_STRUCT part_table[], int size)
{
    int row;

    cout << endl << endl;
    cout << setw(20) << "Part Number"
        << setw(20) << "Quantity On Hand"
        << setw(20) << "Unit Price" << endl;
```

```
        for (row = 0; row < size; ++row)
        {
          cout << endl;
          cout << setw(20) << part_table[row].part_no
                << setw(20) << part_table[row].quantity_on_hand
                << setw(20) << part_table[row].unit_price;
        }
    } //End of Display_Part_Table()
```

Program Output

```
Enter the table values as you are prompted:

For row #1 enter:
Part Number (7 Characters): A123456
Quantity On Hand: 123
Unit Price: 12.99

For row #2 enter:
Part Number (7 Characters): A987654
Quantity On Hand: 53
Unit Price: 52.95

For row #3 enter:
Part Number (7 Characters): D001234
Quantity On Hand: 93
Unit Price: 22.95

For row #4 enter:
Part Number (7 Characters): B109897
Quantity On Hand: 44
Unit Price: 13.95

For row #5 enter:
Part Number (7 Characters): A035467
Quantity On Hand: 15
Unit Price: 59.95

For row #6 enter:
Part Number (7 Characters): C837289
Quantity On Hand: 0
Unit Price: 57.99

For row #7 enter:
Part Number (7 Characters): D346246
Quantity On Hand: 35
Unit Price: 25.99

For row #8 enter:
Part Number (7 Characters): C235146
Quantity On Hand: 104
Unit Price: 110.99
```

```
For row #9 enter:
Part Number (7 Characters): B194791
Quantity On Hand: 33
Unit Price: 14.95

For row #10 enter:
Part Number (7 Characters): A826749
Quantity On Hand: 56
Unit Price: 41.95

This is the table you entered.
        Part Number     Quantity On Hand            Unit Price

          A123456              123                      12.99
          A987654               53                      52.95
          D001234               93                      22.95
          B109897               44                      13.95
          A035467               15                      59.95
          C837289                0                      57.99
          D346246               35                      25.99
          C253146              104                     110.99
          B194791               33                      14.95
          A826749               56                      41.95

    Total On Hand:             556
```

The program begins by defining the structure PART_STRUCT as we described earlier. The program uses the function Load_Part_Table() to load the table, and the function Display_Part_Table() to display the table. Both functions return void and have two arguments. In both functions, the first argument is a PART_STRUCT array, that is, a table. The part table is an array of structures. An array of structures can be passed as an argument in exactly the same way as an array of integers or an array of doubles can be passed as an argument. The second argument for both functions is an integer, which will be the size of the array (that is, the number of rows in the table). Note also that the prototypes for these functions must be placed after the declaration of PART_STRUCT because we refer to this structure in the prototypes.

In main(), we define the constant TABLE_SIZE, which holds the number of rows in the table. We also require three variables: the array part_table, and the integer variables row, which we use for the table subscript, and total_on_hand, which we use to accumulate the quantities on hand for the 10 parts.

The program loads the part table by executing Load_Part_Table(). The for loop in the function prompts the user for the table data. One iteration of this loop fills a single table row by prompting for, and obtaining, the part number, the quantity on hand, and the unit price. The cin.get() at the end of the loop body clears the keyboard input buffer of the newline character that the user entered after the unit price. Without this call to cin.get(), on the next loop iteration cin.getline() would obtain only the newline character that was in the keyboard input buffer. Recall that cin.getline() obtains all characters up to and including the next newline character.

If the very first character in the keyboard input buffer is a newline character, the newline character is all that `cin.getline()` will retrieve.

Next, the `for` loop in `main()` accumulates the `quantity_on_hand` members of each row of the table. Then, the program displays a message that the table is about to print and executes `Display_Part_Table()`. The `for` loop in this function displays the contents of the table. One iteration of the loop displays one row of the table. Finally, the last `cout` in `main()` displays the value of the total quantity on hand.

In addition to hard coding a table and interactively loading a table, table values can be loaded from a file. We shall see how to do this in the chapter on files.

9.3.3 Sorting a Table

There are many techniques for sorting a table. We shall employ the bubble sort, which we used in Chapter 6 to sort an array of numbers. It might be a good idea at this point to review Section 6.3. We shall assume that we want to sort our tables in **ascending order**. Ascending order means that the row with the lowest table key value is in row 0, the row with the next higher table key value is in row 1, and so on. In the experiments at the end of this section, we ask you to adjust the programs in this section to sort the tables into descending order.

There are several differences between sorting an array of numbers and sorting a table. First, we have to know which column of the table is to serve as the table key. When the sort procedure decides if two rows are out of order, it must compare the values in the table key columns. Second, if the table key is a string, as is the part-number column of the table we built in dem09-3.cpp, then we must use `strcmp()` to do the comparisons. Third, when two rows are out of order, we must swap the entire rows.

Following is dem09-4.cpp, which loads and displays a part table exactly as dem09-3.cpp. Then, the program uses the bubble sort to sort the table in ascending order on the part number and then displays the sorted table.

```
// dem09-4.cpp

// This program interactively loads and displays a table (see
// dem09-3.cpp) and then uses the bubble sort to sort the table
// on the part number.  Finally, the program displays the sorted
// table.

#include <iostream>
#include <iomanip>
#include <cstring>

using namespace std;

struct PART_STRUCT
{
  char    part_no[8];
  int     quantity_on_hand;
  double unit_price;
};

void Load_Part_Table(PART_STRUCT [], int);
void Display_Part_Table(PART_STRUCT [], int);
```

```cpp
void Sort_Table(PART_STRUCT [], int);

int main()
{
  const int TABLE_SIZE = 10;

  PART_STRUCT part_table[TABLE_SIZE];

  int row,
      total_on_hand = 0;

  cout << setprecision(2)
       << setiosflags(ios::fixed)
       << setiosflags(ios::showpoint);

  // Load the table
  Load_Part_Table(part_table, TABLE_SIZE);

  // Display the table
  cout << endl << endl;
  cout << "This is the table you entered.";

  Display_Part_Table(part_table, TABLE_SIZE);

  // Calculate the total on hand
  for (row = 0; row < TABLE_SIZE; ++row)
    total_on_hand += part_table[row].quantity_on_hand;

  cout << endl <<endl;
  cout << setw(20) << "Total On Hand:"
       << setw(20) << total_on_hand;

  // Sort the table using the bubble sort
  Sort_Table(part_table, TABLE_SIZE);

  // Display the sorted table
  cout << endl << endl;
  cout << "The table sorted on Part Number is:";

  Display_Part_Table(part_table, TABLE_SIZE);

  cout << endl << endl;
  cout << setw(20) << "Total On Hand:"
       << setw(20) << total_on_hand << endl;

  return 0;
} //End of main()

void Load_Part_Table(PART_STRUCT part_table[], int size)
{
  int row;

  cout << endl;
  cout << "Enter the table values as you are prompted:"
       << endl << endl;
```

```
  for (row = 0; row < size ; ++row)
  {
    cout << endl;
    cout << "For row #" << row + 1 << " enter:" << endl;
    cout << "Part Number (7 Characters): ";
    cin.getline(part_table[row].part_no, 8);

    cout << "Quantity On Hand: ";
    cin >> part_table[row].quantity_on_hand;

    cout << "Unit Price: ";
    cin >> part_table[row].unit_price;

    cin.get();   //remove the newline character from the input buffer
  }
} //End of Load_Part_Table()
void Sort_Table(PART_STRUCT part_table[], int size)
{
  int row,
      pass,
      limit;
  PART_STRUCT temp_part;

  limit = size - 2;

  for (pass = 1; pass <= size - 1; ++pass)
  {
    for (row = 0; row <= limit; ++row)
      if (strcmp(part_table[row].part_no,
                          part_table[row + 1].part_no) > 0)
      {
        temp_part = part_table[row];
        part_table[row] = part_table[row + 1];
        part_table[row + 1] = temp_part;
      }

      --limit;
  }
} //End of Sort_Table()
void Display_Part_Table(PART_STRUCT part_table[], int size)
{
  int row;

  cout << endl << endl;
  cout << setw(20) << "Part Number"
       << setw(20) << "Quantity On Hand"
       << setw(20) << "Unit Price"
       << endl;
```

```
    for (row = 0; row < size; ++row)
    {
      cout << endl;
      cout << setw(20) << part_table[row].part_no
           << setw(20) << part_table[row].quantity_on_hand
           << setw(20) << part_table[row].unit_price;
    }
  } //End of Display_Part_Table()
```

Program Output

Enter the table values as you are prompted:

For row #1 enter:
Part Number (7 Characters): **A123456**
Quantity On Hand: **123**
Unit Price: **12.99**

For row #2 enter:
Part Number (7 Characters): **A987654**
Quantity On Hand: **53**
Unit Price: **52.95**

For row #3 enter:
Part Number (7 Characters): **D001234**
Quantity On Hand: **93**
Unit Price: **22.95**

For row #4 enter:
Part Number (7 Characters): **B109897**
Quantity On Hand: **44**
Unit Price: **13.95**

For row #5 enter:
Part Number (7 Characters): **A035467**
Quantity On Hand: **15**
Unit Price: **59.95**

For row #6 enter:
Part Number (7 Characters): **C837289**
Quantity On Hand: **0**
Unit Price: **57.99**

For row #7 enter:
Part Number (7 Characters): **D346246**
Quantity On Hand: **35**
Unit Price: **25.99**

For row #8 enter:
Part Number (7 Characters): **C235146**
Quantity On Hand: **104**
Unit Price: **110.99**

```
For row #9 enter:
Part Number (7 Characters): B194791
Quantity On Hand: 33
Unit Price: 14.95

For row #10 enter:
Part Number (7 Characters): A826749
Quantity On Hand: 56
Unit Price: 41.95

This is the table you entered.

        Part Number     Quantity On Hand              Unit Price
          A123456             123                       12.99
          A987654              53                       52.95
          D001234              93                       22.95
          B109897              44                       13.95
          A035467              15                       59.95
          C837289               0                       57.99
          D346246              35                       25.99
          C253146             104                      110.99
          B194791              33                       14.95
          A826749              56                       41.95

     Total On Hand:           556

The table sorted on Part Number is:
        Part Number     Quantity On Hand              Unit Price
          A035467              15                       59.95
          A123456             123                       12.99
          A826749              56                       41.95
          A987654              53                       52.95
          B109897              44                       13.95
          B194791              33                       14.95
          C253146             104                      110.99
          C837289               0                       57.99
          D001234              93                       22.95
          D346246              35                       25.99

     Total On Hand:           556
```

This program uses the same PART_STRUCT structure that we used in dem09-3.cpp. In main(), we declare the part_table array of structures that stores the part table. As in dem09-3.cpp, the variable row serves as the table subscript and total_on_hand is the accumulator that totals the quantity-on-hand amounts in each row of the table.

The functions that load and display the table are exactly as they were in dem09-3.cpp. The program sorts the table using the function Sort_Table(). Like the other two functions, the first argument to Sort_Table() is an array of type PART_STRUCT and the second argument is an integer that represents the number of rows in the table.

The function Sort_Table() works as follows. First, the variable limit is initialized to two less than the size of the table, which is 8. This allows the table subscript to range from 0 to 8 in the first pass over the table. The program uses the variable temp_part, which is of type PART_STRUCT, to swap rows of the table when they are not in order. The variables pass and limit have the same purpose as they had in dem06-4.cpp—pass keeps track of the number of the pass over the table and limit keeps track of how far down the table to go on the current pass. Recall that on each pass over the table, the bubble sort moves the row with the greatest key value to the upper part of the table.

The nested for loops do the actual sorting. The outer for loop counts the number of passes over the table, which is one less than the table size. On each pass, the inner for loop compares the keys of pairs of adjacent table rows. The if statement compares the part_no member of adjacent table rows using the strcmp() library function. If the part number of a row follows the part number of the next row, the rows are out of order. See Figure 9.7. In this case, the program interchanges the rows. To interchange the rows requires that one row be stored temporarily in the structure variable temp_part. Then, the second row is assigned to the first. Finally, the row stored in temp_part is placed into the second row. See Figure 9,8. These assignments are valid because the rows and temp_part are all of type PART_STRUCT. In the case that the table rows are not out of order, the sort does nothing to the rows. After comparing all pairs of adjacent rows, the row with the greatest part number has "bubbled" to the top of the table. Then, the variable limit is decreased by one in preparation for the next inner loop pass. The last part of dem09-4.cpp redisplays the table, which is now sorted on the part number.

9.3.4 Searching a Table

There are two very common ways to search a table: the sequential search and the binary search. The simpler and easier to code is the sequential search. To do a **sequential search** on a dictionary for the word rodomontade (remember that a dictionary is a table), begin at the first dictionary entry and compare it to rodomontade. If the first entry is rodomontade, stop; if it is not, go to the second entry. Continue in this manner until you find the word rodomontade or come to the end of the dictionary (at which point, you would have looked at every word in the dictionary!).

	part_no	quantity_on_hand	unit_price
0	A123456	123	12.99
1	A987654	53	52.95
2	D001234	93	22.95
3	B109897	44	13.95
4	A035467	15	59.95
5	C837289	0	57.99
6	D346246	35	25.99
7	C253146	104	110.99
8	B194791	33	14.95
9	A826749	56	41.95

rows 2 and 3 are out of order { 2, 3

Comparing adjacent rows in the
bubble sort

Figure 9.7

	part_no	quantity_on_hand	unit_price
0	A123456	123	12.99
1	A987654	53	52.95
2	D001234	93	22.95
3	B109897	44	13.95
4	A035467	15	59.95
5	C837289	0	57.99
6	D346246	35	25.99
7	C253146	104	110.99
8	B194791	33	14.95
9	A826749	56	41.95

Store row 2 in `temp_row`

Then copy row 3 to row 2 and copy `temp_row` to row 3.

temp_part

Swapping two rows in the bubble sort

Figure 9.8

A **binary search** of the dictionary takes advantage of the alphabetical order of the entries in the dictionary—the dictionary is sorted on the word member. To do a binary search, first go to the middle word (approximately) of the dictionary and compare it to rodomontade. If this middle word is rodomontade, stop. If it is not, you can tell which half of the dictionary contains rodomontade by determining whether rodomontade comes alphabetically before or after the middle word. Once this is decided, you take the half of the dictionary that contains rodomontade, divide it in half, and proceed as before. Each step of the search divides the part of the dictionary still under consideration into two equal parts (see Figure 9.9)—therefore, the name binary search. Eventually, you either find the entry for rodomontade or the search fails.

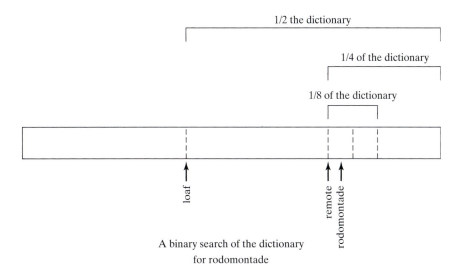

1/2 the dictionary

1/4 of the dictionary

1/8 of the dictionary

loaf

remote

rodomontade

A binary search of the dictionary for rodomontade

Figure 9.9

As a rule, a binary search is much faster than a sequential search. This is especially true when the table has 50 or more rows or when the table must be searched frequently. However, to do a binary search, the table must be sorted on its table key. We shall show how to do both a sequential and a binary search.

9.3.5 Sequential Search

The following pseudocode describes the heart of the sequential search. It assumes that the user has input a value for the search key.

```
for (each table row)
    if (the table key for the row equals the search key)
        break
    endif
endfor

if (search was not successful)
    display search not successful
else
    extract data from table row
    process the extracted data
endif
```

The pseudocode is in two sections. The first section contains a for loop that tests each table row. If the table key of the tested row equals the value of the search key, the search is successful. Then, a break statement takes control out of the loop because there is no need to test the rest of the table. If the table key of the tested row never equals the value of the search key, the search is not successful.

The for loop in the first section of pseudocode can end in one of two ways—the search can be successful or not. The second part of the pseudocode tests why the for loop stopped. If the search was not successful, an appropriate message is displayed. If the search was successful, the row number of the row being tested at the time the break statement in the for loop was executed is the row number that contains the search key. We then extract and process the appropriate data from that row.

The program dem09-5.cpp shows how to do a sequential search of an unsorted table.

```
// dem09-5.cpp

// This program shows how to do a sequential search of a table.

#include <iostream>
#include <iomanip>
#include <cctype>
#include <cstring>

using namespace std;

struct PART_STRUCT
{
    char    part_no[8];
```

```
    int     quantity_on_hand;
    double unit_price;
};

void Load_Part_Table(PART_STRUCT [], int);
void Display_Part_Table(PART_STRUCT [], int);

int main()
{
    const int TABLE_SIZE = 10;

    PART_STRUCT part_table[TABLE_SIZE];
    int         row;
    char        part_key[8];       // The table search key
    char        response[2];

    cout << setprecision(2)
         << setiosflags(ios::fixed)
         << setiosflags(ios::showpoint);

    // Load the table
    Load_Part_Table(part_table, TABLE_SIZE);

    // Display the table
    cout << endl << endl;
    cout << "This is the table you entered.";

    Display_Part_Table(part_table, TABLE_SIZE);

    cout << endl << endl;
    cout << "Do you want to search the table?(Y/N): ";
    cin.getline(response, 2);

    // Do the table search
    while (toupper(*response) == 'Y')
    {
        cout << endl;
        cout << "Enter the part number: ";
        cin.getline(part_key, 8);

        for (row = 0; row < TABLE_SIZE; ++row)
            if (strcmp(part_table[row].part_no, part_key) == 0)
                break;

        if (row == TABLE_SIZE)   //search not successful
        {
            cout << endl;
            cout << "The search for " << part_key
                 << " was not successful." << endl;
        }
        else                         //search successful
        {
            cout << endl;
            cout << "Data for " << part_key << ":" << endl << endl;
            cout << "Quantity On Hand: " << setw(10)
```

```
            << part_table[row].quantity_on_hand << endl;
        cout << "Unit Price:      " << setw(10)
            << part_table[row].unit_price << endl;
      }

    cout << endl << endl;
    cout << "Do you want to search the table?(Y/N): ";
    cin.getline(response, 2);

  }

  return 0;
} //End of main()

void Load_Part_Table(PART_STRUCT part_table[], int size)
{
  int row;

  cout << endl;
  cout << "Enter the table values as you are prompted:"
       << endl << endl;

  for (row = 0; row < size ; ++row)
  {
    cout << endl;
    cout << "For row #" << row + 1 << " enter:" << endl;
    cout << "Part Number (7 Characters): ";
    cin.getline(part_table[row].part_no, 8);

    cout << "Quantity On Hand: ";
    cin >> part_table[row].quantity_on_hand;

    cout << "Unit Price: ";
    cin >> part_table[row].unit_price;

    cin.get();  //remove the newline character from the input buffer
  }
} //End of Load_Part_Table()

void Display_Part_Table(PART_STRUCT part_table[], int size)
{
  int row;

  cout << endl << endl;
  cout << setw(20) << "Part Number"
       << setw(20) << "Quantity On Hand"
       << setw(20) << "Unit Price" << endl;

  for (row = 0; row < size; ++row)
  {
    cout << endl;
    cout << setw(20) << part_table[row].part_no
         << setw(20) << part_table[row].quantity_on_hand
         << setw(20) << part_table[row].unit_price;
  }
} //End of Display_Part_Table()
```

Program Output

Enter the table values as you are prompted:

For row #1 enter:
Part Number (7 Characters): **A123456**
Quantity On Hand: **123**
Unit Price: **12.99**

For row #2 enter:
Part Number (7 Characters): **A987654**
Quantity On Hand: **53**
Unit Price: **52.95**

For row #3 enter:
Part Number (7 Characters): **D001234**
Quantity On Hand: **93**
Unit Price: **22.95**

For row #4 enter:
Part Number (7 Characters): **B109897**
Quantity On Hand: **44**
Unit Price: **13.95**

For row #5 enter:
Part Number (7 Characters): **A035467**
Quantity On Hand: **15**
Unit Price: **59.95**

For row #6 enter:
Part Number (7 Characters): **C837289**
Quantity On Hand: **0**
Unit Price: **57.99**

For row #7 enter:
Part Number (7 Characters): **D346246**
Quantity On Hand: **35**
Unit Price: **25.99**

For row #8 enter:
Part Number (7 Characters): **C235146**
Quantity On Hand: **104**
Unit Price: **110.99**

For row #9 enter:
Part Number (7 Characters): **B194791**
Quantity On Hand: **33**
Unit Price: **14.95**

For row #10 enter:
Part Number (7 Characters): **A826749**
Quantity On Hand: **56**
Unit Price: **41.95**

```
This is the table you entered.
          Part Number      Quantity On Hand              Unit Price
             A123456                 123                    12.99
             A987654                  53                    52.95
             D001234                  93                    22.95
             B109897                  44                    13.95
             A035467                  15                    59.95
             C837289                   0                    57.99
             D346246                  35                    25.99
             C253146                 104                   110.99
             B194791                  33                    14.95
             A826749                  56                    41.95
Do you want to search the table?(Y/N): Y

Enter the part number: D001234

Data for D001234:

Quantity On Hand:          93
Unit Price:             22.95

Do you want to search the table?(Y/N): y

Enter the part number: C012345

The search for C012345 was not successful.

Do you want to search the table?(Y/N): Y

Enter the part number: A826749

Data for A826749:

Quantity On Hand:          56
Unit Price:             41.95

Do you want to search the table?(Y/N): N
```

We declare the table in the usual way using the structure data type PART_STRUCT. The variable row is the table subscript. The program uses the character array part_key[] to hold the value of the search key, which the user inputs. The character array response[] holds the user's response to the question about whether he or she wishes to make a search of the table.

The program begins in the same way as dem09-3.cpp by inputting the table values and displaying the table. Next, the program asks the user if he or she wants to search the table. The while loop does the search for as long as the user responds 'Y' to the prompt. The condition in the while statement converts to uppercase the character that the user enters in response to the prompt. (Recall that the identifier response is a pointer to the first character in the array.) If the resulting character equals 'Y', then the search begins.

In the while loop's body, the user is prompted to enter a part number. This is the value of the search key—the part number whose value we wish to locate in the table. The for loop then proceeds to locate the row containing a match to the search key. For each row of the table, the for loop's if statement compares the part_no member to the value in part_key using the strcmp() library function. Recall that strcmp() returns zero if the two strings that it compares are equal. Thus, if the search key matches the part number of the current row, the appropriate row has been found and the break statement ends the for loop. If the search key is not in the table, the for loop ends because row becomes equal to TABLE_SIZE.

The next if statement tests why the for loop ended. If the value of row equals TABLE_SIZE, the search was not successful and the program displays an appropriate message. If row is not equal to TABLE_SIZE, then the for loop ended because of the break statement, which means that the search was successful. The value of row is then the row number of the matching part number. Thus, the program displays the data corresponding to the search key.

Finally, the program asks the user if he or she wants to do another search. If the user responds 'Y', then the program proceeds to do another search. If not, the program ends.

9.3.6 Binary Search

The logic of a binary search is more complex than that of a sequential search. To explain the binary search, we first assume that the search key value is in the table. That is, we first assume that the search will be successful.

As we mentioned previously, the binary search successively divides the table in half, zeroing in on the row that contains the search key. Thus, the search must have a way of keeping track of which part of the table it is currently searching. We do this using the variables lower and upper, which always contain the row numbers of the first and last rows of the part of the table currently being searched. Initially, the value of lower is 0 and the value of upper is one less than the table size. See Figure 9.10. Thus, the value of lower should never be greater than the value of upper.

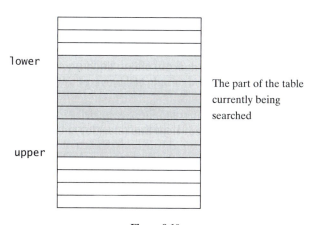

Figure 9.10

The basic idea of the binary search is the following: compare the search key to the table key of the middle row of the part of the table currently being searched. The variable middle, which equals the average of lower and upper, gives the row number of the middle of the part of the table currently being searched. If the search key equals the table key of row middle, the search is successful and the search can stop.

If the search key is less than the table key of row middle, then the row we want is between row lower and row middle - 1. See Figure 9.11. Thus, on the next pass of the search, we want the new value of upper to be middle - 1. If the search key is greater than the table key of row middle, then the row we want is between row middle + 1 and row upper. On the next pass of the search, we want the new value of lower to be middle + 1. In either case, the new values of lower and upper will be closer.

Because we are assuming that the search will be successful, this process must eventually stop. At that point, row middle is the row we want. We can then process the data contained in that row.

Now, suppose that the search key value is not in the table. How can we decide that the search is not successful? The search would still proceed as we have described. At each pass of the search, we increase lower and decrease upper. If the search key is not in the table, the procedure eventually will make the value of lower greater than the value of upper. This contradiction signals an unsuccessful search.

The following pseudocode summarizes the essential parts of a binary search.

```
lower = 0, upper = tablesize − 1, middle = (lower + upper)/2
while (lower <= upper and search key unequal to table key)
  if (search key < table key)
    upper = middle − 1
  else
    lower = middle + 1
  endif
  middle = (lower + upper) / 2;
endwhile
```

Figure 9.11

```
if (lower > upper)
  display unsuccessful search
else
  extract table data from row middle
  process table data from row middle
endif
```

The `while` loop is the heart of the binary search. Its condition says to continue the search as long as the search is not unsuccessful (`lower <= upper`) and as long as we have not yet found the search key (search key unequal to table key). The loop body tests the part of the table that contains the search key and adjusts either `upper` or `lower`. In either case, it calculates the new value for `middle` for the next loop pass.

The second part of the pseudocode decides why the `while` loop ended. The `while` loop ended because a condition in its compound condition was false. If `lower > upper`, the search was not successful. Otherwise, the other condition was false and so the search key must be equal to the table key of row `middle`.

The program dem09-6.cpp shows how to do a binary search of a table. The program is based on dem09-4.cpp, which sorts the table that the user inputs.

```cpp
// dem09-6.cpp

// This program loads a table, sorts it using the bubble sort, and
// then uses a binary search to search the table.

#include <iostream>
#include <iomanip>
#include <cstring>
#include <cctype>

using namespace std;

struct PART_STRUCT
{
  char    part_no[8];
  int     quantity_on_hand;
  double unit_price;
};

void Load_Part_Table(PART_STRUCT [], int);
void Display_Part_Table(PART_STRUCT [], int);
void Sort_Table(PART_STRUCT [], int);

int main()
{
  const int TABLE_SIZE = 10;

  PART_STRUCT part_table[TABLE_SIZE];

  int middle,
      lower,
      upper;
```

```
char part_key[8];         // The table search key
char response[2];

cout << setprecision(2)
     << setiosflags(ios::fixed)
     << setiosflags(ios::showpoint);

// Load the table
Load_Part_Table(part_table, TABLE_SIZE);

// Sort the table using the bubble sort
Sort_Table(part_table, TABLE_SIZE);

// Display the sorted table
cout << endl << endl;
cout << "The table sorted on Part Number is:";

Display_Part_Table(part_table, TABLE_SIZE);

// Do the table search
cout << endl << endl;
cout << "Do you want to search the table?(Y/N): ";
cin.getline(response, 2);

while (toupper(*response) == 'Y')
{
  cout << endl;
  cout << "Enter the part number: ";
  cin.getline(part_key, 8);

  // Do the binary search
  lower = 0;
  upper = TABLE_SIZE - 1;
  middle = (lower + upper) / 2;

  while ( (strcmp(part_table[middle].part_no,part_key))
                && (lower <= upper) )
  {
    if (strcmp(part_key,part_table[middle].part_no) < 0)
      upper = middle - 1;
    else
      lower = middle + 1;

    middle = (lower + upper) / 2;
  }

  if (lower > upper)
  {
    cout << endl;
    cout << "The search for " << part_key
         << " was not successful." << endl;
  }
  else
  {
    cout << endl;
    cout << "Data for " << part_key << ":" << endl << endl;
```

```cpp
         cout << "Quantity On Hand: " << setw(10)
              << part_table[middle].quantity_on_hand << endl;
         cout << "Unit Price:       " << setw(10)
              << part_table[middle].unit_price << endl;
    }

    cout << endl << endl;
    cout << "Do you want to search the table?(Y/N): ";
    cin.getline(response, 2);
  }

  return 0;
} //End of main()

void Load_Part_Table(PART_STRUCT part_table[], int size)
{
  int row;

  cout << endl;
  cout << "Enter the table values as you are prompted:"
       << endl << endl;

  for (row = 0; row < size ; ++row)
  {
    cout << endl;
    cout << "For row #" << row + 1 << " enter:" << endl;
    cout << "Part Number (7 Characters): ";
    cin.getline(part_table[row].part_no, 8);

    cout << "Quantity On Hand: ";
    cin >> part_table[row].quantity_on_hand;

    cout << "Unit Price: ";
    cin >> part_table[row].unit_price;

    cin.get();  //remove the newline character from the input buffer
  }
} //End of Load_Part_Table()

void Sort_Table(PART_STRUCT part_table[], int size)
{
  int row,
      pass,
      limit;
  PART_STRUCT temp_part;

  limit = size - 2;

  for (pass = 1; pass <= size - 1; ++pass)
  {
    for (row = 0; row <= limit; ++row)
      if (strcmp(part_table[row].part_no,
                             part_table[row + 1].part_no) > 0)
      {
        temp_part = part_table[row];
```

```
                part_table[row] = part_table[row + 1];
                part_table[row + 1] = temp_part;
            }

            --limit;
        }
    } //End of Sort_Table()

    void Display_Part_Table(PART_STRUCT part_table[], int size)
    {
        int row;

        cout << endl << endl;
        cout << setw(20) << "Part Number"
                << setw(20) << "Quantity On Hand"
                << setw(20) << "Unit Price"
                << endl;

        for (row = 0; row < size; ++row)
        {
            cout << endl;
            cout << setw(20) << part_table[row].part_no
                    << setw(20) << part_table[row].quantity_on_hand
                    << setw(20) << part_table[row].unit_price;
        }
    } //End of Display_Part_Table()
```

Program Output

Enter the table values as you are prompted:

For row #1 enter:
Part Number (7 Characters): **A123456**
Quantity On Hand: **123**
Unit Price: **12.99**

For row #2 enter:
Part Number (7 Characters): **A987654**
Quantity On Hand: **53**
Unit Price: **52.95**

For row #3 enter:
Part Number (7 Characters): **D001234**
Quantity On Hand: **93**
Unit Price: **22.95**

For row #4 enter:
Part Number (7 Characters): **B109897**
Quantity On Hand: **44**
Unit Price: **13.95**

For row #5 enter:
Part Number (7 Characters): **A035467**

```
Quantity On Hand: 15
Unit Price: 59.95

For row #6 enter:
Part Number (7 Characters): C837289
Quantity On Hand: 0
Unit Price: 57.99

For row #7 enter:
Part Number (7 Characters): D346246
Quantity On Hand: 35
Unit Price: 25.99

For row #8 enter:
Part Number (7 Characters): C235146
Quantity On Hand: 104
Unit Price: 110.99

For row #9 enter:
Part Number (7 Characters): B194791
Quantity On Hand: 33
Unit Price: 14.95

For row #10 enter:
Part Number (7 Characters): A826749
Quantity On Hand: 56
Unit Price: 41.95

The table sorted on Part Number is:

            Part Number     Quantity On Hand              Unit Price

                A035467                   15                   59.95
                A123456                  123                   12.99
                A826749                   56                   41.95
                A987654                   53                   52.95
                B109897                   44                   13.95
                B194791                   33                   14.95
                C253146                  104                  110.99
                C837289                    0                   57.99
                D001234                   93                   22.95
                D346246                   35                   25.99

Do you want to search the table?(Y/N): Y

Enter the part number: D001234

Data for D001234:

Quantity On Hand:          93
Unit Price:            22.95

Do you want to search the table?(Y/N): y

Enter the part number: C012345
```

```
The search for C012345 was not successful.

Do you want to search the table?(Y/N): Y

Enter the part number: A826749

Data for A826749:

Quantity On Hand:          56
Unit Price:             41.95

Do you want to search the table?(Y/N): N
```

The first part of the program closely follows dem09-4.cpp; it loads the table and sorts it on the part number. The next part of the program follows the pseudocode for the binary search. Note that the `while` loop's condition contains the following.

```
strcmp(part_table[middle].part_no, part_key)
```

Recall that `strcmp()` returns a nonzero number, which C++ considers true, if the result of the comparison is that the strings are not equal. Thus, this tests that the table key is unequal to the search key.

Similarly, in the `while` loop's body, the `if` statement tests the following.

```
strcmp(part_key,part_table[middle].part_no) < 0
```

If this condition is true, `part_key` precedes the value of `part_table[middle].part_no`. Thus, the search key is in the lower part of the table and an adjustment is made to the value of `upper`. If the condition is false, the search key is in the upper part of the table and an adjustment is made to the value of `lower`.

Exercises 9.3

Use the following declarations in Exercises 1–6.

```
struct ITEM_STRUCT
{
   char name[21];
   double quantity,
          price;
};

ITEM_STRUCT item = {"Hard Disk", 17, 345.99};
ITEM_STRUCT* item_ptr = &item;

ITEM_STRUCT inventory[100];
```

1. What is the value of `item.name[3]`?
2. What is the value of `item.name + 2`?
3. Is the reference `inventory[14].name` legal? If so, to what does it refer?
4. Is the reference `inventory.name` legal? If so, to what does it refer?
5. How would you refer to the `quantity` member of row 37 of the inventory table?

6. **(a)** Use the STUDENT_STRUCT structure type defined in Exercise 1, Section 9.2, to declare a table that will store the information about 100 students.

   (b) Write a for loop that prompts the user to enter the data necessary to load the table declared in part (a).

7. **(a)** Use the JUROR_STRUCT structure type defined in Exercise 2, Section 9.2, to declare a table that will store the information about 30 jurors.

   (b) Write a for loop that prompts the user to enter the data necessary to load the table declared in part (a).

8. **(a)** Use the EMPLOYEE_STRUCT structure type defined in Exercise 3, Section 9.2, to declare a table that will store the data about 20 employees.

   (b) Write a for loop that prompts the user to enter the data necessary to load the table declared in part (a).

Experiments 9.3

1. Omit the call to cin.get() at the end of the first for loop in dem09-3.cpp. Compile and execute the resulting program. Explain what happens.
2. Recode dem09-3.cpp by hard coding the parts table. Explain what happens.
3. Change dem09-4.cpp so that it sorts the table in descending order.
4. Recode dem09-6.cpp so that it sorts the parts table in descending order and does a binary search to search the table.

Programming Problems 9.3

1. The following table contains the post office abbreviations and names of five states in the Northeast.

   TABLE 9.2

State Name	State Code
New York	NY
New Jersey	NJ
Pennsylvania	PA
Connecticut	CT
Rhode Island	RI

   Write a program in which you hard code a similar table that contains the state names and abbreviations of all 50 states. (You can find this table in an encyclopedia or almanac.) The program should prompt the user to enter a state name. Let the program do a sequential search to find the corresponding state postal code. The program should display the postal code.

2. Redo Programming Problem 1 but let the program do a binary search of the table.
3. See Programming Problems 1 and 2. We mentioned in the text that the binary search is faster than the sequential search when the table is about size 50. This

programming problem shows how to test this statement. We can measure the efficiency of a search technique by how many table key comparisons the technique makes. In your solutions to Programming Problems 1 and 2, declare a counter variable, which you should initialize to zero in its declaration. Increment the counter for each execution of the `strcmp()` function in the search part of the program. Have each program display the value of this counter before the program ends. Run the sequential search program ten times and total the number of key compares that the sequential search makes. Now do the same for the binary search program using the same input data that you used for the sequential search program. How do the total number of key comparisons compare? Is the binary search more efficient than the sequential search?

4. A car rental company uses the following table to help compute rental fees.

TABLE 9.3

Car Type	Rate per Day	Rate per Mile
Chevrolet	50.00	0.27
Corvette	85.00	0.45
Pontiac	53.00	0.32
Buick	60.00	0.32
Oldsmobile	60.00	0.35
Cadillac	70.00	0.40

Write a program to calculate car rental fees based on this table. The program should prompt the user to enter the name of the type of car that was rented, the number of days the car was rented, and the number of miles the car was driven. The program should search the table for a match on the car type. If there is a match, the rental fee is the number of days rented, times the rate per day, plus the number of miles traveled, times the rate per mile. The program should display the type of car, the number of days rented, the number of miles driven, and the rental fee. If the table search cannot find the car type in the table, display an appropriate error message. Write the program to process any number of rentals.

5. The marketing department of a large book club wants to analyze the geographical distribution of its customers by categorizing customers by zip code. Write a program that prompts the user to enter the five-digit zip code of a customer. Store the customer information in an array of structures that have two integer members: the first member stores a zip code and the second stores the count of the customers who have that zip code. Assume a maximum of 100 different zip codes. When a zip code is entered, search the zip code table for the zip code. If it is not in the table, add it to the end of the table and set the corresponding count to one. If the entered zip code is in the zip code table, increment the corresponding count.

When the user completes entering zip codes, the program should display a table that lists the zip codes with their corresponding counts and the percent that count is of the total number of customers. The total number of customers should display at the bottom of the table.

6. Write a program that creates a telephone book. Each telephone book entry is to consist of a name and a 10-digit telephone number. Implement a table entry by a structure with two members—a character pointer called `name` and an array of 11 characters called `tel_no` that stores the telephone number as a string. The program should allow for, at most, 100 names. The program should ask the user to enter the letter 'I' to insert a name in the directory, 'R' to retrieve a telephone number from the directory, 'P' to display the contents of the directory, or 'Q' to exit the program. If the user enters 'I', the program should prompt the user for a last name and store the name in a character array buffer. Then, the program should dynamically allocate enough space for the name and assign the name member of the next available row to the allocated space. Next, the program should copy the name, which is stored in the buffer, to the allocated space. The program should then prompt for the corresponding telephone number. If the user enters 'R', the program should search the directory for the corresponding name. If the name is found, display the corresponding telephone number. If the name is not found, display an error message. If the user enters 'P', display the contents of the directory in tabular form with appropriate column headings. If the user enters 'Q', display an ending message and end the program.

9.4 STRUCTURES, FUNCTIONS, AND POINTERS

Because a structure is a data type, a function can return a structure to a calling function. We can also pass a structure to a function as a function argument. However, a structure is usually a large aggregate of data. Pointers, therefore, can make manipulating structures more efficient. This section discusses how to use structures with functions and how to use pointers to structures.

9.4.1 Functions and Structures

A structure can be a function argument and a function can return a structure. For example, suppose that we need a function to convert a character string that represents a date of the form mm/dd/yyyy into three integers. The first integer represents the month, the second integer represents the day, and the third integer represents the year. The function will return the three integers in a variable of the following structure type.

```
struct DATE_STRUCT
{
  int month,
      day,
      year;
};
```

Once this function converts the date, we want to verify that the date is valid. For example, the date 7/53/2004 is invalid. We will verify the date using a function whose argument is a date of type DATE_STRUCT. For a date to be valid, the day number must be within the valid range of days for the associated month, taking leap years into account.

Also, to be valid, the year must be 1980 or later. The program dem09-7.cpp converts and validates a date and illustrates how to use structures with functions. The program uses the function atoi(), which we discussed in Section 8.5.

```cpp
// dem09-7.cpp

//This program demonstrates the use of structures as function
//arguments and function return values.

#include <iostream>
#include <iomanip>
#include <cstdlib>
#include <cctype>

using namespace std;

struct DATE_STRUCT
{
   int month,
       day,
       year;
};

DATE_STRUCT String_To_MDY(char*);
bool        Validate_Date(DATE_STRUCT);
char*       Strchcpy(char*, char*, int);

int main()
{
   char date_string [11];
   DATE_STRUCT mdy_date;
   char response[2];

   cout << endl << endl;
   cout << "Do you want to convert and validate a date?(Y/N): ";
   cin.getline(response, 2);

   while (toupper(*response) == 'Y')
   {
      cout << endl;
      cout << "Enter the date in mm/dd/yyyy form: ";
      cin.getline(date_string, 11);

      mdy_date = String_To_MDY (date_string);

      cout << endl;
      cout << "The converted date is the following:" << endl << endl;
      cout << "Month: " << setw(4) << mdy_date.month << endl;
      cout << "Day:   " << setw(4) << mdy_date.day << endl;
      cout << "Year:  " << setw(4) << mdy_date.year << endl;

      if ( Validate_Date(mdy_date) )
      {
         cout << endl;
         cout << "The date is valid." << endl;
      }
```

```
    else
    {
      cout << endl;
      cout << "The date is invalid." << endl;
    }

    cout << endl << endl;
    cout << "Do you want to convert and validate a date?(Y/N): ";
    cin.getline(response, 2);
  }

  return 0;
} // End of main()
DATE_STRUCT String_To_MDY(char* date_ptr)
{
  DATE_STRUCT mdy_date;
  char month[3],
       day[3],
       year[5];
  char* ch_ptr;

  ch_ptr = date_ptr;

  ch_ptr = Strchcpy(month, ch_ptr, '/');
  ++ch_ptr;
  ch_ptr = Strchcpy(day, ch_ptr, '/');
  ++ch_ptr;
  Strchcpy(year, ch_ptr, '\0');

  mdy_date.month = atoi(month);
  mdy_date.day   = atoi(day);
  mdy_date.year  = atoi(year);

  return mdy_date;

} // End of String_To_MDY()
char* Strchcpy(char* target, char* source, int ch)
{
  while (*source != ch && *source != '\0')
  {
    *target = *source;
    ++target;
    ++source;
  }

  *target = '\0';

  return source;

} // End of Strchcpy()
bool Validate_Date(DATE_STRUCT date)
{
  int ny_days [13] = {0, 31, 28, 31, 30, 31, 30, 31, 31, 30, 31, 30, 31};
  int ly_days [13] = {0, 31, 29, 31, 30, 31, 30, 31, 31, 30, 31, 30, 31};
```

```
if (date.month < 1 || date.month > 12)
    return false;

if (date.day < 1)
    return false;
if (date.year % 4 == 0)
{
    if (date.day > ly_days[date.month])
        return false;
}
else
    if (date.day > ny_days[date.month])
        return false;
if (date.year < 1980)
    return false;

return true;

} // End of Validate_Date()
```

Program Output

Do you want to convert and validate a date?(Y/N): **y**

Enter the date in mm/dd/yyyy form: **6/9/1993**

The converted date is the following:

```
Month:       6
Day:         9
Year:     1993
```
The date is valid.

Do you want to convert and validate a date?(Y/N): **Yes**

Enter the date in mm/dd/yyyy form: **2/29/1996**

The converted date is the following:

```
Month:       2
Day:        29
Year:     1996
```

The date is valid.

Do you want to convert and validate a date?(Y/N): **Y**

Enter the date in mm/dd/yyyy form: **13/14/1983**

The converted date is the following:

```
Month:      13
Day:        14
Year:     1983
```

The date is invalid.

```
Do you want to convert and validate a date?(Y/N): y

Enter the date in mm/dd/yyyy form: 3/33/1995

The converted date is the following:

Month:      3
Day:       33
Year:    1995

The date is invalid.

Do you want to convert and validate a date?(Y/N): y

Enter the date in mm/dd/yyyy form: 9/23/1976

The converted date is the following:

Month:      9
Day:       23
Year:    1976

The date is invalid.

Do you want to convert and validate a date?(Y/N): n
```

The program begins with the definition of the DATE_STRUCT structure type, which the program uses to store the date as a set of three integers. The program uses three user-defined functions. String_To_MDY() converts the date, which the user enters as a string of the form mm/dd/yyyy, into a date of type DATE_STRUCT. Thus, the return type of String_To_MDY() is DATE_STRUCT. Validate_Date() validates the date passed to it as an argument of type DATE_STRUCT. It returns true if the date is valid and returns false if the date is invalid. We shall explain the purpose of the third function, Strchcpy(), when we discuss the String_To_MDY() function.

The logic of the main processing loop of dem09-7.cpp should, by now, be familiar. It asks the user if he or she wants to convert and validate a date. If the response is yes, the program enters the loop. Inside the loop, the program asks the user to enter a date in the form mm/dd/yyyy. First, cin.getline() retrieves the string and stores it in the character array date_string[]. Next, the program passes date_string to the function String_To_MDY(), which converts it into a date stored as a structure of type DATE_STRUCT. The assignment statement stores the returned structure in the structure variable mdy_date. The cout statements display the converted date.

The condition in the if statement calls the function Validate_Date(). Then, an appropriate message is displayed depending on whether the date is valid or invalid. Finally, the program prompts the user again to see if he or she wants to process another date.

The heart of dem09-7.cpp is the function String_To_MDY(), which converts the date as a string into a date as a DATE_STRUCT structure. The function first separates the month, day, and year digits from the string. The month digits are the first digits in the string up to, but not including, the slash. The day digits are the digits from the digit after the first slash up to, but not including, the second slash. The year digits are the digits from the digit after the second slash to the end of the string. In all three cases, we must obtain characters in the date string from a certain position up to a specific character (the slash in the first two cases, the '\0' in the third case). Because this is essentially the same operation in all three cases, it is appropriate to use a function, which we call Strchcpy(), to do the job.

The function Strchcpy() has three arguments. The first argument is the target string, which is the string into which the function places the result. The second argument is a character pointer, which points to the character in the source string where the copying begins. The third argument is the character that determines when the copying is to stop. The function returns a pointer to the character that makes the copying stop. Thus, the function copies characters from the position determined by its second argument to the string that is its first argument. The copying stops when the function encounters the character that is the function's third argument. To see how the function works, we explain its uses in String_To_MDY().

The parameter date_ptr points to the first character of the string that contains the date in mm/dd/yyyy form. The first assignment statement in String_To_MDY() initializes the character pointer to the value of date_ptr. The right side of the next assignment calls the function Strchcpy(). We want to copy the digits that specify the month into the character array month. Thus, we want to copy the digits up to the first '/' from the string pointed to by ch_ptr into the array month. This is exactly what Strchcpy(month, ch_ptr, '/') does. See Figure 9.12. The function returns a pointer to the '/' character. To make the next call to Strchcpy() work correctly, we increment the pointer ch_ptr so that it points to the first character after the '/'.

The next assignment statement is similar to the previous one. It copies the day digits into the array day. Finally, the third call to Strchcpy() copies the year digits into the array year. The delimiting character is now the null character '\0'.

The digits representing the month, day, and year are separately stored in three character arrays. Now we must convert the three character strings into the corresponding integer values. Therefore, the next three assignments use the standard library function atoi() to convert the numeric character strings into the corresponding integers.

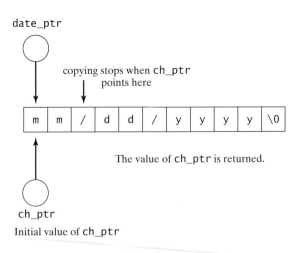

Figure 9.12

Finally, `String_To_MDY()` returns the structure in which the numeric date is stored. (The operation of `String_To_MDY()` depends on the character string that the user enters being in the mm/dd/yyyy form. What if the user incorrectly enters the date? See Programming Problem 1.)

The function `Strchcpy()` copies characters as follows. The `while` loop in `Strchcpy()` copies one character at a time from the source string to the target string. `Strchcpy()`continues copying until it either finds the delimiter character, which is stored in `ch`, or the end of the source string. Once the `while` loop ends, the function places the null character at the end of the target string. Finally, the function returns the value of the pointer `source`, which points to the character that caused the copying to stop.

Once `main()` obtains the date in numeric form in the structure `mdy_date`, it displays the resulting date. Then, `main()`executes an `if` statement. The `if`'s condition tests the value returned from the function `Validate_Date()` and displays an appropriate message.

`Validate_Date()`validates the date. The only part of the function that we shall explain is the test to see if the day is too large. The day must be checked against the number of days in the month. The number of days in February depends on whether the year is a leap year—29 days for a leap year, 28 days otherwise. Therefore, we begin by testing the year. The expression `date.year % 4` is the remainder when the year is divided by four. If the remainder is zero, the year is divisible by four and is, therefore, a leap year. (This test will be valid until the year 2100. See Programming Problem 2.) Then, we check the value of `date.day` against `ly_days[date_month]`. The integer array `ly_days` holds the number of days in each month in a leap year. We place zero in the first element of this array so that the month number corresponds to the correct subscript value. Thus, if `date.day` is greater than `ly_days[date.month]`, the date is invalid and the function returns zero. Note that the inner `if` is enclosed in braces. Without these braces, the compiler would pair the following `else` with the second `if` and not the first `if`, which is what we want.

If the year is not a leap year, the value of `day` is compared to the number of days in the corresponding month for a normal year. This number is stored in the integer array `ny_days[]`. Finally, if the date passes all the tests, it is valid and the function returns the value `true`.

9.4.2 Pointers to Structures

Recall that, by default, C++ passes the arguments to a function by value. Thus, when dem09-7.cpp, calls the function `Validate_Date()`, it passes a copy of the structure variable `mdy_date`. Similarly, when `String_To_MDY()` converts the date into three integers, it passes a copy of a `DATE_STRUCT` variable back to `main()`. A variable of type `DATE_STRUCT` is not very large. However, if we were to pass a much larger structure back and forth between functions, it could become very inefficient. It is usually more efficient to pass a structure pointer to a function instead of a copy of the structure itself. All pointers are the same size and small (usually 4 bytes). Therefore, using pointers minimizes the cost of processing structures in functions.

Note 9.5 Using Structure Pointers in Functions

Use structure pointers to pass structures between functions if the structure contains 8 or more bytes.

In C++, pointers are very versatile. A pointer can point to virtually anything, including a structure variable. For example, if mdy_date is a variable of type DATE_STRUCT, as it was in dem09-7.cpp, we can declare the pointer date_struct_ptr and initialize it to point to mdy_date as follows.

    DATE_STRUCT* date_struct_ptr = &mdy_date;

Figure 9.13 shows the pointer and its target.

To access the entire structure through the pointer, we can use the indirection operator: *date_struct_ptr. To access a particular structure member through the pointer, we can use a reference such as the following.

    (*date_struct_ptr).day

Using Note 9.3, read this reference from right to left as "the day member of the target of date_struct_ptr" or "date_struct_ptr's target's day." In Figure 9.13, this would have the value 10. The parentheses are necessary around the *date_struct_ptr because the dot operator has higher precedence than the dereference operator *.

Referencing a structure member through a pointer is so common that C++ has a special operator for this purpose. The "to" operator, ->, which is a hyphen followed by a greater-than symbol, can be used to reference a structure member through a pointer. To reference the day member of the structure mdy_date through the pointer date_struct_ptr, we can use the following.

    date_struct_ptr -> day

Note 9.6 Reading the "to" operator

Read the "to" operator, ->, as "the X member of the target of" or as a possessive of the target, where X is the name of the structure's member.

Figure 9.13

Therefore, read the previous reference from right to left as "the day member of the target of `date_struct_ptr`" or "`date_struct_ptr`'s target's day."

The program dem09-8.cpp is a second version of dem09-7.cpp. Its functions use structure pointers to access the DATE_STRUCT variables.

```cpp
// dem09-8.cpp

// This program demonstrates the use of structure pointers
// in functions.

#include <iostream>
#include <iomanip>
#include <cstdlib>
#include <cctype>

using namespace std;

struct DATE_STRUCT
{
  int month,
      day,
      year;
};

void    String_To_MDY(char*, DATE_STRUCT*);
bool    Validate_Date(DATE_STRUCT*);

char*   Strchcpy(char*, char*, int);

int main()
{
  char date_string [11];
  DATE_STRUCT mdy_date;
  char response[2];

  cout << endl << endl;
  cout << "Do you want to convert and validate a date?(Y/N): ";
  cin.getline(response, 2);

  while (toupper(*response) == 'Y')
  {
    cout << endl;
    cout << "Enter the date in mm/dd/yyyy form: ";
    cin.getline(date_string, 11);

    String_To_MDY (date_string, &mdy_date);

    cout << endl;
    cout << "The converted date is the following:" << endl << endl;
    cout << "Month: " << setw(4) << mdy_date.month << endl;
    cout << "Day:   " << setw(4) << mdy_date.day << endl;
    cout << "Year:  " << setw(4) << mdy_date.year << endl;

    if ( Validate_Date(&mdy_date) )
    {
      cout << endl;
```

```
       cout << "The date is valid.";
     }
     else
     {
       cout << endl;
       cout << "The date is invalid.";
     }

     cout << endl << endl;
     cout << "Do you want to convert and validate a date?(Y/N): ";
     cin.getline(response, 2);
   }

   cout << endl;
   return 0;
} // End of main()

void String_To_MDY(char* date_ptr, DATE_STRUCT* date_struct_ptr)
{
   char month[3],
        day[3],
        year[5];
   char* ch_ptr;

   ch_ptr = date_ptr;

   ch_ptr = Strchcpy(month, ch_ptr, '/');
   ++ch_ptr;
   ch_ptr = Strchcpy(day, ch_ptr, '/');
   ++ch_ptr;
   Strchcpy(year, ch_ptr, '\0');
   date_struct_ptr -> month = atoi(month);
   date_struct_ptr -> day   = atoi(day);
   date_struct_ptr -> year  = atoi(year);

   return;

} // End of String_To_MDY()

char* Strchcpy(char* target, char* source, int ch)
{
   while (*source != ch && *source != '\0')
   {
     *target = *source;
     ++target;
     ++source;
   }

   *target = '\0';

   return source;

} // End of Strchcpy()

bool Validate_Date(DATE_STRUCT* date_struct_ptr)
{
```

```
int ny_days [13] = {0, 31, 28, 31, 30, 31, 30, 31, 31, 30, 31, 30, 31};
int ly_days [13] = {0, 31, 29, 31, 30, 31, 30, 31, 31, 30, 31, 30, 31};

if (date_struct_ptr -> month < 1 || date_struct_ptr -> month > 12)
   return false;

if (date_struct_ptr -> day < 1)
      return false;
if (date_struct_ptr -> year % 4 == 0)
{
   if (date_struct_ptr -> day > ly_days[date_struct_ptr -> month])
     return false;
}
else
   if (date_struct_ptr -> day > ny_days[date_struct_ptr -> month])
     return false;

if (date_struct_ptr -> year < 1980)
   return false;

return true;

} // End of Validate_Date()
```

The logic and output of dem09-8.cpp are exactly those of dem09-7.cpp. Therefore, we shall discuss only the uses the program makes of structure pointers. In dem09-8.cpp, String_To_MDY() is a void function because its second argument is a pointer to a variable of type DATE_STRUCT. Instead of returning a copy of the date in a structure, we pass a pointer to such a structure to the function. The function then manipulates the structure variable in main(). Similarly, we pass a DATE_STRUCT pointer to the function Validate_Date() instead of a copy of the structure.

After obtaining the date and placing it into the array date_string, main() calls the function String_To_MDY(). The function main() passes two pointers to String_To_MDY()—date_string, which points to the beginning of the array containing the date in mm/dd/yy form, and &mdy_date, which is the address of the structure variable mdy_date. Therefore, in the function String_To_MDY(), the parameter date_struct_ptr points to the structure mdy_date in main(). See Figure 9.14.

Most of the function String_To_MDY() is the same as it was in dem09-7.cpp except the last three assignments. In this version of the function, we use the member operator to refer to the members of the target of date_struct_ptr. Thus, for example, the following assignment places the integer form of the month into the month member of the target of date_struct_ptr, which is the month member of mdy_date in main(). See Figure 9.14.

```
date_struct_ptr -> month = atoi(month);
```

The parameter date_struct_ptr in Validate_Date() also points to the structure variable mdy_date in main(). Therefore, all references to the members of the structure must use the member operator. For example, in the first if statement, we refer to the month member of date as follows.

```
date_struct_ptr -> month
```

As before, this references the month member of the structure mdy_date in main().

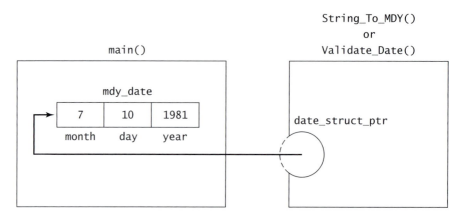

Figure 9.14

9.4.3 Structure References

You can also pass a structure reference to a function. Using structure references combines the ease of passing a structure by value with the efficiency of using references, which are essentially the same as pointers. Following is dem09-9.cpp, which is still another version of dem09-7.cpp.

```cpp
// dem09-9.cpp

// This program demonstrates the use of structure references
// in functions.

#include <iostream>
#include <iomanip>
#include <cstdlib>
#include <cctype>

using namespace std;

struct DATE_STRUCT
{
   int month,
       day,
       year;
};

void   String_To_MDY(char*, DATE_STRUCT&);
bool   Validate_Date(DATE_STRUCT&);
char* Strchcpy(char*, char*, int);

int main()
{
   char date_string [11];
   DATE_STRUCT mdy_date;
   char response[2];
```

```cpp
  cout << endl << endl;
  cout << "Do you want to convert and validate a date?(Y/N): ";
  cin.getline(response, 2);

  while (toupper(*response) == 'Y')
  {
    cout << endl;
    cout << "Enter the date in mm/dd/yyyy form: ";
    cin.getline(date_string, 11);

    String_To_MDY (date_string, mdy_date);

    cout << endl;
    cout << "The converted date is the following:" << endl << endl;
    cout << "Month: " << setw(4) << mdy_date.month << endl;
    cout << "Day:   " << setw(4) << mdy_date.day << endl;
    cout << "Year:  " << setw(4) << mdy_date.year << endl;

    if ( Validate_Date(mdy_date) )
    {
      cout << endl;
      cout << "The date is valid.";
    }
    else
    {
      cout << endl;
      cout << "The date is invalid.";
    }

    cout << endl << endl;
    cout << "Do you want to convert and validate a date?(Y/N): ";
    cin.getline(response, 2);
  }

  cout << endl;
  return 0;
} // End of main()

void String_To_MDY(char* date_ptr, DATE_STRUCT& date_struct)
{
  char month[3],
       day[3],
       year[5];
  char* ch_ptr;

  ch_ptr = date_ptr;

  ch_ptr = Strchcpy(month, ch_ptr, '/');
  ++ch_ptr;
  ch_ptr = Strchcpy(day, ch_ptr, '/');
  ++ch_ptr;
  Strchcpy(year, ch_ptr, '\0');
```

```
  date_struct.month = atoi(month);
  date_struct.day   = atoi(day);
  date_struct.year  = atoi(year);

  return;
} // End of String_To_MDY()

char* Strchcpy(char* target, char* source, int ch)
{
  while (*source != ch && *source != '\0')
  {
    *target = *source;
    ++target;
    ++source;
  }

  *target = '\0';

  return source;

} // End of Strchcpy()

bool Validate_Date(DATE_STRUCT& date_struct)
{
  int ny_days [13] = {0, 31, 28, 31, 30, 31, 30, 31, 31, 30, 31, 30, 31};
  int ly_days [13] = {0, 31, 29, 31, 30, 31, 30, 31, 31, 30, 31, 30, 31};

  if (date_struct.month < 1 || date_struct.month > 12)
    return false;

  if (date_struct.day < 1)
    return false;
  if (date_struct.year % 4 == 0)
  {
    if (date_struct.day > ly_days[date_struct.month])
      return false;
  }
  else
    if (date_struct.day > ny_days[date_struct.month])
      return false;

  if (date_struct.year < 1980)
    return false;

  return true;

} // End of Validate_Date()
```

The only differences between this program and dem09-8.cpp are that the structure arguments in the functions String_to_MDY() and Validate_Date() are references instead of pointers. In the code of these functions, this allows us to use the
member operator on the structure parameters instead of the to operator on the structure pointers. This makes coding the functions a little easier.

Exercises 9.4

Use the following declarations in Exercises 1–4.

```
struct ITEM_STRUCT
{
   char name[21];
   double quantity,
   price;
};
ITEM_STRUCT item = {"Hard Disk", 17, 345.99};

ITEM_STRUCT* item_ptr = &item;

ITEM_STRUCT inventory[100];
```

1. What is the value of item_ptr -> price?
2. What is the value of item_ptr -> name + 2?
3. What is the value of *(item_ptr -> name +2)?
4. Write a statement that makes item_ptr point to the 54th row of the inventory table.
5. **(a)** Refer to Exercise 6, Section 9.3. Write a function Get_Student_Data_1() that prompts for, and obtains, the data for one student. The function should not have any arguments and should pass a copy of the filled student structure back to the calling program. Rewrite the for loop of Exercise 6 to use Get_Student_Data_1().

   (b) Write another version of the function of part (a), Get_Student_Data_2(), that uses pointers. The function should not return a value and should have one argument, which is a pointer to a variable of type STUDENT_STRUCT. Rewrite the for loop of Exercise 6 to use Get_Student_Data_2().
6. Repeat Exercise 5 for the structure defined in Exercise 7, Section 9.3.
7. Repeat Exercise 5 for the structure defined in Exercise 8, Section 9.3.

Experiments 9.4

1. The standard library function strchr() is a string handling function. It takes two arguments. The first argument is a character pointer and the second is a character. The function returns the address of the first occurrence of the character that is its second argument in the string that is its first argument. If the character does not occur in the string, the function returns the NULL pointer. Recode dem09-7.cpp using the function strchr() instead of the user-defined function Strchcpy().
2. In dem09-7.cpp, we made the first element of the day number arrays zero so that the month number equaled the subscript number of the number of days in the month. Recode dem09-7.cpp so that the first element of both day number arrays is 31, the number of days in January.

Programming Problems 9.4

In the following programming problems, use `typedef`, enumerated types, structures, and structure pointers where appropriate.

1. The function `String_To_MDY()` assumes that the user correctly enters the date in the form mm/dd/yyyy. Recode this function to include the following test. Test the string that the user enters to see if it consists of two digits, followed by a slash, followed by two more digits and a slash, followed by four digits. If the string is invalid, issue an error message and exit the program.

2. The test for a leap year that we used in dem09-7.cpp is not quite correct. A year is a leap year if the year number is divisible by four except if the year number is divisible by 100. Of the years that are divisible by 100, the only ones that are leap years are those divisible by 400. Thus, the year 1900 was not a leap year, but the year 2000 was a leap year. Recode the function `Validate_Date()` to incorporate the correct test for a leap year.

3. Dates are sometimes provided in the conventional form of month name, day of the month, and year (in the form yyyy), for example, January 1, 2005. Some applications use such dates in computations (for example, calculating how many days a bill is past due). In these cases, it is convenient to convert the dates from conventional form to Julian form before the computations that use the dates. (A date's Julian date is the number days the date is from January 1. Thus, January 1 is day 1, January 2 is day 2, and so on). Write a function that has one argument—a pointer to a structure that contains the date in conventional form. (You must define this structure.) The function should return the Julian date equivalent of the conventional date that is passed to it. Be sure to take leap year into account. The function should use the following table.

TABLE 9.4

Month	Number of First Day (non-leap year)
January	1
February	32
March	60
April	91
May	121
June	152
July	182
August	213
September	244
October	274
November	305
December	335

Write a short program that tests this function.

4. A professor of marketing keeps the following information on each student in her Marketing 101 class: student last name, student first name, social security number,

telephone number, grades for five quizzes, grade for the final exam, and the final grade average.

(a) Design a structure that will store the information about a student.

(b) Write a function that prompts the user for all the information for one student except the final grade. The function's only argument should be a pointer to a structure of the type defined in part (a).

(c) Write a function whose only argument is a pointer to a structure of the type defined in part (a) and which computes the final grade of the student as follows: the final grade is 75% of the quiz average plus 25% of the final exam.

(d) Write a program that prompts the user to input data about as many as 25 students, which should be stored in a table. The program should use the function of part (b) to input the data. Once the table is loaded, the program should use the function of part (c) to compute the final grade average of each student. Finally, the program should display a report that lists the students in alphabetical order. For each student, display the quiz average, the final exam grade, and the final quiz average.

5. (a) A small airline company needs a program to keep track of the seat availability of its flights. Design the structure type FLIGHT to store a four-digit flight number, the departure date in mm/dd/yy form, the three-character departure airport code, the three-character arrival airport code, and an array SEATS of row structures to store the seating data. The array of row structures is to have 20 elements, one for each row in the airplane. The row structure ROW is to have four integer members called a, b, c, and d, corresponding to the four seats in the row. If a seat is occupied, the corresponding member in the seating array should be one. Otherwise, the member should be zero.

(b) Declare an array of five elements of type FLIGHT. Write a function that initializes the array. The function should prompt the user to enter the flight information (flight number, departure date, departure city code, and arrival city code) for all five flights. The function should initialize all the members of the SEATS arrays to zero. Pass the address of the flight array to the function.

(c) Write a function that displays a list of all the empty seats on a flight. Pass the flight number to the function and a pointer to the flight array. The display should be in tabular form for easy reading. The function should indicate when a flight has no available seats.

(d) Write a seat reservation program. The program should use the function of part (b) to initialize the array of flights. The program should do the following in a loop. Display a list of the flight numbers. Ask the user to enter a flight number. Display a list of all the empty seats on that flight using the function in part (c). Ask the user to pick an available seat(s) from the list of seats. Mark the seat(s) as occupied.

CHAPTER REVIEW

TERMINOLOGY

Describe the meanings of the following terms.

`typedef`	table key
`enum`	sorted
enumerated type	search key
structure	table searching
`struct`	"hard coding" a table
structure members	ascending order
member operator	sequential search
table	binary search

SUMMARY

- The statement `typedef old-type new-type` defines a new data type (Note 9.1). You can declare variables of this new type.
- The `enum` statement defines a set of integer constants that are represented by identifiers. The `enum` statement defines a data type. You can declare variables of this new type (Note 9.2).
- A structure, declared with the keyword `struct`, defines a data type consisting of data items of different types. A structure is a new data type. You can declare variables of this new type.
- Use the member operator, ., to access a member of a structure (Note 9.3).
- The data type of a structure member reference is the same as the type of the right-most element of that reference (Note 9.4).
- A structure can have a member that is a structure.
- You can assign a structure variable to a structure variable of the same type. The assignment is done on a member-by-member basis.
- You can define a table as an array of structures.
- A sequential table search tests each row, in sequence, until there is a match to the search key or until the search fails.
- A binary search repeatedly divides that table in half until there is a match to the search key or until the search fails.
- If a table has 50 or more rows, a binary search is more efficient than a sequential search.
- A function can have a structure as an argument.
- A function can return a structure.
- Instead of passing a structure as an argument by value, it is usually more efficient to pass a pointer to the structure (Note 9.5).
- Use the `->` operator to access a structure member through a pointer (Note 9.6). The expression `str_ptr -> member` is equivalent to `(*str_ptr).member`.
- You can use a reference to a structure as a function argument.

REVIEW EXERCISES

1. What C++ statement allows you to define a data type in terms of existing data types? Give an example of how you might use this statement.

2. What is an enumerated type? Which C++ statement can you use to declare an enumerated type?

3. What is a structure and how do you declare one?

4. Does a structure declaration reserve computer storage?

5. Which operator can you use to access a structure member?

6. How can you initialize a structure variable?

7. How is one structure variable assigned to another of the same type?

8. How can you declare a table?

9. What is meant by a table key?

10. Describe how a binary search works.

11. How can you declare and define a function that returns a structure?

12. How can you declare and define a function that has a structure as an argument?

13. How can you declare and define a function that has a structure pointer as an argument?

14. What operator can you use to access a structure member through a pointer? Give an example of its use.

Part II **Object-Oriented Programming**

Chapter 10

The `string` Class: An Introduction to Classes and Objects

OBJECTIVES

- To understand the object-oriented concepts of object, class, instance, state, and method
- To understand the principle of information hiding
- To use, declare, and initialize `string` class objects
- To understand the concept of a constructor
- To use `cin.getline()` and `cout` for `string` object input and output
- To use =, +, +=, and the relational operators on `string` objects
- To understand the concept of operator overloading
- To use `string` class methods such as `length()`, `at()`, `empty()`, `find()`, `find_first_of()`, `substr()`, `replace()`, `insert()`, and `append()` to manipulate `string` objects
- To use `string` objects as function arguments and return values
- To use references and pointers to `string` objects
- To define and manipulate arrays of `string` objects

In the first nine chapters, we used structured techniques to solve programming problems. We developed a procedural solution to each problem by dividing the problem into a series of steps. Beginning in Chapter 5, we used a top-down approach to solve more complicated problems. Some steps in the problem solutions were handled by functions. The functions, in turn, completed their steps procedurally. In this and the following chapters, we discuss a different way of approaching problems: object-oriented programming.

10.1 OBJECTS, CLASSES, AND OBJECT-ORIENTED SYSTEMS

In object-oriented programming, we view an application as a system of interacting **objects**. Each object is responsible for its own actions. The objects interact by sending messages to one another and behaving in certain ways in response to the messages. A message may be accompanied by one or more pieces of data, which might be needed for the object to carry out the action. When an object receives a message, it is the object's responsibility to carry out the action using some method.

To illustrate, suppose you want to withdraw $100 from your savings account at an ATM (automatic teller machine). We can think of the ATM system in terms of a set of interacting objects. You can think of yourself as an object, the ATM machine as an object, and your savings account as an object. To withdraw the $100, you send a message to the ATM object (by using a touch screen) to perform a withdrawal of $100. The ATM object then sends a message to your savings account object (which resides in the bank's database) to make a withdrawal of $100. The ATM object might do this by sending the message Withdraw(100.00) to your savings account object. The savings account object is responsible for withdrawing the money. The savings account object now determines if its balance (the amount of money in your savings account) is greater than or equal to $100.00. If so, the object decreases its balance by $100 and sends a message to the ATM object to dispense $100. The ATM machine, in response to that message, dispenses five $20 bills and displays a message on its screen that the money is ready. Your response to that message is to take the money out of the cash drawer and place it in your wallet. (It is important to realize that the account object decides if it can make a withdrawal, not the ATM. Also, the account object decreases its own balance. The ATM cannot directly decrease the balance in the account.) If the savings account object determines that its balance is less than $100.00, it sends a message to the ATM object that there are insufficient funds in the account to make the withdrawal. That message causes the ATM object to display a message that the withdrawal request must be denied because of insufficient funds. You respond to that message by getting embarrassed and walking away!

Let us examine this system more closely. The savings account object that represents your account is one of many such savings accounts. All of these accounts are similar to one another. They all have balances and they all behave in a similar manner. Therefore, we can say that each savings account object is a member of the Savings_Account **class**. In object-oriented programming terminology, we say that a particular savings account is an **instance** of the Savings_Account class. All members of a class must behave in the same way. Therefore, making a withdrawal from my savings account would invoke the same **method** (that is, a series actions) as making a withdrawal from your savings account. What differs from one savings account object to another is its **state**, that is, the data values stored in the object. The state of a savings account object might include the account's ID number, balance, and interest rate.

To make the withdrawal from your account, the ATM machine sends the message Withdraw(100.00) to your savings account object. This message is accompanied by the argument 100.00, which lets your bank account know how much money it should withdraw. From the point of view of the ATM object, that is all it has to do to request that your object withdraw $100.00 from your account. The ATM machine does not have to know the means (that is, the method) by which the account object makes the withdrawal. The details of how the withdrawal is made are hidden from the ATM object (and you). This is the principle of **information hiding**—the sender of the message does not need to know the way in which the receiver carries out the request.

Now, what is the difference between this object-oriented approach of sending messages and the procedural approach that uses functions? First, in object-oriented programming, a message has a receiver. A function does not have a receiver. Functions usually operate on something. For example, in a procedural version of the ATM system, to withdraw your $100, the system would execute a function call similar to the following:

```
Withdraw(your_account, 100.00);
```

Thus, the `Withdraw()` function would actually operate on the account. On the other hand, in object-oriented programming, the ATM object requests your account object to perform a service, namely, to withdraw $100 from its own balance.

The second difference between sending messages and using functions is that, in the object-oriented approach, the receiver determines the interpretation of the message. Therefore, the interpretation can vary with different types of receivers. For example, suppose that you want to make a withdrawal of $100 from your CD (certificate of deposit). The ATM will send the same message, `Withdraw(100.00)`, to your CD object (which is a member of the class `CD_Account`). However, the CD object will not use the same method to withdraw the money as did your savings account object. The rules governing withdrawal from a CD are restrictive because you are not allowed to withdraw the principal of the CD before the CD matures; you can withdraw only the interest that has accrued on the CD. However, you can withdraw any amount up to the full balance in a savings account. Thus, the method the CD object uses in response to the `Withdraw(100.00)` message is different from the method that the savings account object uses to respond to the same message.

10.1.1 Familiar Classes and Objects

We have been working with several classes since the first chapter. In Chapter 1, we introduced the standard input and output streams `cin` and `cout`. The C++ language comes with several predefined classes. Two of these are the input class `istream` and the output class `ostream`. The standard input stream `cin` is an `istream` class object. The definition of the `istream` and `ostream` classes and the definitions of `cin` and `cout` are contained in the header file `iostream`.

In a program, we can obtain data from the keyboard by applying the extraction operator `>>` to the `cin` object. We can view the statement

```
cin >> price;
```

as follows: the statement tells the `cin` object to extract a number from the input stream and place the number's value into the variable `price`. Thus, we send a message to the `cin` object and it responds in a certain way to that message. How that message is carried out (that is, the mechanics of extracting the characters and converting them into a number), is immaterial to us (information hiding).

Likewise, we can display data on the monitor by applying the insertion operator << to the `cout` object. We can view the statement

```
cout << "The value is " << price;
```

as sending a message to the `cout` object to display on the monitor screen the string "The value is" followed by the value of the variable `price`.

We have used `get()` with `cin` as follows, where `ch` is a variable of type `char`.

```
ch = cin.get();
```

The function `get()` is a method of the `istream` class. When we code `cin.get()`, we are sending the `get()` message to the `cin` object. In response to this message, the object returns to the program the value of the next character in the input buffer. Note that we use the same dot operator that we use with structures.

The same is true about `getline()`. When we code

```
cin.getline(name, 81);
```

we are sending the `getline()` message to the `cin` object. In response to the message, the `cin` object extracts an entire line of text from the input buffer and places a copy of it into the array `name`. Again, it is no concern to us how the `cin` object obtains the line of characters and places them into the array. That is the responsibility of the object.

In the remainder of this chapter, we shall illustrate these object-oriented concepts by studying the built-in C++ class `string`. In the following chapters, we shall discuss how you can code your own classes and objects and use them in your programs.

Exercises 10.1

1. In the object-oriented ATM system, describe the state (that is, the data possibly stored in) the ATM object. Do the same for a customer object. (You are a customer.)

2. In the object-oriented ATM system, describe the following scenario in terms of the messages that must be sent between objects: After receiving the message that your account object has withdrawn the $100, the ATM object discovers that it does not have enough money in its cash drawer to give to you. In all cases, identify the object sending the message and the object receiving the message. Would you change the description of the ATM method, the savings account method, or both?

3. Suppose that you order a book online through the Online Bookstore. To do so, you fill out a form on a Web page and submit the form. The form contains the book name and price, your name and address, and your credit card number. Describe an object-oriented book-ordering system that will eventually deliver the book to your home in terms of agents (objects) and their responsibilities (methods).

4. Suppose that you are registering for classes next semester at your school. Registration is conducted online. You register by filling out and submitting a form on a Web page that contains a list of the classes you will be taking, your name and student ID number, and your status (full-time or part-time). Describe an object-oriented online registration system in terms of agents (objects) and their responsibilities (methods).

10.2 INTRODUCTION TO string OBJECTS

We have already studied C-strings, which are character arrays. As we shall see, string class objects are much easier, safer, and in many ways, more natural to use than C-strings. It is not important for us to know how string objects or the operations on them are implemented. What is important is that you know how to use string objects. This is in contrast to using C-strings where it is very important that we know that such strings are implemented as character arrays.

The **string class** is built into C++, so there is no need to declare it in any way except that to use the class in your programs you must use the following #include statement.

```
#include <string>
```

10.2.1 Instantiating and Outputting string Objects

Before we learn how to use string objects, we must know how to **instantiate**, or create, them. Although a string object is more, essentially it represents a set of characters. The set of characters a string object represents we shall call the **value of the string object**. This set of characters is stored in the string object, possibly along with other data such as the length of the string. These data comprise the state of the string object. Make sure to keep in mind that a string object is more than just its value.

In C++, any class, including string, is a valid data type. Therefore, you can declare string objects in much the same way as you declare numeric data types. Consider the following declarations.

```
string str1;

string str2 = "Hello";

string str3("Hello");

string str4(50, '*');
```

Note first that the word string is not a C++ keyword—it is the name of a class. (You can easily see this in most C++ editors because the word string will not be highlighted or color-coded as a keyword.) The first declaration defines str1 as an empty, or **null, string**—a string that contains no characters. Therefore, an uninitialized string object is set to the empty string by default. This is in contrast to declaring an uninitialized integer or character pointer, which has a garbage value. When an object is created, it executes a special method, called a **constructor**. The main role of a constructor is to initialize the object. Because no initial value is specified in the first declaration, the object

---

Note 10.1   Uninitialized Strings

A string that is uninitialized in its declaration is automatically set to the empty, or null, string, that is, a string with no characters.

executes the so-called **no-argument constructor**, which initializes the string's value to the empty string. It is called the no-argument constructor because we do not provide any argument (string literal). See Note 10.1.

The second and third declarations define str2 and str3 as a string object having the value "Hello" (without the quotation marks). In both of these cases, a **one-argument constructor** initializes the value of the string to"Hello". Note how enclosing the string "Hello" in parentheses in the third declaration is similar to a function call, although str3 is not the name of a function.

You might wonder if the string literal that you use to initialize a string object has too many characters to fit in the string's value. Although there is a limit to the number of characters that can be stored in a string object, that number is very large. (See Experiment 5 in Section 10.3.) Therefore, there is no practical limit to the number of characters that a string object can store.

The fourth declaration defines str4 as a string of 50 asterisks (*). This declaration uses a **two-argument constructor** to initialize the value of the string. The first argument (an integer) is the number of times the second argument (a character) is to be repeated in the string's value.

We see from these declarations that it is possible to instantiate and initialize a string object in several ways by using different string constuctors. In Chapter 11, you will learn how to write constuctors for the classes that you define.

We can use the fourth type of string declaration to replace some for loop processing in previous programs. For example, in the Display_Greeting() function of prb05-2.cpp in Chapter 5, we used the following for loop to display a line of 70 asterisks:

```
for (position = 1; position <= 70; ++position)
    cout << "*";
```

Instead of using the for loop, we can now declare a string object that contains 70 asterisks as follows (see Experiment 2):

```
string star_line(70, '*');
```

Then, to display the line, we can execute the following.

```
cout << star_line;
```

You can send a string object to cout just as you would send a number. Somehow, cout knows how to output the value of the string object. In Chapter 15, you will learn how to allow cout to output the value (or values) of the objects that you define.

Note 10.2   String Output

You can output the value of a string object by sending the object to cout using the << operator.

The program dem10-1.cpp demonstrates the preceding declarations.

```
//dem10-1.cpp

//This program demonstrates different ways to declare
//string objects and how to output string objects.

#include <iostream>
#include <string>

using namespace std;

int main()
{
  string str1;
  string str2 = "Hello";
  string str3("Hello");
  string str4(50, '*');

  cout << "str1 = " << str1 << endl;
  cout << "str2 = " << str2 << endl;
  cout << "str3 = " << str3 << endl;
  cout << "str4 = " << str4 << endl;

  return 0;
}
```

Program Output

```
str1 =
str2 = Hello
str3 = Hello
str4 = **************************************************
```

When you declare and initialize a string, as done in this program, there is a lot going on. The string "Hello" is not a string object—it is a string literal. Therefore, the one-argument constructor must convert the string literal into an equivalent object. In Chapter 13, we shall learn how such conversions are made.

Because str1 was not initialized, the first line of output shows nothing to the right of the equals sign (str1 is the empty string). Both str2 and str3 have the same value of "Hello" and str4 is a string of 50 asterisks.

10.2.2 String Input

You can also input a string object's value using cin and the >> operator. For example, the following asks for a person's first name and stores it in the string object first_name.

```
string first_name;

cout << "Enter your first name: ";
cin >> first_name;
```

Program dem10-2.cpp shows how this works.

```cpp
//dem10-2.cpp

//This program uses cin to input a first and last name into a program.

#include <iostream>
#include <string>

using namespace std;

int main()
{
  string first_name;
  string last_name;

  cout << "Enter your first name: ";
  cin >> first_name;

  cout << endl;
  cout << "Enter your last name: ";
  cin >> last_name;

  cout << endl << endl;
  cout << "Welcome, " << first_name << " " << last_name << endl;

  return 0;
}
```

Program Output

```
Enter your first name: John

Enter your last name: Molluzzo

Welcome, John Molluzzo
```

In the last cout statement, we place a space as a string literal, " ", into the output stream between the first and last names.

Now, what happens if I enter my first name and my middle initial when prompted to enter my first name? The following shows the output when I do that.

Program Output When Entering Two-Word First Name

```
Enter your first name: John C.

Enter your last name:

Welcome, John C.
```

When hitting the enter key after entering John C., the program does not wait for me to enter my last name, but just goes on to display the welcome message. The program behaves like this because when entering string data, cin uses white space (a blank, an enter, or a tab) to delimit strings. That is, cin can be used to input only *one word at a time*. It cannot be used to input a multi-word string.

To input a multi-word string, we must use the function getline(), but in a way different from the way we used it in Chapter 7. Suppose we want to ask the user in what state he or she lives. Because some state names, such as North Carolina, are two words, we have to use getline() to extract the state name from the input stream. The following code will do that.

```
string state;

cout << "Enter your state of residence: ";

getline(cin, state);
```

Think of the getline() statement as saying the following: "Get a line of text from the cin input stream and place it into the value of the string object state." The getline() function asks cin to retrieve one line from the input stream—that is, everything you type until you hit the enter key. The text you typed (not including the enter character) is then given to the string object state, which takes the text as its value. Note that getline() is not a method of the string class. Following is the program dem10-3.cpp, which demonstrates these concepts.

```
//dem10-3.cpp

//This program illustrates the use of getline()
//to input multi-word strings.

#include <iostream>
#include <string>

using namespace std;

int main()
{
  string full_name;
  string state_name;

  cout << "Enter your full name: ";
  getline(cin, full_name);

  cout << endl;
  cout << "Enter your state of residence: ";
  getline(cin, state_name);

  cout << endl << endl;
  cout << "Welcome, " << full_name << endl;
  cout << state_name << " is a nice place to live." << endl;

  return 0;
}
```

Program Output

Enter your full name: **John C. Molluzzo**

Enter your state of residence: **New York**

Welcome, John C. Molluzzo
New York is a nice place to live.

When running the program, multi-word responses are made to the two prompts. In each case, getline() retrieves the entire line entered and passes a copy of the line to the corresponding string object.

> **Note 10.3   String Input**
>
> Use cin >> str1 to input one word into the string variable str1.
>   Use getline(cin, str1) to input one line from cin into the string variable str1.

C++ string objects can easily be incorporated into the programs of Chapters 1, 2, 3, and 4. For example, consider the program dem10-4.cpp, which is a version of the program prob02-2.cpp. In dem10-4.cpp, in addition to asking for and obtaining the three quiz scores for a student, we also ask for the student's name.

```cpp
//dem10-4.cpp

//This is a version of prob02-2.cpp.
//In addition to calculating the average of three test scores,
//the program asks for the student's name.

#include <iostream>
#include <iomanip>
#include <string>

using namespace std;

int main()
{
    int  quiz1,        // Quiz 1 grade
         quiz2,        // Quiz 2 grade
         quiz3;        // Quiz 3 grade
    double average;    // Average of the three quiz grades
    string name;       // String for storing the student name

    // Setup output stream for one decimal place

    cout << setprecision(1)
         << setiosflags(ios::fixed)
         << setiosflags(ios::showpoint);
```

```
cout << "Enter the name of the Student: ";
getline(cin, name);

cout << endl;
cout << "Enter the grade for Quiz 1: ";
cin >> quiz1;
cout << "Enter the grade for Quiz 2: ";
cin >> quiz2;
cout << "Enter the grade for Quiz 3: ";
cin >> quiz3;

// The type cast double() is required to convert the sum of the
// quiz grades, which is an integer, to a floating point.  Failure
// to convert the expression on the right of the assignment would
// result in the average being truncated to an integer.

average = double (quiz1 + quiz2 + quiz3) / 3;

cout << endl;
cout << "The average of the three quizzes for student "
     << name << " is " << average << endl;
return 0;
}
```

Program Output

Enter the name of the Student: **John C. Molluzzo**

Enter the grade for Quiz 1: **90**
Enter the grade for Quiz 2: **85**
Enter the grade for Quiz 3: **95**

The average of the three quizzes for student John C. Molluzzo is 90.0

Exercises 10.2

1. Declare a string object called my_name and initialize it to your name. Use two different methods to initialize the string object.
2. Write a cout statement that will output the value of the string my_name declared in Exercise 1.
3. Declare a null string object product_name that will hold the name of a product. Write a statement that will input the name of a product and store it in the value of product_name.

Experiments 10.2

1. Write a short program in which you declare an unintitalized string object and an uninitialized character pointer (a C-string), and output both values. What is the output and why?

2. Recode the `Display_Greeting()` function of prb05-2.cpp as follows. Instead of using the `for` loop, declare a `string` object that contains 70 asterisks as follows:

```
string star_line(70, '*');
```

Then, to display the line, execute the following.

```
cout << star_line;
```

Programming Problems 10.2

1. (See Programming Problem 6 in Section 1.4.) Your city's Parking Violation Bureau wants you to write a program to compute fines for parking violations. There are four types of violation: type A carries a fine of $10, type B carries a fine of $20, type C carries a fine of $30, and type D carries a fine of $50. The program should ask for the name of offender, the number of type A violations, the number of type B violations, and so on. Store the offender's name in a `string` object. The program should display the offender's name and the total fine for the person.

2. (See Programming Problem 4 in Section 2.3.) Write a program that asks the user to enter the name of an item, the price of the item, and the sales tax rate as a percent. Store the item name in a `string` object. The program should display the item name and the total price of the item (price plus sales tax). After obtaining the input from the user, the program should use the `*=` operator to calculate the total price of the item using the equivalent of the following formula.

```
price = price * (1 + sales_tax_rate)
```

3. (See Programming Problem 3 in Section 3.3.) A computer science instructor needs a program that averages the grades she receives on a quiz she gives to her class. Each grade is an integer between 0 and 100. She does not know the number of grades at this time. Write a program that asks the user to enter the name of the class and the quiz grades one at a time. Store the name of the class in a `string` object. After the user has completed entering grades, the program should display the name of the class, the number of grades entered, and the sum of the grades entered. The program should also display the average of the grades, rounded to the nearest tenth.

4. A real estate company needs a program to help decide commissions due to an agent when the agent sells a property. Write a program that prompts the user for the name of the real estate agent, the selling price of the property, and the category of the property. Store the name of the agent in a `string` object. If the class equals 1, the commission rate is 4.5%. If the class is 2, the commission rate is 5.0%, and if the class is 3, the commission rate is 6.0%. The commission equals the appropriate commission rate multiplied by the selling price of the property. The program should display then name of the agent, the selling price, the property class, the commission rate, and the commission.

10.3 OPERATIONS ON `string` OBJECTS

The `string` class has many methods that allow you to get information about a string and to manipulate a `string` object's value. Also, you can use many familiar operators on `string` objects in much the same way as you use them on numeric data types.

10.3.1 String Assignment

It is legal to assign one `string` object to another as follows.

```
string str1 = "Hello";
string str2;

str2 = str1;
```

After the assignment, the value of the `string` object `str2` is a copy of the value of the `string` object `str1`. Therefore, assigning one `string` object to another copies the value of the string on the right of the assignment to the value of the string on the left. Contrast this with the way in which you have to assign one string to another using C-strings. See Experiment 1. Note that when you assign one `string` object to another you do not have to worry that the target string (the one on the left of the assignment) can hold a copy of the value of the string on the right (the source string). Automatically, the target string will make enough room to hold the value of the source string.

You can also initialize one `string` object to another in a declaration, as in the following.

```
string str1 = "Hello";
string str2 = str1;
```

You can also initialize one `string` object to another using the following technique:

```
string str1 = "Hello";
string str2(str1);
```

10.3.2 Concatenation

You can also paste (or **concatenate**) two strings together using the + operator, the same operator that we use for the addition of numbers. For example, the following declarations place the string `"Hello, World"` into the value of the `string` object `str3`. See Experiment 2.

```
string str1 = "Hello, ";
string str2 = "World!";
string str3 = str1 + str2;
```

In C++, it is possible to make an operator, such as the addition operator (+), do different things depending on the types of data the operator is working on. This is called **operator overloading**. Thus, the addition operator in the expression i + j, where i and j are integers, will work differently than the addition operator in the expression str1 + str2 of the previous example. In the first case, the + is operating on integers. Therefore, C++ does integer addition. In the second case, the + is operating on `string` objects. Therefore, C++ does concatenation. Overloading addition *is not* done automatically for any combination of objects. The overloading must be coded somewhere. In the case of the `string` class, the overload is coded in the `<string>` header file. In Chapter 15, you will learn how to overload C++ operators.

The += operator also has meaning (that is, is overloaded) for `string` objects and has the effect of appending the value of the string on the right of += to the value of the string on the left of+=. You can read the += when operating on strings as "is appended with." The following code has the same result as the previous example.

```
string str3 = "Hello, ";

str3 += "World!";
```

The declaration initializes `str3` to the string"Hello, ". The second statement is equivalent to the assignment str3 = str3 + "World!";. Thus, the string "World!" is appended to the end of the existing string, which results in `str3` containing the string"Hello, World!".

Note 10.4   Overloaded Operators For string Objects

The assignment operator, =, the + operator, and the compound assignment operator += are overloaded for `string` objects. The assignment operator assigns the value of one string to the value of another. The + operator concatenates together the string values of its operands. The compound assignment operator += appends the value of the string on the right of the operator to the end of the value of the string on the left of the operator.

10.3.3 Length of a String

To find the number of characters in the value of a `string` object (that is, the length of the string), use the `length()` method, which is a method of the `string` class. Recall that a method represents a message, or request, that is sent to an object to do something. To apply a method to an object, you must use the **dot (.) operator** as follows.

```
str1.length()
```

This statement sends the `length()` message to the `string` object `str1`: "Compute your length and return its value." Therefore, the value of this expression would be the length of the value of the `string` object `str1`. We do not know the actual code that the `string` object uses to calculate the length of its value (remember: information hiding), nor should we even want to know. What is important to us is that we know which message to send to a `string` object to have the object return its length. For a more specific example, consider the following code.

```
string full_name;
int chars_in_name;

cout << "Enter your full name: ";
getline(cin, full_name);
```

```
chars_in_name = full_name.length();

cout << "Your name has " << chars_in_name << " characters" << endl;
```

The `getline()` function retrieves the user's name from the input stream and places it into the string `full_name`. The expression `full_name.length()` requests that the `string` object `full_name` execute its `length()` method to find the number of characters in its value and return that value. The value of the expression `full_name.length()`is, therefore, the number of characters in the name. So, if the user enters Jane Smith as the name, the program will display 10 as the number of characters in the name. Note that the `length()` method counts all the characters entered, including the space between the first and last names.

Note 10.5   Applying a Class Method

To apply a class method to an object, use the dot (.) operator as follows:

`class_object.method_name()`

This sends a message, namely `method_name`, to the object `class_object`, which in turn executes the method.

Following is program dem10-5.cpp, which illustrates the operations we have discussed so far.

```
//dem10-5.cpp

//This program illustrates string assignment, concatenation,
//and the length() method.

#include <iostream>
#include <string>

using namespace std;

int main()
{
    string first_name;
    string last_name;
    string full_name;

    int name_length;

    cout << "Enter your first name: ";
    getline(cin, first_name);

    cout << endl;
    cout << "Enter your last name: ";
    getline(cin, last_name);

    full_name = first_name + " " + last_name;

    name_length = full_name.length() - 1;
```

```
cout << endl <<endl;
cout << "Hello, " << full_name << endl;
cout << "Your name contains " << name_length << " characters." << endl;

    return 0;
}
```

Program Output

Enter your first name: **John**

Enter your last name: **Molluzzo**

Hello, John Molluzzo
Your name contains 12 characters.

The program asks for the first and last name of the user and retrieves each with the getline() function. Then, the program pastes the entire name together by concatenating the first name, a space, and the last name into the string object full_name. The program subtracts 1 from the number of characters in full_name, full_name.length() - 1, to adjust for the space that was added. See Experiment 3.

10.3.4 Accessing Individual Characters in a String

Sometimes you may want to access an individual character in the value of a string object. To understand how to do so, you must know that the characters in a string object's value are numbered starting at zero from the first character. Figure 10.1 shows how the characters are numbered in the string"Hello". These numbers are called the **indices** of the characters.

Thus, the character 'H' has index 0, the character 'e' has index 1, and so on. The last character in a string has index equal to one less than the length of the string.

To retrieve or change an individual character in a string object, use the **at()** string class method. If str1 is a string, then executing str1.at(i) asks the string object str1 to return the character at index i in the string's value.

Consider the following code.

```
string str1 = "Hippopotamus";
int last_index = str1.length() - 1;
cout << "The first character in the string is " << str.at(0) << endl;
cout << "The last character in the string is" << str.at(last_index)
        << endl;
```

```
 0  1  2  3  4
 H  e  l  l  o
```

Figure 10.1

The `string` object `str1` is initialized to"Hippopotamus". Then, `last_index` is initialized to one less than the length of the string, which is the highest index of any character in the string. The two `cout` statements then display the first character (at index 0) and the last character (at `last_index`).

You can also use the `at()` method to change a character in a `string` object because it is legal to have the expression `str1.at(i)` on the left side of an assignment. (That is, `str1.at(i)` is a l-value.) For example, the following assignment will change the first character in the string `str` to the character X:

```
str.at(0) = 'X';
```

This statement essentially asks the `string` object `str` to replace the character at index position 0 (the first character) by the character X. The program dem10-5A.cpp illustrates the preceding discussion.

```
//dem10-5A.cpp

//This program illustrates the use of the at()
//string class method.

#include <iostream>
#include <string>

using namespace std;

int main()
{
   string str = "Hippopatamus";

   int last_index = str.length() - 1;

   cout << "The first character in the string is " << str.at(0) << endl;
   cout << "The last character in the string is " << str.at(last_index)
        << endl;

   str.at(0) = 'X';

   cout << "The new string is " << str << endl;
   return 0;
}
```

Program Output

```
The first character in the string is H
The last character in the string is s
The new string is Xippopatamus
```

The `at()` method automatically checks to verify that the index used as its argument is valid, that it is between 0 and one less than the length of the string. See Experiment 4. Contrast this with the situation for C-strings. When you use a C-string, there is no built-in check to see if you used a valid subscript to access a C-string character. If you do not use a valid subscript on a C-string, the program will continue and possibly process bad data. If the `at()` method argument is an invalid index, the program will terminate.

Experiments 10.3

1. Write the C-string statements that would do the equivalent of the following statements that use `string` objects.

   ```
   string str1 = "Hello";
   string str2;

   str2 = str1;
   ```

2. Write the C-string statements that would do the equivalent of the following statements that use `string` objects.

   ```
   string str1 = "Hello, "
   string str2 = "World!"
   string str3 = str1 + str2;
   ```

3. Recode dem10-5.cpp using the method `size()` in place of the `length()` method. These methods always return the same value.

4. Recode dem10-5A.cpp by replacing

   ```
   int last_index = str.length() - 1;
   ```

   by the following.

   ```
   int last_index = str.length();
   ```

   Compile and execute the resulting program. What happens and why?

5. You can find the maximum number of characters that can be stored in a `string` object's value by using the `string` class method `max_size()`. Write a short program that declares a `string` object and then uses the `max_size()` method to display the maximum number of characters in a `string` object's value on your computer system.

6. When a `string` object is initialized to a string literal, a certain amount of space is allocated to hold the `string` object's value. You can find out how many characters are allocated by using the `string` class method `capacity()`. Write a simple program that declares and initializes a `string` object to the string "Hello". Use the `capacity()` method to find out how many character positions have been allocated for the value of the `string` object. After that, keep increasing the size of the initialization string to find out how many characters have to be in the initialization string to make the `string` object's capacity increase. To what does it increase?

Programming Problems 10.3

1. Recode dem09-2.cpp as follows. In the structure PART_STRUCT, replace the eight-character `part_no[]` array by a `string` object. Be careful to use the appropriate

statement to input the part number. Make sure that the user enters exactly eight characters. If not, issue an error message and allow the user one more try. If the user still enters an incorrect number, display an error message and end the program. If the user enters an eight-character part number, the program should behave as dem09-2.cpp. Compile, execute, and test your program.

10.4 MAKING DECISIONS WITH STRINGS

In this section, we show how to make decisions that involve `string` objects. The operators that we discussed in Chapter 3 for comparing numbers are overloaded for use with `string` objects.

10.4.1 Equality

You can use the equals operator, `==`, to test to see if two strings are equal. *Two* `string` *objects are equal only if their values (that is, the character strings they contain) are identical, character-by-character.* (Remember that upper-and lowercase characters are different.) Suppose the following declarations

```
string str1 = "Hello";

string str2 = str1;
```

Then, the test

```
if (str1 == str2)
```

would be true.

10.4.2 Inequality

The testing for inequality between two `string` objects can be done by using the usual operators `!=`, `>`, `<`, `>=`, and `<=`. However, what do we mean by saying that one `string` object is less than or greater than another? These operators should be viewed as operating on the values of the `string` objects involved. Therefore, if `str1` and `str2` are `string` objects, then the expression `str1 < str2` compares the values of `str1` and `str2`.

For `string` objects, the operator `<` should be read as "precedes" and the operator `>` should be read as "follows". The string object values are compared using the ASCII collating sequence as described in Section 8.4 of Chapter 8.

The following program, dem10-6.cpp, uses many of the `string` class concepts we have discussed so far. The program asks the user to enter his or her first and last names. Then the program concatenates the first and last names to form the full name. Finally, the program asks the user to enter his or her full name. If the full name that the user enters equals the full name that the program constructed, the program displays a congratulatory message. Otherwise, the program asks the user to execute the program again. Dem10-6.cpp is a `string` class version of dem08-9.cpp.

```cpp
//dem10-6.cpp
// This program uses several string concepts

#include <iostream>
#include <string>

using namespace std;

int main()
{
   string first_name;
   string last_name;
   string full_name;
   string full_name_chk;

   cout << "Please enter your first name: ";
   getline(cin, first_name);

   cout << endl;
   cout << "Please enter your last name: ;
   getline(cin, last_name);

   full_name = first_name + " " + last_name;

   cout << endl << endl;
   cout << "Hello " << full_name << ". Welcome to the program."
        << endl << endl;
   cout << "Your first name has " << first_name.length()
        << " characters in it." << endl << endl;
   cout << "Your last name has "<< last_name.length()
        << " characters in it." << endl << endl;

   cout << "Now please enter your first and last names" << endl;
   cout << "separated by one space: ";

   getline(cin, full_name_chk);

   if (full_name == full_name_chk)
   {
      cout << endl << endl;
      cout << "Congratulations! You followed the instructions." << endl;
   }
   else
   {
      cout << endl;
      cout << "You did not follow the instructions!" << endl;
      cout << "Please try the program again." << endl;
   }

   return 0;
}
```

Program Output

Please enter your first name: **Adam**

Please enter your last name: **Zapple**

Hello Adam Zapple. Welcome to the program.

Your first name has 4 characters in it.

Your last name has 6 characters in it.

Now please enter your first and last names
separated by one space: **Adam Zapple**

Congratulations! You followed the instructions.

The program begins with the declaration of the four `string` objects that will be used to store the names. The program then prompts for, and obtains, the first and last names of the user, using `getline()`. Then the program constructs the user's full name using concatenation with the + operator. Note that a single blank is placed between the first and last names.

Next, the program uses `full_name` to greet the user and displays the number of characters in the user's first and last names. The program then asks the user to enter his or her first and last names (separated by a blank), and places the name into `full_name_chk`. Then the `if` statement decides if the contents of `full_name_chk` are the same as the contents of `full_name`, which the program constructed earlier. The program issues an appropriate message depending on the outcome of this test.

Programming Problems 10.4

1. When you have to set a password at a Web site, you usually have to enter the password and then reenter it so that the system can verify the password. Write a program that asks the user to enter an eight-character password. Store the password in a `string` object. If the user enters a password that is not exactly eight characters long, ask the user to enter the password again. After the user correctly enters an eight-character password, ask the user to reenter the password. If the passwords match, display an appropriate message. If the passwords do not match, allow the user one more try. If the user still does not enter a matching password, display an appropriate message and end the program.

10.5 FUNCTIONS AND `string` OBJECTS

Because a class is a valid data type in C++, a `string` object can be used as a function argument and a function can return a `string` object. In this section, we discuss such functions in the context of validating user input.

10.5.1 Testing for an Empty String

Sometimes you might want to test to see if a string object's value is empty (null), that is, its value has no characters. For example, in the program dem10-6.cpp, you might want to be sure that the user has entered something in response to the prompt. Applying the string class method empty() to a string object asks the object if its value is the empty string. If the string is empty (or null), the method returns true; otherwise, it returns false. For example, suppose we have the following declaration.

```
string str1;
```

As mentioned earlier, if a string object is not initialized, it has an empty, or null, value. Therefore, the value of str1.empty() would be true. On the other hand, suppose we have the following declaration.

```
string str2 = "Hello";
```

Then, str2.empty() would be false.

10.5.2 Functions that Use string Objects

The program dem10-7.cpp, which is an extension of dem10-6.cpp, uses a data validation function, similar to those developed in Chapter 5, to validate the names that the user enters. Recall that those data validation functions prompted for the data and then returned valid data to the program for processing. Therefore, the data validation function we use in this program returns a string object. Because we want to test for the same error for both the first and last names, it makes sense to use the same validation function. Because we want different prompts for each name, we will pass the prompt to the validation function as a string argument. Following is the program code for dem10-7.cpp.

```
//dem10-7.cpp

//This program, uses a data validation function that has a string
//argument and that returns a string to validate that user input
//is not null, or empty.

#include <iostream>
#include <string>

using namespace std;

string Get_Name(string);

int main()
{
  string first_name;
  string last_name;
  string full_name;
  string full_name_chk;
  string first_initial;
  string last_initial;
```

```
first_name = Get_Name("Please enter your first name: ");

last_name = Get_Name("Please enter your last name: ");

full_name = first_name + " " + last_name;
first_initial = first_name.at(0);
last_initial = last_name.at(0);

cout << endl << endl;
cout << "Hello " << full_name << ". Welcome to the program."
     << endl << endl;
cout << "Your first name has " << first_name.length()
     << " characters in it." << endl << endl;
cout << "Your last name has "<< last_name.length()
     << " characters in it." << endl << endl;
cout << "Your initials are " << first_initial + last_initial
     << endl << endl;

cout << "Now please enter your first and last names" << endl;
cout << "separated by one space: ";

getline(cin, full_name_chk);

if (full_name == full_name_chk)
{
   cout << endl << endl;
   cout << "Congratulations! You followed the instructions." << endl;
}
else
{
   cout << endl;
   cout << "You did not follow the instructions!" << endl;
   cout << "Please try the program again." << endl;
}

   return 0;
}

string Get_Name(string prompt)
{
   string name;

   bool invalid_data;

   do
   {
      cout << endl << prompt;
      getline(cin, name);
      cout << endl;

      if (name.empty())
      {
         cerr << "You did not enter a name - Please try again." << endl;
         invalid_data = true;
      }
```

```
        else
           invalid_data = false;
    }
    while(invalid_data);

    return name;
}
```

Program Output

Please enter your first name: **John**

Please enter your last name:

You did not enter a name - Please try again.

Please enter your last name: **Molluzzo**

Hello John Molluzzo. Welcome to the program.

Your first name has 4 characters in it.

Your last name has 8 characters in it.

Your initials are JM

Now please enter your first and last names
separated by one space: **John Molluzzo**

Congratulations! You followed the instructions.

The prototype for the function Get_Name()

```
string Get_Name(string);
```

shows that the function will return a string object and that the function takes a single string object argument. The value that the function returns is a non empty string object. The string object that we pass to the function is the prompt that the function will use to obtain the name. Therefore, to use the function to obtain a non empty first name requires that we pass the prompt as the argument of the function.

```
first_name = Get_Name("Please enter your first name: ");
```

The string object that we use as the argument then gets assigned to the string object prompt in the function Get_Name(). The cout statement in the function's do loop then uses the string object prompt to display the appropriate message. The getline() function then obtains the name the user enters and places it in the string object name. The if statement that follows tests to see if the string object name is empty. If it is, an error message is displayed on the cerr output stream and the flag invalid_data is set to true. If the string name is not empty, then invalid_data is set to `false`, the do loop ends, and the function returns the value of the string name. In `main()`, the value returned by `Get_Name()` is then assigned to the string object `first_name`. The `Get_Name()` function is also used, with a different prompt, to obtain a nonempty string object for the `last_name`.

A `string` object that is used as an argument to a function is passed by value, just as ordinary numeric variables are passed by value. Therefore, the called function works with a copy of the `string` object. The original `string` object in the calling function cannot be changed by the called function.

We do not choose to use `Get_Name()` to obtain a nonempty string from the user for the full name because if the user enters an empty string at that point, we consider that the user did not follow instructions. That error is handled by the code in `main()`.

Note that you can also pass `string` objects to a function by reference. In that case, the `string` object can be changed by the function. The following program, dem10-7A.cpp, illustrates passing strings by reference. It uses a function, `Swap_Strings()`, that takes two string reference arguments. It works essentially the same as the `Swap_Int()` function of dem08-3R.cpp.

```
//dem10-7A.cpp

//This program illustrates passing string objects by reference.
//It swaps the values of two string objects using a function.

#include <iostream>
#include <string>

using namespace std;

void Swap_Strings(string&, string&);

int main()
{
  string str1;
  string str2;

  cout << "Enter string 1: ";
  getline(cin, str1);

  cout << "Enter string 2: ";
  getline(cin, str2);

  cout << endl;

  cout << "Before the swap:" << endl;
  cout << "String 1 = " << str1 << endl;
  cout << "String 2 = " << str2 << endl;

  Swap_Strings(str1, str2);

  cout << endl;
  cout << "After the swap:" << endl;
  cout << "String 1 = " << str1 << endl;
  cout << "String 2 = " << str2 << endl;

  return 0;
}
```

```
void Swap_Strings(string& s1, string& s2)
{
   string temp;

   temp = s1;
   s1 = s2;
   s2 = temp;
}
```

Program Output

Enter string 1: **Hello**
Enter string 2: **Goodbye**

Before the swap:
String 1 = Hello
String 2 = Goodbye

After the swap:
String 1 = Goodbye
String 2 = Hello

You can also pass a string object pointer to a function. See Experiment 1.

Experiments 10.5

1. Recode the program dem10-7A.cpp as follows. Pass string object pointers to the function Swap_Strings() rather than references. This will mean changing main() as well as the function. Compile, execute, and test your program.

2. There is a string class method called swap() that swaps the values of two string objects. If str1 and str2 are two string objects, then str1.swap(str2) swaps the values of the string objects. Recode dem10-7A.cpp using the swap() method.

10.6 MANIPULATING string OBJECTS

In this section, we discuss some useful string class methods that allow you to manipulate string objects.

Recall that the character positions in a string object's value are numbered from 0 to one less than the number of characters in the string's value. Figure 10.2 shows a string object's value with the character positions numbered.

0	1	2	3	4	5	6	7	8	9	10	11	12	13	14	15	16	17	18	19	20	21	22	23	24
T	h	i	s		i	s		a	n		e	x	a	m	p	l	e		s	t	r	i	n	g

Figure 10.2

We will now discuss several string class methods that we will use to manipulate the string in Figure 10.2.

10.6.1 Finding a String in a String

The first string manipulation method that we will consider is find(). The find() method locates the position of a substring of a string. For example, suppose the following declarations.

```
string str1 = "This is an example string";
int position;
```

The string object str1 would have a value as depicted in Figure 10.2. Then, the statement

```
position = str1.find("an");
```

does the following. It asks the string object str1 to find the first occurrence of the substring "an" in its value and return the index value of that position. Therefore, the statement would place the integer 8 into the variable position, because the substring "an" starts in location 8 in the string str1.

Any search can result in failure—that is, the search may not find what is being searched for. Applying find() to a string may not find the substring being searched for. When using find(), if the string object does not locate the substring being searched for, it returns –1. For example, if we want to locate the substring "Hello" in the value of the string object str1 of Figure 10.2, then str1.find("Hello") would return –1 because the "Hello" is not a substring of str1.

To be safe when using find(), you should always test to see if the method returned –1. For example,

```
position = str1.find("Hello");

if (position == -1)
    cerr << endl << endl << "Substring not found." << endl << endl;
```

Another version of the find() method allows you to start looking for the location of a substring after a given position. Consider, for example, the following, which finds the location of the first blank in str1 at or after position 11.

```
position = str1.find(" ", 11)
```

The statement places the number 18 into the variable position because the next blank at or after position 11 in the value of str1 is in position 18. See Experiment 1.

This version of find() also returns –1 if the substring is not found.

Both versions of find() begin searching a string from left to right in the string's value. The string class method rfind() (think of the r in rfind as meaning "reverse") allows you to search a string's value from right to left, that is, from the end of the string forward to the beginning. For example, executing the following will return 5.

```
str1.rfind("is") ;
```

(Note that executing str1.find("is"); returns 2.)

The `rfind()` method starts searching from the end of the string to the left until it encounters the substring it is searching for. If the substring is not found, `rfind()` returns –1.

There is also a version of `rfind()` that searches a string in reverse beginning from any specified location in the string. For example, the following statement returns 2.

```
str1.rfind("is", 4);
```

10.6.2 Searching for any Character from a Given List

Sometimes it is necessary to find the first character in a string from among a set of characters. For example, suppose you want to find a punctuation character in a string. In this case, the characters you might be looking for are any of the characters , . : ; ! ?. The string method that can find the first occurrence of any of a set of characters is `find_first_of()`. For example, consider the following declarations.

```
string str2 = "Hello, my name is John.";
string punctuation = ",.:;!?";
```

Then `str2.find_first_of(punctuation);` would return 5, the location of the comma in the string. If `find_first_of()` does not find any of the characters it is searching for, it returns –1.

There is a version of `find_first_of()` that starts searching the string from a given position in the string. For example, using the previous declarations,

```
str2.find_first_of(punctuation, 7);
```

returns 22, which is the position of the period in the string.

There are other functions similar to `find_first_of()`, which are covered in the experiments at the end of this section. See Experiments 2, 3, and 4.

10.6.3 Extracting a Substring from a String

The method `substr()` extracts a substring of a given number of characters from a `string` object's value starting at a certain position. For example, suppose the following declaration.

```
string str2;
```

Then the following statement will place the substring `"is"` into `str2`.

```
str2 = str1.substr(5, 2);
```

The first argument in the `substr()` method is the position at which the substring will *start* to become extracted. The second argument is the *number of characters* to extract. Thus, `str1.substr(5,2)` extracts two characters from the value of `str1` beginning at location 5.

10.6.4 Combining `string` Methods

You can combine the `string` methods we have discussed to do more-complex things. For example, the following statements will extract the first word from the string `str` and place that word into the string first_word.

```
int first_blank = str.find(" ");
first_word = str.substr(0, first_blank);
```

The statement str.find(" ") returns the position of the first blank character in the string object str and places it into first_blank. The second statement then extracts a substring of length first_blank (remember the characters begin at location 0, so this is the correct number of characters to extract) starting from the first character in the string (location 0). See Experiment 5.

10.6.5 Inserting and Removing Substrings

There are string methods that allow you to insert and remove substrings from a string. The string method replace() allows you to replace one substring by another. For example, the following statement replaces four characters (the second argument) beginning at location 0 (the first argument) by the string "Here" (the third argument).

```
str1.replace(0, 4, "Here");
```

See Experiment 6 for what happens when the replacement string is smaller or larger than the number of characters to replace.

The **insert()** method can be used to insert a string into the value of a string object. This differs from replace(). The replace() method replaces a substring of a string by another string. On the other hand, insert() places a string at a certain location in another string with the characters that follow being moved to the right. For example, if str1 is the string whose value is shown in Figure 10.2, then executing

```
str1.insert(19, "of a ");
```

would make the string's value the following.

```
"This is an example of a string"
```

The append() method allows you to add a string to the end of the string to which you apply the append() method. For example, the following statement appends the string "." to the end of str1.

```
str1.append(".");
```

The result would be the following string: "This is an example string." Using the append() method is equivalent to using the overloaded += operator discussed previously.

The string method **erase()** can erase a substring from a string. For example, the following erases the word "is" from str1. Note that we are also erasing the blank after the letter s.

```
str1.erase(5, 3);
```

The first argument is the starting position and the second argument is the number of characters to erase. After executing the previous statement, str1 would contain the string

```
"This an example string".
```

The method erase() can be used with one argument. The statement str1.erase(10) erases all characters from the string from position 10 to the end of the string.

10.6.6 Program dem10-8.cpp

Program dem10-8.cpp illustrates all of the methods discussed in this section.

```cpp
//dem10-8.cpp

//This program illustrates some of methods that are available
//to manipulate string objects.

#include <iostream>
#include <string>

using namespace std;

int main()
{
    string str1 = "This is an example string";
    string str2 = "sample";
    string str3;
    string punctuation = ".,:;!?";

    int position;

    cout << "The original string, str1, is : "
        << str1 << endl << endl;

    //Finds the first occurrence of "is" in str1
    position = str1.find("is");

    cout << "The first occurrence of \"is\" is at position "
        << position << endl << endl;

    //Finds the first occurrence of "is" in str1 after position 3
    position = str1.find("is", 3);

    cout << "The first occurrence of \"is\" after position 3 is "
        << "at position " << position << endl << endl;

    //Finds the first occurrence of "is" from the end of str1
    position = str1.rfind("is");

    cout << "The first occurrence of \"is\" from the end of str1 is "
        << "at position " << position << endl << endl;

    //Try to find a substring that is not in str1.
    position = str1.find("Hello");

    if (position == -1)
        cerr << "The substring \"Hello\" was not found in str1."
            << endl << endl;

    //Extracts a 8-character substring from str1 beginning at position 11
    str3 = str1.substr(11, 8);
```

```
cout << "The 8-charater substring of str1 beginning at position 11 is: "
     << str3 << endl << endl;

//Replace 7 characters beginning at position 11 with the string str2
str1.replace(11, 7, str2);

cout << "After replacing the word \"example\" " << endl
     << "by the word \"sample\", in str1 the string is: "
     << str1 << endl << endl;

//Erases a 7-character substring from str1 beginning at position 11
str1.erase(11, 7);

cout << "After erasing the word \"sample \", in str1 the string is: "
     << str1 << endl << endl;

//Insert the string "example " into the string beginning at position 11
str1.insert(11, "example ");

cout << "After putting back the word \"example \", in str1 the string is: "
     << endl << str1 << endl << endl;

//Append a period at the end of the string
str1.append(".");

cout << "After appending a period, the string str1 is: "
     << str1 << endl << endl;

//Finds the first occurrence of a punctuation mark in str1
position = str1.find_first_of(punctuation);

cout << "The first punctuation mark in str1 is "
     << "at position " << position << endl << endl;

    return 0;
}
```

Program Output

```
The original string, str1, is : This is an example string

The first occurrence of "is" is at position 2

The first occurrence of "is" after position 3 is at position 5

The first occurrence of "is" from the end of str1 is at position 5

The substring "Hello" was not found in str1.

The 8-charater substring of str1 beginning at position 11 is: example

After replacing the word "example"
by the word "sample", in str1 the string is: This is an sample string

After erasing the word "sample ", in str1 the string is: This is an string
```

After putting back the word "example ", in str1 the string is:
This is an example string

After appending a period, the string str1 is: This is an example string.

The first punctuation mark in str1 is at position 25

The program comments and output explain the code. Note that the program uses the escape sequence \" several times to allow cout to display the quotes character, ", inside a quoted string.

Experiments 10.6

1. The two-argument version of the find() method allows you to start looking for the location of a substring after a given position. What if that starting position is greater than the length of the string? Write a small program to find out what happens.

2. In dem10-8.cpp, replace each use of the append() method by the operator +=. Compile, execute, and test the resulting program.

3. The string class method find_last_of() finds the last character in a string from among a set of characters. It is used similarly to find_first_of(). Write a program that tests this method. Compile, execute, and test your program.

4. The string class method find_first_not_of() finds the first character in a string that is not from among a set of characters. It is used similarly to find_first_of(). Write a program that tests this method. Compile, execute, and test your program.

5. The string class method find_last_not_of() finds the last character in a string that is not from among a set of characters. It is used similarly to find_first_of(). Write a program that tests this method. Compile, execute, and test your program.

6. Write a short program to verify that the following code extracts the first word from a string of words.

```
int first_blank = str.find(" ");
first_word = str.substr(0, first_blank);
```

7. Write a short program that tests what happens when the replacement string used in the replace() method contains fewer or more than the number of characters to be replaced.

Programming Problems 10.6

1. Write a program that asks the user to enter a string. The program should erase the first word in the string and then output the resulting string. Compile, execute, and test the resulting program.

2. Write a program that asks the user to enter a string. The program should erase the last word in the string and then output the resulting string. Compile, execute, and test the resulting program.

3. Write a program that asks the user to enter a string. The program should replace all blanks in the string by asterisks and output the resulting string. Compile, execute, and test the resulting program.

4. (See Programming Problem 4, Section 8.4.) Write a program that constructs a user ID number from the user's first name, last name, and social security number. The program should prompt the user to enter his/her first name, last name, and social security number, entered with the usual dashes. All should be stored in string objects. Construct the ID number by taking the first two letters of the last name, followed by the second letter of the first name, followed by the middle three digits of the social security number. All characters are to be converted to uppercase. (For example, the ID number of Justin Case, who has social security number 123456789, is CAU456.) The program should then display the newly constructed ID number. Finally, the program should prompt the user to enter the ID number. If the user correctly enters the number, congratulate the user and end the program. If the user does not enter the correct ID number, display it again and ask the user to memorize the ID number. Then end the program.

5. Write a program that asks the user to enter a URL (a Web page address). The program should extract from the URL the substring up to and including one of the following: .com, .gov, .edu, or .net, and display that part of the address.

6. Sometimes, telephone numbers are entered by a user without dashes in the usual places. For example, if asked to enter her telephone number on a Web form, a user might enter 1115551234. Write a program that asks the user to enter a telephone number. The program should place dashes in the correct places in the phone number and display the result. Therefore, if 1115551234 is input, the program should display 111-555-1234.

7. An e-mail address consists of two parts, the user ID and the e-mail server separated, by the @ character. For example, an e-mail address might be wsmith@ mail.isp.com. The user ID is wsmith and the e-mail server is mail.isp.com. Write a program that asks the user to enter his or her e-mail address. The program should separate the e-mail address into its user ID and e-mail server and display them on separate lines. The program should do this using two functions. The function Get_ID() should take as its one argument the entire e-mail address and return the user ID as a string object. The function Get_Server() should take as its only argument the entire e-mail address and return the e-mail server as a string object.

10.7 PUTTING STRINGS TO WORK

In this section, we discuss two programs that involve more complex string manipulation.

10.7.1 Problem 10.1—Removing and Printing Words from a String

Sometimes text processing requires parsing text into words. The individual words can then be processed separately. In this problem, we discuss how to divide a string into individual words. The only processing we will do at this point is to display the words, one word per line.

Program Design   Before we can divide a string into its constituent words, we need
to agree on how words are separated. To keep matters simple, we shall assume that one
or more spaces separate words. Therefore, to find a word, we must first ignore any
spaces we encounter at the beginning of the string until a non-space character is met.
Then, all the non-space characters until the next space constitute a word. The process is
then repeated until the end of the string.

The way in which we shall accomplish this is by successively removing one word
at a time from the string. The string, therefore, becomes shorter as we progress through
the procedure.

For example, suppose that the string we enter is

```
" Hello, my name is    John."
```

Note that there is a space before the H in the word "Hello" and that there are
three spaces before the word "John". The program skips the initial space. It then
finds the next space (after the comma). The program then removes the word "Hello,"
from the string and displays the word. The string that the program will now be working
with is, therefore,

```
" my name is    John."
```

Next, the program skips all initial spaces until it gets to the next non-space, which
indicates the beginning of the next word—"my". The program then finds the next
space (after the word "my"). It then removes the word "my" from the string and displays the word. Continuing in this manner, the program displays each word in the
string.

Following is the program code, prb10-1.cpp.

```cpp
//prb10-1.cpp

//This program asks the user to input a string of words
//and then prints the words one word per line.
//The program uses the find(), length(), substr() and erase()
//string-class methods.

#include <iostream>
#include <string>

using namespace std;

int main()
{
  string the_string;
  string word;

  int space_location;

  cout << "Enter a string. Separate words by spaces: " << endl << endl;
  getline(cin, the_string);

  cout << endl;
  cout << "Following are the words in the string - one word per line: "
       << endl << endl;
```

```
//Find first space.
//If no space, output the entire one-word string

space_location = the_string.find(" ", 0);
if (space_location == -1)
  cout << the_string << endl << endl;

//Process as long as there is a space
while (space_location != -1)
{
  if (space_location == 0) //If initial space, skip it
    if (the_string.length() == 1) //If the string is a single space
      break;
    else
      the_string = the_string.substr(1, the_string.length());
  else
  {
    //otherwise, capture the first word and display it
    word = the_string.substr(0, space_location);
    cout << word << endl;

    //Remove the word
    the_string.erase(0, word.length());
  }

  //Find the next space
  space_location = the_string.find(" ", 0);

  //If there is no space, output the string.
  if (space_location == -1)
    cout << the_string << endl << endl;
}
  return 0;
}
```

Program Output

```
Enter a string. Separate words by spaces:
Hello, my name is    John.

Following are the words in the string - one word per line:

Hello,
my
name
is
John.
```

10.7.2 Discussion of prb10-1.cpp

The program begins by asking the user to enter a string. The getline() function obtains the string and places it into the string variable, the_string. After displaying the first line of output, the program finds the first space by applying the find() method to the_string. The index of the location of the first space in the string is placed into the integer variable space_location. If the find() method returns –1, there are no spaces in the string. Therefore, the string contains only one word. In this case, the string is displayed immediately. Because there are no spaces in the string, the body of the following while loop is never executed and the program ends.

If there is a space in the string, space_location will not equal –1 and the body of the while loop executes. If space_location equals 0 (the outer if), the space that was found is the first character in the string. There are now two possibilities: either the string is a single space or it is not. The inner if statement tests to see if the length of the string is 1. If so, the string consists of just a single space. In this case, there is nothing to do. Therefore, the break statement is executed, which ends the while loop and the program. If the string does not consist of a single space (the inner else), then the_string is replaced by the substring consisting of the second character (at index 1) to the end of the string. In other words, we have removed the first space character from the string.

If space_location is not zero (the outer else), that means that the string begins with a non-space character. Therefore, the program is at the start of a word. The first statement in the outer if uses the substr() method to extract the word and place it into the variable word. Note that the substring starts at location 0 (because the first character is not a space). The number of characters to extract is exactly the value of space_location. Now, because the variable word contains the word just extracted, the program displays the value of word. Finally, the word is removed from the string using the erase() method.

Outside the if statement, space_location is set to the location of the next space character. If there is no space character, there is only one word in the string and the cout statement displays the final word in the string.

10.7.3 Problem 10.2—The Palindrome Problem Revisited

The palindrome problem of Chapter 8 was solved using character pointers. In this section, we discuss another solution to the palindrome problem that uses string objects. First we review some concepts.

The words "otto" and "mom" are **palindromes**—they read the same forward and backward. A string can also be a palindrome if we ignore spacing, case, and punctuation. For example, the string "Madam, I'm Adam" is a palindrome.

We will use the same principle to decide if a word is a palindrome as we used in Chapter 8. Check to see if the first and last characters are the same. If they are not equal, the string is not a palindrome. If they are equal, check the second and next-to-last characters. If they are unequal, the string is not a palindrome. If they are equal, move to the next pair of characters and continue checking. If you arrive at the middle of the word and all pairs of characters are equal, the word is a palindrome. See Figure 10.3.

When checking a string to see if it is a palindrome, we must be aware that the string can contain blanks, mixed case letters, and punctuation characters. Therefore, to test a string, we must first rid the string of all blanks and punctuation characters, and then change all the characters to a common case. The pseudocode for the palindrome problem follows.

Characters are equal, so   All pairs are equal, so
move to the next pair.   word is a palindrome.

Figure 10.3

Prompt for and obtain a string.
Copy only the alphabetic characters to form a new string.
Convert the new string, which is a single word, to lowercase.
Test the resulting word for a palindrome.

The only major difference between the palindrome program in this section and the one in Chapter 8 is that we use string objects and string methods rather than character pointers. The techniques are essentially the same as that of prb08-1.cpp. Following is the program. We have already discussed all the string class concepts contained in this program except for the form of the append() method that we use, which we discuss after the program and output listing.

```
// prb10-2.cpp

// This program uses string objects and character library functions to
// decide whether a string entered by the user is a palindrome.
// A palindrome is a string that, disregarding case and punctuation,
// reads the same backward and forward.

#include <iostream>
#include <cctype>
#include <string>

using namespace std;

void Copy_Alpha(string&, string);
void Convert_To_Lower(string&);
bool  Palindrome(string);

int main()
{
  string line;
  string buffer;

  // Prompt for and obtain a string

  cout <<"\nEnter a string:\n";
  getline(cin, line);
  // Copy only the alphabetic characters

  Copy_Alpha(buffer, line);

  // Convert the string to all lowercase

  Convert_To_Lower(buffer);
```

```cpp
    // Test the result for a palindrome

    if ( Palindrome(buffer) )
      cout <<"\nThe string you entered is a palindrome.";
    else
      cout <<"\nThe string you entered is not a palindrome.";

    cout << endl;
    return 0;
} // End of main()

void Copy_Alpha(string& target, string source)
{
  for (int i = 0; i < source.length(); ++i)
    if (isalpha(source.at(i)))
        target.append(1, source.at(i));

  return;

} // End of Copy_Alpha()

void Convert_To_Lower(string& source)
{
  for (int i = 0; i < source.length(); ++i)
    source.at(i) = tolower(source.at(i));

  return;

}  // End of Convert_To_Lower()

bool Palindrome (string source)
{
  int end = source.length() - 1;
  int start = 0;

  while (start < end)
    if (source.at(start) != source.at(end))
      return false;
    else
      {
          ++start;
          --end;
      }

  return true;

} // End of Palindrome()
```

Program Output

```
Enter a string:
Madam, I'm Adam!

The string you entered is a palindrome.
```

This program works in essentially the same manner as prb08-1.cpp. After obtaining the string from the user using `getline()`, the program executes `Copy_Alpha (buffer, line)`, which copies only the alphabetic characters from the input string into the `string` object buffer. The first argument of `Copy_Alpha()` must be a reference because the function changes that argument. The `Copy_Alpha()` function consists of a `for` loop that tests each character of the source string to see if it is alphabetic. If it is, the character is appended to the end of the target string, thus changing the target string. To do this, we use a form of the `append()` method of the `string` class that allows the appending of one or several copies of a character to the end of a string. The statement

```
target.append(1, source.at(i))
```

appends one copy of the character referenced by `source.at(i)` to the end of `target`. (The statement `target.append(9, source.at(i))` would append nine copies of the character referenced by `source.at(i)` to the end of `target`.)

`Convert_To_Lower()` has one `string` object reference argument because the function has to change its argument. The `for` loop in the function replaces each character in the string by the lowercase version of the character using the function `tolower()`.

Finally, the function `Palindrome()` tests a word to see if it is a palindrome using the method described previously.

10.7.4 Problem 10.3—Sorting a Table Revisited

Following is prb10-3.cpp, which is based on dem09-6.cpp. It asks the user to enter data, which is then loaded into a table. The table is sorted on the part number, which is now a `string` object. (Because `string` is a valid data type, a `string` object can be a member of a structure.) Then the program asks the user if he or she wants to search the table. If the user responds yes, the program asks the user to enter a part number. The program then searches the table for the corresponding data.

```
//prb10-3.cpp

// This program loads a table, sorts it using the bubble sort, and
// then uses a binary search to search the table.

#include <iostream>
#include <iomanip>
#include <string>

using namespace std;

struct PART_STRUCT
{
   string part_no;
   int    quantity_on_hand;
   double unit_price;
};

void Load_Part_Table(PART_STRUCT [], int);
void Display_Part_Table(PART_STRUCT [], int);
```

```
void Sort_Table(PART_STRUCT [], int);

int main()
{
  const int TABLE_SIZE = 10;

  PART_STRUCT part_table[TABLE_SIZE];

  int middle,
      lower,
      upper;
  string part_key;       // The table search key
  string response;

  cout << setprecision(2)
       << setiosflags(ios::fixed)
       << setiosflags(ios::showpoint);

  // Load the table
  Load_Part_Table(part_table, TABLE_SIZE);

  // Sort the table using the bubble sort
  Sort_Table(part_table, TABLE_SIZE);

  // Display the sorted table
  cout << endl << endl;
  cout << "The table sorted on Part Number is:";

  Display_Part_Table(part_table, TABLE_SIZE);

  // Do the table search
  cout << endl << endl;
  cout << "Do you want to search the table?(Y/N): ";
  getline(cin, response);

  while (response == "Y" || response == "y")
  {
    cout << endl;
    cout << "Enter the part number: ";
    getline(cin, part_key);

    // Do the binary search
    lower = 0;
    upper = TABLE_SIZE - 1;
    middle = (lower + upper) / 2;

    while ( (part_table[middle].part_no != part_key)&& (lower <= upper) )
    {
      if (part_key < part_table[middle].part_no)
        upper = middle - 1;
      else
        lower = middle + 1;

      middle = (lower + upper) / 2;
    }
```

```
if (lower > upper)
{
  cout << endl;
  cout << "The search for " << part_key
          << " was not successful." << endl;
}

else
{
  cout << endl;
  cout << "Data for " << part_key << ":" << endl << endl;
  cout << "Quantity On Hand: " << setw(10)
          << part_table[middle].quantity_on_hand << endl;
  cout << "Unit Price:        " << setw(10)
          << part_table[middle].unit_price << endl;
}

cout << endl << endl;
cout << "Do you want to search the table?(Y/N): ";
getline(cin, response);

}

return 0;
} //End of main()
void Load_Part_Table(PART_STRUCT part_table[], int size)
{
  int row;

  cout << endl;
  cout << "Enter the table values as you are prompted:"
          << endl << endl;

  for (row = 0; row < size ; ++row)
  {
    cout << endl;
    cout << "For row #" << row + 1 << " enter:" << endl;
    cout << "Part Number (7 Characters): ";
    getline(cin, part_table[row].part_no);

    cout << "Quantity On Hand: ";
    cin >> part_table[row].quantity_on_hand;

    cout << "Unit Price: ";
    cin >> part_table[row].unit_price;

    cin.get();  //remove the newline character from the input buffer

  }
} //End of Load_Part_Table()

void Sort_Table(PART_STRUCT part_table[], int size)
{
  int row,
```

```
      pass,
      limit;
  PART_STRUCT temp_part;

  limit = size - 2;

for (pass = 1; pass <= size - 1; ++pass)
  {
    for (row = 0; row <= limit; ++row)
      if (part_table[row].part_no > part_table[row + 1].part_no)
      {
        temp_part = part_table[row];
        part_table[row] = part_table[row + 1];
        part_table[row + 1] = temp_part;
      }

      --limit;
  }
} //End of Sort_Table()

void Display_Part_Table(PART_STRUCT part_table[], int size)
{
  int row;

  cout << endl << endl;
  cout << setw(20) << "Part Number"
       << setw(20) << "Quantity On Hand"
       << setw(20) << "Unit Price"
       << endl;

  for (row = 0; row < size; ++row)
  {
    cout << endl;
    cout << setw(20) << part_table[row].part_no
         << setw(20) << part_table[row].quantity_on_hand
         << setw(20) << part_table[row].unit_price;
  }
} //End of Display_Part_Table()
```

Program Output

Enter the table values as you are prompted:

For row #1 enter:
Part Number (7 Characters): **A123456**
Quantity On Hand: **123**
Unit Price: **12.99**

For row #2 enter:
Part Number (7 Characters): **A987654**
Quantity On Hand: **53**
Unit Price: **52.95**

```
For row #3 enter:
Part Number (7 Characters): D001234
Quantity On Hand: 93
Unit Price: 22.95

For row #4 enter:
Part Number (7 Characters): B109897
Quantity On Hand: 44
Unit Price: 13.95

For row #5 enter:
Part Number (7 Characters): A035467
Quantity On Hand: 15
Unit Price: 59.95

For row #6 enter:
Part Number (7 Characters): C837289
Quantity On Hand: 0
Unit Price: 57.99

For row #7 enter:
Part Number (7 Characters): D346246
Quantity On Hand: 35
Unit Price: 25.99

For row #8 enter:
Part Number (7 Characters): C235146
Quantity On Hand: 104
Unit Price: 110.99

For row #9 enter:
Part Number (7 Characters): B194791
Quantity On Hand: 33
Unit Price: 14.95

For row #10 enter:
Part Number (7 Characters): A826749
Quantity On Hand: 56
Unit Price: 41.95

The table sorted on Part Number is:

           Part Number     Quantity On Hand        Unit Price

              A035467              15                 59.95
              A123456             123                 12.99
              A826749              56                 41.95
              A987654              53                 52.95
              B109897              44                 13.95
              B194791              33                 14.95
              C253146             104                110.99
              C837289               0                 57.99
              D001234              93                 22.95
              D346246              35                 25.99
```

```
Do you want to search the table?(Y/N): Y

Enter the part number: D001234

Data for D001234:

Quantity On Hand:          93
Unit Price:             22.95

Do you want to search the table?(Y/N): y

Enter the part number: C012345

The search for C012345 was not successful.

Do you want to search the table?(Y/N): Y

Enter the part number: A826749

Data for A826749:

Quantity On Hand:          56
Unit Price:             41.95

Do you want to search the table?(Y/N): N
```

The major difference between this program and dem09-6.cpp is that the string member of PART_STRUCT is a `string` object. This means that we can use the relational operators `!=` and `>` in `main()` and `Sort_Table()` to test strings rather than using the C-string function `strcmp()`.

Experiments 10.7

1. In the program prb10-1.cpp, add a counter that counts the number of words as they are processed. Have the program display the number of words in the string.
2. The program prb10-1.cpp changes the string that the user inputs. Rewrite the program so that a copy of the original string is saved. The program should also output the original string.
3. In prb10-1.cpp, replace the use of the `find()` method by the `find_first_of_method()`.

Programming Problems 10.7

1. In prb10-1.cpp, the comma was left at the end of the word "Hello." Rewrite the program so that if a comma, exclamation point, colon, or semicolon is found at the end of a word, the punctuation mark is removed before the word is displayed.
2. Write a program that asks the user to input a string of words. The program should replace each occurrence of a multiple space (two or more blanks in a row) by a single space. The program should output the resulting string.
3. Student e-mail IDs at Pace University consist of the first and last initials of the student, followed by five digits, followed by either the letter n or the letter p.

Write a program that asks the user to enter a Pace e-mail ID. The program should then validate the form of the ID as just described. If the ID is invalid, the program should tell the user which part (or parts) of the ID is invalid. If the ID is valid, the program should display an appropriate message.

10.8 ARRAYS OF STRINGS

In C++, a class is a valid data type. Therefore, you can declare an array of objects, so long as the objects are of the same type. This means that we can declare an array of string objects. The following declares an array of string objects and initializes the array to the names of the days of the week.

```
string day_names [] = {"Monday", "Tuesday", "Wednesday", "Thursday",
                       "Friday", "Saturday",  "Sunday"};
```

The following program, dem10-9.cpp, illustrates the use of an array of strings. It is a version of prb07-1.cpp. We repeat the problem statement here:

A sales manager wants to total the sales for each salesperson in her department and find the day of the week on which the salesperson had the highest sales. Write a program to perform this task. The program should ask the user for the sales of the salesperson for each day of the week. The prompt should include the name of the day of the week. The program should then total the weekly sales. Finally, the program should display the total weekly sales, the name of the day of the week that the salesperson had the highest sales, and the highest sales amount.

Following is a pseudocode solution to the problem.

Prompt for and get the name of the salesperson
Prompt for and get the sales amounts for each day
Calculate the total sales
Find the highest sales amount
Display the total sales, name of the day of the highest
    sales, and the highest sales amount

```
//dem10-9.cpp

// This program totals weekly sales amounts and finds the highest
// sales for the week.  It uses an array of strings to store the
// names of the days of the week.

#include <iostream>
#include <iomanip>
#include <string>

using namespace std;

int main()
{
   string day_names [] = {"Monday", "Tuesday", "Wednesday", "Thursday",
                          "Friday", "Saturday",  "Sunday"};
```

```
  double sales[7];
  string salesperson;

  double max_sales,
         total_sales;
  int    day,
         max_day;

  cout << setprecision(2)
       << setiosflags(ios::fixed)
       << setiosflags(ios::showpoint);

  cout << "Enter the name of the salesperson: ";
  getline(cin, salesperson);

  for (day = 0; day < 7; ++day)
  {
    cout << endl << endl;
    cout << "Enter the sales for "<< day_names[day]<< ": ";
    cin >> sales[day];
  }

  total_sales = 0;
  max_day = 0;
  max_sales = sales[0];

  for (day = 0; day < 7; ++day)
  {
    if (sales[day] > max_sales)
    {
      max_sales = sales[day];
      max_day = day;
    }
      total_sales += sales[day];
  }

  cout << endl << endl;
  cout << "The total sales for " << . salesperson
       << " is " << total_sales << "." << endl << endl;
  cout << "The highest sales was " << max_sales << "." << endl << endl;
  cout << "The highest sales occurred on "
       << day_names[max_day]<< ".";

  cout << endl;
  return 0;
}
```

Program Output

Enter the name of the salesperson: **Joseph Harris**

Enter the sales for Monday: **379.90**

Enter the sales for Tuesday: **2877.95**

```
Enter the sales for Wednesday: 2661.90

Enter the sales for Thursday: 178.45

Enter the sales for Friday: 3066.20

Enter the sales for Saturday: 0.00

Enter the sales for Sunday: 2904.77

The total sales for Joseph Harris is 12069.17.

The highest sales was 3066.20.

The highest sales occurred on Friday.
```

The declarations begin with the array of string objects day_names[], which is initialized to the names of the days of the week. The array sales[] stores the seven sales amounts. The string object salesperson stores the name of the salesperson. The double variable max_sales stores the highest sales and the variable total_sales is the accumulator for totaling the sales amounts. The integer variable day acts as the subscript for both the day_names[] array and the sales[] array.

The program begins by prompting for, and obtaining, the name of the salesperson. Next, a for loop prompts for and obtains the seven sales amounts and stores them in the array sales[]. The cout statement displays the name of the day of the week by displaying day_names[day], which is the name of the day corresponding to the day number.

The program prepares to total the sales amounts and find the day of the highest sales by initializing three variables. The accumulator total_sales is initialized to zero. To begin the process of finding the highest sales amount, we assume that the highest sale occurs on day zero. Therefore, the program initializes max_day to zero and max_sales to the sales on the first day, namely sales[0].

The next for loop totals the sales and finds the highest sales amount. For each of the seven days, the loop tests the sales of the day being processed, sales[day], against max_sales, the highest sales found so far. If sales[day] is greater than max_sales, the current day's sales is greater than the highest sales seen so far. Therefore, the program replaces the value of max_sales by the value of sales[day] and replaces the value of max_day by the value of the current day, namely day. If the value of sales[day] is not greater than max_sales, no adjustment needs to be made to either max_sales or max_day. In either case, the value of total_sales is increased by the value of sales[day]. When the program exits the for loop, total_sales contains the sum of the seven days' sales, max_sales contains the highest sales amount, and max_day contains the number of the day on which the highest sales occurred.

The cout statements display the results of the program. The first cout displays the salesperson's name and the total sales for the week. The second cout displays the value of the highest sales. The third cout displays the name of the day on which the highest sales occurred. The name of the day is accessed by day_names[max_day] because max_day is the number of the day of the highest sales.

Programming Problems 10.8

1. (See Programming Problem 6, Section 8.4.) Write a program that validates a date entered by the user. The program should ask the user to enter separately the month, day, and year. All should be stored in `string` objects. The month is to be entered by name and the day and year as integers. For example, the user might enter March, 30, and 2005 for the month, day, and year. The function `Validate_Date()` should determine if the entered date is valid by returning `true` if the date is valid and `false` otherwise. For example, the date March 30, 1999 is valid, but the date February 29, 2006 is not. Store the month names in an array of `string` objects. The program should display an appropriate message. Recall that a leap year is a year that is divisible by four. Remember to validate the month name.

2. (See dem06-4.cpp.) Write a program that asks the user to input 10 strings. Store the strings in an array of `string` objects. The program should use the bubble sort to sort the strings into ascending order and then output the strings in order.

CHAPTER REVIEW

TERMINOLOGY

Describe the meaning of the following terms.

object	concatenate
class	operator overloading
instance	`length()`
method	dot (.) operator
state	indices
information hiding	`at()`
istream	`empty()`
ostream	`find()`
instantiate	`rfind()`
no-argument constructor	`find_first_of()`
one-argument constructor	`substr()`
two-argument constructor	`replace()`
`string` class	`insert()`
value of the string object	`append()`
null string	`erase()`
constructor	palindromes
`getline()`	

SUMMARY

- An object is an agent responsible for its own actions.
- Every object is an instance of some class.
- One object communicates with another by sending messages.

- The receiving object responds to a message by executing a method.
- The state of an object is the data stored in the object.
- The principle of information hiding is that the sender of a message does not need to know the way in which the receiver carries out the request.
- All objects of the same class use the same method in response to a particular message.
- The receiver of a message determines the interpretation of that message. Therefore, objects of different classes might interpret the same message differently (that is, execute different methods in response to the same message).
- The string class is a built-in class in C++. To use the string class, your program must use #include <string>.
- A class, in particular string, is a valid data type.
- The set of characters stored in a string object is the value of the string.
- A constructor is a class method that executes when an object of that class is instantiated.
- The null string is a string object whose value has no characters.
- Use cout to output the value of a string object.
- Use cin to input a string consisting of a single word. Use getline() to input an entire line of text into a string object.
- The assignment operator (=), concatenation (+), and appending (+=) are all overloaded for string objects.
- All of the relational operators (==, !=, >, >=, <, <=) are overloaded for string objects.
- You apply a class method to an object by using the dot (.) operator.
- The length() method returns the number of characters in the value of a string object.
- The characters in the value of a string object are numbered starting from 0 to one less than the length of the string. These numbers are the indices of the characters.
- The at(i) method returns the character at index i of the string object to which it is applied.
- The at() method is a l-value, so it can be on the left side of an assignment. Therefore, at() can also be used to replace a single character in a string at a particular index.
- The empty() method returns true if the string object to which it is applied is the null string. It returns false otherwise.
- You can use a string object as a function argument. A function can return a string object.
- The find() method locates the first position (starting from the left end of the string's value) of a substring of a string object's value. The rfind() method starts searching the string from the right end of the string's value.
- The method find_first_of() finds the location in a string object's value of the first occurrence of any of a set of characters.
- The method substr() extracts a substring of a given number of characters from a string object's value starting at a given position in the string.
- The replace() method replaces a substring of a string object's value by another substring.
- The insert() method inserts a string into the value of a string object.
- The append() method adds a string to the end of the string to which it is applied.
- The erase() method erases a substring from a string.
- Because string is a valid data type, you can declare an array of string objects.

REVIEW EXERCISES

1. What is an object? What is a class?
2. How do objects communicate?
3. What is a method?
4. What is meant by the state of an object?
5. Explain the concept of information hiding.
6. What is the difference between the object-oriented approach of sending messages and the procedural approach that uses functions?
7. Why is the object that sends a message sometimes called a receiver? Why is the object that receives the message sometimes called the client?
8. In what way is an object similar to a special-purpose computer?
9. Give examples of three ways in which you can instantiate a `string` object.
10. What is meant by the value of a `string` object? How is the value of a `string` object different from the `string` object itself?
11. What is the null string?
12. What is a constructor?
13. How do you use `getline()` to input a line of text into the value of a `string` object?
14. When inputting a string into a `string` object, do you have to worry that you will input too many characters? Why or why not?
15. Give examples of two ways in which you can add a string to the end of a given string.
16. What is operator overloading? What operators are overloaded for `string` objects?
17. What method can you use to find the number of characters in a `string` object's value?
18. What operator do you use to apply a method to an object?
19. How are the characters in a `string` object's value numbered?
20. What operator would you use to test whether one `string` object's value follows that of a second `string` object?
21. How can you test a `string` object to see if its value is null?
22. How can you use a `string` object as a function argument?
23. Can you pass a `string` object argument by reference or by pointer? If so, how?
24. How can you find the location of a substring in the value of a `string` object?
25. How can you find the first occurrence of any of a set of characters in a `string` object's value?
26. How can you extract a substring from a `string` object's value?
27. What is the difference between inserting and replacing in a `string` object's value?
28. Is it valid to declare an array of `string` objects? Why or why not?

Chapter 11

Programmer-Defined Classes and Objects

OBJECTIVES

- To define a class and instantiate objects in a program
- To code class member functions
- To use the scope resolution operator to define a class member function outside the class declaration
- To access a class member using the "dot" notation
- To differentiate between accessor and mutator functions
- To code a class constructor
- To code a class destructor
- To assign one object to another
- To overload class constructors
- To use default arguments in a function
- To code and use function templates

In the last chapter, we introduced the concepts of objects and classes through the study of the C++ built-in `string` class. In this chapter, you will learn how to define your own classes and instantiate class objects. You will also learn, in this and the following chapters, how to manipulate objects of your own classes in ways similar to what we learned how to do for `string` class objects.

11.1 DECLARING OBJECTS AND CLASSES

In the introduction to Chapter 10, we discussed an object-oriented view of an ATM system. In that example, we spoke about the user as an **object**, the ATM as an object,

and your savings account as an object. Your savings account was an object in the
`Savings_Account` class. In this section, we show how to declare the `Savings_Account`
class and **instantiate** `Savings_Account` objects. We also discuss the various issues surrounding the declaration of a class and class members. Before continuing, you might
want to reread the introductory section of Chapter 10.

11.1.1 Defining a Class

Consider the following class definition:

```
class Savings_Account
{
  private:
    string id_no;
    double balance;
    double rate;

  public:
    Savings_Account(string, double, double);
    double Calc_Interest();
};

Savings_Account::Savings_Account(string id, double bal, double rt)
{
  id_no = id;
  balance = bal;
  rate = rt;
}

double Savings_Account::Calc_Interest()
{
  return balance * rate;
}
```

The class definition begins with the keyword `class` followed by the name of the
class. As you see, we capitalize the first letter of the name of a class. Although it is not
required to capitalize the first letter of a class name, it is a common convention to do
so. Following the name of the class is the definition of the class enclosed in braces. Note
that you *must* follow the closing brace by a semicolon. See Experiment 1.

The items declared in the class are the **class members**. The class has three data
members, or **instance variables**, `id_no`, `balance`, and `rate`. These are called instance
variables because each `Savings_Account` object that we instantiate contains its own
copies of these three data members. The values of the instance variables for a particular object determine the **state** of that object. The `Savings_Account` class also contains
two **methods**, `Savings_Account()`, a class **constructor**, and `Calc_Interest()`. Recall
that class methods determine the behavior of all the objects of that class—every object
in the class has the same behavior.

There are two new keywords in the class definition. The access specifiers
`private` and `public` determine the visibility of the class members. Class members declared after the `private` label can be accessed only by the methods of that class. Thus,
`id_no`, `balance`, and `rate`, being private instance variables, are accessible only to the

methods `Savings_Account()` and `Calc_Interest()`. No other functions have access to `id_no`, `balance`, or `rate`. Thus, if we declare an `Account` object in `main()`, we cannot directly refer to that object's private instance variables because `main()` is not a method of `Savings_Account`. Therefore, the following statement in `main()` is illegal. See Experiment 2.

```
cout << acc1.rate;
```

Private class members are C++'s way to enforce the principle of **information hiding**, which we discussed in Chapter 10. The things that make an object what it is, the object's state, are kept hidden from the outside world. The only way to change a private instance variable of an object is through the use of the class's methods. Information hiding tightly controls how we may use objects, we can use them only through the class's methods.

All class members that follow the label `public`, in our example `Calc_Interest()` and `Savings_Account()`, are accessible to all functions. By public accessibility we mean that `main()`, or any other function or class, can *use* the public methods to send corresponding messages to the objects of that class. (In fact, sometimes the public methods of a class are called the **public interface** of the class.) However, *how* the methods work, that is, the actual code of the methods, is not known outside the class. This, therefore, also enforces the principle of information hiding.

Why do we need two types of access? We do not want just anyone to be able to change the ID number, balance, or interest rate of an account. Therefore, it makes sense to make these items private. Similarly, we want objects (perhaps the ATM) to be able to request the creation and initialization of an account, and to send a message to an account object for it to calculate interest due the account. Therefore, we make the methods public.

Almost always, the instance variables of a class are private and the class methods are public. It is possible, although unusual, to have a public instance variable; remember, we want to enforce information hiding. However, we shall see in later examples that it is sometimes desirable to have a private class method. Private class methods are also accessible to all other methods of that class.

Note that `private` is the default access specifier. Thus, the following declaration is equivalent to the previous class declaration.

```
class Account
{
    string id_no;      //These are private by default
    double balance;
    double rate;

    public:
        Savings_Account(string, double, double);
        double Calc_Interest();
};
```

It is common practice, and we shall do so, to keep all the `public` items together and all the `private` items together. However, it is not necessary. The following is legal, but not desirable.

```
class Savings_Account
{
   private:
      string id_no;
   public:
      Savings_Account(string, double, double);
   private:
      double balance;
   public:
      double Calc_Interest();
   private:
      double rate;
};
```

As you can see, we declare the methods `Calc_Interest()` and `Savings_Account()` in the class definition, but define them outside the class definition. It is possible to define a class method inside the class definition. We shall do so in a few examples later in the book. However, in either case, the method must be *declared* inside the class declaration.

Note 11.1   Declaring Class Methods

All class methods must be declared inside the class definition, including those methods that are defined outside the class declaration.

11.1.2 Class Methods

Any method that is defined outside the class declaration must use the **scope resolution operator**, ::, in its definition header. Note 11.2 describes how to use the scope resolution operator.

Note 11.2   The Scope Resolution Operator

If you define a class method outside the class definition, you must use the scope resolution operator, ::, in the method definition header as follows:

`return-type ClassName::MethodName(parameter-list)`

Read the operator :: as the possessive "'s ".

Thus, read the definition header of `Calc_Interest()` as "`Savings_Account`'s `Calc_Interest()`." Why is the scope resolution operator necessary? There are situations in which it is necessary to declare several classes. In this case, it is possible that two or more of the classes will have methods with the same name. Suppose, for example, that we also declare a `CD_Account` class, which also has a `Calc_Interest()` method. If the `Calc_Interest()` methods of the two classes are defined inside their respective class definitions, there would be no confusion about which method is being defined. However, if the methods are defined outside the class definitions, as we did for the `Calc_Interest()` method, then it is necessary to specify to which class each method the `Calc_Interest()` method belongs. The definition `Savings_Account::Calc_Interest()` would be for `Savings_Account`'s `Calc_Interest()` method, and the definition `CD_Account::Calc_Interest()` would be for `CD_Account`'s `Calc_Interest()` method. See Experiment 3. A common practice is to define short methods (one or two statements) within the class definition and longer methods outside the class declaration.

It is very important to remember that class methods have access to all the instance variables of the class. There is no need to declare the class instance variables inside a class method—just use the instance variables in the method.

Note 11.3   Instance Variables Inside Methods

All instance variables of a class are accessible inside all methods of the class. Therefore, you can code a class method as though the class instance variables have been declared inside the method definition.

In the definition of the `Calc_Interest()` method, we do not re-declare the instance variables. The methods automatically have access to all the class's instance variables. The method computes the interest earned by the account, that is, the balance multiplied by the interest rate. Therefore, the statement in the method body returns the product of the data members `balance` and `rate`.

11.1.3 The Class Constructor

A constructor is a class method that automatically executes when an object of that class is instantiated. The name of the constructor *must* be the same as the name of the class and the constructor cannot have a return type (because it always results in creating a class object). If a constructor is not explicitly declared in the class definition, by default, C++ provides the **default constructor**. The default constructor only creates the object—it does not initialize the object's data members.

Note 11.4   The Name of a Constructor

If a constructor is explicitly declared in a class declaration, the constructor must have the same name as the class. The constructor cannot have a return type and must be `public`.

The scope resolution operator must be used in the definition of the constructor because the definition is outside the class declaration. Note also that if we declare a constructor that has one or more arguments (as the `Savings_Account()` constructor with three arguments) the default no-argument constructor is no longer available to the program. In this case, every object that is declared *must* be initialized. Therefore, the following declaration, if included in a program that uses the `Savings_Account` class, would be illegal. See Experiment 4.

```
Savings_Account acc1;
```

If there is need for the no-argument constructor, you can, of course, code your own.

Note 11.5   Initializing Objects

In a class, if you declare a constructor with one or more arguments, the default no-argument constructor is no longer available to the program. Therefore, in this case, you must initialize every object you declare by providing the proper number of arguments. If necessary, you can regain the no-argument constructor by coding it yourself.

Inside the definition of `Savings_Account()` we can refer to the instance variables of the class as though they were declared inside the method itself. (See Note 11.3.) The purpose of the constructor is to initialize an account with its basic data—an ID number, balance, and interest rate.

To use the constructor in `main()`, therefore, we would proceed as follows.

```
void main()
{
    int id;
    double bal;
    double rt;

    cout << "\nEnter Account ID: ";
    cin >> id;

    cout << "\nEnter Balance: ";
    cin >> bal;

    cout << "\nEnter Interest Rate: ";
    cin >> rt;

    Savings_Account acc1(id, bal, rt);

        .

        .

        .
}
```

The statement `Savings_Account acc1(id, bal, rt);` instantiates the `acc1` object and gives its instance variables specific values. Note that the constructor is not explicitly invoked; when the object is declared, the constructor is automatically applied to the object using the provided arguments. Therefore, the arguments `id`, `bal`, and `rt` are passed to the `Savings_Account` constructor. The constructor assigns the value of the `id` parameter to `id_no`, the value of the `bal` parameter to `balance`, and the value id_no balance   rate

5678	200.00	0.07

acc as created by the Account_Class constructor

Figure 11.1

of rt to rate. Figure 11.1 shows the object as created by the constructor if the user enters 5678, 200.00, and 0.07 in response to the prompts.

11.1.4 Methods

In earlier chapters, we saw how to apply methods to objects. As mentioned in Chapter 10, cin is an object in the istream class. The functions get() and getline() are public methods of the istream class. When we code cin.get() or cin.getline(), we are applying these member functions to the cin object. Thus, we use the "dot" operator to apply a method to an object. This technique also applies to classes that we declare in our programs. Once we have declared a Savings_Account object, we can use the dot operator with the class's methods to manipulate the object.

> **Note 11.6   How a Method Works**
>
> When a method is applied to an object, all class instance variable references in the method definition are to the instance variables of the object to which the method is applied.

In the statement

```
cout << "The interest on the account is " << acc1.Calc_Interest() << endl;
```

we apply the method Calc_Interest() to the acc1 object, in effect sending a message to the acc1 object to calculate its interest. Recall that the definition of the Calc_Interest() method contained just one statement, namely

```
return balance * rate;
```

When applied to acc1, Calc_Interest() takes the values of the balance and rate members of acc1, multiplies those values, and returns that value (the interest on the account) to main(). It is this value that is output by the cout statement.

We now put the pieces together to form a complete program.

11.1.5 The Program dem11-1.cpp

```
//dem11-1.cpp

//This program illustrates the use of a simple class and member functions

#include <iostream>
#include <iomanip>
#include <string>
```

```cpp
using namespace std;

class Savings_Account
{
  private:
    string id_no;
    double balance;
    double rate;

  public:
    Savings_Account(string, double, double);
    double Calc_Interest();
};

Savings_Account::Savings_Account(string id, double bal, double rt)
{
  id_no   = id;
  balance = bal;
  rate    = rt;
}

double Savings_Account::Calc_Interest()
{
  return balance * rate;
}

int main()
{
  cout << setprecision(2)
       << setiosflags(ios::fixed)
       << setiosflags(ios::showpoint);

  string id;      //Varaibles to store input data
  double bal;
  double rt;

  //Obtain Account information from the user

  cout << "\nEnter Account ID: ";
  getline(cin, id);

  cout << endl;
  cout << "Enter Balance: ";
  cin >> bal;

  cout << endl;
  cout << "Enter Interest Rate: ";
  cin >> rt;

  Savings_Account acc1(id, bal, rt);    //Initialize the object

  cout << endl;
  cout << "The interest on the account is " << acc1.Calc_Interest() << endl;

  return 0;
}
```

Program Output

```
Enter Account ID: 1234
Enter Balance: 100.00
Enter Interest Rate: 0.06
The interest on the account is 6.00
```

The order in which we place the parts of the program can be important. Remember that to use something in a program, it must have been previously declared. In main(), we declare an object, acc1, which is a member of Savings_Account. Therefore, we must place the declaration of Savings_Account before main(). In general, we will use the following outline for all our simple programs that use classes.

Note 11.7   The Structure of a Program that Uses Classes

For simple programs that use classes, we shall use the following program structure:

```
//Preprocessor directives
//Class declarations
//Method definitions
//Definition of main()
```

We emphasize that Note 11.7 applies to simple programs. For more complex programs we can divide the program code into several files, one file containing main() and the others each containing one class definition. After compiling the source files, the linker combines the object files into one executable program. For now, however, we shall stay with the simple program structure described in Note 11.7.

11.1.6 Discussion of dem11-1.cpp

Within main(), we declare the variables id, bal, and rt to use as storage locations for the data input by the user. After prompting for and obtaining the input values from the user, the program instantiates the acc1 object using the three-argument constructor. (Recall that in C++, you can declare a variable or object anywhere in the program.)

The last cout statement in main() contains the reference acc1.Calc_Interest(). The Calc_Interest() method returns a value. Just as with ordinary functions, the name of a method applied to an object represents the value returned by the method. In the case of class methods that return a value, the method name must be prefixed by the dot operator and the name of the object to which the method is being applied, in our case acc1.Calc_Interest(). The value of this expression is, therefore, the value returned by the method when it is applied to acc1. Thus, the cout statement displays the value of the interest, 6.00.

11.1.7 The Relation between `class` and `struct`

A class, like a structure, is an aggregate data type in the sense that its data members can be of different types. See Chapter 9. In fact, in C++, there is little difference between a class and a structure. Although we did not do so in Chapter 9, in C++, structures can have member functions, just as a class does. What, then, is the difference between a class and a structure? As mentioned previously, the default access in a class is `private`. The default access in a structure, on the other hand, is `public`. Therefore, dem11-1.cpp can be written using a structure instead of a class. See Experiment 7. However, in keeping with common practice, we shall use a class when we want to define a class—that is, when we need to use objects in our program. We shall use structures for aggregate data structures, like a three-part address, which we would not consider as separate objects.

Note that in C, unlike C++, a structure cannot have member functions and there are no such things as the access specifiers `public` and `private`. Also, the keyword `class` is not available in C because there are no such things as classes in the C language.

Exercises 11.1

Design a class for the objects in Exercises 1—5. In each case, state possible instance variables and methods. Think about what data characterize each object. Think about what you would want to do to each object and what behavior you would expect from each object. Do not worry at this point about how to represent the instance variables, how many instance variables you think of, or how to code the methods.

1. A stock on the New York Stock Exchange.
2. A customer for a roofing contractor.
3. A supplier for an office equipment store.
4. A building in a database of buildings to be used by a local real estate company.
5. A course in a database of courses used by the registrar at a university.
6. Using the class declaration of dem10-5.cpp, which of the following are incorrect declarations of a `Savings_Account` object? Correct any errors.

   ```
   Savnigs_Account acc1("1234", 200.00);

   Savnigs_Account acc2(0,0,0);

   Savnigs_Account acc3("3333", 300.00, 0.03)

   Savnigs_Account acc4("4444", 400, 0.04);
   ```

7. **(a)** Code a declaration for the class `Rectangle`. The class has two private double data members: `length` and `width`. The class has two methods, which you should declare but not define. The constructor, `Rectangle()`, has two arguments representing the length and width of a rectangle. The second method, `Area()`, has no arguments, but returns the area of the rectangle.

   (b) Define the `Rectangle()` constructor. The constructor assigns its first argument to the `length` instance variable and its second argument to the `width` instance variable.

   (c) Define the `Area()` method. The method returns the area of the rectangle.

8. **(a)** Code a declaration for the class `DigitalClock`. The class has three private integer instance variables: `hours`, `minutes`, and `ampm`. The class has three methods, which you should declare but not define. The constructor, `DigitalClock()`, has three arguments. The first argument represents the hour (an integer between 1 and 12), the second argument represents the minutes (an integer between 0 and 59), and the third argument represents either A.M. or P.M. (0 for A.M., 1 for P.M.). The class also has a method, `ShowTime()`, that displays the time in an appropriate format. The third method `Tick()` advances the time by one minute.

    (b) Define the `DigitalClock()` constructor. The method assigns its first argument to the `hour` instance variable, its second argument to the `minutes` instance variable, and the third argument to the `ampm` instance variable.

    (c) Define the `ShowTime()` method. The method displays the time in the following format: Hour:Minutes AM or PM. For example, 1:23 P.M.

Experiments 11.1

1. In dem11-1.cpp, omit the semicolon after the closing brace in the declaration of `Savings_Account`. Compile the resulting program. What message does the compiler issue?

2. In dem11-1.cpp, place in `main()` the statement `cout << acc1.rate;`. Compile the program. Explain any error messages.

3. In dem11-1.cpp, remove `Savings_Account::` from the definition header of the `Calc_Interest()` method. Compile the resulting program. Explain any error messages.

4. In dem11-1.cpp, change the declaration of `acc1` to the following.

   `Savings_Account acc1;`

   Compile and execute the program. What happens and why?

5. In dem11-1.cpp, place the statement `acc1.id_no = id;` after the declaration

   `Savings_Account acc1;`

   Compile the resulting program. What message does the compiler issue?

6. In dem11-1.cpp, change the declaration of `Savings_Account` to include the constructor method in the `private` section. Compile the resulting program. What message does the compiler issue?

7. Recode dem11-1.cpp using a structure rather than a class. Compile, execute, and test the resulting program. Is there any difference in how the program executes?

Programming Problems 11.1

NOTE: The following programming problems are all continued in the remaining sections of this chapter and in Chapter 12. Whichever ones you try, you should plan on continuing with the corresponding problems in the later sections and in Chapter 12. By the end of Chapter 12, you will have a program that contains most of the C++ elements covered in these chapters.

1. Write a program in which you declare a `WebPage` class. The class includes the following integer instance variables: the number of hits on the Web page (that is, the number of times the page is visited), the number of messages posted on the page site, and the number of downloads from the Web page. Include a constructor that initializes all instance variables to zero. Your `main()` function should just instantiate a `WebPage` object. Compile and test the program. Note: We will continue this exercise in the next section.

2. Write a program in which you declare an `OilTank` class. The class has the following instance variables: tank ID number (a string), tank capacity in gallons (an integer), and current number of gallons in the tank (that is, the tank's contents, also an integer). The methods include a three-argument constructor that assigns its arguments, in turn, to the tank number, capacity, and contents. Your `main()` function should just instantiate an `OilTank` object. Compile and test the program. Note: We will continue this exercise in the next section.

3. Write a program in which you declare a `VehicleService` class. The class has the following instance variables: the vehicle's service number (a string), the number of hours (a double) of labor used to service the vehicle, the cost of parts (a double) to perform the service, and the total cost (a double) of the service. Include a one-argument constructor that sets the vehicle's service number to its argument and that sets the other data members to zero. Compile and test the program. Note: We will continue this exercise in the next section.

4. Write a program in which you declare a class `HotelRoom`. The class has the following private instance variables: the room number (a string), the room capacity (an integer representing the maximum number of people the room can accommodate), the occupancy status (an integer, 0 if the room is not occupied, otherwise the number of occupants in the room), and the daily rate (a double). Include a three-argument constructor that sets the room number to its first argument, the room capacity to the second argument, the room rate to the third argument, and that sets the room occupancy status to 0. Compile and test the program. Note: We will continue this exercise in the next section.

5. Write a program that incorporates and tests the `Rectangle` class of Exercise 7. Declare a `Rectangle` object having width 3 and length 5 and display its area.

6. Write a program that incorporates and tests the `DigitalClock` class of Exercise 8. Declare a `DigitalClock` object having a time of 3:53 P.M. and display the clock's time.

11.2 A MORE USEFUL CLASS – ACCESSOR AND MUTATOR METHODS

The `Savings_Account` class of the previous section is not very useful for several reasons. First, the `Calc_Interest()` method calculates only the interest. The method does not apply the interest to the account balance, which is what we would want it to do in an actual application. Also, there is no way of adding or subtracting money from an account after the account is created. Finally, there is no way to find out how much money is in an account. We now redefine the method `Calc_Interest()` and add to the class the methods `Get_Balance()`, `Deposit()`, and `Withdraw()`.

```
class Savings_Account
{
  private:
    string id_no;
    double balance;
    double rate;

  public:
    Savings_Account(string, double, double);
    double Calc_Interest();
    double Get_Balance();
    void Deposit(double);
    bool Withdraw(double);
};
```

The new version of Calc_Interest() will not only calculate the interest due the account, but will also apply the interest to the account's balance. Each of Deposit() and Withdraw() has one argument, which is a double. We pass to the Deposit() method the amount of money that we want to deposit. We pass to the Withdraw() method the amount of money we want to withdraw.

The new definition of Calc_Interest() follows.

```
double Savings_Account::Calc_Interest()
{
  double interest;

  interest = balance * rate;
  balance += interest;
  return interest;
}
```

The definition of Calc_Interest() contains the declaration of the local variable interest. Local variables that are declared inside a class method obey the same scope and duration rules as all other local variables. Therefore, a local variable is known only inside the method in which it is declared. A local variable comes into existence at the point of declaration in the method and goes out of existence when the method ends. The variable interest is given a value by the first assignment statement in the method. The second assignment statement increases the instance variable balance by the value of interest. As in the original version of the method, the method returns the value of the interest.

The method Get_Balance() is very simple.

```
double Savings_Account::Get_Balance()
{
  return balance;
}
```

Suppose that `acc1` is a `Savings_Account` object that has a `balance` member whose value is 100.00. Then the following statement displays the value of the `balance` member of `acc1`.

```
cout << "The balance in the account is " << acc1.Get_Balance() << endl;
```

A method whose only purpose is to access the value of a private instance variable of the class is sometimes called an **accessor method**. `Get_Balance()` is an example of an accessor method whose purpose is to access the `balance` member of an `Account` object. Accessor methods are necessary because `private` instance variables are hidden from all functions except that class's own methods.

We now define the `Deposit()` method.

```
void Savings_Account::Deposit(double amount)
{
    balance += amount;
}
```

Again we emphasize that all `class` instance variables are accessible to a class method without the need for re-declaration. Therefore, `Deposit()` has access to the instance variable `balance`. The statement in the method definition increases the `balance` by the `amount` of the deposit. To apply a deposit of $55.42 to an account, say `acc1`, we would code the following.

```
acc1.Deposit(55.42);
```

When this statement executes, the method's `amount` parameter is assigned the value 55.42. Then the `balance` instance variable of `acc1` (which we will assume has the value 100.00) is increased by the value of `amount` (55.42), making the new value of `acc1`'s `balance` 155.42. `Deposit()` is an example of a method that changes the value of an instance variable. Such a method is sometimes called a **mutator method**.

The definition of `Withdraw()` must take into account that a withdrawal cannot be made on an account if the amount of the withdrawal exceeds the balance in the account. Therefore, if the withdrawal can be made, the method will make the withdrawal and return `true`. If the withdrawal cannot be made, the method will leave the balance as it is and return `false`. Following is the definition of `Withdraw()`.

```
bool Savings_Account::Withdraw(double amount)
{
    bool result;

    if (amount <= balance)
    {
        balance -= amount;
        result = true;
    }
    else
        result = false;

    return result;
}
```

The method tests the value of amount, which is the amount that we want to withdraw from the account. If the value of amount is less than or equal to the balance in the account, the withdrawal is made and the value of result is set to true. Otherwise, that is, if the amount to withdraw is greater than the balance, result is set to false. In either case, the method returns the value of result.

You may wonder why we do not have Withdraw() display an error message to the user in the case where amount is greater than balance. The decision not to do so is essentially a design decision that was made for the following reason. The Withdraw() method should be concerned with just making a withdrawal and should not be concerned with interfacing with the user. That should be the province of the function that uses Withdraw(). The Withdraw() method should signal only the action it takes—that is the purpose of returning either true or false.

We now use our new class definition in a program.

```cpp
//dem11-2.cpp

//This program uses an expanded version of the Savings_Account
//class introduced in dem11-1.cpp.

#include <iostream>
#include <iomanip>
#include <string>

using namespace std;

class Savings_Account
{
  private:
    string id_no;
    double balance;
    double rate;

  public:
    Savings_Account(string, double, double);
    double Calc_Interest();
    double Get_Balance();
    string Get_ID();
    void Deposit(double);
    bool Withdraw(double);
};

Savings_Account::Savings_Account(string id, double bal, double rt)
{
  id_no   = id;
  balance = bal;
  rate    = rt;
}

double Savings_Account::Get_Balance()
{
  return balance;
}
```

```cpp
string Savings_Account::Get_ID()
{
  return id_no;
}
double Savings_Account::Calc_Interest()
{
  double interest;

  interest = balance * rate;
  balance += interest;

  return interest;
}
void Savings_Account::Deposit(double amount)
{
  balance += amount;
}
bool Savings_Account::Withdraw(double amount)
{
  bool result;

  if (amount <= balance)
  {
    balance -= amount;
    result = true;
  }
  else
    result = false;

  return result;
}
int main()
{
  cout << setprecision(2)
       << setiosflags(ios::fixed)
       << setiosflags(ios::showpoint);

  string id;
  double bal;
  double rt;
  double amount;

  cout << endl;
  cout << "Enter Account ID: ";
  getline(cin, id);

  cout << endl;
  cout << "Enter Balance: ";
  cin >> bal;

  cout << endl;
  cout << "Enter Interest Rate: ";
  cin >> rt;
```

```
Savings_Account acc1(id, bal, rt);

cout << endl;
cout << "Account ID Number is " << acc1.Get_ID() << endl << endl;

cout << "The balance in the account is now " << acc1.Get_Balance()
     << endl << endl;

cout << "Enter an amount to deposit: ";
cin >> amount;

acc1.Deposit(amount);

cout << endl << endl;
cout << "A deposit of " << amount << " was made." << endl;
cout << "The balance in the account is now " << acc1.Get_Balance();

acc1.Calc_Interest();

cout << endl << endl;
cout << "Interest was applied to the account." << endl;
cout << "The balance in the account is now " << acc1.Get_Balance();

cout << endl << endl;
cout << "Enter an amount to withdraw: ";
cin >> amount;

if (acc1.Withdraw(amount))
{
   cout << endl << endl;
   cout << "A withdrawal of " << amount << " was made.";
}
else
{
   cout << endl << endl;
   cout << "WITHDRAWAL NOT MADE: Insufficient funds.";
}

cout << endl;
cout << "The balance in the account is now " << acc1.Get_Balance() << endl;

return 0;
}
```

Program Output

Enter Account ID: **1234**

Enter Balance: **100.00**

Enter Interest Rate: **0.06**

Account ID Number is 1234

The balance in the account is now 100.00

Enter an amount to deposit: **55.42**

```
A deposit of 55.42 was made.
The balance in the account is now 155.42

Interest was applied to the account.
The balance in the account is now 164.75

Enter an amount to withdraw: 120.00

A withdrawal of 120.00 was made.
The balance in the account is now 44.75
```

Exercises 11.2

1. Identify and correct any syntax errors in the following declaration of
   Savings_Account.

```
class Savings_Account
{
    string id_no;
    double balance,
    double rate;

  public;
    Savings_Account(string, double, double);
    Calc_Interest();
    double Get_Balance();
    void Deposit(double);
    bool Withdraw(double);
}

void Savings_Account::Savings_Account(string id, double bal, int rt)
{
  id_no   = id;
  balance = bal;
  rate    = rt;
}

double Savings_Account:Get_Balance()
{
  return balance;
}

double Savings_Account::Calc_Interest()
{
  double interest;

  interest = balance * rate;
  balance += interest;
  return interest;
}

void Account;;Deposit(double amount)
{
  balance += amount;
}
```

```
bool Withdraw(double amount)
{
  bool result;

  if amount <= balance
  {
    balance -= amount;
    result = true;
  }
  else
    result = true;

  return result;
}
```

Experiments 11.2

1. In dem11-2.cpp, we did not take into account the possible error of trying to deposit or withdraw a negative amount from an account. Change the Deposit() function so that it tests the parameter amount to see if it is negative. If so, the function should not make the deposit and should return false. If the amount is nonnegative, the function should make the deposit and return false. Make the necessary changes in main() to reflect the change in Deposit(). Change the Withdraw() member function similarly: if the amount of the withdrawal is negative, do not change the balance and return false; if the amount to withdraw is nonnegative, the function should behave as it does in dem10-2.cpp. Make the necessary changes to main() to reflect the change in Withdraw(). Note that there are now two reasons why a withdrawal might not be possible.

Programming Problems 11.2

1. Refer to Programming Problem 1 in Section 11.1. Add the following methods to the WebPage class: an accessor method for each instance variable of the class (Get_Hits(), Get_Messages(), and Get_Downloads()) that returns the value of that instance variable; a method for each instance variable that increases that variable by one (Inc_Hits(), Inc_Messages(), and Inc_Downloads()); a method Activity() that returns that total activity for the site (hits + messages + downloads).

   Write a main() that declares and initializes a WebPage object. Write statements that increase the number of hits by 2, messages by 3, and downloads by 1. Display the number of hits, messages, and downloads for the page as well as the total activity for the page.

2. Refer to Programming Problem 2 in Section 11.1. Add the following methods to the OilTank class: an accessor method for each instance variable of the class (Get_Number(), Get_Capacity(), and Get_Contents()) that returns the value of the variable; a one-argument method Add_Oil() that increases the number of gallons in a tank by the amount that is its argument; a one-argument method

Remove_Oil() that decreases the number of gallons in a tank by the amount that is its argument.

Write a main() that declares an OilTank object and that initializes it to represent an empty oil tank with ID number 1234 having a capacity of 1000 gallons. Have the program ask the user to enter the number of gallons to be added to the tank. Add this number of gallons to the tank and then display the tank number, capacity, and new contents of the tank. Next, ask the user to enter the number of gallons to remove from the tank. Remove this number of gallons from the tank and then display the tank number, capacity, and new contents of the tank.

3. Refer to Programming Problem 3 in Section 11.1. Add the following methods to the VehicleService class: an accessor method for each instance variable of the class (Get_Number(), Get_Hours(), Get_Parts(), and Get_Cost()) that returns the value of the variable; for each of hours and parts, a one-argument method (Set_Hours(), and Set_Parts()) that sets the value of the corresponding instance variable to the value of its argument. In the case of Set_Hours(), the method should also calculate the labor cost of those hours by multiplying the number of hours by 70.00 and adding this amount to the total cost of service. In the case of Set_Parts(), the method should add the cost of the parts to the total cost of service.

Write a main() that declares a VehicleService object that represents a vehicle with a service number of 432. The program should ask the user to enter the number of hours of labor spent on the vehicle and for the cost of parts to repair the vehicle. The program should apply that number of hours and cost of parts to the vehicle. Finally, the program should display a report that lists the vehicle service number, the number of hours spent repairing the vehicle, the cost of labor, the cost of parts and the total cost of repair.

4. Refer to Programming Problem 4 in Section 11.1. Add the following methods to the HotelRoom class: an accessor method for each instance variable of the class (Get_Number(), Get_Capacity(), Get_Status(), and Get_Rate()); a one-argument method Change_Status() that changes the occupancy status of the room to the value of its argument. The method should verify that the argument value does not exceed the room capacity. If it does, the method should return –1. Finally, add this method to the Hotel Room class: a one-argument method Change_Rate() that sets the room rate to the value of its argument.

Write a main() that creates a hotel room with room number 123, with a capacity of 4, and a rate of 150.00. Suppose a person checks in. The program should ask the user to enter the number of guests to occupy the room. Change the status of the room to reflect the number of guests that just checked in. Display the information about the room in a nicely formatted way. Now assume that the guests check out. Change the status of the room appropriately and display the information about the room. Next, change the room rate to 175.00. Finally, assume that another person checks in. Ask the user to enter the number of guests to occupy the room. Change the room's status accordingly and display the new information about the room.

5. Refer to Programming Problem 5 in Section 11.1. Add the following methods to the Rectangle class: accessor methods Length() and Width() that return the values of the respective instance variables; the method Perimeter() that returns

the perimeter of the object (twice the sum of the length and width.); the method Grow() that doubles both the length and width of the object to which it is applied.

Write a main() that declares a rectangle object of width 3 and length 7. Display its dimensions, area, and perimeter. Then apply the Grow() method to the object and again display its dimensions, area, and perimeter.

6. Refer to Programming Problem 6 in Section 11.1. Add the following methods to the DigitalClock class: accessor methods that return the value of hours, minutes, and A.M. or P.M; the method Tick() that adds one to the minute instance variable, unless minute is 59. In that case, set minute to zero, and increase hour by one (if hour is 11, appropriately change ampm), unless hour is 12. In that case, set hour to 1.

Write a main() that declares a DigitalClock object with an initial time of 3:58 P.M. Display the hours, minutes, and either A.M. or P.M. for the clock. Then, apply the Tick() method to the object several times and verify that the clock's time does in fact change.

11.3 CONSTRUCTOR OVERLOADING AND DESTRUCTORS

In the last section, we used a three-argument constructor in the definition of the Savings_Account class. We now discuss using multiple constructors in a class, and the **destructor**, which executes when an object is destroyed.

11.3.1 Constructor Overloading

C++ allows you to define several constructors for a class. This is called **function overloading** and will be discussed in a more general context later in Section 11.5. Overloading allows us to have constructors for different sets of circumstances.

In Savings_Account, we have a constructor that allows us to create a savings account by giving an account ID number, a balance, and an interest rate. We might also want a constructor that allows us to create a savings account by giving only the account number, with the balance and interest rate being assigned default values of 0.00 and 0.02. We might also want a constructor that allows us to create an account by giving the account number and the balance with the interest rate being assigned a default value of 0.02. You must declare all three constructors in the class definition as follows.

```
class Savings_Account
{
    .
    .
    .
  public:
    Savings_Account(string, double, double);
    Savings_Account(string, double);
    Savings_Account(string);
    .
    .
    .
};
```

The constructor is now overloaded because we have three different constructors depending on the number of arguments given in a Savings_Account object declaration. The three constructor definitions follow.

```
Savings_Account::Saivings_Account(string id, double bal, double rt)
{
   id_no = id;
   balance = bal;
   rate = rt;
}

Savings_Account::Savings_Account(string id, double bal)
{
   id_no = id;
   balance = bal;
   rate = 0.02;
}

Savings_Account::Savings_Account(string id)
{
   id_no = id;
   balance = 0.0;
   rate = 0.02;
}
```

In main(), we can now write the following declarations.

```
Savings_Account acc3("3333", 100.00, 0.06);

Savings_Account acc2("2222", 200.00);

Savings_Account acc1("1111");
```

The C++ compiler distinguishes among the three constructors by the number and type of arguments provided in the declaration of an object. The first declaration uses the three-argument constructor and creates the account 3333 with a balance of 100.00 and interest rate of 0.06. The second declaration creates the account 2222 with an opening balance of 200.00 and the default interest rate of 0.02. The third declaration uses the one-argument constructor and creates the account 1111 with a default balance of 0.00 and a default interest rate of 0.02.

The program dem11-3.cpp demonstrates constructor overloading. We have added a cout statement to each constructor to verify that the corresponding constructor executes. Note that main() has only one cout statement that announces the end of the program. The other output comes from the constructors.

```
//dem11-3.cpp

//This program uses an expanded version of the Savings_Account
//class introduced in dem11-1.cpp.
//It demonstrates overloaded constructor methods

#include <iostream>
#include <iomanip>
#include <string>
```

```cpp
using namespace std;

class Savings_Account
{
  private:
    string id_no;
    double balance;
    double rate;

  public:
    Savings_Account(string, double, double);
    Savings_Account(string, double);
    Savings_Account(string);
    double Calc_Interest();
    double Get_Balance();
    string Get_ID();
    void Deposit(double);
    bool Withdraw(double);
};

Savings_Account::Savings_Account(string id, double bal, double rt)
{
  id_no   = id;
  balance = bal;
  rate    = rt;

  cout << "Three-arg constuctor for " << id_no << endl;
}

Savings_Account::Savings_Account(string id, double bal)
{
  id_no = id;
  balance = bal;
  rate = 0.02;

  cout << "Two-arg constuctor for " << id_no << endl;

}

Savings_Account::Savings_Account(string id)
{
  id_no = id;
  balance = 0.0;
  rate = 0.02;

  cout << "One-arg constuctor for " << id_no << endl;

}

double Savings_Account::Get_Balance()
{
  return balance;
}

string Savings_Account::Get_ID()
```

```cpp
{
  return id_no;
}
double Savings_Account::Calc_Interest()
{
  double interest;

  interest = balance * rate;
  balance += interest;

  return interest;
}
void Savings_Account::Deposit(double amount)
{
  balance += amount;
}
bool Savings_Account::Withdraw(double amount)
{
  bool result;

  if (amount <= balance)
  {
    balance -= amount;
    result = true;
  }
  else
    result = false;

  return result;
}
int main()
{
  Savings_Account acc3("3333", 100.00, 0.06);
  Savings_Account acc2("2222", 200.00);
  Savings_Account acc1("1111");

  cout << endl;
  cout << "*** End of Program ***" << endl;

  return 0;
}
```

Program Output

```
Three-arg constuctor for 3333
Two-arg constuctor for 2222
One-arg constuctor for 1111

*** End of Program ***
```

11.3.2 Destructors

When an object goes out of scope, C++ destroys the object. For example, if we declare an object inside a function, it is a local object and, therefore, its storage class is automatic. When the function ends, the object is destroyed. A class, by default, is given a **default destructor**, which is a method that destroys the object. Like a constructor, the default destructor is not called explicitly—it is automatically executed when the object goes out of scope. As is the case for a constructor, we can write our own destructor for a class. The name of a destructor is the same as the name of the class prefixed by the "tilde" character ~. A destructor cannot have arguments and cannot have a return type. A destructor cannot be overloaded. See Experiments 1 through 3.

Note 11.8   The Name of a Destructor

If a destructor is explicitly declared in a class definition, the destructor must have the same name as the class prefixed by ~. The destructor cannot have a return type, cannot have arguments, and must be `public`. A destructor cannot be overloaded.

Following is dem11-4.cpp, which illustrates how a destructor works.

```
//dem11-4.cpp

//This program uses an expanded version of the Savings_Account
//class introduced in dem11-1.cpp.

//It illustrates the use of a destructor.

#include <iostream>
#include <iomanip>
#include <string>

using namespace std;

class Savings_Account
{
  private:
    string id_no;
    double balance;
    double rate;

  public:
    Savings_Account(string, double, double);
    Savings_Account(string, double);
    Savings_Account(string);
    ~Savings_Account();
    double Calc_Interest();
    double Get_Balance();
    string Get_ID();
    void Deposit(double);
```

```cpp
    bool Withdraw(double);
};

Savings_Account::Savings_Account(string id, double bal, double rt)
{
  id_no   = id;
  balance = bal;
  rate    = rt;

  cout << "Three-arg constuctor for " << id_no << endl;
}

Savings_Account::Savings_Account(string id, double bal)
{
  id_no = id;
  balance = bal;
  rate = 0.02;

  cout << "Two-arg constuctor for " << id_no << endl;

}

Savings_Account::Savings_Account(string id)
{
  id_no = id;
  balance = 0.0;
  rate = 0.02;

  cout << "One-arg constuctor for " << id_no << endl;

}

Savings_Account::~Savings_Account()
{
  cout << "Destructor executed for " << id_no << endl;
}

double Savings_Account::Get_Balance()
{
  return balance;
}

string Savings_Account::Get_ID()
{
  return id_no;
}

double Savings_Account::Calc_Interest()
{
  double interest;

  interest = balance * rate;
  balance += interest;

  return interest;
}
```

DUBLIN BUSINESS SCHOOL LIBRARY

```
void Savings_Account::Deposit(double amount)
{
   balance += amount;
}
bool Savings_Account::Withdraw(double amount)
{
   bool result;

   if (amount <= balance)
   {
      balance -= amount;
      result = true;
   }
   else
      result = false;

   return result;
}

int main()
{
   Savings_Account acc3("3333", 100.00, 0.06);
   Savings_Account acc2("2222", 200.00);
   Savings_Account acc1("1111");

   cout << endl;
   cout << "*** End of Program ***" << endl;

   return 0;
}
```

Program Output

```
Three-arg constuctor for 3333
Two-arg constuctor for 2222
One-arg constuctor for 1111

*** End of Program ***
Destructor executed for 1111
Destructor executed for 2222
Destructor executed for 3333
```

The order of the displayed messages is important. When acc3 is declared, the constructor executes for that object. When acc2 is declared, the constructor executes for that object and likewise for acc1. All three objects remain in existence until main() ends. Therefore, main() displays the message that the program ends. Then the destructor executes for each object in the reverse order of object creation. Thus, C++ executes the destructor for acc1, then acc2, and finally for acc3.

Experiments 11.3

1. Recode the destructor of dem11-4.cpp to include the return type of void. Compile the resulting program. What message does the compiler issue?
2. Recode the destructor of dem11-4.cpp to include an argument of type string. Compile the resulting program. What message does the compiler issue?
3. Recode dem11-4.cpp by making the declaration of the destructor private. Compile the resulting program. What message does the compiler issue?

Programming Problems 11.3

1. In the WebPage class of Programming Problem 1, Section 11.2, in addition to the no-argument constructor, code a three-argument constructor that initializes the data members of the object being created (hits, messages, and downloads) to its arguments. Also, add a destructor that displays a message that it executed. Recode the main() that you wrote to include use of the constructors. Compile, execute, and test the resulting program.

2. In the OilTank class of Programming Problem 2, Section 11.2, add a two-argument constructor that initializes the tank contents to zero. Also, add a one-argument constructor that initializes the capacity to 1000 and the tank contents to zero. Also, add a destructor that displays a message that it executed. Recode the main() that you wrote to include use of the constructors. Compile, execute, and test the resulting program.

3. In the VehicleService class of Programming Problem 3, Section 11.2, add a three-argument constructor in which the arguments are set to, in turn, the service number, number of hours, and the cost of parts. Also, add a destructor that displays a message that it executed. Recode the main() that you wrote to include use of the constructors. Compile, execute, and test the resulting program.

4. In the HotelRoom class of Programming Problem 4, Section 11.2, add a two-argument constructor that sets the room number to its first argument, the room capacity to its second argument, and that defaults the room rate to 129.00 and the room occupancy to zero. Also, add a destructor that displays a message that it executed. Recode the main() you wrote to include the use of the constructor. Compile, execute, and test the resulting program.

5. In the Recatangle class of programming Problem 5, Section 11.2, add a no-argument constructor that sets the length and width each to one. Recode the main() you wrote to include the use of the constructor. Also, add a destructor that displays a message that it executed. Compile, execute, and test the resulting program.

6. In the DigitalClock class of Programming Problem 6, Section 11.2, add a no-argument constructor that sets the time to 12:00AM. Also, add a destructor that displays a message that it executed. Recode the main() you wrote to include the use of the constructor. Compile, execute, and test the resulting program.

11.4 DEFAULT ARGUMENTS AND OBJECT ASSIGNMENT

11.4.1 Default Arguments

In the previous section, we overloaded the `Savings_Account` constructor to allow us to declare a `Savings_Account` object in any of three ways. Sometimes we can achieve the effect of overloading a constructor by using a single constructor with **default arguments**. You must specify the default arguments in the constructor's declaration, not in its definition. See Note 11.9, which follows. Thus, in the class declaration, you must code the following.

```
public:
    Savings_Account(string id, double bal = 0.00, double rt = 0.02);
                        //Three-argument constructor with default values
                        //which serves as a one-argument constructor
                        //and a two-argument constructor
```

This declaration means that if we omit the last two arguments when declaring a `Savings_Account` object, the default value of 0.00 will be used for the second argument and the default value 0.02 for the third argument. Thus, the following declaration creates a `Savings_Account` object with an ID of 1111, a balance of 0.00, and a rate of 0.02.

```
    Savings_Account acc1("1111");
```

When defaulting arguments in a constructor, only the trailing arguments can be defaulted. See Note 11.9, which follows. Therefore, if we declare a `Savings_Account` object with two specific arguments as follows,

```
    Savings_Account acc2("2222", 0.05);
```

the last argument, that is, the interest rate, defaults to 0.02. The value of the second argument, 0.05, is therefore the opening balance of the account.

Note that the following declaration is illegal because (see Note 11.7) the no-argument constructor is not available.

```
    Savings_Account acc0;
```

Note 11.9 summarizes the two rules you must follow when using default arguments in a constructor.

Note 11.9   Default Arguments in a Constructor

· Default arguments must be specified in the declaration of the function.
· Only trailing arguments can be omitted.

Thus, according to Note 11.9, the following declaration is illegal because there is a non-default argument after a default argument. See Experiment 1.

```
Account(string id, double bal = 0.00, double rt);   //Illegal declaration
```

The program dem11-5.cpp illustrates using default arguments in a constructor in the `Savings_Account` class.

```cpp
//dem11-5.cpp

//This program uses an expanded version of the Savings_Account
//class introduced in dem11-1.cpp.

//The program illustrates default arguments in constructor declarations

#include <iostream>
#include <iomanip>
#include <string>

using namespace std;

class Savings_Account
{
  private:
    string id_no;
    double balance;
    double rate;

  public:
    Savings_Account(string id, double bal = 0.00, double rt = 0.02);
    ~Savings_Account();
    double Calc_Interest();
    double Get_Balance();
    string Get_ID();
    void Deposit(double);
    bool Withdraw(double);
};

Savings_Account::Savings_Account(string id, double bal, double rt)
{
  id_no   = id;
  balance = bal;
  rate    = rt;

  cout << "Default-argument constuctor for " << id_no << endl;
  cout << "Value of balance is " << balance << endl;
  cout << "Value of rate is " << rate << endl << endl;
}

Savings_Account::~Savings_Account()
{
  cout << "Destructor executed for " << id_no << endl;
}

double Savings_Account::Get_Balance()
{
  return balance;
}

string Savings_Account::Get_ID()
{
  return id_no;
}
```

```
double Savings_Account::Calc_Interest()
{
  double interest;

  interest = balance * rate;
  balance += interest;

  return interest;
}
void Savings_Account::Deposit(double amount)
{
  balance += amount;
}
bool Savings_Account::Withdraw(double amount)
{
  bool result;

  if (amount <= balance)
  {
    balance -= amount;
    result = true;
  }
  else
    result = false;

  return result;
}
int main()
{
  cout << setprecision(2)
       << setiosflags(ios::fixed)
       << setiosflags(ios::showpoint);

  Savings_Account acc3("3333", 100.00, 0.06);
  Savings_Account acc2("2222", 200.00);
  Savings_Account acc1("1111");

  cout << endl;
  cout << "*** End of Program ***" << endl;

  return 0;
}
```

Program Output

```
Default-argument constuctor for 3333
Value of balance is 100.00
Value of rate is 0.06

Default-argument constuctor for 2222
Value of balance is 200.00
```

```
Value of rate is 0.02

Default-argument constuctor for 1111
Value of balance is 0.00
Value of rate is 0.02

*** End of Program ***
Destructor executed for 1111
Destructor executed for 2222
Destructor executed for 3333
```

The default arguments in the constructor declaration allow us to declare Savings_Account objects in the same way as we did in dem11-4.cpp, in which we had three overloaded constructors. We added cout statements in the constructor to verify the values of the instance variables.

11.4.2 Assigning One Object to Another

It is possible to assign one object to another object as long as they belong to the same class. In this case, the assignment is done on a member-by-member basis. For example, consider the following.

```
Savings_Account acc1("1111", 100.00, 0.03);

Savings_Account acc2("2222", 200.00);

acc2 = acc1;
```

The object acc1 has its id, balance, and rate members initialized to "1111", 100.00, and 0.03, respectively. The object acc2 has its id and balance initialized to "2222" and 200.00. The rate for object acc2 defaults to 0.02. When the assignment executes, the id member of acc1 is copied to the id member of acc2; the balance member of acc1 is copied to the balance member of acc2; the rate member of acc1 is copied to the rate member of acc2.

We illustrate these points in the following program. The program is based on dem11-5.cpp. Note that we have removed the destructor and the cout statements from the constructor. We also added a Get_Rate() method so we could display the values of all the instance variables.

```
//dem11-6.cpp

//This program uses an expanded version of the Savings_Account
//class introduced in dem11-1.cpp.
//The program illustrates object assignment

#include <iostream>
#include <iomanip>
#include <string>

using namespace std;
```

```cpp
class Savings_Account
{
  private:
    string id_no;
    double balance;
    double rate;

  public:
    Savings_Account(string id, double bal = 0.00, double rt = 0.02);
    double Calc_Interest();
    double Get_Balance();
    double Get_Rate();
    string Get_ID();
    void Deposit(double);
    bool Withdraw(double);
};

Savings_Account::Savings_Account(string id, double bal, double rt)
{
  id_no   = id;
  balance = bal;
  rate    = rt;
}

double Savings_Account::Get_Balance()
{
  return balance;
}

string Savings_Account::Get_ID()
{
  return id_no;
}

double Savings_Account::Get_Rate()
{
  return rate;
}

double Savings_Account::Calc_Interest()
{
  double interest;
  interest = balance * rate;
  balance += interest;

  return interest;
}

void Savings_Account::Deposit(double amount)
{
  balance += amount;
}
```

```cpp
bool Savings_Account::Withdraw(double amount)
{
    bool result;

    if (amount <= balance)
    {
        balance -= amount;
        result = true;
    }
    else
        result = false;
    return result;
}

int main()
{
    cout << setprecision(2)
         << setiosflags(ios::fixed)
         << setiosflags(ios::showpoint);

    Savings_Account acc1("1111", 100.00, 0.03);
    Savings_Account acc2("2222", 200.00);

    acc2 = acc1;

    cout << "The new values for acc2 are: " << endl << endl;
    cout << "ID = " << acc2.Get_ID() << endl;
    cout << "Balance = " << acc2.Get_Balance() << endl;
    cout << "Rate = " << acc2.Get_Rate() << endl;

    return 0;
}
```

Program Output

```
The new values for acc2 are:

ID = 1111
Balance = 100.00
Rate = 0.03
```

The Savings_Account constructor executes twice—once for acc1 and once for acc2. The program then assigns the value of acc1 to acc2. The assignment is done on a member-by-member basis. Therefore, the data members of acc1 are copied to the data members of acc2. The program verifies the assignment when it displays the values of the data members of acc2.

Note that an object of one class can be assigned to an object of another class if you define (by overloading the assignment operator) how the assignment is to be carried out. We shall discuss how this can be done in Chapter 15.

Exercises 11.4

1. Assume the following declarations.

   ```
   Savings_Account acc7("7777", 100.00, 0.07);
   Savings_Account acc8("8888", 200.00, 0.08);
   ```

   What are the values of the data members of acc8 after executing the following?

   ```
   acc8 = acc7;
   ```

Experiments 11.4

1. In dem11-5.cpp, replace the declaration of the Savings_Account constructor by the following:

   ```
   Savings_Account(string id, double bal = 0.00, double rt);
   ```

   Compile the resulting program. What message does the compiler issue?

2. Any function can have default arguments. Compile and execute the following program. What are the results and why?

   ```
   #include <iostream>
   using namespace std:
   int Sum(int i = 1, int j = 2);
   int main()
   {
      cout << Sum(3, 4) << endl;
      cout << Sum(6) << endl;
      cout << Sum() << endl;
      return 0;
   }
   int Sum(int i, int j)
   {
      return i + j;
   }
   ```

Programming Problems 11.4

1. In the WebPage class of Programming Problem 1, Section 11.3, replace the constructors by a constructor with default arguments. Recode the main() that you wrote to include use of the constructor. Compile, execute, and test the resulting program.

2. In the OilTank class of Programming Problem 2, Section 11.3, replace the constructors by a constructor with default arguments. Recode the main() that you

wrote to include use of the constructor. Compile, execute, and test the resulting program.

4. In the `VehicleService` class of Programming Problem 3, Section 11. 3, replace the constructors by a constructor with default arguments. Recode the `main()` that you wrote to include use of the constructor. Compile, execute, and test the resulting program.

3. In the `HotelRoom` class of Programming Problem 4 of Section 11.3, replace the constructors by a constructor with default arguments. Recode the `main()` you wrote to include use of the constructor. Compile, execute, and test the resulting program.

4. In the `Recatangle` class of Programming Problem 5 of Section 11.3, replace the constructors by a constructor with default arguments. Recode the `main()` you wrote to include use of the constructor. Compile, execute, and test the resulting program.

5. In the `DigitalClock` class of Programming Problem 6 of Section 11.3, replace the constructors by a constructor with default arguments. Recode the `main()` you wrote to include use of the constructor. Compile, execute, and test the resulting program.

11.5 GENERAL FUNCTION OVERLOADING AND FUNCTION TEMPLATES[1]

In this section, we discuss several ways to make any function in C++, not just constructors, more powerful and useful.

11.5.1 General Function Overloading

Any function, not only constructors, can be overloaded in C++. The overloaded versions of a function must have the same return type and must differ in the number and/or the types of arguments. The following function interchanges its two integer arguments. See dem08-3R.cpp in Chapter 8.

```
void Swap(int& i, int& j)
{
   int temp;

   temp = i;
   i = j;
   j = temp;
}
```

If we were not allowed to overload `Swap()` and we wanted to write a function that interchanges two doubles, we would have to code a separate function, say `Swap_Double()`. However, in C++ we can overload the integer version of `Swap()` with the following double version of `Swap()`.

```
void Swap(double& x, double& y)
{
   double temp;
```

---

[1]This section is optional.

```
   temp = x;
   x = y;
   y = temp;
}
```

When used in a program, the C++ compiler distinguishes between the two versions of Swap() by the data types of its arguments. Following is dem11-7.cpp, which illustrates function overloading.

```
//dem11-7.cpp

//This program demonstrates function overloading.

#include <iostream>

using namespace std;

void Swap(int&, int&);
void Swap(double&, double&);

int main()
{
   int    n = 3,
          m = 9;
   double d = 5.7,
          e = 3.14 ;

   cout << "n = " << n << " m = " << m << endl;
   cout << "d = " << d << " e = " << e << endl;

   Swap(n, m);
   Swap(d, e);

   cout << endl << endl;
   cout << "After swapping:" << endl;
   cout << "n = " << n << " m = " << m << endl;
   cout << "d = " << d << " e = " << e << endl;

   return 0;
}

void Swap(int& i, int& j)
{
   int temp;

   temp = i;
   i = j;
   j = temp;
}

void Swap(double& x, double& y)
{
   double temp;

   temp = x;
   x = y;
   y = temp;
}
```

Program Output

```
n = 3 m = 9
d = 5.7 e = 3.14

After swapping:

n = 9 m = 3
d = 3.14 e = 5.7
```

Two versions of Swap() are declared, one for integers and one for doubles. In main() the compiler decides which version of Swap() to use by the type of its arguments. Thus, the first execution of Swap() uses the integer version and the second uses the double version. We leave as an exercise which version of Swap() is used in the following statement. See Experiment 1.

```
Swap(n, d);     //Which version is used?
```

11.5.2 Function Templates

The overloaded Swap() function of the previous section can be overloaded further for arguments that are floats, longs, shorts, and so on. We would, of course, have to code a different function for each argument type. A **function template** allows the programmer to code a function whose definition is independent of the data type of its arguments and/or its return type. Thus, a function template, in essence, makes the compiler automatically create overloaded functions as needed by the program. A function template for the Swap() function is as follows.

```
template <class Type>
void Swap(Type& x, Type& y)
{
   Type temp;
   temp = x;
   x = y;
   y = temp;
}
```

The definition begins with the keyword `template` followed by the keyword `class` and an identifier both enclosed in angle brackets. The word `template` tells the compiler that a template definition is being made. The angle bracket part of the definition tells the compiler that the identifier, in our case Type, is being used as the name of an arbitrary class or data type. Thus, Type acts as a variable whose value can be any class or data type.

Following the template declaration is the definition of the function. The only rule to remember when writing the function is to use the identifier Type whenever we wish to refer to the data type of a parameter or when declaring a variable. See the program that follows. Thus, in the function header we have Swap(Type& x, Type& y) instead of declaring the parameters of any specific type. Also in the function body we declare the variable temp as follows.

```
Type temp;
```

If the compiler sees Swap(n, m), where n and m are integer variables, it creates a Swap() function having two int arguments. If the compiler sees Swap(d, e), where d and e are double variables, it creates a Swap() function having two double arguments. Following is the program dem11-8.cpp, which contains several examples of function templates.

```cpp
//dem11-8.cpp

//This program demonstrates function templates.

#include <iostream>

using namespace std;

template <class Type>
Type Max(Type x, Type y)
{
   return (x > y)? x: y;
}

template <class Type>
void Swap(Type& x, Type& y)
{
   Type temp;
   temp = x;
   x = y;
   y = temp;
}

template <class TypeA, class TypeB>
TypeA Func(TypeA x, TypeB y)
{
   TypeA r;

   r = 3 * x + 2 * y;

   return r;
}

template <class Type>
Type Sum(Type a[], int n)
{
   Type t = 0;

   for (int i = 0; i < n; ++i)
      t += a[i];

   return t;
}

int main()

{
   int i = 3,
       j = 5;
```

```
double d = 8.62,
       e = 4.14;
float f_arr[6] = {1.2, 2.3, 3.4, 4.5, 5.6, 6.7};
int   i_arr[4] = {4, 5, 6, 7};

cout << "i = " << i << " and j = " << j << endl;
cout << "d = " << d << " and e = " << e << endl << endl;

cout << "The larger of i and j is " << Max(i, j) << endl;
cout << "The larger of d and e is " << Max(d, e) << endl << endl;

Swap(i, j);
Swap(d, e);

cout << "i = " << i << " and j = " << j << endl;
cout << "d = " << d << " and e = " << e << endl << endl;

cout << "Func() applied to i and d is " << Func(i, d) << endl;
cout << "Func() applied to d and i is " << Func(d, i) << endl << endl;

cout << "The sum of f_arr[] is " << Sum(f_arr, 6) << endl;
cout << "The sum of i_arr[] is " << Sum(i_arr, 4) << endl;

return 0;
}
```

Program Output

```
i = 3 and j = 5
d = 8.62 and e = 4.14

The larger of i and j is 5
The larger of d and e is 8.62

i = 5 and j = 3
d = 4.14 and e = 8.62

Func() applied to i and d is 23
Func() applied to d and i is 22.42

The sum of f_arr[] is 23.7
The sum of i_arr[] is 22
```

The function templates are defined before main(), which is required by most compilers. Because the function Max() returns the value of the larger of its arguments, its template uses Type for the function return type as well as for the parameter type.

The second template function, Swap(), is the function we discussed previously. In the program, we use Swap() to interchange the values of two integers and two doubles. If we were not using a template function, we would have needed two separate functions to do the same job.

The function template Sum() shows that two different generic data types can be used in a function template. In main(), we apply Sum() twice, first using an integer-double argument pair, Sum(i, d) and, in the second, a double-integer argument pair,

Sum(d, i). In each case, we obtain a result that is compatible with the data type of the first argument because the function Sum() declares a local variable r, whose type is that of the first argument, and returns the value of r.

The function Total() shows that a template can include an array argument. In fact, a template can include arguments of any type. The function Func() shows that the return type of a template function can depend on the type of one of the function's arguments.

If you attempt to use a function template for which the compiler cannot match types, the program will not compile. See Experiment 2.

Exercises 11.5

1. Write a function template Square() that returns the square of its only argument.
2. Write a function template Power() that takes two arguments. The first argument should be of arbitrary type. The second argument is an integer. The function should return the first argument raised to the power indicated by its second argument. The return type should be that of its first argument.
3. Write a function template Find() that takes two arguments and returns an integer. The first argument is an array of arbitrary type. The second argument is an ordinary variable of the same type as the first argument. The function should return the array subscript of the first array element that exceeds the second argument. If no such element is found, the function should return –1.

Experiments 11.5

1. In dem11-7.cpp, add the following line in main() before return 0.

   Swap(n, d);

   Compile the resulting program. What happens?
2. In dem11-8.cpp, add the following lines in main() before return 0.

   Sum(i, d);

   Swap(i, d);

   Compile the resulting program. What happens? Which line causes an error and why?

Programming Problems 11.5

1. Write, compile, execute, and test a program that uses the function templates Square(), Power(), and Find() of Exercises 1, 2, and 3.

CHAPTER REVIEW

TERMINOLOGY

Describe the meanings of the following terms.

object	scope resolution operator, `::`
instantiate	`istream`
instance variables	accessor method
state	mutator method
methods	constructor
constructor	default constructor
class	destructor
information hiding	default destructor
public interface	function overloading
`class`	default arguments
`public`	function template
`private`	template
class members	function template

SUMMARY

- An object is one or more data values, which define the state of the object, and a set of methods that can be applied to the object.
- A class is a general category that defines the characteristics of the instance variables of objects of that class and that defines the methods that can be applied to objects of that class.
- Use the `class` keyword to define a class.
- Class members can be `public` or `private`. Private members are accessible only to class methods. Public members are accessible to all functions.
- All class methods must be declared inside the class definition even if they are defined outside the class (Note 11.1).
- If you define a class method outside the class definition, in the method definition header you must qualify the name by the class name followed by the scope resolution operator, `::`, followed by the method name (Note 11.2).
- All class instance variables are accessible without qualification or declaration inside all class methods (Note 11.3).
- When a class method is applied to an object, all class instance variable references in the method definition are to the instance variables of the object to which the method is being applied (Note 11.6).
- In C++, the only difference between a structure and a class is that in a class the default access specifier is `private`, whereas in a structure the default access specifier is `public`.
- A class method is an accessor method if it does not change the value of any class instance variable.
- A class method is a mutator method if it changes one or more class instance variables.
- A constructor is a class method that executes when an object of that class is instantiated. A constructor must have the same name as the class name, cannot have a return type, and must be public (Note 11.4).

- If no constructor is explicitly declared for a class, C++ automatically provides the default no-argument constructor.
- If you explicitly declare a constructor, the default no-argument constructor is no longer available (Note 11.5).
- The class destructor method executes automatically when an object goes out of scope. An explicitly declared destructor's name is the same as the class name prefixed by the ~, cannot have a return type, and cannot have arguments. If no destructor is explicitly declared, C++ provides a default destructor (Note 11.8).
- An object can be assigned to another object provided the objects are of the same class. In this case, the assignment proceeds on a member-by-member basis.
- Several constructors can be provided for a class by using function overloading—functions having the same name and return type but a different number and/or types of arguments.
- A constructor (indeed any function) can have default arguments, which must be specified in the function declaration. Only trailing arguments can be omitted (Note 11.9).
- Any function in C++ can be overloaded. The overloaded versions must have the same name and return type, and must differ in the number and/or types of arguments.
- Generic, or type-independent, functions can be defined using function templates.

REVIEW EXERCISES

1. What is the difference between an object and a class?
2. What do the instance variables of a class and the methods of a class represent?
3. Give two places in a program where you can define a class method. Are there any differences in the way a class method is defined depending on where it is defined?
4. How do you use a class method?
5. How do you refer to the instance variables of the object to which a method is applied?
6. What is the difference between an accessor method and a mutator method? Which methods should be made accessor methods?
7. What is a constructor? What is a constructor used for in a program? How must a constructor be named? Why can't a constructor have a return type? When is a constructor executed? Must you explicitly code a constructor for a class? What is the default constructor?
8. What is a destructor? How must a destructor be named? When is a destructor executed? Must you explicitly code a destructor for a class? What is the default destructor?
9. Under what circumstances can you assign one object to another? How is the assignment made?
10. What is function overloading? How does the compiler distinguish between uses of an overloaded function?
11. Which arguments in a constructor can be defaulted? Where do you specify the default values—in the prototype or in the definition?
12. What is a function template? How do you code a template function?

Chapter 12

Manipulating Objects

OBJECTIVES

- To use arrays and character pointers as class data members
- To code a constructor that uses dynamic memory allocation
- To code a destructor that deallocates space that was allocated by a constructor
- To code a copy constructor
- To code an accessor function using `const` so it can be applied to a constant object
- To use `const` in a pointer declaration
- To use `const` arguments in a function
- To code an accessor function that returns a `const` pointer
- To code a function that returns an object
- To code a function that passes an object by value
- To know when the copy constructor is used
- To use the `->` operator to access an object's members through a pointer
- To code a function that passes an object by pointer
- To code a function that passes an object by reference
- To dynamically allocate space for objects
- To code and use static data and function member

This chapter discusses several techniques that allow you to manipulate objects in your programs. Section 12.1 shows you how to include array and pointer data members in a class. Section 12.2 covers the important topic of the copy constructor. Several uses of the keyword `const` are discussed in Section 12.3. Some of this material can be omitted at first reading. You should *not* omit the sections on "Constant Arguments in Functions" and "Constant Arguments and the Copy Constructor." Section 12.4 shows how to write functions that use objects and how to pass objects by value, by pointer, and by reference. Section 12.5 shows how to dynamically allocate objects. This section is important to the

519

material in Chapter 13 and, therefore, can be postponed until then. Finally, Section 12.6 discusses static data members and functions, which allow you to define instance-independent class data members and functions. This entire section may be omitted without loss of continuity.

12.1 USING ARRAYS, POINTERS, AND DYNAMIC MEMORY ALLOCATION

To make the `Savings_Account` class of Chapter 11 more realistic, we now change the data type of `id_no`, the data member that stores the account number. We also include a pointer data member to store the account owner's name.

12.1.1 Array and Pointer Class Members

So far, we have assumed that the account number member of class `Savings_Account`, `id_no`, is a string. Therefore, the account number could be 4, or 73, or 12324, or 34567. In most applications, however, an account number or ID has a specific number of characters. We shall require our account ID to be four characters. Therefore, the account ID number should be stored in a character array of size five (remember that we must have a position for the null character, `'\0'`.) Suppose we declare the following in the `private` section of the definition of `Savings_Account`.

```
char id_no[5];
```

As we shall see, redefining `id_no` in this way will cause us to change how we assign a value to `id_no` in the constructor for `Savings_Account`. We shall also add to the definition of `Savings_Account` an instance variable, `name`, that represents the name of the person holding the account. We could store the name in a string. However, to illustrate certain features of C++, we shall make the `name` data member a character pointer (that is, a C-string) and dynamically allocate exactly enough space for the account owner's name when we create the account. See Experiment 1.

```
char* name;
```

Following is the new declaration of `Savings_Account`, which includes the declaration of a new four-argument constructor with two default arguments and the declaration of a destructor. We also add methods to display the `id_no` and `name` instance variables. We shall see later why these functions do not return the `id_no` and `name` members and we will discuss a better way to handle the output of C-string instance variables of a class.

```
class Savings_Account
{
  private:
    char    id_no[5];
    char*   name;
    double  balance;
    double  rate;

  public:
    Savings_Account(char id[], char* n_p, double bal = 0.00, double rt = 0.04);
    ~Savings_Account();
```

```
double Calc_Interest();
double Get_Balance();
void Deposit(double);
int Withdraw(double);
void Display_ID();
void Display_Name();
};
```

The new constructor assumes that the first and second arguments are character strings. (Recall that an array name, without the brackets, is a pointer to the first element in the array.) We shall treat the first of these strings as a fixed-size character array, and the second as a character pointer. Thus, to create an account with ID number 1111 belonging to Jane Doe with an opening balance of 200.00 and the default rate of 0.04, we would declare the following.

```
Account acc("1111", "Jane Doe", 200.00);
```

The constructor must copy the first argument, "1111", into the member array id_no[], and make the pointer member, name, point to the character string, "Jane Doe". Accomplishing these requires using C-string manipulation functions and the use of dynamic memory allocation. Following is the code for the constructor.

```
Savings_Account::Savings_Account(char id[], char* n_p, double bal, double rt)
{
  strcpy(id_no, id);  //copy first argument into id_no[]

  name = new char[strlen(n_p) + 1]; //create space for the name

  strcpy(name, n_p);  //copy second argument into new space

  balance = bal;
  rate    = rt;
}
```

The first statement in the constructor uses the library function strcpy() to copy the first argument into the five-character member array id_no[]. To make the member name point to the string that is the second argument requires two statements. The first statement uses the new operator to allocate enough space for a character array that will hold the second argument and assigns to name the pointer returned by new. (Note the use of the string function strlen(), which returns the number of characters in the second argument. We add one to the number returned by strlen() to have room for the null character.) After executing the assignment, name points to a character array that is exactly large enough to hold the string that is the second argument of the constructor. See Figure 12.1a. The second statement copies the second argument, which is pointed to by n_p, into the space pointed to by name. See Figure 12.1b.

The definition of the destructor function follows.

```
Savings_Account::~Savings_Account()
{
  cout << "\nAccount " << id_no << " terminated.";
  delete [] name;
}
```

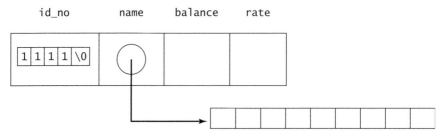

name points to space allocated on the heap

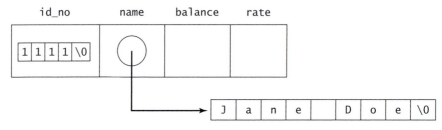

After the second argument is copied into the space pointed to by name

Figure 12.1

When a program creates a Savings_Account object, the constructor allocates space on the heap for the account holder's name. When an object goes out of scope, that is, when the object is destroyed, we must deallocate that heap space by executing the delete statement in the class's destructor function. The process of deallocating heap space when it is no longer needed is sometimes called **garbage collection**. Failure to deallocate heap space causes the space to remain allocated but unusable because the pointer to that space, name, will no longer exist. If this happens for many Savings_Account objects, there will be a great deal of unusable space in main memory. Taken to the extreme, this could cause a program to run out of usable heap space memory. See Experiment 2.

We now incorporate the changed class into a program.

```
//dem12-1.cpp

//This program uses an expanded version of the Savings_Account.
//The program uses a constructor with default arguments.
//The ID number is stored as an array and the name of the
//Savings_Account holder is a character pointer. The constructor uses
//dynamic memory allocation.

#include <iostream>
#include <iomanip>
#include <string>

using namespace std;
```

```
class Savings_Account
{
  private:
    char    id_no[5];
    char*   name;
    double balance;
    double rate;

  public:
    Savings_Account(char id[], char* n_p, double bal = 0.00, double rt = 0.04);
    ~Savings_Account();
    double Calc_Interest();
    double Get_Balance();
    void Deposit(double);
    bool Withdraw(double);
    void Display_ID();
    void Display_Name();
};

Savings_Account::Savings_Account(char id[], char* n_p, double bal, double rt)
{
  strcpy(id_no, id);   //copy first argument into id_no[]

  name = new char[strlen(n_p) + 1]; //create space for the name

  strcpy(name, n_p);   //copy second argument into new space

  balance = bal;
  rate    = rt;
}

Savings_Account::~Savings_Account()
{
  cout << endl << endl;
  cout << "Account " << id_no << " terminated." << endl;
  delete [] name;
}

double Savings_Account::Get_Balance()
{
  return balance;
}

double Savings_Account::Calc_Interest()
{
  double interest;

  interest = balance * rate;
  balance += interest;

  return interest;
}

void Savings_Account::Deposit(double amount)
{
  balance += amount;
}
```

```cpp
bool Savings_Account::Withdraw(double amount)
{
  bool result;

  if (amount <= balance)
  {
    balance -= amount;
    result = true;
  }
  else
    result = false;

  return result;
}

void Savings_Account::Display_ID()
{
  cout << id_no;
}

void Savings_Account::Display_Name()
{
  cout << name;
}

int main()
{
  cout << setprecision(2)
       << setiosflags(ios::fixed)
       << setiosflags(ios::showpoint);

  char   id[5];
  char   buffer[81];   //Temporarily stores the name
  double bal;
  double rt;
  double amount;

  cout << endl;
  cout << "Enter Account ID: ";
  cin.getline(id, 5);

  cout << endl;
  cout << "Enter Account Holder's Name: ";
  cin.getline(buffer, 81);

  cout << endl;
  cout << "Enter Balance: ";
  cin >> bal;

  cout << endl;
  cout << "Enter Interest Rate: ";
  cin >> rt;
```

```cpp
Savings_Account acc1(id, buffer, bal, rt);

cout << endl;
cout << "The Account number is ";
acc1.Display_ID();
cout << endl;
cout << "The owner of the Account is ";
acc1.Display_Name();

cout << endl << endl;
cout << "The balance in the Account is now " << acc1.Get_Balance();

cout << endl << endl;
cout << "Enter an amount to deposit: ";
cin >> amount;

acc1.Deposit(amount);
cout << endl << endl;
cout << "A deposit of " << amount << " was made." << endl;
cout << "The balance in the Account is now "
     << acc1.Get_Balance() << endl;

acc1.Calc_Interest();

cout << endl;
cout << "Interest was applied to the Account." << endl;
cout << "The balance in the Account is now "
     << acc1.Get_Balance() << endl << endl;

cout << "Enter an amount to withdraw: ";
cin >> amount;

if (acc1.Withdraw(amount))
{
  cout << endl <<endl;
  cout << "A withdrawal of " << amount << " was made.";
}
else
{
  cout << endl << endl;
  cout << "WITHDRAWAL NOT MADE: Insufficient funds.";
}

cout << endl;
cout << "The balance in the Account is now " << acc1.Get_Balance() << endl;

return 0;
}
```

Program Output

Enter Account ID: **1234**

Enter Account Holder's Name: **Larrabee Maxwell**

```
Enter Balance: 100.00

Enter Interest Rate: 0.06

The account number is 1234
The owner of the account is Larrabee Maxwell

The balance in the account is now 100.00

Enter an amount to deposit: 200.00

A deposit of 200.00 was made.
The balance in the account is now 300.00

Interest was applied to the account.
The balance in the account is now 318.00

Enter an amount to withdraw: 175.00

A withdrawal of 175.00 was made.
The balance in the account is now 143.00

Account 1234 terminated.
```

The program is fairly straightforward. Note that the destructor displays a message when the program ends.

Experiments 12.1

1. Recode dem12-1.cpp by making the name instance variable a string object. Change the appropriate methods. Compile and execute the resulting program.

2. Remove the destructor from Savings_Account in dem12-1.cpp. Use the following main().

```cpp
void main()
{
    for (long i = 1; i <= 10000; ++i)
    {
        Account acc("1111", "John Doe", 100.00, 0.05);
    }
}
```

Compile and execute the resulting program. Does the program run out of heap space? If not, replace the 10000 by 100000 and try again. Note: The program may take a while to execute. Why does this program waste heap space?

Programming Problems 12.1

1. In the WebPage class of Programming Problem 1, Section 11.3, add the character pointer instance variable page_url that represents the URL of the Web page (for example, www.cpp.edu). Replace the three-argument constructor by a four-argument constructor. The first argument should be a character pointer representing the URL of the Web page. The second, third, and fourth arguments represent the

hits, messages, and downloads of the page. These last three arguments should all default to zero. Use dynamic memory allocation to reserve space for the URL. Code a destructor for the class that deallocates space for the URL that was allocated in the constructor. The destructor should also display a message that indicates that it executed. Add a method Display_URL() that displays the URL member. Recode the main() that you wrote to include use of the constructor, destructor, and the new display method. Compile, execute, and test the resulting program.

2. Recode the OilTank class of Programming Problem 2, Section 10.3 as follows. Replace the string tank number instance variable by a five-character array that represents the tank number. Add the character pointer instance variable company_name that represents the name of the company that owns the tank. Replace the three-argument constructor by a four-argument constructor. The first argument should be a string that represents the name of the company that owns the tank. The second argument should be a character string that represents the five-digit tank number. The third argument should be the capacity of the tank, and the fourth argument should represent the contents of the tank (which should default to zero). Use dynamic memory allocation to reserve space for the company name. Code a destructor that deallocates the space for the company name that was allocated in the constructor. The destructor should also display a message that indicates that it executed. Replace the Get_Number() method by the method Display_Number() that displays the id-no member, and add the method Display_Company() that displays the company_name member. Recode the main() that you wrote to include use of the constructor, destructor, and new display methods. Compile, execute, and test the resulting program.

3. Recode the VehicleService class of Programming Problem 3, Section 10.3, as follows. Replace the string service number by a 6-character array. Add a character pointer, owner, that represents the name of the owner of the vehicle. Replace the four-argument constructor by a five argument constructor. The first argument should be a string that represents the service number. The second argument should be a string that represents the owner of the vehicle. The last three arguments (hours, parts, and total) default to zero. Add a destructor that deallocates the space for the owner member that was allocated in the constructor. The destructor should also display a message that indicates that it executed. Replace the Get_Number() method by the method Display_Number() that displays the service number, and add the method Display_Owner() that displays the owner name. Recode the main() that you wrote to include use of the constructor, destructor, and new display methods. Compile, execute, and test the resulting program.

4. Recode the HotelRoom class of Programming Problem 4, Section 10.3 as follows. Replace the string room number by a character array that stores a 3-character room number. Add the character pointer instance variable guest, which stores the name of the guest occupying the room. Replace the Get_Number() method by the method Display_Number(), which displays the room number, and add the method Display_Guest(), which displays the guest member. Replace the four-argument constructor by a five-argument constructor in which the first argument is the room number, the second argument is the room capacity, the third argument is the room rate (defaulting to 89.00), the fourth argument is the guest

name (defaulting to the NULL pointer), and the fifth argument is the occupancy status (defaulting to zero). Use dynamic memory allocation to reserve space for the guest name. Code a destructor that deallocates the space allocated by the constructor. The destructor should also display a message that it executed. Re-code the main() that you wrote to include use of the constructor, destructor, and new display methods. Compile, execute, and test the resulting program.

12.2 THE COPY CONSTRUCTOR

We mentioned in Chapter 11 that an object can be assigned to another object. You can also assign one object to another when you create an object, such as in the following.

```
Savings_Account acc1("1111", "Larrabee Maxwell", 100.00, 0.02);
Savings_Account acc2  = acc1;
```

As we shall see, when an object is created through initialization (such as the preceding acc2 object), the class constuctor is not executed. The method that is executed during initialization is the copy constuctor. In this section, we discuss the copy constructor and the circumstances under which you need to code a copy constructor for a class. Section 12.4 discusses two more uses of the copy constructor.

12.2.1 The Copy Constructor: A Simple Example

In C++, there is a difference between assignment and initialization. In the operation of assignment, the receiving object must exist prior to the assignment. In initialization, the object is initialized during the process of creation. For example, consider the following.

```
int i = 7,
    j;

j = i;
```

The integer i is declared and initialized to 7. When i is created, it is created with the value 7. There is no time during which i exists without a valid value. On the other hand, when j is declared, it does not receive a value. Therefore, it has a garbage value until a valid value is assigned to it. The assignment operation copies the value of i into the already existing object j, giving j a valid value.

This difference between assignment and initialization is also true of objects. Consider dem12-2.cpp.

```
//dem12-2.cpp

//This program illustrates assigning one object to another.
//Note that initializing an object does not use the
//one-argument constructor.

#include <iostream>

using namespace std;

class Test_Class
{
  private:
    int n;
```

```cpp
  public:
    Test_Class(int);
    ~Test_Class();
    int Get_Value();
};
Test_Class::Test_Class(int i)
{
  n = i;

  cout << endl;
  cout << "Constructor Executed: Data member initialized to " << n << endl;
}

Test_Class::~Test_Class()
{
  cout << endl;
  cout << "Destructor Executed for object with data member " << n << endl;
}

int Test_Class::Get_Value()
{
  return n;
}

int main()
{
  Test_Class tc_object1(4);
  Test_Class tc_object2(0);

  cout << endl;
  cout << "After object creation:" << endl <<endl;
  cout << "Object 1: " << tc_object1.Get_Value() << endl;
  cout << "Object 2: " << tc_object2.Get_Value() << endl << endl;

  tc_object2 = tc_object1;

  cout << "After object assignment:" << endl << endl;
  cout << "Object 1: " << tc_object1.Get_Value() << endl;
  cout << "Object 2: " << tc_object2.Get_Value() << endl << endl;

  Test_Class tc_object3 = tc_object1;

  cout << "After initializing object 3:" << endl << endl;
  cout << "Object 3: " << tc_object3.Get_Value() << endl;

  return 0;
}
```

Program Output

```
Constructor Executed: Data member initialized to 4
Constructor Executed: Data member initialized to 0

After object creation:

Object 1: 4
Object 2: 0
```

```
After object assignment:

Object 1: 4
Object 2: 4

After initializing object 3:

Object 3: 4

Destructor Executed for object with data member 4

Destructor Executed for object with data member 4

Destructor Executed for object with data member 4
```

The Test_Class constructor executes twice—once for tc_object1 and once for tc_object2. After creating the objects, the program displays the values of the data members of the objects. The program then assigns the value of tc_object1 to tc_object2. The assignment is done on a member-by-member basis. Therefore, the n data member of tc_object1 is copied to the n data member of tc_object2. The program verifies the assignment when it displays the values of the data members of the objects. Note that the one-argument constructor does not execute when the program creates and initializes tc_object3 by executing the following statement.

```
Test_Class tc_object3 = tc_object1;
```

The constructor's message does not display at this point in the program! The value of tc_object3 is displayed by main(), but not by the constructor. Finally, at the end of the program, the destructor executes three times, once for each of the objects created by the program.

Because the operation of initialization is different than that of assignment, a special constructor is used by C++ for initialization, namely, the **copy constructor**. Just as for the ordinary constructor, if you do not explicitly code a copy constructor, your class is given the **default copy constructor**. The initialization of tc_object3 in dem12-2.cpp is successful because the default copy constructor is used in the initialization. The default copy constructor copies the data members from tc_object1 and initializes them, on a member-by-member basis, to the corresponding data members of tc_object3.

To code your own copy constructor, use Note 12.1.

For example, we can declare and code a copy constructor for Test_Class as follows.

```
class Test_Class
{
    .
    .
    .
    public:
        Test_Class(Test_Class&);     //Copy Constructor declaration
    .
    .
    .
};
```

Note 12.1   Coding the Copy Constructor

- The copy constructor must, like other constructors, have the same name as the class.
- The copy constructor is distinguished from other constructors by the form of its argument, which is a reference to an object of the class for which it is the copy constructor.
- The syntax of the copy constructor declaration is as follows:

      Class_Name (Class_Name& r_object);

- When coding a copy constructor, think of the constructor's argument as the object on the right side of the = in an initialization. In the copy constructor's code, to refer to the members of this object, use the parameter name r_object, followed by the dot operator, followed by the instance variable name.
- The copy constructor is applied to the object being created. Therefore, it is applied to the object on the left of the = in an initialization. To refer to the members of this object in the copy constructor's code, use unqualified instance variable names.

```
Test_Class::Test_Class(Test_Class& tc_r)
{
   n = tc_r.n;   //Copies the n data member of the object to the right
                 //of the = in an initialization to the n data member
                 //of the object being created.

   cout << endl << endl;
   cout << "Copy Constructor executed: "
        << "Data member initialized to " << n << endl;
}
```

The copy constructor is invoked when an object is initialized in a declaration. Therefore, the second declaration that follows causes the copy constructor to execute.

```
Test_Class tc_object1(3);            //the regular constructor executes

Test_Class tc_object2 = tc_object1;  //the copy constructor executes
```

Using Note 12.1, think of the parameter tc_r in the copy constructor definition as representing the right side of the = in an initialization (in the preceding second declaration, tc_object1). Thus, the copy constructor assigns to the n data member of the new object being created (the object tc_object2 in this initialization) the corresponding data member of the object on the right side of the =, namely, tc_r.n (which represents the n data member of tc_object1).

We shall explain in Section 12.4 why the argument of the copy constructor must be a reference. The following program illustrates the use of the copy constructor.

```
//dem12-3.cpp

//This program illustrates the use of a copy constructor.

#include <iostream>

using namespace std;

class Test_Class
{
  private:
    int n;

  public:
    Test_Class(int);   //One-argument constructor
    Test_Class(Test_Class&);   //Copy constructor
    ~Test_Class();
    int Get_Value();
};

Test_Class::Test_Class(int i)
{
  n = i;

  cout << endl;
  cout << "Constructor Executed: Data member initialized to " << n << endl;
}

Test_Class::Test_Class(Test_Class& tc_r)
{
  n = tc_r.n;

  cout << endl << endl;
  cout << "Copy constructor executed: "
               << "Data member initialized to " << n << endl << endl;
}

Test_Class::~Test_Class()
{
  cout << endl << endl;
  cout << "Destructor Executed for object with data member " << n << endl;
}

int Test_Class::Get_Value()
{
  return n;
}

int main()
{
  Test_Class tc_object1(4);
  Test_Class tc_object2(0);

  cout << "After object creation:" << endl << endl;
  cout << "Object 1: " << tc_object1.Get_Value() << endl;
  cout << "Object 2: " << tc_object2.Get_Value() << endl << endl;

  tc_object2 = tc_object1;
```

```
cout << "After object assignment:" << endl << endl;
cout << "Object 1: " << tc_object1.Get_Value() << endl;
cout << "Object 2: " << tc_object2.Get_Value() << endl << endl;

Test_Class tc_object3 = tc_object1;

cout << "After initializing object 3:" << endl << endl;
cout << "Object 3: " << tc_object3.Get_Value() << endl;

return 0;
}
```

Program Output

```
Constructor Executed: Data member initialized to 0

After object creation:

Object 1: 4
Object 2: 0

After object assignment:

Object 1: 4
Object 2: 4

Copy constructor executed: Data member initialized to 4

After initializing object 3:

Object 3: 4

Destructor Executed for object with data member 4

Destructor Executed for object with data member 4

Destructor Executed for object with data member 4
```

Note that the copy constructor executes when the program creates and initializes tc_object3.

12.2.2 A Copy Constructor For Savings_Account

Although it is not necessary to code a copy constructor for Test_Class in dem12-3.cpp (the default copy constructor works just as well), it is important to code your own copy constructor whenever the class contains a pointer as an instance variable. To see why, consider Savings_Account, which has a character pointer, name, as an instance variable. Because the class does not have an explicitly coded copy constructor, the class's default copy constructor will be used in any object initialization. Suppose that, in a program that uses Savings_Account, we make the following declarations. (We might make such an assignment to experiment with a copy of acc1 without changing the original.)

```
Account acc1("1111", "Maxwell Larrabee");

Account acc2 = acc1;
```

Because the default copy constructor is used in the initialization, acc2 is a member-by-member copy of acc1. Therefore, the pointer acc1.name that points to the string "Maxwell Larrabee" gets copied into the pointer acc2.name. Note that the pointer, that is, the address, is copied, not the string that the pointer points to. Thus, we have the name pointer in two different objects pointing to the same area of the heap. See Figure 12.2. It follows that a change to the target of either of these pointers results in a change for both of them. Thus, if we change the string that the name member of acc2 points to, we also change the string that the name member of acc1 points to. This is exactly what we did not want to happen!

To correct this problem, we write a copy constructor for Savings_Account that copies the target of the name pointer.

```
Savings_Account::Savings_Account(Savings_Account& acc_r)
{
    strcpy(id_no, acc_r.id_no);   //copy first argument into id_no[]

    name = new char[strlen(acc_r.name) + 1]; //create space for the name

    strcpy(name, acc_r.name);   //copy second argument into new space

    balance = acc_r.balance;

    rate    = acc_r.rate;
}
```

Remember (see Note 12.1) that the argument in the copy constructor is the object on the right side of the = in an initialization and that the copy constructor is applied to the object being created. Therefore, within the copy constructor code, unqualified

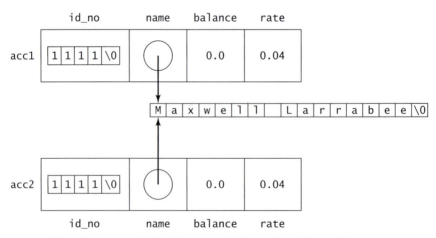

The pointer gets copied, so the name members point to the same heap space

Figure 12.2

names refer to the object being created. Note the similarity between the code of the four-argument constructor and the copy constructor. First, the id_no member of the object being copied is copied into the id_no member of the object being created. Then space is allocated on the heap for a string exactly large enough to hold a copy of the name member of the object being copied. After copying the name into the new heap space, the balance and rate members of the object being copied are copied to the corresponding members of the object being created. Thus, if we make the preceding copy constructor a member of Savings_Account, the following declarations result in the situation depicted in Figure 12.3.

```
Savings_Account acc1("1111", "Maxwell Larrabee");

Savings_Account acc2 = acc1;
```

Following is a program that illustrates the use of the copy constructor in the Savings_Account class.

```
//dem12-4.cpp

//This program illustrates the use of the copy constructor
//in a class that has a pointer as a data member.

#include <iostream>
#include <iomanip>
#include <string>

using namespace std;

class Savings_Account
{
```

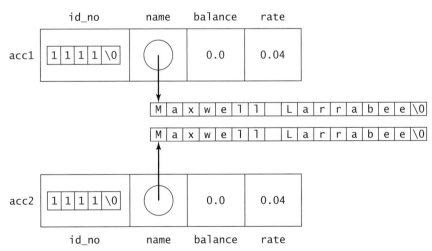

The initialization uses the copy constructor, so the name member in each object points to a different area of heap space.

Figure 12.3

```
private:
  char    id_no[5];
  char*   name;
  double balance;
  double rate;

public:
  Savings_Account(char id[], char* n_p, double bal = 0.00, double rt = 0.04);
  Savings_Account(Savings_Account&);
  ~Savings_Account();
  double Calc_Interest();
  double Get_Balance();
  void Deposit(double);
  bool Withdraw(double);
  void Display_ID();
  void Display_Name();
};

Savings_Account::Savings_Account(char id[], char* n_p, double bal, double rt)
{
  strcpy(id_no, id);   //copy first argument into id_no[]

  name = new char[strlen(n_p) + 1]; //create space for the name

  strcpy(name, n_p);   //copy second argument into new space

  balance = bal;
  rate    = rt;

  cout << endl << endl;
  cout << "Constructor executed." << endl;
}

Savings_Account::Savings_Account(Savings_Account& acc_r)
{
  strcpy(id_no, acc_r.id_no);   //copy first argument into id_no[]

  name = new char[strlen(acc_r.name) + 1]; //create space for the name

  strcpy(name, acc_r.name);   //copy second argument into new space

  balance = acc_r.balance;
  rate    = acc_r.rate;

  cout << endl << endl;
  cout << "Copy constructor executed." << endl;
}

Savings_Account::~Savings_Account()
{
  cout << endl << endl;
  cout << "Account " << id_no << " terminated." << endl;
  delete [] name;
}
```

```
double Savings_Account::Get_Balance()
{
  return balance;
}
double Savings_Account::Calc_Interest()
{
  double interest;

  interest = balance * rate;
  balance += interest;

  return interest;
}
void Savings_Account::Deposit(double amount)
{
  balance += amount;
}
bool Savings_Account::Withdraw(double amount)
{
  bool result;

  if (amount <= balance)
  {
    balance -= amount;
    result = true;
  }
  else
    result = false;

  return result;
}
void Savings_Account::Display_ID()
{
  cout << id_no;
}
void Savings_Account::Display_Name()
{
  cout << name;
}
int main()
{
  cout << setprecision(2)
       << setiosflags(ios::fixed)
       << setiosflags(ios::showpoint);

  char id[5];
  char buffer[81];   //Temporarily stores the name
  double bal;
  double rt;
```

```
cout << "Enter Account ID: ";
cin.getline(id, 5);

cout << endl;
cout << "Enter Account Holder's Name: ";
cin.getline(buffer, 81);

cout << endl;
cout << "Enter Balance: ";
cin >> bal;

cout << endl;
cout << "Enter Interest Rate: ";
cin >> rt;

Savings_Account acc1(id, buffer, bal, rt);

cout << endl << endl;
cout << "Account created with Account number ";
acc1.Display_ID();
cout << endl;
cout << " and owner name ";
acc1.Display_Name();

cout << endl << endl;
cout << "Account now being created by initialization.";

Savings_Account acc2 = acc1;

cout << endl << endl;
cout << "Initialized Account created with Account number ";
acc2.Display_ID();
cout << endl;
cout << "\n and owner name ";
acc2.Display_Name();

cout << endl;

return 0;
}
```

Program Output

Enter Account ID: **1234**

Enter Account Holder's Name: **Maxwell Larrabee**

Enter Balance: **100.00**

Enter Interest Rate: **0.06**

Constructor executed.

Account created with account number 1234
 and owner name Maxwell Larrabee

Account now being created by initialization.

Copy constructor executed.

Initialized account created with account number 1234
 and owner name Maxwell Larrabee

Account 1234 terminated.

Account 1234 terminated.

Exercises 12.2

1. How would the default copy constructor handle copying of the id_no data member in Savings_Account?

2. Add a copy constructor to the Rectangle class of Programming Problem 5, Section 11.3.

3. Add a copy constructor to the DigitalClock class of Programming Problem 6, Section 11.3

Experiments 12.2

1. Remove the copy constructor from the declaration of Savings_Account. Use the following main().

```
void main()
{
    Savings_Account acc1("1111", "Maxwell Larrabee");

    cout << endl;
    cout << "Owner of the Account is ";
    acc1.Display_Name();
    cout << endl;

    {
        Savings_Account acc2 = acc1;
    }

    Savings_Account acc3("3333", "Jane Doe");

    cout << endl;
    cout << "Owner of the Account is ";
    acc1.Display_Name();
    cout << endl;
}
```

What is the output of the resulting program? Explain what happened.

Programming Problems 12.2

1. Add a copy constructor to the WebPage class of Programming Problem 1, Section 12.1. The copy constructor should display a message that it executed. Test the copy constructor by initializing a WebPage object in main().

2. Add a copy constructor to the OilTank class of Programming Problem 2, Section 12.1. The copy constructor should display a message that it executed. Test the copy constructor by initializing an OilTank object in main().

3. Add a copy constructor to the `VehicleService` class of Programming Problem 3, Section 12.1. The copy constructor should display a message that it executed. Test the copy constructor by initializing a `VehicleService` object in `main()`.

4. Add a copy constructor to the `HotelRoom` class of Programming Problem 4, Section 12.1. The copy constructor should display a message that it executed. Test the copy constructor by initializing a `HotelRoom` object in `main()`.

12.3 USING const WITH CLASSES

The keyword `const` has several important uses relative to objects and class methods.

12.3.1 Constant Objects and Methods

It is possible to declare constant objects, just as it is possible to declare constant integers, doubles, and so on. A constant object is one whose instance variable values cannot be changed. For example, consider `Test_Class`, defined in the previous section with the additional method `Change_Value()`.

```
#include <iostream.h>

using namespace std;

class Test_Class
{
  private:
    int n;

  public:
    Test_Class(int i = 0);     //One-argument constructor with default value
    int Get_Value();
    void Change_Value(int);
};

Test_Class::Test_Class(int i)
{
  n = i;

  cout << "\n\nConstructor Executed: Data member initialized to " << n;
}

int Test_Class::Get_Value()
{
  return n;
}

void Test_Class::Change_Value(int i)
{
  n = i;
}
```

Suppose we declare the following in `main()`.

```
const Test_Class  tc_object1(4);

Test_Class tc_object2(7);
```

The following assignment statement is illegal because `tc_object1` is constant and we cannot modify a constant object in `main()`.

```
tc_object1 = tc_object2;    //Illegal - cannot modify a const object
```

Because the object is constant, we cannot change the value of its instance variable, n. There is no way for the compiler to know the difference between an accessor method (one that does not change an instance variable value) and a mutator method (one that changes an instance variable value). Therefore, the compiler will complain (with a Warning or an Error message) if you apply any of the methods of `Test_Class` to `tc_object1`. See Experiment 1.

```
tc_object1.Get_Value();    //Compiler complains

tc_object.Change_Value();  //Compiler complains
```

Not allowing any method at all to operate on a constant object is too severe a restriction. We want to be able to apply an accessor method to a constant object because such a method does not attempt to change the instance variables of the class. To tell the compiler that a method is an accessor method and should be allowed to operate on constant objects, it should be declared constant. This is done by adding the keyword `const` after the parentheses that follow the accessor method's name in both the declaration and definition of the function.

Note 12.2   Constant Methods

Any class method that is an accessor (that is, does not change the value of any instance variable) should be declared as constant. This is done by adding the keyword `const` after the parentheses that follow the method's name in both its declaration and definition. This allows such a method to be applied to a constant object.

Following is a corrected version of the declaration of `Test_Class`.

```
#include <iostream.h>

using namespace std;

class Test_Class
{
  private:
    int n;

  public:
    Test_Class(int i = 0);     //One-argument constructor with default value
    int Get_Value() const;     //Accessor function declared as const
    void Change_Value(int);
};

Test_Class::Test_Class(int i)
{
  n = i;
```

```
   cout << "\n\nConstructor Executed: Data member initialized to " << n;
}

int Test_Class::Get_Value() const              //const required
{
   return n;
}

void Test_Class::Change_Value(int i)
{
   n = i;
}
```

The following program illustrates the use of constant methods. Note that if you include the statement in main() that is commented out, the compiler will issue an error
message because the statement attempts to change a constant object. See Experiment 2.

```
//dem12-5.cpp

//This program illustrates constant member functions.
//Note that the commented statement in main() causes
//a compiler error message.

#include <iostream>

using namespace std;

class Test_Class
{
   private:
   int n;

   public:
      Test_Class(int i = 0);      //One-argument constructor with default value
      int Get_Value() const;
      void Change_Value(int);
};

Test_Class::Test_Class(int i)
{
   n = i;

   cout << endl;
   cout << "Constructor Executed: Data member initialized to "
        << n << endl << endl;

}

int Test_Class::Get_Value() const
{
   return n;
}

void Test_Class::Change_Value(int i)
{
   n = i;
}
```

```
int main()
{
    const Test_Class tc_object1(4);

    cout << "The value of the object is " << tc_object1.Get_Value() << endl;

    //Adding the following statement would cause a compiler error message
    //tc_object1.Change_Value(7);

    return 0;
}
```

Program Output

```
Constructor Executed: Data member initialized to 4
The value of the object is 4
```

12.3.2 const in Pointer Declarations

The keyword const can be used in two ways in a pointer declaration—one way declares the pointer itself to be a constant; the other way declares the target of the pointer to be a constant. If const immediately precedes the name of the pointer variable, then the pointer variable is a constant. Therefore, once initialized, its value cannot be changed; that is, it cannot point to anything else. Consider, for example, the following declarations.

```
int i = 4,
    j = 7;
int* const i_p = &i;        //i_p is constant. Therefore, its value, &i, cannot
                            //be changed. It must always point to i.
```

The declaration of i_p declares the pointer variable to be a constant. Thus, once initialized in the declaration, the pointer value cannot be changed. The following assignment is, therefore, illegal.

```
        i_p = &j;        //Illegal because i_p is a constant
```

However, it is legal to change the value of the target of i_p.

```
        *i_p = 5;        //Legal - the target of i_p is NOT constant.
```

If the keyword const appears before the data type in a pointer declaration, the target of the pointer is a constant. This means that the target of the pointer cannot be changed through the pointer. Consider the following declarations.

```
        int n = 3,
            m = 5;

        const int* n_p = &n;        //The target of n_p, namely n, cannot be
                                    //changed through n_p.
```

The declaration of n_p declares the target of the pointer to be a constant; that is, n_p is a pointer to a constant data object. Because the target of n_p is a constant, you can think of n_p as a "read-only" pointer. Therefore, the following assignment is illegal.

```
*n_p = m;     //Illegal - the target of n_p is a constant
```

On the other hand, n_p is not itself a constant. Therefore, we can make the following assignment.

```
n_p = &m;     //Legal - the pointer itself is not constant
```

Although we have changed what the pointer is pointing to, n_p is still a pointer to a constant object. Therefore, it is illegal to change the target of n_p.

```
*n_p = 6;   //Illegal:cannot change target of pointer to a
constant object.
```

However, we can still change the value of m as follows.

```
m = 6;
```

Note 12.3   Reading Constant Pointer Declarations

- If const immediately precedes the pointer variable name in a declaration, the pointer is a constant.
- If const precedes the data type in a pointer declaration, the target of the pointer is constant.

12.3.3 Mixing Constant and Nonconstant Pointers

An important principle to remember is the following.

Note 12.4   Mixing Pointers

A declaration can impose a constant restriction, but cannot remove one.

Consider the following declarations.

```
int i = 9;
int* i_p = &i;
const int* j_p = i_p;     //Legal
```

The pointer i_p is not a constant and neither is its target. However, the declaration of j_p, which initializes j_p to i_p, states that the target of j_p is a constant. The restriction that is imposed on j_p is that its target is a constant, a restriction that is not true for i_p. Therefore, it is valid to change i, the target if i_p, through i_p but not through j_p.

```
*i_p = 2;     //Legal: the target of i_p, namely i, is not constant
*j_p = 1;     //Illegal: the target of j_p, namely i, is a constant
              //when referenced through j_p
```

On the other hand, consider the following declarations.

```
int n = 8;
const int* n_p = &n;
int* m_p = n_p;     //Illegal - cannot remove a constant restriction
```

The last declaration is illegal. The pointer n_p was declared as a pointer to a constant data object. The declaration of m_p is as an ordinary pointer. Therefore, initializing m_p, a non-constant pointer, to n_p, a constant pointer, is illegal.

12.3.4 Constant Arguments in Functions

The keyword const can also appear with pointer and reference arguments in a function. For example, consider the following function declaration.

```
void Func(char* p, const char* q);
```

In this case, the const in the second argument means that the target of q is a constant. Therefore, the data pointed to by the argument q cannot be changed through the pointer.

Note 12.5   A const Pointer Function Argument

The keyword const appearing before a data type of a pointer argument in a function declaration means that the pointer's target is a constant. Therefore, the pointer's target cannot be changed in the body of the function.

For example, consider the following program, dem12-6.cpp, which is a version of dem08-4.cpp. The only way the programs differ is that in this version we declare the array argument of the function Avg() to be const. This assures that the function cannot change the elements in the array. See Experiment 3.

```
// dem12-6.cpp

// This program shows how to find the average of the elements
// in an array.  It finds the average by passing the array
// to a function that computes the average.

#include <iostream>
#include <iomanip>

using namespace std;

double Avg(const int [], int);
```

```cpp
int main()
{
   const int NUM_QUIZZES = 10;
   int    grade[NUM_QUIZZES]; // The array to store the quiz grades
   int    quiz;               // The array subscript
   double grade_avg;

   cout << setiosflags(ios::fixed)
        << setiosflags(ios::showpoint)
        << setprecision(1);

   cout << "Please enter " << NUM_QUIZZES << " integer quiz grades."
        << endl << endl;

   for (quiz = 0; quiz < NUM_QUIZZES; ++quiz)
   {
      cout << endl;
         cout << "Enter grade for quiz " << quiz + 1 << ": ";
      cin >> grade[quiz];
   }

   grade_avg = Avg(grade, NUM_QUIZZES);

   cout << endl;
   cout << "The average quiz grade is " << grade_avg << endl;

   return 0;
}    // End of main()

double Avg(const int arr[], int size)
{
   int    i,             // The array subscript
          sum = 0;       // The accumulator
   double avg;           // The array average

   for (i = 0; i < size; ++i)
      sum += arr[i];

   avg = double(sum) / size;

   return avg;
}    // End of Avg()
```

Program Output

```
Please enter 10 integer quiz grades.

Enter grade for quiz 1: 67

Enter grade for quiz 2: 55

Enter grade for quiz 3: 83

Enter grade for quiz 4: 75

Enter grade for quiz 5: 57
```

```
Enter grade for quiz 6: 86

Enter grade for quiz 7: 58

Enter grade for quiz 8: 100

Enter grade for quiz 9: 86

Enter grade for quiz 10: 96

The average quiz grade is 76.3
```

12.3.5 Constant Arguments and the Copy Constructor

If you include a copy constructor in a class definition, the argument should be declared const to ensure that the copy constructor code does not change anything in the argument. This is desirable because the copy constructor should just copy and do nothing else. The declaration and definition of the copy constructor for Savings_Account are, therefore, more safely coded as follows.

> Declaration: Savings_Account(const Savings_Account&);
> Defintion Header: Savings_Account::Savings_Account
> (const Savings_Account& acc_r)

12.3.6 Accessor Methods that Return Constant Pointers

In the versions of the Savings_Account class we developed in this chapter, we do not have accessor functions that return the id_no or the name members of the class. Instead we used the functions Display_ID() and Display_Name(), which simply displayed the corresponding data member. If we code an accessor function for the name as follows

```
char* Savings_Account::Get_Name()
{
    return name;
}
```

then, when main() applies this to a Savings_Account object, main() would have access to the name member of the object through the pointer returned by Get_Name(). This would violate the principle of data hiding and subvert the fact that name is declared as private in the class declaration. For example, in the program dem12-7.cpp, main() uses the pointer returned by Get_Name()to change the name of the object to the string "XXX".

```
//dem12-7.cpp

//This program illustrates the use of the copy constructor
//in a class that has a pointer as a data member.
//The class contains accessor functions that return a const pointer.

#include <iostream>
#include <iomanip>
#include <string>
```

```cpp
using namespace std;

class Savings_Account
{
  private:
    char    id_no[5];
    char*   name;
    double balance;
    double rate;

  public:
    Savings_Account(char id[], char* n_p, double bal = 0.00, double rt = 0.04);
    Savings_Account(const Savings_Account &);
    ~Savings_Account();
    double Calc_Interest();
    double Get_Balance();
    char*  Get_Name();
    void Deposit(double);
    bool Withdraw(double);
};

Savings_Account::Savings_Account(char id[], char* n_p, double bal, double rt)
{
  strcpy(id_no, id);  //copy first argument into id_no[]

  name = new char[strlen(n_p) + 1]; //create space for the name

  strcpy(name, n_p);  //copy second argument into new space

  balance = bal;
  rate    = rt;

  cout << endl << endl;
  cout << "Constructor executed." << endl << endl;
}

Savings_Account::Savings_Account(const Savings_Account& acc_r)
{
  strcpy(id_no, acc_r.id_no);  //copy first argument into id_no[]

  name = new char[strlen(acc_r.name) + 1]; //create space for the name

  strcpy(name, acc_r.name);  //copy second argument into new space

  balance = acc_r.balance;
  rate    = acc_r.rate;

  cout << endl << endl;
  cout << "Copy constructor executed." << endl << endl;
}

Savings_Account::~Savings_Account()
{
  cout << endl << endl;
  cout << "Account " << id_no << " terminated." << endl;
  delete [] name;
}
```

```cpp
double Savings_Account::Get_Balance()
{
  return balance;
}

char* Savings_Account::Get_Name()
{
  return name;
}

double Savings_Account::Calc_Interest()
{
  double interest;

  interest = balance * rate;
  balance += interest;

  return interest;
}

void Savings_Account::Deposit(double amount)
{
  balance += amount;
}

bool Savings_Account::Withdraw(double amount)
{
  bool result;

  if (amount <= balance)
  {
    balance -= amount;
    result = true;
  }
  else
    result = false;

  return result;
}

int main()
{
  cout << setprecision(2)
       << setiosflags(ios::fixed)
       << setiosflags(ios::showpoint);

  char id[5];
  char buffer[81];   //Temporarily stores the name
  double bal;
  double rt;

  cout << "Enter Account ID: ";
  cin.getline(id, 5);
```

```
cout << endl;
cout << "Enter Account Holder's Name: ";
cin.getline(buffer, 81);

cout << endl;
cout << "Enter Balance: ";
cin >> bal;

cout << endl;
cout << "Enter Interest Rate: ";
cin >> rt;

cout << endl << endl;
cout << "Account now being created." << endl << endl;

Savings_Account acc1(id, buffer, bal, rt);

cout << "Account Owner: " << acc1.Get_Name() << endl << endl;

char* name = acc1.Get_Name();
strcpy(name, "XXX");

cout << "Account Owner: " << acc1.Get_Name() << endl;

return 0;
}
```

Program Output

Enter Account ID: **1234**

Enter Account Holder's Name: **Maxwell Larrabee**

Enter Balance: **1000.00**

Enter Interest Rate: **0.06**

Account now being created.

Constructor executed.

Account Owner: Maxwell Larrabee

Account Owner: XXX

Account 1234 terminated.

To code a safe accessor method that returns a pointer, we make the method return a constant pointer. This assures that the object being pointed to cannot be changed through the pointer by the calling function.

Note 12.6   Coding an Accessor Function that Returns a Pointer

If an accessor method returns a pointer to a private instance variable of the class, declare the method so that it returns a const pointer.

For example, in the class `Savings_Account`, a safe method that returns the value of the ID number is the following.

```
const char* Get_Name()
{
    return name;
}
```

In `main()`, we could then code the following, but we would then not be allowed to change the name of `acc1` through the pointer. See Experiment 3.

```
const char* name_p = acc1.Get_Name();
```

Note that the following statement is illegal because it would remove a constant restriction. The pointer returned by `Get_Name()` is a pointer to a constant, whereas `name_p` is a nonconstant pointer.

```
char* name_p = acc1.Get_Name();
```

The following program, dem12-8.cpp, illustrates this idea. We also code a similar accessor method for the ID number.

```
//dem12-8.cpp

//This program illustrates the use of the copy constructor
//in a class that has a pointer as a data member.
//The class contains accessor functions that return a const pointer.

#include <iostream>
#include <iomanip>
#include <string>

using namespace std;

class Savings_Account
{
    private:
        char    id_no[5];
        char*   name;
        double balance;
        double rate;

    public:
        Savings_Account(char id[], char* n_p, double bal = 0.00, double rt = 0.04);
        Savings_Account(const Savings_Account&);
        ~Savings_Account();
        double Calc_Interest();
        double Get_Balance();
        const char* Get_Id();
        const char* Get_Name();
        void Deposit(double);
        bool Withdraw(double);
};
```

```
Savings_Account::Savings_Account(char id[], char* n_p, double bal, double rt)
{
  strcpy(id_no, id);   //copy first argument into id_no[]

  name = new char[strlen(n_p) + 1]; //create space for the name

  strcpy(name, n_p);   //copy second argument into new space

  balance = bal;
  rate    = rt;

  cout << endl << endl;
  cout << "Constructor executed." << endl;
}

Savings_Account::Savings_Account(const Savings_Account& acc_r)
{
  strcpy(id_no, acc_r.id_no);   //copy first argument into id_no[]

  name = new char[strlen(acc_r.name) + 1]; //create space for the name

  strcpy(name, acc_r.name);   //copy second argument into new space

  balance = acc_r.balance;
  rate    = acc_r.rate;

  cout << endl << endl;
  cout << "Copy constructor executed." << endl;
}

Savings_Account::~Savings_Account()
{
  cout << endl << endl;
  cout << "Account " << id_no << " terminated." << endl;
  delete [] name;
}

double Savings_Account::Get_Balance()
{
  return balance;
}

const char* Savings_Account::Get_Id()
{
  return id_no;
}

const char* Savings_Account::Get_Name()
{
  return name;
}

double Savings_Account::Calc_Interest()
{
  double interest;

  interest = balance * rate;
```

```cpp
    balance += interest;

    return interest;
}
void Savings_Account::Deposit(double amount)
{
    balance += amount;
}
bool Savings_Account::Withdraw(double amount)
{
    bool result;

    if (amount <= balance)
    {
        balance -= amount;
        result = true;
    }
    else
        result = false;

    return result;
}
int main()
{
    cout << setprecision(2)
         << setiosflags(ios::fixed)
         << setiosflags(ios::showpoint);

    char id[5];
    char buffer[81];   //Temporarily stores the name
    double bal;
    double rt;

    cout << "Enter Account ID: ";
    cin.getline(id, 5);

    cout << endl;
    cout << "Enter Account Holder's Name: ";
    cin.getline(buffer, 81);

    cout << endl;
    cout << "Enter Balance: ";
    cin >> bal;

    cout << endl;
    cout << "Enter Interest Rate: ";
    cin >> rt;

    cout << endl <<endl;
    cout << "Account now being created." << endl <<endl;

    Savings_Account acc1(id, buffer, bal, rt);

    cout << endl << endl;
```

```
cout << "Account ID: " << acc1.Get_Id() << endl <<endl;
cout << "Account Owner: " << acc1.Get_Name() << endl <<endl;

cout << "Account now being created by initialization." << endl;

Savings_Account acc2 = acc1;

return 0;
}
```

Program Output

Enter Account ID: **1234**

Enter Account Holder's Name: **Maxwell Larrabee**

Enter Balance: **1000.00**

Enter Interest Rate: **0.06**

Account now being created.

Constructor executed.

Account ID: 1234

Account Owner: Maxwell Larrabee

Account now being created by initialization.

Copy constructor executed.

Account 1234 terminated.

Account 1234 terminated.

The accessor methods Get_Id() and Get_Name() return const char*. This guarantees that the calling function, main() in this case, cannot alter the target of the pointer that is returned by each method. Therefore, the id_no and name members of the class cannot be changed through these pointers.

Exercises 12.3

1. Write a statement that declares c_p as a constant character pointer and that initializes the pointer to the address of the character variable ch.
2. Write a statement that declares d_p as a pointer whose target, the double db, is a constant.

Suppose the following declarations in Exercises 3–9.

```
long r = 6;
long s = 19;
long* k_p = &s;
long const l_p = &r;
const long* m_p = &r;
```

Which of the following statements is legal?

3. r = 9;

4. *1_p = 4;

5. 1_p = &s;

6. m_p = &s;

7. *m_p = 27;

8. long * n_p = m_p;

9. const long * q_p = k_p;

Experiments 12.3

1. Remove the keyword const in the declaration and definition of Get_Value() in dem12-5.cpp. Compile the resulting program. What messages does the compiler issue?

2. Remove the comment from the statement in main() in dem12-5.cpp. Compile the program. What message does the compiler issue?

3. In dem12-6.cpp, place the following statement before the return statement in function Avg().

```
arr[0] = 0;
```

Compile the resulting program. What happens and why?

4. In dem12-8.cpp, place the following statements at the end of main().

```
const char* name_p = acc1.Get_Name();
*name_p = 'X';
```

Compile the resulting program. What happens and why?

Programming Problems 12.3

1. Make the following changes to the WebPage class of Programming Problem 1, Section 12.2. Recode the copy constructor using const as described in this section. Replace the Display_URL() method with a Get_URL() method that returns a pointer to the URL. Recode main() as necessary. Compile, execute, and test the resulting program.

2. Make the following changes to the OilTank class of Programming Problem 2, Section 12.2. Recode the copy constructor using const as described in this section. Replace the Display_Number() method and the Display_Company() method by the methods Get_Number() and Get_Company(), respectively, so that each returns a pointer to the corresponding instance variable. Recode main() as necessary. Compile, execute, and test the resulting program.

3. Make the following changes to the VehicleService class of Programming Problem 3, Section 12.2. Recode the copy constructor using const as described in this section. Replace the Display_Number() and Display_Owner() methods by the methods Get_Number() and Get_Owner(), respectively, so that each returns a pointer to the corresponding instance variable. Recode main() as necessary. Compile, execute, and test the resulting program.

4. Make the following changes to the HotelRoom class of Programming Problem 4, Section 12.2. Recode the copy constructor using const as described in this section. Replace the Display_Number() and Display_Guest() methods by the methods Get_Number() and Get_Guest(), respectively, so that each returns a pointer to the corresponding instance variable. Recode main() as necessary. Compile, execute, and test the resulting program.

12.4 OBJECTS, FUNCTIONS AND POINTERS

A class is a data type. Therefore, a function can return an object and we can pass an object to a function as an argument. For example, we might want to write a function Get_Account() that prompts for all the data necessary to create a Savings_Account object and then returns a copy of the created object to the calling program. As another example, we might want a function Display_Account() that displays the account information of a Savings_Account object, which we pass to the function as an argument.

There are three ways in which we can pass an object to a function—by value, by pointer, or by reference. In this section, we discuss functions that return objects and the three methods of passing an object to a function.

12.4.1 Functions that Return an Object

In most of the programs that used Savings_Account, we prompted for the data to create an account by coding the necessary statements in main(). We now code a function Get_Account() that does the prompting for us and returns to main() a Savings_Account object.

In the definition header of Get_Account(), there is no need to use the class name and the scope resolution operator, ::, because the function is not a member of Savings_Account. The function returns a Savings_Account object, which is the reason for the identifier Savings_Account appearing before the function name.

```
Savings_Account Get_Account()
{
    char id[5];
    char buffer[81];
    double bal;
    double rt;

    cout << endl;
    cout << "Enter Account ID: ";
    cin.getline(id, 5);

    cout << endl;
    cout << "Enter Account Holder's Name: ";
    cin.getline(buffer, 81);
```

```
        cout << endl;
        cout << "Enter Balance: ";
        cin >> bal;

        cout << endl;
        cout << "Enter Interest Rate: ";
        cin >> rt;

        Savings_Account acc(id, buffer, bal, rt);

        return acc;
}
```

This function contains most of the prompting code that appeared in main() in the programs that used Savings_Account.

Get_Account() creates a local Savings_Account object, acc, using the data input by the user. Therefore, the name member of acc points to space that is allocated on the heap by the Savings_Account constructor. The return statement sends a temporary copy of acc to the calling function. We shall say more about this momentarily. When the function ends, the local object acc goes out of scope and is, therefore, destroyed. This causes the Savings_Account destructor to be executed, which deallocates the space that the name member of acc was pointing to. Now, if the return statement had sent a member-by-member copy of acc back to the calling function, the name member of that copy would be pointing to unallocated space. See Figure 12.4a. This corrupted pointer could cause the program to crash. To ensure that this does not happen, C++ uses

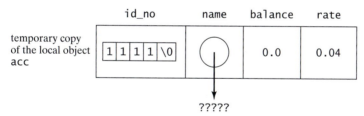

(a) The temporary copy of the local variable acc would have a name member that points to unallocated heap space.

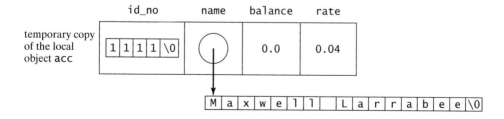

(b) Because the copy constructor is used to make the temporary copy of the local variable acc, the copy's name member points to a valid location on the heap that contains a copy of the name input by the user.

Figure 12.4

the Savings_Account copy constructor to make the temporary copy of acc. Therefore, the name member of the temporary copy is pointing to a different place on the heap than was the name member of acc. See Figure 12.4b.

Following is a complete program that uses the new function. Before reading the paragraph that follows the output, take a careful look at the program output.

```
//dem12-9.cpp

//This program illustrates the use of the copy constructor
//in a class that has a pointer as a data member.
//The copy constructor is used to make a temporary copy
//of the returned object in function Get_Account().

#include <iostream>
#include <iomanip>
#include <string>

using namespace std;

class Savings_Account
{
  private:
    char   id_no[5];
    char*  name;
    double balance;
    double rate;

  public:
    Savings_Account(char id[], char* n_p, double bal = 0.00, double rt = 0.04);
    Savings_Account(const Savings_Account&);
    ~Savings_Account();
    double Calc_Interest();
    double Get_Balance();
    void Deposit(double);
    bool Withdraw(double);
};

Savings_Account::Savings_Account(char id[], char* n_p, double bal, double rt)
{
  strcpy(id_no, id);   //copy first argument into id_no[]

  name = new char[strlen(n_p) + 1]; //create space for the name

  strcpy(name, n_p);   //copy second argument into new space

  balance = bal;
  rate    = rt;

  cout << endl << endl;
  cout << "Constructor executed." << endl;
}

Savings_Account::Savings_Account(const Savings_Account& acc_r)
{
  strcpy(id_no, acc_r.id_no);   //copy first argument into id_no[]
```

```cpp
  name = new char[strlen(acc_r.name) + 1]; //create space for the name
  strcpy(name, acc_r.name);   //copy second argument into new space
  balance = acc_r.balance;
  rate    = acc_r.rate;

  cout << endl << endl;
  cout << "Copy constructor executed." << endl;
}
Savings_Account::~Savings_Account()
{
  cout << endl <<endl;
  cout << "Account " << id_no << " terminated." << endl;
  delete [] name;
}
double Savings_Account::Get_Balance()
{
  return balance;
}
double Savings_Account::Calc_Interest()
{
  double interest;

  interest = balance * rate;
  balance += interest;

  return interest;
}
void Savings_Account::Deposit(double amount)
{
  balance += amount;
}
bool Savings_Account::Withdraw(double amount)
{
  bool result;

  if (amount <= balance)
  {
    balance -= amount;
    result = true;
  }
  else
    result = false;

  return result;
}
Savings_Account Get_Account();    //Prototype for Get_Account()

int main()
```

```
{
  cout << setprecision(2)
       << setiosflags(ios::fixed)
       << setiosflags(ios::showpoint);

  cout << endl << endl;
  cout << "Account now being created.";

  Savings_Account acc1 = Get_Account();

  cout << endl << endl;
  cout << "Account now being created by initialization." << endl;

  Savings_Account acc2 = acc1;

  return 0;
}
Savings_Account Get_Account()
{
  char id[5];
  char buffer[81];
  double bal;
  double rt;

  cout << endl;
  cout << "Enter Account ID: ";
  cin.getline(id, 5);

  cout << endl;
  cout << "Enter Account Holder's Name: ";
  cin.getline(buffer, 81);

  cout << endl;
  cout << "Enter Balance: ";
  cin >> bal;

  cout << endl;
  cout << "Enter Interest Rate: ";
  cin >> rt;

  Savings_Account acc(id, buffer, bal, rt);

  return acc;
}
```

Program Output

```
Account now being created.
Enter Account ID: 1111

Enter Account Holder's Name: John Molluzzo

Enter Balance: 100.00

Enter Interest Rate: 0.06

Constructor executed.
```

```
Copy constructor executed.
Account 1111 terminated.
Account now being created by initialization.
Copy constructor executed.
Account 1111 terminated.
Account 1111 terminated.
```

The message "Constructor executed" is produced by the constructor when the local object acc is created in the function Get_Account(). When the return statement executes, it makes a temporary copy of acc, which executes the copy constructor. The first "Account 1111 terminated" message executes as the local object acc is destroyed when the function ends. Back in main(), the temporary copy of acc that was created by the function is assigned to the object acc1. *Note that this does not cause the copy constructor to execute.* Think of acc1 becoming the temporary copy that was returned by the function. The next step in main() is the creation by initialization of acc2. This causes the copy constructor to execute. Finally, when main() ends, acc1 and acc2 are destroyed, which causes the destructor to execute for each of them.

> **Note 12.7   The Copy Constructor and Functions that Return an Object**
>
> If you define a function that returns an object of a user-defined class, provide the class with a copy constructor.

12.4.2 Passing an Object by Value

Suppose we want to pass an object by value to the function Display_Account() in such a way that executing Display_Account(acc1) will display the account information for the object acc1. Assume the function definition header for Display_Account() is the following. We will supply the function code later.

    Display_Account(Savings_Account acc)

When the program executes Display_Account(acc1), the function's parameter acc is *initialized* to the value of acc1. Therefore, the copy constructor for Savings_Account, which performs initializations, is used in passing the argument to the function. Recall that you should code your own copy constructor whenever the class has a data member that is a pointer. Therefore, because we are passing an object by value, we must make sure that our class contains a copy constructor.

> **Note 12.8   The Copy Constructor and Passing an Object by Value**
>
> If you pass an object by value to a function, make sure that you code a copy constructor for the class.

Following is program dem12-10.cpp, which illustrates the use of a copy constructor when passing an object by value.

```
//dem12-10.cpp

//This program illustrates passing an object by value.
//A copy constructor is required to ensure that a correct
//copy of the object is passed to the function.

#include <iostream>
#include <iomanip>
#include <string>

using namespace std;

class Savings_Account
{
  private:
    char    id_no[5];
    char*   name;
    double balance;
    double rate;

  public:
    Savings_Account(char id[], char* n_p, double bal = 0.00, double rt = 0.04);
    ~Savings_Account();
    Savings_Account(const Savings_Account&);
    const char* Get_Id() const;
    const char* Get_Name() const;
    double Calc_Interest();
    double Get_Balance();
    void Deposit(double);
    bool Withdraw(double);
};

Savings_Account::Savings_Account(char id[], char* n_p, double bal, double rt)
{
  strcpy(id_no, id);  //copy first argument into id_no[]

  name = new char[strlen(n_p) + 1]; //create space for the name

  strcpy(name, n_p);  //copy second argument into new space

  balance = bal;
  rate    = rt;
}

Savings_Account::Savings_Account(const Savings_Account& acc_r)
{
  strcpy(id_no, acc_r.id_no);  //copy first argument into id_no[]

  name = new char[strlen(acc_r.name) + 1]; //create space for the name

  strcpy(name, acc_r.name);  //copy second argument into new space

  balance = acc_r.balance;
  rate    = acc_r.rate;
```

```cpp
  cout << endl << endl;
  cout << "Copy constructor executed." << endl;
}
Savings_Account::~Savings_Account()
{
  cout << endl << endl;
  cout << "Account " << id_no << " terminated." << endl;
  delete [] name;
}
const char* Savings_Account::Get_Id() const
{
  return id_no;
}
const char* Savings_Account::Get_Name() const
{
  return name;
}
double Savings_Account::Get_Balance()
{
  return balance;
}
double Savings_Account::Calc_Interest()
{
  double interest;

  interest = balance * rate;
  balance += interest;

  return interest;
}
void Savings_Account::Deposit(double amount)
{
  balance += amount;
}
bool Savings_Account::Withdraw(double amount)
{
  bool result;

  if (amount <= balance)
  {
    balance -= amount;
    result = true;
  }
  else
    result = false;

  return result;
}
```

```cpp
void Display_Account(Savings_Account);      //Function prototype

int main()
{
  cout << setprecision(2)
       << setiosflags(ios::fixed)
       << setiosflags(ios::showpoint);

  char id[5];
  char buffer[81];   //Temporarily stores the name
  double bal;
  double rt;
  double amount;

  cout << endl;
  cout << "Enter Account ID: ";
  cin.getline(id, 5);

  cout << endl;
  cout << "Enter Account Holder's Name: ";
  cin.getline(buffer, 81);

  cout << endl;
  cout << "Enter Balance: ";
  cin >> bal;

  cout << endl;
  cout << "Enter Interest Rate: ";
  cin >> rt;

  Savings_Account acc1(id, buffer, bal, rt);

  Display_Account(acc1);

  cout << endl << endl;
  cout << "Enter an amount to deposit: ";
  cin >> amount;

  acc1.Deposit(amount);

  cout << endl << endl;
  cout << "A deposit of " << amount << " was made.";

  Display_Account(acc1);

  acc1.Calc_Interest();

  cout << endl << endl;
  cout << "Interest was applied to the account.";

  Display_Account(acc1);

  cout << endl << endl;
  cout << "Name: " << acc1.Get_Name();

  cout << endl << endl;
  cout << "Enter an amount to withdraw: ";
  cin >> amount;
```

```
  if (acc1.Withdraw(amount))
  {
    cout << endl << endl;
    cout << "A withdrawal of " << amount << " was made.";
  }
  else
  {
    cout << endl << endl;
    cout << "WITHDRAWAL NOT MADE: Insufficient funds.";
  }

  cout << endl << endl;
  cout << "Name: " << acc1.Get_Name();

  Display_Account(acc1);

  cout << endl;
  return 0;
}
void Display_Account(Savings_Account acc)
{
  cout << endl << endl;
  cout << "Data for Account# " << acc.Get_Id();

  cout << endl << endl;
  cout << "Owner's Name: " << acc.Get_Name();

  cout << endl << endl;
  cout << "Account Balance: " << acc.Get_Balance();
}
```

Program Output

```
Enter Account ID: 1234

Enter Account Holder's Name: Maxwell Larrabee

Enter Balance: 100.00

Enter Interest Rate: 0.06

Copy constructor executed.

Data for Account# 1234

Owner's Name: Maxwell Larrabee

Account Balance: 100.00

Account 1234 terminated.

Enter an amount to deposit: 50.00

A deposit of 50.00 was made.
```

```
Copy constructor executed.

Data for Account# 1234

Owner's Name: Maxwell Larrabee

Account Balance: 150.00

Account 1234 terminated.

Interest was applied to the account.

Copy constructor executed.

Data for Account# 1234

Owner's Name: Maxwell Larrabee

Account Balance: 159.00

Account 1234 terminated.

Name: Maxwell Larrabee

Enter an amount to withdraw: 60.00

A withdrawal of 60.00 was made.

Name: Maxwell Larrabee

Copy constructor executed.

Data for Account# 1234

Owner's Name: Maxwell Larrabee

Account Balance: 99.00

Account 1234 terminated.

Account 1234 terminated.
```

Note that, immediately before the lines displayed by Display_Account(), the program displays the message from the copy constructor. The copy constructor executes when the parameter in Display_Account() is initialized to the value of the account being passed to the function. When the function ends, the function's parameter, which is a Savings_Account object, goes out of scope. Therefore, the parameter is destroyed and the class's destructor executes, which is the cause of the displays of the destructor's message.

What would happen if the programmer did not provide a copy constructor and, instead, relied on the default copy constructor? When the function Display_Account() is called for the first time, the default constructor would make a member-by-member copy of the argument and place it into the function's parameter. Therefore, the name member of the parameter would be pointing to the same heap space as the argument. The problem arises when the function ends because the class destructor is executed.

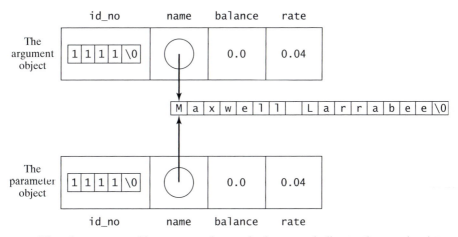

When the parameter object goes out of scope, the destructor deallocates the space it points to. Therefore, the argument's name member will then point to deallocated heap space.

Figure 12.5

This causes the space pointed to by the parameter's name member to be deallocated. But this is exactly the same space pointed to by the argument's name member. See Figure 12.5. The result is that the argument's name member is pointing to non-protected heap space—that is, space that can be reused by the system. See Experiment 1.

We have now identified several ways in which the copy constructor is used in C++.

Note 12.9   When the Copy Constructor Is and Is Not Used

The copy constructor is used when:

- An object is created from an existing object of that class through initialization.
- An object is passed by value to a function.
- A temporary copy of an object is created to hold the return value of an object in a function that returns an object of that class.

The copy constructor is not used when:

- An object is assigned to another object of the same class.

The last point of Note 12.9 is important to keep in mind. If acc1 and acc2 are Savings_Account objects, the assignment acc1 = acc2 does not execute the copy constructor because an object is not being created by the assignment. The assignment results in a member-by-member copy of acc2 into acc1. We shall see how to code a safe assignment of an object that contains a pointer when we discuss how to overload the assignment operator in Chapter 15.

12.4.3 Pointers to Objects

You can declare a pointer to an object in the same way that you declare any other type of pointer. For example, consider `Test_Class`.

```
class Test_Class
{
  private:
    int n;
  public:
    Test_Class(int i = 0);    //One-argument constructor with default value
    int Get_Value() const;
    void Change_Value(int);
};
```

In `main()`, we can make the following declarations, which are illustrated in Figure 12.6.

```
Test_Class tc_object(5);

Test_Class* tc_p = &tc_object;
```

Methods can be applied to the target of an object pointer by using the **indirect member operator** `->` that we used for pointers to structures. Therefore, `tc_p ->` `Get_Value()` applies the `Get_Value()` method to the target of `tc_p`. Recall that `tc_p -> Get_Value()` is equivalent to `(*tc_p).Get_Value()`. Recall that we must use parentheses around `*tc_p` because the dot operator has higher precedence than the dereference operator`*`.

The following will display the value of the target of `tc_p`, change the value of the target to 7, and display the new value.

```
cout << "The value of the object is " << tc_p -> Get_Value();

tc_p -> Change_Value(7);

cout << end;

cout << "\nThe new value of the object is " << tc_p -> Get_Value();
```

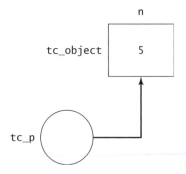

Figure 12.6

In the program dem12-11.cpp, we use an object pointer to display the value of the object, change its value, and then display the new value.

```cpp
//dem12-11.cpp

//This program demonstrates the use of pointers to objects
//and the use of the -> operator to call methods.

#include <iostream>

using namespace std;

class Test_Class
{
  private:
    int n;

  public:
    Test_Class(int i = 0);    //One-argument constructor with default value
    int Get_Value() const;
    void Change_Value(int);
};

Test_Class::Test_Class(int i)
{
  n = i;

  cout << endl << endl;
  cout << "Constructor Executed: Data member initialized to " << n << endl;
}

int Test_Class::Get_Value() const
{
  return n;
}

void Test_Class::Change_Value(int i)
{
  n = i;
}

int main()
{
  Test_Class tc_object(5);
  Test_Class* tc_p = &tc_object;

  cout << "The value of the object is " << tc_p -> Get_Value();

  tc_p -> Change_Value(7);    //Change the value of the pointer's target

  cout << endl;

  cout << "The new value of the object is " << tc_p -> Get_Value();

  cout << endl;
  return 0;
}
```

Program Output

```
Constructor Executed: Data member initialized to 5
The value of the object is 5
The new value of the object is 7
```

12.4.4 Passing an Object by Pointer

In the previous section, we used the function Display_Account() to display in a nicely formatted way the data in a Savings_Account object. The object whose data we wanted to display was passed to the function using call by value. Therefore, when we call the function, a copy of the object is passed to the function. Call by value can be very inefficient because a Savings_Account object is fairly large. It is more efficient if, instead, we pass to the function a pointer to the object. Following is program dem12-12.cpp, which is a new version of dem12-10.cpp that uses pointers in the definition of Display_Account().

```
//dem12-12.cpp

//This program uses an expanded version of Savings_Account.
//The program uses a constructor with default arguments.
//The ID number is stored as an array and the name of the
//account holder is a character pointer. The constructor uses
//dynamic memory allocation.

//A Savings_Account object is passed by pointer to the function
//Display_Account()

#include <iostream>
#include <iomanip>
#include <string>

using namespace std;

class Savings_Account
{
  private:
    char    id_no[5];
    char*   name;
    double balance;
    double rate;

  public:
    Savings_Account(char id[], char* n_p, double bal = 0.00, double rt = 0.04);
    ~Savings_Account();
    const char* Get_Id() const;
    const char* Get_Name() const;
    double Calc_Interest();
    double Get_Balance();
    void Deposit(double);
    bool Withdraw(double);
};
```

```
Savings_Account::Savings_Account(char id[], char* n_p, double bal, double rt)
{
  strcpy(id_no, id);   //copy first argument into id_no[]

  name = new char[strlen(n_p) + 1]; //create space for the name

  strcpy(name, n_p);   //copy second argument into new space

  balance = bal;
  rate    = rt;
}

Savings_Account::~Savings_Account()
{
  cout << endl << endl;
  cout << "Account " << id_no << " terminated." << endl;
  delete [] name;
}

const char* Savings_Account::Get_Id() const
{
  return id_no;
}

const char* Savings_Account::Get_Name() const
{
  return name;
}

double Savings_Account::Get_Balance()
{
  return balance;
}

double Savings_Account::Calc_Interest()
{
  double interest;

  interest = balance * rate;
  balance += interest;

  return interest;
}

void Savings_Account::Deposit(double amount)
{
  balance += amount;
}

bool Savings_Account::Withdraw(double amount)
{

  bool result;

  if (amount <= balance)
  {
```

```
    balance -= amount;
    result = true;
  }
  else
    result = false;

  return result;
}

void Display_Account(Savings_Account*);     //Function prototype

int main()
{
  cout << setprecision(2)
       << setiosflags(ios::fixed)
       << setiosflags(ios::showpoint);

  char id[5];
  char buffer[81];   //Temporarily stores the name
  double bal;
  double rt;
  double amount;

  cout << "Enter Account ID: ";
  cin.getline(id, 5);

  cout << endl;
  cout << "Enter Account Holder's Name: ";
  cin.getline(buffer, 81);

  cout << endl;
  cout << "Enter Balance: ";
  cin >> bal;

  cout << endl;
  cout << "Enter Interest Rate: ";
  cin >> rt;

  Savings_Account acc1(id, buffer, bal, rt);

  Display_Account(&acc1);

  cout << endl << endl;
  cout << "Enter an amount to deposit: ";
  cin >> amount;

  acc1.Deposit(amount);

  cout << endl <<endl;
  cout << "A deposit of " << amount << " was made." << endl;

  Display_Account(&acc1);

  acc1.Calc_Interest();

  cout << endl << endl;
  cout << "Interest was applied to the account." << endl;
```

```
   Display_Account(&acc1);

   cout << endl << endl;
   cout << "Name: " << acc1.Get_Name();

   cout << endl << endl;
   cout << "Enter an amount to withdraw: ";
   cin >> amount;

   if (acc1.Withdraw(amount))
   {
      cout << endl << endl;
      cout << "A withdrawal of " << amount << " was made." << endl;
   }
   else
   {
      cout << endl << endl;
      cout << "WITHDRAWAL NOT MADE: Insufficient funds." << endl;
   }

   cout << endl << endl;

   Display_Account(&acc1);

   cout << endl;
   return 0;
}
void Display_Account(Savings_Account* acc_p)
{
   cout << endl;

   cout << "Data for Account# " << acc_p -> Get_Id() << endl << endl;

   cout << "Owner's Name: " << acc_p -> Get_Name() << endl << endl;

   cout << "Account Balance: " << acc_p -> Get_Balance();
}
```

Program Output

```
Enter Account ID: 1234

Enter Account Holder's Name: Maxwell Larrabee

Enter Balance: 100.00

Enter Interest Rate: 0.06

Data for Account# 1234

Owner's Name: Maxwell Larrabee

Account Balance: 100.00

Enter an amount to deposit: 50.00
```

A deposit of 50.00 was made.

Data for Account# 1234

Owner's Name: Maxwell Larrabee

Account Balance: 150.00

Interest was applied to the account.

Data for Account# 1234

Owner's Name: Maxwell Larrabee

Account Balance: 159.00

Name: Maxwell Larrabee

Enter an amount to withdraw: **90**

A withdrawal of 90.00 was made.

Data for Account# 1234

Owner's Name: Maxwell Larrabee

Account Balance: 69.00

Account 1234 terminated.

12.4.5 References to Objects

You can define reference variables for objects in the same way that you define reference variables for the native data types. Consider the following declaration.

```
Savings_Account acc1("1111", "Maxwell Larrabee", 100.00, 0.06);
Savings_Account& acc_r  = acc1;
```

The variable acc_r is a reference, that is, an alias, for the variable acc1. Manipulating acc_r is equivalent to manipulating acc1. Therefore,

```
acc_r.Deposit(50.00);
```

deposits $50.00 into acc1.

12.4.6 Passing an Object by Reference

We can also pass an object to a function by reference. References have all the advantages with objects that they have with other data types. Following is the program dem12-13.cpp, which is a version of dem12-12.cpp that uses references rather than pointers.

```
//dem12-13.cpp
```

```
//This program uses an expanded version of the Savings_Account class.
```

```
//The program uses a constructor with default arguments.
//The ID number is stored as an array and the name of the
//account holder is a character pointer. The constructor uses
//dynamic memory allocation.
//A Savings_Account object is passed by reference to the function
//Display_Account()

#include <iostream>
#include <iomanip>
#include <string>

using namespace std;

class Savings_Account
{
  private:
    char    id_no[5];
    char*   name;
    double balance;
    double rate;

  public:
    Savings_Account(char id[], char* n_p, double bal = 0.00, double rt = 0.04);
    ~Savings_Account();
    const char* Get_Id() const;
    const char* Get_Name() const;
    double Calc_Interest();
    double Get_Balance();
    void Deposit(double);
    bool Withdraw(double);
};

Savings_Account::Savings_Account(char id[], char* n_p, double bal, double rt)
{
  strcpy(id_no, id);   //copy first argument into id_no[]

  name = new char[strlen(n_p) + 1]; //create space for the name

  strcpy(name, n_p);   //copy second argument into new space

  balance = bal;
  rate    = rt;
}

Savings_Account::~Savings_Account()
{
  cout << endl << endl;
  cout << "Account " << id_no << " terminated." << endl;
  delete [] name;
}

const char* Savings_Account::Get_Id() const
{
  return id_no;
}
```

```
const char* Savings_Account::Get_Name() const
{
  return name;
}

double Savings_Account::Get_Balance()
{
  return balance;
}

double Savings_Account::Calc_Interest()
{
  double interest;

  interest = balance * rate;
  balance += interest;

  return interest;
}

void Savings_Account::Deposit(double amount)
{
  balance += amount;
}

bool Savings_Account::Withdraw(double amount)
{
  bool result;

  if (amount <= balance)
  {
    balance -= amount;
    result = true;
  }
  else
    result = false;

  return result;
}

void Display_Account(Savings_Account&);    //Function prototype

int main()
{
  cout << setprecision(2)
       << setiosflags(ios::fixed)
       << setiosflags(ios::showpoint);

  char id[5];
  char buffer[81];  //Temporarily stores the name
  double bal;
  double rt;
  double amount;
```

```
cout << "Enter Account ID: ";
cin.getline(id, 5);

cout << endl;
cout << "Enter Account Holder's Name: ";
cin.getline(buffer, 81);

cout << endl;
cout << "Enter Balance: ";
cin >> bal;

cout << endl;
cout << "Enter Interest Rate: ";
cin >> rt;

Savings_Account acc1(id, buffer, bal, rt);

Display_Account(acc1);

cout << endl << endl;
cout << "Enter an amount to deposit: ";
cin >> amount;

acc1.Deposit(amount);

cout << endl << endl;
cout << "A deposit of " << amount << " was made." << endl;

Display_Account(acc1);

acc1.Calc_Interest();

cout << endl << endl;
cout << "Interest was applied to the account." << endl;

Display_Account(acc1);

cout << endl << endl;
cout << "Name: " << acc1.Get_Name();

cout << endl << endl;
cout << "Enter an amount to withdraw: ";
cin >> amount;

if (acc1.Withdraw(amount))
{
   cout << endl << endl;
   cout << "A withdrawal of " << amount << " was made." << endl;
}
else
{
   cout << endl << endl;
   cout << "WITHDRAWAL NOT MADE: Insufficient funds." << endl;
}

cout << endl << endl;
```

```
   Display_Account(acc1);

   cout << endl;
   return 0;
}
void Display_Account(Savings_Account& acc)
{
   cout << endl;
   cout << "Data for Account# " << acc.Get_Id() << endl << endl;

   cout << "Owner's Name: " << acc.Get_Name() << endl << endl;

   cout << "Account Balance: " << acc.Get_Balance();
}
```

Program Output

Enter Account ID: **1234**

Enter Account Holder's Name: **Maxwell Larrabee**

Enter Balance: **100.00**

Enter Interest Rate: **0.06**

Data for Account# 1234

Owner's Name: Maxwell Larrabee

Account Balance: 100.00

Enter an amount to deposit: **50.00**

A deposit of 50.00 was made.

Data for Account# 1234

Owner's Name: Maxwell Larrabee

Account Balance: 150.00

Interest was applied to the account.

Data for Account# 1234

Owner's Name: Maxwell Larrabee

Account Balance: 159.00

Name: Maxwell Larrabee

Enter an amount to withdraw: **90.00**

A withdrawal of 90.00 was made.

Data for Account# 1234

Owner's Name: Maxwell Larrabee

Account Balance: 69.00

Account 1234 terminated.

Exercises 12.4

Consider the following class declaration and object declaration in `main()`:

```
class ExerClass
{
    private:
        int p1;
        int p2;
    public:
        ExerClass (int a, int b) {p1 = a; p2 = b;}
        int Get_P1() {return p1;}
        int Get_P2() {return p2;}
        void Combine(int a) {p1 = p1 + p2 + a;}
};
void main()
{
    ExerClass ex1(3, 4);
    ExerClass* ex_p = &ex1;
    ExerClass ex2(7, 8);
    ExerClass& ex_r = ex2;
    .
    .
    .
}
```

What is the output in each of Exercises 1–4? Work each independently of the others.

1. `cout << ex_p -> Get_P1();`
2. `ex_p -> Combine(6);`

   `cout << ex_p -> Get_P1();`

3. `cout << ex_r.Get_P2();`
4. `ex_p = &ex_r;`

   `ex_p -> Combine(5);`

   `cout -> ex2.Get_P1();`

5. Write a void function `Display_Exer()` that displays in a nicely formatted way the data members of an `ExerClass` object. Pass the object to the function by value.
6. Write a void function `Display_Exer()` that displays in a nicely formatted way the data members of an `ExerClass` object. Pass the object to the function by pointer.
7. Write a void function `Display_Exer()` that displays in a nicely formatted way the data members of an `ExerClass` object. Pass the object to the function by reference.
8. Code a `Display_Rectangle()` function for the `Rectangle` class. The function should display the length and the width of the rectangle in a nicely formatted way. Pass a `Rectangle` object to the function by pointer.

9. Code a `Display_Time()` function for the `DigitalClock` class. The function should display the time in the format hh:mm AM or PM. Pass a `DigitalClock` object to the function by reference.

Experiments 12.4

1. Remove the copy constructor from dem12-10.cpp. Compile and execute the resulting program, if necessary several times, noting the name that is displayed by `Display_Account()`. When prompted for a name for the account, enter a name of at least eight characters. Does the program execute correctly? If not, explain why.

Programming Problems 12.4

1. Code a display function that displays the data members of the `WebPage` class in a nicely formatted way. Use the function in a program to display the information about a Web page. Pass a `WebPage` object to the function by one of the following:
   (a) value
   (b) pointer
   (c) reference
   Compile, execute, and test the resulting program.
2. Code a display function that displays the data members of the `OilTank` class in a nicely formatted way. Use the function in a program to display the information about an oil tank object. Pass an `OilTank` object to the function by one of the following:
   (a) value
   (b) pointer
   (c) reference
   Compile, execute, and test the resulting program.
3. Code a display function that displays the data members of the `VehicleService` class in a nicely formatted way. Use the function in a program to display the information about a vehicle. Pass a `VehicleService` object to the function by one of the following:
   (a) value
   (b) pointer
   (c) reference
   Compile, execute, and test the resulting program.
4. Code a display function that displays the data members of the `HotelRoom` class in a nicely formatted way. Use the function in a program to display the information about a hotel room. Pass a `HotelRoom` object to the function by one of the following:
   (a) value
   (b) pointer
   (c) reference
   Compile, execute, and test the resulting program.

12.5 DYNAMIC ALLOCATION OF OBJECTS

Recall that integers, doubles, and other built-in data objects can be created and destroyed dynamically using the new and delete operators. We can also use these operators to dynamically create and destroy objects.

12.5.1 Using new and delete with Objects

Objects can be dynamically allocated using the new operator. For example, the following statements dynamically allocate a Test_Class object and a Savings_Account object. Recall from Note 8.6 that to code a new statement, you code a declaration for the object and then remove the name of the object.

```
Test_Class* t_p = new Test_Class(5);

Savings_Account* acc_p = new Savings_Account("3456", "Smith", 250.00, 0.062);
```

The first statement declares a Test_Class pointer and sets it equal to the address of a Test_Class object with an n data member value of 5. The one-argument constructor is called when the object is created on the heap by the new operator. The second statement declares a Savings_Account pointer and sets it equal to the address of a Savings_Account object with an ID number of 3456, a name of Smith, a balance of $250.00, and a rate of 0.062. The four-argument constructor is called when the object is created on the heap by the new operator.

Suppose we want to write a program that prompts the user to create up to 10 Savings_Account objects. One way to handle the problem is to declare an array of 10 Savings_Account objects, each of which is not initialized with meaningful data. When the user decides to create an account, the program fills the next available account object with data. See Figure 12.7. This approach works but wastes space. Each of the Savings_Account objects requires at least 25 bytes of main storage, not including the heap space needed to store the names of the owners of the accounts. If the user decides to create only three accounts, the other seven Savings_Account objects will occupy 175 bytes, which will remain unused. Although this does not seem to be a large amount of space, in a "real-world" problem, an array of accounts might have to be of size 10,000 or greater. If such an array is only one-quarter filled, there would be a great deal of wasted space.

Instead of using an array of 10 Savings_Account objects, we can use an array of 10 Savings_Account object pointers. Such an array requires only about 40 bytes of storage. When the user creates an account, the program can dynamically allocate a Savings_Account object.

See Figure 12.8. This approach uses only as many Savings_Account objects as are needed, thus avoiding the wasted space of the first approach.

An array of 10 Account_Class objects

Figure 12.7

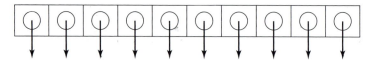

An array of 10 `Savings_Account` pointers

Figure 12.8

Following is program dem12-14.cpp, which illustrates using an array of object pointers. See Experiment 1 for an alternative solution that uses an array of objects.

```cpp
//dem12-14.cpp

//This program illustrates the use of dynamically allocated
//objects.

#include <iostream>
#include <iomanip>
#include <string>
#include <cctype>

using namespace std;

class Savings_Account
{
  private:
    char   id_no[5];
    char*  name;
    double balance;
    double rate;

  public:
    Savings_Account(char id[], char* n_p, double bal = 0.00, double rt = 0.04);
    ~Savings_Account();
    const char* Get_Id() const;
    const char* Get_Name() const;
    double Calc_Interest();
    double Get_Balance();
    void Deposit(double);
    bool Withdraw(double);
};

Savings_Account::Savings_Account(char id[], char* n_p, double bal, double rt)
{
  strcpy(id_no, id);  //copy first argument into id_no[]

  name = new char[strlen(n_p) + 1]; //create space for the name

  strcpy(name, n_p);  //copy second argument into new space

  balance = bal;
  rate    = rt;
}
```

```cpp
Savings_Account::~Savings_Account()
{
  cout << endl << endl;
  cout << "Account " << id_no << " terminated." << endl;
  delete [] name;
}
const char* Savings_Account::Get_Id() const
{
  return id_no;
}
const char* Savings_Account::Get_Name() const
{
  return name;
}
double Savings_Account::Get_Balance()
{
  return balance;
}
double Savings_Account::Calc_Interest()
{
  double interest;

  interest = balance * rate;
  balance += interest;

  return interest;
}
void Savings_Account::Deposit(double amount)
{
  balance += amount;
}
bool Savings_Account::Withdraw(double amount)
{
  bool result;
  if (amount <= balance)
  {
    balance -= amount;
    result = true;
  }
  else
    result = false;

  return result;
}
void Display_Account(Savings_Account&);     //Function prototypes
Savings_Account* Create_Account();

int main()
{
```

```cpp
cout << setprecision(2)
     << setiosflags(ios::fixed)
     << setiosflags(ios::showpoint);

Savings_Account* account_table[10];

int count = 0;
char response;

cout << endl;
cout << "Do you want to create an account?(Y/N): ";
response = cin.get();
cin.get();                //Clear the input buffer

while (toupper(response) == 'Y' && count < 10)
{
   account_table[count] = Create_Account();
   ++count;
   cout << endl;
   cout << "Do you want to create an account?(Y/N): ";
   response = cin.get();
   cin.get();                //Clear the input buffer
}

//Display the accounts

for (int i = 0; i < count; ++i)
   Display_Account(*account_table[i]);

//Clean up

for (i = 0; i < count; ++i)
   delete account_table[i];

cout << endl;
return 0;
}
void Display_Account(Savings_Account& acc)
{
   cout << endl << endl << endl;
   cout << "Data for Account# " << acc.Get_Id() << endl << endl;

   cout << "Owner's Name: " << acc.Get_Name() << endl << endl;

   cout << "Account Balance: " << acc.Get_Balance();
}
Savings_Account* Create_Account()
{
   char id[5];
   char buffer[81];
   double bal;
   double rt;

   Savings_Account* acc_ptr;
```

```
    cout << endl;
    cout << "Enter Account ID: ";
    cin.getline(id, 5);

    cout << endl;
    cout << "Enter Account Holder's Name: ";
    cin.getline(buffer, 81);

    cout << endl;
    cout << "Enter Balance: ";
    cin >> bal;

    cout << endl;
    cout << "Enter Interest Rate: ";
    cin >> rt;

    cin.get();    //Clear the input buffer of newline character

    acc_ptr = new Savings_Account (id, buffer, bal, rt);

    return acc_ptr;
}
```

DUBLIN BUSINESS SCHOOL LIBRARY

Program Output

Do you want to create an account?(Y/N): **y**

Enter Account ID: **1111**

Enter Account Holder's Name: **Maxwell Larrabee**

Enter Balance: **1000.00**

Enter Interest Rate: **0.06**

Do you want to create an account?(Y/N): **y**

Enter Account ID: **2222**

Enter Account Holder's Name: **Adam Zapple**

Enter Balance: **2000.00**

Enter Interest Rate: **0.07**

Do you want to create an account?(Y/N): **y**

Enter Account ID: **3333**

Enter Account Holder's Name: **Poly Ester**

Enter Balance: **4444**

Enter Interest Rate: **0.07**

Do you want to create an account?(Y/N): **n**

```
Data for Account# 1111
Owner's Name: Maxwell Larrabee
Account Balance: 1000.00
Data for Account# 2222
Owner's Name: Adam Zapple
Account Balance: 2000.00
Data for Account# 3333
Owner's Name: Poly Ester
Account Balance: 4444.00
Account 4444 terminated.
Account 3333 terminated.
Account 2222 terminated.
Account 1111 terminated.
```

The program begins in main() with the declaration of the array account_table[] of 10 Savings_Account pointers. The variable count is used as a subscript for the array and, thus, is initialized to zero. After prompting the user, the program enters the while loop to create an account. The first statement in the loop body assigns the Savings_Account pointer returned by the function Create_Account() to the next available account_table pointer. Then count is incremented by one and the user is prompted again. The while loop continues creating accounts until either the user responds no or until 10 accounts are created. See Figure 12.9. When the program exits the while loop, a for loop displays the information for the created accounts by executing the function Display_Account() for each account created by the program. Note the argument in the function call. The identifier account_table[i] is a pointer to a Savings_Account object. Therefore, *account_table[i], the target of that pointer, is a Savings_Account object. The function Display_Account() requires the name of a

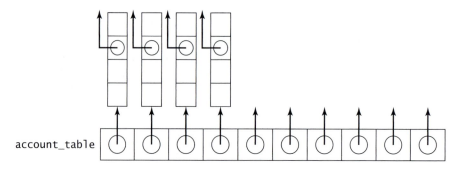

Each member of account_class is a pointer to a Savings_Account object.

Figure 12.9

Savings_Account object as its argument because its argument is a Savings_Account reference. Finally, the last for loop deletes the dynamically allocated accounts.

Exercises 12.5

1. Declare a Rectangle class pointer that points to a dynamically allocated Rectangle object that has length 5 and width 8.
2. Declare a DigitalClock class pointer that points to a dynamically allocated DigitalClock object that is initialized to 8:47 PM.
3. Declare an array of 20 Rectangle objects.
4. Declare an array of 15 DigitalClock pointers.

Experiments 12.5

1. Suppose you declare an array of objects such as the following.

   Savings_Account account_objects[10];

   This declaration is equivalent to declaring 10 Savings_Account objects, each with a no-argument constructor. Define a no-argument constructor for Savings_Account. The id_no member should contain the NULL string and the name member should be the NULL pointer. Initialize the values of balance and rate to 0.00. Now, with the no-argument constructor added to the class, recode dem12-14.cpp so it uses the account_objects[] array instead of an array of Savings_Account pointers.

Programming Problems 12.5

1. Using the WebPage class of Programming Problem 1, Section 12.4, write a program that uses an array web_site[] of 20 WebPage pointers to store information about a set of Web pages. The program should ask the user to enter information about a Web page. The program should dynamically allocate space for a WebPage object and set an element of web_site[] to point to the WebPage object. After the user decides not to enter any more WebPage objects, the program should display all data in all the objects created by the program.
2. Using the OilTank class of Programming Problem 2, Section 12.4, write a program that uses an array tank_farm[] of 100 OilTank pointers to store information about a set of oil tanks. The program should ask the user to enter information about an oil tank. The program should dynamically allocate space for an OilTank object and set an element of tank_farm[] to point to the OilTank object. After the user decides not to enter any more OilTank objects, the program should display all data in all the objects created by the program.
3. Using the VehicleService class of Programming Problem 3, Section 12.4, write a program that uses an array customer[] of 10 VehicleService pointers to store information about a set of vehicles. The program should ask the user to enter information about a vehicle. The program should dynamically allocate space for a VehicleService object and set an element of customer[] to point to the VehicleService object. After the user decides not to enter any more

VehicleService objects, the program should display all data in all the objects created by the program.

4. Using the HotelRoom class of Programming Problem 1, Section 12.4, write a program that uses an array Hotel[] of 200 HotelRoom pointers to store information about a set of hotel rooms. The program should ask the user to enter information about a room. The program should dynamically allocate space for a HotelRoom object and set an element of hotel[] to point to the HotelRoom object. After the user decides not to enter any more HotelRoom objects, the program should display all data in all the objects created by the program.

12.6 STATIC DATA MEMBERS AND FUNCTIONS

Sometimes it is necessary to have a class instance variable whose existence is independent of any object in that class. To manipulate such a class member requires a class method that can be executed independently of any object in the class. In this section, we show how to define such instance variables and methods.

12.6.1 Static Data Members

Suppose that in the Savings_Account class we want all accounts to have the same interest rate. We could assign each Savings_Account object's rate member the same value, say 0.04. However, this is inadvisable for two reasons. First, if each object has its own rate member, it might be possible for a method to change an individual account's rate. Then not all accounts would have the same rate. In addition, if we want to change the rate, we would have to make sure to change to the new value the rate member of every Savings_Account object that exists. Finally, it is not very efficient for each Savings_Account object to have its own rate member if the rate is to be the same for all accounts. All objects should share the same memory location for the rate.

A possible solution would be to declare a variable in main() or, perhaps, a global variable, that holds the common value for the rate. This solution, however, is not acceptable because the rate for Savings_Account objects should be part of the class—it is a property of a Savings_Account object. The rate should also be a private member to assure that only a Savings_Account class method can change its value.

The solution that C++ offers is to declare the rate data member to be static. A **static** data member of a class is instance independent. That is, no matter how many class objects are created in the program, there is only one copy of the static data member. Therefore, its value is independent of the existence of any object. Thus, if we declare the rate member of class Savings_Account to be static, all Savings_Account objects will share this one value. If we change the value of rate, all Savings_Account objects will use this new value automatically.

Because a static data member exists independently of any object, when does it get created and how does it get a value? Like all static variables (class members or not), a static class data member is created at compile time, prior to the execution of main(), and receives an initial value of zero. When we declare a data member as static in a class declaration, it is only a declaration, not a definition. (Remember that a class declaration is simply a blueprint for the structure of a class object. You cannot give a class data member a value in the class declaration.) Therefore, we must define a static member and, if necessary, give it an initial value outside the class definition. Following is the declaration of the class `Savings_Account` with the `rate` data member declared as static.

```
class Savings_Account
{
  private:
    char    id_no[5];
    char*   name;
    double balance;
    static double rate;   //rate is declared static

  public:
    Savings_Account(char id[], char* n_p, double bal = 0.00);

    ~Savings_Account();

    const char* Get_Id() const;

    const char* Get_Name() const;

    double Calc_Interest();

    double Get_Balance();

    void Deposit(double);

    int Withdraw(double);

};
//Static data member definition

double Savings_Account::rate = 0.040;
```

Note that `rate` still remains private. Also, when we define `rate` outside the class definition, we do not use the keyword `static` again and we must qualify its name by the name of the class using the scope resolution operator. Finally, we have also changed the declaration of the constructor. You no longer need to include the rate in the constructor because all objects will now use the common static `rate` member.

Note 12.10   Static Class Data Members

- Declare a class data member static by beginning its declaration with the keyword `static`.
- A static data member is instance independent. All objects of the class share a static data member.
- Define a static data member outside the class definition. In the definition, you must qualify the name of the data member by the name of the class.

12.6.2 Static Methods

Another common use for a static class data member is to count the number of objects that are created by a program. For example, in the class Savings_Account we can declare a static integer variable number_accounts and initialize the variable to zero in its definition. When a Savings_Account object is created, we increment number_accounts, and when a Savings_Account object is destroyed, we decrement number_accounts. Therefore, we include the statement ++number_accounts; in the Savings_Account class constructor and include the statement --number_accounts; in the Savings_Account class destructor.

If we keep count of the number of objects using the static data member number_accounts, we would want to access this variable at certain times to see how many accounts exist. As usual, we would want to define a method that returns the value of number_accounts. However, how would we use this method? We apply a method through an object. But if number_accounts is static, it exists independently of any object. We should be able to access its value even if no Savings_Account objects exist. To access a static data member, you should use a **static method**. Following is another declaration of class Savings_Account that includes the static data member number_accounts. We also show the new definitions of the constructor, the destructor, and the definition of the static method, Total_Accounts(). Note that in the definition of Total_Accounts(), you do not use the keyword static.

```
class Savings_Account
{
  private:
    char    id_no[5];
    char*   name;
    double balance;
    static double rate;
    static int number_accounts;

  public:
    Savings_Account(char id[], char* n_p, double bal = 0.00);
    ~ Savings_Account();
    const char* Get_Id() const;
    const char* Get_Name() const;
    double Calc_Interest();
    double Get_Balance();
    void Deposit(double);
    bool Withdraw(double);

    static int Total_Accounts();   //static method
};

//Static data member definitions

double Savings_Account::rate = 0.040;
int Savings_Account::number_accounts = 0;

Savings_Account:: Savings_Account(char id[], char* n_p, double bal)
{
```

```
    strcpy(id_no, id);   //copy first argument into id_no[]
    name = new char[strlen(n_p) + 1]; //create space for the name
    strcpy(name, n_p);   //copy second argument into new space
    balance = bal;
    ++number_accounts;
}
Savings_Account::~ Savings_Account()
{
    cout << endl << endl;
    cout << "Account " << id_no << " terminated." << endl;
    delete [] name;

    --number_accounts;

    cout << endl;
    cout << "Number Accounts Remaining: " << number_accounts << endl;
}
int Savings_Account::Total_Accounts()
{
    return number_accounts;
}
```

A static method, like a static data member, is instance independent. Thus, it can be executed independently of any object in the class. To execute such a method, you must qualify the method name with the class name and the scope resolution operator. Thus, to display the number of existing accounts, we can code the following statement.

```
    cout << "Number Existing Accounts: "
         << Savings_Account::Total_Accounts() << endl;
```

Note 12.11   Static Class Member Functions

- Use a static method to access a static data member.
- Declare a static class method in the class declaration by preceding its declaration by the keyword static.
- A static method is instance independent.
- To execute a static method, qualify the method name by the name of the class followed by the scope resolution operator.

Following is the program dem12-15.cpp, which illustrates the use of static data members and static methods.

```
//dem12-15.cpp

//This program illustrates the use of static data members
//and functions.
```

```
#include <iostream>
#include <iomanip>
#include <string>
#include <cctype>

using namespace std;

class Savings_Account
{
  private:
    char    id_no[5];
    char*   name;
    double balance;
    static double rate;          //static data member
    static int number_accounts;  //static data member

  public:
    Savings_Account(char id[], char* n_p, double bal = 0.00);
    ~Savings_Account();
    const char* Get_Id() const;
    const char* Get_Name() const;
    double Calc_Interest();
    double Get_Balance();
    void Deposit(double);
    bool Withdraw(double);

    static int Total_Accounts();   //static method declaration
};

//Static data member definitions

double Savings_Account::rate = 0.040;
int Savings_Account::number_accounts = 0;

Savings_Account::Savings_Account(char id[], char* n_p, double bal)
{
  strcpy(id_no, id);  //copy first argument into id_no[]

  name = new char[strlen(n_p) + 1]; //create space for the name

  strcpy(name, n_p);  //copy second argument into new space

  balance = bal;

  ++number_accounts;
}

Savings_Account::~Savings_Account()
{
  cout << endl << endl;
  cout << "Account " << id_no << " terminated." << endl;
  delete [] name;

  --number_accounts;

  cout << endl;
  cout << "Number Accounts Remaining: " << number_accounts << endl;
}
```

```cpp
const char* Savings_Account::Get_Id() const
{
  return id_no;
}

const char* Savings_Account::Get_Name() const
{
  return name;
}

double Savings_Account::Get_Balance()
{
  return balance;
}

double Savings_Account::Calc_Interest()
{
  double interest;
  interest = balance * rate;
  balance += interest;

  return interest;
}

void Savings_Account::Deposit(double amount)
{
  balance += amount;
}

bool Savings_Account::Withdraw(double amount)
{
  bool result;

  if (amount <= balance)
  {
    balance -= amount;
    result = true;
  }
  else
    result = false;

  return result;
}

int Savings_Account::Total_Accounts()
{
  return number_accounts;
}

void Display_Account(Savings_Account&);    //Function prototypes
Savings_Account* Create_Account();

int main()
{
  cout << setprecision(2)
       << setiosflags(ios::fixed)
       << setiosflags(ios::showpoint);
```

```
Savings_Account* account_table[10];

int count = 0;
char response;

cout << endl;
cout << "Do you want to create an account?(Y/N): ";
response = cin.get();
cin.get();                  //Clear the input buffer
while (toupper(response) == 'Y' && count < 10)
{
   account_table[count] = Create_Account();
   account_table[count] -> Calc_Interest();
   ++count;

   cout << endl;
   cout << "Do you want to create an account?(Y/N): ";
   response = cin.get();
   cin.get();               //Clear the input buffer
}

//Display the accounts
for (int i = 0; i < count; ++i)
   Display_Account(*account_table[i]);

//Clean up

for (i = 0; i < count; ++i)
   delete account_table[i];

cout << endl;
return 0;
}
void Display_Account(Savings_Account& acc)
{
   cout << endl << endl << endl;
   cout << "Data for Account# " << acc.Get_Id() << endl << endl;

   cout << "Owner's Name: " << acc.Get_Name() << endl << endl;

   cout << "Current Account Balance: " << acc.Get_Balance();
}
Savings_Account* Create_Account()
{
   char id[5];
   char buffer[81];
   double bal;

   Savings_Account* acc_ptr;

   cout << endl;
   cout << "Enter Account ID: ";
   cin.getline(id, 5);

   cout << endl;
   cout << "Enter Account Holder's Name: ";
   cin.getline(buffer, 81);
```

```
    cout << endl;
    cout << "Enter Balance: ";
    cin >> bal;

    cin.get();      //Clear the input buffer of newline character

    acc_ptr = new Savings_Account (id, buffer, bal);

    cout << endl << endl;
    cout << "Number Existing Accounts: "
                << Savings_Account::Total_Accounts() << endl;
    return acc_ptr;
}
```

Program Output

Do you want to create an account?(Y/N): **y**

Enter Account ID: **1111**

Enter Account Holder's Name: **Adam Zapple**

Enter Balance: **100.00**

Number Existing Accounts: 1

Do you want to create an account?(Y/N): **y**

Enter Account ID: **2222**

Enter Account Holder's Name: **Sal Monella**

Enter Balance: **200.00**

Number Existing Accounts: 2

Do you want to create an account?(Y/N): **y**

Enter Account ID: **3333**

Enter Account Holder's Name: **Polly Ester**

Enter Balance: **300.00**

Number Existing Accounts: 3

Do you want to create an account?(Y/N): **n**

Data for Account# 1111

Owner's Name: Adam Zapple

Current Account Balance: 104.00

Data for Account# 2222

Owner's Name: Sal Monella

Current Account Balance: 208.00

Data for Account# 3333

```
Owner's Name: Polly Ester

Current Account Balance: 312.00

Account 1111 terminated.
Number Accounts Remaining: 2

Account 2222 terminated.
Number Accounts Remaining: 1

Account 3333 terminated.
Number Accounts Remaining: 0
```

Class Savings_Account has two static data members, rate and number_accounts, and one static method, Total_Accounts(). As described previously, the definitions of the two static data members must made outside the class declaration. The rate member is given the initial value 0.040 and the member number_accounts is given the initial value zero. The counter number_accounts is incremented in the class constructor and is decremented in the class destructor. We also display the value of number_accounts in the destructor after decrementing the counter. The definition of Total_Accounts() is similar to the definitions of the other methods. It simply returns the value of number_accounts. Note that although rate is a static data member, any class method can use rate. Thus, the method Calc_Interest() uses rate in its calculation of the interest.

In main(), after soliciting a response from the user to create an account, the while loop body first executes the function Create_Account() to create an account. In addition to obtaining the data and dynamically creating a Savings_Account object, Create_Account() also displays the value of number_accounts by using the static method Total_Accounts(). Note that to call the method, we must qualify its name by the class name and the scope resolution operator. The program's output shows that each time we create an account, the Create_Account() function displays the number of accounts currently in existence. After creating the accounts, the first for statement displays the data for all the accounts. Finally, the second for statement deletes all the Savings_Account objects that the program created. The program's output shows that the destructor displays the ID number of the account that is destroyed and the number of remaining accounts.

Experiments 12.6

1. In dem12-15.cpp, remove the definitions (not the declarations) of the static data members rate and number_accounts. Compile the resulting program. What happens?

2. In dem12-15.cpp, remove the class name and scope resolution operator in the call to method Total_Account() that occurs in the function Create_Account(). Compile the resulting program. What happens?

3. Add the static public method Change_Rate() to class Savings_Account in dem12-15.cpp. The method should assign its only argument to the static data member rate.

The method should return void. Test Change_Rate() by including in main() statements that change the rate data member to a new value that is input by the user. Compile, execute, and test the resulting program.

4. Add a copy constructor to class Savings_Account in dem12-15.cpp. In addition to the assignment statements, the copy constructor should increment the static data member number_accounts. Test the constructor by creating a Savings_Account object in main() by initialization. Compile, execute, and test the resulting program.

5. A static data member can be a constant. For example, suppose we want the bank ID number to be a class data member. Because each account will have this bank ID number, it makes sense to declare it static so that all accounts can share the same memory location. However, the bank ID will not change, so it also makes sense to declare it a constant. Add the constant static data member BANK_ID to the Savings_Account class. To declare it constant, start the declaration of BANK_ID with the keyword const, but do not give it a value in the declaration. Also, begin the definition of BANK_ID with the keyword const and assign the constant its value, say 342. In addition to the data member BANK_ID, add a static method, Get_Bank_Id(), that returns the value of BANK_ID. Write a main() to test the data member and the method Get_Bank_Id(). Compile, execute, and test the resulting program.

Programming Problems 12.6

1. In Programming Problem 1, Section 12.5, add a static data member number_pages to the WebPage class to count the number of pages created by the program. Increment the counter in the class constructor and decrement it in the class destructor. Also, add a static method that returns the value of number_pages. Make sure the resulting program displays the value of number_pages as each page is created and destroyed.

2. In Programming Problem 2, Section 12.5, add the static data member number_tanks to class OilTank. Increment number_tanks in the class constructor and decrement it in the class destructor. Also, add a static method that returns the value of number_tanks. The resulting program should display the number of tanks in the tank farm as they are created and destroyed.

3. In Programming Problem 3, Section 12.5, add the static data member number_vehicles to the VehicleService class. Increment number_vehicles in the class constructor and decrement it in the class destructor. Also, add a static method that returns the value of number_vehicles. The resulting program should display the number of vehicles being serviced as VehicleClass objects are being created and destroyed.

4. In Programming Problem 4, Section 12.5, add the static data member number_rooms to the HotelRoom class. Increment number_rooms in the class constructor and decrement it in the class destructor. Also, add a static method to the class that returns the value of number_rooms. The resulting program should display the number of rooms occupied as guests check in and check out.

CHAPTER REVIEW

TERMINOLOGY

Describe the meanings of the following terms.

garbage collection

copy constructor

default copy constructor

`const` pointer

indirect member operator, ->

`static`

static method

SUMMARY

- Arrays and pointers can be class data members.
- If a character pointer is a class instance variable, the class constructor should dynamically allocate space for the target of the pointer.
- If space is allocated for a pointer's target in a constructor, the space must be deallocated in the class destructor.
- A class's copy constructor executes when an object is created by initialization.
- A copy constructor must have the same name as the class, must have no return type, and its only argument is a reference to an object of that class. The copy constructor's argument refers to the object on the right side of an initialization. The copy constructor is applied to the object being created (Note 12.1).
- If a class has a character pointer instance variable, its copy constructor should dynamically allocate space for the target of the pointer.
- You can create `const` objects. The only methods that can be applied to such objects are accessor methods declared as `const` (Note 12.2).
- If `const` precedes a pointer name in a declaration, the pointer is constant (Note 12.3).
- If `const` precedes the data type in a pointer declaration, the target of the pointer is constant (Note 12.3).
- A declaration can impose a constant restriction, but cannot remove one (Note 12.4).
- The keyword `const` preceding the data type of a pointer in a function's argument means that the target of the pointer is a constant. Thus, the function cannot change the target of the pointer.
- The argument in a copy constructor should be `const`.
- An accessor method that returns a pointer data member should return a `const` pointer (Note 12.6).
- A function can return an object. If you define such a function, provide a copy constructor for the class (Note 12.7).
- You can pass an object to a function by value. If you define such a function, provide a copy constructor for the class (Note 12.8).
- The copy constructor is used in object initialization, when an object is passed to a function by value, and when a temporary is created on return of an object by a function that returns an object (Note 12.9).
- The copy constructor is not used when one object is assigned to another (Note 12.9).
- You can access a member of an object through a pointer using the -> operator.

- An object can be passed to a function by pointer.
- An object can be passed to a function by reference.
- Objects can be allocated dynamically using new.
- A static data member is instance independent. Use the keyword static in its declaration in the class. A static data member must be defined outside the class declaration using the class name and the scope resolution operator (Note 12.10).
- Use a static method to access a static data member. Such a method is instance independent. Declare the method inside the class declaration using the keyword static. Define the method as you would a normal method. To execute the method independently of any class object, qualify the method name by the class name and scope resolution operator (Note 12.11).

REVIEW EXERCISES

1. If a class contains a pointer member, explain why it is necessary to have an explicitly defined destructor.

2. What is the syntax of a copy constructor? When does C++ use the copy constructor? Why must a reference to the class be the argument of a copy constructor?

3. Which methods are allowed to operate on a const object? How do you declare and define such methods?

4. Explain the difference between the following declarations:

   ```
   double* const d_p1 = &d1;

   const double* d_p1 = &d2;
   ```

5. Explain when it is advisable to have a const argument in a function.

6. Explain when it is advisable to have a method return a constant pointer.

7. Why should you provide a class with a copy constructor if you define a function that returns an object of that class?

8. Why should you provide a class with a copy constructor if you pass an object of that class to a function by value?

9. If you pass an object obj to a function Func() by pointer, what operator must you use to apply the class member functions to obj within the body of Func()?

10. What are the differences between passing an object to a function by pointer and by reference?

11. What method is automatically executed when an object is created dynamically by the new operator? How do you use the new operator to create an object?

12. Explain why a static data member is sometimes needed in a class. What is meant by saying that a static data member is instance independent? Why must such a data member be defined outside the class declaration?

13. Explain why a static method is sometimes needed in a class. Describe how to declare and define a static method. How do you execute a static method?

Chapter 13

Inheritance

OBJECTIVES

- To be familiar with the terminology of inheritance—object, class, base class, derived class, indirect and direct derivation, the "is a" relation
- To derive a class from a base class using direct derivation
- To use the `protected` access specifier
- To know the accessibility of `public`, `private`, and `protected` class members of a base class in both publicly derived and privately derived classes
- To know which functions are and are not inherited
- To code a constructor for a derived class
- To code the destructor for a derived class
- To code a copy constructor for a derived class
- To understand function overriding and when it takes place
- To use the scope resolution operator to use an overridden base class function on a derived class object
- To understand and use polymorphism
- To correctly use pointers in a class hierarchy
- To declare a virtual function
- To apply a function polymorphically through a pointer
- To declare virtual destructors
- To use pure virtual functions to create an abstract base class

If I tell you that I am in the market to buy a sheltie, you might not know what I am talking about. You might think that a sheltie is a bird or maybe a car. Suppose that now I tell you that a sheltie is a dog. Immediately, you know some properties of the object that I want to buy—it has four legs, it is furry, it has a tail and a wet nose. You make these deductions because you know that, being a dog, a sheltie inherits the properties that all dogs possess. In this chapter, we will apply the ideas of inheritance to classes that we define in our programs.

A program may have more than one class. For example, in Chapter 11, we discussed a set of classes in an example ATM system that contained the `Customer` class, the ATM class and the `Savings_Account` class. When a system contains several classes, it is necessary to consider how the various classes are related and to include those relationships in your program solution. The most important way in which classes can be related is through **inheritance**. For example, we can define an `Account` class from which we can derive, through inheritance, the `Savings_Account` class and a `Checking_Account` class. Each `Savings_Account` object and `Checking_Account` object inherits all the instance variables and all the methods of the `Account` class. Classes related this way embody the **"is a" relation**. Thus, a `Savings_Account` object "is an" `Account` object and a `Checking_Account` object "is an" `Account` object. In this chapter, we discuss how to derive one class from another and the implications of inheritance on class data members and functions.

13.1 INHERITANCE

One of the most important concepts in object-oriented programming is that of inheritance. Inheritance allows us to define a class in terms of another class, which makes it easier to create and maintain an application. We begin by discussing several examples.

13.1.1 Examples of Inheritance and Basic Terminology

So far, we have considered problems in which there is only one class. Generally speaking, "real world" problems involve many classes. It is possible that some classes in a problem are not directly related in the sense that they do not share any member data or methods. For example, if we were designing a drawing program, we might define the classes `Rectangle` and `Circle` in such a way that they do not have any common data members or any common methods. A rectangle would be described in terms of its length and width, and a circle in terms of its radius. Each class would have its own `Area()` and `Perimeter()` methods.

However, there are times when classes are related in a hierarchy that moves from the general to the specific. Such a hierarchy implements the "is a" relation in the sense that an object in a class that is below another class in the hierarchy "is an" object of the type in the class above. For example, in a banking application there might be three types of interest-bearing accounts: savings accounts, money market accounts, and certificates of deposit (CD). Each type of account "is an" interest-bearing account. The three account types have some common attributes (that is, data). For example, all three types of accounts have an ID number, owner's name, balance, and interest rate. The three account types also have some common methods. For example, all three would have a `Calc_Interest()` method. Although all would have a `Withdraw()` method, each class's version of that method would behave differently. For example, a premature withdrawal from a CD requires that the bank impose a penalty on the interest earned.

The three types of accounts could be defined as separate classes, each with its own ID number, name, balance, and interest rate. However, this would not embody the fact that the three account types are specialized versions of a general type of account, the interest-bearing account. It would be better program design to arrange the classes

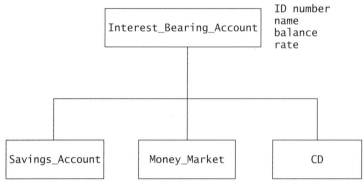

Figure 13.1

in a hierarchy as shown in Figure 13.1. The relationship of classes in such a hierarchy, in which classes go from the general to the specific, is known as **inheritance**. The `Interest_Bearing_Account` class is known as the **base class** (sometimes called the **parent class** or **super class**). The classes below the base class in the hierarchy are the **derived classes** (sometimes called **child classes** or **subclasses**).

When we declare such a class hierarchy in a program, `Interest_Bearing_Account` will include the ID number, name, balance, and rate members (shown to the right of the class in the figure). The derived classes **inherit** these members from the base class. We declare in a derived class only those members that are specific to that class. For example, the CD class would contain the data member `term` that stores the term of the CD. (A CD is purchased for a specific number of months, the term of the account, at which time the owner has the option of withdrawing all or part of the balance. If the CD is renewed, a new interest rate would be in effect for the new term.) We shall see later that methods can also be inherited.

As another example, suppose a video store requires us to write an inventory program that stores data about the videos stocked by the store. The store sells several types of items—movies, specialized videos (exercise, sports, and so on), and video games for three types of game systems (System X, System Y, and System Z). We could design a program that uses five different, unrelated classes (`Movie`, `SpecialVideo`, `SysXGame`, `SysYGame`, and `SysZGame`). However, such a design would not reflect the fact that all the items are videos of some type (we are including VCRs, DVDs, and game cartridges as "videos"), that some are movies and some are games, that the three types of games are all game videos and not movies, and so on. If we arrange the classes in an inheritance hierarchy (Figure 13.2), we can more clearly see the relationships among the different inventory types. Again we show to the right of each class the data members of the class.

As mentioned previously, the idea of inheritance implements the "is a" relationship. For example, a movie is a video, a System X game is a video game, and so on. Therefore, it makes sense that derived classes inherit data from their base class. Because a movie is a video, it should have all the characteristics of a video. Likewise, because a System X game is a video game, it should have all the characteristics of a video game. In the same manner, because a movie is a video, which in turn is an inventory item, a movie should also have all the characteristics of an inventory item.

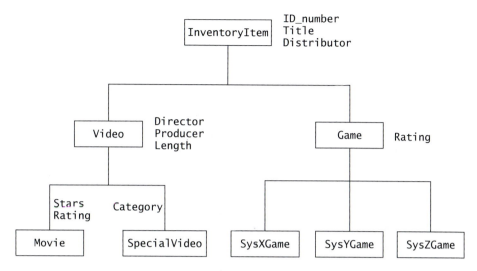

Figure 13.2

The Video class, therefore, inherits all the data from the InventoryItem class. This means that all the members (ID_number, Title, Distributor) of the base class InventoryItem are also members of the derived Video class. It can happen, as it does in the hierarchy of Figure 13.2, that a class, which is derived from a base class, can itself serve as the base class of another class. This is the case for Video class, which is derived from InventoryItem, but is itself the base class for Movie and SpecialVideo. Both Movie and SpecialVideo inherit all the members of Video class, including the members that Video inherits from InventoryItem class. We say that Video and Game are **directly derived** from InventoryItem; Movie and SpecialVideo are directly derived from Video, but are **indirectly derived** from InventoryItem (through the Video class). See Exercises 2 and 3. Thus, the Movie class has the following data members: ID_Number, Title, Distributor (indirectly derived from InventoryItem), Director, Producer, Length (directly derived from Video), and Stars and Rating.

Most methods are also inherited in the hierarchy. (We shall mention the exceptions later in the chapter.) Once again, this should make sense because inheritance implements the "is a" relation. Suppose we have a method Get_Title() that is a member of the InventoryItem class. This method is inherited by all the classes derived from InventoryItem. Therefore, all the classes in the hierarchy have this same Get_Title()method as a member. Thus, for example, because a Movie object is an InventoryItem object, by means of inheritance, we can apply the Get_Title() method to the Movie object.

Note that the classes SysXGame, SysYGame, and SysZGame do not have any data members that are specific to those classes. Why, then, are they separate classes? The reason is that these classes may behave differently when they are acted upon by the same method. For example, if a SysXGame class object receives the message to display itself, it may behave differently than when a SysYGame class object receives the same message. We shall see how to do this later in this chapter.

13.1.2 Defining Derived Classes

For simplicity, we shall work first with `Test_Class`, which we used in the previous chapter. We want `Test_Class` to serve as a base class for `Derived_Test_Class`, which will also have a single data member, m. See Figure 13.3.

Below is the definition of `Test_Class` from the previous chapter. We have re-moved the `Get_Value()`method to keep the class as simple as possible.

```
class Test_Class
{
  private:
    int n;

  public:
    Test_Class(int i = 0);      //One-argument constructor
    Test_Class(Test_Class&);    //Copy constructor
    ~Test_Class();              //Destructor
};
```

As we mentioned in the previous section, any class that we derive from `Test_Class` inherits all the instance variables of `Test_Class`, including the `private` members and most of the methods. Therefore, a `Derived_Test_Class` object will have an n instance variable. However, because n is a `private` member of `Test_Class`, it is not accessible to any function outside `Test_Class`. It follows that although a `Derived_Test_Class` object has an n instance variable by means of inheritance, the object does not have access to that variable. Thus, a method of `Derived_Test_Class` does not have access to the n instance variable, even though n is a member of `Derived_Test_Class`. This is a bit awkward—the object does not have access to one of its own members. We could remedy this situation by declaring the access category of the n instance variable of `Test_Class` to be `public`. This, however, would violate the principle of data hiding because every function would then have access to the n instance variable of every `Test_Class` object. The answer that C++ provides to this dilemma is a third access category, `protected`. An item in a base class, whether an instance variable or a method, that has access category `protected` behaves as though it is a `private` item to all functions except methods in classes derived from the base class. Methods in a derived class have access to all `protected` items in the base class.

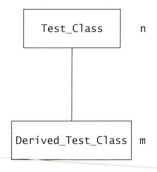

Figure 13.3

Note 13.1   The protected Access Specifier

- A protected item in a base class behaves as though it is private to all functions except to methods in classes derived from the base class.
- Methods in a derived class have access to all protected members in the base class.
- Table 13.1 summarizes access in base and derived classes for class members that are public, protected, and private.

TABLE 13.1

	If base class member is		
	public	protected	private
Access in derived class method?	Yes	Yes	No
Access in non-related method? (not in base or derived class)	Yes	No	No

Therefore, if we want the methods of Derived_Test_Class to have access to the n instance variable of Test_Class, we must change the access category of n to protected.

```
class Test_Class
{
  protected:      //Data accessible to derived classes
     int n;

  public:
     Test_Class(int i = 0);   //One-argument constructor
     Test_Class(Test_Class&);   //Copy constructor
     ~Test_Class();
};
```

Now, how do we encode the fact that Derived_Test_Class is derived from Test_Class? To define Derived_Test_Class as derived from Test_Class, follow the name of the derived class with a colon followed by the keyword public and the name of the base class.

```
class Derived_Test_Class : public Test_Class
{
  protected:
       int m;

  public:
       Derived_Test_Class(int j = 0);
       Derived_Test_Class(Derived_Test_Class&);
       ~Derived_Test_Class();
};
```

In this use, the keyword `public` means that we are publicly deriving this class from the base class. **Public derivation** means that the `protected` and `public` members of the base class are considered `protected` and `public` members of the derived class. The default type of deriving is `private` rather than `public`. Therefore, if we omit the keyword `public`, the derived class will be **privately derived** from the base class. (We could also use the keyword `private` to indicate `private` derivation.) This would mean that the `protected` and `public` members of the base class would be considered `private` members of the derived class. Therefore, no method in a class derived from such a privately derived class would have access to the instance variables of the base class. It is common practice to include the word `public` or `private` and not use the default.

We use `public` derivation if we want users of the derived class to have access to the `public` methods of the base class. We use `private` derivation if we want to block users of the derived class from using the `public` methods of the base class. Because `private` derivation is very unusual, we shall not use it in this book.

Note 13.2   Deriving a Class and Accessibility in Public and Private Derivation

To derive a class from a base class, in the declaration of the derived class, follow the derived class's name by a colon, the keyword `public` or the keyword `private`, and the name of the base class. The Table 13.2 summarizes accessibility in `public` and `private` derivation.

Consider the third row, where we see the words `public`, `public`, `private` going from left to right. This means that an instance variable that is `public` in the base class (the word `public` in the first column) is considered `public` (the word `public` in the second column) in a class that is publicly derived from it. Likewise, a variable that is `public` in the base class is considered `private` (the word in the third column) in a class that is privately derived from the base class.

In a publicly derived class (the middle column), an instance variable or method has the same access category that it has in the base class. In a privately derived class (the right-most column), all instance variables and methods are `private`, no matter what their access category in the base class.

TABLE 13.2

Base Class Member Access Category	Derived Class Public Base Class	Derived Class Private Base Class
`private`	`private`	`private`
`protected`	`protected`	`private`
`public`	`public`	`private`

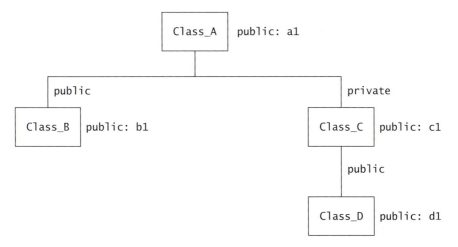

Figure 13.4

For example, consider the class hierarchy of Figure 13.4. The variable a1 is a public instance variable of the base class Class_A. By inheritance, instance variable a1 is also an instance variable of Class_B. What is the access category of instance variable a1 as a member of Class_B? According to the third row of Table 13.2, because Class_B is publicly derived from Class_A, the variable a1 is also a public variable of Class_B. On the other hand, variable a1, by inheritance, is also an instance variable of Class_C. However, from the third row of Table 13.2, a1 is a private member of Class_C because Class_C is privately derived from Class_A. The two instance variables of Class_C, c1 (which is public in Class_C) and the derived a1 (which is private in Class_C) are inherited by Class_D. Therefore, from Table 13.2, c1 is a public member and a1 is a private member of Class_D because Class_D is publicly derived from Class_C. Note also that a1, being a private member of Class_C, is not accessible to the methods of Class_D.

Note that we make the m instance variable of Derived_Test_Class protected. This ensures that if we derive a class from Derived_Test_Class, the m member will be accessible as a protected member of all publicly derived classes.

13.1.3 Constructors in a Derived Class

Note 13.3 states which methods are not inherited.

Note 13.3   Functions that Are Not Inherited

A derived class inherits all base class methods with the following exceptions:

- constructors and copy constructors
- destructors
- overloaded operators (covered in Chapter 15)
- friend functions (covered in Chapter 15)

Figure 13.5

Thus, we must provide the derived class's constructors, copy constructors, and destructor. They are not inherited.

When we create a `Derived_Test_Class` object `dtc_object`, the object has two instance variables. It has an n member inherited from `Test_Class` and it has an m member from `Derived_Test_Class`. See Figure 13.5.

Suppose we want the following declaration to create a `Derived_Test_Class` object with an m instance variable value of 7 and an n instance variable value of 8.

`Derived_Test_Class dtc_object1(7);`

When we create an object of the class `Derived_Test_Class`, we also create an object of the class `Test_Class`. This is so because a `Derived_Test_Class` object "is a" `Test_Class` object. Therefore, when the constructor for `Derived_Test_Class` executes, the constructor for `Test_Class` also executes. In fact, the constructor for `Test_Class` executes before the constructor for `Derived_Test_Class` because the object must obtain its identity as a `Test_Class` object before it obtains its identity as a `Derived_Test_Class` object. The definition of the constructor for `Derived_Test_Class` reflects this.

```
Derived_Test_Class::Derived_Test_Class(int j) : Test_Class(j+1)
{
   m = j;
   cout << endl;
   cout << "Derived_ Test_Class Constructor Executed: "
       << "Data member initialized to "
       << m << endl;
}
```

After the closing parenthesis in the constructor definition header is a colon followed by an explicit call to the one-argument constructor of the base class. This is called an **initialization list**. Items in the initialization list of a constructor are executed as the object is being created. Thus, the act of creating a `Derived_Test_Class` object with an initial value of j causes the one-argument constructor for the base class to execute with an initial value of j+1. That causes the creation of a `Test_Class` object with an n instance variable having a value of j+1. These things happen before the execution of the body of the `Derived_Test_Class` constructor.

Note 13.4   Derived Class Constructors

- The constructor for a derived class should explicitly call the constructor of the base class.
- Call the base class constructor in an initialization list.

The initialization list is not limited to calling the constructor of a base class. We can use it in any constructor to initialize data members. For example, following is the definition of the Test_Class constructor that we used in Chapter 12.

```
Test_Class::Test_Class(int i)
{
  n = i;

  cout << endl;
  cout << "Test_Class Constructor Executed: Data member initialized to "
       << n << endl;
}
```

When we declare a Test_Class object, the object is created with an n instance variable that has a garbage value. When the constructor executes, the assignment statement in the constructor places the value of i (or the default value of 0) into n. There is, therefore, an instant of time when the n instance variable does not have a valid value. The following definition of the Test_Class constructor uses an initialization list to place the value of i into n.

```
Test_Class::Test_Class(int i) : n(i)
{
  cout << endl;
  cout << "Test_Class Constructor Executed: Data member initialized to "
       << n << endl;
}
```

Note that the assignment operator is not used in the initialization list. The expression n(i) says to initialize the value of n to i. With the initialization list as noted, when a Test_Class object is created, the n instance variable is actually created with the value of i. Therefore, the n instance variable always has a valid value. There is no time during which n has a garbage value. Because this is a safer and more efficient way to initialize a data member in a constructor, we shall do so in the following programs.

If we apply this to the Derived_Test_Class constructor, we have the following.

```
Derived_Test_Class::Derived_Test_Class(int j) : Test_Class(j+1), m(j)
{
  cout << endl;
  cout << "Derived_ Test_Class Constructor Executed: "
       << "Data member initialized to "
       << m << endl;
}
```

The initialization list for the constructor contains two statements separated by a comma. The first statement in the initialization list, which executes first, is the explicit call to the base class constructor. The second statement initializes the m data member to the value of j.

13.1.4 The Destructor in a Derived Class

When an object in a derived class (Derived_Test_Class) is destroyed, we also destroy an object in the base class (Test_Class) because, by inheritance, the object is

also a base class (Test_Class) object. When the destructor for the derived class executes, the destructor for the base class should also execute. However, the destructor for
the derived class should execute before the destructor for the base class. Unlike what
we must do for constructors, we do not need to do anything special in the destructor's
code for the system to call the destructor of the base class. The C++ system does this
automatically. Following is dem13-1.cpp, which demonstrates how the constructors and
destructors execute in a class hierarchy.

```cpp
//dem13-1.cpp

//This program illustrates how constructors and destructors
//execute in a base class.

#include <iostream>

using namespace std;

class Test_Class
{
  protected:
    int n;

  public:
    Test_Class(int i = 0);   //One-argument constructor
    ~Test_Class();
};

Test_Class::Test_Class(int i) : n(i)

{
  cout << endl;
  cout << "Test_Class Constructor Executed: Data member initialized to "
       << n << endl;
}

Test_Class::~Test_Class()
{
  cout << endl;
  cout << "Test_Class Destructor Executed for object with data member "
       << n << endl;
}

class Derived_Test_Class : public Test_Class
{
  protected:
    int m;

  public:
    Derived_Test_Class(int j = 0);
    ~Derived_Test_Class();
};

Derived_Test_Class::Derived_Test_Class(int j) : Test_Class(j+1), m(j)
{
  cout << endl;
```

```
  cout << "Derived_Test_Class Constructor Executed: "
      << "Data member initialized to "
      << m <<endl;
}
Derived_Test_Class::~Derived_Test_Class()
{
  cout << endl;
  cout << "Derived_Test_Class Destructor Executed "
      << "for object with data member "
      << m << endl;
}
int main()
{
  cout << "Test_Class object being created:" << endl;
  Test_Class tc_object1(4);
  cout << endl;
  cout << "Derived_Test_Class object being created:" << endl;
  Derived_Test_Class dtc_object1(7);

  return 0;
}
```

Program Output

Test_Class object being created:

Test_Class Constructor Executed: Data member initialized to 4

Derived_Test_Class object being created:

Test_Class Constructor Executed: Data member initialized to 8

Derived_Test_Class Constructor Executed: Data member initialized to 7

Derived_Test_Class Destructor Executed for object with data member 7

Test_Class Destructor Executed for object with data member 8

Test_Class Destructor Executed for object with data member 4

Note the order of execution of the constructors. When the Test_Class object tc_object1 is created, the constructor for Test_Class executes. When the Derived_Test_Class object dtc_object1 is created, the Derived_Test_Class constructor is invoked. However, before any of its statements execute, a call is made to the base class constructor, Test_Class(). After executing and displaying its message, the Test_Class constructor ends. At that point, the body of the constructor for Derived_Test_Class executes and displays its message. When the program ends, the objects are destroyed in the reverse order of creation. Therefore, dtc_object1 is destroyed first. The destructor for Derived_Test_Class executes and then the destructor for Test_Class executes. Finally, the Test_Class object tc_object1 is destroyed. Therefore, the Test_Class destructor executes for this object.

13.1.5 The Copy Constructor in a Derived Class

If a derived class has a copy constructor, it should be treated in the same manner as an ordinary constructor. Therefore, the derived class's copy constructor definition should call the base class's copy constructor in an initialization list. Following is dem13-2.cpp, which illustrates how to code a copy constructor.

Note 13.5   The Copy Constructor in a Derived Class

- The copy constructor of a derived class should explicitly call the copy constructor of its base class.
- Call the base class's copy constructor in an initialization list.

```
//dem13-2.cpp

//This program illustrates the copy constructor in a derived class.

#include <iostream>

using namespace std;

class Test_Class
{
  protected:
    int n;

  public:
    Test_Class(int i = 0);   //One-argument constructor
    Test_Class(const Test_Class &);   //Copy constructor
    ~Test_Class();
};

Test_Class::Test_Class(int i) : n(i)
{
  cout << endl;
  cout << "Test_Class Constructor Executed: Data member initialized to "
       << n << endl;
}

Test_Class::Test_Class(const Test_Class & tc_r) : n(tc_r.n)
{
  cout << endl;
  cout << "Test_Class Copy constructor executed: "
       << "Data member initialized to " << n << endl;
}

Test_Class::~Test_Class()
{
  cout << endl;
  cout << "Test_Class Destructor Executed for object with data member "
       << n << endl;
}
```

```
class Derived_Test_Class : public Test_Class
{
  protected:
    int m;

  public:
    Derived_Test_Class(int j = 0);
    Derived_Test_Class(const Derived_Test_Class &);
    ~Derived_Test_Class();
};

Derived_Test_Class::Derived_Test_Class(int j) : Test_Class(j+1), m(j)
{
  cout << endl;
  cout << "Derived_Test_Class Constructor Executed: "
       << "Data member initialized to "
       << m << endl;
}

Derived_Test_Class::Derived_Test_Class(const Derived_Test_Class & dtc_r)

                    : Test_Class(dtc_r), m(dtc_r.m)
{
  cout << endl;
  cout << "Derived_Test_Class Copy constructor executed: "
       << "Data member initialized to " << m << endl;
}

Derived_Test_Class::~Derived_Test_Class()
{
  cout << endl;
  cout << "Derived_Test_Class Destructor Executed "
       << "for object with data member "
       << m << endl;
}

int main()
{
  Derived_Test_Class dtc_object1(7);
  Derived_Test_Class dtc_object2 = dtc_object1;
  cout << endl;
  return 0;
}
```

Program Output

Test_Class Constructor Executed: Data member initialized to 8

Derived_Test_Class Constructor Executed: Data member initialized to 7

Test_Class Copy constructor executed: Data member initialized to 8

Derived_Test_Class Copy constructor executed: Data member initialized to 7

Derived_Test_Class Destructor Executed for object with data member 7

Test_Class Destructor Executed for object with data member 8

Derived_Test_Class Destructor Executed for object with data member 7

Test_Class Destructor Executed for object with data member 8

The code for the copy constructors is similar to the code for the constructors. Note that in the definition of the copy constructor for Test_Class, we use the expression n(tc_r.n) in the initialization list. This initializes the n instance variable of the object being initialized to the value of the n instance variable of the object that is on the right side of the initialization. The definition of the copy constructor for Derived_Test_Class calls the copy constructor, Test_Class(dtc_r), in its initialization list, and initializes the m instance variable of the object being initialized to the value of the m instance variable of the right side of the initialization, m(dtc_r.m).

Once again, note the order of execution of the constructors and destructors. The program first declares the Derived_Test_Class object dtc_object1. Therefore, the constructor for Test_Class executes first, followed by the execution of the constructor for Derived_Test_Class. Next, the program declares and initializes the Derived_Test_Class object dtc_object2. Because the object is initialized, the copy constructor is used. Just as in the case for the ordinary constructor, the copy constructor for the base class executes first. Therefore, we see that the copy constructor for Test_Class executes first, followed by the execution of the copy constructor for Derived_Test_Class.

When the program ends, the destructors are invoked for the objects in the reverse order of object creation. First the destructor for dtc_object2 executes, which, in turn, automatically executes the destructor for the base class, Test_Class. The destructors for dtc_object1 execute in a similar manner.

Exercises 13.1

Use the following class declarations to answer Exercises 1–16.

```
class Class_A
{
  private:
    int A_private;
  protected:
    int A_protected;
  public:
    Class_A(int, int);
    void A_Pub_Func();
};
```

```
class Class_B : public Class_A
{
  private:
    int B_private;
  protected:
    int B_protected;
  public:
    Class_B(int, int);
    void B_Pub_Func();
};
class Class_C : private Class_A
{
  private:
    int C_private;
  protected:
    int C_protected;
  public:
    Class_C(int, int);
    void C_Pub_Func();
};
class Class_D : public Class_B
{
  private:
    int D_private;
  protected:
    int D_protected;
  public:
    Class_D(int, int);
    void D_Pub_Func();
};
class Class_E : public Class_C
{
  private:
    int E_private;
  protected:
    int E_protected;
  public:
    Class_E(int, int);
    void E_Pub_Func();
};
```

1. Draw the class hierarchy diagram for the classes.
2. Which classes are directly derived from Class_A?
3. Which classes are indirectly derived from Class_A?
4. Which classes can you call base classes?
5. Using Table 13.2, list all the private, protected, and public members of Class_B, including those inherited from the base class.

6. Using Table 13.2, list all the private, protected, and public members of Class_C, including those inherited from the base class.

7. Using Table 13.2, list all the private, protected, and public members of Class_D, including those inherited from the base class.

8. Using Table 13.2, list all the private, protected, and public members of Class_E, including those inherited from the base class.

9. Write the code for the two-argument constructor for Class_A. The constructor should assign its first argument to the class's private instance variable and the second argument to its protected instance variable.

10. Write the code for the two-argument constructor for Class_B. The constructor should assign its first argument to the class's private instance variable and the second argument to its protected instance variable. Pass the same two arguments to the base class constructor using an initialization list.

11. Write the code for the two-argument constructor for Class_C. The constructor should assign its first argument to the class's private instance variable and the second argument to its protected instance variable. Pass the same two arguments to the base class constructor using an initialization list.

12. Write the code for the two-argument constructor for Class_D. The constructor should assign its first argument to the class's private instance variable and the second argument to its protected instance variable. Pass the same two arguments to the base class constructor using an initialization list.

13. Write the code for the two-argument constructor for Class_E. The constructor should assign its first argument to the class's private instance variable and the second argument to its protected instance variable. Pass the same two arguments to the base class constructor using an initialization list.

Assume the constructors of Exercises 9–13 and the following declarations, which are made in main().

```
Class_A a_object(1,1);
Class_B b_object(2,2);
Class_C c_object(3,3);
Class_D d_object(4,4);
Class_E e_object(5,5);
```

14. List the values of all the instance variables of a_object, b_object, c_object, d_object, and e_object.

15. Code a destructor for each of Class_A, Class_B, Class_C, Class_D, and Class_E.

16. Code a copy constructor for each of Class_A, Class_B, Class_C, Class_D, and Class_E.

17. Write class declarations for the classes depicted in Figure 13.2. Choose how each class should be derived from its base class (public or private) based on how you think that the class instance variables should be accessible. Code only the instance variables of each class.

Experiments 13.1

1. In dem13-1.cpp, remove the call `Test_Class(j+1)` from the initialization list of the constructor of `Derived_Test_Class`. Compile, execute, and test the resulting program. What are the results?
2. In dem13-2.cpp., remove the call `Test_Class(dtc_r)` from the initialization list of the copy constructor of `Derived_Test_Class`. Compile, execute, and test the resulting program. What are the results?

Programming Problems 13.1

1. A Web page is one of several types of document that can constitute a Web site. Code a class `Document` from which you should derive the `WebPage` class of previous Programming Problems. The `Document` class should have a `url` instance variable, which is a string that represents the URL of the document, and an integer member `downloads`. Because `url` and `downloads` are members of `Document`, they and all associated methods should be removed from the `WebPage` class and placed into the `Document` class. In addition to `WebPage`, derive from `Document` the classes `DataFile` and `MultimediaFile`. The class `DataFile` should contain the integer instance variable `num_records`, which represents the number of data records in the file, and the integer instance variable `record_size`, which represents the size in bytes of each record in the file. The class `MultimediaFile` should contain the integer instance variable `file_type`, which represents the type of multimedia file, and the integer instance variable `size`, which represents the size in KB of the file. Code all appropriate constructors, copy constructors, and destructors for the classes. Code a function `main()` to test the classes. Make sure to create objects of all types.

2. An `OilTank` is just one of several types of storage tanks that can be maintained at a storage facility. Code a class `StorageTank` from which you should derive the class `OilTank` of previous Programming Problems. `StorageTank` should have two instance variables, a string `company_name`, which represents the name of the company that owns the tank, and a five-character array `id_no[]`, which represents the tank number. `OilTank` will inherit these instance variables, so you should remove the `company_name` and `id_no` from the class declaration of `OilTank`. The methods `Get_Name()` and `Get_ID()` should now be members of `StorageTank`. Also, derive from `StorageTank` the class `GasTank`. A `GasTank` object represents a tank that stores natural gas. `GasTank` should contain the double instance variable `volume`, which represents the volume in cubic feet of the tank, and the double instance variable `contents`, which represents the current volume of gas in the tank. `GasTank` should also have an `Add()` and a `Remove()` method. Code all appropriate constructors, copy constructors, and destructors for the classes. Code a function `main()` to test the classes. Make sure to create objects of all types.

3. The `VehicleService` class of previous Programming Problems was not very specific about the type of vehicle being serviced. Different types of vehicles might be serviced according to different rate schedules. Change each of `Set_Parts()` and `Set_Hours()` methods so that it sets only the value of the corresponding data

member to the argument of the function. Neither method should change the value of the total cost of service. Derive from `VehicleService` the classes `PrivateVehicle` and `Truck`. `PrivateVehicle` should have no additional instance variables. `Truck` should have an integer instance variable, `num_axles`, which represents the number of axles on the truck. Code all appropriate constructors, copy constructors, and destructors for the classes. Code a function `main()` to test the classes. Make sure to create objects of all types.

4. There are several types of rooms in a hotel. The `HotelRoom` class of previous Programming Problems was not specific regarding the type of room. Assume that a hotel has guest rooms and meeting rooms. Modify the `HotelRoom` class as follows: remove the `capacity` and `status` instance variables and associated methods. Change the class's constructor, copy constructor, and destructor accordingly. Derive from `HotelRoom` the classes `GuestRoom` and `MeetingRoom`. `GuestRoom` contains the following data members: the integer instance variable `capacity`, which represents the maximum number of guests that can occupy the room; the integer instance variable `status`, which represents the number of guests in the room (0 if unoccupied); and the integer instance variable `days`, which represents the number of days the guest occupies the room. `MeetingRoom` has the integer instance variable `seats`, which represents the number of seats in the room, and the integer instance variable `status` (1 if the room is booked for a meeting; 0 otherwise). Code all appropriate constructors, copy constructors, and destructors for the classes. Code a function `main()` to test the classes. Make sure to create objects of all types.

13.2 FUNCTIONS IN CLASS HIERARCHIES

According to Note 13.3, all functions are inherited except constructors, copy constructors, destructors, overloaded operators, and `friend` functions. This section discusses those functions that are inherited.

13.2.1 Inheriting a Function

Suppose `Test_Class` contains the following method `Get_Value()`.

```
int Test_Class::Get_Value()
{
    return n;
}
```

`Get_Value()` is inherited by the derived class `Derived_Test_Class`. Therefore, we can apply `Get_Value()` to any `Derived_Test_Class` object as follows.

```
Derived_Test_Class dtc_object(7);

cout << endl << endl;

cout << "The value returned by Get_Value() is "
    << dtc_object.Get_Value() << endl;
```

When a method is applied to an object of a certain class, the compiler checks to see if the method is a method of that class. If the method is a class member, the compiler applies that method to the object. If the method is not a class member, the compiler checks to see if the method is a member of a base class (if there is one) of the class. If the method is a member of the class's base class, then it applies that method to the object, and so on. In our case, the compiler sees that the method is not a member of Derived_Test_Class and so looks in the base class Test_Class. Because Get_Value() is a method of Test_Class, the compiler applies the base class's Get_Value()method to dtc_object. It makes sense to do this because, by means of inheritance, dtc_object is also a Test_Class object. The object dtc_object has an m instance variable of value 7 and an n instance variable of value 8. Thus, the previous cout statement will display

> The value returned by Get_Value() is 8

The program dem13-3.cpp verifies this.

```cpp
//dem13-3.cpp

//This program illustrates how a function is inherited.

#include <iostream>

using namespace std;

class Test_Class
{
  protected:
    int n;

  public:
    Test_Class(int i = 0);   //One-argument constructor
    ~Test_Class();
    int Get_Value();
};

Test_Class::Test_Class(int i) : n(i)
{
  cout << endl;
  cout << "Test_Class Constructor Executed: Data member initialized to "
       << n << endl;
}

Test_Class::~Test_Class()
{
  cout << endl;
  cout << "Test_Class Destructor Executed for object with data member "
       << n << endl;
}

int Test_Class::Get_Value()
{
  return n;
}
```

```
class Derived_Test_Class : public Test_Class
{
  protected:
    int m;

  public:
    Derived_Test_Class(int j = 0);
    ~Derived_Test_Class();
};

Derived_Test_Class::Derived_Test_Class(int j) : Test_Class(j+1), m(j)
{
  cout << endl;
  cout << "Derived_Test_Class Constructor Executed: "
       << "Data member initialized to " << m << endl;
}

Derived_Test_Class::~Derived_Test_Class()
{
  cout << endl;
  cout << "Derived_Test_Class Destructor Executed "
       << "for object with data member " << m << endl;
}

int main()
{
  Derived_Test_Class dtc_object(7);

  cout << endl;
  cout << "The value returned by Get_Value() is "
       << dtc_object.Get_Value();

  cout << endl;
  return 0;
}
```

Program Output

```
Test_Class Constructor Executed: Data member initialized to 8

Derived_Test_Class Constructor Executed: Data member initialized to 7

The value returned by Get_Value() is 8

Derived_Test_Class Destructor Executed for object with data member 7

Test_Class Destructor Executed for object with data member 8
```

13.2.2 Method Overriding

What happens if Derived_Test_Class and Test_Class each has its own Get_Value() method? Consider the following program in which we have added a Get_Value() method to *both* Test_Class and Derived_Test_Class.

```cpp
//dem13-4.cpp

//This program illustrates method overriding.

#include <iostream>

using namespace std;

class Test_Class
{
  protected:
    int n;

  public:
    Test_Class(int i = 0);  //One-argument constructor
    Test_Class(Test_Class &);  //Copy constructor
    ~Test_Class();
    int Get_Value();
};

Test_Class::Test_Class(int i) : n(i)
{
  cout << endl;
  cout << "Test_Class Constructor Executed: Data member initialized to "
       << n << endl;
}

Test_Class::Test_Class(Test_Class & tc_r) : n(tc_r.n)
{
  cout << endl;
  cout << "Test_Class Copy constructor executed: "
       << "Data member initialized to " << n << endl;
}

Test_Class::~Test_Class()
{
  cout << endl;
  cout << "Test_Class Destructor Executed for object with data member "
       << n << endl;
}

int Test_Class::Get_Value()
{
  return n;
}

class Derived_Test_Class : public Test_Class
{
  protected:
    int m;

  public:
    Derived_Test_Class(int j = 0);
    Derived_Test_Class(Derived_Test_Class &);
    ~Derived_Test_Class();
```

```
     int Get_Value();
};
Derived_Test_Class::Derived_Test_Class(int j) : Test_Class(j+1), m(j)
{
   cout << endl;
   cout << "Derived_Test_Class Constructor Executed: "
        << "Data member initialized to " << m << endl;
}
Derived_Test_Class::Derived_Test_Class(Derived_Test_Class & dtc_r)

                                 : Test_Class(dtc_r), m(dtc_r.m)
{
   cout << endl;
   cout << "Derived_Test_Class Copy constructor executed: "
        << "Data member initialized to " << m << endl;
}
Derived_Test_Class::~Derived_Test_Class()
{
   cout << endl;
   cout << "Derived_Test_Class Destructor Executed "
        << "for object with data member " << m << endl;
}
int Derived_Test_Class::Get_Value()
{
   return m;
}
int main()
{
   Test_Class tc_object(3);
   Derived_Test_Class dtc_object(7);

   cout << endl;
   cout << "The n value of the Test_Class object is "
        << tc_object.Get_Value() << endl <<endl;

   cout << "The m value of the Derived_Test_Class object is "
        << dtc_object.Get_Value();

   cout << endl;
   return 0;
}
```

Program Output

Test_Class Constructor Executed: Data member initialized to 3

Test_Class Constructor Executed: Data member initialized to 8

Derived_Test_Class Constructor Executed: Data member initialized to 7

The n value of the Test_Class object is 3

The m value of the Derived_Test_Class object is 7

Derived_Test_Class Destructor Executed for object with data member 7

Test_Class Destructor Executed for object with data member 8

Test_Class Destructor Executed for object with data member 3

In main, we apply Get_Value() to two objects in different classes. The C++ compiler knows which Get_Value() method to use by the object to which the method is applied. In the first case, Get_Value() is applied to a Test_Class object. Therefore, the Get_Value()method from Test_Class is used. In the second case, Get_Value() is applied to a Derived_Test_Class object. Therefore, the Get_Value()method from Derived_Test_Class is used. This is known as **method overriding**; when a method is applied to an object in a derived class, the method in the derived class overrides the method of the same name and signature (i.e., same number and types of arguments) in the base class.

If the method names are the same and the signatures are different, overriding does not take place. For example, suppose Derive_Test_Class's Get_Value() method is defined as follows.

```
int Get_Value(int i)
{
   return m + i;
}
```

Then, the method call dtc_object.Get_Value() uses the Get_Value() method of Test_Class and the method call dtc_object.Get_Value(4) uses the Get_Value() method of Derived_Test_Class. See Experiment 1.

13.2.3 Using the Scope Resolution Operator

Suppose again that Test_Class and Derived_Test_Class have their own Get_Value()methods and that we want to apply the Get_Value()method of the base class to a Derived_Test_Class object to access its n instance variable.

To apply the base class's Get_Value()method to an object in the derived class, you must qualify the name of the method with the name of the class followed by the scope resolution operator ::. Thus, the expression dtc_object.Test_Class::Get_Value() applies Test_Class's Get_Value() method to dtc_object. The scope resolution operator can also be used to access a global variable when there is a local variable of the same name. See Experiment 2.

The following program, dem13-5.cpp, illustrates this use of the scope resolution operator.

```
//dem13-5.cpp

//This program illustrates the scope resolution operator.

#include <iostream>
```

```cpp
using namespace std;

class Test_Class
{
  protected:
    int n;

  public:
    Test_Class(int i = 0);  //One-argument constructor
    Test_Class(const Test_Class &);  //Copy constructor
    ~Test_Class();
    int Get_Value();
};

Test_Class::Test_Class(int i) : n(i)
{
  cout << endl;
  cout << "Test_Class Constructor Executed: Data member initialized to "
       << n << endl;
}

Test_Class::Test_Class(const Test_Class & tc_r) : n(tc_r.n)
{
  cout << endl;
  cout << "Test_Class Copy constructor executed: "
       << "Data member initialized to " << n << endl;
}

Test_Class::~Test_Class()
{
  cout << endl;
  cout << "Test_Class Destructor Executed for object with data member "
       << n << endl;
}

int Test_Class::Get_Value()
{
  return n;
}

class Derived_Test_Class : public Test_Class
{
  protected:
    int m;

  public:
    Derived_Test_Class(int j = 0);
    Derived_Test_Class(const Derived_Test_Class &);
    ~Derived_Test_Class();
    int Get_Value();
};
```

```
Derived_Test_Class::Derived_Test_Class(int j) : Test_Class(j+1), m(j)
{
   cout << endl;
   cout << "Derived_Test_Class Constructor Executed: "
        << "Data member initialized to " << m << endl;
}

Derived_Test_Class::Derived_Test_Class(const Derived_Test_Class & dtc_r)
                   :Test_Class(dtc_r), m(dtc_r.m)
{
   cout << endl;
   cout << "Derived_Test_Class Copy constructor executed: "
        << "Data member initialized to " << m << endl;
}

Derived_Test_Class::~Derived_Test_Class()
{
   cout << endl;
   cout << "Derived_Test_Class Destructor Executed "
        << "for object with data member " << m << endl;
}

int Derived_Test_Class::Get_Value()
{
   return m;
}

int main()
{
   Test_Class tc_object(3);
   Derived_Test_Class dtc_object(7);

   cout << endl << endl;
   cout << "The n value of the Test_Class object is "
        << tc_object.Get_Value() << endl << endl;

   cout << "The m value of the Derived_Test_Class object is "
        << dtc_object.Get_Value() << endl << endl;

   cout << "The n value of the Derived_Test_Class object is "
        << dtc_object.Test_Class::Get_Value();

   cout << endl;

   return 0;
}
```

Program Output

```
Test_Class Constructor Executed: Data member initialized to 3

Test_Class Constructor Executed: Data member initialized to 8

Derived_Test_Class Constructor Executed: Data member initialized to 7

The n value of the Test_Class object is 3

The m value of the Derived_Test_Class object is 7
```

```
The n value of the Derived_Test_Class object is 8

Derived_Test_Class Destructor Executed for object with data member 7

Test_Class Destructor Executed for object with data member 8

Test_Class Destructor Executed for object with data member 3
```

Note 13.6 summarizes the results of this section.

Note 13.6   Methods in a Class Hierarchy

· A base-class method is inherited by all classes derived from it either directly or indirectly.

· If a derived class contains a method of the same name and signature as a
method of the base class, the derived class's version of the method overrides the base class's version.

· To apply an overridden base class method to a derived class object, qualify
the method name with the base class name followed by the scope resolution operator : :.

Exercises 13.2

Use the following declarations to answer Exercises 1–7. They are the same classes used
in Exercises 13.1 with the code provided for the public methods.

```
class Class_A
{
  private:
    int A_private;
  protected:
    int A_protected;
  public:
    Class_A(int, int);
    void A_Pub_Func() {cout << endl<< "Class_A's method";}
};

class Class_B : public Class_A
{
 private:
    int B_private;
  protected:
    int B_protected;
```

```
  public:
    Class_B(int, int);
    void B_Pub_Func(){cout << endl << "Class_B's method";}
    void A_Pub_Func(){cout << endl << "Class_B' A method";}
};

class Class_C : private Class_A
{
 private:
    int C_private;
 protected:
    int C_protected;
 public:
    Class_C(int, int);
    void C_Pub_Func(){cout << endl << "Class_C's method";}
};
class Class_D : public Class_B
{
 private:
    int D_private;
 protected:
    int D_protected;
 public:
    Class_D(int, int);
    void D_Pub_Func(){cout << endl << "Class_D's method";}
    void A_Pub_Func(){cout << endl << "Class_D's A method";}
};

class Class_E : public Class_C
{
 private:
    int E_private;
 protected:
    int E_protected;
 public:
    Class_E(int, int);
    void E_Pub_Func(){cout << endl << "Class_E's method";}
};
```

Now assume that the following declarations have been made in main().

```
Class_A a_object(1,1);
Class_B b_object(2,2);
Class_C c_object(3,3);
Class_D d_object(4,4);
Class_E e_object(5,5);
```

Which of the statements in Exercises 1–6 are legal? For those that are legal, state what each will display.

1. `a_object.A_Pub_Func();`
2. `b_object.A_Pub_Func();`
3. `d_object.A_Pub_Func();`
4. `b_object.C_pub_Func();`
5. `e_object.C_Pub_Func();`
6. `e_object.A_Pub_Func();`
7. How would you apply `Class_A`'s `A_Pub_Func()` to `b_object`? to `d_object`?

Experiments 13.2

1. In dem13-4.cpp, redefine `Get_Value()` as follows.

   ```
   int Get_Value(int i) {return m + i;}
   ```

   Include in `main()` the following statements.

   ```
   Derived_Test_Class dtc_object(5);

   cout << dtc_object.Get_Value() << endl;

   cout << dtc_object.Get_Value(4) << endl;
   ```

   What do the `cout` statements display?

2. The scope resolution operator can be used to access a global variable when there is a local variable of the same name. For example, consider the following declarations. In the function `Func()`, `::n` refers to the global variable `n`.

   ```
   int n = 6;
   void Func()
   {
      int n = 17;

      cout << "The local n = " << n << endl;
      cout << "The global n = " << ::n << endl;
   }
   ```

   Write a program that uses these declarations and tests the method `Func()`.

Programming Problems 13.2

1. In the `Document` class hierarchy of Programming Problem 1 in Section 13.1, do the following. Code an `Activity()` method for class `DataFile` that returns the number of bytes downloaded (downloads multiplied by `num_records` multiplied by `record_size`). Code an `Activity()` method for class `MultimediaFile` that returns the number of bytes downloaded (`downloads` multiplied by `size`). For each of `WebPage`, `DataFile`, and `MultimediaFile`, code an appropriate `Display()` method, which displays in a nicely formatted way the values of the instance variables (even the inherited ones). Write a `main()` in which you create objects from each of the three classes and apply the `Activity()` and `Display()` methods.

2. In the StorageTank class hierarchy of Programming Problem 2, Section 13.1, do the following. Code a Display() method for each of the classes OilTank and GasTank, which displays in an appropriately formatted way the values of the instance variables of the class (including the inherited ones). Code a Remainder()method for OilTank, which returns the capacity minus the contents of a tank. Code a Remainder() method for GasTank that which returns the volume minus the contents of a tank. Write a main() in which you create objects from each class and apply the Display() and Remainder()methods.

3. Using the VehicleService class hierarchy of Programming Problem 3, Section 13.1, do the following: PrivateVehicle should have a method, CalculateBill(), which returns a double and has no arguments. The method should calculate the bill as follows: the number of hours multiplied by 70.00, plus the cost of parts. Truck should also have a CalculateBill() method, which computes the bill as follows: the number of hours multiplied by 85.00, plus the cost of parts, plus the number of axles multiplied by 100.00. Code a Display() method for each of PrivateVehicle and Truck, which displays in an appropriately formatted way the values of the instance variables of the class (including the inherited ones). Code a main() in which you create objects of each type, compute the bill for each object, and display each object's information.

4. Using the HotelRoom class hierarchy of Programming Problem 4, Section 13.1, do the following: GuestRoom contains the method CalculateBill(), which returns the amount of the guest's bill. The bill is calculated as follows: the room rate (this is inherited from HotelRoom) multiplied by the number of days of the stay, multiplied by the status (which represents the number of guests, is also inherited from HotelRoom). MeetingRoom also contains the method CalculateBill(), which returns the amount of the bill for renting the room for one day. The method calculates the bill as follows: the number of seats multiplied by 10.00, plus 500.00. Code a Display() method for each of GuestRoom and MeetingRoom, which displays in an appropriately formatted way the values of the instance variables of the class (including the inherited ones). Code a main() in which you create objects of each type, compute the bill for each object, and display each object's information.

13.3 POLYMORPHISM

In a class hierarchy, several classes may each contain its own version of a method. When using pointers to access objects, polymorphism allows the data type of the object to determine which of these methods is applied.

13.3.1 The Class Hierarchy

To focus on the important concepts in this section, we shall use a very simple class hierarchy based on familiar geometric figures and their areas. Suppose we are developing a drawing application that needs to define and manipulate simple geometric figures and compute their areas. The figures are rectangles, circles, and trapezoids. Because these are geometric shapes, we decide to derive them from the class Shape. Figure 13.6

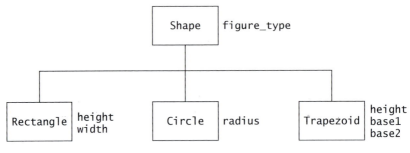

Figure 13.6

shows the class hierarchy. To the right of each class in the figure are the private instance variables of the class. Each class will have a constructor, a destructor, and a method, Area(), that computes the area of the figure using the appropriate formula.

Problem: Suppose we want to enable the user to create a series of shapes of his or her own choosing. Thus, the user can first decide to create a rectangle of a certain size, then a circle with a certain radius, and so on. After the user has created the shapes, we want the program to display the areas of all the figures. How can we do this? The way you might think of approaching the problem is to create an array of shapes. However, all the elements in an array must be of the same type. We cannot place a rectangle object and a circle object into the same array because they are of different data types. The answer, as we shall see, is to use an array of Shape pointers and to employ the concept of polymorphism.

13.3.2 Defining the Classes

Following are the class declarations for the classes Shape, Rectangle, Circle, and Trapezoid. For simplicity, we define all methods in the class declarations. When this is done, you do not have to prefix the class name and scope resolution operator to the method name in the method definition. Because the method is defined inside the class declaration, the compiler knows to which class the method belongs.

```
class Shape
{
  protected:
    string figure_type;
  public:
    Shape(string ft = "Default Figure") : figure_type(ft)
            {cout << endl << "Shape Constructor" << endl;}
    string Get_Type() {return figure_type;}
    ~Shape() {cout << endl << "Shape Destructor" << endl;}
    double Area() {return 0.0;}
};

class Rectangle : public Shape
{
  protected:
    double height, width;
```

```
public:
    Rectangle(double h, double w): Shape("Rectangle"), height(h),width(w)
            {cout << endl << "Rectangle Constructor" << endl;}
    ~Rectangle() {cout << endl << "Rectangle Destructor" << endl;}
    double Area() {return height * width;}
};
class Circle : public Shape
{
  protected:
    double radius;
  public:
    Circle(double r) : Shape("Circle"), radius(r)
            {cout << endl << "Circle Constructor" << endl;}
    ~Circle() {cout << endl << "Circle Destructor" << endl;}
    double Area() {return 3.1416 * radius * radius;}
};

class Trapezoid : public Shape
{
  protected:
    double base1, base2, height;
  public:
    Trapezoid(double b1, double b2, double h)
               : Shape("Trapezoid"), base1(b1), base2(b2), height(h)
            {cout << endl << "Trapezoid Constructor" << endl;}
    ~Trapezoid() {cout << endl << "Trapezoid Destructor" << endl;}
     double Area() {return 0.5 * height * (base1 + base2);}
};
```

The base class Shape has one data member, the string object figure_type, whose value is the name of the type of figure (Rectangle, Circle, or Trapezoid). We also include an accessor method Get_Type() that returns the figure name. Both figure_type and Get_Type() are inherited by the Rectangle, Circle, and Trapezoid classes. The constructors perform initialization in their initialization lists. The body of each constructor and destructor displays an identification message.

Note that in the initialization list for the Shape constructor is figure_type(ft). An entry in an initialization list is equivalent to an initialization. Therefore, figure_type(ft) is equivalent to the following,

```
string figure_type = ft;
```

We define a dummy Area() method in the Shape class that returns the value zero. Each of the other classes is derived publicly from class Shape. The constructors for Rectangle, Circle, and Trapezoid call the constructor for the base class Shape and pass to that constructor the name of the object being created. The Area() method for each class returns the area based on the formula for the area of that shape.

13.3.3 Pointers in a Class Hierarchy

We can declare a Rectangle pointer, or a Circle pointer, or a Trapezoid pointer and have each point to an object of the appropriate type. For example, we could make the following declarations.

```
Rectangle r1(3, 5);
Circle c1(7);
Trapezoid t1(4, 2, 6);

Rectangle* r_p = &r1;
Circle* c_p = &c1;
Trapezoid* t_p = &t1;
```

A Shape pointer can point to a Rectangle object, or a Circle object, or a Trapezoid object because, by inheritance, each of these is a Shape object. Thus, continuing from the previous declarations, the following are legal.

```
Shape* s_p1;
Shape* s_p2;
Shape* s_p3;

s_p1 = &r1;
s_p2 = &c1;
s_p3 = &t1;
```

Although s_p1, s_p2, and s_p3 are Shape pointers, they are allowed to point to objects in any derived class. Note, however, that the converse is not true. That is, a Rectangle pointer (or a Circle pointer or a Trapezoid pointer) cannot point to a Shape object.

Note 13.7 Base Class Pointers

- In a class hierarchy, a base class pointer can point to an object of any class derived (either directly or indirectly) from the base class.
- The converse is not true: a derived class pointer cannot point to a base class object.

That a base class pointer can point to an object from a derived class brings up an interesting question. Using the previous declarations and assignments, suppose we now code the following.

```
cout    << "The area of the rectangle is " << s_p1 -> Area() << endl;
```

The pointer s_p1 is a Shape pointer, but it points to a Rectangle object. Whose Area() method will this statement execute: that of the Rectangle class or that of the base class Shape? The output of the following program answers the question.

```
//dem13-6.cpp

//This program demonstrates the use of pointers and methods
//in a class hierarchy.

#include <iostream>
#include <iomanip>
#include <string>
```

```cpp
using namespace std;
class Shape
{
  protected:
    string figure_type;
  public:
    Shape(string ft = "Default Figure") : figure_type(ft)
             {cout <<    endl << "Shape Constructor" << endl;}
    string Get_Type() {return figure_type;}
    ~Shape() {cout << endl << "Shape Destructor" << endl;}
    double Area() {return 0.0;}
};
class Rectangle : public Shape
{
  protected:
    double height, width;
  public:
    Rectangle(double h, double w): Shape("Rectangle"), height(h),width(w)
             {cout << endl << "Rectangle Constructor" << endl;}
    ~Rectangle() {cout << endl << "Rectangle Destructor" << endl;}
    double Area() {return height * width;}
};

class Circle : public Shape
{
  protected:
    double radius;
  public:
    Circle(double r) : Shape("Circle"), radius(r)
             {cout << endl << "Circle Constructor" << endl;}
    ~Circle() {cout << endl << "Circle Destructor" << endl;}
    double Area() {return 3.1416 * radius * radius;}
};

class Trapezoid : public Shape
{
  protected:
    double base1, base2, height;
  public:
    Trapezoid(double b1, double b2, double h)
               : Shape("Trapezoid"), base1(b1), base2(b2), height(h)
             {cout << endl << "Trapezoid Constructor" << endl;}
    ~Trapezoid() {cout << endl << "Trapezoid Destructor" << endl;}
    double Area() {return 0.5 * height * (base1 + base2);}
};

int main()
{

  cout << setprecision(4)
       << setiosflags(ios::fixed)
```

```
        << setiosflags(ios::showpoint);
    Shape* s_p1;
    Circle* c_p1;
    Circle c1(5);

    s_p1 = &c1;                 //Shape pointer points to a Circle object

    c_p1 = &c1;                 //Circle pointer points to a Circle object

    cout << endl;
    cout << "Area() applied through Circle pointer: "
         << c_p1 -> Area() << endl << endl;

    cout << "Area() applied through Shape pointer: "
         << s_p1 -> Area() << endl << endl;

    cout << endl;
    return 0;
}
```

Program Output

```
Shape Constructor.

Circle Constructor.

Area() applied through Circle pointer: 78.5400

Area() applied through Shape pointer: 0.0000

Circle Destructor.

Shape Destructor.
```

From the two lines displayed by cout in main(), we see that the Area() method applied to the Circle object through the Circle pointer yields the correct area of 78.5400. However, the Area() method that is applied to the Circle object through the Shape pointer is the Area() method from the Shape class. Although s_p1 points to a Circle object, the base class method is invoked when it is applied to the object through a base class pointer. Thus, method overriding does not work in this case.

13.3.4 Virtual Methods and Polymorphism

The concept of **polymorphism** (literally, "many forms") extends method overriding to the case of objects in a derived class accessed through a base class pointer. To implement polymorphism, the method that is to be overridden must be declared to be **virtual**. The keyword virtual must appear in the declaration of the method in the base class. The following program demonstrates the difference that declaring Area() as a virtual method makes to the output of the previous program.

```
//dem13-7.cpp

//This program demonstrates the use of a virtual function
//in a class hierarchy.
```

```cpp
#include <iostream>
#include <iomanip>
#include <string>

using namespace std;

class Shape
{
  protected:
    string figure_type;
  public:
    Shape(string ft = "Default Figure") : figure_type(ft)
      {cout << endl << "Shape Constructor" << endl;}
    string Get_Type() {return figure_type;}
    ~Shape() {cout << endl << "Shape Destructor" << endl;}
    virtual double Area() {return 0.0;}
};

class Rectangle : public Shape
{
  protected:
    double height, width;
  public:
    Rectangle(double h, double w): Shape("Rectangle"), height(h),width(w)
      {cout << endl << "Rectangle Constructor" << endl;}
    ~Rectangle() {cout << endl << "Rectangle Destructor" << endl;}
    double Area() {return height * width;}
};

class Circle : public Shape
{
  protected:
    double radius;
  public:
    Circle(double r) : Shape("Circle"), radius(r)
        {cout << endl << "Circle Constructor" << endl;}
    ~Circle() {cout << endl << "Circle Destructor" << endl;}
    double Area() {return 3.1416 * radius * radius;}
};

class Trapezoid : public Shape
{
  protected:
    double base1, base2, height;
  public:
    Trapezoid(double b1, double b2, double h)
            : Shape("Trapezoid"), base1(b1), base2(b2), height(h)
        {cout << endl << "Trapezoid Constructor" << endl;}
    ~Trapezoid() {cout << endl << "Trapezoid Destructor" << endl;}
    double Area() {return 0.5 * height * (base1 + base2);}
};
```

```
int main()
{
  cout << setprecision(4)
       << setiosflags(ios::fixed)
       << setiosflags(ios::showpoint);

  Shape* s_p1;
  Circle* c_p1;

  Circle c1(5);

  s_p1 = &c1;                //Shape pointer points to a Circle object

  c_p1 = &c1;                //Circle pointer points to a Circle object

  cout << endl;
  cout << "Area() applied through Circle pointer: "
       << c_p1 -> Area() << endl << endl;

  cout << "Area() applied through Shape pointer: "
       << s_p1 -> Area() << endl << endl;

  cout << endl;

  return 0;
}
```

Program Output

Shape Constructor.

Circle Constructor.

Area() applied through Circle pointer: 78.5400

Area() applied through Shape pointer: 78.5400

Circle Destructor.

Shape Destructor.

This time, the second cout statement executes the Area() method of the target of the Shape pointer s_p1. It does so because we declared the Area() method in the base class Shape as a virtual method.

Polymorphism allows the choice of method to depend on the data type of the target of the pointer rather than on the data type of the pointer. For polymorphism to work, follow the guidelines of Note 13. 8.

13.3.5 Virtual Destructors

Now consider the following program, dem13-8.cpp, in which we have replaced the statically declared object c1 of the previous program by a dynamically allocated object pointed to by s_p1.

Note 13.8   Polymorphism

Polymorphism allows the choice of method to depend on the data type of the target of the pointer rather than on the data type of the pointer.

- For polymorphism to work, objects in the class hierarchy must be accessed through pointers.
- Only class methods can be `virtual`.
- For a method in the derived class to override a `virtual` method in the base class, the method in the derived class must have the same name and signature (number and type of arguments) as the base class method.
- A method in a derived class with the same name and signature as a `virtual` method in a base class is also `virtual`, whether or not the `virtual` keyword appears in its declaration. (Thus, the `Area()` methods in the derived classes in the previous program are also `virtual`.)

```cpp
//dem13-8.cpp

//This program demonstrates the incorrect use of destructors
//in a class hierarchy.

#include <iostream>
#include <iomanip>
#include <string>

using namespace std;

class Shape
{
  protected:
    string figure_type;
  public:
    Shape(string ft = "Default Figure") : figure_type(ft)
      {cout << endl << "Shape Constructor" << endl;}
    string Get_Type() {return figure_type;}
    ~Shape() {cout << endl << "Shape Destructor" << endl;}
    virtual double Area() {return 0.0;}
};
class Rectangle : public Shape
{
  protected:
    double height, width;
  public:
    Rectangle(double h, double w): Shape("Rectangle"), height(h),width(w)
      {cout << endl << "Rectangle Constructor" << endl;}
    ~Rectangle() {cout << endl << "Rectangle Destructor" << endl;}
    double Area() {return height * width;}
};
```

```cpp
class Circle : public Shape
{
  protected:
    double radius;
  public:
    Circle(double r) : Shape("Circle"), radius(r)
      {cout << endl << "Circle Constructor" << endl;}
    ~Circle() {cout << endl << "Circle Destructor" << endl;}
    double Area() {return 3.1416 * radius * radius;}
};

class Trapezoid : public Shape
{
  protected:
    double base1, base2, height;
  public:
    Trapezoid(double b1, double b2, double h)
          : Shape("Trapezoid"), base1(b1), base2(b2), height(h)
      {cout << endl << "Trapezoid Constructor" << endl;}
    ~Trapezoid() {cout << endl << "Trapezoid Destructor" << endl;}
    double Area() {return 0.5 * height * (base1 + base2);}
};

int main()
{
  cout << setprecision(4)
       << setiosflags(ios::fixed)
       << setiosflags(ios::showpoint);

  Shape* s_p1 = new Circle (5);

  cout << endl;
  cout << "Area() applied through Shape pointer: "
       << s_p1 -> Area() << endl;

  delete s_p1;

  cout << endl;

  return 0;
}
```

Program Output

Shape Constructor.

Circle Constructor.

Area() applied through Shape pointer: 78.5400

Shape Destructor.

When the `delete` statement is executed for `s_p1`, which points to a `Circle` object, only the destructor for the base class executes. This is because the destructor is applied to the object through the pointer. Because the base class destructor is not declared as virtual, applying the destructor to the target of s_p1 executes the base class destructor and not the destructor of the derived class.

To properly execute the destructors, that is, to execute the destructor for the derived class and then execute the destructor for the base class, make the destructor of the base class a virtual method.

Note 13.9   Virtual Destructors

To ensure the proper execution sequence of destructors for dynamically allocated objects in a class hierarchy, declare the base class destructor as a virtual method.

The following program, dem13-9.cpp, uses virtual destructors.

```cpp
//dem13-9.cpp

//This program demonstrates the correct use of destructors
//in a class hierarchy.

#include <iostream>
#include <iomanip>
#include <string>

using namespace std;

class Shape
{
  protected:
    string figure_type;
  public:
    Shape(string ft = "Default Figure") : figure_type(ft)
      {cout << endl << "Shape Constructor" << endl;}
    string Get_Type() {return figure_type;}
    virtual ~Shape() {cout << endl << "Shape Destructor" << endl;}
    virtual double Area() {return 0.0;}
};

class Rectangle : public Shape
{
  protected:
    double height, width;
  public:
    Rectangle(double h, double w): Shape("Rectangle"), height(h),width(w)
      {cout << endl << "Rectangle Constructor" << endl;}
    virtual ~Rectangle() {cout << endl << "Rectangle Destructor" << endl;}
    double Area() {return height * width;}
};

class Circle : public Shape
{
  protected:
    double radius;
```

```
  public:
    Circle(double r) : Shape("Circle"), radius(r)
      {cout << endl << "Circle Constructor" << endl;}
    virtual ~Circle() {cout << endl << "Circle Destructor" << endl;}
    double Area() {return 3.1416 * radius * radius;}
};
class Trapezoid : public Shape
{
  protected:
    double base1, base2, height;
  public:
    Trapezoid(double b1, double b2, double h)
          : Shape("Trapezoid"), base1(b1), base2(b2), height(h)
        {cout << endl << "Trapezoid Constructor" << endl;}
    virtual ~Trapezoid() {cout << endl << "Trapezoid Destructor" << endl;}
    double Area() {return 0.5 * height * (base1 + base2);}
};
int main()
{
  cout << setprecision(4)
       << setiosflags(ios::fixed)
       << setiosflags(ios::showpoint);

  Shape* s_p1 = new Circle (5);

  cout << endl;

  cout << "Area() for the " << s_p1 -> Get_Type()
       << " applied through Shape pointer: "
       << s_p1 -> Area() << endl;

  delete s_p1;

  cout << endl;

  return 0;
}
```

Program Output

Shape Constructor

Circle Constructor

Area() for the Circle applied through Shape pointer: 78.5400

Circle Destructor

Shape Destructor

Now, the destructors for the target of s_p1 are executed correctly. First, the destructor for the derived class is executed, and then the destructor for the base class is executed. Note that we have also used the accessor method Get_Type(), which is also applied through the pointer.

13.3.6 Putting Polymorphism to Work

The following program solves the problem that we posed at the beginning of this section and which we repeat here. Suppose we want to enable the user to create a series of shapes of his or her own choosing. Thus, the user can first choose to create a rectangle of a certain size, then a circle with a certain radius, and so on. After the user has created the shapes, we want the program to display the areas of all the figures. How can we do this? The answer lies in creating an array of Shape pointers and using polymorphism with the Area() method. The following program solves our problem.

```cpp
//dem13-10.cpp

//This program demonstrates the use of polymorphism.

#include <iostream>
#include <iomanip>
#include <string>

using namespace std;

class Shape
{
  protected:
    string figure_type;
  public:
    Shape(string ft = "Default Figure") : figure_type(ft) {}
    string Get_Type() {return figure_type;}
    virtual ~Shape() {}
    virtual double Area() {return 0.0;}
};

class Rectangle : public Shape
{
  protected:
    double height, width;
  public:
    Rectangle(double h, double w): Shape("Rectangle"), height(h),width(w) {}
    virtual ~Rectangle() {}
    double Area() {return height * width;}
};

class Circle : public Shape
{
  protected:
    double radius;
  public:
    Circle(double r) : Shape("Circle"), radius(r) {}
    virtual ~Circle() {}
    double Area() {return 3.1416 * radius * radius;}
};

class Trapezoid : public Shape
{
```

```
  protected:
    double base1, base2, height;
  public:
    Trapezoid(double b1, double b2, double h)
          : Shape("Trapezoid"), base1(b1), base2(b2), height(h) {}
    virtual ~Trapezoid() {}
    double Area() {return 0.5 * height * (base1 + base2);}
};

Shape* Get_Shape();

int main()
{
  cout << setprecision(4)
       << setiosflags(ios::fixed)
       << setiosflags(ios::showpoint);

  const int num_shapes = 5;

  Shape* shapes[num_shapes];

  for (int i = 0; i < num_shapes; ++i)
    shapes[i] = Get_Shape();

  cout << endl;

  for (i = 0; i < num_shapes; ++i)
    cout << "\nThe area of the " << shapes[i] -> Get_Type() << " is "
         << shapes[i] -> Area();

  cout << endl;

  for (i = 0; i < num_shapes; ++i)
    delete shapes[i];

  cout << endl;

  return 0;
}

Shape* Get_Shape()
{
  Shape* s_p;     //To be returned by the function

  double height,
         width,
         radius,
         base1,
         base2;

  cout << endl;
  cout << "Enter the number of the shape you want to create:"
       << endl << endl;
  cout << "For a Rectangle, enter 1" << endl;
  cout << "For a Circle, enter 2" << endl;
  cout << "For a Trapezoid, enter 3" << endl << endl;
```

```
cout << "Please make your selection: ";

int response;

cin >> response;

switch (response)
{
  case 1:
     cout << endl << endl;
     cout << "Enter the height of the rectangle: ";
     cin >> height;
     cout << endl << endl;
     cout << "Enter the width of the rectangle: ";
     cin >> width;

     s_p = new Rectangle(height, width);

     break;

  case 2:

     cout << endl << endl;
     cout << "Enter the radius of the circle: ";
     cin >> radius;

     s_p = new Circle(radius);

     break;

  case 3:
     cout << endl << endl;
     cout << "Enter the first base of the trapezoid: ";
     cin >> base1;
     cout << endl << endl;
     cout << "Enter the second base of the trapezoid: ";
     cin >> base2;
     cout << endl << endl;
     cout << "Enter the height of the trapezoid: ";
     cin >> height;

     s_p = new Trapezoid(base1, base2, height);

     break;

  default:
     cout << endl << endl;
     cout << "Invalid selection. Creating default object.";

     s_p = new Shape();

     break;
}
  return s_p;
}
```

Program Output

Enter the number of the shape you want to create:

For a Rectangle, enter 1
For a Circle, enter 2
For a Trapezoid, enter 3

Please make your selection: **1**

Enter the height of the rectangle: **3**

Enter the width of the rectangle: **5**

Enter the number of the shape you want to create:

For a Rectangle, enter 1
For a Circle, enter 2
For a Trapezoid, enter 3

Please make your selection: **2**

Enter the radius of the circle: **5.6**

Enter the number of the shape you want to create:

For a Rectangle, enter 1
For a Circle, enter 2
For a Trapezoid, enter 3

Please make your selection: **3**

Enter the first base of the trapezoid: **7**

Enter the second base of the trapezoid: **8**

Enter the height of the trapezoid: **9**

Enter the number of the shape you want to create:

For a Rectangle, enter 1
For a Circle, enter 2
For a Trapezoid, enter 3

Please make your selection: **5**

Invalid selection. Creating default object.

Enter the number of the shape you want to create:

For a Rectangle, enter 1
For a Circle, enter 2
For a Trapezoid, enter 3

Please make your selection: **1**

Enter the height of the rectangle: **1**

Enter the width of the rectangle: **1**

```
The area of the Rectangle is 15.0000
The area of the Circle is 98.5206
The area of the Trapezoid is 67.5000
The area of the Default Figure is 0.0000
The area of the Rectangle is 1.0000
```

Note that we deleted the cout statements in the constructors and destructors to make the program's output shorter. All destructors are declared as virtual methods to allow the proper sequence of execution of the class destructors. Also, the Area() method in class Shape is declared to be virtual. This allows the appropriate Area() method to be applied through a Shape pointer. In main(), we declare an array shapes[] of Shape pointers. The first for loop assigns to each element of shape[] a Shape pointer returned by the function Get_Shape().

When Get_Shape() executes, it presents the user with a menu of choices to create a Rectangle, a Circle, or a Trapezoid. The switch statement determines the action taken based on the user's response. If, for example, the user wants to create a Rectangle, the function asks for the height and width of the rectangle. Then, a new Rectangle object is created, dynamically using the new operator. Although this returns a Rectangle pointer, it is legal to assign it to s_p, which is a Shape pointer. If the user enters a number other than 1, 2, or 3, the default case in the switch statement creates a default Shape object.

Thus, the first for loop initializes the Shape pointers in shapes[] to point to some combination of Rectangle, Circle, Trapezoid, and default objects. The elements of an array must all be of the same type, as are the elements of shapes[]—they are all Shape pointers. However, the elements of the array shapes[] *point* to objects of different types. For this reason, such an array is sometimes called a **heterogeneous array**.

The second for loop uses polymorphism. On each iteration of this for loop, the Area() method is applied through the shapes[i] pointer. The Area() method that the loop uses depends entirely on the type of shape the pointer is pointing to (polymorphism). By contrast, the method Get_Type() is not polymorphically applied. There is only one Get_Type() method, which is a member of the Shape class, and which the other classes inherit.

It is important to realize that when the program is compiled, the compiler has no idea which Area() method the loop will use when the program executes. In fact, on each iteration, a different Area() method can be applied. C++ decides which method to use when the loop executes, not when the program compiles. This behavior is called **late** (or **dynamic**) **binding**; that is, which method to use in the call shapes[i] -> Area() is not decided until the code executes. This is in contrast to how the compiler handles the call to the Get_Shape() function in the first for loop. There, the compiler knows which function will be executed at compile time (known as **early**, or **static, binding**).

Finally, the third for loop in main() cleans up by deleting the objects that were created in the first for loop.

Exercises 13.3

Use the following class declarations to answer Exercises 1–11. *Note that some of the declarations are incomplete.*

```
class Class_A
{
  protected:
    int a;
  public:
    Class_A(int i);        //See Exercise 2
    int Func();            //See Exercise 6
};

class Class_B : public Class_A
{
  protected:
    int b;
  public:
    Class_B(int i);        //See Exercise 3
    int Func();            //See Exercise 7
};

class Class_C : public Class_B
{
  protected:
    int c;
  public:
    Class_C(int i);        //See Exercise 4
    int Func();            //See Exercise 8
};

class Class_D : public Class_A
{
  protected:
    int d;
  public:
    Class_D(int i);        //See Exercise 5
    int Func();            //See Exercise 9
};
```

1. Draw the hierarchy diagram for the classes.
2. Define the one-argument constructor for Class_A. The constructor should initialize the data member a to the value of the constructor's argument.
3. Define the one-argument constructor for Class_B. The constructor should initialize the data member b to the value of the constructor's argument and call the base class constructor with the same argument.
4. Define the one-argument constructor for Class_C. The constructor should initialize the data member c to the value of the constructor's argument and call the base class constructor with the same argument.
5. Define the one-argument constructor for Class_D. The constructor should initialize the data member d to the value of the constructor's argument and call the base class constructor with the same argument.

6. Declare the method Func() in Class_A so that it is a virtual method. The method should return the value of its protected instance variable.

7. Declare the method Func() in Class_B so that it returns the sum of its protected instance variables.

8. Define the method Func() of Class_C so that it returns the sum of all its protected instance variables.

9. Define the method Func() of Class_D so that it returns the product of its protected instance variables.

10. Define destructors for all the classes.

11. Declare a class, Class_E, that is derived publicly from Class_D and that has one protected integer instance variable e. Define an appropriate one-argument constructor for the class that is similar to the constructor of the other derived classes. Define a method Func() that returns the product of all the classes protected instance variables.

Assume the classes from Exercises 1–10. Now consider the following declarations, which are made in main().

```
Class_C c_object(3);
Class_D d_object(4);
Class_A* a_p;
Class_B* b_p;
```

Use the preceding declarations to answer Exercises 12–16.

12. What does the following display?

```
a_p = &c_object;

cout << a_p -> Func();
```

13. What does the following display?

```
a_p = &d_object;

cout << a_p -> Func();
```

14. What does the following display?

```
a_p = &b_object;

cout << a_p -> Func();
```

15. What does the following display?

```
b_p = &c_object;

cout << b_p -> Func();
```

16. What does the following display?

```
cout << d_object.Func() << endl;

cout << c_object.Func() << endl;
```

Experiments 13.3

1. The output of dem13-10.cpp displays the area of each figure but does not give the dimensions of the figure. Use a `virtual Show_Dimension()` method in each class to display the dimensions of each figure. Compile, execute, and test the resulting program.

Programming Problems 13.3

1. Add the class `Square` to the hierarchy of Figure 13.6 by deriving it publicly from class `Rectangle`. Class `Square` should have a one-argument constructor that represents the side of the square. The `Area()` method for class `Square` should return the square of its side. Also, add the class `RightTriangle` by deriving it publicly from `Shape`. `RightTriangle` should have two instance variables—base and `height`. The `Area()` method for `RightTriangle` should return $0.5 * base * height$. Now extend the program dem13-10.cpp by adding these classes. The `Get_Shape()` function should have a `switch` statement to accommodate the five classes in the hierarchy.

2. In the `Document` class hierarchy of Programming Problem 1, Section 13.2, do the following: Add the `virtual` methods `Activity()` and `Display()` to the `Document` class. `Activity()` should return 0 and `Display()` should display the word "Document." Declare all destructors as `virtual` methods. Code a *nonmember* function `Get_Document()` that asks the user to choose a document type. Depending on the user's choice, the function should create an appropriate object and return a `Document` pointer. Code a `main()` in which you declare an array of 20 `Document` pointers. Assign values to the pointers in the array by obtaining a set of documents from the user using `Get_Document()`. Then print the activity of each document and display all the information of each document.

3. In the `StorageTank` class hierarchy of Programming Problem 2, Section 13.2, do the following. Add the `virtual` method `Display()` to the `StorageTank` class. The method should display the words "Storage Tank." Declare all destructors as `virtual`. Code a *nonmember* function `Get_Tank()` that asks the user to choose a tank type. Depending on the user's choice, create an appropriate object and return a `StorageTank` pointer. Code a `main()` in which you declare an array of 20 `StorageTank` pointers. Assign values to the pointers in the array by obtaining a set of tanks from the user using `Get_Tank()`. Then display the data for all the storage tanks.

4. In the `VehicleService` class hierarchy of Programming Problem 3, Section 13.2, do the following. Add the `virtual` methods `CalculateBill()` and `Display()` to the `VehicleService` class. `CalculateBill()` should return 0.00 and `Display()` should display the word "Vehicle." Declare all destructors as `virtual`. Code a *nonmember* function `Get_Vehicle()` that asks the user to choose a vehicle type. Depending on the user's choice, create an appropriate object and return a `VehicleService` pointer. Code a `main()` in which you declare an array of 20 `VehicleService` pointers. Assign values to the pointers in the array by obtaining a set of vehicles from the user using `Get_Vehicle()`. Apply the `CalculateBill()` function to all the vehicles. Then display the data for all the vehicles.

5. In the HotelRoom class hierarchy of Programming Problem 4, Section 13.2, do the following. Add the virtual methods CalculateBill() and Display() to the HotelRoom class. CalculateBill() should return 0.00 and Display() should display the words "Hotel Room." Declare all destructors as virtual. Code a *nonmember* function Get_Room() that asks the user to choose a room type. Depending on the user's choice, create an appropriate object and return a HotelRoom pointer. Code a main() in which you declare an array of 20 HotelRoom pointers. Assign values to the pointers in the array by obtaining a set of rooms from the user using Get_Room(). Apply the CalculateBill() function to all the rooms. Then display the data for all the rooms.

13.4 ABSTRACT BASE CLASSES

The class hierarchy presented in the previous section has Shape as the base class for three other classes. The way in which we defined class Shape made it possible to declare a Shape object even though such an object has no dimensions. (This in fact could be done in dem13-10.cpp by entering a number other than 1, 2, or 3 when the menu is displayed.) Although it does not quite make sense to declare a Shape object, it is possible and sometimes desirable to do so.

13.4.1 Pure virtual Methods and Abstract Base Classes

In C++, we can define a class in such a way as to make it impossible to declare an object of that type. We do so by making the class an **abstract base class**, or **ABC**. To make a class an ABC, declare *any one* of its methods as a **pure virtual method**. You can make a virtual method a pure virtual method by following Note 13.10.

Note 13.10   Abstract Base Classes and Pure virtual Methods

To declare a virtual method as a pure virtual method, thereby making the class an abstract base class, do the following:

- Place = 0 after the method's argument list in the method's declaration in the class.
- Do not define the method.

Because a pure virtual method has no definition, it does not make sense to declare an object that would make use of such a method. Therefore, it is reasonable to call such a class "abstract" because you cannot create any "concrete" objects of that type. An ABC provides a standard interface (i.e., pure virtual methods) for the derived classes. The derived classes must specify the implementation of the interface (i.e., the definition of the those methods). By providing the definitions of all pure virtual methods in a derived class, we specify the class's interface. Therefore, it would be possible to create objects in that derived class.

We can make the Shape class an abstract base class as follows.

```
class Shape
{
  protected:
        string figure_type;
  public:
        Shape(string ft = "Default Figure") : figure_type(ft) {}
        const char* Get_Type() {return figure_type;}
        virtual ~Shape() {}
        virtual double Area() = 0;
};
```

Note that the = 0 is placed after the right parenthesis of the argument list of Area(). The method is not defined anywhere in the program. Making Area() a pure virtual method implies that we expect the derived classes to provide their own definitions of Area(). The following declarations in main() would now be illegal.

```
Shape s;                //Illegal object

Shape Func();           //Illegal return value

double Func(Shape s);   //Illegal value parameter
```

Because Shape is an abstract base class, you cannot create an object of type Shape. Therefore, the first declaration is illegal. The second declaration is illegal because it implies that the function Func() contains a return statement that returns a Shape object. That implies that a Shape object is created by the return mechanism, which is illegal. Likewise, the third declaration is illegal because use of the function requires passing a Shape object by value, again requiring that a Shape object be created.

However, because pointers and references do not require object creation, the following declarations are legal.

```
Rectangle r(3, 5);

Shape& s_ref = r;

Shape* s_ptr = &r;

double Func(Shape*);
```

Recall that a Shape reference is an alias, or another name, for a Shape object. Because a Rectangle object is, by inheritance, a Shape object, we can use a Shape reference for it. We have already discussed why it is legal for a Shape pointer to point to a Rectangle object.

The presence of just one pure virtual method makes the class an abstract base class. The class can contain other pure virtual methods, ordinary virtual methods, or non-virtual methods. See Experiment 1. If you now try to declare a Shape object, the compiler will issue an error message. See Experiment 2.

The following Note is important.

> **Note 13.11   Abstract Base Classes**
>
> - In each class derived from an abstract base class (ABC), each pure `virtual` method *must* either be defined or re-declared as a pure `virtual` method. See Experiment 3.
> - In the latter case, the derived class also becomes an ABC. See Experiment 4.
> - In a class hierarchy that is based on an ABC, the only way for a derived class to yield objects is to define an overriding method for each pure `virtual` method that it would inherit.

13.4.2 The Loan Class

Suppose a banker wants to compute the monthly payment on loans. The bank grants two types of loan. A simple interest loan is one in which interest is computed using the following simple interest formula.

```
interest = principal * rate * term
```

The `principal` is the amount of money borrowed. The `rate` is the yearly rate as a decimal. The `term` is the number of years of the loan. The total amount of the loan is the `principal` plus the `interest`.

```
loan_amount = principal + interest
```

To pay off the loan in equal monthly installments, divide the `loan_amount` by the number of months (`term * 12`) of the loan.

```
payment = loan_amount / (term * 12)
```

The second type of loan is an amortized loan. In this type of loan, the interest is computed monthly on the basis of the unpaid loan balance. Suppose you borrow $1000.00 at a yearly rate of 12%. This means that each month you must pay 1% interest (12% divided by the number of months) on the unpaid balance. Suppose that your monthly payment is $100.00. In the first month, you must pay 1% interest ($10), on the full $1000.00. Of the $100.00 payment, therefore, $90.00 is paid toward the principal and $10.00 is paid in interest. Therefore, at the end of the first month, you owe the bank $910.00. Of your second $100.00 payment, $9.10 (1% of 910.00) is for interest and the remainder ($90.90) is paid toward the principal. Therefore, at the end of the second month you owe the bank $819.10. This continues until the loan is repaid. Deriving the formula for the payment amount for an amortized loan is beyond the scope of this book. The reader is referred to almost any text that covers the mathematics of finance. We can, however, use the formula for the payment of an amortized loan, which follows. In the formula, P represents the principal, R the rate as a decimal, and T the term.

$$payment = \frac{P * R * (1 + R)^T}{(1 + R)^T + 1}$$

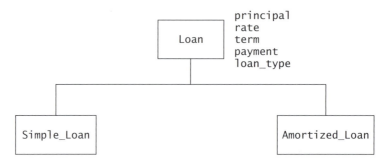

Figure 13.7

All loans, both simple and amortized, have common data. For example, all loans have a principal, rate, term, and payment. What differs is the way in which the interest is computed. Therefore, we might decide to have a Loan class from which we can derive the classes Simple_Loan and Amortized_Loan. Figure 13.7 shows the class hierarchy. The Loan class contains all the data members mentioned previously and the data member loan_type, which is a string equal to either "Simple Loan" or "Amortized Loan". Because it is meaningless to create a Loan object (how would you calculate its payments?), we make Loan an abstract base class. We shall make the method   Payment() a pure virtual method in class Loan and specify how the payment is to be computed in each derived class.

Following are the definitions for the classes Loan, Simple_Loan, and Amortized_Loan.

```
class Loan
{
  protected:
        double principal;
        double yearly_rate;       //rate as a percent
        int    term_in_years;
        double payment;
        string loan_type;
  public:
        Loan (double prin, double rt, int term, const char* lt) :
                  principal(prin), yearly_rate(rt),term_in_years(term),
                  loan_type(lt), payment(0.0) {};
        virtual ~Loan() {}
        virtual void Payment() = 0;    //pure virtual function
        void Display_Loan_Info();
};
void Loan::Display_Loan_Info()
{
  cout << "\n\nLoan Type: " << loan_type;
  cout << "\nPrinciple: " << principal;
  cout << "\nYearly Rate: " << yearly_rate;
  cout << "\nNumber of Years: " << term_in_years;
```

```
    cout << "\n\nMonthly Payment: " << payment;
}

//End of Class Loan       ********************************************

class Simple_Loan : public Loan
{
  public:
      Simple_Loan(double prin, double rt, int term)
          : Loan(prin, rt, term, "Simple Loan") {}
      ~Simple_Loan() {}
      void Payment();
};

void Simple_Loan::Payment()
{
  double interest = principal *  term_in_years * (yearly_rate / 100);
  double loan_amount = principal + interest;

  payment = loan_amount / (term_in_years * 12);
}

//End of Class Simple_Loan *********************************************

class Amortized_Loan : public Loan
{
  public:
      Amortized_Loan(double prin, double rt, int term)
          : Loan(prin, rt, term, "Amortized Loan") {}
      ~Amortized_Loan() {}
      void Payment();
};

void Amortized_Loan::Payment()
{
  double monthly_rate = yearly_rate / 12 / 100;
  int term_in_months = term_in_years * 12;
  double power = pow(1 + monthly_rate, term_in_months);
  payment = (principal * monthly_rate * power) / (power - 1);
}

//End of Class Amortized_Loan *********************************************
```

The class Loan contains declarations of the protected instance variables mentioned previously. The member loan_type is declared as a string. The Loan constructor has four arguments—the principal, rate, term, and loan_type. All the work of the constructor is done in its initialization list. Note that the payment defaults to 0.0. The Loan destructor, declared as a virtual method, is an empty method included for completeness. The Payment() method is declared as a pure virtual method. This makes the Loan class an abstract base class. Each derived class has its own definition of Payment(). Finally, Display_Loan_Info() displays all the information about a loan. All the derived classes inherit this method.

Class `Simple_Loan` is publicly derived from `Loan`. The `Simple_Loan` constructor has three arguments—the `principal`, `rate`, and `term`. However, the constructor's initialization list calls the `Loan` constructor with four arguments. (Recall from the previous paragraph that the fifth argument, the payment, defaults to 0.0.) The fourth argument is the string "`Simple Loan`". The `Payment()` method for class `Simple_Loan` computes the payment using the simple interest formula as described previously.

The class `Amortized_Loan` is similar to `Simple_Loan`. The three-argument `Amortized_Loan` constructor calls the four-argument `Loan` constructor with the fourth argument equal to the string "`Amortized Loan`". The `Payment()` method of class `Amortized_Loan` computes the payment according to the formula described previously. To raise `1 + monthly_rate` to a power, we use the standard math library function `pow()`. The function `pow()`, which returns a `double`, has two arguments both of which must be doubles. The first is the base and the second the exponent. Therefore, for example, `pow(2.0, 5.0)` returns 2^5, or 32.0. To use `pow()`, or any other function in the math library, you must include the header file `cmath`.

The following program, dem13-11.cpp, tests the classes by creating three loans.

```cpp
//dem13-11.cpp

#include <iostream>
#include <iomanip>
#include <string>
#include <cmath>

using namespace std;

class Loan
{
  protected:
    double principal;
    double yearly_rate;      //rate as a percent
    int    term_in_years;
    double payment;
    string loan_type;
  public:
    Loan (double prin, double rt, int term, const char * lt) :
        principal(prin), yearly_rate(rt),term_in_years(term),
        loan_type(lt), payment(0.0) {};
    virtual ~Loan() {}
    virtual void Payment() = 0;    //pure virtual function
    void Display_Loan_Info();
};
void Loan::Display_Loan_Info()
{
  cout << endl << endl;
  cout << "Loan Type: " << loan_type << endl;
  cout << "Principle: " << principal << endl;
  cout << "Yearly Rate: " << yearly_rate <<endl;
  cout << "Number of Years; " << term_in_years << endl << endl;
```

```cpp
    cout << "Monthly Payment: " << payment << endl;
}
//End of Class Loan
    ***********************************************

class Simple_Loan : public Loan
{
  public:
    Simple_Loan(double prin, double rt, int term)
        : Loan(prin, rt, term, "Simple Loan") {}
    ~Simple_Loan() {}
    void Payment();
};

void Simple_Loan::Payment()
{
  double interest = principal *  term_in_years * (yearly_rate / 100);
  double loan_amount = principal + interest;

  payment = loan_amount / (term_in_years * 12);
}

//End of Class Simple_Loan
    ***********************************************

class Amortized_Loan : public Loan
{
  public:
    Amortized_Loan(double prin, double rt, int term)
        : Loan(prin, rt, term, "Amortized Loan") {}
    ~Amortized_Loan() {}
    void Payment();

};
void Amortized_Loan::Payment()
{
  double monthly_rate = yearly_rate / 12 / 100;
  int term_in_months = term_in_years * 12;

  double power = pow(1 + monthly_rate, term_in_months);

  payment = (principal * monthly_rate * power) / (power - 1);
}

//End of Class Amortized_Loan
    ***********************************************

Loan* Get_Loan_Data();   //Prototype for function used by main()

int main()
{
  cout << setprecision(2)
       << setiosflags(ios::fixed)
       << setiosflags(ios::showpoint);
```

```
  const int num_loans = 3;

  Loan* loans[num_loans];

  for (int i = 0; i < num_loans; ++i)
    loans[i] = Get_Loan_Data();

  for (i = 0; i < num_loans; ++i)
    loans[i] -> Payment();

  for (i = 0; i < num_loans; ++i)
    loans[i] -> Display_Loan_Info();

  for (i = 0; i < num_loans; ++i)
    delete loans[i];

  cout << endl;

  return 0;
} //End of main()

Loan* Get_Loan_Data()
{
  double principal;
  double rate;
  int term_in_years;

  Loan* l_p;

  cout << endl << endl;
  cout << "Enter the first letter of the loan type." << endl << endl;
  cout << "(S)imple" << endl;
  cout << "(A)mortized" << endl << endl;
  cout << "Enter your choice: ";
  char response = cin.get();

  cout << endl << endl;
  cout << "Principal: ";
  cin >> principal;
  cout << endl;
  cout << "Yearly Rate as a Percent: ";
  cin >> rate;
  cout << endl;
  cout << "Term in Years: ";
  cin >> term_in_years;

  cin.get();                    //clear the input buffer

  switch (response)
  {
    case 'S': case 's':
      l_p = new Simple_Loan(principal, rate, term_in_years);
      break;
    case 'A': case 'a':
      l_p = new Amortized_Loan(principal, rate, term_in_years);
      break;
  }

  return l_p;
}    //End of Get_Loan_Data()
```

Program Output

```
Enter the first letter of the loan type.

(S)imple
(A)mortized

Enter your choice: s

Principal: 1000

Yearly Rate as a Percent: 12

Term in Years: 3

Enter the first letter of the loan type.

(S)imple

(A)mortized

Enter your choice: A

Principal: 1000

Yearly Rate as a Percent: 12

Term in Years: 3

Enter the first letter of the loan type.

(S)imple
(A)mortized

Enter your choice: A

Principal: 150000

Yearly Rate as a Percent: 8.5

Term in Years: 30

Loan Type: Simple Loan
Principle: 1000.00
Yearly Rate: 12.00
Number of Years: 3

Monthly Payment: 37.78

Loan Type: Amortized Loan
Principle: 1000.00
Yearly Rate: 12.00
Number of Years: 3

Monthly Payment: 33.21

Loan Type: Amortized Loan
Principle: 150000.00
Yearly Rate: 8.50
Number of Years: 30

Monthly Payment: 1153.37
```

The program uses the function Get_Loan_Data(), which returns a Loan pointer. The function asks the user to choose between a simple interest loan and an amortized loan. Then the function prompts for, and obtains, the principal, rate, and term of the loan. A switch statement then uses the new operator to create either a Simple_Loan object or an Amortized_Loan object, depending on the user's response, and assigns the resulting pointer to a Loan pointer l_p. The function returns the value of l_p.

An array of Loan pointers is declared in main(). The processing in main() is accomplished in four for loops. The first executes Get_Loan_Data() for each pointer in the loans[] array. This assigns to each pointer either a Simple_Loan object or an Amortized_Loan object. The second for loop polymorphically applies the appropriate Payment() method through the loans[] pointers. Therefore, the correct payment formula will be applied to each loan, depending on the loan type. In the third for loop, the inherited Display_Loan_Info() method is applied to each loan through the loans[] pointer. Finally, the fourth for loop deletes the space that was dynamically allocated in the first for loop.

Exercises 13.4

Use the following declarations to answer Exercises 1–5. Note that some of the declarations are incomplete.

```
class Class_A
{
  protected:
    int a;
  public:
    Class_A(int i) : a(i) {}
    int Func()              //See Exercise 1
};

class Class_B : public Class_A
{
  protected:
    int b;
  public:
    Class_B(int i) : b(i), Class_A(i) {}
    int Func()              //See Exercise 2
};

class Class_C : public Class_B
{
  protected:
    int c;
  public:
    Class_C(int i) : c(i), Class_B(i) {}
    int Func()              //See Exercise 3
};
```

```
class Class_D : public Class_A
{
  protected:
    int d;
  public:
    Class_D(int i) : d(i), Class_A(i) {}
    int Func()            //See Exercise 4
};
```

1. Declare `Func()` in `Class_A` so that `Class_A` becomes an abstract base class.
2. Declare `Func()` in `Class_B` so that `Class_B` becomes an abstract base class.
3. Define `Func()` in `Class_C` so that it returns the sum of the protected instance variables of the class.
4. Define `Func()` in `Class_D` so that it returns the product of the protected instance variables of the class.
5. Define destructors for the classes.

Based on the previous class declarations and the results of Exercises 1–5, which of the declarations in Exercises 6–10 are legal?

6. `Class_C Func6(int);`
7. `Class_B b_object;`
8. `Class_B * b_ptr;`
9. `int Func9(Class_A);`
10. `int Func10(Class_A &);`
11. In the `Shape` class hierarchy, add the class `Square`, which is derived from class `Rectangle`. The class should have one `double` instance variable, s, representing the side of the square. The class should also have an `Area()` method that returns the value of s*s. The class should have a constructor that displays "Square Constructor" and calls the `Rectangle` constructor. The class should also have a destructor that displays "Square Destructor".
12. See Exercise 11. Write a program that declares a `Shape` pointer and sets it to a dynamically allocated `Square` object with a side of 6.5. Make the program display the area of the square by applying the `Area()` method through the pointer. In what sequence are the constructors and destructors executed? Which `Area()` method is executed?

Experiments 13.4

1. Change the declaration of the `Shape` class of dem13-10.cpp in Section 13.3 to make `Shape` an abstract base class. Compile, execute, and test the resulting program.
2. See Experiment 1. Replace `main()` in dem13-10.cpp by one in which you declare a `Shape` object. Compile the resulting program. What message does the compiler issue?
3. See Experiment 1. Change the `Rectangle` class as follows: do not define the `Area()` method and do not declare it as a pure `virtual` method. Compile the resulting program. What message does the compiler issue?

4. See Experiment 1. Change the Rectangle class as follows: declare the Area() method so that it is a pure virtual method. Replace main() by one in which you declare a Rectangle object. Compile the resulting program. What message does the compiler issue?

Programming Problems 13.4

1. Recode Programming Problem 1, Section 13.3, in such a way that Shape is an abstract base class by making Area() a pure virtual method.

2. Recode Programming Problem 2, Section 13.3, in such a way that Document is an abstract base class. Recode the MultimediaFile class so that it becomes an abstract base class by making Activity() and Display()pure virtual methods. Derive from MultimediaFile two classes, GraphicsFile and AudioFile. GraphicsFile contains the integer instance variables graphics_type and AudioFile contains the integer instance variable audio_type. Code appropriate constructors, copy constructors, and destructors for the new classes. Code appropriate Activity() and Display() methods for the new classes. Code a main() that is similar to the one in Programming Problem 1, Section 13.3.

3. Recode Programming Problem 3, Section 13.3, in such a way that StorageTank is an abstract base class. Recode the GasTank class to make it an abstract base class by making Remainder() and Display()pure virtual methods. Add the string instance variable, tank_type, to the class. Derive from GasTank the two classes, PropaneTank and MethaneTank. Code appropriate constructors, copy constructors, and destructors for the new classes. Code appropriate Remainder() and Display() methods for the new classes. Code a main() that is similar to the one in Programming Problem 2, Section 13.3.

4. Recode Programming Problem 4, Section 13.3, in such a way that VehicleService is an abstract base class. Recode the PrivateVehicle class to make it an abstract base class by making Display() and CalculateBill() pure virtual methods. Add the string instance variable, vehicle_type, to the class. Derive from PrivateVehicle the two classes, FamilyVehicle and RecreationalVehicle. Code appropriate constructors, copy constructors, and destructors for the new classes. Also, code Display() and CalculateBill() methods for the new classes. To calculate the bill for a family vehicle, add to the cost of the parts the product of the hours and 70.00. To calculate the bill for a recreational vehicle, add to the cost of parts the product of the hours and 75.00. Code a main() that is similar to the one in Programming Problem 3, Section 13.3.

5. Recode Programming Problem 5, Section 13.3, in such a way that HotelRoom is an abstract base class. Make GuestRoom an abstract base class by making Display() and CalculateBill() pure virtual methods. Add the string instance variable, room_type, to the class. Derive from GuestRoom the two classes, SingleRoom and Suite. Code appropriate constructors, copy constructors, and destructors for the new classes. Also, code Display() and CalculateBill() methods for the new classes. Calculate the bill for a single room in the normal way. Calculate the bill for a suite by calculating the bill in the normal way and then adding a luxury tax of 6% of the regular bill. Code a main() that is similar to the one in Programming Problem 4, Section 13.3.

CHAPTER REVIEW

TERMINOLOGY

Explain the meanings of the following terms.

"is a" relation	protected
inheritance	public derivation
base class	privately derived
parent class	initialization list
super class	method overriding
derived class	polymorphism
child classes	virtual
subclasses	heterogeneous array
inherit	late (or dynamic) binding
directly derived	abstract base class
indirectly derived	pure virtual method

CHAPTER REVIEW

- Classes can be related by means of inheritance. Inheritance embodies the "is a" relation.
- If a class inherits from another, the first class is derived from the other, which in turn called the base class.
- A derived class inherits all the instance variables and methods of the base class.
- Private members of a base class, although members of a derived class, are inaccessible to the methods of the derived class. A protected member of a base class behaves as though it is private to all functions except methods in a derived class. Thus, methods in a derived class have access to all protected members in the base class (Note 13.1).
- To derive a class from a base class, in the declaration of the derived class, follow the derived class's name by a colon, the keyword public or the keyword private, and the name of the base class (Note 13.2).
- All private, protected, and public base class members remain private, protected, and public as members of a publicly derived class. All base class members, regardless of their access category, are private members of a privately derived class (Table 13.2).
- A derived class with the following exceptions inherits all base class methods: constructors, copy constructors, destructors, overloaded operators, and friend functions (see Chapter 15) (Note 13.3).
- The constructor of a derived class should explicitly call the base class constructor in an initialization list. (Note 13.4) Properly coded, the base class constructor completes execution before the derived class constructor completes execution.
- Nothing special needs to be done to the code of derived class destructors. The derived class destructor completes execution before the base class destructor completes execution.
- The copy constructor of a derived class should explicitly call the copy constructor of its base class in an initialization list (Note 13.5).
- A method in a base class can be applied to a derived class object because the derived class inherits the base class method. However, if the derived class has a method of the same name and signature (number and types of arguments) as a method of the base class, when that function

is applied to a derived class object, the method in the derived class overrides the method of the base class (Note 13.6).

- To apply an overridden base class method to a derived class object, qualify the method name with the base class name followed by the scope resolution operator, :: (Note 13.6).

- In a class hierarchy, a base class pointer can point to an object of any derived class. The converse is not true: a derived class pointer cannot point to a base class object (Note 13.7).

- The concept of polymorphism extends method overriding to the case of objects in a derived class accessed through base class pointers. Polymorphism allows the choice of method to depend on the target of the pointer rather than on the type of the pointer. C++ decides which method to use when the program executes. This is called late binding.

- For polymorphism to work, (a) objects must be accessed through pointers, (b) the method to be overridden must be declared virtual in the base class, and (c) the overriding method in the derived class must have the same name and signature as the base class method. Such a method is also virtual by default (Note 13.8).

- To ensure the proper execution sequence of destructors for dynamically allocated objects in a class hierarchy, declare the base destructor as a virtual method (Note 13.9).

- A heterogeneous array is an array of base class pointers. The pointers in such an array can point to any object in any class derived from the base class.

- An abstract base class is one for which it is impossible to instantiate an object. To make a class an abstract base class, declare one of its virtual methods a pure virtual method.

- To declare a virtual method a pure virtual method, place = 0 after the method's argument list in the method's declaration in the class, and do not define the method (Note 13.10).

- In each class derived from an abstract base class, each pure virtual method must be either defined or re-declared as a pure virtual method. In the latter case, the derived class becomes an abstract base class (Note 13.11).

- In a class hierarchy that is based on an abstract base class, the only way for a derived class to yield objects is to define an overriding method for each pure virtual method that it inherits (Note 13.11).

REVIEW EXERCISES

1. Explain what it means to say that inheritance embodies the "is a" relation.
2. If class D is derived from class B, exactly what is and is not inherited by D from B? Include instance variables and methods.
3. Why is the protected access category needed?
4. Explain the difference between public and private class derivation.
5. Explain how a derived class's constructors must be coded relative to the base class constructors.
6. What is the difference between initializing an instance variable in the body of a constructor and initializing it in the constructor's initialization list?
7. In what order are the base class constructor and derived class constructor executed when a derived class object is instantiated?
8. In what order are the base class destructor and derived class destructor executed when a derived class object goes out of scope?
9. What is method overriding and how does it differ from function overloading?
10. How can you apply an overridden base class method to a derived class object?

11. Why does it make sense for a base class pointer to point to a derived class object?
12. What is polymorphism? What is a `virtual` method?
13. Why should class destructors in a class hierarchy be declared `virtual`?
14. What is a heterogeneous array and how is it useful?
15. Explain the difference between late and early binding.
16. What is an abstract base class and how do you declare one? What is the purpose of an abstract base class?

Chapter 14

Files

Most "real world" applications of C++ involve the use of files. Data is read from a file and/or written to a file by such programs. This chapter discusses how C++ views files and how to process files in your programs. It covers both sequential and random access processing, and how to process files either one character at a time or one record at a time.

14.1 INPUT/OUTPUT STREAMS

Files are handled differently in different programming languages. In C++, a file is treated as a stream of characters. See Figure 14.1. The characters in the file are made available to the program one at a time, in sequence. Thus, input and output in C++ are known as **stream I/O**. The C++ language does not assume any organization to a file except its structure as a stream. To give a file an additional logical structure, the programmer must write program instructions to do so.

14.1.1 The Standard I/O Streams: Revisiting cin, cout, and cerr

Since Chapter 1, you have been using the standard output stream cout and the standard input stream cin. Later, we introduced the standard error stream, cerr. By default, the standard input stream is "attached" to the keyboard. Therefore, cin receives its input from the keyboard. Likewise, the standard output streams, cout and cerr, are "attached" to the monitor display. Any data inserted into the cout or cerr output streams appear on the monitor. The standard input and output streams are automatically made available to every C++ program that contains the preprocessor directive #include <iostream>. We are now in a position to explain more fully the nature of cin, cout, and cerr.

We have already mentioned that cin is an object of the class istream and that cout and cerr are objects of the class ostream. These two classes are actually part of a complex hierarchy of classes for doing input and output that are part of the C++ language. Figure 14.2 shows part of the hierarchy.

The header file <iostream> contains the definition of the class **iostream**, which derives from both istream and ostream. A class such as iostream, which is derived from two or more parent classes, is an example of **multiple inheritance**. In multiple inheritance, the derived class inherits all the members from all the classes from which it is derived. Thus, class iostream inherits all the members from istream, ostream and

Figure 14.1

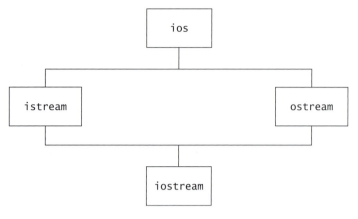

Figure 14.2

also, indirectly, from the class ios, the class from which both istream and ostream are derived.

The istream class handles input and includes the definition of the extraction operator, >>. The object cin is a member of the class istream. The get() and getline() methods are members of the class istream. Therefore, they can be applied to an istream object such as cin. This is, in fact, how we have been using these methods.

```
ch = cin.get();
cin.getline(buffer, 81);
```

Likewise, the ostream class handles output and includes the definition of the insertion operator, <<. The object cout is a member of the ostream class. The I/O manipulators that we have been using to control the form of the output to our programs are actually methods that use ostream and ios methods to manipulate the output stream. For example, the method setprecision(), when sent to cout, determines the precision of the decimal numbers that are displayed by cout. Similarly, the statement setiosflags(ios::showpoint), when sent to cout, sets a one-bit flag in an instance variable of the class ios that determines that the output stream will display the decimal point when a decimal number is output. (The scope resolution operator, ::, is necessary to ensure that the reference is to a member of the parent class.) See Experiment 1.

14.1.2 Text Files

For now, we shall assume that the files we are processing are text files. A **text file** consists of letters of the alphabet, digits, and special characters, such as the comma, hyphen, and period. At the end of each line of a text file is a newline ('\n') character. Text files are produced using what is sometimes called an ASCII text editor or, simply, a text editor. Examples of such editors are Notepad in Windows and the VI editor in UNIX. Also, the editors that accompany C++ compilers, such as Visual C++, are text editors. Any text editor can create the text files used for input to the programs of this chapter. Note that files produced by a word processor, such as Microsoft Word, are not text files. The .doc files produced by Word, for example, contain special formatting codes and other information about the document that are not visible to the user. It is possible in most word processors, however, to choose to save a file as a text file. See your word processor's documentation for details. We shall further discuss text files and another type of file, binary files, in Section 14.3.

14.1.3 User-Declared Files

C++ allows the programmer to declare I/O streams, that is, files, other than the standard ones. To perform input and output on named files requires that we instantiate file objects in classes that are designed for performing file operations. To work with a file in C++, we must follow the steps of Note 14.1

Note 14.1   To Work with a File in C++

· Declare a file object of the appropriate mode (i.e., input or output or both).
· Open the file object and associate the object with a named file on your system.
· Perform operations on the file (i.e., read data from or write data to the file).
· Close the file.

14.1.4 Declaring the File Object

To accomplish the first step of Note 14.1 (that is, to declare a file object), we must learn about the three classes that support file I/O. Use the class **ifstream** (see Figure 14.3) to create input files. (Figure 14.3 contains a more complete picture of the classes in the C++ I/O class hierarchy.) The class ifstream is derived from istream and a class called **fstreambase**. The class fstreambase, which is derived from class ios, provides facilities for handling named files. Use the class **ofstream** to create output files. This class is derived from ostream and fstreambase. Finally, use the class **fstream** to create files that can be both input and output files. This class is derived from iostream and fstreambase. In Figure 14.3, the classes above the dotted line are declared in the header file <iostream> and the classes below the dotted line are declared in the header file <fstream>.

To use a file, first declare a file object of the appropriate type, as shown in the following declarations.

```
ofstream out_file;      //Declares an output file object called out_file
ifstream in_file;       //Declares an input file object called in_file
fstream io_file;  //Declares a file object io_file for either input or output
```

The first statement declares out_file as an ofstream object, that is, as an output file stream. This means that our program can place data into the out_file stream in much the same manner as we place data into the standard output stream,cout. The second statement declares in_file as an ifstream object. Therefore, our program

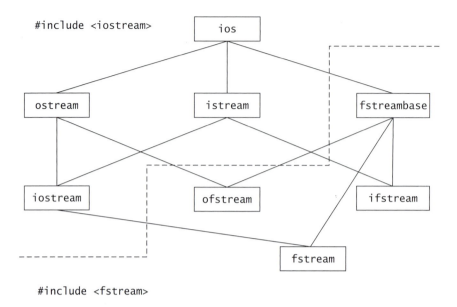

Figure 14.3

can extract data from the in_file stream in much the same manner as we extract data from the standard input stream, cin. The third statement declares io_file as an object of the fstream class. Our program can use io_file as either an input stream or an output stream, depending on the circumstances within the program and how we choose to open the file.

14.1.5 Opening the File

After declaring a file object, we must, as mentioned in Note 14.1, open the file and associate the file object with an actual physical file that resides on a computer system. The first of the previous file declarations, for example, declares out_file as an ofstream object. However, the output stream out_file has not yet been associated with, or attached to, an actual file. This situation is similar to declaring an integer variable and not assigning it a value. To use the variable meaningfully, you must assign it a value. Likewise, once we have declared a file object, we must associate that object with a file. We do this by opening the file using the open() method. The following statement opens the out_file stream and attaches it to the file outdata.dat.

```
out_file.open("outdata.dat");
```

From this point on in the program, all operations on the file object out_file will be performed on the file outdata.dat. Note that the argument of the open() method must be a string. Therefore, the name of the file must be enclosed in quotes. In the absence of a directory path, the file will be opened in the folder in which the program is executed. The name of the file can include the path to the file on the computer system.

In that case, the program will open the file in the appropriate folder. For example, the following statement opens the file outdata.dat in the root directory of the a: drive.

```
out_file.open("a:\outdata.dat");
```

A second way to create and open a file is by using the one-argument ofstream constructor. The following declaration creates in one step the ofstream object out_file and attaches it to the fileoutdata.dat.

```
ofstream out_file("outdata.dat");
```

The act of opening a file has several implications, which are mentioned in Note 14.2.

Note 14.2   Opening a File

Opening a file (either by using the open() method or by using the one-argument constructor when declaring the file object):

- Associates a real file on the computer system with the file object being opened.
- Opens the file in a mode appropriate to the type of file object.
- Creates a variable, which is part of the file object, called the **file position indicator,** or **FPI,** that keeps track of the program's position in the file. The value of the FPI is the program's displacement into the file, that is, the number of bytes from the first byte in the file.

Some explanation of the file position indicator is in order. The FPI helps your program keep track of where it is in the file. For example, when you open an ofstream file object, if the file that you are associating with the object does not exist, it is created automatically by the system. If the file does already exist, it is opened for output. In either case, the FPI is set to 0, that is, the first byte position in the file. The first data your program writes to the file are placed beginning at that position. If the first write operation places seven characters in the file, the system automatically increases the FPI by 7. The next write operation will then cause data to be placed starting at displacement 7 bytes from the beginning of the file. See Figure 14.4.

Figure 14.4

When you open an ifstream file object, that is, an input file, the file that you are associating with the object must already exist. If it does not, an error occurs. We will address how to handle this error shortly. Assuming the file to be opened exists, the file's FPI is set to 0. The first data that we read from the file is extracted beginning at displacement 0. If we read 5 characters from the file, the FPI is increased by 5. Therefore, the next reading of data from the file begins at displacement 5. See Figure 14.5.

When we cover fstream file objects, we shall discuss how the FPI works for those files.

14.1.6 Processing the File

We now know how to complete the first two steps of Note 14.1. For the third step, processing the file, the power of inheritance comes to the rescue! Once the ofstream object is created and opened, we can use any of the file output operations that we have used in this book, including the insertion operator<<. Recall that the insertion operator is declared in the class ostream, which is a class from which ofstream is derived. See Figure 14.3 again. Operators are essentially methods (functions) and are treated as such by C++. Therefore, the class ofstream inherits the insertion operator. This allows us to do the following to write the string "Hello, World!" onto the file outdata.dat followed by a newline character. Remember that the file object out_file represents the file outdata.dat.

```
out_file << "Hello, World!" << endl;
```

14.1.7 Closing the File

After the program finishes processing the file, it should close the file. The C++ system automatically closes any open file when the program ends. However, it is good practice to close files using the **close()** method. For example, the following statement closes out_file.

```
out_file.close();
```

The following program illustrates the simple use of an output file.

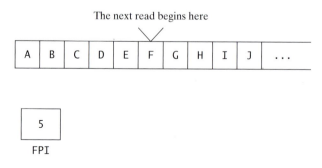

The next read begins here

| A | B | C | D | E | F | G | H | I | J | ... |

| 5 |

FPI

Figure 14.5

```
//dem14-1.cpp

//This program demonstrates simple file output

#include <fstream>
#include <iostream>

using namespace std;

int main()
{
    char buffer[81];

    ofstream out_file("outdata.dat");

    cout << "Enter your name: ";
    cin.getline(buffer, 81);

    out_file << buffer << endl;

    cout << endl;
    cout << "Enter the first line of your address: ";
    cin.getline(buffer, 81);
    out_file << buffer << endl;

    out_file.close();

    cout << endl;
    cout << "Program Terminated" << endl;

    return 0;
}
```

Program Output

Enter your name: **John Molluzzo**

Enter the first line of your address: **Pace University**

Program Terminated

Other than the message Program Terminated, the program does not display any results on the monitor because the program places the user's name and address into the file outdata.dat. Following is a listing of the output file.

Listing of File outdata.dat

John Molluzzo

Pace University

Recall that the insertion operator is inherited by the ofstream class. It is meaningful, therefore, to apply the operator to an ofstream object such as out_file, so we use the insertion operator << to output our data to the file. We place data onto the out_file stream in the same way that we place data onto the standard output stream, cout.

Note that we use C-strings (that is, character arrays) in this and in the subsequent programs in this chapter, rather than string objects. You can, in dem14-1.cpp, declare buffer as a string object and the program will work in the same way. However, we will refrain from using objects with cout because we do not want to give the impression that you can do so with arbitrary objects. For example, you cannot code for the Savings_Account object acc1:

```
cout << acc1;
```

Doing so will result in a compiler error. The only way to make such a statement work is by overloading the << operator. See Chapter 15. As we have mentioned, the << operator is already overloaded for string objects.

14.1.8 Checking for Errors When Opening a File

The program dem14-1.cpp does not check for errors when the file is opened. Possible output file errors include disk errors and writing to a file on a nonexistent disk.

> **Note 14.3   Errors When Opening a File**
>
> If an error occurs when a file is opened, the value of the file object is zero.

The following program shows how to check for such an error. The first run of the program outputs to a file, outdata.dat, which is created in the folder in which the program executes. The second program run attempts to output to a file on disk M, which did not exist on the system on which the program was executed. (If you run this program on your system, you may have to change the drive letter. Choose a drive letter that is not in use on your system.)

```
//dem14-2.cpp

//This program demonstrates simple file output
//The program checks the file open for errors

#include <fstream>
#include <iostream>
#include <cstdlib>

using namespace std;

int main()
{
    char buffer[81];
    char file_name[81];

    cout << "Enter the name of the file you want to write to: ";
    cin.getline(file_name, 81);
```

```
        ofstream out_file(file_name);

        if (!out_file)
        {
          cerr << endl;
          cerr << "ERROR: File could not be opened." << endl;
          cerr << "Program Terminated" << endl;
          exit(1);
        }

        cout << endl;
        cout << "Enter your name: ";
        cin.getline(buffer, 81);

        out_file << buffer << endl;

        cout << endl;
        cout << "Enter the first line of your address: ";
        cin.getline(buffer, 81);

        out_file << buffer << endl;

        out_file.close();

        cout << endl;
        cout << "Program Terminated" << endl;

        return 0;
      }
```

Program Output–Run 1

Enter the name of the file you want to write to: **outdata.dat**

Enter your name: **John Molluzzo**

Enter the first line of your address: **Pace University**

Program Terminated

Program Output–Run 2

Enter the name of the file you want to write to: **m:outdata.dat**

ERROR: File could not be opened.
Program Terminated

In this program, we allow the user to enter the name of the file to which the name and address will be written. The program obtains the file name from the user and places it into the array file_name[]. When the file object out_file is declared, we use as the argument to the constructor the array name file_name, which is a character pointer, or string.

To check for errors when the file is opened, we test the file object as follows:

```
if (!out_file)
{
  cerr << endl;
  cerr << "ERROR: File could not be opened.";
  cerr << "Program Terminated" << endl;
  exit(1);
}
```

If the file is not opened properly, the value of out_file is zero. Therefore, testing !out_file is, in effect, saying "if out_file failed to open properly". In this case, an error message is sent to the standard error stream and the program is ended with the exit(1) statement. In the second program run, we entered the name of a file on disk M, which did not exist on the system on which the program was executed. Therefore, the second program run resulted in the error message.

14.1.9 Creating a Text File of Records

Although C++ treats all files as streams of characters, we can impose a logical structure on the file. A **record** is the set of data, or facts, concerning a particular entity. Each fact within a record is a **field**. For example, if we were to write a program to process the inventory for a small manufacturing company, we might design a part record. Each such record might consist of three fields: the ID number field, the quantity-on-hand field, and the price field. The entire set of part records is the inventory parts file.

There are several ways in which to construct records in C++. Because we are, for now, only considering text files, we shall construct records as follows. Each record in the file is a line of text. Therefore, in the stream of characters that constitutes the file, the newline character separates records. The fields within each record are separated by one or more spaces. The fields in such a record are sometimes called **space-separated**. The position within the record identifies the field. In the part record described in the previous paragraph, the ID number field would be first in the record, followed by the quantity on hand, followed by the price. Thus, a three-record parts inventory file, when viewed using a text editor, might look like the following.

```
23 145 24.95
15  46 67.99
65 230 11.95
```

The preceding file is an example of a **sequential file**, which is a file whose records are stored in sequence one after the other. The program, prb14-1.cpp, creates a sequential text parts inventory file. It asks the user to enter data for a record in the file. Then the program writes the record to the parts file.

```
//prb14-1.cpp

//This program demonstrates the creation of a simple text data
//inventory file in which the data items are space separated.

#include <fstream>
#include <iostream>
```

```
#include <cstdlib>
#include <iomanip>

using namespace std;

int main()
{
  char file_name[81];

  int     id_no;
  int     qoh;
  double price;

  int response;

  cout << "Enter the name of the new inventory file: ";
  cin.getline(file_name, 81);

  ofstream inventory_file(file_name);

  if (!inventory_file)
  {
    cerr << endl;
    cerr << "ERROR: File could not be opened." << endl;
    cerr << "Program Terminated" << endl;
    exit(1);
  }

  inventory_file << setprecision(2)
                 << setiosflags(ios::fixed)
                 << setiosflags(ios::showpoint);

  cout << endl;
  cout << "Create an inventory record? (1 for Yes/0 for No): ";
  cin >> response;

  while (response)
  {
      // Get data for inventory record

    cout << endl;
    cout << "ID Number: ";
    cin >> id_no;
    cout << endl;
    cout << "Quantity On Hand: ";
    cin >> qoh;

    cout << endl;
    cout << "Price: ";
    cin >> price;

        //Write inventory record

    inventory_file << id_no << " " << qoh << " " << price << endl;

    cout << endl;
    cout << "Create an inventory record? (1 for Yes/0 for No): ";
```

```
        cin >> response;
    }
    cout << endl << endl;
    cout << "Inventory File " << file_name << " created." << endl;

    inventory_file.close();

    return 0;
}
```

Program Output

Enter the name of the new inventory file: **invent.dat**

Create an inventory record? (1 for Yes/0 for No): **1**

ID Number: **10**

Quantity On Hand: **100**

Price: **10.00**

Create an inventory record? (1 for Yes/0 for No): **1**

ID Number: **20**

Quantity On Hand: **200**

Price: **20.00**

Create an inventory record? (1 for Yes/0 for No): **1**

ID Number: **30**

Quantity On Hand: **300**

Price: **30.00**

Create an inventory record? (1 for Yes/0 for No): **1**

ID Number: **40**

Quantity On Hand: **4**

Price: **400.00**

Create an inventory record? (1 for Yes/0 for No): **1**

ID Number: **50**

Quantity On Hand: **500**

Price: **500.00**

Create an inventory record? (1 for Yes/0 for No): **0**

Inventory File invent.dat created.

Listing of File invent.dat

```
10 100 10.00
20 200 20.00
30 300 30.00
40 4 400.00
50 500 500.00
```

The program first asks the user to enter the name for the inventory file. After obtaining the name from the user, the program opens the file as the ofstream file object inventory_file and tests to see if the file was opened properly. Next, the program sends to inventory_file the setprecision() and setiosflags() statements that we usually send to cout. This ensures that each value for the price field will retain the decimal point and have two digits to the right of the decimal when written to the output file. See Experiment 4.

The program then enters a while loop that creates the output file. In the loop body, the program asks, in turn, for the ID number, quantity on hand, and price of an item. Then it writes an inventory record onto the file. Note that the program places a space between each field, and ends the record with a newline character. Then the program asks the user if he or she wants to create another record. After exiting the loop, the program displays a message that it is done and closes the file. See Experiment 5 for an extension to the program.

14.1.10 File Input

Now that we have created several files, how can we use these files for input to a program and read their contents? As mentioned previously, to create an input file, declare an ifstream file object and then open the file. For example, to open the file outdata.dat for input, we can execute the following statements.

```
ifstream in_file;
in_file.open("outdata.dat");
```

Alternatively, we can create and open the file at the same time using the one-argument constructor as follows.

```
ifstream in_file("outdata.dat");
```

When we read data from a file, we must always check for the **end-of-file condition**. The end-of-file condition means that the program, in processing the file, has come to the end of the file. Therefore, there is no more data to read from the file. The method **eof()** returns 1 (that is, true) if the FPI is at the end of the file (what numeric value would the FPI have in this case?), and returns 0 otherwise. Therefore, assuming that in_file is an ifstream object that has been opened, if the value returned by in_file.eof() is 1, the end-of-file condition has been reached. Otherwise, it has not and the file contains more data that the program can process.

The following program illustrates how we can read and display the data that the program dem14-2.cpp placed into outdata.dat.

```
//dem14-3.cpp

//This program demonstrates simple file input

#include <fstream>
#include <iostream>
#include <cstdlib>

using namespace std;

int main()
{
  char buffer[81];
  char file_name[81];

  cout << "Enter the name of the file you want to display: ";
  cin.getline(file_name, 81);
  ifstream in_file(file_name);

  if (!in_file)
  {
    cerr << endl;
    cerr << "ERROR: File could not be opened." << endl;
    cerr << "Program Terminated" << endl;
    exit(1);
  }

  cout << endl;

  while (!in_file.eof())
  {
    in_file.getline(buffer, 81);
    cout << buffer << endl;
  }

  in_file.close();

  cout << endl << endl;
  cout << "Program Terminated" << endl;

  return 0;
}
```

Program Output

Enter the name of the file you want to display: **outdata.dat**

John Molluzzo
Pace University

Program Terminated

We check for an error when opening the file in exactly the same way as we did for an output file, by checking for a zero value for the ifstream object in_file. The copy and display of the file is done in the while loop. The loop condition checks for the end-of-file on the input file. If it is not the end-of-file, (that is, `!in_file.eof()` is true) the program executes the loop body. In the loop body, the `getline()` method reads a line from the input file in exactly the same way as it reads lines entered at the keyboard using the standard input stream `cin`. (Recall that the `getline()` is inherited from the class `istream`.) The `cout` statement then displays the line on the monitor.

14.1.11 Processing a Text File of Records

The following program, prb14-2.cpp, shows how to process the sequential text file of records that was created in prb14-1.cpp. The program reads through the inventory part file and displays only those part records for which the total value of that part (quantity on hand multiplied by the price) exceeds $3000.00.

```
//prb14-2.cpp

//This program demonstrates reading a text file of records
//whose data are space separated.

#include <fstream>
#include <iostream>
#include <iomanip>
#include <cstdlib>

using namespace std;

int main()
{
  char file_name[81];

  int    id_no;
  int    qoh;
  double price;
  double total;

  cout << setprecision(2)
       << setiosflags(ios::fixed)
       << setiosflags(ios::showpoint);

  cout << "Enter the name of the inventory file: ";
  cin.getline(file_name, 81);

  ifstream inventory_file(file_name);
  if (!inventory_file)
  {
    cerr << endl;
    cerr << "ERROR: File could not be opened." << endl;
    cerr << "Program Terminated" << endl;
    exit(1);
  }

  cout << endl << endl;
  cout << setw(8) << "ID No." << setw(10) << "Quantity"
       << setw(10) << "Price" << setw(12) << "Total"
       << endl << endl;
```

```
//Obtain the first inventory record
inventory_file >> id_no >> qoh >> price;
while (!inventory_file.eof())
{
  total = qoh * price;
  if (total > 3000.00)
  {
    cout << setw(8) << id_no << setw(10) << qoh
         << setw(10) << price << setw(12)<< total
         << endl;
  }

    //obtain the next inventory record
  inventory_file >> id_no >> qoh >> price;
}
inventory_file.close();

cout << endl;
return 0;
}
```

Program Output

```
Enter the name of the inventory file: invent.dat
ID No.  Quantity      Price      Total
  20       200        20.00     4000.00
  30       300        30.00     9000.00
  50       500       500.00   250000.00
```

The program begins by obtaining the name of the inventory file from the user and opening the file as the ifstream file object inventory_file. Then, the program displays a line of column headings.

When reading a file of records sequentially, that is, one at a time, you must take care that your program processes the last record in the file and that it processes the record only once. Note 14.4 explains how to read a sequential input file of records.

Note 14.4   The Read Ahead Rule

To read properly all the records in a sequential input file:

1. Read the first record of the file immediately after opening the file.

2. Read the input file again as soon as the program completes processing the input data.

Thus, a typical program that processes such a file and uses eof() to detect the end of the file should have the following format, which is written in pseudocode.

```
open the input_file
read the first record
while (!input_file.eof())
   process the record
   read the next record
endwhile
```

The program code for prb14-02.cpp follows this outline. After the inventory file is opened, the program reads the first record by executing

```
inventory_file >> id_no >> qoh >> price;
```

This statement reads the first three numbers in the file, which represent the ID number, quantity on hand, and price, and places them into three variables. Then, the program enters the processing loop. If the program has not reached the end of the file, the while loop body calculates the total and tests to see if it exceeds 3000.00. If so, the program displays the values of id_no, qoh, and price. This finishes processing the record so, by the Read Ahead Rule of Note 14.4, the program obtains the next record. When the end of file is reached, the program exits the loop, closes the inventory file, and ends. See Experiment 6.

14.1.12 File Input/Output

We can use a file for both input and output in the same program. To do this, we need a file object that can serve as both an output and an input stream. The class fstream, which inherits from iostream, which in turn inherits from both ostream and istream (see Figure 14.3), is just what we need. Because a member of the fstream class can be used for either input or output, when the file is opened, you must specify an opening mode as the open() method's second argument, or the constructor's second argument. (The open() method and the file constructors are overloaded—they can take either one or two arguments.) You indicate the opening mode by using **access mode constants**, which are defined in the ios class and, therefore, available to fstream, ifstream, and ofstream. Note 14.5 shows some common opening modes.

Note 14.5   Access Mode Constants

ios::in	Opens the file for input (or reading). This mode can also be used with ifstream file objects.
ios::out	Opens the file for output (or writing). This mode can also be used with ofstream file objects.
ios::app	Opens the file for output beginning at the end of the file (or appending). This mode can be used only with ofstream objects.

To open a file outdata.dat for input, we can code the following.

```
fstream file("outdata.dat", ios::in);
```

When opening a file in either the ios::in or ios::out modes, the FPI is set to 0. Therefore, extracting data or inserting data into the stream begins at the first character position in the file. When an output file is opened in the ios::app, or the **append mode**, the FPI is set to the number of bytes in the file. Therefore, if we insert data into the file, it begins inserting at the end of the file. Therefore, the new data is added to the original file contents.

The program dem14-4.cpp allows the user to enter his/her name and address and stores them in a text file. The program then displays the contents of the file.

```cpp
//dem14-4.cpp

//This program demonstrates simple file input and output.
//The file is opened in ios::in and ios::out modes.

#include <fstream>
#include <iostream>
#include <cstdlib>

using namespace std;

int main()
{
   char buffer[81];
   char file_name[81];

   cout << "Enter the name of the file you want to write to: ";
   cin.getline(file_name, 81);
   fstream file(file_name, ios::out);

   if (!file)
   {
      cerr << endl;
      cerr << "ERROR: File could not be opened." << endl;
      cerr << "Program terminated" << endl;
      exit(1);
   }

   cout << endl;
   cout << "Enter your name: ";
   cin.getline(buffer, 81);

   file << buffer << endl;

   cout << endl;
   cout << "Enter the first line of your address: ";
   cin.getline(buffer, 81);

   file << buffer << endl;

   file.close();

   cout << endl;
   cout << "The file you created is the following:"
                  << endl << endl;

   file.open(file_name, ios::in);
```

```
          if (!file)
          {
            cerr << endl;
            cerr << "ERROR: File could not be opened." << endl;
            cerr << "Program Terminated" << endl;
            exit(1);
          }
          while (!file.eof())
          {
            file.getline(buffer, 81);
            cout << buffer << endl;
          }
          file.close();

          cout << "Program Terminated." << endl;

          return 0;
     }
```

Program Output

Enter the name of the file you want to write to: **dem14-4.txt**

Enter your name: **John C. Molluzzo**

Enter the first line of your address: **Pace University**

The file you created is the following:

John C. Molluzzo
Pace University

Program Terminated.

The program first asks for the name of the file that the user wants to create. The first time we open the file, we create the `fstream` file object in the declaration and open the file in `ios::out` mode. The program next asks for the user's name and address, which the program writes to the file. The program then closes the file and opens the same file in the `ios::in` mode. The `while` statement then displays the contents of the file. Note that, after each time, the file is opened with the `open()` method, we check for an error condition.

The next program, dem14-5.cpp, opens the file created in dem14-4.cpp and appends one line to the file. To open a file in `ios::app` mode, the file object representing the file, `file_app` in the program, should be an `ofstream` object. After appending the line to the file, the program closes the file and then opens it again as an `ifstream` file, `file_in` in the program, so the file contents can be displayed.

```
//dem14-5.cpp

//This program demonstrates simple file input and output.
//The file is opened in in, out, and app modes.
```

```
#include <fstream>
#include <iostream>
#include <cstdlib>

using namespace std;

int main()
{
    char buffer[81];
    char file_name[81];

    cout << "Enter the name of the file you want to append to: ";
    cin.getline(file_name, 81);

    cout << endl;
    cout << "Enter the city, state, and zip code in which you live: ";
    cin.getline(buffer, 81);

    cout << endl;
    cout << "The information will be appended to your file." << endl;

    ofstream file_app(file_name, ios::app);

    if (!file_app)
    {
        cerr << endl;
        cerr << "ERROR: File could not be opened in append mode." << endl;
        cerr << "Program terminated" << endl;
        exit(1);
    }

    file_app << buffer << endl;

    file_app.close();

    cout << endl;
    cout << "Your complete name and address is the following:"
                << endl << endl;

    ifstream file_in(file_name);

    if (!file_in)
    {
        cerr << endl;
        cerr << "ERROR: File could not be opened." << endl;
        cerr << "Program terminated" << endl;
        exit(1);
    }

    while (!file_in.eof())
    {
        file_in.getline(buffer, 81);
        cout << buffer << endl;
    }

    file_in.close();
```

```
    cout << endl;
    cout << "Program Terminated" << endl;

    return 0;
}
```

Program Output

Enter the name of the file you want to append to: **dem14-4.txt**

Enter the city, state, and zip code in which you live: **New York, NY 10038**

The information will be appended to your file.

Your complete name and address is the following:

John C. Molluzzo
Pace University
New York, NY 10038

Program Terminated

Exercises 14.1

In Exercises 1–9 write appropriate C++ statements.

1. Declare and open an output file object and attach it to the file `a:\file1.txt`.
2. Write your name and address onto the file of Exercise 1 on three separate lines.
3. Close the file of Exercise 1.
4. Declare and open an input file object and attach it to the file `c:\data\file2.txt`.
5. Read the first line of the file of Exercise 4 into a character array called `buffer[]`.
6. Close the file of Exercise 4.
7. In a new program, declare and open the file of Exercise 1 in the append mode.
8. Write your age onto the end of the file.
9. Close the file of Exercise 7.
10. Explain the difference between opening a file in the output mode and opening a file in the append mode.

Experiments 14.1

1. Take any program you have written that includes the manipulator `setiosflags()` and remove the `ios::` qualifier from the argument. Compile the resulting program. What happens and why?
2. In dem14-3.cpp, enter the name of a nonexistent file. How does the program behave?
3. In dem14-3.cpp, remove the `if` statement that tests for an error when the file is opened. Recompile and execute the resulting program. When prompted for a file name, enter the name of a nonexistent file. How does the program behave?

4. In prb14-1.cpp, remove the statement that sends `setprecision()` and `setiosflags()` messages to `inventory_file`. Compile, execute, and test the resulting program with the same data used in testing prb14-01.cpp. Examine the file created by the program. Does the data for the price contain decimal points?

5. In prb14-1.cpp, add a record counter to the program that is incremented each time a record is written to the inventory part file. After the program closes the inventory part file, the program should display the value of the record counter.

6. Verify that the Read Ahead Rule of Note 14.4 is needed. Remove the first read of the inventory file that is outside the `while` loop in prb14-2.cpp. Then move the read of the inventory file from the end of the `while` loop body to the beginning of the `while` loop body. Compile, execute, and test the resulting program. Does the program process the file correctly?

Programming Problems 14.1

1. Write a program that combines the processing of programs prb14-1.cpp and 14-2.cpp. Thus, the program should create the parts inventory file by obtaining the data from the user. After creating the file, the program should then search through the file and display those records whose quantity on hand multiplied by price exceeds 3000.00. Declare the file as an `fstream` object so you can perform both input and output on the file.

2. A small business wants to create a file to store its customer information. Each record in the file is to contain the following data: customer ID number (an integer 01–50), first name, last name, city, zip code, and account balance. Write a program to create such a customer file. Set up the file as a sequential text file with space-separated fields.

3. Write a program that displays the file of Programming Problem 2 in column form with appropriate column headings.

4. The National Bank credit card company wishes to issue a new type of card, the Platinum Card, to its preferred customers. Write a program that prints a report that lists all customers who will or can receive a Platinum Card. The customer data is contained in a text file. Each line of the text file contains the following space-separated fields: the customer ID number (a four-digit integer), credit limit, and account balance. If a customer has a credit limit of at least $2000.00 and an account balance of $500.00 or less, the customer will receive a Platinum Card. If a customer's credit limit is at least $2000.00 and account balance is greater than $500.00, the customer will be sent a letter. The letter will state that if the customer's balance becomes $500.00 or less, he or she will receive a Platinum Card.

   Each line of the report should list the customer ID number, credit limit, account balance, and the word APPROVED, LETTER, or DISAPPROVED. The report should contain appropriate column headings. At the end of the report, print the number of customers in each category.

14.2 PROCESSING A FILE ONE CHARACTER AT A TIME

In the previous section, we used the insertion operator to place data onto a text file, and the extraction operator and the `getline()` method to extract data from a text file.

In some cases, it is either necessary or more efficient to extract and/or insert one character at a time onto a text file. In this section, we discuss how to do this.

14.2.1 The get() and put() Methods

To read and write one character to a file, you can use the **get()** and **put()** methods. These methods are faster than using the insertion and extraction operator. The get() method extracts and returns one character from an input file. (We have already used the get() method with the standard input stream, cin.) If in_file is an open ifstream object, in_file.get() returns the next available object from the in_file stream. The get() method retrieves whichever character is indicated by the FPI. Thus, if the FPI is 6, in_file.get() retrieves the character that is 6 characters from the beginning of the file (that is, the seventh character in the file). Then, the get() method increases the FPI by one (7). Therefore, the next exccution of the get() method for the stream will retrieve the next character. See Figure 14.6a.

In addition, the get() method always detects the end-of-file condition, whereas the extraction operator >> does not. (Recall that, in dem14-3.cpp and dem14-4.cpp, we used the eof() method to detect the end-of-file condition.) The get() method returns **EOF** (end-of-file, a constant defined in the iostream header file) if the end-of-file is reached in the input file.

If out_file is an open output stream, then out_file.put(ch) places a copy of the character stored in the variable ch at the position indicated by the FPI. Then the put() method increases the FPI by one. See Figure 14.6b. The program dem14-6.cpp copies one text file to another, one character at a time.

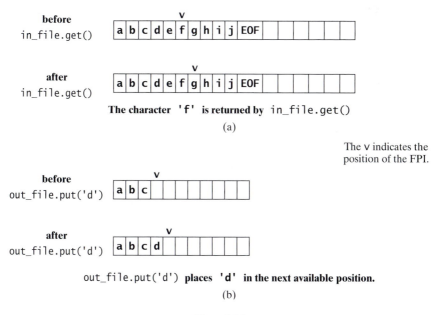

before
in_file.get()

after
in_file.get()

The character 'f' is returned by in_file.get()

(a)

The v indicates the position of the FPI.

before
out_file.put('d')

after
out_file.put('d')

out_file.put('d') places 'd' in the next available position.

(b)

Figure 14.6

```
//dem14-6.cpp

//This program copies one file to another using get() and put()

#include <fstream>
#include <iostream>
#include <cstdlib>

using namespace std;

int main()
{
  char file_name[81];
  char ch;

  cout << "Enter the name of the source file: ";
  cin.getline(file_name, 81);
  ifstream source_file(file_name);

  if (!source_file)
  {
    cout << endl;
    cout << "ERROR: File cannot be opened.";
    exit(1);
  }

  cout << endl;
  cout << "Enter the name of the target file: ";
  cin.getline(file_name, 81);

  ofstream target_file(file_name);

  if (!target_file)
  {
    cout << endl;
    cout << "ERROR: File cannot be opened.";
    exit(1);
  }

  while ( (ch = source_file.get()) != EOF )
    target_file.put(ch);

  source_file.close();
  target_file.close();

  cout << endl << endl;
  cout << "Program Terminated." << endl;

  return 0;
}
```

Program Output

Enter the name of the source file: **outdata.dat**

Enter the name of the target file: **outdata.cpy**

Program Terminated.

from the source file and prints them on the printer. The if statement in the loop tests the character read by get() to see if it is a newline character. If it is, the character is printed again, which achieves double spacing.

Exercises 14.2

1. Declare and open an output file object test_file and attach it to the file testfile.dat.
2. Write a for loop that places all the lowercase letters on this file, one character per line, using put().
3. Close the file.
4. Open the file created in Exercise 14.2 as an input file.
5. Declare and open an output file object, printer_file, attached to the printer.
6. Write a for loop that uses get() and put() to read characters from the input file and places the uppercase version on the printer_file.
7. Close the files test_file and printer_file.

Experiments 14.2

1. Recode dem14-2.cpp using put() instead of cout.
2. Recode dem14-3.cpp using get() instead of cin.
3. Recode dem14-6.cpp using cin and cout.
4. Recode prb14-2.cpp by making the program print its output on the printer rather than displaying it on the monitor.

Programming Problems 14.2

1. Many grammar-checking programs include a utility that computes statistics about a file. Write a program that asks the user for the name of a text file. The program should then count the number of characters, words, and sentences in the file. The program should display the number of characters, words, and sentences in the file, the average word length and the average sentence length. Assume that white space (blanks, tabs, newline characters) separates words. Also, assume that a period ends a sentence.
2. Write a program that compares the contents of two text files. If the files are identical, the program should display a message to that effect. If the files differ, the program should display an appropriate message and the number of bytes from the beginning of the files where the files first differ.
3. Sometimes, when a compiler produces a source-code listing, it numbers the lines of the source code consecutively from 1. Write a program that accepts the name of a text file and numbers its lines beginning at 1. The output of the program should be a file with the same name as the source file and with the extension .lst. Remember to first remove any extension the file name has before adding the .lst.
4. The cloze procedure test is a quick way for a teacher to estimate the difficulty of a textbook. The procedure consists of deleting every fifth word from a passage

from the book. While reading the passage, the student is expected to replace the deleted words. Write a program that reads words from a text file and prepares a cloze test. For purposes of the test, a word is any sequence of alphabetic characters. Therefore, do not delete things such as hyphens and punctuation. Leave the first and last sentences intact. Begin at the second word in the second sentence and replace every fifth word by 15 underscores until 50 words are deleted.

The following table gives the suitability of the text.

Percent Correct	Suitability of Text
Below 40%	Too Hard
Between 40% and 60%	Appropriate for Instruction
Above 60%	Too Easy

(Daniel R. Hittleman, *Developmental Reading*, Rand McNally College Publishing Co., Chicago, 1978.)

14.3 RANDOM FILE ACCESS

In Sections 14.1 and 14.2, we **processed files sequentially**, one character or record at a time. It is also possible to **process** the characters in a **file randomly**. Thus, a program can begin processing a file at any desired location within the file, then go to another location in the file, and so on, at random.

14.3.1 Text and Binary Files

As we discussed in Section 14.1, all the files we have processed so far are **text files**. A text file, for example a C++ source-code program, is a sequence of characters that occasionally includes a newline character. In some operating systems, most notably Windows, when a program places a newline character into a file, the newline character is physically stored as two characters: a carriage return and a line feed (CRLF). Similarly, when a program reads the CRLF pair from a text file, the system converts them into a single newline character. Although the program "sees" only one character, the newline character, the operating system is actually processing the CRLF pair.

When randomly processing a file, a program must know its exact position in the file. If we attempt to process randomly a file that is opened as a text file (which is the default when using the opening modes previously discussed), the program can lose its place in the file. This can occur because of the conversion of the newline character into the CRLF pair. Therefore, when we process a file randomly, we should not open the file as a text file.

When a program opens a file as a **binary file**, none of the characters is ever changed when read or written by the program. Thus, the program will process the newline character, if it is stored as the CRLF pair, as a pair of characters instead of as a single character. To open a file in binary mode, you must use the opening mode **ios::binary** together with one of the opening modes previously discussed. To do this requires the use of |, the **bitwise OR** operator. Do not confuse the logical OR operator, ||, with bitwise OR. Logical OR returns true, that is, numeric 1, if either of its operands is true. Bitwise

OR works at the *bit level* between its operands. If either of two bits is 1, then the bitwise OR of them is 1. The only time bitwise OR results in a 0 bit is when the bits are both 0. Following is an example. Note that the only time we obtain a 0 is when both bits are 0.

```
1010 1010     First operand
0010 0111     Second Operand
---------
1010 1111     Bitwise OR
```

Bitwise OR is used to set (that is, make 1) particular bits. Note, in the preceding example, that if a bit in the first operand is 0, the result of the bitwise OR is to copy the corresponding bit of the second operand into the result. On the other hand, if a bit in the first operand is 1, the result of the bitwise OR is a 1 in the corresponding position of the result, no matter what the bit in the second operand. Thus, to set a bit to 1, bitwise OR it with 1. Bitwise ORing with 0 leaves the bit unchanged. For example, consider the following bitwise OR in which we do not know the second operand.

```
0010 0000     First Operand
???? ????     Second Operand
---------
??1? ????     Bitwise OR
```

No matter what the bit value of the second operand, the third bit from the left must be a 1 in the result. The remaining seven bits are copied to the result.

The opening modes for files, for example `ios::in` and `ios::binary`, actually refer to specific bits in a status variable defined in the `ios` class. For illustrative purposes, suppose that opening a file in the `ios::in` mode results in setting the second bit of that variable to 1.

```
0100 0000
```

Also suppose that opening the file in `ios::binary` mode results in setting the fifth bit to 1.

```
0000 1000
```

Now, if we open the file in `ios::in | ios::binary` mode, the resulting bitwise OR of the two modes would be as follows:

```
0100 0000     ios::in
0000 1000     ios::binary
---------
0100 1000     ios::in | ios::binary
```

The file would be opened in both the input and binary modes because both the input and binary bits are 1. The following statement would, therefore, open the file `bindata.dat` as a binary input file.

```
fstream in_file ("bindata.dat", ios::in | ios::binary);
```

It is also possible to open a file using three of the opening modes as follows.

```
fstream iofile("bindata.dat", ios::in | ios::out | ios::binary);
```

The file `bindata.dat` is open in the binary mode as both an input and an output file. Therefore, the program can read and write data to the file without having to close and open the file between file operations.

14.3.2 Random-Access Member Functions

The C++ I/O classes contain several methods that enable a program to access a file randomly. Each of these methods manipulates the file's File Position Indicator, or FPI. Recall that the methods `getc()` and `putc()` determine where to access the file by using the FPI. Therefore, if we can manipulate the FPI, we can read or write characters to any desired location in the file.

The methods of Note 14.6 are available for stream objects.

Note 14.6   Random-Access Methods

The following methods are available to perform random file access.

seekg(*offset, mode*) // for input files - move to *offset* as indicated by mode.

seekp(*offset, mode*) // for output files - move to offset as indicated by mode.

tellg()// for input files - returns the current value of the FPI (a long).

tellp()// for output files - returns the current value of the FPI (a long).

Note that you can think of the suffix "p" in the function names as meaning "put" and the suffix "g" as meaning "get."

The *offset* must be a long integer (positive or negative). The *mode* can be any of the following:

ios::beg   //Places the FPI at the beginning of the file.

ios::cur   //Places the FPI at the current position in the file.

ios::end   //Places the FPI at the end of the file.

A few examples will illustrate the uses of these methods. Figure 14.7 shows the eight-character file, `"fpitest.dat"`, which is opened as a binary file as follows.

```
fstream in_file("fpitest.dat", ios::in | ios::binary);
```

Opening the file in `ios::in` mode sets its FPI to zero, as Figure 14.7a shows. The caret shows the character that the FPI indicates. Figure 14.7b shows the FPI after executing `in_file.seekg(3L, ios::cur)`. (The suffix L causes the computer to store the integer 3 as a `long` instead of the default type `int`. You can also use a type cast `(long)3` or `long(3)` in place of the suffix L.) Because the second argument of **seekg()** is `ios::cur`, the method initially does nothing to the value of the FPI. Because the first

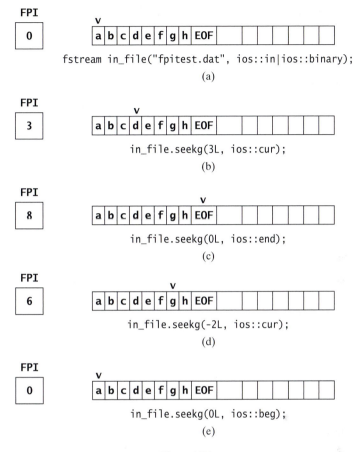

Figure 14.7

argument is 3L, seekg() adds three to the FPI. Thus, the value of the FPI is 3 and the character it indicates is 'd'.

Figure 14.7c shows how to move the FPI to the end of the file by executing in_file.seekg(0L, ios::end). Figure 14.7d shows that the first argument in seekg() can be negative. The statement in_file.seekg(-2L, ios::cur) subtracts two from the current value of the FPI. Therefore, the statement "backs up" the FPI to the character 'g'. Finally, as shown in Figure 14.7e, the statement in_file.seekg (0L, ios::beg) sets the FPI back to zero, which makes the FPI indicate the first character in the file.

You can use the method tellg() to find the value of the FPI at any point in your program. For example, the following statements calculate the size of a file in bytes.

```
long file_size;

in_file.seekg(0L, ios::end);

file_size = in_file.tellg();
```

The program dem14-8.cpp illustrates these concepts. The program asks the user for the name of a file. The program then uppercases all the characters in the file. Note that the program does not make an uppercase copy of the file while leaving the original intact. It opens the file, uppercases its characters, and closes the file.

```cpp
//dem14-8.cpp

#include <iostream>
#include <fstream>
#include <cstdlib>
#include <cctype>
#include <iomanip>

using namespace std;

int main()
{
  char file_name [51];
  char ch;

  cout << "Enter the file you want to uppercase: ";
  cin.getline(file_name, 51);

  fstream file(file_name, ios::in | ios::out | ios::binary);

  if (!file)
  {
    cout << endl;
    cout << "ERROR: Could not open file.";
    exit(1);
  }
  while ( (ch = file.get()) != EOF)
  {
    ch = toupper(ch);
    file.seekg(-1L, ios::cur);
    file.put(ch);
    cout << file.tellg() << setw(6) << ch << endl;
  }

  cout << endl;
  cout << "Program Terminated." << endl;
  cout << endl;

  file.close();

  return 0;
}
```

Program Input File

abC De
fg

Program Output - Monitor

```
Enter the file you want to uppercase: text.txt
1      A
2      B
3      C
4
5      D
6      E
7
8

9      F
10      G
11
12

Program Terminated.
```

Program Output - Output File

```
ABC DE
FG
```

The program begins by asking the user to enter the name of the file to be upper-cased. The program stores the name of the file in the array file_name[]. The program then creates an fstream object called file, which is opened as a binary file for both input and output. After checking that the file was opened correctly, the program enters the while loop. The while loop's test gets a character from the file and tests for the end-of-file condition. If a character is read, the first statement in the loop body stores the uppercase version of the character in the variable ch. Because file.get()increased the FPI by one, the next statement in the loop body subtracts one from the FPI. This ensures that the next file operation, namely file.put(ch), places the character back into its original position in the file. Note that executing file.put(ch) again increases the FPI by one, so the next file.get() will retrieve the next character in the file. The last statement in the loop body displays the current value of the FPI using file.tellg() and the current value of ch. Can you explain why there is a blank line between the line that is numbered 8 and the line that is numbered 9?

Exercises 14.3

In Exercises 1–5, assume that the file alpha.dat contains only the 26 lowercase letters of the alphabet (abcd … wxyz). In each exercise, state the letter of the alphabet that the FPI indicates after executing the given instruction. Assume that the statements are executed in sequence.

1. `fstream input_file("alpha.dat", ios::in | ios::binary);`
2. `input_file.seekg(5L, ios::cur);`
3. `input_file.seekg(3L, ios::cur);`
4. `input_file.seekg(-3L, ios::end);`
5. `input_file.seekg(5L, ios::beg);`

In Exercises 6–15, assume that the file `alpha.dat` contains only the 26 lowercase letters of the alphabet (abcd … wxyz). In each exercise, either give the letter that the FPI indicates or state the change made to the file and the resulting value of the FPI. Assume that the statements are executed in sequence.

6. `fstream input_file("alpha.dat", ios::in | ios::out | ios::binary);`
7. `input_file.seekg(7L, ios::beg);`
8. `ch = input_file.get();`
9. `input_file.seekg(3L, ios::cur);`
10. `ch = input_file.get();`
11. `input_file.seekg(-5L, ios::end);`
12. `input_file.put('*');`
13. `ch = input_file.get();`
14. `input_file.seekg(-1L, ios::cur);`
15. `ch = input_file.get();`

In Exercises 16–19, suppose that byte b contains the bits 1010 0101. Give the result of bitwise ORing b with the indicated byte.

16. 0000 0000
17. 1111 1111
18. 0101 1010
19. b

Experiments 14.3

1. Write a program that asks the user for the name of a file and then prints a capitalized version of the file on the printer.
2. Remove the `ios:binary` from the file opening mode in dem14-8.cpp. Compile and execute the resulting program. What happens? Carefully explain the resulting output.
3. A student writes the executable part of `main()` in dem14-8.cpp as follows. Does this version of the program work? If not, explain why.

```
cout << "Enter the file you want to uppercase: ";
cin.getline(file_name, 51);

fstream input_file(file_name, ios::in | ios::out | ios::binary);

while ( !file.eof() )
    {
```

```
      ch = input_file.get();
      input_file.seekg(- 1L, ios::cur);
      input_file.put(toupper(ch));
      input_file.seekg(0L, ios::cur);
   }

   input_file.close();
```

4. The **bitwise AND** operator, & (not to be confused with the logical AND operator, &&), is defined as follows. If both of two bits are 1, then the bitwise AND of them is 1. Otherwise, the bitwise AND of them is 0. Therefore, if either bit is 0, the bitwise AND of them is 0. Following is an example. Note that the only time we obtain a 1 is when both bits are 1.

1010 1010	First operand
0010 0111	Second Operand

0010 0010	Bitwise AND

Whereas the bitwise OR is used to turn on a bit, the bitwise AND is used to turn off a bit. Note that no matter what a bit is set to, ANDing it with a 0 results in a 0. ANDing a bit with a 1 leaves the bit unchanged. Now, suppose that byte b contains the bits 1010 0101. Give the result of bitwise ANDing b with the indicated byte.

   (a) 0000 0000

   (b) 1111 1111

   (c) 0101 1010

   (d) b

Programming Problems 14.3

1. Write a program that asks the user to enter the name of a file. The program should display the number of characters in the file.

2. Write a program that asks the user to enter the name of a text file. The program should display on the monitor the contents of the file in reverse order, that is, from the last character to the first.

3. Write a program that asks the user to enter the name of a text file. The program should display on the monitor the middle character in the file if there is an odd number of characters in the file. If there is an even number of characters in the file, the program should display the middle two characters.

4. Write a program that asks the user to enter the name of a text file and a positive integer, n. The program should display on the monitor the n-th character in the file. If n exceeds the number of characters in the file, the program should display an error message.

14.4 BINARY SEQUENTIAL FILE PROCESSING

In Section 14.1, we created and processed a text file of records in which each **record** was a line of text terminated by a newline character. The fields in the file's records were text fields separated by one or more spaces. When processing such a file, each record is not read or written as a unit. To write a record to such a file requires writing each field separately. Likewise, to read a record from such a file requires reading each field separately. In C++, we can store and process all the data in a record as a unit by using a structure to implement the records in a file. For example, we could use the following structure for the part record of the inventory file of Section 14.1. Recall that each record in the part inventory file consists of three fields: the ID number field, the quantity-on-hand field, and the price field. The members of the structure are the fields of the record.

```
struct Part_Record
{
   char    id_no[3];
   int     qoh;
   double  price;
};
```

The `Part_Record` structure is in binary form. Although the first member of the structure, `id_no`, is character data, it is of fixed size—3 bytes. The qoh and `price` members are binary data, not text data. To illustrate the difference, suppose that the value of qoh for a specific record is 23450. If this is stored as text, it requires 5 bytes of memory. However, because 23450 is an integer, if stored as an integer (that is, in binary), it requires as little as 2 bytes on some systems. In fact, on a given computer system, all integers require the same amount of storage (4 bytes on either Windows or UNIX/Linux systems) no matter what their values. The same is true of doubles (8 bytes on most systems). Because each field in `Part_Record` is a fixed size (3 bytes for id_no, 4 bytes for qoh, and 8 bytes for `price`), there is no need to separate the fields by spaces. Also, when we write such records to a binary sequential file, the newline character *will not* separate one record from the next. Instead, any program that processes this file distinguishes one record from the next by the length of the record. This is possible because all records in the file are the same size.

In this section, we discuss how to create and process binary **sequential files** that consist of sequences of structures. That is, we discuss how to create and process a sequential binary file of records.

14.4.1 Creating a Binary Sequential File of Records

We first consider binary files that are created and accessed sequentially. Suppose that we have a data file of inventory records that was created using a text editor or by a program such as prb14-1.cpp in Section 14.1. Each record is a line in the file. Each line consists of a two-digit part number, an integer quantity on hand, and a decimal-valued unit price. Spaces separate each of these fields from the others. The following is an example inventory file. The first field in each record is a two-character ID number. The second field is an integer representing the quantity on hand for the part. The third field is the price of the item.

```
23 145    24.95
15 46     67.99
65 230    11.95
```

```
56 37      73.95
59 1074     3.95
12 26     104.99
84 19      55.95
03 81      18.95
44 39      31.95
```

We wish to write a program that reads records from this file and writes them to a binary sequential file. We assume that the records of the binary sequential file are Part_Record structures, as described previously. One way to read records from the input text file is to use the extraction operator <<. Because we must obtain three fields from the file for each record, we use the function Read_Part_Record() to read a record from the file. The definition of the function is as follows.

```
void Read_Part_Record(ifstream& ifs, Part Record& pr)
{
   ifs >> pr.id_no;
   ifs >> pr.qoh;
   ifs >> pr.price;
}
```

The function takes two arguments. The first argument is a reference to an ifstream object. Therefore, we shall pass the input file object name as the first argument. The second argument is a reference to a Part_Record structure. Therefore, we shall pass the name of a Part_Record structure as the second argument. The function reads three data items from the ifstream object, ifs, and places them into the three members of the part structure. The program can then manipulate the part structure.

Assume the following declarations in our program.

```
Part_Record part;
```

```
ifstream input_file(input_file_name);
```

Then to read a data from the input file, we could execute the following statement, which reads a record from input_file and places a copy of the record into the structure part.

```
Read_Part_Record(input_file, part);
```

Now that we can read data from the input file, we want to write it onto a binary file as a structure. To do this requires the method **write()**, whose syntax is given in Note 14.7.

We cast the structure pointer as (char*) for the following reason. The people who coded the write() method could not know the data type of the first argument. The first argument could be a pointer to any structure that you choose. To allow write() to be used with any pointer, the method assumes its first argument to be a character pointer. Then, to use the method, the programmer simply casts the first argument as a character pointer.

The operator **sizeof()**—yes, sizeof() is an operator, not a function—returns the number of bytes required to store a variable of the type that is its argument. You use the sizeof() operator in much the same way as you use a function. Place the name of a data type (one of C++'s built-in types or a user-defined type) in parentheses

---

Note 14.7   The Syntax of the Method `write()`

The method `write()`, which can be applied to any output file object opened in binary mode, has the following syntax.

```
write( (char*) ptr, item_size)
```

In the preceding syntax, `ptr` is a pointer to the data that is to be written. The pointer must be cast as a character pointer because generally it will be pointing to some kind of structure. (See the discussion following this note.) The second argument, `item_size`, is the number of bytes to be written, which is usually the size of the structure that is being written to the file. Use the operator `sizeof()`, which we soon discuss, to have the system determine the number of bytes in the structure.

---

after `sizeof()`. The value returned by the operator is the number of bytes required to store a variable of that type. Thus, `sizeof(int)` is the number of bytes required to store an integer in the system on which the function is evaluated. On Windows or UNIX/Linux systems, `sizeof(int)` is four.

To write a copy of the structure variable `part` onto the file `input_file`, we execute the following statement.

```
input_file.write( (char*) &part, sizeof(Part_Record) );
```

In the first argument, `&part` is the address of (that is a pointer to) the area of storage that is to be copied onto the file. As required by the method, `(char*)` casts the `Part_Record` pointer as a character pointer. The second argument is the number of bytes to copy.

Program dem14-9.cpp reads records from a text file and writes structures onto a binary sequential file of records.

```
//dem14-9.cpp

//This program creates a sequential file of structures from a text
//data file. It uses >> to obtain data from the text file
//and uses the write() method to write structures
//onto the output file.

#include <iostream>
#include <fstream>
#include <cstdlib>

using namespace std;

struct Part_Record
{
   char    id_no[3];
   int     qoh;
   double  price;
};
```

```cpp
void Read_Part_Record(ifstream&, Part_Record&);

int main()
{
  int record_count = 0;

  char input_file_name[51];
  char output_file_name[51];

  Part_Record part;

  cout << "Enter the name of the text file: ";
  cin.getline(input_file_name, 51);

  ifstream input_file(input_file_name);

  if (!input_file)
  {
    cout << endl;
    cout << "ERROR: Could not open text file.";
    exit(1);
  }

  cout << endl;
  cout << "Enter the name of the sequential file: ";
  cin.getline(output_file_name, 51);

  ofstream output_file(output_file_name, ios::binary);

  if (!output_file)
  {
    cout << endl;
    cout << "ERROR: Could not open sequential file: ";
    exit(1);
  }

  //Read the first record

  Read_Part_Record(input_file, part);

  while (!input_file.eof())
  {
    output_file.write( (char *)&part, sizeof(Part_Record) );
    ++record_count;

    Read_Part_Record(input_file, part);
  }

  cout << endl << endl << record_count << " records written.";

  input_file.close();
  output_file.close();

  cout << endl;

  return 0;
}

void Read_Part_Record(ifstream& ifs, Part_Record& pr)
```

```
{
    ifs >> pr.id_no;
    ifs >> pr.qoh;
    ifs >> pr.price;
}
```

Program Output - Monitor

Enter the name of the text file: **dem14-9.in**

Enter the name of the sequential file: **dem14-9.out**

9 records written.

Input File: dem14-9.in

```
23 145     24.95
15 46      67.99
65 230     11.95
56 37      73.95
59 1074     3.95
12 26     104.99
84 19      55.95
03 81      18.95
44 39      31.95
```

In the program, we first declare a counter, record_count, which counts the number of records the program processes. Two character arrays store the system names of the input and output files. The Part_Record structure part is where the program will place the data. The program then obtains the names of the input and output files and opens associated file objects. Note that the input file is opened, by default, as a text file, and the output file is opened as a binary file.

When reading a file sequentially, you must take care that your program processes the last input record, and that it processes it exactly once. Note 14.4, the Read Ahead Rule, applies here also: read the first record after opening the file; read the next record as soon as the program completes processing the input data.

The program code of dem14-9.cpp follows this outline. After the input file is opened, the program reads the first record using the function Read_Part_Record(). The program passes as reference arguments to the function the name of the file and the Part_Record structure part. In the body of the function, the extraction operator obtains the three fields and place each into the corresponding data member of the structure. The while loop then tests the end-of-file condition. If it is not the end-of-file, the loop body executes and processes the record. The processing is simply to write a copy of the record onto the sequential output file and increment the record counter. Then the input file is read again. The program exits the loop when the end-of-file is reached. Then the program displays the number of records that were processed and closes the files.

14.4.2 Reading a Sequential File of Records

To read the records of the sequential file created by dem14-8.cpp, we need the member function **read()** whose syntax is given in Note 14.8.

Note 14.8   The Syntax of the Member Function read()

The method read(), which can be applied to any input file object that is opened as a binary file, has the following syntax.

```
read( (char*) ptr, item_size)
```

In this syntax, ptr is a pointer to the location where the read data is to be stored. The pointer must be cast as a character pointer because it will, generally, be pointing to some kind of structure. The second argument, item_size, is the number of bytes to be read, which is usually the size of the structure that is being read from the file. Use the operator **sizeof()** to have the system determine the number of bytes in the structure.

Program dem14-10.cpp shows how to read the records from a sequential file of structures and write them onto a file that is suitable for printing.

```cpp
//dem14-10.cpp

//This program shows how to read a sequential file of structures.
//It uses the member function read() to read records from the file
//and uses << to print records to a disk text file in a form
//suitable for later printing. The program assumes that the input file
//has been previously created by the program dem14-8.cpp

#include <iostream>
#include <iomanip>
#include <fstream>
#include <cstdlib>

using namespace std;

struct Part_Record
{
   char    id_no[3];
   int     qoh;
   double price;
};

int main()
{
   Part_Record part;

   char input_file_name[51];
   char output_file_name[51];
```

```
   int record_count = 0;

   cout << "Enter the name of the printable file: ";
   cin.getline(output_file_name, 51);

   ofstream output_file(output_file_name);

   if (!output_file)
   {
     cout << "ERROR: Could not open printable file.";
     exit(1);
   }

   output_file << setw(15) << "Part Number" << setw(15) << "Quan on Hand"
               << setw(15) << "Price" << endl << endl;

   cout << "Enter the name of the sequential file: ";
   cin.getline(input_file_name, 51);

   ifstream input_file(input_file_name, ios::binary);

   if (!input_file)
   {
     cout << "ERROR: Could not open sequential file.";
     exit(1);
   }

   input_file.read( (char*) &part, sizeof(Part_Record) );

   while (!input_file.eof())
   {
     ++record_count;
     output_file << setw(15) << part.id_no << setw(15) << part.qoh
                 << setw(15) << part.price << endl;

     input_file.read( (char *) &part, sizeof(Part_Record) );
   }

   cout << endl << endl << record_count << " records read.";

   input_file.close();
   output_file.close();

   return 0;
}
```

Program Output - Monitor

Enter the name of the printable file: **dem14-10.out**

Enter the name of the sequential file: **dem14-9.out**

9 records read.

Listing of dem14-10.out

```
Part Number    Quan on Hand              Price
        23             145              24.95
        15              46              67.99
        65             230              11.95
        56              37              73.95
        59            1074               3.95
        12              26             104.99
        84              19              55.95
        03              81              18.95
        44              39              31.95
```

First, the program obtains the name of the printable file and opens it. Then it writes column headings onto the file using the insertion operator. Next, the program obtains the name of the sequential input file and opens it in binary mode. Using the Read Ahead Rule of Note 14.4 again, the program reads the first record from the input file using the read() method. It then enters the while loop, where it increments record_count and writes the three structure members (the ID number, quantity in hand, and price) onto the output file. Because this completes processing the current record, the program then reads the next input record using read(). When the program reaches the end-of-file, the loop ends and the program displays the number of records processed. Finally, the program closes both files. Shown after the program code is the output that the program displays on the monitor and a listing of the output file. You can also view the output file in a text editor.

Exercises 14.4

Suppose a text file contains on each line, separated by spaces, a decimal number and an integer representing a price and a quantity.

1. Code a structure declaration Item for a structure to contain the price and quantity as members.
2. Code a function Read_Item() that reads a record from the file previously described into a structure variable of type Item.
3. Code a write() statement that writes an Item structure onto the binary file item_file, which is opened for output.
4. Code a read() statement that reads an Item structure from the binary file item_file, which is opened for input.

Experiments 14.4

1. In dem14-9.cpp, omit the opening mode ios::binary in the declaration of output_file. Compile the resulting program. What happens and why?
2. In dem14-9.cpp, declare output_file as an fstream object. Make the appropriate changes to the program. Compile, execute, and test the resulting program. Do these changes make any difference?

3. In dem14-9.cpp, omit the first call to the function Read_Part_Record(). Compile, execute, and test the resulting program. What happens and why?

4. In dem14-9.cpp, omit the type cast (char*) in the write() method inside the while loop. Compile the resulting program. What happens and why? If the program compiles without error, execute the program. Do any run-time errors occur?

5. In dem14-10.cpp, omit the opening mode ios::binary from the declaration of input_file. Compile, execute, and test the resulting program. Explain the results.

Programming Problems 14.4

1. (See Programming Problem 2, Section 14.1.) A small business wants to create a file to store its customer information. Each record in the file is to contain the following data: customer ID number (a two-digit integer), first name, last name, city, zip code, and account balance. Design a record structure for the records of this file. Write a program to create a binary sequential customer file. The program should prompt the user for the information on each record and then create and store the record as a structure in the file.

2. Write a program that displays the file of Programming Problem 1 in column form with appropriate column headings on the printer and a system report file.

3. Write a program that creates a sequential binary file of account records. Each record in the file contains an ID number (a four-digit integer), a customer name, credit limit, and account balance. The program should ask the user to enter the data for each account. Then the program should write the data as a structure onto the account file.

4. (See Programming Problem 4, Section 14.1.) The National Bank credit card company wishes to issue a new type of card, the Platinum Card, to its preferred customers. Write a program that prints a report that lists all customers who will or can receive a Platinum Card. The customer data is contained in the sequential file created in Programming Problem 3. Each record in the file contains the following fields: the customer ID number (a four-digit integer), the customer name, credit limit, and account balance. If a customer has a credit limit of at least $2000.00 and an account balance of $500.00 or less, the customer will receive a Platinum Card. If a customer's credit limit is at least $2000.00 and account balance is greater than $500.00, the customer will be sent a letter. The letter will state that if the customer's balance becomes $500.00 or less, he or she will receive a Platinum Card.

Each line of the report should list the customer ID number, customer name, credit limit, account balance, and the word APPROVED, LETTER, or DISAPPROVED. The report should contain appropriate column headings. At the end of the report, print the number of customers in each category. Output the report to the printer and a system report file.

5. A retail-store owner must submit a monthly report to the city government that lists each of the store's employees, together with each employee's gross pay for the month, city tax, and net pay. Write a program that prompts the user to enter each employee's name and gross pay for the month. If the employee's gross pay is $1000.00 or less, the city tax rate is 5% of the gross pay. If the gross pay exceeds

$1000.00, the city tax is $50.00 plus 7.5% of the gross pay over $1000.00. The net pay is the gross pay less the city tax. The program should print the city tax report on a printer and create a binary sequential employee file. Each record in the file contains the employee's name, gross pay, city tax, and net pay.

6. Write a program that reads the binary sequential employee file created in Programming Problem 5 and displays a list of all employees whose gross pay exceeds $1000.00.

14.5 RANDOM RECORD INPUT/OUTPUT

In this section, we describe how to process a binary random-access file of records. This requires using the techniques and methods of the previous sections. We begin by discussing a problem.

14.5.1 Random-Access File Update

Problem: The accounts receivable department wants a program that will enable them to access randomly a file called `partfile.dat` containing information on parts. Each record in the file contains a two-digit part number (01-99), the quantity on hand for the part, and the unit price of the part. The user must be able to do the following:

1. Add a record to the file.
2. Find a record in the file and change either the quantity on hand or the price, or both.
3. Delete a record from the file.
4. Display the contents of the file.

The program must be able to process the records in any order.

We shall use a type of random file called a **relative file**. In a relative file, a program uses a record's position in the file to access the record. For our problem, we shall use the part number, which is an integer from 01 to 99, as the **relative record number**. Therefore, the record for part 01 is the first record in the file, the record for part 02 is the second record in the file, and so on. The 47th record in the file is the record for part number 47. Conceptually, the records in a relative file are stored sequentially. Therefore, a relative file is analogous to an array. See Figure 14.8.

14.5.2 Creating the File

Before using a relative file, a program must create the file with enough space for the file's records. This file will contain records (structures) that are filled with "null" information.

```
record 1   record 2                    record 47
┌──────┬──────┬         ┬──────┬
│01┊   │02┊   │   . . . │47┊   │   . . .
└──────┴──────┴         ┴──────┴
```

A Relative File

Figure 14.8

For example, all numeric fields will contain zero and any character field will contain blanks. The program dem14-11.cpp creates a file of 99 "null" structures of type Part_Record.

```
//dem14-11.cpp

//This program creates a file of empty part records.
//The file is used by the program prb14-4.cpp.

#include <fstream>
#include <iostream>

using namespace std;

struct Part_Record
{
  char    id_no[3];
  int     qoh;
  double price;
};

int main()
{
  fstream part_file("partfile.dat", ios::out | ios::binary);
  Part_Record null_part = {"  ", 0, 0.0};

  for (long rec_num = 1L; rec_num <= 99L; ++rec_num)
    part_file.write( (char *) &null_part, sizeof(Part_Record) );

  cout << endl;
  cout << "Null File Created." << endl;

  //Close the file

  part_file.close();

  return 0;
} //End of main()
```

Program Output

```
Null File Created.
```

The program is very simple. The file binary partfile.dat is opened for output. The program then writes 99 "null" part records to the file. Each of these records contains a blank id_no field and qoh and price fields containing numeric zero. The program then closes the file.

14.5.3 Designing the Update Program

The logic of main() in the update program is simple. The program opens the parts file if it exists or terminates with an error message if it does not exist. The program then displays the main menu and takes the appropriate action depending on the user's menu choice. Following is the pseudocode for `main()`.

Pseudocode for `main ()`:

open partfile.dat
do
    get main menu choice
    switch (menu choice)
        case add: add_record
        case delete: delete_record
        case change: change_record
        case display: display_file
        case quit: quit program
        default: display "Invalid Choice"
    endswitch
while(!quit)
close partfile.dat

The designs of the modules for adding, deleting, and changing a record and displaying the file are also straightforward. Following is the pseudocode for adding a record to the file.

Pseudocode for `add_record`:

get record number
validate record number
get rest of record data
find record position in file
if record does not already exist
    write record onto file
else
    display "Part already exists"
endif

The module begins by obtaining the record number from the user and validating the number (remember, the number must be between 01 and 99). If the record number is valid, the module obtains the rest of the record data from the user. Next, the module finds the position of the record in the file—that is, where to place the record in the file based on the record number. If there is no record currently occupying this position in the file, the record does not already exist and the module writes the record to the file. If there is a record occupying the position in the file, the record exists and the record cannot be added to the file. Therefore, the module displays an appropriate error message.

Following is the pseudocode for the `delete_record` module.

Pseudocode for `delete_record`:

get record number
validate record number
find and read record from file
if record position is not occupied

```
   display "Record does not exist"
else
   delete record from file
endif
```

The `delete_record` module gets a record number from the user and then validates that the number is between 01 and 99. If the record number is in the valid range, the module finds that record position in the file and reads the contents of that position. If the record position is not occupied (remember, a "null" record contains null information), the record does not exist and the module displays an appropriate error message. If the record position is occupied, the module deletes the record.

Following is the pseudocode for `change_record`.

Pseudocode for `change_record`:

```
get record number
validate record number
find and read record from file
if record position is not occupied
   display "Record does not exist"
else
   display current record contents
   do
     get change menu choice
     switch (change menu choice)
        case change q_o_h:  get new q_o_h
        case change price:  get price
        case quit and write: write changed record onto file
        default:            display "Invalid Choice"
     endswitch
   while ( !quit )
```

The `change_record` module obtains and validates the number of the record to change. Then, it finds and reads that record from the file. If the record position is unoccupied, the record does not exist. Therefore, the module displays an error message.

If the record position is occupied, the module makes the changes in a do loop. The module obtains a menu choice from the user. If the user chooses to change the quantity on hand field in the record, the module obtains the new quantity on hand from the user. If the user chooses to change the price field in the record, the module obtains the new price from the user. When satisfied with the changes to the record, the user can choose to write the record changes and quit the change module.

The design of the `display_file` module follows.

Pseudocode for `display_file`:

```
move to start of the file
display column headings
for (rec_num = 1; rec_num <= 99; ++rec_num)
   read record
   if record is not empty
     print record
```

```
        increment record count
      endif
    endfor
    print record count
```

The `display_file` module begins by moving to the start of the file and display-ing the column headings. The `for` loop then displays the file. For each record in the file, if the record is not empty, the module displays the record and increments the record count. After the module exits the `for` loop, it displays the record count.

To fully explain the rest of the program logic, we now discuss the program itself.

14.5.4 Program Code

Following is the code of prb14-3.cpp, our program solution to the random-file update problem.

```cpp
//prb14-3.cpp

//This program does a random update of a relative file
//of part records. The initial file of empty records is
//created by the program dem14-11.cpp. This program assumes
//that file exists.

#include <iostream>
#include <iomanip>
#include <fstream>
#include <cstdlib>
#include <string>

using namespace std;

struct Part_Record
{
   char   id_no[3];
   int    qoh;
   double price;
};

int Get_Menu_Choice();
void Add_Record(fstream&);
void Delete_Record(fstream&);
void Change_Record(fstream&);
int Get_Change();
void Display_File(fstream&);
bool Valid_Rec_Num(long);

int main()
{
   int choice;
   bool quit = false;

   cout << setprecision(2)
        << setiosflags(ios::fixed)
        << setiosflags(ios::showpoint);
```

```
fstream part_file;

Part_Record null_part = { "   ", 0, 0.0};

//Open the file for reading to see if file exists

part_file.open("partfile.dat", ios::in | ios::binary);

//If the file does not exist,
//display message and end program

if (part_file.fail())
{
  cerr << "Part File does not exist." << endl;
  cerr << "Run Part File Creation Program." << endl;
  part_file.close();
  exit(1);
}

//Close the file

part_file.close();

//Open the file for both input and output

part_file.open("partfile.dat", ios::in | ios::out | ios::binary);

//Processing loop

do
{
  choice = Get_Menu_Choice();
  switch (choice)
  {
    case 1:
      Add_Record(part_file); break;
    case 2:
      Delete_Record(part_file); break;
    case 3:
      Change_Record(part_file); break;
    case 4:
      Display_File(part_file); break;
    case 5:
      quit = true; break;
    default:
      cout << endl << endl;
      cout << "Invalid Choice. Try Again." << endl << endl; break;
  }
}
while (!quit);

part_file.close();

cout << endl;
cout << "Program Ended" << endl;
```

```
    return 0;
} //End of main()

int Get_Menu_Choice()
{
    int choice;
    cout << endl << endl;
    cout << "Main Menu" << endl << endl;
    cout << "1 - Add a Record" << endl
         << "2 - Delete a Record" << endl
         << "3 - Change a Record" << endl
         << "4 - Display the File" << endl
         << "5 - Quit the Program" << endl << endl;

    cout << "Enter your choice: ";
    cin >> choice;

    return choice;
}   //End Get_Menu_Choice()

void Add_Record(fstream& file)
{
    Part_Record part;
    Part_Record temp_part;

    long rec_num;

    cin.get();

    cout << endl;
    cout << "Enter the data for a part:" << endl << endl;
    cout << "Part Number (01-99): ";
    cin.getline(part.id_no, 3);

    rec_num = atol(part.id_no);
    if ( !Valid_Rec_Num(rec_num) )
      return;

    cout << endl;
    cout << "Quantity On Hand: ";
    cin >> part.qoh;

    cout << endl;
    cout << "Price: ";
    cin >> part.price;

    file.seekg( (rec_num - 1) * sizeof(Part_Record), ios::beg);

    file.read( (char *)&temp_part, sizeof(Part_Record) );

    if ( strcmp(temp_part.id_no, "  ") == 0)
    {
      file.seekg( -(long)sizeof(Part_Record), ios::cur);
      file.write( (char *)&part, sizeof(Part_Record) );
      cout << endl;
      cout << "Record " << part.id_no << " added to file." << endl;
```

```
  }
  else
  {
    cout << endl;
    cout << "Part already exists. Make another selection." << endl;
  }
} //End of Add_Record

void Delete_Record(fstream& file)
{
  Part_Record part;
  Part_Record null_part = {"   ", 0, 0.0};

  long rec_num;

  cout << endl;
  cout << "Enter the number of the record to delete: ";
  cin >> rec_num;

  if (!Valid_Rec_Num(rec_num))
    return;

  file.seekg( (rec_num - 1) * sizeof(Part_Record), ios::beg);
  file.read( (char *) &part, sizeof(Part_Record) );

  if ( strcmp(part.id_no, "   ") == 0)
  {
    cout << endl;
    cout << "The record does not exist. Make another selection.";
  }
  else
  {
    file.seekg(-(long)sizeof(Part_Record), ios::cur);
    file.write( (char *) &null_part, sizeof(Part_Record) );
    cout << endl;
    cout << "Record " << rec_num << " deleted from file.";
  }
}  //End of Delete_Record

void Change_Record(fstream& file)
{
  Part_Record part;
  long rec_num;
  int change;
  bool quit = false;

  cout << endl;
  cout << "Enter number of record to change: ";
  cin >> rec_num;

  if (!Valid_Rec_Num(rec_num))
    return;
```

```
file.seekg( (rec_num - 1) * sizeof(Part_Record), ios::beg);
file.read( (char *) &part, sizeof(Part_Record) );

if ( strcmp(part.id_no, "  ") == 0)
{
   cout << endl;
   cout << "The record does not exist. Make another selection.";
   return;
}

cout << endl;
cout << "The current record contents are:" << endl << endl;
cout << setw(20) << "Part Number"
     << setw(20) << "Quantity On Hand"
     << setw(20) << "Price" << endl << endl;
cout << setw(20) << part.id_no
     << setw(20) << part.qoh
     << setw(20) << part.price << endl;

do
{
   change = Get_Change();
   switch (change)
   {
     case 1:
       cout << endl;
       cout << "Enter Quantity On Hand: ";
       cin >> part.qoh;
       break;
     case 2:
       cout << endl;
       cout << "Enter Price: ";
       cin >> part.price;
       break;
     case 3:
       quit = true;
       file.seekg(-(long)sizeof(Part_Record), ios::cur);
       file.write( (char *) &part, sizeof(Part_Record) );
       cout << endl;
       cout << "Changes made to record " << rec_num;
       break;
     default:
       cout << endl;
      cout << "Invalid Choice. Try Again.";
       break;
   }
}
while (!quit);
} //End of Change_Record()

int Get_Change()
```

```cpp
{
  int change;

  cout << endl << endl;
  cout << "Change Menu" << endl << endl;
  cout << "1 - Change Quantity On Hand" << endl
       << "2 - Change Price" << endl
       << "3 - Write Changes and return to Main Menu" << endl << endl;
  cout << "Enter your choice: ";
  cin >> change;

  return change;
}   //End Get_Change()

void Display_File(fstream& file)
{
  Part_Record part;
  long rec_num;
  long rec_count = 0L;

  file.seekg( 0L, ios::beg);

  cout << endl;
  cout << setw(20) << "Part Number"
       << setw(20) << "Quantity On Hand"
       << setw(20) << "Price" << endl << endl;

  for (rec_num = 1L; rec_num <= 99L; ++rec_num)
  {
    file.read( (char*) &part, sizeof(Part_Record) );
    if (strcmp(part.id_no, "  ") != 0)
    {
      cout << setw(20) << part.id_no
           << setw(20) << part.qoh
           << setw(20) << part.price << endl;
      ++rec_count;
    }
  }

  cout << endl << endl;
  cout << "File contains " << rec_count << " records." << endl;

}   //End of Display_File()

bool Valid_Rec_Num(long rec_num)
{
  if ( rec_num < 1L || rec_num > 99L )
  {
    cout << endl << endl;
    cout << "ERROR: Invalid record number. Try again." << endl;
    return false;
  }
  else
    return true;

}   //End of Valid_Rec_Num()
```

The function `Main()` follows the logic of the pseudocode we developed in the last section. First, `main()` determines if the file exists by attempting to open the file for input. If the file does not exist, the open operation fails. The `if` statement uses the **`fail()`** method. The `fail()` method returns 1, that is, true, if the attempted operation on the file fails. If you attempt to open a nonexistent file for input, the open fails. Therefore, the `if` statement tests true. In that case, the program displays an error message. Whether the file does not exist or if it already exists, the program then closes the file. To process the file randomly, the program now opens the file in both the input and output modes.

In the processing loop, `main()` obtains a menu choice from the user using the `Get_Menu_Choice()` function. Then a `switch` statement executes the function appropriate to the user's menu selection. The processing loop continues until the user selects the fifth menu choice.

`Get_Menu_Choice()` displays the menu of choices, one choice on a line, and obtains the choice using `cin`. Note that one `cout` displays the entire menu.

`Add_Record()` begins by using `cin.get()` to flush the `stdin` keyboard input buffer of the newline character that was left in the buffer after the user made a menu choice. This is necessary because the first input done by `Add_Record()` is by using `cin.getline()`. If we did not flush the keyboard input buffer, `cin.getline()` would retrieve the newline character instead of the part number. The function obtains the part number and places it into the `id_no` member of the `part` structure variable. Then, the function uses `atol()` to convert the `id_no` string into the equivalent `long int`. Next, an `if` statement uses the function `Valid_Rec_Num()` to check that the record number is between 01 and 99. If `rec_num` is invalid, the function returns to `main()`. If `rec_num` is valid, the function obtains the quantity on hand and price from the user.

`Add_Record()` can now attempt to place the record onto the file. First, `seekg()` adjusts the FPI to indicate the beginning of the record with record number `rec_num`. Each record in the file contains `sizeof(Part_Record)` bytes. Therefore, the first byte of the record with record number `rec_num` is

```
(rec_num - 1) * sizeof(Part_Record)
```

bytes from the beginning of the file (Figure 14.9.)

The `read()` then reads the record that it finds at this location into the structure variable `temp_part`. (Recall that this `read()` moves the FPI to the beginning of the next record.) If the `id_no` member of the record contains blanks, the record is null. Therefore, we can add the new record. The `seekg()` backs up the FPI to the beginning of the record we just read. The `write()` then writes the new record onto the file. If the `id_no` member of the record is not blank, the record already exists. Therefore, the function cannot add the record to the file, so it displays an error message.

`Delete_Record()` first asks for and obtains the record number of the record to delete. Then, it uses `Valid_Rec_Num()` to verify that the record number is between 01 and 99. Next, `seekg()` adjusts the FPI to indicate the beginning of the record to delete and `read()` places a copy of the record into the structure variable `part`. Before deleting the record, `Delete_Record()` checks to see if the record is empty. If the record is empty, the `if` statement displays an error message. Otherwise, `seekg()` backs up the FPI to the beginning of the record to delete and `write()` writes a null record in its place.

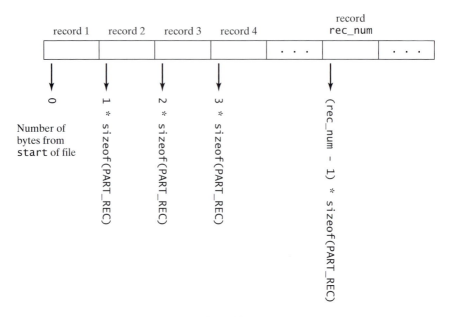

Figure 14.9

Change_Record() obtains and validates the record number in the same way as Delete_Record(). Next, it adjusts the FPI to indicate the beginning of the record to change and reads a copy of the record into the structure variable part. Because, we cannot change a record that does not exist, the if statement checks to see if the record just read is null. If it is null, the function displays an error message and returns to main(). If the record is not null, the function displays the contents of the record and executes a do statement to make the changes.

The first statement in the do loop body obtains the field to be changed from the user by executing Get_Change(), which is similar in form and content to Get_Menu_Choice(). The switch statement then acts on the value of change. If change is 1 or 2, the function obtains the appropriate data. If change is 3, the user wants to write the change onto the file. The seekg() method backs up the FPI to the beginning of the record and the write() method places a copy of the changed record onto the file.

The last function main() uses is Display_File(). After positioning the FPI to the beginning of the file, the function displays the column headings. Then, a for loop reads each record in the file. If the record is not null, the if statement displays the record and increments rec_count. After the for loop ends, a cout displays the number of records in the file.

Following is a sample output for the program. See Experiment 2 for suggestions on testing the program.

Program Output

```
Main Menu

1 - Add a Record
```

```
2 - Delete a Record
3 - Change a Record
4 - Display the File
5 - Quit the Program

Enter your choice: 1

Enter the data for a part:

Part Number (01-99): 11

Quantity On Hand: 123

Price: 45.99

Record 11 added to file.

Main Menu

1 - Add a Record
2 - Delete a Record
3 - Change a Record
4 - Display the File
5 - Quit the Program

Enter your choice: 1

Enter the data for a part:

Part Number (01-99): 22

Quantity On Hand: 234

Price: 67.95

Record 22 added to file.

Main Menu

1 - Add a Record
2 - Delete a Record
3 - Change a Record
4 - Display the File
5 - Quit the Program

Enter your choice: 1

Enter the data for a part:

Part Number (01-99): 33

Quantity On Hand: 345

Price: 67.89

Record 33 added to file.

Main Menu
```

```
1 - Add a Record
2 - Delete a Record
3 - Change a Record
4 - Display the File
5 - Quit the Program

Enter your choice: 4
```

Part Number	Quantity On Hand	Price
11	123	45.99
22	234	67.95
33	345	67.89

```
File contains 3 records.

Main Menu

1 - Add a Record
2 - Delete a Record
3 - Change a Record
4 - Display the File
5 - Quit the Program

Enter your choice: 3

Enter number of record to change: 22

The current record contents are:
```

Part Number	Quantity On Hand	Price
22	234	67.95

```
Change Menu

1 - Change Quantity On Hand
2 - Change Price
3 - Write Changes and return to Main Menu

Enter your choice: 1

Enter Quantity On Hand: 203

Change Menu

1 - Change Quantity On Hand
2 - Change Price
3 - Write Changes and return to Main Menu

Enter your choice: 3

Changes made to record 22

Main Menu

1 - Add a Record
2 - Delete a Record
3 - Change a Record
```

```
4 - Display the File
5 - Quit the Program

Enter your choice: 4

        Part Number      Quantity On Hand                    Price
             11               123                            45.99
             22               203                            67.95
             33               345                            67.89

File contains 3 records.

Main Menu

1 - Add a Record
2 - Delete a Record
3 - Change a Record
4 - Display the File
5 - Quit the Program

Enter your choice: 3

Enter number of record to change: 33

The current record contents are:

        Part Number      Quantity On Hand                    Price
             33               345                            67.89

Change Menu

1 - Change Quantity On Hand
2 - Change Price
3 - Write Changes and return to Main Menu

Enter your choice: 2

Enter Price: 70.89

Change Menu

1 - Change Quantity On Hand
2 - Change Price
3 - Write Changes and return to Main Menu

Enter your choice: 3

Changes made to record 33

Main Menu

1 - Add a Record
2 - Delete a Record
3 - Change a Record
4 - Display the File
5 - Quit the Program
```

```
Enter your choice: 4
        Part Number      Quantity On Hand                    Price
               11                123                         45.99
               22                203                         67.95
               33                345                         70.89
File contains 3 records.

Main Menu

1 - Add a Record
2 - Delete a Record
3 - Change a Record
4 - Display the File
5 - Quit the Program

Enter your choice: 2

Enter the number of the record to delete: 11

Record 11 deleted from file.

Main Menu

1 - Add a Record
2 - Delete a Record
3 - Change a Record
4 - Display the File
5 - Quit the Program

Enter your choice: 4
         Part Number     Quantity On Hand                    Price
                22                203                         67.95
                33                345                         70.89
File contains 2 records.

Main Menu

1 - Add a Record
2 - Delete a Record
3 - Change a Record
4 - Display the File
5 - Quit the Program

Enter your choice: 5

Program Ended
```

Experiments 14.5

1. Write a program that uses the operator `sizeof()` to find the number of bytes needed on your computer system to store a variable of the following types: `char`, `short`, `int`, `long`, `float`, `double`. Also, use `sizeof()` to determine the number of bytes in a `Part_Record` structure.

2. Test prb14-3.cpp. First run dem14-11.cpp to create the file. Then add at least five records to the file `partfile.dat`. Display the current file. Now try the following to test the program. After each, display the file to verify the file's contents.

   (a) Try to add a record that already exists.
   (b) Change an existing record's quantity-on-hand field.
   (c) Change an existing record's price field.
   (d) Try to change a nonexistent record.
   (e) Enter an invalid choice when asked which field to change.
   (f) Delete an existing record.
   (g) Try to delete a nonexistent record.
   (h) Enter an invalid record number (say, 101) when asked for the record number of the record to delete.
   (i) Make an invalid main menu choice.

3. Change prb14-03.cpp to allow the user to enter a record number and have that record displayed on the monitor. If the record does not exist, display an appropriate error message.

4. In the `Add_Record` module of prb14-3.cpp (see the pseudocode for `add_record`), it is probably more efficient to move "get rest of record data" into the `if` part of the module's `if` statement. Recode prb14-03.cpp appropriately.

5. In prb14-3.cpp, change the `Get_Menu_Choice()` function so that the user can enter A, D, C, L, or Q (allow lowercase also) instead of 1, 2, 3, 4, and 5. Also, change the `Get_Change()` function to allow the user to enter Q, P, or W (allow lowercase also) instead of 1, 2, and 3.

6. What changes would you have to make to prb14-3.cpp if the `id_no` member of the `Part_Record` structure were stored as type `int` instead of a two-character string?

7. Change prb14-3.cpp as follows. Change the main menu that prb14-3.cpp displays so the user can choose to copy the file in one of several forms. This menu choice should lead to another menu. In the second menu, the user can choose to display the file on the monitor, print the file on the printer, or copy the file to a disk file.

8. Use enumerated types for the menu choices in prb14-3.cpp. For example, you might use the following `typedef` for the main menu choices.

```
typedef enum {add = 1, delete, change, display, quit} CHANGE;
     CHANGE change;
```

Then, use the enumerated type values in the `switch` statement in `main()`. Define a similar `typedef` for the submenu choices in the function `Change_Record()`.

Programming Problems 14.5

1. In the relative file that we created in dem14-11.cpp, blanks placed in the id_no member of the record identified an empty record. Another method of marking a record as empty is to place a one-character status field at the beginning of the record. If the field contains a blank, the record position in the file is empty. Otherwise, the record contains valid data. Change the Part_Record structure type to incorporate this idea and make all necessary changes to dem14-11.cpp and prb14-3.cpp. Add a one-character status member to the structure. When creating the file, place a blank into the status member of each record. When writing a record to the file, place a non-blank character, for example 'x', in status to indicate the record is active.

2. A small business wants to create a file to store information about its customers. Each record in the file is to contain the following data: customer ID number (an integer 01–50), first name, last name, street address, city, zip code, account balance. Write a program to create such a customer file. Set up the file as a relative file with the customer ID number as the relative record number.

3. Write a menu-driven program that allows the user to add, change, or delete a record from the customer file created in Programming Problem 2.

4. Write a program that asks the user for a specific zip code and then displays a list of all customers in the customer file created in Programming Problem 2 who have the given zip code. Be sure to format and appropriately label the output.

5. Write a program that asks the user for an account balance level and then displays a list of all customers in the customer file created in Programming Problem 2 who have an account balance greater than that entered. Be sure to format and appropriately label the output.

6. A small mutual fund company wants you to create a program to randomly access the data on stocks it holds. Presently, the data are stored in a text file, each line of which contains the following: a stock code, which is an integer between 100 and 999; the stock's current price; the change in the stock's price since the last trading day; the highest price for the stock during the past year; the lowest price for the stock during the past year.

   Write a program that uses the text file to create a corresponding relative file. Translate the stock code to an appropriate relative record address.

7. Write a program that allows the user to randomly access the relative file created by Programming Problem 6. The program should allow the user to do the following:

   (a) Enter a stock code and then display all the information about the stock, appropriately labeled.

   (b) Add a new stock to the relative file.

   (c) Delete a stock from the relative file.

   (d) Change any of the data on a stock.

8. Periodically, usually at the end of a trading day, the mutual fund company of Programming Problem 6 wants to update the relative file of stock data. Assume that the new data on the stocks is in a transaction file (stored as a text file), each line of which has the following data: the stock code and the new closing price. Write a program that updates the relative file. Do the following for each record in the transaction file:

(a) Make the current price of the corresponding record in the relative file equal to the new closing price.

(b) In the corresponding relative file record, make the price change equal to the difference between the old current value and the new current value.

(c) If the new current value is greater than the year's highest price, replace the year's highest price with the new current value.

(d) If the new current value is less than the year's lowest price, replace the year's lowest price with the new current value.

9. A personal computer manufacturing company keeps a relative file in which it stores data on the parts it uses to manufacture computers. Each record in the file contains the following data: part ID number (100–999), part name, quantity on hand, reorder quantity, and, at most, two ID numbers (01–99) of companies that supply the part. The manufacturing company also keeps a relative file of all suppliers of parts. Each record in that file contains the following data: supplier ID number (01–99), supplier name, street address, city, zip code. Write a program that allows the user to enter a part number and then displays the suppliers of that part, including their addresses. Be sure to label the output appropriately.

10. As we mentioned in Chapter 9, you can load a table's values from a file. Recode dem09-03.cpp (specifically, recode the `Load_Part_Table()` function) so that the values for part table are loaded from a file. Assume the file containing the table data is a text file called `table.dat` stored in the same directory as the program. Each line of the text file contains the data for one table row: a seven-character part number, the quantity on hand, and the unit price.

CHAPTER REVIEW

TERMINOLOGY

Describe the meanings of the following terms.

stream I/O	end-of-file condition
iostream	eof()
multiple inheritance	access mode constants
text file	ios::in
ifstream	ios::out
fstreambase	ios::app
ofstream	append mode
fstream	get()
open()	put()
file position indicator (FPI)	EOF
close()	sequential file processing
record	random file processing
field	ios::binary
space-separated	bitwise AND &
sequential file	bitwise OR |

binary file   `ios::end`
`seekg()`   `write()`
`seekp()`   `sizeof()`
`tellg()`   `read()`
`tellp()`   relative file
`ios::beg`   relative record number
`ios::cur`   `fail()`

SUMMARY

- All I/O in C++ is stream I/O. To give a file an additional structure, the programmer must write program instructions to do so.
- The class `iostream` is derived from classes `istream` and `ostream`.
- `cin` is a member of class `istream` and `cout` is a member of `ostream`.
- The methods `get()` and `getline()` are members of class `istream` and, therefore, can be applied to `cin`.
- A text file consists of character data. At the end of each line in a text file is the newline character.
- To declare an output file, declare an `ofstream` file object. The class `ofstream` derives from `ostream` and `fstreambase`.
- To open an `ofstream` object (an output file) and attach it to a system file, use either the `open()` method or the one-argument constructor of the `ofstream` class.
- Opening a file object attaches the object to a system file in an appropriate mode and creates the file's File Position Indicator (FPI) (Note 14.2).
- Every read and write operation changes the FPI.
- The insertion operator `<<` can be used to place data onto an `ofstream` file object.
- The `close()` method can be used to close a file object.
- If an error occurs when opening a file, the value of the file object is zero (Note 14.3).
- A record is a set of data concerning a particular entity. Each fact within a record is a field.
- In a text file of records, spaces separate fields and the newline character separates records.
- A sequential file is one whose records are stored in sequence.
- To declare an input file, declare an `ifstream` object. The class `ifstream` derives from `istream` and `fstreambase`.
- To open an `ifstream` object (input file) and attach it to a system file, use either the `open()` method or the one-argument constructor of the `ifstream` class.
- You can use the extraction operator `>>` as well as the `get()` and `getline()` methods to read data from an `ifstream` object.
- When reading an `ifstream` object, you must test for the end-of-file condition. The method `eof()` returns one if the program reaches the end-of-file.
- Use the Read Ahead Rule to correctly process a sequential input file (Note 14.4). Read the first record after opening the file; read the file again as soon as the program completes processing the input record.
- To declare a file that can be used for both input and output, declare an `fstream` file object. The `fstream` class derives from `iostream` (therefore, also from `istream` and `ostream`) and from `fstreambase`.
- When opening an `fstream` file object, specify its opening mode using `ios::in`, `ios::out`, or `ios::app` (Note 14.5).

- The get() and put() methods can be used to read and write one character to a file.
- You can output to the printer by attaching an output file object to your system's printer name ("prn" in DOS/Windows systems).
- In a text file on some systems (Windows), the newline character is actually stored as a pair of characters—the carriage-return/line-feed (CRLF) pair. This pair is processed as though it were a single character. In a binary file, none of the characters are ever changed when read or written by the program.
- To open a file in binary mode, use the access mode ios::binary.
- The seekg() and seekp() methods move the FPI to an indicated position in the file (Note 14.6).
- The tellg() and tellp() methods return the value of the FPI (Note 14.6).
- A structure can be used to store a record.
- A sequential binary file of records is a sequential file of structures.
- The write() method can be used to write a structure onto a file (Note 14.7).
- The read() method can be used to read a structure from a file (Note 14.8).
- A relative file is one in which a record's position in the file is used to access the record.
- A relative file can be processed randomly.

REVIEW EXERCISES

1. How are input and output accomplished in C++?
2. Exactly what are cin and cout in terms of the classes ostream and istream?
3. Explain how to create and open a file object in C++.
4. What are the basic I/O classes and how are they related?
5. What is the File Position Indicator (FPI) and how is it affected by the various I/O functions?
6. If you do not explicitly close a file, what will C++ do when the program ends?
7. What is the end-of-file condition and how can your program detect it?
8. How can you declare a file so that it can be used for both input and output?
9. What are the three basic opening modes for a file and how do they affect the processing of the file?
10. What method can you use to read a single character from a file? to write a character to a file?
11. How can you do output to a printer?
12. Explain the difference between sequential and random file access.
13. Explain the difference between text and binary files. How do you declare a text file? a binary file?
14. What is the bitwise OR and how is it used to set file opening modes?
15. What are the two basic random file–access methods and how are they used?
16. What is a record? What is a field?
17. Explain the differences in how the records and fields are stored in text files and binary files.
18. What method can place a record onto a file? Why should you use the sizeof() operator in this function?
19. What method can read a record from a file? Why should you use the sizeof() operator in this function?
20. What is the Read Ahead Rule and why is it helpful?
21. What is a relative file?

Special Topics: Friends, Operator Overloading, Macros, and Inline Functions

OBJECTIVES

- To declare and code a `friend` function for a class
- To decide when an overloaded operator should be a class member function or a `friend`
- To know which operators cannot be overloaded
- To know which overloaded operators must be class members
- To overload the basic arithmetic operators
- To know the meaning of the `this` pointer
- To overload the assignment operator
- To overload the insertion and extraction operators
- To overload the compound assignment operators
- To overload the relational operators
- To overload the unary operators ++ and −−

This chapter covers several topics that supplement material in earlier chapters. Sections 15.1 through 15.8 extend the material of Chapter 12. They show how to use `friend` functions and how to expand the use of many operators through overloading. Section 15.8 extends the material of Chapter 5 by discussing inline functions and the use of macros.

15.1 friend FUNCTIONS

So far, we have learned that the class methods are the only functions that have access to the private instance variables of that class. However, there are times when it is desirable for a function that is not a class method to have access to the private instance variables of a class.

15.1.1 Defining a friend Function

Suppose that in a system that uses the Savings_Account class, we want to implement a function that transfers money from one account into another. A possible solution would be to write a Savings_Account method,Transfer_Method. The method would have two arguments: the first is the account we are transferring funds from, and the second argument would be the amount of money to transfer. The account to which we apply the method would be the account to which we are transferring funds. For example, if acc1 and acc2 are accounts, the following statement would transfer $100.00 from acc2 to acc1.

```
acc1.Transfer_Method(acc2, 100.00);
```

Although this approach works, the way in which we use the method might seem a bit awkward. Another approach would be to define a nonmember function Transfer1() that takes three arguments: the first is the account receiving the funds, the second is the account giving the funds, and the third is the amount of the transfer. Thus, to transfer $100.00 from acc2 to acc1, we would code the following statement.

```
Transfer1(acc1, acc2, 100);
```

We can use the methods of Savings_Account to code such a function. The function returns true if the transfer is successfully made and false otherwise.

```
bool Transfer1(Savings_Account acc1, Savings_Account acc2, double amount)
{
  if (!acc2.Withdraw(amount))
    return false;

  acc1.Deposit(amount);

  return true;
}
```

Recall that Withdraw() returns true if the withdrawal is made and false otherwise. The if statement in Transfer1() returns false if the withdrawal is not made. An objection to this implementation of a transfer function is that the function requires executing two other functions, namely, Withdraw() and **Deposit()**. The function would be more efficient if it could directly access the instance variables of the parameters acc1 and acc2.

The solution is to create a **friend function**. A **friend** function of a class has the same access privileges as the class methods, but is not itself a method. Therefore, a friend function of a class has access to all the private members of the class just as though it were a class method. It is important to note that a class must declare a function to be a friend, not the other way around. It would violate the principle of data hiding if any function could declare itself a friend of a class! To create a friend function, follow the procedure of Note 15.1.

Note 15.1   How to Write a friend Function

To declare a function to be a friend function of a class:

- Declare the function inside the class declaration and precede the return type of the function with the keyword friend. It does not matter in which access category you define the function (public or private).
- When you define the function outside the class, *do not* repeat the keyword friend. The keyword friend can appear only in a class declaration.

Thus, in the declaration of Savings_Account, we would code the following.

```
class Savings_Account
{
  friend bool Transfer(Savings_Account&, Savings_Account&, double);

  private:
  .
  .
  .
  public:
  .
  .
  .
};
```

Note that we place the declaration of the friend function before either access specifier. We pass the two accounts to the function by reference because the function must change both Account objects that are passed as arguments. If we pass the Savings_Account objects by value, the changes made by the function would be made to the function's parameters (which are copies of the arguments) and not to the arguments themselves. See Experiment 1. The code for the function follows.

```
bool Transfer(Savings_Account& acc_r1, Savings_Account& acc_r2,
              double amount)
{
  //If amount exceeds acc_r2's balance, do nothing and return false

  if (amount > acc_r2.balance)
    return false;

  //Otherwise, make the transfer and return true

  acc_r2.balance -= amount;   //decrease acc_r2's balance by amount
  acc_r1.balance += amount;   //increase acc_r1's balance by amount

  return true;
}
```

This function is somewhat longer than Transfer1(), but it is more efficient because it does not have to execute functions to perform its task. Note that we can directly access the private data members of both accounts because Transfer() is a friend of Savings_Account. We must use the dot **operator** to access the data members of both parameters because Transfer() is not a class method.

Following is a complete program that uses the Transfer() function. It is based on program dem12-13.cpp. To simplify the program, we have removed the Calc_Interest(), Deposit(), and Withdraw() methods.

```cpp
//dem15-1.cpp

//This program illustrates a friend function.

//It is based on dem12-13.cpp.
//To simplify the program the Calc_Interest(), Deposit()
//and Withdraw() methods have been removed.

#include <iostream>
#include <iomanip>
#include <string>

using namespace std;

class Savings_Account
{
   friend bool Transfer(Savings_Account&, Savings_Account&, double);

   private:
      char     id_no[5];
      char*    name;
      double   balance;
      double   rate;

   public:
      Savings_Account(char id[], char* n_p, double bal = 0.00,
                     double rt = 0.04);
      ~Savings_Account();
      const char* Get_Id() const;
      const char* Get_Name() const;
      double Get_Balance();
};

Savings_Account::Savings_Account(char id[], char* n_p, double bal, double rt)
{
   strcpy(id_no, id);   //copy first argument into id_no[]

   name = new char[strlen(n_p) + 1]; //create space for the name

   strcpy(name, n_p);   //copy second argument into new space

   balance = bal;
   rate    = rt;
}
```

```cpp
Savings_Account::~Savings_Account()
{
  cout << endl << endl;
  cout << "Account " << id_no << " terminated." << endl;
  delete [] name;
}

const char* Savings_Account::Get_Id() const
{
  return id_no;
}

const char* Savings_Account::Get_Name() const
{
  return name;
}

double Savings_Account::Get_Balance()
{
  return balance;
}

bool Transfer(Savings_Account& acc_r1, Savings_Account& acc_r2,
              double amount)
{
  //If amount exceeds acc_r2's balance, do nothing and return 0

  if (amount > acc_r2.balance)
    return false;

  //Otherwise, make the transfer and return 1

  acc_r2.balance -= amount;   //decrease acc_r2's balance by amount
  acc_r1.balance += amount;   //increase acc_r1's balance by amount

  return true;
}

void Display_Account(Savings_Account&);     //Function prototype

int main()
{
  cout << setprecision(2)
       << setiosflags(ios::fixed)
       << setiosflags(ios::showpoint);

  double amount;

  Savings_Account acc1("1111", "Adam Zapple", 100.00, 0.08);
  Savings_Account acc2("2222", "Poly Ester", 200.00, 0.06);
  Display_Account(acc1);
  Display_Account(acc2);

  cout << endl;
  cout << "Enter an amount to transfer from the second account "
       << "to the first: ";
```

```
  cin >> amount;
  if (Transfer(acc1, acc2, amount))
  {
    cout << endl;
    cout << "Transfer made. Updated Account Information:" << endl;
    Display_Account(acc1);
    Display_Account(acc2);
  }
  else
  {
    cout << endl;
    cout << "Transfer could not be made." << endl;
  }
  return 0;
}
void Display_Account(Savings_Account& acc)
{
  cout << endl;
  cout << "Data for Account# " << acc.Get_Id() << endl << endl;

  cout << "Owner's Name: " << acc.Get_Name() << endl << endl;

  cout << "Account Balance: " << acc.Get_Balance() << endl << endl;
}
```

Program Output–Run 1

```
Data for Account# 1111

Owner's Name: Adam Zapple

Account Balance: 100.00

Data for Account# 2222

Owner's Name: Poly Ester

Account Balance: 200.00

Enter an amount to transfer from the second account to the first: 40.50

Transfer made. Updated Account Information:

Data for Account# 1111

Owner's Name: Adam Zapple

Account Balance: 140.50

Data for Account# 2222
```

```
Owner's Name: Poly Ester

Account Balance: 159.50

Account 2222 terminated.

Account 1111 terminated.
```

Note how main() uses the function Transfer(). The if statement tests to see if the transfer was successful. If so, the program displays a message and the new account information. If the transfer was not successful, the program displays an appropriate message. Following is a program run in which we try to transfer more money from the first account than is in the account.

Program Output–Run 2

```
Data for Account# 1111

Owner's Name: Adam Zapple

Account Balance: 100.00

Data for Account# 2222

Owner's Name: Poly Ester

Account Balance: 200.00

Enter an amount to transfer from the second account to the first: 201.00

Transfer could not be made.

Account 2222 terminated.

Account 1111 terminated.
```

15.1.2 Inheritance and friend Functions

friend functions are not inherited in a class hierarchy. If a function is a friend of the base class in a class hierarchy, it is not a friend of any derived class. If you want such a function to be a friend of the derived class, you must declare it as such in the derived class. See Experiment 7.

Exercises 15.1

1. Code the Savings_Account method, Transfer_Method(), that was discussed at the beginning of this section, which can be used to transfer money between accounts.

2. Code a friend function Switch() for the Rectangle class. See Exercise 7 in Section 11.1. The function should have two Rectangle reference arguments. The function should interchange the dimensions of its arguments. Why must the arguments be passed by reference?

3. Code a `friend` function `Synchronize()` for the `DigitalClock` class. See Exercise 8 in Section 11.1. The function should have two `DigitalClock` reference arguments. The function should reset the time of its first argument to that of its second argument. Must both of the arguments be passed by reference?

4. Code a `friend` function `Merge()` for the `Rectangle` class. See Exercise 7 in Section 11.1. The function should have two `Rectangle` arguments passed by value. The function should dynamically create a `Rectangle` object whose length is the sum of the lengths of its arguments, and whose width is the sum of the widths of its arguments. The function should return a `Rectangle` pointer, which points to the new object. Why is it safe to pass the arguments to `Merge()` by value rather than by reference?

Experiments 15.1

1. Change the `Transfer()` function of dem15-1.cpp so that it passes its arguments by value rather than by reference. Recompile and execute the resulting program. Does the new `Transfer()` function work? Explain.

2. Rewrite dem15-1.cpp using the member function `Transfer_Method()` of Exercise 1. Recompile and execute the resulting program. Does the program work as it did using the `Transfer()` function?

3. Rewrite dem15-1.cpp using the function `Transfer1()` that was discussed in this section, rather than the `friend` function `Transfer()`. Recompile and execute the resulting program. Does the program work as it did using the `Transfer()` function?

4. Omit the keyword `friend` in the declaration of `Savings_Account`. Recompile the program. Explain what happens.

5. Recode the `Transfer()` `friend` function of dem15-1.cpp by passing the arguments by pointer rather than by reference. Recode `main()` to reflect this change. Compile, execute, and test the resulting program.

6. Recode the `Display_Account()` function of dem15-1.cpp as a `friend` function of `Savings_Account`. Therefore, it will not have to use the `Get_` methods to access the instance variables of the `Savings_Account` class. Recode `main()` to reflect this change. Compile, execute, and test the resulting program.

7. Code a class, `Class_A`, and a derived class, `Class_B`, of `Class_A`. Write a program that shows that a `friend` function of `Class_A` is not a `friend` function of `Class_B`.

Programming Problems 15.1

1. In the `OilTank` class of Chapters 11 and 12, add a `friend` function `Transfer()` that transfers oil from one tank to another. The function should have three arguments. The first argument is the ID number of the tank you are transferring oil from; the second argument is the ID number of the tank you are transferring oil to; the third argument is the amount of oil being transferred. Be sure that the function checks to see if there is enough oil in the tank you are transferring oil from and that there is enough room in the tank to which you are transferring oil to hold the oil that is being transferred. Code a `main()` that tests the new `friend` function.

2. It sometimes happens at a hotel that a guest wants to be transferred from one room to another. In the HotelRoom class of Chapters 11 and 12, add a friend function Transfer() that transfers a guest from one room to another. The function should have two arguments. The first argument should be the number of the room you are transferring guests from; the second argument should be the room number you are transferring guests to. The function should make appropriate changes to the occupancy status of both rooms. Code a main() to test the new friend function.

15.2 OVERLOADING BASIC ARITHMETIC OPERATORS

We noted in Chapter 11 that C++ allows us to overload constructors. C++ also allows the programmer to overload operators. We can, therefore, extend the meaning of the sum operator +, the insertion operator <<, and most other C++ operators. In this section, we discuss how to overload the basic arithmetic operators. In the following sections, we discuss overloading the other arithmetic operators, assignment, the insertion and extraction operators, and the relation operators.

15.2.1 Adding Two Objects

Consider Test_Class, which we have used in previous chapters.

```
class Test_Class
{
  private:
    int n;

  public:
    Test_Class(int i = 0);  //One-argument constructor
    Test_Class(Test_Class&);  //Copy constructor
    ~Test_Class();
    int Get_Value();
};

Test_Class::Test_Class(int i)
{
  n = i;

  cout << endl;
  cout << "Constructor Executed: Data member initialized to "
       << n << endl;
}

Test_Class::Test_Class(Test_Class& tc_r)
{
  n = tc_r.n;
  cout << endl << endl;
  cout << "Copy constructor executed: "
       << "Data member initialized to " << n << endl;
}

Test_Class::~Test_Class()
```

```
{
    cout << endl << endl;
    cout << "Destructor Executed for object with data member "
        << n << endl;
}
int Test_Class::Get_Value()
{
    return n;

}
```

Suppose we make the following declarations in main().

```
Test_Class tc_object1(4);

Test_Class tc_object2(7);

Test_Class tc_object3;
```

Because a Test_Class object has only one data member, we might want to make the following assignment.

```
tc_object3 = tc_object1 + tc_object2;
```

For this statement to have meaning, the operation of addition would have to be extended to include adding two objects of type Test_Class to yield another object of type Test_Class. It would be appropriate for the assignment to assign the value 11 (the sum of the data members of tc_object1 and tc_object2) to the data member of tc_object3. We can, in fact, extend the meaning of addition in exactly this way by overloading the + operator.

With the following few exceptions listed, an operator can be overloaded as a class method or as a friend function. Some overloaded operators should be defined as class methods, while others are better defined as friend functions. Although there are no iron-clad rules for deciding which overloaded operators should be class methods and which should be friends, we shall use the convention of Note 15.2. See Exercise 15.3.

Note 15.2   friend and Member Operator Overloads

An overloaded operator that changes one of its operands should be defined as a method of the class. All other overloaded operators should be defined as friend functions. However, the following operators *must* be overloaded as class methods. See Section 15.3.

   assignment (=), function call (()), subscript ([]), and indirect member operator (->).

According to Note 15.2, therefore, operators such as addition, subtraction, multiplication, and division, as well as the insertion and deletion operators, should be declared as friend functions. Operators such as the compound assignment operators (+=, -=, and so on) should be declared as class methods.

We shall begin with the case of operators that are defined as `friend` functions. Such operators include the arithmetic operators and the insertion and extraction operators. To declare an overloaded `friend` operator, use the following syntax.

```
friend return-type operator operator-symbol (argument-list);
```

The keyword **operator** is mandatory and must immediately precede the symbol for the operator. For example, following is the declaration for an overload of addition for `Test_Class`, which must, of course, appear in the class declaration.

```
friend Test_Class operator + (const Test_Class&, const Test_Class&);
```

The two arguments in the function represent the two operands in the binary operation of addition. The first argument always represents the operand to the left of the operator and the second argument always represents the operand to the right of the operator.

Note 15.3   Arguments in an Overloaded `friend` Operator

In an overload of a binary operator as a `friend` function, the first argument of the overload always represents the left operand and the second argument of the overload always represents the right operand.

Following is the code of the overloaded addition operator.

```
Test_Class operator + (const Test_Class& left_op, const Test_Class& right_op)
{
   Test_Class temp_obj;     //Uses the default value of 0 for n

   temp_obj.n = left_op.n + right_op.n;

   return temp_obj;
}
```

We use the names `left_op` and `right_op` for the first and second arguments because they represent the left and right operands of the operator. Thus, if we code the expression `tc_object1 + tc_object2`, `tc_object1` is the value of `left_op` because it is to the left of the operator, and `tc_object2` is the value of `right_op` because it is to the right of the operator.

The overloaded addition operator returns a `Test_Class` object. Therefore, the first statement in the function declares a temporary `Test_Class` object, `temp_obj`, whose value the function will return to the calling program. The next statement in the function assigns to `temp_obj`'s n instance variable, the sum of the n instance variables of `left_op` and `right_op`. Finally, the function returns a copy of `temp_obj` to the calling program.

15.2.2 Adding an Object and an Integer

We might also decide that we want to be able to add an ordinary integer constant or integer variable to a `Test_Class` object. For example, consider the following declarations and assignment.

```
Test_Class tc_object1(4);
Test_Class tc_object2;

tc_object2 = tc_object1 + 15;
```

It would be reasonable for the assignment to assign 19 (the sum of the n instance variable of tc_object1 and the integer constant 15) to the n instance variable of tc_object2. Note that in the assignment, the left operand to the addition is a Test_Class object and the right operand is an integer. Therefore, we want to overload the addition operator with the left operand a Test_Class object and the right operand an integer. Following is the declaration and code of the overloaded addition operator.

```
friend Test_Class operator + (const Test_Class& left_op, const int right_op);

    Test_Class operator + (const Test_Class& left_op, const int right_op)
    {
      Test_Class temp_obj;

      temp_obj.n = left_op.n + right_op;

      return temp_obj;
    }
```

With the preceding overload of addition, the following statement would not be allowed because the left operand is an integer and the right operand is a Test_Class object.

```
        tc_object2 = 7 + tc_object1;
```

We leave for the exercises the coding of the overloaded addition operator with the left operand an integer and the right operand a Test_Class object. See Exercise 1.

Following is a complete program that uses the two overloads of addition. Note that we have commented out the cout statements in the constructor, copy constructor, and destructor to make the output simpler. See Experiment 1, which asks you to run the program with the cout statements put back into the program and to explain the resulting output.

```
//dem15-2.cpp

//This program illustrates overloading of the addition operator.

#include <iostream>

using namespace std;

class Test_Class
{
  friend Test_Class operator + (const Test_Class&, const Test_Class&);
  friend Test_Class operator + (const Test_Class&, const int);

  private:
    int n;

  public:
    Test_Class(int i = 0);   //One-argument constructor
    Test_Class(Test_Class&);   //Copy constructor
```

```
     ~Test_Class();
     int Get_Value();
};
Test_Class::Test_Class(int i)
{
   n = i;

   //cout << endl;
   //cout << "Constructor Executed: Data member initialized to "
   //      << n << endl;
}
Test_Class::Test_Class(Test_Class& tc_r)
{
   n = tc_r.n;

   //cout << endl << endl;
   //cout << "Copy constructor executed: "
   //      << "Data member initialized to " << n << endl;
}
Test_Class::~Test_Class()
{
   //cout << endl << endl;
   //cout << "Destructor Executed for object with data member "
   //      << n <<endl;
}
int Test_Class::Get_Value()
{
   return n;
}
Test_Class operator + (const Test_Class& left_op, const Test_Class& right_op)
{
   Test_Class temp_obj;

   temp_obj.n = left_op.n + right_op.n;

   return temp_obj;
}
Test_Class operator + (const Test_Class& left_op, const int right_op)
{
   Test_Class temp_obj;

   temp_obj.n = left_op.n + right_op;

   return temp_obj;
}
int main()
```

```
{
  Test_Class tc_object1(4);
  Test_Class tc_object2(7);
  Test_Class tc_object;

  cout << endl << endl;
  cout << "Prior to adding the objects, the value of tc_object is "
       << tc_object.Get_Value() << endl;

  tc_object = tc_object1 + tc_object2;

  cout << endl << endl;
  cout << "After adding the objects, the value of tc_object is "
       << tc_object.Get_Value() << endl;

  tc_object = tc_object1 + 15;

  cout << endl << endl;
  cout << "After adding 15 to tc_object1, the value of tc_object is "
       << tc_object.Get_Value() << endl;

  return 0;
}
```

Program Output

Prior to adding the objects, the value of tc_object is 0

After adding the objects, the value of tc_object is 11

After adding 15 to tc_object1, the value of tc_object is 19

The object tc_object begins with the n instance variable having the default value of 0. After adding the objects tc_object1 (with instance variable value 4) and tc_object2 (with instance variable value 7) and assigning the result to tc_object, the value of the instance variable of tc_object is 11. Finally, after adding the integer 15 to tc_object1 (with instance variable value 4) and assigning the result to tc_object, the instance variable of tc_object has the value 19.

Note that making the overloaded addition operator return a Test_Class object makes statements such as the following possible.

```
tc_object = tc_object1 + tc_object2 + tc_object3 + 6;
```

The first addition results in a temporary Test_Class object, which then is added to tc_object3, resulting in another Test_Class object. The third addition then adds this temporary object and the integer 6, resulting in still another temporary object. This last temporary object is assigned to tc_object.

15.2.3 Operator Overloading Rules

The following rules must be observed when overloading operators.

Note 15.4   Rules for Operator Overloading

- All operators can be overloaded except the following:

.	direct member (dot)
::	scope resolution
?:	conditional
sizeof	size operator
new	allocation
delete	deallocation
.*	direct pointer-to-member

- The following operators *must* be class methods

=	assignment
()	function call
[]	subscript
->	indirect member

- You cannot change the unary/binary nature of an operator. Thus, division must remain a binary operator. If an operator is both unary and binary (for example, +), then it can be overloaded either or both ways.
- You cannot override the predefined operator precedence rules.

Exercises 15.2

1. Code the prototype and the definition of an overload of addition for Test_Class in which the first argument is an integer and the second argument is an object of type Test_Class. The overloaded operator should return a Test_Class object whose n instance variable is the sum of the first argument and the n instance variable of the second.

2. Code the prototype and the definition of an overload of subtraction for Test_Class in which both arguments are of type Test_Class. The overloaded operator should return a Test_Class object whose n instance variable is the n instance variable of the first argument minus the n instance variable of the second.

3. Code prototypes and definitions of overloaded subtraction operators for Test_Class that allow the subtraction of an integer from a Test_Class object and that allow the subtraction of a Test_Class object from an integer.

4. Do Exercise 2 with multiplication replacing subtraction.

5. Do Exercise 3 with multiplication replacing subtraction.

6. Do Exercise 2 with division replacing subtraction. Be sure to check for division by zero and take appropriate action if such an attempt is made.

7. Do Exercise 3 with division replacing subtraction. Be sure to check for division by zero and take appropriate action if such an attempt is made.

8. Replace the `Merge()` `friend` function for the `Rectangle` class of Exercise 4, Section 15.1, by an overload of addition.

Experiments 15.2

1. Remove the commented-out statements in the constructor, the copy constructor, and the destructor of program dem15-2.cpp. Compile and execute the program. Explain the resulting output.

2. Place the following statement at the end of `main()` in dem15-2.cpp.

```
tc_object = 7 + tc_object1;
```

Describe the error message and explain why it is issued.

Programming Problems 15.2

1. Write a program that uses `Test_Class` and all the operator overloads that you coded in Exercises 2 through 7. Compile, execute, and test the resulting program.

2. Write a program that uses the `Rectangle` class and the overload of addition from Exercise 8. Compile, execute, and test the resulting program.

15.3 OVERLOADING ASSIGNMENT AND THE this POINTER

In this section, we discuss how to overload the assignment operator. To make the overloaded assignment work in the same way as assignment of the built-in types, we must use a special pointer, called `this`, that is available to every class method.

15.3.1 Overloading Assignment

We mentioned several times that we can assign an object to another object of the same class. In doing so, the assignment is made on a member-by-member basis. This type of assignment is appropriate for `Test_Class` objects, which have a single integer instance variable. However, member-by-member copying is not appropriate for a class that has one or more pointers as instance variables. For example, if acc1 and acc2 are `Savings_Account` (here we use the `Savings_Account` class as defined in Section 12.1) objects, they each have a `name` instance variable that points to the name of the person holding the account. See Figure 15.1. Suppose we make the assignment acc1 = acc2. Because the copy is made on a member-by-member basis, the `name` members of both objects are now pointing to the name associated with acc2. Thus, both are pointing to the same physical space on the heap. It follows that a change to the name of either account would cause that change to occur in both. To avoid this, we must overload the assignment operator.

You should code the overload of an operator in such a way that the overloaded operator behaves as much as possible like the operator behaves for the corresponding native C++ data types. For an overload of the assignment operator, this means that the following should make sense for `Savings_Account` objects.

```
acc1 = acc2 = acc3;
```

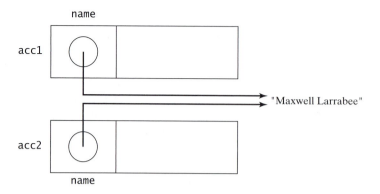

Figure 15.1

Recall that in C++, every expression has a value. The value of an assignment is the left side of the assignment operator. Therefore, because assignment associates from right to left, the value of the first assignment, acc2 = acc3, is the object acc2. Then the second assignment assigns acc2 to acc1. To make the overloaded assignment operator behave like the usual assignment operator, we would even want the following to work correctly.

```
(acc1 = acc2) = acc3;
```

In this case, the left assignment is executed first. The result is the object acc1, which is then assigned the value of acc3. See Experiment 1.

To make these multiple assignments work the way we want them to, our overload of assignment must return the object to which the operator is being applied. Therefore, the operator must return a reference to the first argument and not a copy of the first argument.

Assignment is a binary operator—it has a left and a right operand. Unlike when we overloaded addition, the assignment operation changes the left operand. Therefore, it is best to think of assignment as operating on the left operand. Using Note 15.2, it follows that we should make the overloaded assignment operator a method of Savings_Account and not a friend function.

Note 15.5   Arguments in an Overloaded Member Operator

When overloading a binary operator as a class method, the object to which the function is applied represents the left operand and the one argument of the operator represents the right operand.

The declaration of the operator follows. The one argument to the overloaded operator is the right side of the assignment operator. The left side of the assignment operator is the object to which the assignment is applied.

```
Savings_Account& operator = (const Savings_Account&);
```

15.3.2 The this Pointer

Remember that each object has its own copies of the class instance variables, but there is only one copy of each class method for all the objects a program might create. A method knows on which object it is working by means of a special pointer that the system automatically provides and that you can use as you see fit. Within the code of any class method, the pointer **this**, which is a keyword, always refers to the object to which the method is applied. When the C++ compiler translates the code of a method, it precedes each reference to an instance variable by this ->. Although it is not necessary, if you wish, you can place the expression this -> before each instance variable name in a method and the program will compile and execute correctly. For example, following is the original code for the constructor of Test_Class.

```
Test_Class::Test_Class(int i)
{
  n = i;

  //cout << "\nConstructor Executed: Data member initialized to " << n;
}
```

We can replace the preceding code by the following equivalent code. See Experiment 2.

```
Test_Class::Test_Class(int i)
{
  this -> n = i;

  //cout << "\nConstructor Executed: Data member initialized to " << n;
}
```

Because the this pointer points to the object on which the method is operating, *this refers to the object itself. We therefore make the overloaded assignment operator return *this, namely, the left side of the equals sign.

Note 15.6   The Meaning of the this Pointer

Within the code of a class method, the pointer this points to the object to which the method is applied. Therefore, within the code of a class method, *this represents the object to which the method is applied.

Following is the code for the overloaded assignment operator.

```
Savings_Account& Savings_Account::operator =
                              (const Savings_Account& right_op)
{
  if (&right_op == this)
    ;                       //Self assignment - do nothing
  else
  {
    strcpy(id_no, right_op.id_no);  //copy id of right_op into id_no[]
```

```
    delete [] name;

    name = new char[strlen(right_op.name) + 1]; //create space for the name

    strcpy(name, right_op.name);   //copy second argument into new space
    balance = right_op.balance;
    rate    = right_op.rate;
  }

  return *this;
}
```

Because the overloaded assignment operator is a method, within the method an unqualified instance variable refers to the instance variable of the object on which the method is operating, namely, the operand to the left of the assignment operator. The object to the right of the assignment operator is represented by the parameter in the method definition, left_op in the preceding method. The instance variables of this object must be referenced using the dot operator.

Most of the method's code consists of an if statement. The condition in the if statement tests whether the right operand in the assignment equals the first operand. Thus, we are checking for a so-called self assignment such as acc1 = acc1. If this condition is true, there is nothing to do, so the null statement is executed. Otherwise, the members of the right operand are copied to the left operand in much the same way as is done in the code of the constructor and copy constructor.

Note that it is necessary to deallocate the space pointed to by the name instance variable of the left operand. Failure to do so would leave that space allocated but unusable by the program. The program that follows tests the overloaded assignment operator.

```
//dem15-3.cpp

//This program demonstrates overloading the assignment operator.

#include <iostream>
#include <iomanip>
#include <string>

using namespace std;
class Savings_Account
{
  private:
    char    id_no[5];
    char*   name;
    double balance;
    double rate;

  public:
    Savings_Account(char id[], char* n_p,
                    double bal = 0.00, double rt = 0.04);
    Savings_Account(const Savings_Account &);
    ~Savings_Account();
    double Calc_Interest();
    double Get_Balance();
    const char* Get_Id() const;
```

```
      const char* Get_Name() const;
      void Deposit(double);
      bool Withdraw(double);

      Savings_Account& operator = (const Savings_Account&);
};
Savings_Account::Savings_Account(char id[], char* n_p, double bal, double rt)
{
   strcpy(id_no, id);   //copy first argument into id_no[]

   name = new char[strlen(n_p) + 1]; //create space for the name

   strcpy(name, n_p);   //copy second argument into new space

   balance = bal;
   rate    = rt;
}

Savings_Account::Savings_Account(const Savings_Account& acc_r)
{
   strcpy(id_no, acc_r.id_no);   //copy first argument into id_no[]

   name = new char[strlen(acc_r.name) + 1]; //create space for the name

   strcpy(name, acc_r.name);   //copy second argument into new space

   balance = acc_r.balance;
   rate    = acc_r.rate;
}

Savings_Account::~Savings_Account()
{
   delete [] name;
}

double Savings_Account::Get_Balance()
{
   return balance;
}

double Savings_Account::Calc_Interest()
{
   double interest;

   interest = balance * rate;
   balance += interest;

   return interest;
}

const char* Savings_Account::Get_Name() const
{
   return name;
}
```

```
const char* Savings_Account::Get_Id() const
{
  return id_no;
}

void Savings_Account::Deposit(double amount)
{
  balance += amount;
}

bool Savings_Account::Withdraw(double amount)
{
  bool result;

  if (amount <= balance)
  {
    balance -= amount;
    result = true;
  }
  else
    result = false;

  return result;
}

Savings_Account& Savings_Account::operator = (const Savings_Account& right_op)
{
  if (&right_op == this)
      ;                         //Self assignment - do nothing
  else
  {
    strcpy(id_no, right_op.id_no);  //copy id of right_op into id_no[]

    delete [] name;

    name = new char[strlen(right_op.name) + 1]; //create space for the name

    strcpy(name, right_op.name);  //copy second argument into new space

    balance = right_op.balance;
    rate    = right_op.rate;
  }

  return *this;
}

Savings_Account Get_Account();     //Prototype for Get_Account()

void Display_Account(Savings_Account&);     //Prototype for Display_Account()

int main()
{
  cout << setprecision(2)
       << setiosflags(ios::fixed)
       << setiosflags(ios::showpoint);
```

```
   Savings_Account acc1 = Get_Account();

   cout << endl;

   Display_Account(acc1);

   Savings_Account acc2 = Get_Account();

   cout << endl;

   Display_Account(acc2);

   acc1 = acc2;

   cout << endl << endl;
   cout << "After the assignment:" << endl << endl;

   Display_Account(acc1);
   Display_Account(acc2);

   return 0;

}
Savings_Account Get_Account()
{
   char id[5];
   char buffer[81];
   double bal;
   double rt;

   cout << endl;
   cout << "Enter Account ID: ";
   cin.getline(id, 5);

   cout << endl;
   cout << "Enter Account Holder's Name: ";
   cin.getline(buffer, 81);

   cout << endl;
   cout << "Enter Balance: ";
   cin >> bal;

   cout << endl;
   cout << "Enter Interest Rate: ";
   cin >> rt;

   cin.get();    //clear the newline character from the buffer

   Savings_Account acc(id, buffer, bal, rt);

   return acc;
}
void Display_Account(Savings_Account& acc_r)
{
   cout << endl;
   cout << "Data for Account# " << acc_r.Get_Id() << endl << endl;
```

```
    cout << "Owner's Name: " << acc_r.Get_Name() << endl << endl;
    cout << "Account Balance: " << acc_r.Get_Balance() << endl;
}
```

Program Output

```
Enter Account ID: 1111
Enter Account Holder's Name: Adam Zapple
Enter Balance: 100.00
Enter Interest Rate: 0.06
Data for Account# 1111
Owner's Name: Adam Zapple
Account Balance: 100.00
Enter Account ID: 2222
Enter Account Holder's Name: Poly Ester
Enter Balance: 200.00
Enter Interest Rate: 0.08
Data for Account# 2222
Owner's Name: Poly Ester
Account Balance: 200.00
After the assignment:
Data for Account# 2222
Owner's Name: Poly Ester
Account Balance: 200.00
Data for Account# 2222
Owner's Name: Poly Ester
Account Balance: 200.00
```

The program creates two accounts using the Get_Account() function and displays the contents of both accounts using Display_Account(). Then the program assigns acc2 to acc1 and displays the contents of both accounts to show that the accounts are indeed the same.

15.3.3 Inheritance and Overloaded Operators

Like friend functions, overloaded operators are not inherited in a class hierarchy. Therefore, if you overload an operator in a base class, you must overload it again in any derived class. See Experiments 3, 4, and 5.

Exercises 15.3

1. Recode the declaration of Test_Class in dem15-2.cpp by making the overload of the addition operator a method rather than a friend function.
2. Code an overloaded subtraction operator for Test_Class that is a method of the class. See Exercise 2 of Section 15.2.
3. Code an overloaded multiplication operator for Test_Class that is a method of the class. See Exercise 4 of Section 15.2.
4. Code an overloaded division operator for Test_Class that is a method of the class. See Exercise 6 of Section 15.2.
5. See Chapter 11. Code an overload of assignment for the Rectangle class.
6. See Chapter 11. Code an overload of assignment for the DigitalClock class.

Experiments 15.3

1. Write a small program using the Savings_Account class to verify that the assignment

   ```
   (acc1 = acc2) = acc3;
   ```

   assigns the object acc3 to the object acc1.
2. In dem15-2.cpp, recode the constructor for Test_Class, replacing the assignment n = i by the assignment this -> n = i. Does the program behave any differently?
3. Code an overload of the assignment operator for Test_Class. Write a program to test the overload.
4. Code Derived_Test_Class, which is derived from the version of Test_Class of Experiment 3. Write a program that shows that the assignment operator for Test_Class is not overloaded for Derived_Test_Class.
5. Code an overload of assignment for the Derived_Test_Class of Experiment 4. Write a program to test the overloaded operator.

Programming Problems 15.3

1. Write a program using Test_Class that tests the overloaded subtraction, multiplication, and division operators of Exercises 2–4.
2. See Chapter 11. Overload the assignment operator for the WebPage class. Compile, execute, and test the class in a program.
3. See Chapter 11. Overload the assignment operator for the OilTank class. Compile, execute, and test the class in a program.
4. See Chapter 11. Overload the assignment operator for the VehicleService class. Compile, execute, and test the class in a program.
5. See Chapter 11. Overload the assignment operator for the HotelRoom class. Compile, execute, and test the class in a program.

15.4 OVERLOADING THE INSERTION AND EXTRACTION OPERATORS

The insertion and extraction operators can also be overloaded. In this section, we discuss how to overload the insertion operator for `Savings_Account` and how to overload the extraction operator for `Test_Class`.

15.4.1 Overloading the Insertion Operator

In dem15-3.cpp, we used the function `Display_Account()` to display account information. We can simplify displaying data associated with an object by overloading the insertion operator `<<`. The insertion operator is already overloaded. You can send integers, doubles, strings, and so on to the output stream using `<<`. The operator behaves differently, depending on the type of data that is sent to `cout`.

The insertion operator is a binary operator. The left operand, as we have used the operator, is `cout`, which is an object in the class `ostream`. The right operand is the data that we send to the output stream. As is the case with all C++ operators, the insertion operator has a value, which is the operator's left operand. Therefore, the value of the expression

```
cout << "Hello";
```

is the object `cout`. This is why it is possible to "cascade" the insertion operator. For example, the statement

```
cout << "The value of i is " << i;
```

works because the insertion operator associates from left to right. Therefore, the first insertion is done, sending the string "`The value of i is` " to `cout`. The result of this operation is the first operand, namely `cout`. Therefore, the second insertion sends the value of `i` to `cout`.

We must, therefore, take into account the fact that insertion returns its left operand if we want to be able to cascade insertion with `Savings_Account` objects. In addition, because insertion does not change the value of any object, it is better to code the overloaded insertion as a `friend` function. Following is the declaration of an overloaded insertion operator for `Savings_Account`.

```
friend ostream& operator << (ostream& , const Savings_Account&);
```

The return type of the operator is `ostream&` because, as noted previously, the value of the insertion operator should be the first argument, which is of type `ostream`. The first argument, as in overloading addition, is the left operand, which is an `ostream` object (`cout` in most cases). See Note 15.3. The second argument is the right operand, which is a `Savings_Account` object. Following is the code for the operator.

```
ostream& operator << (ostream& os, const Savings_Account& right_op)
{
  os << endl;
  os << "Data for Account# " << right_op.id_no << endl << endl;

  os << "Owner's Name: " << right_op.name << endl << endl;

  os << "Account Balance: " << right_op.balance << endl;

  return os;
}
```

Make sure you understand how this function works. If acc1 is a Savings_Account object, we would code

```
cout << acc1;
```

This statement would call the version of << that is overloaded for Savings_ Account. When the function is called, the parameter os becomes an alias for cout and the parameter right_op becomes an alias for acc1. Therefore, the uses of << in the function send output to cout. The instance variable references are to the instance variables of acc1. Finally, the function returns os, the first operand, namely cout.

The following program illustrates the overloaded insertion operator.

```cpp
//dem15-4.cpp

//This program demonstrates overloading the assignment operator.

#include <iostream>
#include <iomanip>
#include <string>

using namespace std;

class Savings_Account
{
  private:
    char    id_no[5];
    char*   name;
    double balance;
    double rate;

  public:
    Savings_Account(char id[], char* n_p, double bal = 0.00,
                                          double rt = 0.04);
    Savings_Account(const Savings_Account &);
    ~Savings_Account();
    double Calc_Interest();
    double Get_Balance();
    const char* Get_Id() const;
    const char* Get_Name() const;
    void Deposit(double);
    bool Withdraw(double);

    Savings_Account& operator = (const Savings_Account&);

    friend ostream& operator << (ostream&, const Savings_Account&);
};

Savings_Account::Savings_Account(char id[], char* n_p, double bal, double rt)
{
  strcpy(id_no, id);  //copy first argument into id_no[]

  name = new char[strlen(n_p) + 1]; //create space for the name

  strcpy(name, n_p);  //copy second argument into new space

  balance = bal;
  rate    = rt;
}
```

```
Savings_Account::Savings_Account(const Savings_Account& acc_r)
{
  strcpy(id_no, acc_r.id_no);  //copy first argument into id_no[]

  name = new char[strlen(acc_r.name) + 1]; //create space for the name

  strcpy(name, acc_r.name);  //copy second argument into new space

  balance = acc_r.balance;
  rate    = acc_r.rate;
}
Savings_Account::~Savings_Account()
{
  delete [] name;
}
double Savings_Account::Get_Balance()
{
  return balance;
}
double Savings_Account::Calc_Interest()
{
  double interest;

  interest = balance * rate;
  balance += interest;

  return interest;
}
const char* Savings_Account::Get_Name() const
{
  return name;
}
const char* Savings_Account::Get_Id() const
{
  return id_no;
}
void Savings_Account::Deposit(double amount)
{
  balance += amount;
}
bool Savings_Account::Withdraw(double amount)
{
  bool result;

  if (amount <= balance)
  {
    balance -= amount;
    result = true;
  }
```

```
    else
      result = false;
    return result;
}
Savings_Account& Savings_Account::operator = (const Savings_Account& right_op)
{
    if (&right_op == this)
        ;                       //Self assignment - do nothing
    else
    {
      strcpy(id_no, right_op.id_no);   //copy id of right_op into id_no[]

      delete [] name;

      name = new char[strlen(right_op.name) + 1]; //create space for the name

      strcpy(name, right_op.name);   //copy second argument into new space

      balance = right_op.balance;
      rate    = right_op.rate;
    }

    return *this;
}
ostream& operator << (ostream& os, const Savings_Account& right_op)
{
    os << endl;
    os << "Data for Account# " << right_op.id_no << endl << endl;

    os << "Owner's Name: " << right_op.name << endl << endl;

    os << "Account Balance: " << right_op.balance << endl;

    return os;
}
Savings_Account Get_Account();      //Prototype for Get_Account()

int main()
{
    cout << setprecision(2)
         << setiosflags(ios::fixed)
         << setiosflags(ios::showpoint);

    Savings_Account acc1 = Get_Account();

    cout << acc1;

    Savings_Account acc2 = Get_Account();

    cout << acc2;

    cout << endl << endl;
    cout << "Assigning acc2 to acc1." << endl;

    acc1 = acc2;
```

```
   cout << acc1 << acc2;

   cout << endl;

   return 0;

}
Savings_Account Get_Account()
{
   char id[5];
   char buffer[81];
   double bal;
   double rt;

   cout << endl;
   cout << "Enter Account ID: ";
   cin.getline(id, 5);

   cout << endl;
   cout << "Enter Account Holder's Name: ";
   cin.getline(buffer, 81);

   cout << endl;
   cout << "Enter Balance: ";
   cin >> bal;

   cout << endl;
   cout << "Enter Interest Rate: ";
   cin >> rt;

   cin.get();    //clear the newline character from the buffer

   Savings_Account acc(id, buffer, bal, rt);

   return acc;
}
```

Program Output

Enter Account ID: **1111**

Enter Account Holder's Name: **Adam Zapple**

Enter Balance: **100.00**

Enter Interest Rate: **0.06**

Data for Account# 1111

Owner's Name: Adam Zapple

Account Balance: 100.00

Enter Account ID: **2222**

Enter Account Holder's Name: **Poly Ester**

Enter Balance: **200.00**

```
Enter Interest Rate: 0.08

Data for Account# 2222

Owner's Name: Poly Ester

Account Balance: 200.00

Assigning acc2 to acc1.

Data for Account# 2222

Owner's Name: Poly Ester

Account Balance: 200.00

Data for Account# 2222

Owner's Name: Poly Ester

Account Balance: 200.00
```

Note that in the program, we have one instance of cascading.

```
cout << acc1 << acc2;
```

Because the overload of << returns the left operand, the result of the first insertion is cout. Therefore, the second insertion sends acc2 to cout using the overload of << again.

15.4.2 Overloading the Extraction Operator

The extraction operator can be overloaded in much the same way as we overloaded the insertion operator with a few important differences. The prototype for an extraction operator for Test_Class follows. Note that the function returns an istream object and the first operand is a reference to an istream object because we are doing input. Also, we do not declare the second operand as const because the operator will change the value of the data member of the object. Although the extraction operator changes one of its operands, we choose to declare it as a friend because the insertion operator is usually declared as a friend. See Exercises 1 and 2.

```
friend istream& operator >> (istream& , Test_Class&);
```

The code for the overloaded extraction operator is also similar to that of the code for the overload of the insertion operator. In fact, the function is simpler because we have only one data member to assign a value to. Note also that we use the parameter is as the name of the first operand because it represents the input stream.

```
istream& operator >> (istream& is, Test_Class& right_op)
{
    is >> right_op.n;

    return is;
}
```

The first argument is the left operand of the extraction operator, which will be the istream object cin. The function returns this operand so we can cascade the operator. Following is the program dem15-5.cpp that uses the overloaded insertion operator. We leave as an exercise the overloading of the insertion operator for Test_Class.

```cpp
//dem15-5.cpp

//This program illustrates the overloading of the extraction operator.

#include <iostream>

using namespace std;

class Test_Class
{
   friend Test_Class operator + (const Test_Class &, const Test_Class &);
   friend Test_Class operator + (const Test_Class &, const int);
   friend istream & operator >> (istream &, Test_Class &);

   private:
      int n;

   public:
      Test_Class(int i = 0);   //One-argument constructor
      Test_Class(Test_Class &);   //Copy constructor
      ~Test_Class();
      int Get_Value();
};

Test_Class::Test_Class(int i)
{
   n = i;
}

Test_Class::Test_Class(Test_Class & tc_r)
{
   n = tc_r.n;
}

Test_Class::~Test_Class()
{

}

int Test_Class::Get_Value()
{
   return n;
}

Test_Class operator + (const Test_Class & left_op,
                       const Test_Class & right_op)
{
   Test_Class temp_obj;

   temp_obj.n = left_op.n + right_op.n;

   return temp_obj;
}
```

```
Test_Class operator + (const Test_Class & left_op, const int right_op)
{
  Test_Class temp_obj;

  temp_obj.n = left_op.n + right_op;

  return temp_obj;
}

istream & operator >> (istream & is, Test_Class & right_op)
{
  is >> right_op.n;

  return is;
}

int main()
{
  Test_Class tc_object1;
  Test_Class tc_object2;
  Test_Class tc_object3;

  cout << endl;
  cout << "Enter a value for the first object: ";
  cin >> tc_object1;

  cout << endl;
  cout << "Enter two values for the next two objects: ";
  cin >> tc_object2 >> tc_object3;

  cout << endl;
  cout << "The data values for the three objects are: " << endl;
  cout << tc_object1.Get_Value() << endl;
  cout << tc_object2.Get_Value() << endl;
  cout << tc_object3.Get_Value() << endl;
  cout << endl;
  return 0;
}
```

Program Output

Enter a value for the first object: **1**

Enter two values for the next two objects: **2 3**

The data values for the three objects are:
1
2
3

Note that we cascade the insertion operator in the program. The result of cin >> tc_object2 is the object cin. Therefore, the second extraction is equivalent to cin >> tc_object3.

Exercises 15.4

1. Code an overload of the insertion operator for Test_Class.
2. Code the overload of the extraction operator as a friend function of Test_Class.
3. See Chapter 11. Code an overload of the insertion operator for the Rectangle class. The output should be nicely formatted.
4. See Chapter 11. Code an overload of the extraction operator for the Rectangle class. Executing cin >> rec; allows the user to enter two numbers separated by a space, the first for the length and the second for the width.
5. See Chapter 11. Code an overload of the insertion operator for the DigitalClock class. The output should be nicely formatted.
6. See Chapter 11. Code an overload of the extraction operator for the DigitalClock class. Executing cin >> clock; should allow the user to enter three numbers separated by spaces; the first for the hour, the second for the minutes, and the third for AM(0) or PM(1).

Experiments 15.4

1. Recode dem15-5.cpp using the overload of the insertion operator of Exercise 1. The program should not use the Get_Value() function.
2. Recode dem15-5.cpp using the overload of the extraction operator as a member function. Does the program behave differently?

Programming Problems 15.4

1. See Chapter 11. Overload the insertion operator for the WebSite class so it displays the values of the instance variables of the class in a nicely formatted way. Write a program that tests the operator. Compile, execute, and test the resulting program.
2. See Chapter 11. Overload the insertion operator for the OilTank class so it displays the values of the instance variables of the class in a nicely formatted way. Overload the extraction operator for the class. The overload should prompt the user for the required information. Write a program that tests the operators. Compile, execute, and test the resulting program.
3. See Chapter 11. Overload the insertion operator for the VehicleService class so it displays the values of the instance variables of the class in a nicely formatted way. Write a program that tests the operator. Compile, execute, and test the resulting program.
4. See Chapter 11. Overload the insertion operator for the HotelRoom class so it displays the values of the instance variables of the class in a nicely formatted way. Overload the extraction operator for the class. The overload should prompt the user for the required information. Write a program that tests the operators. Compile, execute, and test the resulting program.

15.5 OVERLOADING COMPOUND ASSIGNMENT OPERATORS

The compound assignment operators can also be overloaded.

15.5.1 Overloading += and −=

You can think of withdrawing money from an account as decreasing the account and of making a deposit as increasing an account. In Savings_Account, it would, therefore, be reasonable to replace the Deposit() method by an overload of += and to replace the Withdraw() method by an overload of −=. Because making either a deposit or withdrawal to an account changes the object to which it is applied, we code the overloads of these operators as methods.

Both the += and −= operators are considered assignment operators. Therefore, as we did for our overload assignment, the value of each of these operators will be the object to which the operator is applied. Each overload will return a reference to the object to which the operator is applied, namely, the left operand. Therefore, each operator returns *this.

```
Savings_Account& Savings_Account::operator += (const double right_op)
{
   balance += right_op;

   return *this;
}

Savings_Account& Savings_Account::operator -= (const double right_op)
{
   balance -= right_op;

   return *this;
}
```

Following is dem15-6.cpp, which uses overloads of += and −=.

```
//dem15-6.cpp

//This program demonstrates overloading the assignment operator.

#include <iostream>
#include <iomanip>
#include <string>

using namespace std;

class Savings_Account
{
   private:
      char   id_no[5];
      char*  name;
      double balance;
      double rate;
```

```
public:
    Savings_Account(char id[], char* n_p, double bal = 0.00,
                                          double rt = 0.04);
    Savings_Account(const Savings_Account &);
    ~Savings_Account();
    double Calc_Interest();
    double Get_Balance();
    const char* Get_Id() const;
    const char* Get_Name() const;
    Savings_Account& operator += (const double);
    Savings_Account& operator -= (const double);
    Savings_Account& operator = (const Savings_Account&);

    friend ostream& operator << (ostream&, const Savings_Account&);
};

Savings_Account::Savings_Account(char id[], char* n_p, double bal, double rt)
{
    strcpy(id_no, id);  //copy first argument into id_no[]

    name = new char[strlen(n_p) + 1]; //create space for the name

    strcpy(name, n_p);  //copy second argument into new space
    balance = bal;
    rate    = rt;
}

Savings_Account::Savings_Account(const Savings_Account& acc_r)
{
    strcpy(id_no, acc_r.id_no);   //copy first argument into id_no[]

    name = new char[strlen(acc_r.name) + 1]; //create space for the name

    strcpy(name, acc_r.name);   //copy second argument into new space

    balance = acc_r.balance;
    rate    = acc_r.rate;
}

Savings_Account::~Savings_Account()
{
    delete [] name;
}

double Savings_Account::Get_Balance()
{
    return balance;
}

double Savings_Account::Calc_Interest()
{
    double interest;
    interest = balance * rate;
    balance += interest;
```

```
   return interest;
}
const char* Savings_Account::Get_Name() const
{
   return name;
}
const char* Savings_Account::Get_Id() const
{
   return id_no;
}
Savings_Account& Savings_Account::operator += (const double right_op)
{
  balance += right_op;

  return *this;
}
Savings_Account& Savings_Account::operator -= (const double right_op)
{
  balance -= right_op;

  return *this;
}
Savings_Account& Savings_Account::operator = (const Savings_Account&
                                               right_op)
{
  if (&right_op == this)
      ;                        //Self assignment - do nothing
  else
  {
    strcpy(id_no, right_op.id_no);  //copy id of right_op into id_no[]

    delete [] name;

    name = new char[strlen(right_op.name) + 1]; //create space for the name

    strcpy(name, right_op.name);  //copy second argument into new space

    balance = right_op.balance;
    rate    = right_op.rate;
  }

  return *this;
}
ostream& operator << (ostream& os, const Savings_Account& right_op)
{
  os << endl;
  os << "Data for Account# " << right_op.id_no << endl << endl;

  os << "Owner's Name: " << right_op.name << endl << endl;

  os << "Account Balance: " << right_op.balance << endl;
```

```
    return os;
}

Savings_Account Get_Account();      //Prototype for Get_Account()

int main()
{
  cout << setprecision(2)
       << setiosflags(ios::fixed)
       << setiosflags(ios::showpoint);

  double amount;

  Savings_Account acc1 = Get_Account();

  cout << acc1;

  cout << endl;
  cout << "Enter an amount to deposit: ";
  cin >> amount;

  acc1 += amount;

  cout << endl;
  cout << "After the deposit:" << endl << endl << acc1;

  cout << endl;
  cout << "Enter an amount to withdraw: ";
  cin >> amount;

  acc1 -= amount;

  cout << endl;
  cout << "After the withdrawal:" << endl << endl << acc1;

  cout << endl;
  return 0;

}

Savings_Account Get_Account()
{
  char id[5];
  char buffer[81];
  double bal;
  double rt;

  cout << endl;
  cout << "Enter Account ID: ";
  cin.getline(id, 5);

  cout << endl;
  cout << "Enter Account Holder's Name: ";
  cin.getline(buffer, 81);

  cout << endl;
  cout << "Enter Balance: ";
  cin >> bal;
```

```
    cout << endl;
    cout << "Enter Interest Rate: ";
    cin >> rt;

    cin.get();    //clear the newline character from the buffer

    Savings_Account acc(id, buffer, bal, rt);

    return acc;

}
```

Program Output

Enter Account ID: **1111**

Enter Account Holder's Name: **Maxwell Larrabee**

Enter Balance: **200.00**

Enter Interest Rate: **0.08**

Data for Account# 1111

Owner's Name: Maxwell Larrabee

Account Balance: 200.00

Enter an amount to deposit: **50.00**

After the deposit:

Data for Account# 1111

Owner's Name: Maxwell Larrabee

Account Balance: 250.00

Enter an amount to withdraw: **100.00**

After the withdrawal:

Data for Account# 1111

Owner's Name: Maxwell Larrabee

Account Balance: 150.00

Exercises 15.5

1. Code the prototype and definition of an overload of += for Test_Class. The operator should increase the value of the instance variable n of the object to which it is applied by the value of the integer that is the right operand.

2. Code the prototype and definition of an overload of -= for Test_Class. The operator should decrease the value of the instance variable n of the object to which it is applied by the value of the integer that is the right operand.

3. Code the prototype and definition of an overload of *= for `Test_Class`. The operator should multiply the value of the instance variable n of the object to which it is applied by the value of the integer that is the right operand.

4. Code the prototype and definition of an overload of /= for `Test_Class`. The operator should divide the value of the instance variable n of the object to which it is applied by the value of the integer that is the right operand. Be sure to test for division by zero.

5. Recode the overload of += given in this section for `Savings_Account` as a `friend` function rather than as a class method.

6. Recode the overload of -= given in this section for `Savings_Account` as a `friend` function rather than as a class method.

Programming Problems 15.5

1. See Chapter 11. In the `WebPage` class, add an overload of += that increases the number of hits on the page. Write a program to test the new operators. Compile, execute, and test the resulting program. Write a program to test the new operators. Compile, execute, and test the resulting program.

2. See Chapter 11. In the `OilTank` class, replace the method `Add_Oil()` by an overload of the += operator and the method `Remove_Oil()` by an overload of the -= operator. Write a program to test the new operators. Compile, execute, and test the resulting program.

3. See Chapter 11. In the `VehicleService` class, code an overload of += that increases the number of hours of labor done on the vehicle. Write a program to test the new operator. Compile, execute, and test the resulting program.

4. See Chapter 11. In the `HotelRoom` class, add an overload of += to add guests to a room and an overload of -= to remove guests from a room. Write a program to test the new operators. Compile, execute, and test the resulting program.

15.6 OVERLOADING RELATIONAL OPERATORS

The relational operators, ==, >, <, and so on, sometimes can also be overloaded in a meaningful way.

15.6.1 Overloading ==

What if we want to see if two savings account objects, say `acc1` and `acc2`, contain the same information? We could make such a test by using the accessor methods to get the values of the instance variables and test them for equality. If the instance variables are equal, on a member-by-member basis, then the accounts contain the same information. This approach works (see Exercise 1), but it would be nice if we could simply code an `if` statement as follows.

```
if (acc1 == acc2)

. . .

else

. . .
```

The problem with the preceding solution is that the expression `acc1 == acc2` is illegal. See Experiment 1. There is no default test for equality that extends to objects in the same way as there is a default assignment that extends to objects. If we want to use a relation operator to test a relation between two objects, we must overload the operator. Because a relation operator does not change the objects involved, we shall code the overload of the equals operator as a `friend` function. Following are the prototype and code of the overloaded equals operator.

```
friend int operator == (Account&, Account&);

int operator == (Account& acc_left, Account& acc_right)
{
  if (strcmp(acc_left.id_no, acc_right.id_no))
    return 0;

  if (strcmp(acc_left.name, acc_right.name))
    return 0;

  if (acc_left.balance != acc_right.balance)
    return 0;

  if (acc_left.rate != acc_right.rate)
    return 0;

  return 1;
}
```

To make the overloaded equals operator behave as the equals operator does when comparing the native data types, we code the overload so that the operator returns one if the operands are equal, and zero otherwise. Recall that the function `strcmp()` returns a nonzero, that is, true, value if the strings it compares are not equal. Thus, the first `if` statement causes the function to return zero if the `id_no` members of the objects being compared are not equal. Likewise, the second `if` statement causes the function to return zero if the `name` members of the objects being compared are not equal. The next two `if` statements cause the function to return zero if the `balance` or the `rate` members of the objects being compared are not equal. Thus, if the two objects differ in any of their instance variables, the operator returns zero. Otherwise, the operator returns one.

Following is program dem15-7.cpp, which illustrates the use of the overloaded `==` operator.

```
//dem15-7.cpp

//This program demonstrates overloading the assignment operator.

#include <iostream>
#include <iomanip>
#include <string>

using namespace std;

class Savings_Account
{
```

```
  private:
    char    id_no[5];
    char*   name;
    double balance;
    double rate;

  public:
    Savings_Account(char id[], char* n_p, double bal = 0.00,
                                          double rt = 0.04);
    Savings_Account(const Savings_Account &);
    ~Savings_Account();
    double Calc_Interest();
    double Get_Balance();
    const char* Get_Id() const;
    const char* Get_Name() const;
    Savings_Account& operator += (const double);
    Savings_Account& operator -= (const double);
    Savings_Account& operator = (const Savings_Account&);
    friend ostream& operator << (ostream&, const Savings_Account&);
    friend int operator == (Savings_Account&, Savings_Account&);
};

Savings_Account::Savings_Account(char id[], char* n_p, double bal, double rt)
{
  strcpy(id_no, id);  //copy first argument into id_no[]

  name = new char[strlen(n_p) + 1]; //create space for the name

  strcpy(name, n_p);  //copy second argument into new space

  balance = bal;
  rate    = rt;
}

Savings_Account::Savings_Account(const Savings_Account& acc_r)
{
  strcpy(id_no, acc_r.id_no);  //copy first argument into id_no[]

  name = new char[strlen(acc_r.name) + 1]; //create space for the name

  strcpy(name, acc_r.name);  //copy second argument into new space

  balance = acc_r.balance;
  rate    = acc_r.rate;
}

Savings_Account::~Savings_Account()
{
  delete [] name;
}

double Savings_Account::Get_Balance()
{
  return balance;
}
```

```
double Savings_Account::Calc_Interest()
{
  double interest;

  interest = balance * rate;
  balance += interest;

  return interest;
}
const char* Savings_Account::Get_Name() const
{
  return name;
}
const char* Savings_Account::Get_Id() const
{
  return id_no;
}
Savings_Account& Savings_Account::operator += (const double right_op)
{
  balance += right_op;

  return *this;
}
Savings_Account& Savings_Account::operator -= (const double right_op)
{
  balance -= right_op;

  return *this;
}
Savings_Account& Savings_Account::operator = (const Savings_Account& right_op)
{
  if (&right_op == this)
       ;                         //Self assignment - do nothing
  else
  {
    strcpy(id_no, right_op.id_no);   //copy id of right_op into id_no[]

    delete [] name;

    name = new char[strlen(right_op.name) + 1]; //create space for the name

    strcpy(name, right_op.name);   //copy second argument into new space

    balance = right_op.balance;
    rate    = right_op.rate;
  }

  return *this;
}
ostream& operator << (ostream& os, const Savings_Account& right_op)
{
```

```
    os << endl;
    os << "Data for Account# " << right_op.id_no << endl << endl;

    os << "Owner's Name: " << right_op.name << endl << endl;

    os << "Account Balance: " << right_op.balance << endl;

    return os;
}
int operator == (Savings_Account& acc_left, Savings_Account& acc_right)
{
    if (strcmp(acc_left.id_no, acc_right.id_no))
        return 0;

    if (strcmp(acc_left.name, acc_right.name))
        return 0;

    if (acc_left.balance != acc_right.balance)
        return 0;

    if (acc_left.rate != acc_right.rate)
        return 0;

    return 1;
}
Savings_Account Get_Account();      //Prototype for Get_Account()

int main()
{
    cout << setprecision(2)
         << setiosflags(ios::fixed)
         << setiosflags(ios::showpoint);

    Savings_Account acc1 = Get_Account();

    cout << acc1;

    cout << endl;
    cout << "Initializing acc2 to the value of acc1.";

    Savings_Account acc2 = acc1;

    if (acc1 == acc2)
    {
        cout << endl << endl;
        cout << "The accounts are equal";
    }
    else
    {
        cout << endl << endl;
        cout << "The accounts are not equal";
    }

    cout << endl << endl;
    cout << "Adding $50.00 to Account 2" << endl;
```

```cpp
   acc2 += 50.00;

   cout << acc2;

   if (acc1 == acc2)
   {
      cout << endl;
      cout << "The accounts are equal";
   }
   else
   {
      cout << endl;
      cout << "The accounts are not equal";
   }

   cout << endl;
   return 0;

}
Savings_Account Get_Account()
{
   char id[5];
   char buffer[81];
   double bal;
   double rt;

   cout << endl;
   cout << "Enter Account ID: ";
   cin.getline(id, 5);

   cout << endl;
   cout << "Enter Account Holder's Name: ";
   cin.getline(buffer, 81);

   cout << endl;
   cout << "Enter Balance: ";
   cin >> bal;

   cout << endl;
   cout << "Enter Interest Rate: ";
   cin >> rt;

   cin.get();   //clear the newline character from the buffer

   Savings_Account acc(id, buffer, bal, rt);

   return acc;
}
```

Program Output

Enter Account ID: **1234**

Enter Account Holder's Name: **John Smith**

```
Enter Balance: 200.00

Enter Interest Rate: 0.07

Data for Account# 1234

Owner's Name: John Smith

Account Balance: 200.00

Initializing acc2 to the value of acc1.

The accounts are equal

Adding $50.00 to Account 2

Data for Account# 1234

Owner's Name: John Smith

Account Balance: 250.00

The accounts are not equal
```

The program asks the user to enter data for an account. Then the program initializes a second account to the first account. Therefore, the accounts are identical. This is verified by the program using the overloaded == operator in an if statement. The program then deposits $50.00 into the second account using the overloaded += operator and then again uses an if statement and the overloaded == operator to test the two accounts for equality. Of course, the accounts are no longer equal, because their balances differ.

Exercises 15.6

1. Recode dem15-7.cpp without using the overloaded == operator. Instead, when the program needs to test for equality, test each of the data members for equality by using the corresponding accessor methods. You will need to code accessor methods to get the balance and the rate for a Savings_Account object.

2. Code an overload of the == operator for Test_Class. Two objects are equal if their n instance variables are equal.

3. Code an overload of the > operator for Test_Class. The object tc_object1 is greater than tc_object2 if its instance variable n is greater than the instance variable n of tc_object2.

4. Code an overload of the < operator for Test_Class. The object tc_object1 is less than tc_object2 if its instance variable n is less than the instance variable n of tc_object2.

5. Code an overload of the != operator for Savings_Account that uses the overload of the == operator that was developed in this section.

6. Code overloads of the <= operator and the >= operator for Test_Class that use the == operator of Exercise 2 and the overloads of > and < of Exercises 3 and 4.

Programming Problems 15.6

1. See Chapter 11. Code an overload of the == operator for the WebPage class. Write a program that tests the new operator. Compile, execute, and test the resulting program.
2. See Chapter 11. Code an overload of the == operator for the OilTank class. Also, overload the > operator. The operator should return true if the oil in the tank, that is, its left operand, exceeds the oil in the tank that is its right operand. Otherwise, it should return false. Write a program that tests the new operator. Compile, execute, and test the resulting program.
3. See Chapter 11. Code an overload of the == operator for the VehicleService class. Write a program that tests the new operator. Compile, execute, and test the resulting program.
4. See Chapter 11. Code an overload of the == operator for the HotelRoom class. Write a program that tests the new operator. Compile, execute, and test the resulting program.

15.7 OVERLOADING UNARY OPERATORS

Unary operators, such as ++, −−, +, and − can also be overloaded. In the case of ++ and −−, however, you must take care to overload the pre- and post-versions of the operators properly.

15.7.1 Overloading ++

In some cases, it makes sense to overload the unary operators. For example, to overload the ++ operator for Test_Class, we might code the following prototype and code.

```
Test_Class& operator ++ ();

Test_Class& Test_Class::operator ++ ()
{
   ++n;

   return *this;
}
```

Note that the operator has no argument. The operator operates on the object to which it is applied. Thus, the n instance variable in the operator definition refers to the instance variable of the object to which the operator is applied. The function returns a reference to that object. Thus, we can code the following in main().

```
Test_Class tc_object(5);

++tc_object;
```

15.7.2 Overloading the Post-Increment ++

The statement ++tc_object increments the data member of tc_object. However, what if we code the following statement?

```
tc_object++;
```

This statement uses ++ as a post-increment operator. The compiler will not use the overload that we just coded. See Experiment 1. The post-increment operator requires a separate overload. To distinguish between the two, the compiler requires a "dummy" integer argument in the prototype and definition of the post-increment operator. There is no need to specify a parameter in the definition because the parameter is never used.

```
Test_Class& operator ++ (int);                    //postincrement

Test_Class& Test_Class::operator ++ (int)
{
    n++;

    return *this;
}
```

When you use the post-increment operator in a program, the compiler uses the version with the dummy integer argument. Following is a program that uses both versions of the ++ operator.

```
//dem15-8.cpp

//This program illustrates overloading the ++ operator.

#include <iostream>

using namespace std;

class Test_Class
{
    friend Test_Class operator + (const Test_Class&, const Test_Class&);
    friend Test_Class operator + (const Test_Class&, const int);
    friend istream& operator >> (istream&, Test_Class&);
    friend ostream& operator << (ostream&, Test_Class&);

    private:
        int n;

    public:
        Test_Class(int i = 0);   //One-argument constructor
        Test_Class(Test_Class&);   //Copy constructor
        ~Test_Class();
        Test_Class& operator ++();      //Prefix overload
        Test_Class& operator ++(int); //Postfix overload
};

Test_Class::Test_Class(int i)
{
    n = i;
}

Test_Class::Test_Class(Test_Class& tc_r)
{
    n = tc_r.n;
}
```

```
Test_Class::~Test_Class()
{
}

Test_Class operator + (const Test_Class& left_op, const Test_Class& right_op)
{
  Test_Class temp_obj;
  temp_obj.n = left_op.n + right_op.n;

  return temp_obj;
}

Test_Class operator + (const Test_Class& left_op, const int right_op)
{
  Test_Class temp_obj;

  temp_obj.n = left_op.n + right_op;

  return temp_obj;
}

istream& operator >> (istream& is, Test_Class& right_op)
{
  is >> right_op.n;

  return is;
}

ostream& operator << (ostream& os, Test_Class& right_op)
{
  os << right_op.n;

  return os;
}

Test_Class& Test_Class::operator ++ ()                  //Preincrement overload
{
  ++n;

  return *this;
}

Test_Class& Test_Class::operator ++ (int)               //Postincrement overload
{
  n++;

  return *this;
}

int main()
{
  Test_Class tc_object(5);

  cout << endl;
  cout << "The current value of the object is " << tc_object;

  ++tc_object;
```

```
cout << endl << endl;
cout << "After a preincrement the value of the object is "
    << tc_object;

tc_object++;

cout << endl << endl;
cout << "After a postincrement the value of the object is "
    << tc_object;

cout << endl;
return 0;
}
```

Program Output

```
The current value of the object is 5

After a preincrement the value of the object is 6

After a postincrement the value of the object is 7
```

Note in the definition of Test_Class that we replace the Get_Value() method by an overload of the << operator, which sends the value of the instance variable of the object to the output stream.

The program creates a Test_Class object with a data member value of 5. Then a pre-increment increases the data member to 6 and then a post-increment increases the data member to 7.

Exercises 15.7

1. Code a prototype and definition for an overload of the -- operator for Test_Class.

2. Code a prototype and definition for overloads of the unary + and - operators for Test_Class. The overload of unary + should place a + in front of the instance variable of the object and return a reference to the object. The overload of unary - should negate the instance variable of the object and return a reference to the object.

3. See Chapter 11. Code a prototype and definition for an overload of the ++ and -- operators for the Rectangle class. Applying ++ to a Rectangle object should increment the length and width by one. Applying -- to a Rectangle object should decrement the length and width by one. If either the length or the width are thereby decreased to zero or less, the default value of 1 should be assigned to that member.

4. See Chapter 11. Code a prototype and definition for an overload of the ++ operator for the DigitalClock class. Applying ++ to a DigitalClock object should increase the minutes instance variable by one. Remember that increasing the minutes instance variable by one can result in an increase in the hour instance variable and a change to the ampm instance variable.

Experiments 15.7

1. Remove the prototype and the definition of the post-increment operator in dem15-8.cpp and keep `main()` as it is in the program. Compile the resulting program. What message does the compiler issue?

2. Add to the definition of `Test_Class` the overloads for −−, unary +, and unary − that you coded in Exercises 1 and 2. Write a program that tests the overloaded operators. Compile, execute, and test the resulting program.

3. See Chapter 11. Add to the `Rectangle` class the overloads of ++ and −− that you coded in Exercise 3. Write a program that tests the overloaded operators. Compile, execute, and test the resulting program.

4. See Chapter 11. Add to the `DigitalClock` class the overload of ++ that you coded in Exercise 4. Write a program that tests the overloaded operator. Compile, execute, and test the resulting program.

Programming Problems 15.7

1. See Chapter 11. Overload the ++ operator for the `WebPage` class. Applying the operator to a `WebPage` object should increment the number of hits on the page. Code both a pre-increment and a post-increment. Write a program that tests the overloaded operator. Compile, execute, and test the resulting program.

2. See Chapter 11. Overload the ++ and −− operators for the `HotelRoom` class. Applying the ++ operator to a `HotelRoom` object increments the number of guests in the room. Applying the −− operator decrements the number of guests in the room. Code pre- and post-versions of both operators. Write a program that tests the overloaded operators. Compile, execute, and test the resulting program.

15.8 MACROS AND INLINE FUNCTIONS

So far, we have defined symbolic constants by declaring them as `const` variables, which is the preferred way in C++. It is also possible to define symbolic constants by using the `#define` preprocessor directive. In fact, you can use the `#define` preprocessor directive to define macros, which can sometimes replace functions.

15.8.1 Symbolic Constants Using #define

Recall that the C++ preprocessor is a text replacement mechanism. The `#define` preprocessor directive allows us to replace any expression by a defined name. For example, in prb05-3.cpp, we could replace the declaration

```
const double COMMISSION_RATE = 0.050;
```

by the definition

```
#define COMMISSION_RATE 0.050
```

This directive defines the symbolic constant `COMMISSION_RATE` as the value 0.050. When the preprocessor scans the program code, it replaces every occurrence of the symbol

COMMISSION_RATE by the value 0.050. Thus, when the preprocessor scans the line

```
straight_commission = sales * COMMISSION_RATE;
```

it replaces the symbol COMMISSION_RATE by its defined value of 0.050.

Note that the preprocessor directive does not end in a semicolon. Doing so would cause the semicolon to be part of the definition, which could cause a syntax or logic error in your program.

Although you can use #define to define symbolic constants in any C++ program, we shall refrain from doing so in the programs in this book. In modern C++ usage, symbolic constants are defined using const.

15.8.2 Macro Definitions

The #define directive also can be used to define macros with parameters. A **macro** is a name that stands for a statement or expression. For example, consider the following.

```
#define SQ(x)   x * x
```

The macro being defined is SQ(x) and its definition is x * x. When the C++ preprocessor sees this #define, it searches the program for all occurrences of the macro name SQ. Suppose, for example, the preprocessor finds SQ(count) in the program. The preprocessor then replaces the macro, SQ(count), by the expression obtained by replacing the parameter x in the macro's definition by count. Thus, the preprocessor would replace the expression

```
s = SQ(count);
```

by

```
s = count * count;
```

Because the preprocessor is a text replacement mechanism, it does not check for correctness in syntax or meaning. For example, you cannot put a space after the macro name and before the left parenthesis. Doing so causes the preprocessor to interpret everything that follows the macro name as part of the definition, even the parentheses. Thus, incorrectly defining SQ as

```
#define SQ (x) x * x
```

results in the preprocessor expanding the assignment

```
s = SQ(count);
```

to the following meaningless expression.

```
s = (x) x * x(count);
```

Also, do not put a semicolon at the end of a macro. Doing so makes the semicolon part of the definition, which could cause a syntax error. For example, incorrectly defining SQ as

```
#define SQ(x) x * x;
```

causes the preprocessor to expand the macro in the following if statement

```
if (count > 3)
   count = SQ(count);
else
   count = 1;
```

as follows

```
if (count > 3)
   count = count * count;;
else
   count = 1;
```

The extra semicolon in the first assignment is a null statement and causes a syntax error.

The given definition of SQ also can cause side effects that result in a change in meaning. Suppose we have the following definitions and assignment.

```
int i = 2,
    j = 4,
    k;
```

```
k = SQ(i + j);
```

The assignment does not assign the value 36 to k as you might first think. The preprocessor expands the macro in the assignment as follows, replacing each occurrence of the parameter x by the string i + j.

```
k = i + j * i + j;
```

Because the computer evaluates multiplication before addition, the right side of the assignment evaluates to 14.

To avoid this **side effect** of macro expansion, enclose each occurrence of the parameter in the macro definition by parentheses.

```
#define SQ(x) (x) * (x)
```

With this definition, in the assignment to k, the preprocessor would replace each occurrence of x in the definition of SQ by the string i + j. This time, however, the parentheses are part of the macro. The macro expands as follows, which correctly evaluates to 36.

```
k = (i + j) * (i + j);
```

There is still another side effect that can occur with this new macro definition. Using the same definitions of i, j, and k as before, consider the following assignment.

```
k = j / SQ(i);
```

The assignment does not assign 1 to k. Instead, the preprocessor replaces the macro in the assignment by (i) * (i), which results in the following assignment.

```
k = j / (i) * (i);
```

Because multiplication and division are on the same precedence level and they associate from left to right, the computer does the division first. This results in the computer assigning 4 to k.

To avoid this side effect, enclose the entire macro definition in parentheses as follows.

```
#define SQ(x)   ((x) * (x))
```

With this new definition, the preprocessor would expand the macro as `((i) * (i))` and the assignment to k would be the following.

```
k = j / ( (i) * (i) );
```

Now the computer evaluates the multiplication first and then the division. This results in the computer assigning 1 to k.

Note 15.7 summarizes the rules for writing macros.

Note 15.7   Rules for Writing Macros

- Do not code a space between the macro name and the left parenthesis that follows the name.
- Do not end the macro definition with a semicolon.
- Enclose each occurrence of each parameter in the macro definition in parentheses.
- Enclose the entire macro definition in parentheses.

Macros can have more than one parameter. For example, the following macro squares the sum of its two parameters.

```
#define SUM_SQ(x, y)   ( ((x) + (y)) * ((x) + (y)) )
```

You also can use a macro in the definition of another macro that has already been defined in the program. For example, the following is legal.

```
#define SQ(x) ( (x) * (x) )
#define SUM_SQ(x, y) ( SQ((x) + (y)) )
```

In the next section, we put macros to work in a program and discuss the relative merits of macros and functions.

15.8.3 An Example Using Macros—The Conditional Operator

The following program, dem15-9.cpp, asks the user to enter several numbers. When the user stops entering the numbers, the program displays the smallest and the largest numbers that the user entered. The program uses two macros, MAX(x, y) and MIN(x, y), that find the larger and smaller of the two parameters. The macro definitions use the **conditional operator** ? : , which is the only operator in C++ that has three operands. The conditional operator has the following form.

conditional-expression ? expression1 : expression2

If the conditional expression is true, the value of the entire operator is expression1. If the conditional expression is false, the value of the entire operator is expression2. Thus, the conditional operator is similar to an if-else statement. If the conditional expression is true, the value of the operator is expression1; otherwise, the value of the operator is expression2. For example, suppose we have the following declarations and assignment.

```
int i = 3,
    j = 4,
    k;
```

```
k = (i == j)? i: j;
```

It helps to read the operator as follows: "i, if i equals j; else j." Thus, the statement assigns the value of i to k if i equals j; otherwise, it assigns the value of j to k. Using the initial values of i and j, the statement assigns 4 to k.

A common use of the conditional operator is in macro definitions. For example, the following macro results in the larger of its two parameters.

```
#define MAX(x, y)   ( ((x) > (y))? (x): (y) )
```

Thus, MAX(x, y) is x if x is greater than y; otherwise, MAX(x, y) is y. The following program, dem15-9.cpp, uses this macro and a similar one MIN(x, y) that finds the smaller of its two parameters.

```
// dem15-9.cpp

// This program uses macros to find the largest and
// smallest of a set of numbers input by the user.
// The macros make use of the conditional operator.

#include <iostream>
#include <iomanip>

using namespace std;

#define MAX(x, y) ( ((x) > (y))? (x): (y) )
#define MIN(x, y) ( ((x) < (y))? (x): (y) )

int main()
{
    int     number_count,
            i;
    double number,
            minimum,
            maximum;

    cout << setprecision(6)
         << setiosflags(ios::fixed)
         << setiosflags(ios::showpoint);

    cout << "This program will find the largest and smallest of "
         << endl;
    cout << "the numbers you enter." << endl << endl;
    cout << "Enter the number of numbers that you will enter: ";
    cin >> number_count;

    cout << endl << endl;
    cout << "Now you will be asked to enter the numbers."
         << endl << endl;
```

```
      cout << "Enter number 1: ";
      cin >> number;

      minimum = maximum = number;

      for (i = 2; i <= number_count; ++i)
      {
         cout << endl;
         cout << "Enter number " << i << ": ";
         cin >> number;
         minimum = MIN(minimum, number);
         maximum = MAX(maximum, number);
      }

      cout << endl << endl;
      cout << "Smallest number: " << minimum << endl << endl;
      cout << "Largest number:  " << maximum << endl;

      return 0;
   }
```

Program Output

This program will find the largest and smallest of
the numbers you enter.

Enter the number of numbers that you will enter: **10**

Now you will be asked to enter the numbers.

Enter number 1: **3.6**

Enter number 2: **-5.0**

Enter number 3: **6.3**

Enter number 4: **9.9**

Enter number 5: **2.1**

Enter number 6: **12.3**

Enter number 7: **-7.8**

Enter number 8: **10.6**

Enter number 9: **-3.4**

Enter number 10: **5.2**

Smallest number: -7.800000

Largest number: 12.300000

The program begins by asking the user for the number of numbers that will be
entered. After placing that value into number_count, the program prompts for the first

number. The program places the number that the user enters into the variable `number`. A multiple assignment then places the value of `number` into the variables `minimum` and `maximum`. The variable `minimum` holds the value of the smallest number that the user has entered so far. The variable `maximum` holds the value of the largest number that the user has entered so far. When the user enters the first number, that number is both the smallest and largest number entered so far.

The program then enters a `for` loop that processes the rest of the numbers that the user enters. Each iteration prompts the user for a number. Then, the first assignment replaces `minimum` by the smaller of `minimum` and the number that the user entered. The second assignment replaces `maximum` by the larger of `maximum` and the number that the user entered. Therefore, when the program exits the loop, `maximum` contains the largest number the user entered, and `minimum` contains the smallest number the user entered.

15.8.4 Functions vs. Macros

There are several advantages to using macros instead of functions. First, because using a macro does not involve a function call or passing parameters, a macro executes faster than a function. Second, the parameters in a macro do not have a type. For example, the MAX macro of dem15-9.cpp will find the larger of two `int` variables, two `long` variables, or two `double` variables. If you use a function to find the larger of two numbers, you must specify the data type of the numbers. Thus, you would need different functions to find the larger of two integers and the larger of two doubles.

There are also disadvantages to using macros instead of functions. First, as we noted, macros can have side effects that lead to incorrect results. Functions are not subject to these side effects. Second, although there is overhead in calling a function and passing parameters, the function mechanism is safer to use. Remember that the compiler uses the function prototype to ensure that you use the function's parameters and return type correctly. The compiler does no such checking for macros.

15.8.5 Inline Functions

In C++, there is a way to combine the efficiency of a macro with the safety of a function by using an **inline function**. If a function is inline, the compiler places a copy of the code of that function at each point where the function is called. Therefore, short functions (one or two lines of code) are ideal candidates for inlining. Because the compiler replaces an inline function's call by the code of the function, it follows that the compiler must know the definition of the function before any calls to the function are made in the program code. To inline a function, place the keyword **inline** before the function name and define the function before any calls are made to the function. This means that you place the function's definition where you usually place the function prototype. In our programs, this means that inline function definitions are placed before `main()`.

For example, in dem15.9.cpp, we used the following macro:

```
#define MAX(x, y) ( ((x) > (y))? (x): (y) )
```

An inline function that is equivalent to this macro is the following.

```
inline double Max(double x, double y) {return (x > y)? x : y;}
```

Note that we do not need to use excessive parentheses, as was necessary in the macro definition to avoid side effects. Suppose `main()` contains the following declarations and function call.

```
double d1 = 4.8,
       d2 = 9.6
       d;
```

```
d = Max(d1, d2);
```

When the compiler encounters the function call to `Max()`, it replaces the function call with the code of the inline function using the values of the arguments as the values of the parameters. Therefore, the assignment is equivalent to the following.

```
d = (d1 > d2)? d1 : d2;
```

We illustrate inline functions by recoding dem15-9.cpp using inline functions in place of macros.

```
// dem15-10.cpp

// This program uses inline functions to find the largest and
// smallest of a set of numbers input by the user.
// The functions make use of the conditional operator.

#include <iostream>
#include <iomanip>

using namespace std;

inline double Max(double x, double y) {return (x > y)? x : y;}
inline double Min(double x, double y) {return (x < y)? x : y;}

int main()
{
    int     number_count,
            i;
    double  number,
            minimum,
            maximum;

    cout << setprecision(6)
         << setiosflags(ios::fixed)
         << setiosflags(ios::showpoint);

    cout << "This program will find the largest and smallest of "
         << endl;
    cout << "the numbers you enter." << endl << endl;
    cout << "Enter the number of numbers that you will enter: ";
    cin >> number_count;

    cout << endl << endl;
    cout << "Now you will be asked to enter the numbers."
         << endl << endl;
    cout << "Enter number 1: ";
    cin >> number;
```

```
    minimum = maximum = number;
    for (i = 2; i <= number_count; ++i)
    {
      cout << endl;
      cout << "Enter number " << i << ": ";
      cin >> number;
      minimum = Min(minimum, number);
      maximum = Max(maximum, number);
    }
    cout << endl << endl;
    cout << "Smallest number: " << minimum << endl << endl;
    cout << "Largest number:  " << maximum << endl;

    return 0;
}
```

Program Output

```
This program will find the largest and smallest of
the numbers you enter.

Enter the number of numbers that you will enter: 3

Now you will be asked to enter the numbers.

Enter number 1: 3.4

Enter number 2: 6.8

Enter number 3: 4.1

Smallest number: 3.400000

Largest number:  6.800000
```

Note 15.8   When and How to Use Inline Functions

- Consider inlining a function if the function has one or two lines of code.
- To inline a function, place the keyword inline before the return type in the function definition. The function's definition must precede any call to the function in the program code.

Inline functions also play a role in where methods are defined in a class declaration. The difference between defining a method inside or outside a class declaration is that a class method that is defined inside the class declaration is, by default, inline. If you define a method outside the class declaration, then to inline the method, you must precede the definition by the keyword inline.

Exercises 15.8

1. Recode the `Calculate_Income()` function in prb05-3.cpp, replacing all the symbolic constants by their equivalents using `#define`. Compile and execute the resulting program.
2. Write a macro `AREA` that finds the area of a rectangle in terms of its length and width.
3. Write an inline function `Area()` that finds the area of a rectangle in terms of its length and width.
4. Write a macro `CELSIUS` that converts a Fahrenheit temperature to the equivalent Celsius temperature.
5. Write an inline function `Celsius()` that converts a Fahrenheit temperature to the equivalent Celsius temperature.
6. Write a macro `SALE_PRICE` that computes the sale price of an item, given the item's list price. The macro should apply a 25% discount on the list price and then add 8.25% sales tax.
7. Write an inline function `Sale_Price()`that computes the sale price of an item, given the item's list price. The function should apply a 25% discount on the list price and then add 8.25% sales tax.
8. Use the macro `SQ` that we developed in the text to define macros `THR` and `FOR` that compute the third and fourth powers of their parameters.
9. Write a macro that finds the largest among three parameters. Feel free to use the macro, `MAX`, that we used in dem15-9.cpp.

Experiment 15.8

1. Redo dem15-9.cpp using functions instead of macros to find the minimum and maximum between two numbers.

CHAPTER REVIEW

TERMINOLOGY

Describe the meanings of the following terms.

friend function	`#define`
`friend`	macro
`operator`	side effect
operator overload	conditional operator
`this`	inline function

SUMMARY

- A `friend` function of a class has the same access privileges as methods of the class, but is not itself a method. Thus, a `friend` function has access to a class's private members. Declare a `friend` function within a class with the keyword `friend` (Note 15.1).

- `friend` functions are not inherited in a class hierarchy.

- An overloaded operator that changes one of its operands should be defined as a method of the class. All other overloaded operators should be `friend` functions (Note 15.2).

- To overload an operator that is a `friend`, use the following syntax for the prototype and function definition header.

  `friend` *return-type* `operator` *operator-symbol* `(argument-list)`

- In an overload of a binary operator as a `friend` function, the first argument of the overload represents the left operand and the second argument represents the right operand (Note 15.3).

- Some operators cannot be overloaded. Some operators must be class methods. You cannot change the unary/binary nature of an operator, nor can you override the operator precedence rules (Note 15.4).

- When overloading an operator that is a class method, use the following syntax in the prototype and method definition header.

  return-type `operator` *operator-symbol* `(argument-list)`

- When overloading a binary operator as a class method, the object to which the function is applied represents the left operand and the one argument of the operator represents the right operand (Note 15.5).

- Within the code of a class method, the `this` pointer points to the object to which the method is being applied. Therefore, within such a method, `*this` represents the object to which the method applies (Note 15.6).

- The assignment operator can be overloaded as a class method as follows.

  class-name`& operator = (const` *class-name*`&` *right-operand*`)`

  In this case, the method should return `*this`.

- The insertion operator can be overloaded as follows.

  `friend ostream& operator << (ostream& os, const` *class-name*`&` *right-operand*`)`

  In this case, the function should return `os`.

- The extraction operator can be overloaded as follows.

  `friend istream& operator >> (istream& is,` *class-name*`&` *right-operand*`)`

  In this case, the function should return `is`.

- The compound assignment operators should be overloaded as class methods. For example, the `+=` operator can be overloaded as follows.

  class-name`& operator += (const` *data-type right-operand*`)`

  In this case, the method should return `*this`.

- The relational operators, for example `==`, can be overloaded as follows.

  `friend int operator == (`*class-name*`&,` *class-name*`&)`

  In this case, the function should return 1 if the objects are equal, and 0 otherwise.

- The unary operators can be overloaded as class methods. For example, the following is the prototype for an overload of the pre-increment `++` operator.

  class-name`& operator ++ ()`

  In this case, the method should return `*this`.

- To overload the post-increment ++ operator, you must use a dummy integer argument as follows.

  class-name & `operator` ++ `(int)`

  In this case, the function should return *`this`.
- Define a symbolic constant or a macro having parameters using the `#define` preprocesor directive.
- Use parentheses in a macro definition to avoid side effects (Note 15.7).
- The conditional operator can replace a simple condition.
- Macros are often more efficient than functions, but functions do not have side effects.
- An `inline` function, defined with the keyword `inline`, can combine the efficiency of a macro with the safety of a function (Note 15.8).

REVIEW EXERCISES

1. What is a `friend` function and how is it declared?
2. Generally speaking, which overloaded operators should be declared as `friend` functions and which should be defined as class methods? Which overloaded operators *must* be declared as methods?
3. Explain the syntax for overloading a binary operator.
4. Explain the syntax for overloading a unary operator.
5. In an overloaded binary operator that is declared as a `friend` function, what does the first operand of the operator represent? What does the second operand of the operator represent?
6. In an overloaded binary operator that is declared as a method, what is the left operand and what does the operand of the operator represent?
7. Can an overloaded unary operator have an argument? Explain.
8. Which operators cannot be overloaded?
9. What is the `this` pointer? When should you use it?
10. Give the syntax for the prototype and definition header of an overload of the insertion operator. Why should the overload return a reference?
11. Is there a default equals operator available for a user-defined class?
12. Explain how to overload the pre- and post-decrement operators.
13. Operators and `friend` functions are not inherited in a class hierarchy. Why do you think this is so?
14. How do you define a symbolic constant using `#define`?
15. How do you define a macro with parameters?
16. What are side effects in a macro and how can you avoid them?
17. Discuss the relative merits of using macros vs. using functions.
18. Explain when and how to use an `inline` function.

Appendix A

Computers and Data

This appendix covers the ideas necessary to understand the first few chapters. First, we discuss a model computer system that will help you to understand many hardware-related ideas in the book. Next, we investigate how a computer stores characters, integers, and decimal numbers.

A.1 A MODEL COMPUTER SYSTEM

In discussing several concepts in this book, we shall use a simplified model of a computer consisting of the following. See Figure A.1

1. Main memory—where programs must be to execute and where data is manipulated
2. Input and output ports—"gateways" through which data is passed to and from the computer
3. Control unit—interprets and executes program instructions
4. Registers—special high-speed memory where the arithmetic/logic unit manipulates data
5. Arithmetic/logic unit—carries out arithmetic and compare operations
6. Operating system—a set of programs that help run the computer hardware and software

Main Memory: The **main memory** of our model computer consists of cells of equal size called **bytes**. One byte is the amount of memory necessary to store one character, such as a letter of the alphabet, a digit, or a special character like a comma, a period, or a blank. We assume that these cells are arranged in a straight line, as Figure A.2 shows.

To keep track of the programs and data that reside in main memory, the computer identifies each byte by a numerical **address**. The first byte in main memory has address zero, the second byte address one, and so on to the last byte in the computer's

Figure A.1

Figure A.2

main memory. See Figure A.2. Do not confuse the contents of a byte with the byte's address. The address of a byte specifies its location in main memory in much the same way as a house's address identifies its location in a city. Just as the contents of a house can change over time, the contents of a byte can change as a program executes. The address of the byte, however, is fixed and cannot change.

Main memory is important because of the following.

1. For a program to execute, it must reside in main memory.
2. For a program to manipulate data, the data must reside in main memory.

For example, suppose we want to execute a program that is stored on a hard disk. Furthermore, suppose the program is to update data that is also stored on disk. To execute the program, you must first load it into main memory and begin its execution. When the program needs to update the data that is stored on disk, the program must transfer the data from the disk into main memory, operate on the data, and then transfer the updated data back onto the disk.

We assume that main memory has enough storage for our largest programs and for all our data.

The Control Unit: The **control unit** of our model computer interprets program instructions and carries them out. It can copy data from the main memory, place the data into the registers, pass the instruction that is to be executed to the arithmetic/logic unit, and copy the results from the registers back to main memory. It can accept data from outside the computer through one of the input ports and place that data into main memory. It can copy a portion of main memory and send it to an output device through one of the output ports. In short, the control unit interprets instructions and moves data from one part of the computer to another.

The Registers and the Arithmetic/Logic Unit: To do arithmetic on two numbers, the control unit must copy the numbers from main memory into special high-speed memory locations called **registers**. We shall assume that our model computer has several registers—enough to enable it to carry out all necessary instructions. Once the control unit places the numbers into the registers, the **arithmetic/logic unit**, or **ALU**, can manipulate them. The ALU of our model computer contains electronic circuits that enable it to do the four basic arithmetic operations—addition, subtraction, multiplication, and division—on the contents of the registers. The ALU also does the logic operation of comparison. It can test the contents of two registers and decide how these data compare: are they equal, is one less than or greater than the other?

The following illustrates how the registers, ALU, and the control unit work together to execute an instruction. Suppose the computer is to carry out an instruction to add the numbers in locations A and B of main memory and place the sum in location C. The control unit makes copies of the numbers in A and B and transfers these values to two of the registers. Then, the control unit sends the ALU an instruction to add the two numbers. The ALU does the addition. The control unit then copies the result, which is in a register, into location C in main memory.

The Operating System: The **operating system** of a computer is a set of programs that helps control (or operate) the computer hardware and manage computer software (files and programs). Thus, the operating system is the interface between the user and the computer system. The operating system keeps track of, and maintains, all input/output devices, main and auxiliary memory (such as floppy disks, CD-ROMs, and hard disks), all current users of the system, and all files stored on the system. Large (or **mainframe**) IBM computers can use the OS, VS, MVS or VM operating systems. Many medium size computers (or **minicomputers**), as well as some mainframes and PCs, use the UNIX or Linux operating systems. The most popular operating system for PCs (personal computers or **microcomputers**) is Windows. The most current version of Windows at this writing is Windows XP.

Input and Output Ports: The computer communicates with its environment through the input and output ports.

An input port is connected to an **input device**, such as a keyboard or disk drive. The operating system supplies the data our programs process to the main memory of the computer through an input port via an input device. The operating system even gives our program to the computer through an input device so the computer can execute the program's instructions.

An output port is connected to an **output device** such as a printer, monitor, or disk drive. The operating system outputs the data our programs produce through an output port and places that data on an output device.

Some devices, such as disk drives, serve as both input and output devices. Therefore, it is possible for both an input and output port to be connected to the same device.

For example, a program can obtain its data (input) from a disk drive and output its results (output) to the same disk.

We shall not be concerned with the characteristics of the different types of input and output devices. We assume that one input port is connected to the keyboard, one output port is connected to the monitor, another output port is connected to a printer, and an input and an output port are connected to a disk drive. This reflects the usual setup for most computers.

A.2 DATA REPRESENTATION—CHARACTERS

Recall from Section A.1 that a **byte** is the amount of computer storage needed to store one character. But how is a character stored in a byte?

The ASCII Code: Typically, a byte is a set of eight miniature electronic switches, called **bits,** each of which is in either of two states—on or off. It is convenient to represent the two states by the digits 1 (for on) and 0 (for off). Thus, a sequence of eight bits, that is, eight 1s and 0s, represents the contents of a byte. We can then interpret a specific eight-bit pattern, such as 01000001, to mean a specific character, such as A. The bit patterns that represent particular letters, digits, and punctuation characters depend on the encoding scheme your computer uses. A common way to encode characters is the **ASCII** code. (IBM mainframe computers use another encoding scheme, the EBCDIC code.)

Table A.1 shows the digits and the letters of the alphabet in the eight-bit ASCII code.

TABLE A.1

0	00110000	M	01001101	i	01101001
1	00110001	N	01001110	j	01101010
2	00110010	O	01001111	k	01101011
3	00110011	P	01010000	l	01101100
4	00110100	Q	01010001	m	01101101
5	00110101	R	01010010	n	01101110
6	00110110	S	01010011	o	01101111
7	00110111	T	01010100	p	01110000
8	00111000	U	01010101	q	01110001
9	00111001	V	01010110	r	01110010
A	01000001	W	01010111	s	01110011
B	01000010	X	01011000	t	01110100
C	01000011	Y	01011001	u	01110101
D	01000100	Z	01011010	v	01110110
E	01000101	a	01100001	w	01110111
F	01000110	b	01100010	x	01111000
G	01000111	c	01100011	y	01111001
H	01001000	d	01100100	z	01111010
I	01001001	e	01100101		
J	01001010	f	01100110		
K	01001011	g	01100111		
L	01001100	h	01101000		

In ASCII code, the word Exam appears as follows, in four consecutive bytes of main memory.

E	x	a	m
01000101	01111000	01100001	01101101

The Binary Number System and Characters: It is difficult to remember the ASCII codes in bit form because there are eight bits for each character. However, we can represent the codes in more compact form by taking advantage of the binary number system.

In the familiar decimal (or base 10) system, each digit position has a place value that is a power of 10. The units position is the right-most position. As you go to the left in the number, each digit position has a place value that is the next power of 10.

$10^3 = 1000$ $10^2 = 100$ $10^1 = 10$ $10^0 = 1$

4	0	6	7

$$= 4(1000) + 0(100) + 6(10) + 7(1) = 4067$$

In the **binary** (or **base 2) number system**, we write numbers in terms of powers of two. Thus, each bit position has a place value that is a power of two. The place values begin with units in the right-most position, and continue with the successive powers of two as you go to the left. Because we are writing numbers as sums of powers of two, we need only two digits, 1 and 0, to represent numbers in the binary system.

We interpret the binary number 1001 as follows.

$2^3 = 8$ $2^2 = 4$ $2^1 = 2$ $2^0 = 1$

1	0	0	1

$= 1(8) + 0(4) + 0(2) + 1(1)$

$= (8) + 0 + 0 + (1)$

$= 9$ in decimal

We can interpret each ASCII code in Table A.1 as an eight-bit binary number. For example, the letter A in the ASCII code is 01000001. As a binary number, this code represents

$2^7 = 128$ $2^6 = 64$ $2^5 = 32$ $2^4 = 16$ $2^3 = 8$ $2^2 = 4$ $2^1 = 2$ 1

0	1	0	0	0	0	0	1

$= 1(64) + 1(1) = 65$

Therefore, the bit pattern that represents the letter A also can represent the decimal number 65. The reader can verify that the ASCII bit pattern for the digit 4, 00110100, also can represent the decimal number 52. Similarly, the bit pattern for the letter s, 01110011, can represent the decimal number 115.

It is very important to realize that a bit pattern has no intrinsic meaning. Viewed as a character, the bit pattern 01000001 represents the letter A. Viewed as a binary number, the same bit pattern 01000001 represents the decimal number 65. It is up to you, the programmer, to decide how the program interprets the contents of a byte.

The Hexadecimal Number System and Characters: We also can use the **hexadecimal (or base 16) number system** to represent the bit patterns that make up the ASCII code. In the hexadecimal system, we write numbers in terms of powers of 16. Thus, the place values are the successive powers of 16.

$16^3 = 4096$ $16^2 = 256$ $16^1 = 16$ $16^0 = 1$

Writing numbers in terms of powers of 16 requires the use of 16 hexadecimal digits. The decimal digits 0 through 9 represent the numbers zero through nine. The first six uppercase letters of the alphabet, A through F, represent the numbers 10 through 15. Thus, the first sixteen hexadecimal numbers are

0, 1, 2, 3, 4, 5, 6, 7, 8, 9, A, B, C, D, E, F.

To find the decimal equivalent of the hexadecimal number 4BAD, proceed as follows.

$16^3 = 4096$ $16^2 = 256$ $16^1 = 16$ $16^0 = 1$

4	B	A	D

= 4(4096) + 11(256) + 10(16) + 13(1)
= 19373 in decimal

Table A.2 shows each hexadecimal digit as a four-bit binary number. Remember that leading zeros in a number have no effect on its value.

TABLE A.2

Decimal	Hexadecimal	Binary
0	0	0000
1	1	0001
2	2	0010
3	3	0011
4	4	0100
5	5	0101
6	6	0110
7	7	0111
8	8	1000
9	9	1001
10	A	1010
11	B	1011
12	C	1100
13	D	1101
14	E	1110
15	F	1111

To represent the contents of an eight-bit byte in hexadecimal, group the eight bits into two sets of four. Then replace each set of four bits by its corresponding hexadecimal digit (see Table A.2). Thus,

```
     (decimal)            (binary)
A --->      65      ---> 0100 0001
                                  (hexadecimal)
                    4  1    --->              41
```

To convert from hexadecimal to binary, reverse the process—expand each hexadecimal digit to its equivalent binary.

```
(hexadecimal)
   6D           --->    6    D
                      0110 1101 --->    109 ---> m
                      (binary)       (decimal)
```

Because there are eight bits in a byte and each bit can have one of two possible values, there are $2^8 = 256$ characters in the ASCII code. Table A.3 lists only the printable character set and the corresponding ASCII decimal and hexadecimal codes.

Using Table A.3, my name in ASCII hexadecimal code is as follows.

```
J o h n    C .    M o l l u z z o
4A6F686E20432E204D6F6C6C757A7A6F
```

Unicode: Because the ASCII code is an 8-bit code, it can represent only 256 $(2^8 = 256)$ different characters. Although 256 characters is enough for the English alphabet, digits, and punctuation characters, it is not nearly enough for the characters in other alphabets (Cyrillic, Greek, Arabic, Chinese, Japanese, and special characters used in European languages). Therefore, today, many computer systems and applications support **Unicode**, which is an extension of the ASCII code. In Unicode, one character is stored in two bytes. An ASCII character is converted to Unicode by placing a byte of all 0 bits before the original ASCII code. Therefore, the letter A in Unicode is

```
character  →  hexadecimal →        binary
    A      →     00 41     →   00000000 01000001
```

Because Unicode uses two bytes to represent a character, it can represent 65,536 $(= 2^{16})$ different characters. That is enough for all the common characters used in most of the world's languages. For example, the uppercase Greek letter sigma, Σ, is 03A3 in hexadecimal Unicode. You can access the Unicode database of characters at *http://www.unicode.org/ucd/*.

A.3 DATA REPRESENTATION—INTEGERS

Binary Integers: Integers $(\dots, -3, -2, -1, 0, 1, 2, 3, \dots)$ are the simplest type of number that you can use in a program. In mathematics, there are an infinite number of integers. However, a computer can represent only a finite number of integers because it has only a finite amount of main memory. A computer stores integers (positive, negative, and zero) in binary form. Depending on the computer and the computer language

TABLE A.3

Decimal	Hex	Symbol	Decimal	Hex	Symbol	Decimal	Hex	Symbol
32	20	(blank)	64	40	@	96	60	`
33	21	!	65	41	A	97	61	a
34	22	"	66	42	B	98	62	b
35	23	#	67	43	C	99	63	c
36	24	$	68	44	D	100	64	d
37	25	%	69	45	E	101	65	e
38	26	&	70	46	F	102	66	f
39	27	'	71	47	G	103	67	g
40	28	(	72	48	H	104	68	h
41	29	)	73	49	I	105	69	i
42	2A	*	74	4A	J	106	6A	j
43	2B	+	75	4B	K	107	6B	k
44	2C	'	76	4C	L	108	6C	l
45	2D	–	77	4D	M	109	6D	m
46	2E	.	78	4E	N	110	6E	n
47	2F	/	79	4F	O	111	6F	o
48	30	0	80	50	P	112	70	p
49	31	1	81	51	Q	113	71	q
50	32	2	82	52	R	114	72	r
51	33	3	83	53	S	115	73	s
52	34	4	84	54	T	116	74	t
53	35	5	85	55	U	117	75	u
54	36	6	86	56	V	118	76	v
55	37	7	87	57	W	119	77	w
56	38	8	88	58	X	120	78	x
57	39	9	89	59	Y	121	79	y
58	3A	:	90	5A	Z	122	7A	z
59	3B	;	91	5B	[	123	7B	{
60	3C	<	92	5C	\	124	7C		
61	3D	=	93	5D	]	125	7D	}
62	3E	>	94	5E	^	126	7E	~
63	3F	?	95	5F	_			

(we shall call the combination of computer and language a **platform**), an integer can occupy two or four bytes of main memory. For example, an older Borland C++ compiler on a PC using Windows stores integers in two bytes. On the same computer with the same operating system, Visual C++ stores integers in four bytes. Most modern platforms store integers in four bytes.

The amount of storage required by an integer determines the range of integer values that the computer can represent. For example, consider a platform that stores an integer in two bytes, that is, 16 bits. Because there are $2^{16} = 65536$ ways of arranging 16 zeros and ones, such a computer can represent 65536 integers (positive, negative, and zero) in two bytes. Half the integers in this range are negative (that is, less than zero) and half are nonnegative (that is, greater than, or equal to, zero). Therefore, on such a platform, a two-byte integer can have a value in the range -32768 (-2^{15}) to $+32767$ $(2^{15} - 1)$.

Similarly, a platform that stores integers in four bytes can represent $2^{32} =$ 4294967296 integers. Therefore, a four-byte integer can have a value in the range $-2^{31} = -2147483648$ (about -2 billion)   to $+2^{31} - 1 = +2147483647$ (about $+$ 2 billion).

All computers store nonnegative integers as binary numbers. Thus, the integer 14160 has the following representation as a two-byte binary number.

00110111 01010000

Negative Integers: Most computers represent negative numbers in **2's complement** form, which allows the computer to do binary arithmetic efficiently. It is not important for our purposes to know how to derive the 2's complement form of a negative number, so we shall not discuss how to do so. For us, it suffices to know that the first bit of a byte that represents a negative integer is one. For example, the two-byte integer 11111110 10011001 represents a negative number, namely, -359.

A.4 DATA REPRESENTATION—REAL NUMBERS

A **real number** is a number that has a decimal point, such as -73.456 and 0.029854. Most computers store real numbers in **floating point** form. To write a number in floating point form, move the decimal point to the right of the number's first significant digit (that is, its first nonzero digit) and multiply by an appropriate power of 10. For example,

$$-73.456 = -7.3456 \times 10^{1}$$

The power of 10 is 1 because we moved the decimal point left one place to put it to the right of the digit 7. Also,

$$0.029854 = 2.9854 \times 10^{-2}$$

The power of 10 is -2 because we moved the decimal point right two places to put it to the right of the digit 2.

The decimal part of a number in floating point form is the number's **mantissa** and the power of 10 is the number's **exponent**.

When you place a real number in a computer's main memory, the computer stores only the mantissa and the exponent (it does not have to store the decimal point because it knows where the decimal point is—to the right of the first digit in the mantissa). The number of bytes the computer uses to store a floating-point number restricts the number of digits that can be in the mantissa and the range of possible exponents. The number of digits that can be in the mantissa is the **precision** of the number. A floating-point number can occupy either four or eight bytes of storage. A typical four-byte floating-point number has a precision of seven digits and an exponent range of -38 to $+38$. A typical eight-byte floating point number has a precision of 15 digits and an exponent range of -308 to $+308$.

EXERCISES APPENDIX A

1. Define the following terms.
   main memory
   byte
   address
   control unit
   ALU (arithmetic/logic unit)
   operating system
   mainframe computer
   minicomputer
   microcomputer
   CPU (central processing unit)
   input device
   output device
   bit
   ASCII
   binary system
   hexadecimal system
   Unicode
   2's complement
   real number
   floating point
   mantissa
   exponent
   precision

Convert the binary numbers in Exercises 2–6 to the equivalent decimal numbers.

2. 1101001
3. 1000111
4. 111001001
5. 101010101
6. 100111010

Convert the hexadecimal numbers in Exercises 7–11 to the equivalent decimal numbers.

7. 3A1
8. 77
9. 10F
10. ABCD
11. 3E6F

12. Use Table A.3 to translate the title of this book into ASCII hexadecimal code.
13. Use Table A.3 to translate your name into ASCII hexadecimal code.
14. Translate the following hexadecimal ASCII message.

   4920686F706520796F7520686176652073756363657373732E20696E20432E

In Exercises 15–19, write each decimal number in floating point form.

15. 528.9923
16. −9234.011
17. 3.677322
18. 0.00004520018
19. −0.00000004562155

In Exercises 20–22, write each floating point number in decimal form.

20. -6.342113×10^5
21. -6.342113×10^{-5}
22. 1.757822×10^0

Appendix B

Program Control

This appendix discusses the standard ways of controlling the flow of control in a program through structured programming.

Structured programming is a technique for writing programs using only three logical control structures—sequence, selection, and iteration—and several derivatives of these three. You can code any proper program using combinations of these three control structures. By restricting the types of control structures, structured programming attempts to reduce program complexity, increase programmer productivity, produce more reliable code, and ease program maintenance.

B.1 SEQUENCE

Sequence refers to doing things in order or sequence, one after the other. Figure B.1 shows a sequence structure in flowchart form and in pseudocode.

Figure B.1 shows that the program first executes statement 1, then statement 2, and, finally, statement 3.

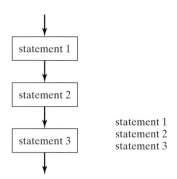

Figure B.1

Sequence is the natural way in which a computer executes instructions. A C++ program begins by executing the first executable statement of main(), followed by the second, and so on, until it encounters a statement that alters the sequential flow of execution. Statements that change the sequential execution of a program fall into two classes—selection statements and iteration statements.

B.2 SELECTION

Frequently, a program must decide between two alternative paths based on the truth or falsity of a condition. This is the **selection** structure of structured programming. In this section, we consider the basic selection structure, the if statement, and two structures derived from the if statement—nested if statements and the case structure.

The if Statement: Figure B.2 shows the flowchart and pseudocode forms of a typical if **statement**. An if statement flowchart tests the condition in the decision box (balance > 500.00). If the condition is true, the program executes the true part (add 1 to large_balance) and then executes the statement following the collector. If the condition is false, the program executes the false part (add 1 to small_balance) and then executes the statement following the collector.

The exits from the decision box are **branches**. Both branches from the decision box meet at a common point, which should be the only exit from the selection structure.

You read the pseudocode if statement of Figure B.2 as follows. If the condition (balance > 500.00) is true, execute the true part, which is everything between the condition and the pseudocode word else. Then, execute the statement that follows endif. The pseudocode word endif is a delimiter that indicates the end of the else part of the if statement and does not represent an executable statement.

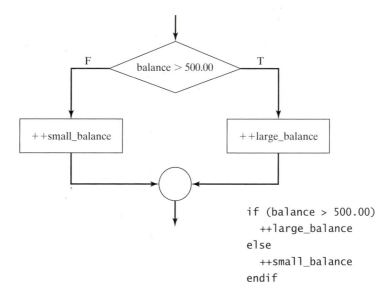

```
if (balance > 500.00)
    ++large_balance
else
    ++small_balance
endif
```

Figure B.2

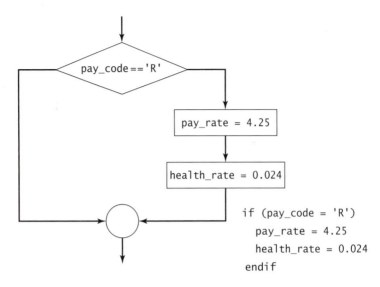

Figure B.3

If the condition is false, execute the false part, which is everything between the pseudocode words else and endif. Then, execute the statement that follows endif.

Both exits from the condition box must lead to a common point. The branches of the flowchart in Figure B.2 meet in the collector. Whichever branch the program takes, control eventually leads to this collector.

The endif in the pseudocode of Figure B.2 acts as the collector in the flowchart. Whichever branch of the if statement the program takes, control eventually passes through the endif and on to the next statement. We indent the true branch and the false branch, and align corresponding if-else-endif directly under each other.

An if statement need not have an else. For example, the flowchart and pseudocode of Figure B.3 have no else part.

The selection structure illustrates the **'straight-through' principle**, which we state in Note B.1.

Note B.1 The Straight-Through Principle

Each control structure has exactly one entrance and one exit.

Therefore, you should not code a condition as shown in Figure B.4

Nested if Statements: Sometimes a program must test a condition only if a previously tested condition is true (or false). To code such a decision structure, you can **nest** if statements; that is, include an if statement in the true part or false part of another if statement.

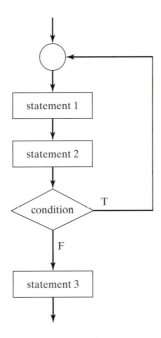

Figure B.4

Figure B.5 shows a nested if in which the program tests state_code only if employee_code equals 'A'.

If employee_code equals 'A', then the program tests state_code. If state_code equals 'Y', then tax is assigned the value of gross_pay multiplied by 0.045. If state_code is unequal to 'Y', then tax is assigned the value of gross_pay multiplied by 0.070. Returning to the first decision, if employee_code is unequal to 'A', then the tax is assigned the value 0.00.

The Case Structure: The if statement provides only a two-way branch. If the condition in an if statement is true, the program takes one path. If the condition is false, the program takes another path. Sometimes, a program requires a **multi-way branch**. That is, depending on the value of a variable, the program can take one of several paths. For example, Table B.1 shows the commission rates that a real estate broker sets for selling properties according to the property code. A property code other than R, M, or C is invalid.

TABLE B.1

Property Type	Code	Rate
Residential	R	0.060
Multi-Dwelling	M	0.050
Commercial	C	0.045

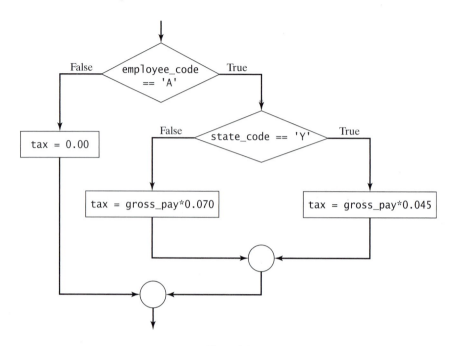

Figure B.5

To select the proper commission rate, a program can test the property code using a nested if, as in the following pseudocode.

```
if (property_code = 'R')
  commission_rate = 0.060
else
  if (property_code = 'M')
    commission_rate = 0.050
  else
    if (property_code = 'C')
      commission_rate = 0.045
    else
      print error message
    endif
  endif
endif
```

Another way of designing the code is as follows. Choosing the proper commission rate requires the program to select one of four possible alternatives, depending on the value of property_code. This is a multi-way decision. Structured programming refers to a multi-way decision that is based on the value of a variable as a **case structure**. Figure B.6 shows the multi-way decision structure that our program requires, flowcharted as a case structure.

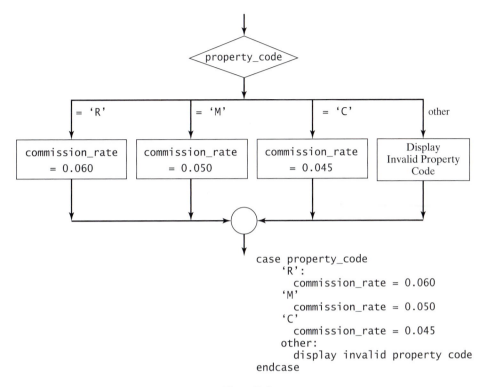

```
case property_code
    'R':
        commission_rate = 0.060
    'M'
        commission_rate = 0.050
    'C'
        commission_rate = 0.045
    other:
        display invalid property code
endcase
```

Figure B.6

In Figure B.6, the decision box contains the variable (property_code) that the program tests. There are as many exits from the decision box (four) as there are possible paths that the program can take. All exits from the decision box meet in a collector.

The case flowchart works as follows. The program first evaluates the variable (property_code) that appears in the decision box. Then the program takes the branch from the decision box that corresponds to the current value of the variable, executes the statements in that branch, and exits the structure at the collector. If the variable does not equal any of the listed values, the program takes the branch labeled other, executes the appropriate statements, and exits the structure at the collector.

The corresponding case pseudocode statement works in the same way. The program evaluates the variable that appears after the pseudocode word case. Then, the program goes to the label that corresponds to the value of the variable, executes the appropriate statements, and exits the structure at the pseudocode word endcase. If the variable does not equal any of the case label values, the program goes to the label other, executes the statements located there, and exits the structure at the pseudocode word endcase.

For example, suppose that the user enters 'M' for property_code when the program prompts for its value. When the program executes the case structure, it tests the value of property_code. Because the value of property_code is 'M', the program takes the 'M' branch of the case structure, assigns the value 0.050 to the variable commission_rate, and then exits the case structure.

B.3 ITERATION

Perhaps the most powerful capability of a computer is its ability to quickly execute the same set of instructions repeatedly (possibly millions of times), without making a mistake. **Iteration**, or **looping**, is repeated execution of the same set of instructions.

Sometimes there is no way to tell in advance how often the same set of instructions is to execute. For example, suppose a program that you are writing for a stockbroker is to process a day's stock transactions. The program is to process each transaction in the same way. When you design the program, there is no way to know how many stock transactions will take place on a given day. Because we do not know how often the program is to repeat the transaction processing instructions, we refer to this type of iteration as **indefinite iteration**.

On the other hand, when designing a program, we sometimes know how often a set of instructions is to execute. For example, suppose a program must print a ten-row tax table. The set of instructions that calculates the tax for a given income and prints the corresponding row of the table must execute exactly ten times. Because we know how often the set of instructions is to execute, we refer to this type of iteration as **definite iteration**.

In this section, we consider three forms of iteration—indefinite iteration with a while loop, indefinite iteration with a do loop, and definite iteration with a for loop.

The while Loop: Figure B.7 shows the structure of a typical while **loop** in flowchart and pseudocode forms. The purpose of the loop is to count the number of times the user responds 'Y' to a prompt. Because we do not know how often the user will respond 'Y', an indefinite iteration is appropriate.

Program execution enters the loop by first testing the **loop condition**, (response == 'Y'). If the loop condition is true (T), the **loop body** executes. In this example, the loop body consists of two statements. Generally, the loop body can consist of zero or more statements.

After executing the loop body, the program returns (or loops) to test the loop condition. Therefore, the loop body repeatedly executes while the loop condition is true. This is why we call the loop of Figure B.7 a while loop. When (indeed, if) the loop condition tests false, control exits the loop. That is, program control proceeds to the statement following the while loop. At this point in the program, the variable num_yeses contains the number of times the user responded 'Y' to the prompt.

The structure of the pseudocode while loop is self-evident except, perhaps, for the word endwhile. Endwhile is a delimiter that indicates the end of the set of statements that make up the loop body and, as such, does not represent an executable statement.

Note B.2 lists two important facts to remember about while loops.

Note B.2 Understanding while Loops

1. When the program encounters a while loop, it tests the loop condition first. Therefore, if the loop condition is false the first time the program tests it, the loop body never executes.

2. Normally, when the program exits a while loop, the loop condition is false.

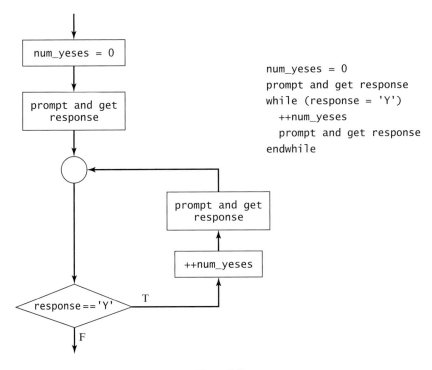

```
num_yeses = 0
prompt and get response
while (response = 'Y')
    ++num_yeses
    prompt and get response
endwhile
```

Figure B.7

Again refer to the example while loop of Figure B.7. If the user enters 'N' in response to the prompt that is immediately before the loop condition test, the loop body never executes. Then, the value of num_yeses is zero, which is correct. The user never responded 'Y'.

Also, when the program exits the while loop, the loop condition must be false. Therefore, when the program takes the false exit from the loop condition, the value of response must be something other than 'Y'.

The do Loop: As Note B.2 stated, the body of a while loop does not execute if the loop condition is false the first time a program executes the while statement. However, program logic sometimes requires the body of a loop to execute at least once, no matter what conditions prevail at the time the program encounters the loop.

For example, suppose we want to design a loop that counts the number of times the user answers a prompt. The while loop of Figure B.7 counts only the number of 'Y' responses because the loop body executes only after the program tests the loop condition. The do **loop** of Figure B.8 is an indefinite iteration loop in which the loop body must execute at least once. This loop counts the total number of responses the user makes.

When the program encounters the do loop, the loop body executes first. (Therefore, the loop counts every answer that the user enters.) Then the program tests the loop condition. If the condition is true, the program executes the loop body again, and so on. When the loop condition tests false, the program exits the loop.

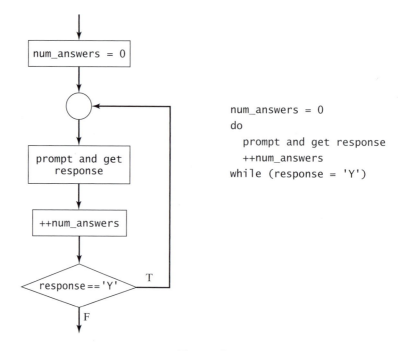

```
num_answers = 0
do
    prompt and get response
    ++num_answers
while (response = 'Y')
```

Figure B.8

Definite Iteration: When you know exactly how often the loop body must execute, it is appropriate to use a definite iteration loop. For example, you may require a program to display a tax table for yearly incomes ranging from $10,000.00 to $100,000.00 in intervals of $10,000.00. This table has exactly ten rows. You could, therefore, design a loop that executes exactly ten times, each time producing one row of the tax table. A variable, called a **counter**, usually controls the number of times that the body of a definite iteration loop executes. Consequently, we also call a definite iteration loop a **counter-controlled loop**.

Figure B.9 shows a typical definite iteration flowchart box and the corresponding pseudocode.

When the program enters the definite iteration box of Figure B.9, it initializes the counter variable row to the value 1. Next, the program tests the counter variable against its maximum value of 10. If the counter is less than or equal to this maximum value, the program executes the loop body once. Next, the program adjusts the loop counter. (In the flowchart of Figure B.9, the counter row is increased by one. However, a program can adjust the loop counter by any amount.) Again, the program tests the counter variable against its maximum value. Therefore, the program stays in the loop until the counter variable exceeds its maximum value.

A program must treat the loop counter in any definite iteration loop as the loop counter in Figure B.9. Note B.3 states these rules.

The pseudocode for statement of Figure B.9 works in essentially the same way as the definite iteration box. Semicolons separate the three things that the program must

Note B.3 Iteration Loop Counters

A program must do the following to a definite iteration loop counter.

    1. Initialize: Before entering the loop body, the program must initialize the loop counter.

    2. Test: The program must test the loop counter. If the counter satisfies the test, the program executes the loop body once. If the counter does not satisfy the test, the program exits the loop.

    3. Adjust: After executing the loop body, the program must adjust the loop counter.

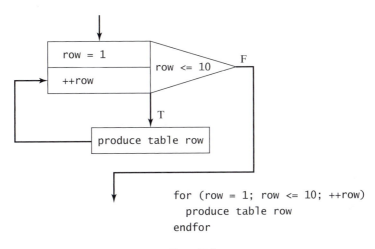

```
for (row = 1; row <= 10; ++row)
    produce table row
endfor
```

Figure B.9

do to the loop counter. When the program encounters the `for` statement, it initializes the counter variable and then tests the value of the counter. If the counter is less than or equal to its maximum allowable value, the program executes the loop body. (The pseudocode word `endfor` delimits the body of the `for` loop.) Then the program adjusts the loop counter and tests the counter variable again.

    Infinite Loops: The loop condition is the most important part of any iteration. Once in a loop, the program (theoretically, at least) can stay in the loop forever, unless there is some mechanism that tells the program to exit the loop. This mechanism is the loop condition. Each time the program executes the loop body, it should execute one or several instructions that *could* alter the truth or falsity of the loop condition.

    For example, in Figure B.10, the integer variable i begins with a value of three. The loop condition is i > 0. The loop body consists of the statement "Decrease i by 1". This is the statement that could affect the loop condition. Because i begins at 3,

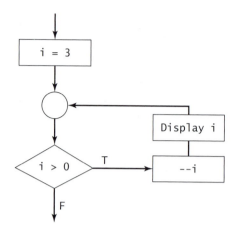

Figure B.10

after three passes through the loop, the loop condition is false and the program exits the loop. The effect of the loop is to display the following:

2 1 0

Note B.4 is important to keep in mind when writing any program.

Note B.4 Infinite Loops

When writing a loop, make sure the loop condition will eventually be false. If the loop condition is always true, the program will cycle the loop indefinitely, causing an **infinite loop**.

Figure B.11 shows an infinite loop. Because the integer variable i begins at three and is increased by one each time through the loop, i is always greater than 0.

Improper Loop Exits: The Straight-Through Principle (see Note B.1) applies to all three iteration control structures. Therefore, never allow a program to exit from a loop at any point other than the loop exit. The loop body should never contain a statement that would cause the program to transfer control outside the loop at a point other than the loop exit. For example, never allow the structure shown in Figure B.12. There are two exits from the iteration: one from condition 1 (which is the loop condition) and one from condition 2.

B.4 COMBINATIONS

You can build complicated control structures by "pasting" together the basic control structures. Be sure to use the Straight-Through Principle to ensure that you correctly

Figure B.11

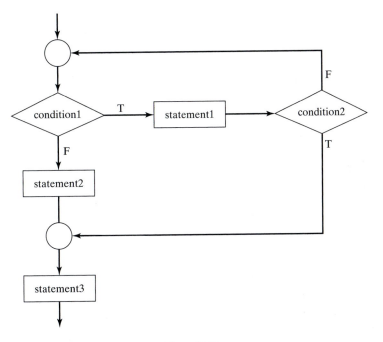

Figure B.12

paste the basic control structures. For example, consider Figure B.13, in which C1, C2, and C3 represent conditions, and P1, P2, P3, P4, and P5 represent processing instructions.

The false branch of the C1 condition leads to another selection structure. The true branch of C1 leads to a sequence structure. The second part of this sequence is an iteration. Whichever branch the program takes out of C1, control eventually comes to the common exit.

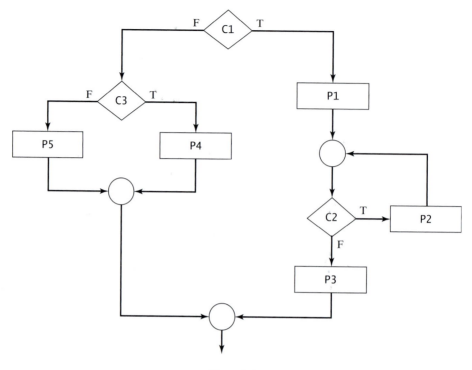

Figure B.13

EXERCISES APPENDIX B

1. Define the following terms.

   structured programming
   sequence
   selection
   if statement
   branch
   Straight-Through Principle
   nested if statement
   multi-way decision
   case structure
   iteration
   looping
   indefinite iteration
   definite iteration
   while loop
   loop condition

loop body
endwhile
do loop
counter
counter-controlled loop
infinite loop

2. Identify the basic control structures (sequence, selection, iteration) of which Figure B.14 is composed.
3. Identify the basic control structures (sequence, selection, iteration) of which Figure B.15 is composed.
4. In Figure B.16, find how often the loop body executes.
5. In Figure B.17, find how often the loop body executes.
6. In Figure B.18, find how often the loop body executes.
7. In Figure B.19, find how often the loop body executes.
8. What is wrong with the flowchart of Figure B.20? Can you correct it? (Adapted from *Techniques of Structured Programming and Design*, Yourdon, p.164, Figure 4.16(a)).

Figure B.14

Figure B.15

Figure B.16

Figure B.17

Figure B.18

Figure B.19

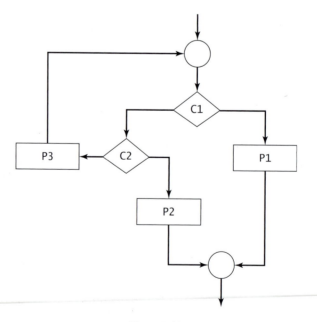

Figure B.20

Index